D1236365

ANNALS OF
THE NEW YORK ACADEMY
OF SCIENCES

Volume 575

EDITORIAL STAFF

Executive Editor
BILL BOLAND

Managing Editor
JUSTINE CULLINAN

Associate Editor
LINDA H. MEHTA

The New York Academy of Sciences
2 East 63rd Street
New York, New York 10021

THE PSYCHOBIOLOGY OF HUMAN EATING DISORDERS: PRECLINICAL AND CLINICAL PERSPECTIVES

ANNALS OF THE NEW YORK ACADEMY OF SCIENCES
Volume 575

THE PSYCHOLOGY OF HUMAN EATING DISORDERS: PRECLINICAL AND CLINICAL PERSPECTIVES

Edited by Linda H. Schneider, Steven J. Cooper, and Katherine A. Halmi

The New York Academy of Sciences
New York, New York
1989

Library of Congress Cataloging in Publication Data

The Psychobiology of human eating disorders: preclinical and clinical perspectives/edited by Linda H. Schneider, Steven J. Cooper, and Katherine A. Halmi.

    p. cm.—(Annals of the New York Academy of Sciences, ISSN 0077-8923 ; v. 575)

    Result of a conference held by the New York Academy of Sciences on Oct. 13–15, 1988 in New York City.

    Includes bibliographical references.

    ISBN 0-89766-541-4 (alk. paper). —ISBN 0-89766-542-2 (pbk., alk. paper)

    1. Eating disorders—Congresses. 2. Biological psychiatry—Congresses. I. Schneider, Linda H. II. Cooper, S. J. III. Halmi, Katherine A. IV. New York Academy of Sciences. V. Series.

    [DNLM: 1. Eating Disorders—psychology—congresses. W1 AN626YL v. 575 / WM 175 P9748 1966]

Q11.N5 vol. 575

[RC552.E16]   600 s—dc20   [616.85'26]   DNLM/DLC

for Library of Congress

CCP

Printed in the United States of America

ISBN 0-89766-541-4 (cloth)

ISBN 0-89766-542-2 (paper)

ISSN 0077-8923

ANNALS OF THE NEW YORK ACADEMY OF SCIENCES

Volume 575
December 18, 1989

THE PSYCHOBIOLOGY OF HUMAN EATING DISORDERS: PRECLINICAL AND CLINICAL PERSPECTIVES[a]

Editors
LINDA H. SCHNEIDER, STEVEN J. COOPER, and KATHERINE A. HALMI

Scientific Advisory Committee
BRIAN L. G. MORGAN, *Chair*, LEON BRADLOW, WILLIAM S. CAIN,
KEVIN KEIM, and PHILIP SIEKEVITZ

CONTENTS

[a] This volume is the result of a conference entitled The Psychobiology of Human Eating Disorders, which was held in New York City on October 13–15, 1988. The conference was held by the New York Academy of Sciences.

Part III. Neurochemistry and Pharmacology of Food Intake in Humans and Animals
ANTHONY SCLAFANI, Chair

Part IV: Neural and Behavioral Responses to Orosensory Stimuli
STYLIANOS NICOLAIDIS, Chair

Financial assistance was received from:

- THE COCA COLA COMPANY
- HOFFMANN-LA ROCHE, INC.
- INSTITUT DE RECHERCHES INTERNATIONALES SERVIER
- KRAFT, INC.
- LILLY RESEARCH LABORATORIES
- M&M/MARS
- MONSANTO COMPANY
- THE NUTRASWEET COMPANY
- PARKE-DAVIS PHARMACEUTICAL RESEARCH DIVISION
    WARNER-LAMBERT COMPANY
- PEPSICO INC., RESEARCH & TECHNICAL SERVICES
- PFIZER CENTRAL RESEARCH
- SOCIETY FOR THE STUDY OF INGESTIVE BEHAVIOR
- THE SUGAR ASSOCIATION, INC.
- THOMPSON MEDICAL

Preface

KATHERINE HALMI AND LINDA SCHNEIDER

Department of Psychiatry
Cornell University Medical College
Cornell Medical Center
White Plains, New York 10605

STEVEN J. COOPER

University of Birmingham
Birmingham, United Kingdom

The human eating disorders of anorexia nervosa and bulimia have become a substantial clinical problem in the population at risk, adolescents and young adults. Within this population, the prevalence of bulimia nervosa varies 3–8%, and that of anorexia nervosa is about one in 200.[1] The first well-described case of anorexia nervosa in the literature was in 1694 by Richard Morton, who noted the characteristic trend of refusal to eat, amenorrhea, and extreme wasting without lassitude.[2] Twenty years earlier, a less complete description of "prodigious abstinence" was made by John Reynolds. The disorder of anorexia nervosa seemed to blossom in the Victorian era, when Sir William Gull proposed its name (1868) and when both he and Laséque (1873) described approaches to treatment.[3,4] Since then, a remarkable variety of therapies has been used to treat this disorder. None of these have been predictably effective. More recently, the related disorder of bulimia nervosa was defined,[5] and again a variety of pharmacological and cognitive–behavioral treatments attempted had limited effectiveness. The study of eating behavior and the interactions of psychological and physiological disturbances in these patients has been neglected. This is an area of investigation that should produce useful information for developing more successful treatment strategies.

Several decades of animal research into the biobehavioral basis of eating has provided a considerable body of empirical data, specific methods, and a comprehensive conceptual framework that could be used to good effect in the experimental investigation of human eating disorder. The purpose of the conference from which this volume was derived was to bring together basic and clinical scientists to review recent developments in research relevant to the psychobiology of human eating disorders and to stimulate future collaborations between preclinical and clinical investigations.

The book is divided into six sections. The first section is a clinical overview of disturbed eating behavior in psychiatric disorders. In the second section, the development and application of animal models to clinical eating disorders considers the perspectives (conditioning, metabolic, ecological) and measurements (microstructural, nutrient specific) that may allow meaningful modeling of eating disorders in animals. The third section is an update on the neurochemistry and pharmacology of food intake in humans and animals and emphasizes the major neurotransmitter–neuromodulator systems which are strongly implicated in the initiation, maintenance, and termination of eating. Neural and behavioral responses to orosensory stimuli is the theme of the fourth section, which focuses upon the mouth–brain axis as it determines eating behavior. In the fifth section, sensory-hedonic aspects in human eating behavior are presented, including the role of taste factors involved in the attraction to foods. The sixth and final section consists of eating behavior studies in anorexia nervosa and bulimia nervosa.

We would like to express our gratitude to those companies and organizations, listed in the Table of Contents, whose generous financial support made this conference possible. We would also like to thank the members of the Scientific Advisory Committee, who gave valuable advice in the early stages of planning. Thanks are also due to Gerri Busacco of the New York Academy of Sciences, who brought considerable administrative skill to the task of organizing the conference.

REFERENCES

1. HALMI, K. A. 1987. Anorexia nervosa and bulimia. *In* Handbook of Adolescent Psychology. Hersen and Van Hassett, Eds.: 265–287. Pergamon Press. New York.
2. MORTON, R. 1694. Phthisiologia: Or, a Treatise of Consumptions. Smith & Walford. London.
3. GULL, W. 1874. Anorexia Nervosa (apepsia hysterica, anorexia hysterica). Trans. Clin. Soc. London. **7:** 22–28.
4. LASÈQUE, E. C. 1873. De l'anorexie hystérique. Arch. Gen. Med. **21:** 385–403.
5. RUSSELL, G. F. M. 1979. Bulimia nervosa: An ominous variant of anorexia nervosa. Psychol. Med. **9:** 429–448.

The Approaches to the Study of Human Disorders in Food Ingestion and Body Weight Maintenance

PAUL R. McHUGH, TIMOTHY H. MORAN,
AND MARIE KILLILEA

Department of Psychiatry and Behavioral Sciences
The Johns Hopkins University School of Medicine
Baltimore, Maryland 21205

INTRODUCTION

Human disorders of food intake and body weight control fall into two distinctively different groups. One group includes all those disorders caused by pathology within the individual that disrupts the normal physiology controlling behavior. These might be called "spanner in the works" conditions. The discovery of these "proximate causes" represents the most natural integration of information from both clinicians and laboratory scientists. A second group of disorders encompasses those distortions or deviations in food intake and weight control that emerge with development and its capacity to direct, reinforce, or hinder behavior. They rest on more "ultimate causes" ranging from genetic differences within populations to sociocultural processes that interact with intrapersonal factors. The discernment of these ultimate causes depends at least initially upon epidemiology and the methods that derive from it. It is our purpose to describe the differences in the study of human feeding disorders by reviewing two conditions from each group: hypothalamic hyperphagia and cancer anorexia from the first, and obesity and anorexia nervosa from the second.

PROXIMATE OR IMMEDIATE FACTOR DISORDERS

Hypothalamic Hyperphagia

The main reason for beginning with the proximate group is that it is here that successful collaboration between clinicians and basic scientists in the study of food intake and weight control first occurred. The first confident recognition of an association between pathological lesions at the base of the brain and abnormal obesity was made in man by Fröhlich in 1901[1-3] and was promptly followed up by Erdheim, who announced in 1904[4] that it was injury to the hypothalamus and not to the underlying pituitary gland that produced such obesity. These remarkable observations from the clinic can be considered the opening events in the collaboration of clinicians and basic scientists in obesity because they eventually prompted Hetherington and Ranson[5] to define specific regions in the hypothalamus that must be destroyed to produce these effects. This could best be addressed in animals and at the laboratory bench and required the redeployment of the Horsley–Clarke instrument for precise placement of lesions. The success at reproducibly evoking obesity with strategically placed lesions in the ventral and medial hypothalamus of the rat was a landmark discovery. On the one hand, it promoted an enthusiasm for the Horsley–Clarke instrument throughout physiological psychology, and on the other hand, it brought into sharp focus the mechanisms of obesity that led to Brobeck's[6] demonstration that the obesity was primarily due to overeating and not to the metabolic factors that had previously been assumed. Hence, he chose to speak of hypothalamic hyperphagia as the fundamental phenomenon.

It is not necessary to go into more detail about this great achievement because we wish primarily to point it out as the classic example of work on the proximate or immediate causes in the control of food intake and body weight where clinicians and basic scientists have collaborated to advantage. Simply, it has cultivated a general appreciation of the existence of localized physiological controls on body weight that generate their effects through behavior. The particular roles within the hypothalamus itself remain to be enunciated. An appreciation of an interaction in behavior between the brain and the physiology and metabolism of the periphery has emerged. The concepts of transmitter-specific neural paths converging within the hypothalamus have opened a view that the behavioral outcomes from lesions depend on injury to both intrinsic hypothalamic mechanisms and fibers of passage. Hypothalamic hyperphagia still remains an intriguing issue, but its pathophysiology is emerging and the stimulus its study gave to the alliance of clinicians and bench scientists remains powerful.

Cancer Anorexia

If hypothalamic hyperphagia and its resultant obesity is the classic example of this collaboration over a proximate factor in the control of food intake, then cancer anorexia and cachexia are the contemporary issues that reveal its intrinsic liveliness. What more clear example of the "spanner in the works" view is there than the behavioral and physiological effects of cancer? The patient with cancer may have a change in his food appetite as the very first sign of his disease. A prompt improvement in appetite may be the best indicator of successful oncologic treatment even before other objective evidence of tumor regression is apparent. This anorexia often appears abruptly, dramatically interrupting the eating patterns of a lifetime, often before any other sign of neoplasm is noted. The associated wasting of body fat and lean body mass may lead to death long before the local or metastatic aspects of tumor growth would have killed, and even the survival period is made miserable by the malaise and weakness that accompany anorexia and cachexia.

The early assumptions that the explanation for this anorexia–cachexia might be sought from the growth characteristics of cancer, as with functional or anatomical derangements to the gastrointestinal tract, cerebral metastases with increased intracranial pressure, pain-induced food suppression, or simply increased metabolic requirements from tumor growth, soon were disproven because these factors, though active in some patients, were not common in the majority. In fact, the incidence and severity of anorexia and weight loss bore no precise relation to the size, site, stage, or histology of the neoplasm.[7] What did seem clear was that inadequate food intake was a partial explanation. Secondary features tied to being a cancer patient, such as depression of mood, surgical experience, or a side effect of chemotherapy, did not explain this anorexia in more than a small minority.

In the study of tumor-bearing experimental animals, it was possible to demonstrate the phenomena of anorexia and cachexia with the induction of cancer. Again, the conditions were not explained by the simple effects of the tumor, and although such standard laboratory approaches as seeking out learned food aversions have offered occasional demonstrations of a role in cancer anorexia, they have not held up as a general explanation.

The most useful results from the behavioral studies in the laboratory were the clear signs that some circulating factor, either from the neoplasm or from the host, was active in cancer anorexia. The best indication was from parabiotic rats in which a tumor in one of the parabiotic pair induced anorexia and weight loss in both, without the spread of cancer to the other rat.[8] The evidence that diminished food intake and body weight depended upon the area postrema in tumor-bearing rats[9] was another indication that some circulating factor (noticed by the chemosensitive trigger zone of the brain) was active in cancer anorexia.

It was with these suggestions that an intriguing set of discoveries has opened up inquiries into the biology of anorexia and of cachexia itself. Cerami and coworkers[10,11] in efforts to determine the cause of endotoxin-induced hypertriglyceridemia in infected animals, identified a circulating factor that suppressed the synthesis of lipoprotein lipase. This factor was produced by the macrophages of the animals and could be garnered from cell cultures. It is one of the cytokines synthesized and released by blood monocytes and tissue macrophages in response to inflammation.[12] These investigators, reasoning that it may be involved in the pathophysiology of progressive bodily wasting in disease, designated this factor as "cachectin" and have demonstrated that the tissue loss it provokes is quite different from that seen in simple caloric restriction and starvation.[13]

Simultaneously, other workers[14] had demonstrated that an antitumor factor could be induced in mice by the same bacterial endotoxin, an idea prompted in part by a set of clinical observations of tumor regression after infection by a New York surgeon made almost a century ago.[15,16] This factor, which killed a variety of murine and human tumor cells *in vitro* and *in vivo*, was also produced by hematopoietic mononuclear cells including macrophages and was designated "tumor necrosis factor" (TNF). Many investigators working with cachectin and TNF demonstrated their comparable molecular weight. Beutler and associates[17] documented recently that purified "cachetin" has a tumor necrosis factor activity *in vitro* and established from inspection of the amino acid sequences and molecular clones of TNF and cachectin that they are homologues of one protein—referred to now as TNF/cachectin.[18]

Recombinant TNF/cachectin is now available and many laboratories have helped to uncover a long list of biological activities affected by TNF/cachectin.[19,20] Crucial to the interest in body-weight regulation is the suppression of anabolic enzymes that gives the factor its ability to deplete body lipid stores and provokes peripheral protein wasting irrespective of caloric intake. It is clear that TNF/cachectin does lead to reduced food intake as well.

Thus with the discovery of this factor, we have come around to new opportunities to appreciate many of the features represented by cancer anorexia and cachexia. This host-derived factor can mediate and provoke many of the metabolic changes associated with cachexia and as well lead to reduced caloric intake in many cancers. The weight loss is likely due to a combination of these two aspects of TNF/cachectin's actions, and thus we understand the rather frequent observation of cancer patients with cachexia in whom the degree of weight loss exceeds what would be expected from the reduction in caloric intake. As well, we can understand the appearance of anorexia in some patients early in their course of illness when their tumor is small and site restricted.

The overriding question is how to make sense out of this combination of body wasting and reduction in food intake tied to a common factor released into the blood circulation in response to a wide range of assaults, from bacterial and parasitic infection to neoplasia. Are the anorexic and cachexic features simply unfortunate side effects of a factor that offers the host some means of eliminating a tumor, or is there some biological utility to the suppression of caloric intake simultaneously with an attack on tumor tissue itself? It has been long known that caloric restriction in animals with advanced tumors will inhibit tumor growth as well as reduce the incidence of spontaneous malignancies in laboratory animals. The metabolic factors that lead to depletion of muscle protein may lead to the preservation of hepatic proteins, a phenomenon that is usually found during an acute illness and may have survival value but can be inappropriately sustained with continuing neoplasia.

Much more is yet to come in addressing the ultimate fitness of this combination of features (metabolic changes associated with cachexia and reduced caloric intake) in TNF/cachectin. It offers great opportunities for investigation to students of food intake and of disease of all kinds. Antagonists for this hormone/factor are presently being sought[20] and will certainly prove useful to clinician scientists concerned with nutritional abnormalities in general and cancer anorexia in particular. The entire realm of biology from generic mechanisms to neural transmission has been opened up by this effort to study a remarkable behavioral phenomenon, cancer anorexia, cachexia, that links body weight control to disease.

ULTIMATE OR DISTAL FACTOR DISORDERS

In contrast to those disorders that depend upon "proximate" pathology, there are others that derive from more "ultimate" features, such as the genetic constitution and its expression in behavior through the shaping influences of life experience. Epidemiologic investigation has proven to be the method to illuminate these conditions and their causes. Epidemiology looks at the distribution of disorders in populations and attempts to discern risk factors that contribute to this distribution. It is of fundamental importance in human behavior studies and has linkages to genetics, ethology, and ecology. The particular focus here is not on the "epidemics" of disease from which epidemiology got its name but upon influences on behavior within a population, as in the behavior of food intake and disorders of its expression. As with the previous section, we begin with a classic line of research and with obesity.

Obesity

The first indication that obesity has a crucial sociocultural aspect came from epidemiology and specifically the Midtown Manhattan Study of mental disorders,[21] in which a clear relationship between social class and obesity was shown. Obesity was much more prevalent among the lower classes. It seemed to be avoided by the upper classes. The fascinating point that subsequently emerged was that this class distinction is a feature of developed societies. Just the reverse relationship is found in underdeveloped nations where the well-to-do tend toward obesity and the poor, perhaps because of caloric starvation, are thin often to the point of emaciation. These observations have held up in many studies and beyond themselves offer intriguing speculations about the meaning of weight regulation within different classes and cultures.

A link across cultures is the emergence of obesity and its complications among peoples who survived famine in prehistory and are transported to or emerge within a calorie-rich contemporary world. These groups may develop obesity and its complications because of a "thrifty genotype rendered detrimental by progress" (see J. V. Neel[22]) — that is, a genetic endowment for fat storage that would have had the survival value of reducing the expenditure of energy during prior times of shortage but would overstore energy as fat as food became plentiful and remained so.

A considerable amount of confirming evidence exists[23-25] for a tendency among the obese to have a reduced energy expenditure as indicated by the metabolic rate at rest. This low 24-hour energy expenditure is a clear risk factor for obesity when calories are abundant. It appears to be a familial trait, and thus directs attention to the search for a genetic basis for human obesity.

A. J. Stunkard has provided two important studies that indicate a strong influence of heredity on human obesity, by employing two standard techniques for revealing a genetic element, an adoption study and a comparison of monozygotic and dizygotic twins. The Danish adoption study[26] employed the birth and health history registers available in that country. Stunkard and colleagues demonstrated a clear correlation (essentially using body mass index, BMI) between the weight of adoptees and their natural parents but no correlation with the weight of the adoptive parents.

In his twin study, Stunkard's group[27] demonstrated a much higher correlation of BMI in monozygotic than in dizygotic twins. In fact, the implications of these data are that as much as 80% of the variance in body mass index can be accounted for in some way from the genetic makeup. This is a remarkable figure, and as he points out, contrasts with data from twin studies in conditions assumed previously to be more strictly tied to heredity such as hypertension (57%) and epilepsy (50%).

The epidemiological question for the study of human obesity is how to put these observations together — that is, the clear evidence of environmental and sociocultural influences on obesity with the equally clear evidence of a genetic contribution. Once again the nature–nurture issue seems to beset us. However, as in every behavior-based disorder (and obesity at its root depends on the behavior of food consumption), the ultimate and crucial issue to comprehend is not the genes alone, nor the environment alone, but the interaction of the two factors. "The action is in the interaction" says Stunkard, and he bases the thought directly on understanding the heritability concept derived from monozygotic and dizygotic twin comparisons. The twin method, intended to discriminate the environmental factors that dizygotic and monozygotic twins may share from the genetic factors that render monozygotic twins identical and dizygotic twins distinct, places all the interactions of genes and environment into the genetic compartment and thus underestimates the environmental contributions.

With behavior-driven disorders such as obesity, it is very likely that not only are there genetic controls on the basic metabolism but also that there is a genetic control on the respnose of individuals to a given environment. This may influence the individual's sensitivity to calories within the environment, may provoke an avoidance of calorie-expending activities such as exercise, and lead to preference for such sedentary behaviors as reading, writing, or television viewing when these are available.

Much of the excitement in obesity research today is in the search for major genes that can interact in this way with the environment. The neatest example is the intriguing genetic differences in sweetness apprehension.[28] People differ in their "sweet worlds"; some live in a "vivid and bright" sweet world because their capacity to perceive and appreciate sweetness is genetically high. Others live in a "pastel" sweet world (I thank Linda Bartoshuk for these metaphors). The potential outcome on body weight from reinforcements for sweet food intake and the powerful interaction of persons with environments that differ in their provision of refined sugar are obvious. It is the capacity for genetic analysis right down to the molecular level that has recently come to light. As well, though, the ultimate explanations for obesity in given individuals and within populations will be found in the interactions of genetic constitution with reinforcing environment such as we have today. These illuminations are the outcome of epidemiologically based studies that focus on behavior and its disorder.

Anorexia Nervosa

If obesity research is emerging into the daylight, the study of anorexia nervosa (AN) remains in the shadow. On first blush, this seems suprising given that obesity seems a "constitutional" issue defined simply by a deviation above the population mean for body weight, whereas anorexia nervosa seems to have a more categorical nature with symptomatic "criteria" like a disease (Table 1). One might expect that a search for proximate causes and mechanisms would be more successful in AN. And yet, there remains, despite a large degree of definitional specificity, not only great ignorance about the fundamental cause of this condition, but real doubts as to whether there are distinctly separate entities of weight control distinguished by food-restricting behavior alone (restrictive AN) that contrasts with a behavior of periods of binging on food followed by purging and vomiting (bulimia nervosa, BN). It is even uncertain whether the food-restricting, perception-altered, emaciated anorexic patient is to be seen as a person deviating to an extreme in food consciousness and body weight but still represented within the normal range of behavior in our society, or whether she represents a clear aberration from normal as the syndromic definition implies.[29] There are champions for all these points of view and this, perhaps more than any other piece of evidence, identifies our ignorance about the fundamentals of the condition.

Whatever is implied about cause in AN, it differs in its onset from obesity, where the increased body weight emerges gradually over the course of development due to some insensible imbalance between food intake and energy consumption. In AN (and BN) the patient is conscious of a struggle to achieve a reduction in her body weight. This struggle is represented by her active efforts to avoid or eliminate caloric intake. It is this behavioral dominance that is the essence of the condition. This behavior and its provocative concerns can often be given a clear onset in time and even an initiating stimulus. The search for an explanation of this behavior, a stubborn rejection of nourishment based on a resolve to be very thin has so far been fruitless. We need such an explanation in order to appreciate the cause, explain the course and its variants, and propose its rational rather than symptomatic treatment and prevention.

TABLE 1. Russell Criteria for Anorexia Nervosa and Bulimia Nervosa

Anorexia Nervosa

1. Self-induced loss of weight (resulting mainly from the studied avoidance of foods considered by the patient to be fattening).
2. A characteristic psychopathology consisting of an overvalued idea that fatness is a dreadful state.
3. A specific endocrine disorder that in the postpubertal girl causes the cessation of menstruation or a delay of events of puberty in the prepubertal or early pubertal female.

Bulimia Nervosa

1. A powerful and intractible urge to overeat resulting in episodes of overeating.
2. Avoidance of "fattening" effects of food by inducing vomiting or abusing purgatives or both.
3. A morbid fear of becoming fat.

Thus, for example, the last decades have seen a great deal of physiological, metabolic, and endocrine research in AN, attempting to identify bodily derangements that might represent the causal elements of the behavior. These studies, often to be construed as attempts to reveal a hypothalamic disorder at the root of anorexia nervosa and thus in essence to identify it as another "spanner" condition, include studies of gonadotrophin secretion behind the suppression of menses, body temperature response failure, gastrointestinal slowing and changes in ovarian anatomy. Every positive observation has proven on follow-up after treatment to be a symptom of the food restriction and starved state and thus a result rather than a cause of the behavior. All anomalies disappear with the return of normal food intake and the restoration of body weight. The suspicion that AN represents a form of the lateral hypothalamic syndrome proves on careful examination to be unlikely.[30]

Anorexia nervosa has so far provided a model of chronic starvation and its consequences. Many of the signs and symptoms of chronic starvation are important to identify when a course of treatment and explanations for distressing features of the disorder are to be offered to the patient. These include the role of reduced gastric emptying in provoking the early sense of fullness and even nausea during refeeding in AN,[31] and the information that there is a need for extra body weight on recovery to restore normal menses and complete reproductive capacity.[32] Other discoveries such as the sonographic identification of ovarian atrophy[33] and its restoration with refeeding have permitted a definition of recovery. But if the aim of research is the discovery of cause, these biological studies have revealed only symptoms and consequences of the behavior of food restriction, avoidance, and weight reduction, and nothing of their generation. What can lie behind this resolve — this drive to be thin — this insistent rejection of nourishment and its natural effects on the body? One turns to seek ultimate factors in frustration from the failures to find proximate ones.

For this reason an epidemiologic approach, with its capacity to identify risk factors, is again the most promising we have. The sense that risk factors derive from the genetic constitution and also from the culture and life experience, and that these interact to produce the disorder is the unifying theme. This has been the approach that at least appears to direct us toward success. The time–place–person triad of epidemiology can be recommended. From this viewpoint, what are the crucial epidemiological rather than syndromic facts about AN? These can be briefly summarized.

Anorexia nervosa is a behavioral disorder that primarily affects (1) youthful females of the (2) upper classes in (3) developed nations in the (4) contemporary era. This is the major set of features. Among the minor features, AN varies in its severity among individuals, and its pattern distinctions (food-restrictive behavior emphasized as against bulimic and purging behaviors) correlate with personality variables in the young women. Family constellations give evidence of a genetic tendency that interacts with environmental features. And finally there is evidence that the struggle for thinness that represents the prime acknowledged aim of the sufferers represents an overvalued idea that emerges from a sense that bodily appearance is crucial for social acceptance, adult roles, and evidence of self-control.

From among these observations it is the major ones that deserve most attention and whose limits are to be appreciated. First, there is the female sex of the afflicted. This is not an absolute exclusion (females outnumber males 10 to 1) but is certainly strong enough to make us devote attention to females primarily and to see the male examples as anomalous and offering perhaps some opportunity to identify a feature that might point up an element provoking or sustaining the behavior that could be shared by the female group. The high incidence of homosexuality among the males[34] with AN might suggest, for example, an extra strength for concerns about sexuality in the provocation of the overvalued ideas at the symptomatic heart of AN.

That it is youthful females — primarily those emerging from puberty — rather than an even distribution of the disease across all ages promotes a focus of attention on the events of puberty and its aftermath in women, not on all of the other psychosocial factors that distinguish the lives of women from men across the life-span. These events of puberty include the biological ones of the establishment of a cyclical program of hormone release as well as an appearance of bodily contour important for the capability and sustenance of procreation. The social impact of these bodily changes is on young women, and this social impact is complicated because it can be both an influence that modifies affective attitudes and one that draws attention from the culture.

Evidence for a constitutional vulnerability beyond female sex has emerged only as suggestions. A genetic contribution to anorexia nervosa is secure; it rests on an increased concordance in monozygotic as compared to dyzygotic twins, and a higher rate among sisters.[35] It is possible that the genetic contribution functions through the personality characteristics.[29] As discussed below, the restricting anorexic tends to a personality of introversion and self reflection that can enhance the influence of sociocultural pressure. There may be more serious obsessional characteristics as well. A major problem for giving personality features a sustaining role for this behavior is the capacity of the food restriction behavior and starvation to alter the sense of self and enhance an introverted, obsessional stance. As with the other features of AN, symptoms and potential causes are difficult to disentangle and may in fact, as in these features of personality, become amplifying, positive feedback features.

Finally, the epidemiological approach has established several other points that may illuminate AN. The condition is increasing in its incidence. The evidence for a sharp rise includes the observations of Theander who noted a fivefold increase in Malmö, Sweden between the 1930s and 1950s,[36] a doubling of incidence in Monroe County in New York State,[37] and a rise in annual incidence from 1.6 to 4.1 per 100,000 population in northeast Scotland between the late 1960s and the early 1980s.[38]

Along with this increased incidence, there is also evidence for a spread of the disorder outside its prime targets. Females both younger and older than the original 14–25 year-old range are now plentiful. The appearance of AN in prepubescent girls can be particularly damaging to growth and development. Older women are often examples of relapses, but all specialists in AN can now report the initial appearance of the disorder in an occasional case over age 30. There is clear evidence that AN is spreading beyond the confines of the upper classes of developed nations and is appearing now among American blacks from impoverished backgrounds and among the upper class of Third World nations.[39] There is even a suggestion that there is an increased appearance of AN in males. Certainly most specialty services now regularly have at least one male patient in the hospital — at any time — a rare phenomenon a decade ago.

All of these results tend to support a view of this disorder as, in part, the outcome of contemporary sociocultural pressures on vulnerable people, with more and more persons succumbing to the disorder as the pressure persists, and, perhaps, as examples of the disorder get described and mimicked. The sociocultural pressure most often mentioned is the increasing ideal of thinness as a bodily shape for women. This certainly matches the clinical symptoms and would perhaps be the best explanation for the increased incidence of the disorder among occupations where thinness is stressed, as in ballet performers and models. However, essentially coincidental with the pressure for thinness has been an increasing sexualization of adolescence in the last several decades in which a preoccupation with the body's appearance may be but one expression. It is not farfetched to assume that some of the features of AN come out of the nexus of choice and demand imposed primarily on developing females by the broadly construed sexual engrossments emerging in a cultural era where freedom from other burdens has been achieved. AN may be a way of reacting to and defending against these demands and preoccupations, a female ascetic response.

The appearance of the new disorder, bulimia nervosa (BN),[40] in which the weight loss is less and the behavior is disturbed by gorging and purging rather than restricting suggests that both AN and BN are pathoplastic responses to a similar cultural pressure on young women. The personal characteristics of the bulimic person are more those of extroversion with histronic features, impulsivity is higher than in the temperament of the anorexic person which is characterized by introversion, obsessionality, and controlling tendencies. A possible way of putting these features together with the sociocultural suggestions is that a pressure for sexuality and for appearance could be felt in the introvert as a threat to control of the future and this pressure could be met by a stance of restriction sustained by self-control. The same pressure felt by the extrovert could be responded to intermittently and impulsively and with a greater sensitivity to signals, both external and internal, that are events of the moment. The sustaining of hunger over time may be more difficult for extroverts than introverts and provoke them to give way to binging when hunger is great or when food is suddenly available.

These suggestions emerge out of an epidemiologic approach to AN. This approach functions to identify high-risk populations and to generate a search for greater specificity in the provocative issues. Epidemiology, however, has an extra problem with disorders of behavior; distinctions between what may initially cause or provoke disorder and what may be sustaining it over time may be obscure. This is particularly so with issues such as food restriction and thinning, where subjective sensations and objective bodily changes are prominent with progress; that which began the behavior may disappear within what maintains it.

What sustains a behavior is likely to be more salient and accessible in the clinic, more critical for treatment, and the source of chronicity if overlooked. Yet an understanding of the initiating factors is very likely more critical for prevention and control of spread of the behavior among the vulnerable. A complete comprehension of the disorder AN and its relative BN awaits the placing of all these factors into an interactive network of provocative and sustaining factors that may explain variations among young women today. It is not difficult, however, to imagine that with such an achievement will come not only methods of treatment and prevention but also a clearer understanding of the particular challenges that young women must grapple with as they emerge into adulthood and how this contemporary era burdens them in the process.

In summary, variations in human food intake and the consequences for body weight, obesity, and anorexia do not derive obviously from disease and the injury to normal bodily mechanisms, but rather from more ultimate factors such as human genetic variation, reinforcing life events, and the role of meaning tied to culturally based values that shape the expression of most behaviors in our species. Although we might all agree that eventually all these influences must pass through the proximate mechanisms discerned in the laboratory, it is also clear that an understanding of the anomalies of feeding behavior in mankind emerging from more ultimate mechanisms are not so easily translated into animal laboratory studies because they are tied to issues of mankind as a species with characteristic features, strengths, and vulnerabilities. They are best illuminated by methods derived from epidemiology — writ large to include genetics.

CONCLUSION

Our major aim in this presentation was not to give an encyclopedic account of the human disorders of feeding and weight control. Rather we wished to emphasize the natural separation among these disorders seen in the clinic, and the different contemporary logics that can be applied to their further study. The sense that there are two major lines of investigation, on the one hand biochemical and physiologic, and on the other hand epidemiologic, based on the genetic, intrapersonal, and sociocultural, that can be distinguished by such terms as the identification of proximate and ultimate factors is clear. We believe that a greater contact is emerging between these two lines of research but they remain, by their nature, relatively separate and distinct. They evoke different questions and must be approached by quite different methods. It is the concept of motivated behaviors — directed toward goals tied to the vital needs of the organism, imbedded in psychoneural systems that function to organize activity and the commerce with surrounds, subject to pathological change from within the organism and to deviant influences from without — that holds this work together.

REFERENCES

1. FRÖHLICH, A. 1901. Ein Fall von Tumor der Hypophysis Cerebri ohne Akromegalie. Wien Klin. Rundschau. **15**: 883–886; 906–908.
2. BRUCH, H. 1939. Progress in pediatrics. The Fröhlich syndrome. Am. J. Dis. Child. **58**: 1282–89.
3. FULTON, J. F. 1939. Introduction: Historical resume. *In* The Hypothalamus and Central Levels of Autonomic Function. Research Publications, Association for Research in Nervous and Mental Disease. **20**: xiii-xxx, Williams and Wilkins, Baltimore.
4. ERDHEIM, J. 1904. Ueber Hypopysenganggeschwulste und Hirncholestratome. Sitzungsb. d. Akad. d. Wissensch. Math.-Naturw. Kl. **113**: 537–726.
5. HETHERINGTON, A. W. & S. W. RANDON. 1940. Hypothalamic lesions and adiposity in the rat. Anat. Rec. **78**: 149–172.
6. BROBECK, J. R., J. TEPPERMAN, & C. N. H. LONG. 1943. Experimental hypothalamic hyperphagia in the albino rat. Yale J. Biol. Med. **15**: 831–853.
7. HOLROYDE, C. P. & G. A. REICHARD. 1986. General metabolic abnormalities in cancer patients. Anorexia and cachexia. Surg. Clinics N. Am. **66**: 947–956.
8. NORTON, J. A., J. F. MOLEY, M. V. GREEN, R. E. CARSON, & S. D. MORRISON. 1985. Parabiotic transfer of cancer anorexia/cachexia in male rats. Cancer Res. **45**: 5547–5552.
9. BERNSTEIN, I. L., C. M. TRENEER & J. N. KOTT. 1985. Area postrema mediates tumor effects on food intake, body weight, and learned aversions. Am. J. Physiol. **249**: R296–R300.
10. ROUZER, C. A. & A. CERAMI. 1980. Hypertriglyceridemia associated with trypanosoma brucei brucei infection in rabbits. Mol. Biochem. Parasitol. **2**: 31–38.
11. CERAMI, A., Y. IKEDA, N. LE TRANG, P. J. HOTEZ & B. BEUTLER. 1985. Weight loss associated with an endotoxin-induced mediator from peritoneal macrophaces: the role of cachectin (tumor necrosis factor). Immun. Lett. **11**: 173–177.
12. TRACEY, K. J., S. F. LOWRY & A. CERAMI. 1987. Physiological-responses to cachetin. *In* Ciba Foundation Symposium, No. 131. 88–108. Wiley. New York.
13. FONG, Y., L. L. MOLDAWER, M. MARANO, H. WEI, A. BARBER, K. MANOGUE, K. J. TRACEY, G. KUO, D. A. FISCHMAN, A. CERAMI & S. F. LOWRY. 1989. Cachectin/TNF or IL-la induces cachexia with redistribution of body proteins. Am. J. Physiol. **256**: R659–R665.
14. CARSWELL, E. A., L. J. OLD, R. L. KASSEL, S. GREEN, N. FIORE & B. WILLIAMSON. 1975. An endotoxin-induced serum factor that causes necrosis of tumors. Proc. Natl. Acad. Sci. USA **72**: 3666–3670.
15. COLEY, W. B. 1893. The treatment of malignant tumors by repeated inoculations of erysipelas: With a report of ten original cases. Am. J. Med. Sci. **105**: 487–511.
16. COLEY, W. B. 1906. Late results of the treatment of inoperable sarcoma by the mixed toxins of erysipelas and *Bacillus prodigiosus*. Am. J. Med. Sci. **131**: 375–430.
17. BEUTLER, B., D. GREENWALD, J. D. HULMES, M. CHANG, Y.-C.E. PAN, J. MATHISON, R. ULEVITCH & A. CERAMI. 1985. Identity of tumour necrosis factor and the macrophage-secreted factor cachectin. Nature **316**: 552–554.
18. BEUTLER, B. & A. CERAMI. 1986. Cachectin and tumour necrosis factor as two sides of the same biological coin. Nature **320**: 584–588.
19. BEUTLER, B. & A. CERAMI. 1987. Cachectin: More than a tumor necrosis factor. N. Engl. J. Med. **316**: 379–385.

20. OLIFF, A. 1988. The role of tumor necrosis factor (cachectin) in cachexia. Cell **54**: 141–142.
21. SROLE, L., T. S. LANGNER & S. T. MICHAEL. 1962. Mental Health in the Metropolis: The Midtown Manhattan Study. McGraw-Hill. New York.
22. NEEL, J. V. 1962. Diabetes mellitus: A "thrifty" genotype rendered detrimental by "progress"? Am. J. Hum. Gen. **14**: 353–362.
23. LEIBEL, R. L. & J. HIRSCH. 1984. Diminished energy requirement in reduced-obese patients. Metabolism **33**:164–170.
24. RAVUSSIN, E., S. LILLIOJA, W. C. KNOWLER, L. CHRISTIN, D. FREYMOND, W. G. H. ABBOTT, V. BOYCE, B. V. HOWARD & C. BOGARDUS. 1988. Reduced rate of energy expenditure as a risk factor for body weight gain. N. Engl. J. Med. **318**: 467–472.
25. ROBERTS, S. B., J. SAVAGE, W. A. COWARD, B. CHEW & A. LUCAS. 1988. Energy expenditure and intake in infants born to lean and overweight mothers. N. Engl. J. Med. **318**: 461–466.
26. STUNKARD, A. J., T. I. A. SORENSON, C. HANIS, T. W. TEASDALE, R. CHAKRABORTY, W. J. SCHULL & F. SCHULSINGER 1986. An adoption study of human obesity. N. Engl. J. Med. **314**: 193–198.
27. STUNKARD, A. J., T. T. FOCH & Z. HRUBEC. 1986. A twin study of human obesity. J. Am. Med. Assoc. **256**: 51–54.
28. BARTOSHUK, L. M. 1979. Bitter taste of saccharin related to the genetic ability to taste the bitter substance 6-*n*-propylthiouracil. Science **205**: 934–935.
29. GARNER, D. M., M. P. OLMSTED & P. E. GARFINKEL. 1983. Does anorexia nervosa occur on a continuum? Int. J. Eating Disord. **2**: 11–20.
30. STRICKER, E. M. & A. E. ANDERSEN. 1980. The lateral hypothalamic syndrome: Comparison with the syndrome of anorexia nervosa. Life Sci. **26**: 1927–1934.
31. ROBINSON, P. H., P. R. MCHUGH, T. H. MORAN, J. D. STEPHENSON. 1988. Gastric control of food intake. Psychosom. Res. **32**: 593–600.
32. FRISCH, R. E. 1985. Fatness, menarche and female fertility. Perspect. Biol. Med. **28**: 611–633.
33. TREASURE, J. L., P. A. GORDON, E. A. KING, M. WHEELER & G. F. RUSSELL. 1984. Cystic ovaries: A phase of anorexia nervosa. Lancet **2**: 1379–1382.
34. HERZOG, D. B., D. K. NORMAN, C. GORDON & M. PEPOSE. Sexual conflict and males. Am. J. Psychiatry. **141**: 989–990.
35. STROBER, M., W. MORRELL, J. BURROUGHS, B. SALKIN & C. JACOBS. 1985. A controlled family study of anorexia nervosa. J. Psychiatr. Res. **19**: 239–246.
36. THEANDER, S. 1970. Anorexia nervosa: A psychiatric investigation of 94 female patients. Acta Psychiatr. Scand. Suppl. **214**: 1–194.
37. JONES, D. J., M. M. FOX, H. M. BABIGAN & H. E. HUTTON. 1980. Epidemiology of anorexia nervosa in Monroe County. Psychosom. Med. **42**: 551–558.
38. SZMUKLER, G. I. 1985. The epidemiology of anorexia nervosa and bulimia. J. Psychiatr. Res. **19**: 143–153.
39. BUHRICH, N. 1981. Frequency of anorexia nervosa in Malaysia. Aust. N. Z. J. Psychiatry **15**: 153–155.
40. RUSSELL, G. F. M. 1979. Bulimia nervosa: An ominous variant of anorexia nervosa. Psychol. Med. **9**: 429–448.

DISCUSSION

DR. P. R. MCHUGH (*Johns Hopkins University School of Medicine, Baltimore, MD*): I hope there are going to be plenty of people in the audience who will fill in the gaps of what was intended only to be a very minor charcoal sketch of contemporary research enterprises between investigators in the clinic and in the laboratory.

DR. J. MORLEY (*Sepulveda VA Medical Center, Sepulveda, CA*): You took Dr. Russell's viewpoint that anorexia nervosa is fundamentally a disease of prepubertal girls.

I suggest that perhaps it's also a disease of the end of life and that we haven't really looked at this situation. If you don't look for something, particularly if you define anorexia nervosa as a disease predominantly of the prepubertal period, we will miss a lot of anorexia nervosa that occurs fairly frequently in both older men and women. Do you have any comments or thoughts about that?

DR. McHUGH: First of all I think it's not a prepubertal condition but a condition of youth. I believe that we're going to have to understand more about the psychological states of individuals who are elderly, and we need to appreciate what is behind their reductions in food intake and weight loss. I await your demonstration that they hold what is for me the crucial aspect of the Russell definition of anorexia nervosa, namely, overvaluing thinness. If you can demonstrate that this also exists among an equal number of males and females in the geriatric population, it will be an intriguing observation, certainly illuminating for me.

DR. J. E. BLUNDELL (*University of Leeds, Leeds County, U.K.*): Paul, you mentioned towards the end of your talk that the preoccupation of thinness among young girls may be a defense against increasing sexualization. I wonder, therefore, if you would predict that the prevalance of AIDS and the increased fearfulness about sexual activity is going to increase the intensity of this feeling.

DR. McHUGH: Yes, John. I'm just proposing what plenty of psychiatrists have proposed, that striving for thinness is not occurring in a vacuum. It's occurring for these young women in a state of contemporary culture that has made sexuality threatening for many of them. Perception of the threatening aspects of sexuality provides a distinction, for example, between the personalities of anorectic individuals, who are restrictors, from bulimics. The obsessional and introverted tendencies of the anorexic restrictor are going to make the AIDS issues even more of a burden for them and may increase their concerns about sexuality. I agree with you.

The Modern History of Anorexia Nervosa

An Interpretation of Why the Illness Has Changed

GERALD F. M. RUSSELL AND JANET TREASURE

Department of Psychiatry
Institute of Psychiatry
De Crespigny Park, Denmark Hill
London, SE5 8AF, England

This article is concerned with the historical development of anorexia nervosa, the lessons taught by historical studies, and the recent advances in knowledge that should facilitate a multidimensional formulation of this illness. The aims are fourfold:

1. To examine the changes undergone by anorexia nervosa during recent decades;
2. To set these changes within the broader historical context of the fasting behavior in women since the 14th century;
3. To assess the role of sociocultural factors in causing anorexia nervosa, shaping the clinical form of the illness, or influencing the content of the patient's psychological concerns;
4. To attempt to integrate sociocultural influences with disturbed biological mechanisms so as to facilitate a multidimensional view of anorexia nervosa.

THE RECENT HISTORY OF ANOREXIA NERVOSA

The view has already been put forward that anorexia nervosa has changed over recent decades.[1] The evidence will be reviewed under three headings (1) the increased incidence of the illness; (2) alterations in its psychopathology; and (3) changes in its form, especially the emergence of bulimia nervosa.

The Increased Incidence of Anorexia Nervosa

Sten Theander[2] was the first investigator to record a rise in the incidence of anorexia nervosa in Malmö, Sweden, between the 1930s and 1950s. Since then, several investigators, in different countries and over different periods, have confirmed this rise in the United Kingdom and the United States,[3,4] in Switzerland,[5] and in Scotland.[6] There is, however, one discrepant finding, that of Lucas and his colleagues,[7] who did not find that anorexia nervosa had increased since the 1940s. They scrutinized the medical records of patients from Rochester, Minnesota, who had been referred to the Mayo Clinic during a 45-year period (1935–79). A possible explanation for this discrepancy is that the Mayo Clinic study was based on general medical as opposed to psychiatric records. In other studies the increased incidence of anorexia nervosa is most evident or only detectable among the patients referred to the psychiatric services.[5,6]

Although Williams and King[8] have also advised caution in interpreting increased admission data, the weight of the evidence favors a rise in the incidence of anorexia nervosa over recent decades.

The Changed Psychopathology of Anorexia Nervosa

The second argument for deducing that anorexia nervosa has undergone transformation during recent years is that the principal psychological disturbance found in these patients has radically changed. It may be said that the "psychopathology" of the illness has altered, but we should note that this term is ambiguous because writers may apply it whether they are referring to the content and nature of the patient's preoccupations (the *form* of the psychological disorder) or to the psychological *causes* of the illness (i.e., its psychogenesis).

If we wish to compare the psychopathology of anorexia nervosa between current and historical times, we should adopt a point of reference. It is probably best to choose the early 1870s, to correspond with the original descriptions by William Gull[9] and Charles Lasègue.[10] Gull used the diagnostic approach of a good general physician: He stressed the association of the emaciation with amenorrhea and excluded known causes of wasting. His approach to the psychiatric assessment was rather simple:

> The want of appetite is, I believe, due to a morbid mental state. That mental states may destroy appetite is notorious, and it will be admitted that young women at the ages named are specially obnoxious to mental perversity.

He was reluctant to be more precise about the form of psychological disorder:

> We might call the state hysterical without committing ourselves to the etymological values of the word, or maintaining that the subjects of it have the more common symptoms of hysteria. I prefer, however, the more general term "nervosa" . . .

Charles Lasègue, while echoing the same view of "perversion mentale," believed the disorder was hysterical in form:

> Après plusieurs mois . . . c'est a ce moment que va se dessiner la perversion mentale, qui à elle seule est presque caractéristique et qui justifie le nom que j'ai proposé faute de mieux, d'anorexie hystérique.

As evidence of the hysterical nature of the illness, he adduced the patient's resistance to eating, her denial of needing more food, an abnormal acceptance of her condition, and (mistakenly) the lack of any fatal outcome.

Until the mid-1960s the recurring theme in the literature was that anorexia nervosa represented a defence against sexuality. For example, in 1940 Waller, Kaufman, and Deutsch[11] viewed the illness psychodynamically as a defence against unconscious fantasies of oral insemination. In 1961 Joachim Meyer[12] indicated that most patients consciously rejected sexuality: The young patient was expressing a reluctance to grow up, to develop into a sexually mature woman, a theme refined and elaborated later by Crisp.[13]

No mention was made of a "disturbance of body image" until 1962 when Hilde Bruch[14] applied this expression to a general "perceptual and conceptual disturbance in these patients." By 1970, the patients seen in clinical practice directly expressed an exaggerated fear of becoming fat. It was therefore an obvious step to look upon "a morbid dread of fatness" as characteristic of the psychopathology of anorexia nervosa, and include it as one of the necessary diagnostic criteria of the illness.[15-17]

These observations were very simple and direct. It is curious that they were only made during the past 15 to 20 years, and it is unlikely that previous generations of able clinicians would have missed these plainly obvious features of the patients' psychopathology. It is more likely that anorexia nervosa has itself changed over the course of years.

Changes in the Form of Anorexia Nervosa — Bulimia Nervosa

The most powerful evidence that anorexia nervosa has undergone a major transformation is the appearance of bulimia nervosa in recent years. The most dramatic feature of this disorder is the way the patient induces vomiting or abuses purgatives, so as to avoid weight gain from episodic overeating. It is unlikely that in earlier times bulimic patients were missed or diagnosed as examples of anorexia nervosa. Earlier reviews of anorexia nervosa had little to say about vomiting or purging.[12,18] It was only in the 1970s that patients who induced vomiting or diarrhea were gradually recognized as increasing clinical problems.[19] Hilde Bruch[20] in 1974 described as "thin fat people" the patients who regurgitated food after eating large meals. Stunkard[21] in 1959 had coined the phrase "the binge-eating syndrome" as applicable to a small group of obese patients who behaved similarly. In 1979, the term "bulimia nervosa" was introduced to characterize patients who experienced episodes of overeating and used devices such as induced vomiting so as to mitigate the fattening effects of food, in keeping with a morbid dread of fatness that was identical with that present in anorexia nervosa.[22]

Bulimia nervosa is now so well recognized that some investigators have argued that it may be clearly distinguished from anorexia nervosa.[23] There are indeed clinical differences and their distinction is often important as a guide to treatment. The most striking difference is with regard to body weight, the anorexic patient showing emaciation, the bulimic patient often having an unremarkable "normal" weight. Amenorrhea is a diagnostic necessity for anorexia nervosa but not for bulimia nervosa. These differences should not obscure the fact that there are important similarities between the two conditions — especially the patients' dread of weight gain.[23] The close relationship between the two disorders is important for the main thesis of this presentation. Historically, bulimia nervosa has "evolved" from anorexia nervosa. In clinical practice it may be hard to distinguish sharply between the two disorders. An individual patient's behavior may best be diagnosed as anorexia nervosa, only to change to that of bulimia nervosa within several months or a few years. It is best to concede that the two disorders overlap.[24]

THE BROADER HISTORICAL CONTEXT OF FASTING BEHAVIOR

The preceding section has been confined to the modern history of anorexia nervosa. It is also appropriate to examine a broader span of history for putative cases of this illness occurring during earlier times.

The Saints

Rudolph Bell[25] has proposed that several saints and pious women from the 13th century onward were cases of "holy anorexia." The first type of "holy anorexia" is exemplified by St. Catherine of Siena whose starvation and other austerities led to her death. Rampling[26] had also concluded that St. Catherine's life of asceticism leading to spiritual fulfillment could be identified as characteristic of severe anorexia nervosa. She had an abhorrence of being looked at by men. The most remarkable feature of her ascetism was her abnormal eating behavior. She regarded her inability to eat as punishment for her sins and a method of expiation. The latter was served by her vomiting, which she achieved by means of a fine straw of some such thing being pushed far down her throat. Catherine had made a vow of virginity when still a child, and she knew that to achieve this it would be helpful to practice abstinence from food and drink. Her body became emaciated, and yet she would frequently, and "like a flash," seize the opportunity to work for the honor of God's name or for the good of souls. Finally starvation induced a state of psychological vigilance conducive to mystical experience. She died at the age of 33.

Bell provides another example in St. Mary Magdalen de' Pazzi (1566–1607). She sensed that God commanded her to subsist on a depleted diet of bread and water. She was tormented by cravings for food; and other nuns reported seeing her (or a devil impersonating her) gobbling food down in secret. Bell concludes that this is the repetitive binge-eating–vomiting pattern typical of "acute anorexic behavior." Bell's thesis is that these pious women exhibited an anorexic behavior pattern in response to the patriarchal social structures in which they were trapped. This thesis has been questioned by Brumberg.[27]

Early Medical Descriptions

To Richard Morton (1689)[28,29] has been attributed the first description of anorexia nervosa by a physician who recognized that the condition was caused by "Sadness and Anxious Cares"; he named it "a Nervous Consumption."[30]

Mr Duke's daughter in St Mary Axe, in the year 1684, and the Eighteenth year of her Age . . . fell into a total suppression of her monthly courses from a multitude of Cares and Passions of her Mind, but without any Symptom of the Green-Sickness following upon it. From which time her Appetite began to abate. . . .

She wholly neglected the care of herself for two full years. . . . I do not remember that I did ever in all my Practice see one, that was conversant with the Living so much wasted with the greatest degree of a Consumption, (like a skeleton only clad with skin). . . ."

Silverman's[20] promotion of Richard Morton as the limner of anorexia nervosa is compelling.

The "Fasting Girls" (16th–19th Centuries)

These were young women (or children) who practiced prolonged abstinence from food, but in whose case there was uncertainty about the causes of the fast. The intentions of the faster often included a wish to attract public attention and sometimes financial gain. They, or their relatives, sometimes claimed that they could subsist for months or years without food—the "miraculous maids" or "Anorexia Mirabilis" (a term also applied to the spiritual fasts of the saints). They were suspected of deception (or hysteria at least) by medical observers.

One such fasting girl was Martha Taylor (1668), described by Silverman[31] as a 19-

year-old girl from Over-Haddon near Bakewell (Derbyshire) who "hath very small left on her but skin and bone" and whose menstruation had previously ceased. She preceded Richard Morton's description of a case of "nervous consumption" by some 20 years. Sarah Jacobs, the Welsh fasting girl, began her fast in October 1867 as a premenstrual 12-year-old. She died during a medical "watch" during which a team of nurses from Guy's Hospital ensured she ate and drank nothing. An autopsy revealed she was not emaciated. Thus she did not die from starvation (or anorexia nervosa) but from water deprivation and renal failure.[32] A notorious case was Mollie Fancher (1848–1916), the "Brooklyn Enigma." She earned the title of "America's most famous invalid" when from the age of 17 she assumed the invalid role and claimed powers of clairvoyance. Later she underwent intermittent fasts and was said to be so thin that her backbone could be felt through the abdomen. She was denounced by medical men as fraudulent or hysterical.[27]

Although they underwent phases of severe illness, the evidence is insufficient to consider these fasting girls as forerunners of anorexia nervosa.

The Promotion of Thinness in Women during the 1920s

If fashionable thinness in the 1960s played a part in the recent increased frequency of anorexia nervosa, was there a similar phenomenon in the 1920s in the wake of the "flapper fashion"? Silverstein et al.[33] found that models shown in women's fashion magazines from 1909 to 1925 had noncurvaceous figures (measured from bust-to-waist ratios). They quote from one contemporary source. "The figures of our flappers . . . shall be slender and slinky and lath-like and the line of grace no longer the curve but the prolonged parallelogram."

They concede that it is not possible to quantify the extent of eating disorders over these years. Nevertheless they suggest that the 1909–1925 noncurvaceous trend in fashion was associated with a fall in weight among college students, and they count increased literary references to self-starvation in schoolgirls, college girls, and office workers.

HISTORICAL INFLUENCES RESPONSIBLE FOR CHANGES IN ANOREXIA NERVOSA

We have already argued that anorexia nervosa has undergone significant changes during recent decades. Nevertheless we need to ascertain, as far as possible, how much latitude to allow before deciding whether two psychiatric disorders, separated by historical time, are fundamentally the same clinical entities. This is why it has been necessary to adopt a point of reference, and we have chosen the clinical descriptions by William Gull and Charles Lasègue. We thus take issue with Brumberg[27] who focuses primarily on the sociocultural nexus that encourages self-starvation, rather than the clinical syndrome itself. She goes too far in the direction of diagnostic latitude when she writes: "We should expect to see anorexia nervosa 'present' differently, in terms of both predisposing psychological factors and actual physical symptoms." [p. 5]

A specific example of excessive diagnostic latitude is the contention by Loudon,[34] in part supported by Parry-Jones,[35] that chlorosis and anorexia nervosa had been two closely related conditions, each representing a psychological reaction to the turbulence of adolescence. Loudon suggested that the disappearance of chlorosis during the early years of the 20th century coincided with the emergence of anorexia nervosa. Neither Richard Morton nor Lasègue had any difficulty in excluding the "green sickness" as the cause of wasting in their patients. Chlorosis was due to iron-deficiency anemia, occurring mainly among poorer working girls who generally remained well nourished.[36] Neither the clinical picture nor the patient's social background justifies any association between the two disorders.

Having set certain limits to diagnostic latitude, we should not be reluctant to consider that mental illnesses may undergo major changes over the course of years, except to wonder at their rapidity in the case of anorexia nervosa. Hare[37] has written about the "evolution" of mental illness over the course of time, and has drawn an analogy with Darwinian evolution, though the differences in rate should warn us against pushing this analogy too far.

> Diseases change much more quickly than species do. And perhaps psychiatric diseases change much more quickly than others because their expression is largely psychological and follows changing fashions.

Neurotic disorders are even more likely to undergo transformation. Karl Jaspers[38] writes:

> ... from (a history of illness) we can learn how the picture of illness shifts though scientifically the illness may be identical; the neuroses in particular have a contemporary style — they flourish in certain situations and are almost invisible in others.

> The older medical literature shows that individual symptoms were known under different names in those times as well. The general impression nowadays regarding neurosis is as follows: hysterias have greatly decreased. . . . the compulsive neuroses on the other hand have greatly increased.

These statements require clarification. Jaspers hints that history may merely lead to changes in the terminology applied to neurotic illnesses. On the other hand he also refers to changes in the form of the neuroses (hysterias, compulsive neuroses). Moreover the clinical picture may shift, but *scientifically* the illness remains identical. These ideas are imprecise, as is Hare's attribution of clinical changes to changing fashions.

Investigators who documented the evidence for an increased incidence of anorexia nervosa during the 1960s explained this change in terms of culturally determined attitudes or behavior patterns causing the illness.[3] Brumberg[27] has written an impressive analysis of the historical influences since the 13th century. Her touchstone is that "from a historical perspective . . . certain social and cultural systems, at different points in time, encourage or promote control of appetite in women, but for different reasons and purposes."

We agree that the symptoms of anorexia nervosa have changed in response to different social and cultural influences. But diagnostic similarities should remain discernible, as in the transition from anorexia to bulimia nervosa; thus a careful balance should be maintained. It is appropriate to examine the reasons why women should elect to fast at different periods of history, but it is also right to retain a measure of clinical diagnostic cohesion.

SOCIOCULTURAL FORCES AND DISTURBED BIOLOGICAL MECHANISMS

Specific Sociocultural Forces

While accepting that sociocultural influences have played an important role in molding the expression of anorexia nervosa, it is more difficult to identify specific causal factors. Brumberg[27] attempts to bridge the gap between the 13th and 20th centuries in an arresting statement. "In the earlier era (13th to 16th centuries) control of appetite was linked to piety and belief; . . . the modern anorectic strives for perfection in terms of society's ideal of physical, rather than spiritual beauty."

The strongest argument for linking recent changes in anorexia nervosa to sociocultural forces is that dieting behavior has become popularized, is prevalent among young women in schools and colleges, and is probably harmful.[39,40]

We therefore agree with Brumberg when she identifies the pernicious role of books and magazines, the fashion industry, films and television, all of which have contributed to fasting behavior. Social factors, collectively leading to fasting behavior, may therefore constitute a specific set of causes.

Far less convincing is Brumberg's adoption of the feminist politician's view that anorexia nervosa is the young woman's protest against the patriarchy. She is surely over-inclusive when she concludes that anorexia has been promoted by "the army of health professionals" and medical researchers, anxious to obtain funding for their work.

Pathoplasticity

In exploring the reasons for anorexia nervosa having undergone transformation, we should consider the role of pathoplastic causal factors. They do not amount to fundamental causes of psychiatric illness, but they may act as triggering agents and shape the form of the illness. They not only influence the content of a psychiatric illness but also its "coloring" and its form.[41,42] Sociocultural forces of the kind previously discussed may thus play an important part in molding the form of anorexia nervosa and its psychological content. Moreover, the cult of thinness in Westernized societies has probably led to neurotic disorders expressing themselves more commonly in the form of anorexia nervosa or bulimia nervosa, without neurotic illnesses as a whole having necessarily become more frequent.

A Multidimensional Causation

The emphasis so far on sociocultural influences over the course of history should not obscure the important role of biological factors in the causation of anorexia nervosa. Moreover, neither set of factors should be seen as operating in isolation: Their interaction is crucial in explaining why only some individuals succumb to anorexia nervosa in spite of pervasive adverse sociocultural influences. Three sets of biological mechanisms operating in anorexia nervosa will now be examined: weight homeostasis, endocrine function, and genetic makeup.

Interference with Weight Homeostasis

Body weight, if displaced from the normally maintained level, will subsequently be restored to its initial level.[43] Adult rats, whose weight has been experimentally reduced by fasts, quickly regain their lost weight and return precisely to the weight appropriate for their age and sex.[44] Effective homeostatic mechanisms were also demonstrated in man by Ancel Keys during his classical studies on volunteers subjected to a semistarvation diet.[45] In most of the subjects body weight was restored to its former level within months of food restriction being lifted. These observations fit in with set-point theory, the "set-point" representing a predetermined and self-restoring weight level,[46] without necessarily requiring that the body weight set-point should always remain the same.[43]

It can be surmised that in anorexia nervosa, whatever the initial causes of the illness, the patient's severe weight loss and the persistence of emaciation represent a disturbance of the normal homeostatic mechanisms. Thus it is possible that some of the weight loss is maintained by a lowering of "physiologically defended" levels.[47] There is tentative evidence that anorexic patients are less able than normal controls to regulate their body weight by physiological mechanisms. In a study on patients with anorexia nervosa whose weight had returned to a near normal level after treatment, they were asked to weigh themselves every morning and chart their own weight. When the weighing scales were gradually misaligned to deceive the patients into the belief that they were losing weight, they reacted by actually gaining weight (presumably by increasing their food intake). When the deception subsequently operated in the reverse direction, the patients lost the weight previously gained. The same procedure in matched normal subjects induced no significant weight change. In anorexic patients, therefore, physiological weight-controlling mechanisms are to some degree overpowered by external cues pertaining to body size.[48] It should be noted that in anorexia nervosa, the postulated lowering of the physiologically defended weight level is congruent with the patient's conscious desire to maintain a low body weight.

In bulimia nervosa, however, the situation is quite different. Whereas the patient is also anxious to maintain her weight at a suboptimal level, the homoeostatic control mechanisms act in a converse direction by inducing cravings for food and corrective overeating, which would restore body weight to the "healthy" level were it not for the patient resorting to self-induced vomiting.[22,49-52] Robinson[53] has proposed that these behavioral responses to caloric deprivation are mirrored through cognitive and biological mechanisms. He has demonstrated abnormal cognitive processes in bulimic patients after a food load. The food load was followed by increased ratings in the urge to eat instead of the reduction that would be expected in normal subjects.[54] This paradoxical response has been named "counter regulation"[55] and occurs in subjects who persist in their attempts to restrict their food intake.

In conclusion, altered body weight homeostasis is likely to play a role in both anorexia and bulimia nervosa. In the former, there may be a lowering of the physiologically defended level; in the latter, corrective homeostatic mechanisms contribute to the episodes of overeating.

Impaired Reproductive Function in Anorexia Nervosa

The hypothalamic–pituitary–gonadal disorder is a fundamental component of anorexia nervosa. In women, it leads to secondary amenorrhea and infertility. In premenarchal girls it causes delayed puberty and primary amenorrhea and may, in more severely protracted instances, result in permanent sequelae such as a shortened stature and underdeveloped breasts.[56] The endocrine disorder is, to a large extent, secondary to weight loss and malnutrition. Whether it is solely attributable to this mechanism has been the subject of a long-standing debate. The possibility that the endocrine disorder is not entirely due to weight loss has previously been proposed.[57-60] Others, however, maintain that starvation and weight loss are solely responsible for the amenorrhea of anorexia nervosa.[61]

This question can be tackled by monitoring the stages of endocrine recovery when effective treatment leads to a progressive weight increase. Endocrine recovery can most readily be followed by demonstrating three stages of ovarian growth and differentiation by means of sequential pelvic ultrasonography.[62,63] The first stage, that of small *amorphous ovaries* occurs in the majority of patients who are severely undernourished. All patients, while they are still of suboptimal weight, go through the second stage—

multifollicular ovaries (containing small cysts 3 to 9 mm in diameter). The third stage is that of a *dominant follicle* (one whose growth exceeds the others with a diameter of 10 mm or more) (FIG. 1 and TABLE 1). This sequence of ovarian growth and differentiation reflects corresponding changes in reproductive hormonal levels, summarized in TABLE 2, and published in detail elsewhere.[63] Weight gain is followed by an augmented secretion of FSH and LH, which in turn leads to increases in ovarian volume and differentiation. The rise of FSH is associated with the transition from an amorphous to a multifollicular ovary, whereas the main rise of LH occurs with the appearance of a dominant follicle. The growth of a dominant follicle corresponds with a

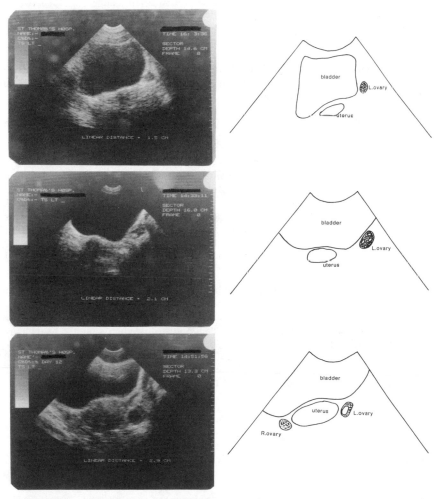

FIGURE 1. Sequential ultrasound appearances, showing from above downwards: (i) small amorphous ovary and small uterus, (ii) multifollicular ovary, and (iii) normal-sized ovary with dominant follicle and normal-sized uterus.

TABLE 1. Anorexia Nervosa: Stages of Ovarian Differentiation

	Amorphous	Multi-follicular	Dominant Follicle no menst.	Dominant Follicle + menst.
No. patients[a] at lowest weight (% PMW)[b]	24 (69%)	12 (78%)	–	–
No. patients at highest weight (% PMW)	–	17 (91%)	8 (98%)	11

NOTE: Total number of patients studied was 36.

[a] Relative number of patients at different stages of ovarian differentiation: (i) at lowest weight when first admitted, and (ii) near optimum weight before discharge from hospital.

[b] PMW = premorbid weight.

maximal increase in estradiol which in turn leads to enlargement of the uterus. The clinical predictive value of sequential ultrasound examination is that ovaries that have increased in size and contain a dominant follicle indicate that in 50% of the patients menstruation will recommence within a month.

No simple way exists of predicting the weight gain required for total reproductive recovery. Measures such as the absolute weight or "ideal body weight" are of little value, presumably because they do not adequately reflect the weight required constitutionally for reproductive recovery in an individual patient. The individual patient's optimum or "healthy" weight should be defined as that needed for reproductive recovery. The use of the body-mass index has become popular and attempts have been made to define optimal weight at an arbitrary cut-off point of the BMI such as above 19.1 kg/m².[64] Our own studies have demonstrated the fallibility of the body-mass index in this regard.[63] We have already demonstrated that the appearance of a dominant follicle on ultrasound is predictive of the resumption of menstruation. Thus we thought it would be revealing to compare the probability of a dominant follicle being associated with a given weight gain during treatment, expressed by two measures:

1. The percentage of "premorbid weight" which is the patient's optimum weight before the onset of her eating disorder and weight loss, and
2. The body-mass index (weight in kg ÷ height in m²). Statistical analyses demonstrated the greater probability of a dominant follicle being related to the percentage of premorbid weight achieved, rather than any given level of BMI (FIG.

TABLE 2. Anorexia Nervosa: Stages of Ovarian Differentiation

Parameter	Amorphous	Multifollicular	Dominant Follicle
% PMW[a]	73	85	98
FSH	–	+ +	+ +
LH	–	+	+ + +
Estradiol	+	+	+ + +
Ovarian volume	+	+ +	+ + +
Uterine area	+	+ +	+ +

NOTE: Hormonal patterns in 36 patients at different body weights and at different stages of ovarian differentiation.

[a] PMW = premorbid weight.

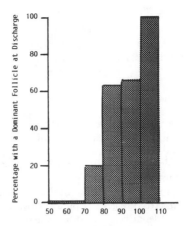

FIGURE 2. Bar charts showing the percentage probability of a dominant follicle developing at different weights expressed (upper half) as percentage of patients' premorbid weight, and (lower half) as body-mass index. (Standard errors omitted for clarity — reprinted from Treasure et al.[63] by permission.)

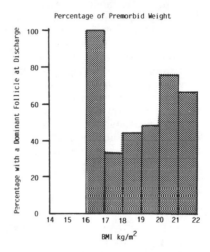

2). This conclusion is reinforced by the finding that multifollicular ovaries — indicating incomplete reproductive recovery — were still frequently present when weight was within the "normal" range of BMI (19–21 kg/m²).[63]

These findings support the view that treatment programs should aim at restoring an individual patient's weight to its premorbid level. In some patients this level cannot readily be determined, for example, in cases of marked obesity before the onset of the illness or when the onset was premenarchal. In these instances, ultrasonography becomes an indispensable method for establishing the patient's optimum weight, namely that weight conducive to reproductive recovery. Until now the return of menstruation has simply been hailed as a sign that the patient's progress was satisfactory, and it has not been a therapeutic goal. The advent of ultrasonography should lead us to question this indifference, and we should try to establish whether an early reproductive recovery might lead to a more favorable long-term outcome. At a more theoretical level we are also better placed to re-examine the question of whether the endocrine disorder is wholly secondary to the loss of weight, given that we can now revise our criterion of what constitutes an optimum weight for the individual. It should become possible to resolve the important issue of the primacy or otherwise of the hypothalamic disorder in anorexia nervosa.[58]

Genetic Contribution to Anorexia Nervosa

In a collaborative study between St. George's and the Maudsley Hospitals in London, 30 female twin pairs were studied, in which the proband had anorexia nervosa. The second twin was more likely to be concordant for anorexia nervosa if the twins were monozygotic (MZ) rather than dizygotic (DZ): 9 out of 16 (55%) MZ pairs were concordant, whereas only one out of 14 (7%) DZ pairs was concordant ($p < 0.01$).[65] In this first twin study the authors considered the most plausible explanation for the findings to be a genetic predisposition to anorexia nervosa, which could become manifest under adverse conditions such as inappropriate dieting. Possible explanations for the genetic vulnerability were a predisposition to a particular personality type, predisposition to psychiatric illness, a disturbance of body image, or a hypothalamic disorder.

In a subsequent study that is still in progress, Holland, Sicotte, and Treasure[66] confirmed the earlier finding on 25 MZ and 20 DZ twin pairs (56% of the MZ twins were concordant for anorexia nervosa, but ony 5% of the DZ twins; $p < 0.004$). These authors also support a multidimensional model for the causation of anorexia nervosa, and conclude that their family and twin data demonstrate that the propensity for anorexia nervosa is significantly genetically determined. Moreover, they put forward the interesting proposal that the genetic vulnerability to anorexia nervosa is a weakness of those homeostatic mechanisms that normally ensure weight restoration after a period of weight loss. Such a model would predict that in a society where dieting is common and weight reduction encouraged, those who are genetically vulnerable would be most likely to develop anorexia nervosa.

CONCLUSIONS

1. During recent decades anorexia nervosa has undergone change: Its incidence has increased, the psychological content has changed, and its clinical form has become more variable. The most important manifestation of the change in form is the emergence of bulimia nervosa.

2. During previous centuries fasting practices have led to disturbances reminiscent of anorexia nervosa. With a few exceptions the evidence is weak, and it is essential to maintain the clinical cohesiveness of the syndrome described by Gull and Lasègue.

3. The expression of anorexia nervosa has been "molded" by sociocultural forces, more specifically by the cult of thinness leading to widespread fasting practices (euphemistically named "dieting").

4. A multidimensional view of causation supports a close interaction between sociocultural forces and disturbed biological mechanisms, especially impaired weight homeostasis, defective control of reproductive function, and a genetic disorder.

REFERENCES

1. RUSSELL, G. F. M. 1985. The changing nature of anorexia nervosa: An introduction to the conference. J. Psychiatr. Res. 19(2/3): 101–109.

2. THEANDER, S. 1970. Anorexia nervosa: A psychiatric investigation of 44 female cases. Acta Psychiatr. Scand. (Suppl) **214:** 1-194.
3. KENDELL, R. E., D. J. HALL, A. HAILEY & H. M. BABIGIAN. 1973. The epidemiology of anorexia nervosa. Psychol. Med. **3:** 200-203.
4. JONES, D. J., M. M. FOX, H. M. BABIGIAN & H. E. HUTTON. 1980. Epidemiology of anorexia nervosa in Monroe County, New York: 1960-1976. Psychosom. Med. **42:** 551-558.
5. WILLI, J. & S. GROSSMANN. 1983. Epidemiology of anorexia nervosa in a defined region of Switzerland. Am. J. Psychiatry. **140(5):** 564-567.
6. SZMUKLER, G., C. MCCANCE, L. MCCRONE & D. HUNTER. 1986. Anorexia nervosa: A psychiatric case register study from Aberdeen. Psychol. Med. **16:** 49-58.
7. LUCAS, A. R., C. M. BEARD, W. M. O'FALLON & L. T. KURLAND. 1988. Anorexia nervosa in Rochester, Minnesota: A 45-year study. Mayo Clin. Proc. **63:** 433-442.
8. WILLIAMS, P. & M. KING. 1987. The "epidemic" of anorexia nervosa: Another medical myth? Lancet **i:** 205-207.
9. GULL, W. W. 1874. Anorexia nervosa (apepsia hysterica, anorexia hysterica). Trans. Clin. Soc. London **7:** 22-28.
10. LASÈGUE, C. 1873. De l'anorexie hystérique. Archives Générales de Médicine. **21**(April): 385-403.
11. WALLER, J. V., M. R. KAUFMAN & F. DEUTSCH. 1940. Anorexia nervosa. A psychosomatic entity. Psychosom. Med. **2:** 3-16.
12. MEYER, J. E. 1961. Das Syndrom der Anorexia Nervosa: Katamnestische Untersuchungen. Arch. Psychiatr. Z. Ges. Neurol **202:** 31-59.
13. CRISP, A. H. 1967. The possible significance of some behavioural correlates of weight and carbohydrate intake. J. Psychosom. Res. **11:** 117-131.
14. BRUCH, H. 1962. Perceptual and conceptual disturbances of anorexia nervosa. Psychosom. Med. **24:** 187-194.
15. RUSSELL, G. F. M. 1970. Anorexia nervosa: Its identity as an illness and its treatment. *In* Modern Trends in Psychological Medicine. J. H. Price, Ed. Vol. **2:** 131-164. Butterworth. London.
16. WORLD HEALTH ORGANIZATION. 1986. Mental, behavioural and developmental disorders. Draft for field trials. *In* Tenth Revision of the International Classification of Diseases. Chapter **V:** 95-98.
17. 1987. Diagnostic and Statistical Manual of Mental Disorders, Third Edition (Revised). American Psychiatric Association. Washington, DC.
18. KAY, D. W. K. & D. LEIGH. 1954. The natural history, treatment, and prognosis of anorexia nervosa, based on a study of 38 patients. J. Ment. Sci. **100:** 411-431.
19. DAHLEM KONFERENZEN. 1975. Life Sciences Research Report 2. T. Silverstone, Ed. Berlin.
20. BRUCH, H. 1974. Eating Disorders: Obesity, Anorexia Nervosa and the Person Within: 283. Routledge Kegan Paul. London.
21. STUNKARD, A. J. 1959. Eating patterns and obesity. Psychiatr. Q. **33:** 284-292.
22. RUSSELL, G. F. M. 1979. Bulimia nervosa: An ominous variant of anorexia nervosa. Psychol. Med. **9:** 429-448.
23. GARNER, D. M. & C. G. FAIRBURN. 1988. Relationship between anorexia nervosa and bulimia nervosa: Diagnostic implications. *In* Diagnostic Issues in Anorexia Nervosa and Bulimia Nervosa. D. M. Garner & P. E. Garfinkel, Eds.: 56-79. Brunner/Mazel. New York.
24. RUSSELL, G. F. M. 1988. The diagnostic formulation in bulimia nervosa. *In* Diagnostic Issues in Anorexia Nervosa and Bulimia Nervosa. D. M. Garner & P. E. Garfinkel, Eds.: 3-25. Brunner/Mazel. New York.
25. BELL, R. M. 1985. Holy Anorexia. The University of Chicago Press. Chicago and London.
26. RAMPLING, D. 1985. Ascetic ideals and anorexia nervosa. J. Psychiatr. Res. **19(2/3):** 89-94.
27. BRUMBERG, J. J. 1988. Fasting Girls: The Emergence of Anorexia Nervosa as a Modern Disease. Harvard University Press. Cambridge, MA and London.
28. MORTON, R. 1689. Phthisiologia, seu Exercitationes de Phthisi. S. Smith. London.
29. MORTON, R. 1694. Phthisiologia: Or, a Treatise of Consumptions. Smith & Walford. London.
30. SILVERMAN, J. A. 1983. Richard Morton, 1637-1698. Limner of anorexia nervosa: His life and times. A tercentenary essay. J. Am. Med. Soc. **250(20):** 2830-2832.
31. SILVERMAN, J. A. 1986. Anorexia nervosa in seventeenth century England as viewed by phy-

sician, philosopher, and pedagogue: An essay. Int. J. Eating Disord. **5(5):** 847–853.

32. CULE, J. 1967. Wreath on the Crown. Gomerian Press. Llandysul.
33. SILVERSTEIN, B., B. PETERSON & L. PERDUE. 1986. Some correlates of the thin standard of bodily attractiveness for women. Int. J. Eating Disord. **5(5):** 895–905.
34. LOUDON, I. S. L. 1980. Chlorosis, anaemia and anorexia nervosa. Br. Med. J. **281:** 1669–1675.
35. PARRY-JONES, W. L. 1985. Archival exploration of anorexia nervosa. J. Psychiatr. Res. **19(2/3):** 95–100.
36. CHRISTIAN, H. A. 1942. Osler's Principles and Practice of Medicine. 14th Edit.: 945–947. D. Appleton-Century. New York.
37. HARE, E. 1981. The two manias: A study of the evolution of the modern concept of mania. Br. J. Psychiatry **138:** 89–99.
38. JASPERS, K. 1959. Allgemeine Psychopathologie, 7th Edit. (Translated by J. Hoenig and M. W. Hamilton, 1962.): 732, 742. Manchester University Press. Manchester, United Kingdom.
39. NYLANDER, I. 1971. The feeling of being fat and dieting in a school population: Epidemiologic, interview investigation. Acta Sociomed. Scand. **3:** 17–26.
40. PATTON, G. C. 1988. The spectrum of eating disorder in adolescence. J. Psychosom. Res. In press.
41. BIRNBAUM, K. 1923. Der Aufbau der Psychose.: 6–7. Springer. Berlin.
42. SHEPHERD, M. 1975. Epidemiologische psychiatrie. *In* Psychiatrie der Gegenwart Forschung und Praxis. Vol. 3, 2nd Edit. K. P. Kisker, J.-E. Meyer, C. Muller & E. Stromgren, Eds.: 119–149. Springer. Berlin.
43. KEESEY, R. E. 1986. A set-point theory of obesity. *In* Handbook of Eating Disorders. K. D. Brownell & J. P. Foreyt, Eds.: 63–87. Basic Books. New York.
44. LEVITSKY, D. A. 1970. Feeding patterns of rats in response to fasts and changes in environmental conditions. Physiol. Behav. **5:** 291–300.
45. KEUS, A., J. BROZEK, A. HENSCHEL, O. MICKELSEN & M. L. TAYLOR. 1950. *In* The Biology of Human Starvation. University of Minnesota Press. Minneapolis, MN.
46. KEESEY, R. E. & S. W. CORBETT. 1984. Metabolic defence of the body weight set-point. *In* Eating and Its Disorders. A. J. Stunkard & A. Stellar, Eds. Vol. 62. Raven Press. New York.
47. MROSOVSKY, N. 1983. Animal anorexias, starvation, and anorexia nervosa: Are animal models of anorexia nervosa possible? *In* Anorexia Nervosa: Recent Developments in Research. P. L. Darby, P. E. Garfinkel, D. M. Garner & D. V. Coscina, Eds.: 199–205. Alan R. Liss. New York.
48. RUSSELL, G. F. M., P. G. CAMPBELL & P. D. SLADE. 1975. Experimental studies on the nature of the psychological disorder in anorexia nervosa. Psychoneuroendocrinology **1:** 45–56.
49. RUSSELL, G. F. M. 1985. Bulimia revisited. Int. J. Eating Disord. **4:** 681–692.
50. GARFINKEL, P. E. & D. M. GARNER. 1982. Anorexia Nervosa: A Multidimensional Perspective. Brunner/Mazel. New York.
51. FAIRBURN, C. G. & P. J. COOPER. 1984. The clinical features of bulimia nervosa. Br. J. Psychiatry **144:** 238–246.
52. WOOLEY, S. C. & A. KEARNEY-COOKE. 1986. Intensive treatment of bulimia and body-image disturbance. *In* Handbook of Eating Disorders. K. D. Brownell & J. P. Foreyt, Eds. Basic Books, Inc. New York.
53. ROBINSON, P. H. 1986. Review: The bulimic disorders. Clin. Neuropharmacol. **9(1):** 14–36.
54. ROBINSON, P. H., S. A. CHECKLEY & G. F. M. RUSSELL. 1985. Suppression of eating by fenfluramine in patients with bulimia nervosa. Br. J. Psychiatry **146:** 169–176.
55. HERMAN, C. P. 1978. Restrained eating. Psychiat. Clin. Am. **1:** 593–607.
56. RUSSELL, G. F. M. 1985. Premenarchal anorexia nervosa and its sequelae. J. Psychiatr. Res. **19(2/3):** 363–369.
57. RUSSELL, G. F. M. 1965. Metabolic aspects of anorexia nervosa. Proc. R. Soc. Med. **58:** 811–814.
58. RUSSELL, G. F. M. 1977. The present status of anorexia nervosa. Psychol. Med. **7:** 363–367.
59. HALMI, K. A. & J. R. FALK. 1983. Behavioral and dietary discriminators of menstrual function in anorexia nervosa. *In* Anorexia Nervosa: Recent Developments in Research. P.

L. Darby, P. E. Garfinkel, D. M. Garner & D. V. Coscina, Eds. Vol. **3**: 323–329. Alan R. Liss. New York.

60. WAKELING, A., V. A. DESOUZA, M. B. R. GORE, M. SABUR, D. LIVINGSTONE & A. M. B. BOSS. 1979. Amenorrhea, body weight and serum hormone concentration, with particular reference to prolactin and thyroid hormones in anorexia nervosa. Psychol. Med. **40:** 499.
61. PLOOG, D. W. & K. M. PIRKE. 1987. Psychobiology of anorexia nervosa. Psychol. Med. **17:** 843–859.
62. TREASURE, J. L., P. A. L. GORDON, E. A. KING, M. J. WHEELER & G. F. M. RUSSELL. 1985. Cystic ovaries: A phase of anorexia nervosa. Lancet **ii:** 1379–1382.
63. TREASURE, J. L., M. WHEELER, E. A. KING, P. A. L. GORDON & G. F. M. RUSSELL. 1988. Weight gain and reproductive function: Ultrasonographic and endocrine features in anorexia nervosa. Clin Endocrinol. **29:** In press.
64. ADAMS, J., S. FRANKS, D. W. POLSON, H. D. MASON, N. ABDULWAHID, M. TUCKER, D. V. MORRIS, J. PRICE & H. S. JACOBS. 1985. Multifollicular ovaries: Clinical and endocrine features and response to pulsatile gonadotrophin releasing hormone. Lancet **ii:** 1375–1378.
65. HOLLAND, A. J., A. HALL, R. MURRAY, G. F. M. RUSSELL & A. H. CRISP. 1984. Anorexia nervosa: A study of 34 twin pairs and one set of triplets. Br. J. Psychiatry **145:** 414–419.
66. HOLLAND, A. J., N. SICOTTE & J. L. TREASURE. 1988. Anorexia nervosa: Evidence for a genetic basis. J. Psychosom. Res. In press.

DISCUSSION

DR. J. WURTMAN (*Massachusetts Institute of Technology, Cambridge, MA*): As you know, Dr. Russell, a number of investigators, such as Walter Kay in Pittsburgh and Pope and Hudson, have suggested that bulimia is actually a heterogenous disorder and that there are anorexic bulimics as opposed to obese bulimics in whom the food cravings seem to be predominant. I wonder what your thoughts are about this and also whether there are now genetic data relating genes to bulimia.

DR. G. F. M. RUSSELL (*The Institute of Psychiatry, University of London, U.K.*): I agree with your main point that bulimia, especially bulimia as defined in DSM III before it was refined in the revised version, is very much a heterogeneous disorder. Evidence is growing that bulimia nervosa, which is related to anorexia nervosa and that's really all I've been talking about, is something that you can identify a bit better than is possible in the mixture of other forms of bulimia that exist. Some cases are associated with other forms of psychiatric disorders — addictive behavior, compulsive behavior, and personality disorders — and in them it's too early to say much more because the situation is so complex. However, I would agree with your sentiment that genetic studies along these lines, perhaps confirming this sense of bulimia's heterogeneity, are very important. My three colleagues (J. Treasure, A. Holland, and N. Sicotte) are in fact also looking at the incidence of concordant bulimia nervosa in twins. The fact that I haven't got a slide to show is evidence of the various difficulties. They've produced ideas that are revised month by month, and the answers are not, it appears, going to be as clear-cut as in anorexia nervosa.

DR. L. SCHNEIDER (*New York Hospital–Cornell Medical Center, White Plains, NY*): I would like to ask you to comment, Dr. Russell, on the 19th century observation that success in treatment of the anorexic required removing the anorexic from the home, how far back in history that observation went, and the consensus about it.

DR. RUSSELL: It certainly went back to Gull. Gull didn't actually say you should remove the anorexic patient from the home, but he said that family and close relatives were really the worst people to be involved in helping the patient, that help should be provided by attendants who have a greater moral influence, meaning a psychological influence, over these patients. This was very much a tradition in France. There, a treatment of separation of the patient from the family was introduced with apparently good results. I think it's difficult nowadays to suggest that this is a good approach. There is evidence that the best method of treatment is to work with the family. Our own studies on the efficacy of family therapy in younger patients showed that you approach the family, the parents and the rest of the household, in such a way that they function as good attendants to insure that the anorexics improve their food intake and that they are handled sensibly. The success of family therapy doesn't mean that the family is pathogenic. It suggests, however, that they normally have difficulty in coping with a daughter who is starving herself, and with help, with family therapy, they can learn how to handle the situation better.

Dr. A. Levine (*Minneapolis VA Medical Center, Minneapolis, MN*): You mentioned that starvation was the cause of effects seen with anorexia. Endocrine and metabolic changes are often related to those effects seen with starvation, and when you mentioned Ancel Keys, it reminded me that he also noted in those fine studies, albeit mostly on males, that associated with these partial starvations were a lot of behavioral changes, such as apathy towards family or apathy about sexual behavior. I was wondering if you could comment on how much of the behavioral changes, as well as the endocrine changes, that are seen in anorexia are associated with starvation rather than just the anorexia.

Dr. Russell: That is a very important question, and I wish I could give you a definite answer. I think the most pertinent observation is that if you admit the patients to a unit where there's intensive treatment aimed at making them gain weight, it appears as if you're flying into the face of their psychopathology. They will tell you the worst thing that can happen to them is to put on weight. You then say, "Right, come into hospital and we shall make you put on weight." Of course they hesitate to come in. However, if they do come in and agree to the treatment, in the majority of patients a startling improvement occurs in their mental state and their attitude. Why this happens isn't entirely clear. The simplest explanation, as you imply, is that as you improve their nutritional state, a great deal of their psychopathology melts away. It may not be as simple as that because the actual process of accepting food and coming to terms with it has an important psychological component.

Dr. K. Halmi (*New York Hospital–Cornell Medical Center, White Plains, NY*): We have been speaking of hypothalamic dysfunction mainly through the eyes of amenorrhea and the hypothalamic pituitary ovarian axis. Hypothalamic dysfunction could be represented, in fact, by abnormal eating behavior. For example, neurotransmitters, such as norepinephrine and serotonin, all affect eating behavior, and we do know that when anorexics return to a normal weight many of them do not engage in normal eating behavior. This can occur for many years after achieving and while maintaining a normal weight. Also in your very interesting work showing the development of the ovary concomitantly with restoration to a premorbid body weight makes me reflect, first of all, on what happens to some of these women who actually menstruate and show normal ovarian development at a normal body weight with regard to population norms and not at their premorbid body weight. Is that possible? Do you have some women in your sample who menstruate and have normal ovarian function at a normal body weight but not at their own premorbid weight, which may have been a little bit over the normal range? Could that reflect that perhaps there are other aspects of this hypothalamic dysfunction than just the menstrual cycle?

DR. RUSSELL: There really are two parts to your question, Kathy. Let me take the second part first. The simple phrase normal weight is so complicated that I never use it now, except in a lapse. I think you have to have some sort of yardstick for recovery, but "normal" as defined by standard tables of weights is virtually useless. At least that's our thesis. In a simple clinical context, you use premorbid weight because you can obtain that from the weight history. In the event that you can't determine premorbid weight for whatever reason, the best guide is reproductive recovery because that's the most definite feature of the hypothalamic disorder. Until and unless research establishes otherwise, I think restoration of reproductive function is going to be the most useful yardstick of recovery, and we found it is mainly related to premorbid weight. I agree that you sometimes get tremendous surprises, young women who tell you that they can menstruate at only 45 or 43 kilos. My response is always to say you are certainly deceiving yourself and perhaps trying to deceive me. To my surprise occasionally she's right, but if you look carefully at her weight history you usually find that she reached menarche at a relatively young age and light weight. Wide ranges can be found, but at the current stage of knowledge I still think reproductive recovery and the weight that corresponds to it provide the best index of recovery.

I agree, of course, with your second point that abnormal attitudes and abnormal eating behavior are the most persistent symptoms, and that many so-called recovered anorexic patients will report that they're still plagued with uncertainty about eating and eating behavior. I prefer for the time being to put that to one side for the reasons that Paul McHugh has already given, that it is very difficult to disentangle bodily functions from the complexities of their psychopathology. Hypothalamic pituitary ovarian disorder, on the other hand, is a tangible thing that can currently be measured.

DR. S. NICOLAIDIS (*College de France CNRS, Paris*): It was shown that food intake affects sleep to a large extent. Also, food deprivation induces insomnia, which by itself is pathogenic in terms of the psychiatric syndrome. Do you think that the abnormalities you were invoking could be due to that deprivation, particularly paradoxical sleep which was also described in those patients?

DR. RUSSELL: You've touched on an area about which, Dr. Nicolaidis, I am very ignorant. I agree with your observation that malnutrition and weight loss are associated with insomnia. Insomnia is one symptom that sometimes enables you to persuade the patient to accept treatment. I also agree that if you restore a patient's weight to normal that patient's insomnia will become relieved. It's complicated to disentangle from that which is due to a depressed mood, which a lot of these patients also have. But I agree, the observations, particularly those of Arthur Crisp regarding the relationship between weight loss and insomnia, are direct and very convincing; however, beyond that I'm unable to answer your question or even to speculate.

DR. D. BOOTH (*University of Birmingham, Birmingham, England*): In the important monozygote twin studies that you presented, you suggested a genetic disorder. I wonder how definite you feel about that compared with the possibility that there might be pathogenetic environmental correlation or even mediation with the differences—although unreliably recognized—between monozygotic and dizygotic twins, differences in the sense of identity crisis or whatever.

DR. RUSSELL: Thank you for that question because it enables to me to emphasize a point that I had to rush over at the end of my presentation. Dr. Holland produces figures I didn't dare to present. They're very much like Paul McHugh's figures, which show enormously high percentages for heritability of anorexia nervosa. Nevertheless even if these percentages are high, one has to wonder what it is about this genetic vulnerability that interacts with environmental factors. The answer to your question is, I'm sure these factors must interact. The hypothesis that we put forward is that in these individuals, whenever they lose weight for one reason or another, the ability to restore the lost weight is impaired. It may be an intercurrent illness that has led to weight loss or it could be a bereavement that's made them depressed and lose weight. Regardless of the cause, the normal response of weight restoration due to weight homeostatic mechanisms is defective, and this is what is genetically determined. That's a guess really, but it's an interesting speculation that fits in with some of the other data.

DR. J. BLUNDELL (*University of Leeds, Leeds County, U.K.*): I want to ask you about the form in which this genetic vulnerability might express itself. I wonder if it's perhaps due to some defect of internal metabolism or a vulnerability to external symptoms. I mention this because I was struck, when I read the work of Salvador Minuchin on family processes in anorexia, that he measured a numer of physiological parameters and that he has worked with diabetic children as well as with anorexics. I was struck by the comparison between those groups and by the possibility that in anorexia there's some defect of carbohydrate metabolism, and the behavior is functional as an attempt to defend the effects of carbohydrate metabolism. You have worked on the linkage between diabetes and anorexia, and I wonder if a theme is emerging here in which the genetic vulnerability is expressed through metabolism rather than through enhanced sensitivity to environmental factors.

DR. RUSSELL: I presume that if we did succeed in going beyond the rather elementary stage we've reached, then the next step would indeed be a search for ways of identifying the individual who has a metabolic disturbance along the lines you suggest. Then you could predict who is vulnerable to weight loss as a result of genetic factors. I'm afraid that we don't have evidence that this is possible. The work we did was mainly to look at patients who have both diabetes mellitus and bulimia nervosa. We were able to demonstrate what a terrible combination these are and how difficult it was to treat these patients. I hope that the work that's been done at the Maudsley will act as a stimulus for the more basic scientists to pursue research along the lines you suggest, John.

Depression, Antidepressants, and Body Weight Change[a]

MADELYN H. FERNSTROM[b]

Department of Psychiatry
Western Psychiatric Institute and Clinic
University of Pittsburgh School of Medicine
Pittsburgh, Pennsylvania 15213

Among the prominent symptoms of major depression are marked alterations in appetite and body weight (most often reductions). During treatment with antidepressants, depressive symptoms disappear, including those associated with weight and appetite. In many patients, however, excessive and problematic weight gain occurs, primarily during treatment with tricyclic antidepressants. This article reviews evidence concerning the behavioral and metabolic changes that occur in depression and recovery, and the effects of antidepressant medication on appetite and body weight.

BODY WEIGHT CHANGE IN DEPRESSION AND RECOVERY: EXTENT OF THE PROBLEM

Major depression is often associated with alterations in body weight: Patients frequently lose weight,[1-3] though some actually gain weight during their depressive episode.[3,5] During treatment, especially with tricyclic antidepressant medications, patients often complain of unwanted and excessive weight gain. This is an important concern to both patient and clinician, as weight gain often results in medication noncompliance. The use of two frequently prescribed drugs, amitriptyline[6-9] and imipramine[9-11] is often associated with increased body weight during treatment (TABLE 1). In our own studies,[7,9,11] however, no relationship was observed between clinical response and weight change. Moreover, observed weight changes following medication were not negatively correlated with those occurring at disease onset. These results suggest that medication-induced changes result from a pharmacologic action of the drug independent of its effect on mood. The mechanism(s) by which tricyclic antidepressants produce alterations in body weight are not understood and could conceivably reflect changes in energy balance produced by alterations in caloric intake or expenditure or both.

[a] The studies described were supported by the National Institute of Mental Health (MH-41644; MH-29618) and the John D. and Catherine T. MacArthur Foundation on the Psychobiology of Depression.
[b] Address for correspondence: Dr. Madelyn Fernstrom, Western Psychiatric Institute and Clinic, 3811 O'Hara Street, Pittsburgh, PA 15213.

TABLE 1. Weight Change in Patients Treated with Antidepressants for One Month

Weight Change[a]	Drug Treatment for One Month[b]			
	Amitriptyline (n = 18)	Nortriptyline (n = 24)	Desipramine (n = 18)	Zimelidine (n = 13)
Very rapid gain (>10 pounds)	5 (28%)	2 (11%)	4 (17%)	0
Rapid gain (7–10 pounds)	8 (44%)	2 (11%)	3 (12%)	0
Moderate gain (3–6 pounds)	3 (17%)	8 (45%)	7 (29%)	1 (8%)
No change (± 2 pounds)	2 (11%)	6 (33%)	9 (38%)	9 (69%)
Moderate loss (3–6 pounds)	0	0	0	3 (23%)
Rapid loss (7–10 pounds)	0	0	0	0
Very rapid loss (>10 pounds)	0	0	1 (4%)	0

[a] Weight change represents the number of pounds gained or lost after one month of treatment. (From Fernstrom & Kupfer.[9] Used by permission.)
[b] Figures given are the number of subjects with the percent of total group in parentheses.

ISSUE ONE: ANTIDEPRESSANT-INDUCED WEIGHT GAIN — A RESULT OF FOOD CRAVINGS?

Abundant anecdotal reports describe the presence of cravings for "sweets" or "carbohydrates" that occur with weight gain in some patients treated with tricyclic antidepressants. The inference from such reports is that weight gain resulted from excessive consumption of these foods. Only an occasional published report, however, has actually attempted to examine this issue with any precision: Paykel et al.[6] (who coined the term "carbohydrate craving") reported a craving for carbohydrates among some amitriptyline-treated patients; Berken et al.[10] observed an increase in "sweets" consumption in some patients treated with antidepressants. Such changes in food preference are reported to be large, and obvious to both the patient and the physician.

A major problem in investigating food preference changes, however, is the absence of a definition of the desired foods. TABLE 2, for example, lists the variety of definitions proposed for "carbohydrate" foods. Such confusion in terminology suggests that preferences for particular nutrients are not single, and perhaps can change during antidepressant treatment. In order to generate a sound database for evaluating food preference changes during treatment, we have embarked on an investigation of the potential changes in food preference occurring during antidepressant treatment using a validated survey, the Pittsburgh Appetite Test© (PAT).[12] Our aim has been to identify, in a systematic way, the extent to which changes in food preference occur during tricyclic antidepressant treatment. The PAT does not attempt to address the question of food intake (i.e., amount of food consumed). Rather, it focuses on the issue of appetite for sweets (carbohydrate- and fat-rich foods with a sweet taste) and carbohydrates (carbohydrate rich, low in fat with or without a sweet taste). It is an instrument that can detect shifts in appetite and food preference and that provides a reasonable index of

TABLE 2. Definitions of Carbohydrates

1.	High-carbohydrate, high-fat, sweet-tasting foods
2.	High-carbohydrate, high-fat, nonsweet-tasting foods
3.	High-carbohydrate, low-fat foods
4.	"Sweets"

eating attitudes and preferences. A description of the food categories used to obtain macronutrient preference is shown in TABLE 3. The food groupings are designed to be easily recognized by the patients, with the PAT listing the food category and examples of food items (macronutrient composition is not provided, as in TABLE 3). Patients complete the survey two to three times during the medication-free period, and then monthly during treatment with the tricyclic antidepressant imipramine. Studies using this instrument provide a useful preliminary to the pursuit of direct food-intake measurements in populations of depressed patients undergoing antidepressant treatment.

Using the PAT, we have observed that by the end of four months of antidepressant treatment, in a group of depressed patients, no differences could be found in preference for the starchy, salty, fruit/vegetable, or meat groups (TABLE 4). A trend toward increased sweet preference was noted, but this difference was not statistically significant. Despite the lack of a significant change in preference toward "sweets" in this imipramine-treated population, a very small percentage (15%) of patients did experience a notable change in preference toward calorically dense, sweet foods, based on this group's response to the "favorite foods" section of the PAT.[13] It is of interest to identify which particular constituents of these foods were appealing. Sweet foods containing *both* carbohydrate *and* fat (TABLE 3) were the commonly preferred items in this sub-

TABLE 3. Definition of Food Categories Used in Pittsburgh Appetite Test

Food Category	Major Nutrient Composition	Examples
Sweets	High carbohydrate High fat	Pastry, candy, ice cream, cake
Salty	High carbohydrate High fat	Nuts, chips, olives
Starches	High carbohydrate Low fat	Breads, pasta, crackers, cereal
Fruits/vegetables	High carbohydrate Low fat	Apples, lettuce, carrots, potatoes
Meat	High protein Low-high fat	Beef, chicken, eggs, fish
Dairy	High protein Low-high fat	Milk, yogurt, cheese

NOTE: Food categories were listed in the survey and examples of specific foods listed beside each food category each time a question was asked. The major nutrient composition was not presented in the questions. Patients responded to the question "During the past week, how often did you eat _____ ?" and rated their frequency of consumption of foods within each category as follows: 0 (never); 1 (once a day); 2 (2–3 times/day; 4 (≥ 4 times/day). (From Fernstrom *et al.*[12] Used by permission.)

TABLE 4. Food Preference in Depressed Patients before and during Four Months of Imipramine Treatment

Food Category	Months of Imipramine Treatment				
	0	1	2	3	4
Sweets	1.1 ± 0.2	2.0 ± 0.1	1.3 ± 0.1	1.2 ± 0.1	1.2 ± 0.2
Starches	1.7 ± 0.2	1.6 ± 0.1	1.5 ± 0.1	1.6 ± 0.1	1.5 ± 0.1
Salty	0.6 ± 0.1	0.5 ± 0.1	0.6 ± 0.1	0.4 ± 0.1	0.4 ± 0.1
Fruits/Vegetables	1.4 ± 0.1	1.7 ± 0.1	1.6 ± 0.1	1.6 ± 0.1	1.8 ± 0.1
Meats	1.2 ± 0.1	1.1 ± 0.1	1.2 ± 0.1	1.0 ± 0.1	1.2 ± 0.1
Dairy	0.9 ± 0.1	1.0 ± 0.1	1.2 ± 0.1	1.1 ± 0.1	1.4 ± 0.1[a]

NOTE: Fifty outpatients completed the Pittsburgh Appetite Test during the second week of a drug-free period, while they were depressed (month 0). They were then treated with imipramine (200–250 mg/day) for the next four months. Data during imipramine treatment represent values obtained during the final week of each month. Values are expressed as the means ± SEM. (From Fernstrom et al.[12] Used by permission.)

Patients were asked "During the past week how often did you eat _____?" The rating scale for frequency of consumption was: 0 (never); 1 (once a day); 2 (2–3 times/day); 4 (> 4 times/day).

[a] $p < 0.01$ versus 0 month (repeated measures analysis of variance and the Newman–Keuls test).

group. Sweet foods containing little or no fat were *not* identified. It thus seems unlikely that sweetness alone is the determinant of choice. Our results suggest that *both* sweetness and fat content motivate preference in these patients. Our observation in depressed patients is thus compatible with results of Drewnowski and Greenwood,[14] who noted a preference for sweetened, high-fat foods in normal subjects.

In our studies, clinical outcome was not correlated with sweet preference when comparing the sweet-cravers ($n = 14$) with the rest of the group ($n = 26$). Weight change was also unassociated with sweet preference: Although substantial weight gain (> 5 pounds) was noted in 43% of patients (and up to 5 pounds in another 30%), neither weight gain nor the presence of obesity predicted who would seek sweet foods. How might these findings be interpreted regarding weight gain during treatment? In general, a craving for sweet, calorically dense foods does not drive weight gain in affected patients, though this association might be claimed in occasional patients.

ISSUE 2: SWEET–FAT PREFERENCE DURING A DEPRESSIVE EPISODE

Almost all published data before 1986 that focus on the issue of food cravings during antidepressant treatment ignore the evolution of the depressive episode itself. We have been particularly interested in investigating potential alterations in food preference that occur when the patient becomes depressed. Accordingly, we examined a group of 50 patients and had them evaluate their food preferences while depressed (using the PAT). This information was compared to food preference recalled by patients when they were feeling well. The food categories are presented in TABLE 3. Patients revealed a significant increase in their preference for sweets (carbohydrate- *and* fat-rich foods) while they were depressed, compared to when they reported feeling well. Because the overall group response was highly significant but the magnitude of the change was actually modest, we further investigated individual responses. An even greater response was observed in 39% of the group: the self-report of "sweet" consumption was in the range of two to three times per week "when well," and increased to two to three times per day when they became depressed (TABLE 5). No additional changes in food preference were noted for any other food categories.[12]

A change in preference for sweets could be of considerable clinical importance; perhaps it is associated with the onset of a depressive episode and could therefore reliably

TABLE 5. Preference for Sweet, Carbohydrate–Fat-Rich Foods in Major Depression Measured by Pittsburgh Appetite Test

Responses	Food Category: Sweets[a]	
	When Well	When Depressed
Group Response:	0.7 ± 0.1	1.1 ± 0.2[a]
	5 times/week	12 times/week
	(< 1 time/day)	(1–2 times/day)
Individual Responses (39% of Patients):	2–3 times/week	14–21 times/week
		(2–3 times/day

NOTE: Patients reported frequency of consumption of "sweets" (carbohydrate–fat-rich foods with a sweet taste) during their depression episode and during periods when they recalled feeling well.

[a] $p < 0.01$.

herald the onset of an episode at least in some patients. We will be able to address this issue more precisely during the longitudinal study of this population, as we anticipate that at least a portion of these patients will experience a recurrence of depressive symptoms.

ISSUE THREE: ALTERED METABOLIC RATE AND WEIGHT CHANGE

An increase in body weight could result not only from a rise in energy intake (increased food ingestion), but also from a reduction in energy expenditure. Depressed patients taking antidepressant drugs might well gain weight by such a mechanism, because typical tricyclic antidepressants might be predicted to alter sympathetic nervous system function and thus metabolic rate. For example, the positive energy balance resulting in weight gain might be accounted for by a decrease in caloric utilization, making a person more energy efficient and promoting weight gain. Resting metabolic rate (RMR), which reflects the number of calories used by a person in a resting state, represents at least 70% of the person's total caloric use;[15] RMR probably accounts for an even greater proportion of calories in hospitalized patients due to their greater inactivity. Therefore, in the event that a reduction in metabolic rate occurs during treatment, RMR determinations are likely to reveal it. In fact, we have found consistent reductions in the resting metabolic rate of patients treated with tricyclic antidepressants.[16]

Our paradigm uses each patient as his/her own control, and compares triplicate measurements obtained during a two-week drug-free period with those taken during the second and fourth weeks of antidepressant treatment. It is important to note that these determinations are very consistent within each testing period. The drug-free determinations (FIG. 1) in all subjects were quite reproducible, and resting metabolic rate values (expressed as kcal/min) were within the normal range for each person's height and weight. During drug treatment, these subjects showed a reduction in metabolic rate, at two and four weeks into treatment (FIG. 1). Similar data have been obtained in twelve additional patients. Such reductions in RMR are remarkably large: they exceed by far changes in RMR produced by any other stimuli. For example, exercise produces a 5–10% change in RMR,[17] an effect considered to be robust. Our results demonstrate that particular antidepressants can elicit a change in RMR that is two to three times greater than other reported values (like exercise), a finding that may have important ramifications in overall metabolic function. These kinds of changes, expressed in kcal/min, predict a reduction in daily caloric need of about 300–400 kcal. Thus, a person might be expected to gain a pound every 9–12 days, independent of any change in caloric intake. Our results support the idea that weight increases occurring during antidepressant treatment may be due, at least in part, to changes in caloric expenditure. Normally, an increase in weight would be expected to increase, not reduce, resting metabolic rate,[15] suggesting further that the effect on the RMR is drug-related.

Recently we have begun to investigate the effects of nontricyclic antidepressants on resting metabolic rate and body weight gain during recovery. For example, a patient treated with the serotonergic reuptake inhibitor fluvoxamine showed a robust *increase* (e.g. 29%) in resting metabolic rate that was associated with a weight loss of 3.5 pounds (FIG. 2).[18] This result is potentially important. It suggests specificity of action of antidepressant drugs in altering body weight through metabolic mechanisms. That is, a drug that promotes weight gain lowers metabolic rate, while a compound that promotes weight loss increases metabolic rate. Although the underlying mechanism(s) eliciting such changes in metabolic rate are presently unstudied, it is apparent that

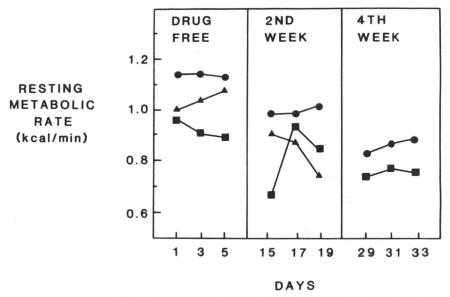

FIGURE 1. Effect of antidepressant treatment on resting metabolic rate in depressed patients. Data represent three separate measurements taken during each time period. Measurements were performed during the drug-free period and during the second and fourth weeks of drug treatment. Differing symbols refer to individual patients. (From Fernstrom *et al.*[16] Used by permission.)

alterations in caloric expenditure contribute to antidepressant-induced weight change. If this effect can be identified as a property of serotonergic reuptake blockers, like fluvoxamine, then serotonergic drugs may become more attractive as antidepressants and lead to better patient compliance.

Interestingly, despite our evidence that RMR falls within a "normal" range for height and weight in the untreated depressed patient, we can not yet ascertain whether the depressed person displays an altered metabolic rate, using the patient as his/her own control. We are now undertaking a study, using matched controls, to examine this possibility.

SUMMARY AND CONCLUSIONS

The excessive weight gain observed during treatment of depression with antidepressant medications is caused in part, at least in some persons, by reductions in resting metabolic rate. Such problematic weight gain appears unrelated to clinical recovery, weight change during the depressive episode, prior weight, or other related factors. Preliminary results suggest that increased energy efficiency (of about 16–24%) during treatment with tricyclic antidepressants could promote weight gain even in the absence of a change in caloric intake. This is not a property of all antidepressants, as demonstrated by the increase in metabolic rate and associated weight loss observed during treatment with the monocyclic antidepressant compound fluvoxamine. Should these serotonergic compounds continue to be effective antidepressants, they may be better accepted by patients, and their use help avoid medication noncompliance.

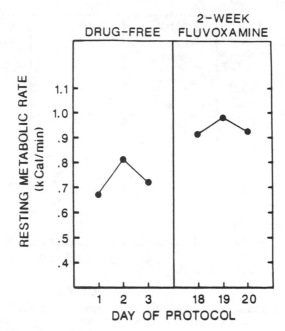

FIGURE 2. Resting metabolic rate in a depressed patient before and during fluvoxamine treatment. (From Fernstrom *et al.*[18] Used by permission.)

In considering energy balance and weight change, our focus has been drawn to altered metabolic rate. Continuing studies do *not* suggest an effect of antidepressants on appetite, particularly the presence of "carbohydrate craving," either during treatment or during a depressive episode. Certainly, a notable preference for highly palatable foods (rich in fats and carbohydrates) occurs during the depressive episode, but not during treatment. These foods cannot be labeled carbohydrates.

REFERENCES

1. ROBINSON, R. G., P. R. McHUGH & M. F. FOLSTEIN. 1975. Measurement of appetite disturbances in psychiatric disorders. J. Psychiatr. Res. **12:** 59–68.
2. PAYKEL, E. S. 1977. Depression and appetite. J. Psychosom. Res. **21:** 401–407.
3. MEZZICH, J. E. & J. S. RAAB. 1980. Depressive symptomology across the Americas. Arch. Gen. Psychiatry **37:** 818–823.
4. STUNKARD, A. J., M. H. FERNSTROM, A. PRICE, E. FRANK & D. J. KUPFER. Direction of weight change in recurrent depression: A possible marker of subtypes of depression. Am J. Psychiatr. Submitted.
5. WEISSENBURGER, J., A. J. RUSH, D. E. GILES & A. J. STUNKARD. 1986. Weight change in depression. Psychiatr. Res. **17:** 275–283.
6. PAYKEL, E. S., P. S. MEULLER & P. M. DE LA VERGNE. 1973. Amitriptyline, weight gain, and carbohydrate craving: A side effect. Br. J. Psychiatry **123:** 501–507.
7. KUPFER, D. J., P. A. COBLE & D. RUBINSTEIN. 1979. Changes in weight during treatment for depression. Psychosom. Med. **41:** 535–543.

8. HARRIS, B., J. YOUNG & B. HUGHES. 1986. Appetite and weight during short-term antidepressant treatment. Br. J. Psychiatry 145: 645–648.
9. FERNSTROM, M. H. & D. J. KUPFER. 1988. Antidepressant-induced weight gain: A comparison study of four medications. Psychiatr. Res. 26: 265–271.
10. BERKEN, G. H., D. WEINSTEIN & W. C. STERN. 1984. Weight gain: A side-effect of tricyclic antidepressants. J. Affect. Dis. 7: 133–138.
11. FERNSTROM, M. H., R. L. KROWINSKI & D. J. KUPFER. 1986. Chronic imipramine treatment and weight gain. Psychiatr. Res. 17: 269–272.
12. FERNSTROM, M. H., R. L. KROWINSKI & D. J. KUPFER. 1987. Appetite and food preference in depression: Effects of imipramine treatment. Biol. Psychiatry 22: 529–539.
13. FERNSTROM, M. H. & D. J. KUPFER. 1988. Imipramine treatment and preference for sweets. Appetite 10: 149–155.
14. DREWNOWSKI, A. & M. R. C. GREENWOOD. 1982. Cream and sugar: Human preferences for high-fat foods. Physiol. Behav. 30: 629–633.
15. GARROW, J. S. 1978. Energy Balance and Obesity in Man, 2nd Edit. Elsevier-North Holland Press. Oxford, England.
16. FERNSTROM, M. H., D. G. SPIKER, L. H. EPSTEIN & D. J. KUPFER. 1985. Resting metabolic rate is reduced in patients treated with antidepressants. Biol. Psychiatry 20: 688–692.
17. MCARDLE, W., F. KATCH & V. KATCH. 1981. Exercise Physiology: Energy, Nutrition and Human Performance. Lea and Fibiger. Philadelphia.
18. FERNSTROM, M. H., M. MASSOUDI & D. J. KUPFER. 1988. Fluvoxamine treatment increases metabolic rate and promotes weight loss. Biol. Psychiatry 24: 948–949.

DISCUSSION

DR. R. WURTMAN (*Massachusetts Institute of Technology, Cambridge, MA*): First, I'd like to congratulate Dr. Fernstrom on what I think is a very compelling piece of work. Hereafter all of us must consider the peripheral metabolic effects of these categories of drugs in trying to interpret their effects on weight.

We've just completed, in our clinical center, a similar study on the effects of another serotonin compound, *d*-fenfluramine, on thermogenesis, both basal and following food consumption. We see exactly what you see with fluvoxamine, and it suggests that the serotonin-specific drugs may be categorically different from the mixed drugs in what they do to thermogenesis. That's very nice.

In terms of carbohydrate craving, our data also tend to agree with yours. There's a big difference between unipolar depressives, the bipolar depressives, and the seasonal depressives that we study. If we bring the patients in, if we measure what they actually eat, we find that in that population the starch craving is every bit as common as the sweet craving and I think, as you've said, that one has to use this dissection of appetitive behaviors as a tool in making different types of homopsychiatric diagnoses with these heterogeneous populations that we face.

One of your slides showed that some of your depressed patients gained weight during their depressive episode and some of them lost weight. I wondered if you took the ones who gained weight, and you put them on amitriptyline or something, (a) did they lose weight, and (b) what did the antidepressant do to their basal metabolic rate?

DR. M. H. FERNSTROM (*University of Pittsburgh School of Medicine, Pittsburgh, PA*): Your question, if I may restate it, is what happens if a patient who had gained weight during the depressive episode were given amitriptyline or another tricyclic antidepressant medication. This raises an interesting point because we have found that there's been an absence of factors that will predict who will gain weight during antidepressant treatment. It's not related to obesity status, body mass index, nor to degree of obesity, or whether the person gained or lost weight during the depressive episode. We still see a reduction in resting metabolic rate in those treated with amitriptyline, which is perhaps not surprising if one is under the premise that the effects that we are seeing are related more to alterations of the drug on sympathetic nervous system function, either centrally or peripherally, rather than related simply to changes in body weight that were seen during the depressive episode.

DR. A. GELIEBTOR (*St. Luke's–Roosevelt Hospital, New York, NY*): Have you also tested MAO inhibitors?

DR. FERNSTROM: The information on that is somewhat incomplete. We tested some monoaminoxidase inhibitors and found a reduction in metabolic rate. These are more problematic in terms of identifying the mechanism simply because they have more complexity of action. They are probably more complex even than the tricyclic antidepressant compounds. Of the MAOIs we have looked at in a few patients, and we don't have a large data base for that, the resting metabolic rate is also reduced.

DR. B. ROLLS (*Johns Hopkins University School of Medicine, Baltimore, MD*): I wonder if you can tell us if the effects of the tricyclics are specific in depressed individuals. Do they only affect depressed individuals, or do you see such effects on resting metabolic rates, diet-induced thermogenesis, in normal individuals given the tricyclics, persons with eating disorders, and so forth?

DR. FERNSTROM: This is a question of great interest to us because the question is are these medications, are these drugs acting only in depression on particular groups of neurons or is it a more ubiquitous effect of these drugs. We're conducting a study in normal individuals. I must tell you, approval to give normal individuals a potent tricyclic antidepressant medication was enormously difficult to get, but we came to a reasonable compromise. I lead into this simply because we are not giving the same dose of amitriptyline that we are giving to the depressed people, yet we do see encouraging results that we're looking at reductions in resting metabolic rate in the normal individual.

The second question is have we looked at this in other psychiatric diseases or eating disorders, and the answer to that is yes, and results actually are very consistent with what we've seen in depression. In normal-weight bulimics treated with imipramine, we find the same pattern of reduced metabolic rate and reduced, diet-induced thermogenesis, indicating increased metabolic efficiency of the body during treatment with these drugs.

DR. J. MORLEY (*Sepulveda VA Medical Center, Sepulveda, CA*): Did the metabolic rate covary with the depressive scores or were they separate? In other words, as the metabolic rate changed were the biggest changes seen in those who have the greatest improvement in their depression, or do you not have a sufficiently large sample to really look at that at this time?

DR. FERNSTROM: We looked at that, and that was another factor that did not seem to predict or correlate at all with the changes we saw in metabolic rate. In fact, the kinds of changes we see might be opposed to what one might expect during recovery, namely, improved mood, increased activity, and restored appetite. These would all increase the metabolic rate rather than reduce it, but, no, we haven't seen that association.

Psychopharmacology of Eating Disorders[a]

JAMES E. MITCHELL

Eating Disorders Program
Department of Psychiatry
University of Minnesota Medical School
Minneapolis, Minnesota 55455

Over the last decade pharmacotherapies have played an increasingly important role in the treatment of patients with anorexia nervosa and bulimia nervosa. This is particularly true of bulimia nervosa, where antidepressant therapy is firmly established as a useful component of treatment for many patients.

Much of the interest in drug therapies for eating disorders grew out of attempts to treat certain target symptoms with drugs that had originally been developed for other diagnoses, for example the use of antipsychotics to treat the "delusional" beliefs of anorectics concerning body weight and shape, and the use of antidepressants to treat the depression associated with bulimia nervosa. More recently, treatment strategies have evolved from basic research findings concerning the mechanisms that control appetite and eating, and it can be anticipated that our rapidly expanding knowledge concerning the biology of eating behavior will continue to offer new, interesting strategies that will be translatable into clinical practice.

In this paper I will review the studies of pharmacological agents in anorexia nervosa and bulimia nervosa, focusing on the controlled treatment literature. We turn first to the treatment of anorexia nervosa.

ANOREXIA NERVOSA

Antidepressants

Depression is commonly seen in patients with anorexia nervosa, and some researchers have argued that anorexia nervosa might actually be regarded as a form of affective disorder,[1] although this notion is a matter of considerable debate.[2] One confounding element in attempting to examine the relationship between anorexia nervosa and affective disorders is the effect of starvation, which causes many symptoms suggestive of depression.

Most of the literature on the antidepressant treatment of anorexia nervosa consists of case reports and series of patients[1,3-7] and is in general supportive of the use of antidepressants in the treatment of this disorder. Only three controlled trials have been reported. Lacey and Crisp[8] in 1980 reported a placebo-controlled, double-blind trial

[a] Supported in part by National Institute of Mental Health Grants MH40377 and MH43296 and a Research Scientist Award from the Joseph P. Kennedy Foundation.

in 13 hospitalized anorexia nervosa subjects who were treated for 10 to 11 weeks with clomipramine at a dosage of 50 mg a day ($n = 6$) or placebo ($n = 7$). There were no significant differences between active drug and placebo. The dosage selected for this study was certainly reasonable given the fact that this was an initial investigation in a group of patients who generally tolerate tricyclics poorly. However, in retrospect the small sample size and low dosage employed make it difficult to generalize from this study. Biederman et al.[9] reported a double-blind, placebo-controlled trial of amitriptyline. Eleven subjects were randomized to active drug and fourteen to placebo. Again, there was no significant advantage for active drug over placebo. The mean dosage at termination was 150 mg with a mean serum level of 140 ± 95 ng/ml (amitriptyline plus nortriptyline).

The third study, by Halmi et al.,[10] was a multicenter study in 72 anorectic subjects and employed a three-cell design: cyproheptadine with dosage increases to a maximum of 32 mg a day, amitriptyline with dosage increases to a maximum of 160 mg a day, and placebo. The results in the cyproheptadine cell will be discussed later. Subjects receiving amitriptyline gained weight more quickly than those treated with placebo, although the side effects of the drug were problematic.

Taken together, these studies provide decidedly mixed results. Overall, we must conclude that the evidence for the use of antidepressants in this population is preliminary, and the side effects of many of the tricyclic antidepressants make them difficult to use with these patients. Some of these problems may be obviated by the use of newer, less anticholinergic compounds in higher dosages.

Lithium Carbonate

A few case reports have suggested the utility of lithium in the treatment of anorexia nervosa.[11-12] However, there has only been one controlled trial, reported by Gross et al. in 1981.[13] The study involved 16 inpatients who were also involved in a behavior-modification program. Serum lithium levels were kept between 0.9 and 1.4 mg/dl and subjects were treated for four weeks. Subjects on active drug had gained more weight at weeks three and four. However, the authors were careful to stress that the use of lithium can be problematic in patients with anorexia nervosa, who frequently have fluid, electrolyte, and cardiovascular problems.

Cyproheptadine

Cyproheptadine is a serotonin and histamine antagonist that has been noted for some time to stimulate appetite in patients being treated with it for various allergic conditions.[14-15] A case report in 1970[16] first suggested the possible utility of the drug in the treatment of anorexia nervosa, and Silverstone and Schuyler[17] reported a small outpatient trial of the drug in 1972, again indicating that the drug might be beneficial in this population.

Three additional double-blind placebo-controlled trials have been reported. In 1977, Vigersky and Loriaux[18] reported that they had treated 13 patients with active drug (12 mg a day) and 11 with placebo for eight weeks in a randomized trial. There were no significant differences between the two groups at outcome. Goldberg et al.[19] reported the results of a multicenter trial that used a four-cell design: cyproheptadine plus behavior therapy, cyproheptadine plus standard ward milieu therapy, placebo plus behavior therapy, placebo plus standard ward milieu therapy. Dosages ranged from 12 to 32 mg a day. There was a small numerical advantage for active drug over placebo, but the difference was not statistically significant.

Halmi et al.[10] reported the results of their multicenter study, which was mentioned previously in the antidepressant section. The target dose of medication for cyproheptadine was 32 mg. The patients taking cyproheptadine achieved their target weight on average 10.5 days earlier than those taking placebo. A particularly interesting finding was a differential effect in subgroups of anorectic patients. Cyproheptadine increased treatment efficiency in the nonbulimic subgroup but seemed to impair treatment efficiency in the bulimic subgroup. This was the first pharmacological finding suggesting a significant biological difference between these two subgroups.

Taken together, the available studies suggest that cyproheptadine may be quite useful in the treatment of anorexia nervosa. The drug is fairly well tolerated by this patient group. If it is to be used, it should be used at higher dosages such as those employed in the Halmi et al.[10] study.

Antipsychotics

Dally et al.[20] reported the first trial of neuroleptics in patients with anorexia nervosa in 1958. Patients were treated with chlorpromazine to a maximum of 1000 mg a day (mean dose 600 mg), combined with insulin, which was used as an appetite stimulant. These authors subsequently summarized their treatment experience with an expanded series of 48 patients.[21] As a control, they used data on 48 patients who had been treated in their facility over the preceding 20 years who had not received chlorpromazine; therefore, treatment was not randomized. The authors concluded that chlorpromazine plus insulin was effective in inducing more rapid weight gain. It is of note that at follow-up there was no significant difference in weight between the two groups.

Crisp and colleagues reported a single case, and subsequently a series of 21 patients with anorexia nervosa, many of whom received chlorpromazine as part of their treatment.[22,23] A few other case reports or uncontrolled trials have appeared.[24,25]

Two placebo-controlled, randomized trials have been reported, both by Vandereycken and colleagues.[26,27] The first study, reported in 1980, involved a double-blind, crossover trial of pimozide in 18 female inpatients who were also involved in a contingency management program.[26] The dosage of pimozide varied from 4 to 6 mg. There was a statistical trend for superiority in the active drug phase. The subsequent trial of 18 patients used the same basic design, but employed the alternative neuroleptic sulpiride at a dosage of 300 to 400 mg a day.[27] No significant advantage was found for active drug over placebo. However, the weight gain was higher in 13 of the 18 patients during the sulpiride treatment phase.

In conclusion there does not appear to be evidence that neuroleptics should be used routinely or even commonly among patients with anorexia nervosa.

Other Treatments

Casper et al. reported a small placebo-controlled, crossover study of the α_2-adrenergic agonist clonidine in four patients with anorexia nervosa.[28] There was no advantage for the active drug over placebo.

Johanson and Knorr[29] have reported open-label trials of L-dopa in patients with anorexia nervosa for up to four months in duration. These authors concluded that five of the nine patients they treated responded well without evidence of adverse effects.

Gross et al.[30] reported a controlled trial of δ-9-tetrahydrocannabinol (THC) in patients with anorexia nervosa. The rationale for this approach was based on a common observation that marijuana stimulates appetite in many users. Eleven hospitalized patients participated in the protocol, which employed a double-blind crossover design. Medication was given before each meal with the dose of δ-9-THC adjusted from 7.5 mg to 30 mg. Diazepam was used as an active control in increasing doses from 3 to 15 mg. There was no evidence for an advantage for δ-9-THC, and several of the patients tolerated the drug poorly.

Patients with anorexia nervosa frequently have markedly delayed gastric emptying time. This is particularly problematic during the period of refeeding, when it is necessary for them to eat large amounts of food in order to gain weight, yet they may have a great deal of abdominal pain and bloating after eating.[31] Because of this, several research groups have attempted to use pharmacological agents to stimulate gastric peristalsis, including metoclopramide[32,33] and domperidone[31] with some success. However, it should be remembered that metoclopramide is a dopamine blocker that crosses the blood–brain barrier and poses the risk of the development of neurological side effects.

Attempts have also been made to modify the endogenous opioid system as a way of modulating appetite in anorexia nervosa. Moore et al.[34] treated inpatients with naloxone and placebo at various intervals, using naloxone dosages of 3.2 to 6.4 mg a day, by continuous infusion. Patients had a significantly greater weight gain during periods of naloxone infusion. Unfortunately the design of this experiment makes interpretation of the results difficult. Recently Luby et al.[35] have also reported improvement in anorectic patients using narcotic antagonists. To my knowledge, a placebo-controlled, double-blind trial in this population has not been reported using this class of drugs.

Other agents that have been reported to be effective in case reports or series of patients include zinc supplementation as a way of stimulating appetite,[36] phenoxybenzamine,[37] and glycerol as a source of glucose and to replenish carbohydrate stores.[38] The administration of ACTH, cortisone,[39] and the anabolic steroid nandrolone[40] can no longer be considered acceptable in these patients given our current knowledge of the systemic effects of these compounds.

BULIMIA NERVOSA

Anticonvulsants

Rau, Green, and their colleagues, in a series of papers published between 1974 and 1979, explored the hypothesis that bulimia might represent a seizure equivalent.[41-44] These authors pointed out certain similarities between binge eating and seizure activity. They reported EEG abnormalities in 64% of a series of 59 patients with compulsive overeating whom they evaluated. The most frequent abnormalities described were a 14 and 6 per second spike pattern. They treated 47 of these patients with the antiepileptic phenytoin open label, and described improvement in symptoms in the majority of cases.

There has been one controlled trial of phenytoin in binge-eating, by Wermuth et al.[45] This double-blind, crossover study involved a total of 20 subjects. The results were confounded by the fact that binge frequency did not increase following the switch to placebo in the active drug–placebo sequence, and overall no significant difference was found between the two active treatments. There also was no relationship between the presence of EEG abnormalities and response.

Kaplan et al.[46] reported a small pilot crossover study in six patients using the anticonvulsant carbamazepine and placebo. Only one of the patients appeared to respond to carbamazepine.

Opioid Antagonists

Jonas and Gold in 1986 reported a six-week, open-label trial of naltrexone in five bulimic women who had failed to respond to antidepressants.[47] The patients tolerated the drug quite well, and all demonstrated a significant reduction in bulimic symptoms. These authors subsequently expanded their series to include 25 subjects treated with naltrexone at dosages of 200 to 300 mg a day.[48] Five subjects were unable to complete the protocol because of gastrointestinal side effects, and one patient required dosage reduction because of liver transaminase elevations. All of the remaining subjects demonstrated significant reductions in bulimic symptoms.

Our group at the University of Minnesota reported a small pilot pharmacological probe study involving infusion of naloxone, CCK-8, or placebo before binge eating episodes in women hospitalized on a research ward.[49] The putative satiety agent CCK-8 failed to suppress binge eating. However, naloxone administration followed by the continuous infusion of naloxone resulted in a significant reduction in the amount of food consumed. Our group subsequently undertook a placebo-controlled, double-blind crossover study of naltrexone in 16 normal-weight bulimic outpatients at a dosage of 50 mg a day.[50] The use of the active drug was not associated with a clinically significant reduction in target symptoms, although there were some trends favoring active drug on target eating variables. Jonas and Gold have subsequently reported a lack of effect for the 50- to 100-mg dose range in seven bulimic patients treated open label, with improvement in four of these patients when they were crossed over to higher dose therapy.[48] Therefore, low-dose naltrexone appears to be ineffective in the treatment of this condition while high-dose therapy may have a significant effect. However, strong consideration must be given to the problem of nausea with this drug at high dosage, and the potential problem of hepatotoxicity, which has been previously summarized in the literature.[51]

Antidepressants

Pope and Hudson were first to report the use of tricyclic antidepressants in patients with bulimia nervosa.[52] Their initial report led to the development and implementation of several controlled, double-blind studies. The initial impetus to employ antidepressants grew from the hypothesis that these agents would improve the depressive symptoms seen so commonly in these patients, and therefore allow them to better control their eating behavior. Subsequent studies have shown that the drugs may work through a different mechanism, and are also effective in many patients who do not have depressive symptoms at baseline.

Pope et al.[52] were the first to report a double-blind, placebo-controlled trial using a parallel design. Several other trials have employed a similar parallel design[53-59] while two studies have employed crossover designs.[60,61] The particulars of these studies and the percent reduction in binge eating frequence pre- to post-treatment are shown in TABLE 1. With the exception of the study by Sabin et al.,[54] all of the studies have demonstrated superiority for active drug over placebo on target eating variables and/or ratings of mood. The studies by Hughes et al.[56] and Horne et al.[59] are of particular interest because these investigators selected nondepressed patients for participation.

TABLE 1. Overview of Controlled Antidepressant Treatment Studies in Bulimia Nervosa

Investigator	Drug	Dosage	Design	Duration	Percent Reduction Binge Eating
Pope et al.[53]	Imipramine	200 mg	Parallel	6 wk	70%
Sabine et al.[54]	Mianserin	60 mg	Parallel	8 wk	
Mitchell & Groat[55]	Amitriptyline	150 mg	Parallel	8 wk	72%
Hughes et al.[56]	Desipramine	200 mg	Parallel	6 wk	91%
Agras et al.[57]	Imipramine	$\bar{x} = 167$ mg	Parallel	16 wk	72%
Walsh et al.[58]	Phenelzine	69–90 mg	Parallel	8 wk	64%
Barlow et al.[60]	Desipramine	150 mg	Crossover	6 wk	
Horne et al.[59]	Bupropion	450 mg	Parallel	8 wk	67%
Blouin et al.[61]	Desipramine	150 mg	Crossover	6 wk	
	Fenfluramine	60 mg			

We have previously published the preliminary results of an antidepressant–psychotherapy comparison study in bulimia nervosa.[62] This protocol employed randomization to one of four cells: active drug plus involvement in an intensive outpatient group psychotherapy program, placebo plus group involvement, active drug alone, and placebo alone. Preliminary results suggested superiority for group therapy, with or without drug, over drug therapy alone.[64] This study raises interesting questions about the place of antidepressant treatment in bulimia nervosa. Although these drugs appear to be quite useful with many patients, there is a question as to whether or not they should be employed as the sole treatment, because certain forms of psychotherapy may be superior. This needs to be studied further.

The only long-term follow-up study of antidepressant treatment of bulimia nervosa was published by Pope et al.[63] They followed 20 bulimic subjects who had originally been treated in their imipramine protocol. Ten (50%) were in remission in follow-up, and nineteen (95%) were improved. However, the authors noted that managing these patients required frequent medication changes and dosage adjustments.

Other Therapies

Hsu[64] has reported the results of a nonblind trial of bulimia nervosa, and has subsequently added an additional 17 patients to the series. Overall, 25 of the 31 subjects had at least a 75% reduction in target symptom frequency.

CONCLUSIONS

Pharmacotherapy is emerging as an important treatment in the management of eating disorders. In anorexia nervosa, cyproheptadine appears to be of particular promise because it improves the rate of weight gain and mood and has a tolerable level of side effects. The antidepressant studies are difficult to interpret given the small number of studies done and the dosages employed. Further protocols in this area may elect to use alternative, less anticholinergic agents and to focus on maintenance strategies as well as acute treatment. In bulimia nervosa, much of the treatment literature has focused on use of antidepressants, which appear to be a very useful treatment for many patients. Preliminary data concerning opioid antagonists are promising, but placebo-controlled, double-blind studies at higher dosages need to be done before this should be an accepted form of therapy, given the possible hepatotoxicity of naltrexone.

REFERENCES

1. HUDSON, J. I., G. P. POPE, J. M. JONAS & D. YURGELUN-TODD. 1985. J. Clin. Psychopharmacol. **5:** 17–23.
2. ALTSHULER, K. Z. & M. F. WEINER. 1985. Am. J. Psychiatry **142:** 328–332.
3. MILLS, I. H. 1976. Lancet **2:** 687.
4. MOORE, D. C. 1977. Am. J. Psychiatry **134:** 1303–1304.
5. NEEDLEMAN, H. L. & D. WABER. 1976. Lancet **2:** 580.
6. NEEDLEMAN, H. L. & D. WABER. 1977. In Anorexia Nervosa. R. A. Vigersky, Ed.: 357–362. Raven Press. New York.
7. WHITE, J. H. & N. L. SCHNAULTZ. 1977. Dis. Nerv. Syst. **38:** 567–571.
8. LACEY, J. H. & A. H. CRISP. 1980. Postgrad. Med. J. **56:** 79–85.
9. BIEDERMAN, J., D. A. HERZOG, T. M. RIVINUS, G. P. HARPER, R. A. FERBER, et al. 1985. J. Clin. Psychopharmacol. **5:** 10–16.
10. HALMI, K. A., E. ECKERT, T. LADU & J. COHEN. 1986. Arch. Gen. Psychiatry **43:** 177–181.
11. BARCAI, A. 1977. Acta Psychiatr. Scand. **55:** 97–101.
12. STEIN, G. S., S. HARTSHORN, J. JONES & D. STEINBERG. 1982. Br. J. Psychiatry **140:** 526–528.
13. GROSS, H. A., M. H. EBERT, V. B. FADEN, S. C. GOLDBERG & W. H. KAYE. 1981. J. Clin. Psychopharmacol. **1:** 376–381.
14. BERGEN, S. S. 1964. Am. J. Dis. Child. **108:** 270–273.
15. STIEL, J. N., G. W. LIDDLE & W. W. LACEY. 1970. Metabolism **19:** 192–200.
16. BENADY, D. R. 1970. Br. J. Psychiatry **117:** 681–682.
17. SILVERSTONE, T. & D. SCHUYLER. 1975. Psychopharmacologia **40:** 335–350.
18. VIGERSKY, R. A. & D. L. LORIAUX. 1977. In Anorexia Nervosa. R. A. Vigersky, Ed.: 346–356. Raven Press. New York.
19. GOLDBERG, S. C., K. A. HALMI, E. D. ECKERT, R. C. CASPER & J. M. DAVIS. 1979. Br. J. Psychiatry **134:** 67–70.
20. DALLY, P. J., G. B. OPPENHEIM & W. SARGANT. 1958. Br. Med. J. **2:** 633–634.
21. DALLY, P. & W. SARGANT. 1966. Br. Med. J. **2:** 793–795.
22. CRISP, A. H. 1965. Br. J. Psychiatry **112:** 505–512.
23. CRISP, A. H. & F. J. ROBERTS. 1962. Postgrad. Med. J. **38:** 350–352.
24. HOES, M. 1980. J. Orthomol. Psychiatry **9:** 48–51.
25. PLANTLEY, F. 1977. Lancet **1:** 1105.
26. VANDEREYCKEN, W. & R. PIERLOTT. 1982. Acta Psychiatr. Scand. **66:** 445–450.
27. VANDEREYCKEN, W. 1984. Br. J. Psychiatry **144:** 288–292.
28. CASPAR, R. C., R. FRANCIS SCHLEMMER, JR. & I. JAVAID. 1987. A placebo-controlled cross-over study of oral clonidine in acute anorexia nervosa. Psychiatr. Res. **20:** 249–260.
29. JOHANSON, A. J. & N. J. KNORR. 1977. In Anorexia Nervosa. R. A. Vigersky, Ed.: 363–372. Raven Press. New York.
30. GROSS, H., M. EBERT, V. B. FADEN, S. C. GOLDBERG, W. H. KAYE, et al. 1983. J. Clin. Psychopharmacol. **3:** 165–171.
31. RUSSELL, D. M., M. L. FREEDMAN, D. H. I. FEIGLIN, K. N. JEEJEEBHOY, R. P. SWINSON, et al. 1983. Am. J. Psychiatry **140:** 1235–1236.
32. LEBWOHL, P. 1980. Am. J. Gastroenterol. **74:** 127–132.
33. MOLDOFSY, H., N. JEUNIEWIC & P. E. GARFINKEL. 1977. In Anorexia Nervosa. R. A. Vigersky, Ed.: 373–375. Raven Press. New York.
34. MOORE, R., I. H. MILLS & A. FORSTER. 1981. J. R. Soc. Med. **74:** 129–131.
35. LUBY, E. D., M. A. MARRAZZI & J. KINZIE. 1987. Case reports — treatment of chronic anorexia nervosa with opiate blockade. J. Clin. Psychopharmacol. **7(1):** 52–53.
36. BRYCE-SMITH, D. & R. I. D. SIMPSON. 1984. Lancet **2:** 350.
37. REDMOND, D. E., A. SWANN & G. R. HENINGER. 1976. Lancet **II:** 307.
38. CAPLIN, H., J. GINSBURG & P. BEACONSFIELD. 1973. Lancet **1:** 319.

39. GREENBLATT, R . B., W. M. E. BARFIELD & S. L. CLARKS. 1951. J. Med. Assoc. Georgia 40: 229-301.
40. TEC, L. 1974. J. M. Med. Assoc. 229: 1423.
41. GREEN, R. S. & J. H. RAU. 1974. Am. J. Psychiatry 131: 428-432.
42. GREEN, R. S. & J. H. RAU. 1977. In Anorexia Nervosa. R. A. Vigersky, Ed.: 377-382. Raven Press. New York.
43. RAU, J. H. & R. S. GREEN. 1975. Compr. Psychiatry 16: 223-231.
44. RAU, J. H., F. A. STRUVE & R. S. GREEN. 1979. Clin. Electroencephalogr. 10: 180-189.
45. WERMUTH, B. M., K. L. DAVIS, L. E. HOLLISTER & A. J. STUNKARD. 1977. Am. J. Psychiatry 134: 1249-1253.
46. KAPLAN, A. S., P. E. GARFINKEL, P. L. DARBY & D. M. GARNER. 1983. Am. J. Psychiatry 140: 1225-1226.
47. JONAS, J. M. & M. S. GOLD. 1986. Naltrexone reverses bulimic symptoms. Lancet 1: 807.
48. JONAS, J. M. & M. S. GOLD. 1987. Treatment of bulimia with opiate antagonist naltrexone: Preliminary data and theoretical implications. In Psychobiology of Bulimia. J. I. Hudson & H. G. Pope, Eds. APA Press.
49. MITCHELL, J. E., D. E. LAINE, J. E. MORLEY & A. S. LEVINE. 1986. Naloxone but not CCK-8 may attenuate binge-eating behavior in patients with the bulimia syndrome. Biol. Psychiatry 21: 1399-1406.
50. MITCHELL, J. E., G. CHRISTENSON, J. JENNINGS, M. HUBER, B. THOMAS, C. POMEROY & J. MORLEY. A placebo-controlled, double-blind crossover study of naltrexone hydrochloride in outpatients with normal weight bulimia.
51. PFOHL, D. N., J. I. ALLEN, R. L. ATKINSON, D. S. KNOPMEN, R. J. MALCOLM, J. D. MITCHELL & J. E. MORLEY. 1985. Naltrexone hydrochloride (Trexan): A review of serum transaminase elevations at high dosage. In Problems of Drug Dependence. NIDA Research Monograph. Bethesda, MD.
52. POPE, H. G. JR. & J. I. HUDSON. 1982. Treatment of bulimia with antidepressants. Psychopharmacology 78: 176-179.
53. POPE, H. G. JR., J. I. HUDSON, J. M. JONAS, et al. 1983. Bulimia treated with imipramine: A placebo-controlled, double-blind study. Am. J. Psychiatry 140: 554-558.
54. SABINE, E. J., A. YONACE, A. J. FARRINGTON, et al. 1983. Bulimia nervosa: A placebo controlled double-blind therapeutic trial of mianserin. Br. J. Clin. Pharmacol. 15: 195S-202S.
55. MITCHELL, J. E. & R. GROAT. 1984. A placebo-controlled, double-blind trial of amitriptyline in bulimia. J. Clin. Psychopharmacol. 4: 186-193.
56. HUGHES, P. L., L. A. WELLS, C. J. CUNNINGHAM, et al. 1986. Treating bulimia with desipramine. Arch. Gen. Psychiatry 43: 182-186.
57. AGRAS, W. S., B. DORIAN, B. G. KIRKLEY, et al. 1987. Imipramine in the treatment of bulimia: A double-blind controlled study. Int. J. Eating Dis. 6: 29-38.
58. WALSH, B. T., M. GLADIS, S. P. ROOSE, et al. 1988. Phenelzine vs. placebo in 50 patients with bulimia. Arch. Gen. Psychiatry 45: 471-475.
59. HORNE, R. L., J. M. FERGUSON, H. G. POPE, et al. 1988. Treatment of bulimia with bupropion: A multicenter controlled trial. J. Clin. Psychiatry 49: 262-266.
60. BARLOW, J., J. BLOUIN, A. BLOUIN, et al. 1988. Treatment of bulimia with desipramine: A double-blind crossover study. Can. J. Psychiatry 33:129-133.
61. BLOUIN, A. G., J. H. BLOUIN, E. L. PEREZ, et al. 1988. Treatment of bulimia with fenfluramine and desipramine. J. Clin. Psychopharmacol. 8: 261-269.
62. MITCHELL, J. E., R. L. PYLE, E. D. ECKERT, D. HATSUKAMI, C. POMEROY & R. ZIMMERMAN. 1988. Preliminary results of a comparison treatment trial of bulimia nervosa. In The Psychobiology of Bulimia Nervosa. K. M. Pirke, V. Vandereycken & D. Ploog, Eds. Springer-Verlag. Berlin/Heidelberg.
63. POPE, H. G., J. I. HUDSON, J. M. JONAS, et al. 1985. Antidepressant treatment of bulimia: A two-year follow-up study. J. Clin. Psychopharmacol. 5: 320-327.
64. HSU, L. K. G. 1984. Treatment of bulimia with lithium. Am. J. Psychiatry 141: 1260-1262.

DISCUSSION

Dr. Silvio Garatini (*Mario Negri, Milan Italy*): You mentioned that metochlopramide and domperidone may be effective agents in treatment of anorexia because they stimulate activity of the gastric functions. These compounds have been recently recognized to have not only antipulmonergic activity but also an antiserotonergic activity in a subset of receptors called 5HT$_3$. There are now specific 5HT$_3$ inhibitors that lack the antipulmonergic activity, such as odansidine and BYM25801. These agents may be candidates for trials. Is there anything going on now?

Dr. J. E. Mitchell (*University of Minnesota, Minneapolis, MN*): I'm not aware of those compounds being investigated in these patients. I didn't mean to imply that they should be used routinely or that they've been demonstrated as efficacious in controlled trials. The reports have been anecdotal in patients with a lot of postprandial bloating.

Dr. K. Halmi (*New York Hospital–Cornell Medical Center, White Plains, NY*): It seems to me a contradiction that we use antidepressants to reduce bulimic behavior, yet from Madelyn Fernstrom's study we know that antidepressants can cause weight gain, and almost all bulimics are very concerned about their body image and their weight. Don't you think eventually patients treated with antidepressants who gain weight will simply continue their bulimic and purging behavior to try to control their weight?

Dr. Mitchell: Certainly an interesting question. As you know, in most of the published antidepressant studies patients did not gain weight. If anything, if we looked at all the studies, we'd find that the typical patient in these protocols lost weight. That may mean that the disadvantages of the antidepressants are offset by the improved nutritional status overall. Also, patients with bulimia nervosa, when they're actively bulimic, have unfortunate consequences in their weight which may improve by virtue of better nutrition. So, a number of factors are involved. What little follow-up work is available would suggest that patients who are maintained on antidepressants don't gain weight. That's certainly true of our six-month follow-up data, and I think that was true of Skip Pope's two-year follow-up data.

Dr. Sarah Leibowitz (*Rockefeller University, New York, NY*): You've been focusing on body weight which is clearly the easiest measure, but what about the long-term effects of the drug treatment in terms of subsequent effects on appetite and eating patterns? As we know, the anorexics as well as bulimics may maintain abnormal eating patterns. Has there been any long-term documentation of that relative to the drug effects?

Dr. Mitchell: Not to my knowledge. We have a limited amount of data on the effects of CBT therapy versus drug therapy on meal patterns in patients with eating disorders, and those data suggest that, even though the patients are on antidepressants and have ceased binging and vomiting, they really don't normalize their eating patterns. Patients who received the CBT approach normalize their meal intake patterns. I think that means that those patients on drugs are at higher risk for relapse, but I can't absolutely prove that now. I think there are real questions about that.

The Anorexia of the Elderly

JOHN E. MORLEY,[a,b] ANDREW J. SILVER,[a]
DOUGLAS K. MILLER,[c] AND
LAURENCE Z. RUBENSTEIN[a]

[a]Geriatric Research, Education and Clinical Center
Sepulveda VA Medical Center
Sepulveda, California 91343
and
Department of Medicine
UCLA School of Medicine
Los Angeles, California 90024

[c]Department of Medicine
St. Louis University School of Medicine
St. Louis, Missouri 63104

INTRODUCTION

Protein calorie malnutrition is not rare in older persons and is correlated with mortality and morbidity.[1,2] In long-term care facilities in the United States, up to 58% of residents have some degree of malnutrition[3]; even in an academic nursing home where special attention was paid to nutritional status, 26% of the patients were malnourished.[4] In our study of medical outpatients 70 years and older, we found that 11 to 22% displayed various forms of undernutrition (unpublished observations). Among elderly persons in hospitals, 17 to 65% have malnutrition.[5,6] The Health and Nutrition Examination Survey (HANES) for the United States population reported that 16% of white and 18% of blacks older than 60 years ingest less than 1000 calories per day.[7] Among those whose incomes fell below the poverty level, these percentages were 27 and 36%, respectively.

Despite the epidemic proportions reached by protein calorie malnutrition in elderly persons in the United States, as attested to by the above statistics, little attention has been paid to the cause or treatment of this problem. Some of the decreased calorie intake that occurs with aging can be accounted for by the decreased basal metabolic rate (due predominantly to the increased adipose tissue mass) and the decrease in physical activity that occurs with aging.[8] However, this cannot explain the development of malnutrition.

Many of the causes of weight loss in older persons are related to either physical or psychiatric diseases[9] (TABLE 1). However, in hospitalized patients with involuntary weight loss, 35% had no identifiable physical cause of weight loss.[10] In some cases this weight loss can be traced to social factors, such as poverty, a need for help with shopping and food preparation, and/or lack of social interaction associated with meals.

[b] Current address: John E. Morley, M.D., Division of Geriatric Medicine, St. Louis University Medical Center, 1402 S. Grand Blvd., Rm. M238, St. Louis, MO 63104.

TABLE 1. Physical and Psychiatric Causes of Weight Loss and Anorexia in Older Subjects

Physical Causes

Infections
- Candidal esophagitis
- Recurrent infections releasing interleukin-1 and cachectin

Cardiovascular
- Cardiac cachexia (severe right-sided heart failure)

Pulmonary
- Chronic obstructive pulmonary disease and increased effort of eating ("pink puffer")

Gastrointestinal
- Abdominal ischemia leading to pain on eating and early satiety
- Nausea
- Poor dentition
- Dysphagia and aspiration leading to a conditioned aversion to eating
- Malabsorption

Cancer
- Nausea
- Ectopic hormones, for example, bombesin
- Increased utilization
- Decreased lipogenesis and increased lipolysis

Endocrine
- Thyrotoxicosis, particularly the apathetic form
- Addison's disease (adrenal insufficiency)
- Hypopituitarism

Muscular and neurological
- Dysphagia
- Immobility
- Inability to feed oneself
- Depression following cerebrovascular accident

Drugs
- Digoxin
- Laxatives

Psychiatric Causes

- Bereavement
- Depression
- Anorexia nervosa
- Dementia
- Sociopathy (food as a weapon)
- Late-life paranoia

However, when all these factors are excluded, we are still left with a substantial proportion of subjects who have no discernible cause for their weight loss. We have previously suggested that these patients should be designated as suffering from the anorexia of the elderly.[9] A similar idiopathic weight loss and anorexia has been seen in old rodents.[11]

In this brief review, we will first discuss some of the psychiatric and psychological factors associated with weight loss in the elderly. We will then turn our attention to the pathogenesis of anorexia in healthy elderly. For these formulations, we will rely heavily on the rapidly emerging data on the causes of anorexia in old rodents.

THE EATING ATTITUDES TEST
AND WEIGHT LOSS IN THE ELDERLY

In an attempt to gain some preliminary insight into the psychological factors associated with weight loss in the elderly, we administered the 26-item Eating Attitudes Test[12] (EAT-26) to 183 male outpatients over the age of 70 years. All subjects also had a nutritional assessment, had their cognitive status assessed by the Mini-Mental State Examination,[13] and answered the Yesavage Geriatric Depression Scale.[14] Eleven percent of patients had a weight below 90% of average based on Master's tables[15] and 19% had a midarm circumference below 10.4 in (Miller *et al.*, manuscript submitted). Depression, but not cognitive dysfunction, was strongly correlated with both low weight and decreased midarm circumference.

In our preliminary analysis of the EAT-26 data, we found that a surprisingly high percentage of individuals who were below 90% of average body weight appear to have a disturbance of body image. In these subjects, 50% answered never or rarely to the question, "other people think I am too thin," and 45% answered similarly to "feel that others would prefer if I ate more."

TABLE 2 lists the percentages of subjects with a midarm circumference below 10.4 in, who answered "sometimes" or "more often" to a series of questions where these answers would seem to be highly unlikely in malnourished subjects. The majority of subjects "displayed self-control around food," nearly one-third "like their stomach to be empty," and one-fifth "avoid eating when hungry." Clearly pathological responses in this malnourished group of subjects were seen in 9% who were "terrified about being overweight" and one subject who felt "extremely guilty after eating."

Using the subscales of the EAT-26 as suggested by Garner *et al.*[16] the malnourished subjects as a group scored lower on Factor I (dieting) and Factor II (bulimia and food preoccupation), and significantly higher on Factor III (oral control) than did either normal weight or overweight subjects. Factor III consists predominantly of items related to self-control concerning food and an acknowledgment of social pressure to gain weight. In younger subjects, it has been suggested that high scores on Factor III would be associated with a favorable outcome.[16]

Overall, these findings demonstrate objectively that some older malnourished subjects have pathological attitudes toward eating and that approximately half of them have a distorted body image. The role that these abnormal attitudes played in the development of their protein-calorie malnutrition cannot be discerned from this study. However, it seems reasonable to suggest that these attitudes may, at least in part, explain the malnutrition seen in this group and in a small percentage of these patients may have been the primary causative factor. In addition, these findings suggest that the EAT-26 may be a useful tool in probing eating attitudes in older persons.

TABLE 2. Percentage of Subjects with a Midarm Circumference below 10.4 Inches Who Answered Sometimes, Often, Usually, or Always to Selected Items on the EAT-26

Display self-control around food	70%
Like my stomach to be empty	30%
Avoid eating when hungry	18%
Engage in dieting behavior	9%
Am terrified about being overweight	9%
Am preoccupied with a desire to be thinner	3%
Feel extremely guilty after eating	3%

DEPRESSION, AGING, AND ANOREXIA

Depression occurs approximately half as often in elderly compared to younger persons.[17] However, in the elderly, the diagnosis of depression is often missed, predominantly because of the ageist viewpoint that the "losses" experienced by the elderly make it reasonable for "them" to be depressed. While, on the whole, depressed elderly demonstrate similar symptoms to younger subjects, weight loss is seen more frequently in depressed elderly than in depressed younger subjects.[18] Zung[19] found that a decreased appetite was one of the most common symptoms reported. Other symptoms in depressed elderly that could reduce nutrient intake include diarrhea and/or constipation, stomach pains, nausea, vomiting, and weakness.[20]

The neurotransmitter alterations associated with anorexia of depression are not fully elucidated. Antidepressants that enhance the catecholamine system increase appetite.[19] Further, much evidence exists for an increased activity of the hypothalamic–pituitary–adrenal axis in depression and corticotropin-releasing factor (CRF) levels are elevated in the cerebrospinal fluid of patients with depression.[21] CRF is a potent inhibitor of food intake in rodents.[22] For these reasons, it has been suggested that CRF plays a role in the pathophysiology of the anorexia associated with depression.

DEMENTIA AND ANOREXIA

In our study of nursing home patients,[4] dementia occurred more commonly in malnourished patients. Sandman et al.[23] found protein-energy malnutrition in the majority of demented patients studied despite a purported sufficient dietary intake (mean 2059 kcal/day). Further carefully controlled studies are needed to determine whether demented patients do, in fact, have an increased energy expenditure. Causes of decreased food intake in cognitively impaired subjects include indifference to food, failure to remember to eat, impairment of recognition of the need to eat, an inability to self feed, and apraxia. The time spent feeding demented patients in an institutional setting has been shown to be inadequate. The neurotransmitter candidates that have been suggested to play a role in the anorexia associated with Alzheimer's disease are neuropeptide Y and norepinephrine.[9]

As pointed out by Fairburn and Hope,[24] besides anorexia, a number of other eating disturbances are observed in cognitively impaired subjects. Of these, increases in eating are probably the most common. Pica, especially coprophagia, is associated with dementia. Ghaziuddin and McDonald[25] reported that nine out of 14 subjects with coprophagia had dementia. Apraxia, the failure to swallow chewed food, has already been alluded to.

ANOREXIA NERVOSA

Since 1936, when Ryle[26] reported a 59-year-old patient in his series of 51 patients with anorexia nervosa, a number of patients over 50 years old with anorexia nervosa have been reported (TABLE 3). Only one of these has been a male and from the details reported, the diagnosis appeared doubtful.[27] The oldest reported patient was 94 years old, but a diagnosis of depression may have been more appropriate.[28] Of the reported cases, only the 70-year-old reported by Launer[29] and the 52-year-old reported by Kellet et al.[30] represented classic cases of anorexia nervosa. Nevertheless, it seems clear that

TABLE 3. Case Reports of Anorexia Nervosa in Patients over 50 years

Author	Year	Age	Differential Diagnosis
Ryle[26]	1936	59	?
Bernstein[28]	1972	94	Depression
Kellett[30]	1976	52	Classic
Launer[29]	1978	70	Classic
Price et al.[31]	1985	68	Bereavement
Price et al.[55]	1986	60	Depression
		62	Depression
Nagaratnam & Ghougassian[27]	1988	70	Anorexia of elderly[a]
Russell et al.[56]	1988	69	Anorexia due to small-cell cancer

[a] Only male.

anorexia nervosa should now be considered in the differential diagnosis of weight loss in the elderly.

FOOD AS A WEAPON AND THE ETHICS OF FOOD WITHDRAWAL IN THE ELDERLY

We have now seen a number of elderly patients who, as their physical condition deteriorates, lose their locus of control and attempt to regain it by abusing their caregivers.[32] In these situations, food may be used as a weapon in an attempt to gain control over the caregivers. Both food refusal and the spitting out of food after chewing it are commonly observed ploys. In our experience, these behaviors often occur in patients with a lifelong sociopathic history and are extremely difficult to treat.

A number of court cases, such as the Brophy, Corbett, Conroy, Jobes, and Peter decisions, have concluded that competent patients have the right to refuse intravenous or tube feeding, and that feeding can also be withheld in incompetent subjects who have earlier made their wishes known (see Steinbruck & Lo[33] for a review). On the basis of the known causes of anorexia in the elderly, it would seem prudent to carefully exclude depression and to fully assess the subject's attitudes toward eating before acceding to such a request. In addition, we have now seen a number of subjects who refuse food but nevertheless request that they should be resuscitated when their heart stops. In these cases, we have taken the attitude that a request for feeding withdrawal must recognize that the logical consequence will be death. Thus, we only accept a withdrawal of feeding request when it is accompanied by an agreement to a do-not-resuscitate order.

THE PATHOGENESIS OF THE ANOREXIA OF AGING

As outlined in TABLE 4 a number of factors have been implicated in the pathogenesis of the anorexia of aging. Numerous studies have clearly demonstrated that the ability to enjoy the hedonic qualities of food is diminished with aging. Both increased taste thresholds and decreased olfaction are associated with aging (see Morley & Silver[9] for a review). Opioids play a role in enhancing the enjoyment of sweet and salty tastes[34]; and in view of the decreased activity of the opioid system with aging, it has been suggested that alterations in opioid activity may play a major role in the reduction of the appreciation of the hedonic qualities of food that occurs with advancing age.[9]

We have previously postulated that the short-term regulation of food intake is dependent upon a peripheral satiety system and a central feeding system.[35] The components of the peripheral satiety system are a number of gastrointestinal hormones that are released during passage of food through the gastrointestinal tract. It appears that it is the interaction of these peptide hormones that is ultimately responsible for the termination of a meal.

The best studied of these satiety hormones is cholecystokinin (CCK).[36] In our studies in 8- and 25-month-old mice, we examined the effects of age on pharmacologically administered gastrointestinal hormones.[37] CCK-octapeptide was significantly more potent at inhibiting feeding in older mice. In addition, circulating levels of CCK have been demonstrated to be elevated in older humans.[38] On the basis of these studies, it would appear that CCK may play a role in the pathogenesis of the anorexia of aging.

In other studies, we demonstrated that the CCK antagonist, L-364,718, enhanced feeding in a number of paradigms (Silver, Flood, and Morley; unpublished observations). We also found marked strain differences, with L-364,718 being much less potent in C57BL/6 mice compared to TAC(SW) mice. L-364,718 was effective at enhancing feeding in 8-month-old mice but not in 25-month-old mice. These studies would suggest that, while CCK may play a role in the early satiety seen with aging, it does not appear to play a role in tonically reducing food intake in older animals.

Studies by Hinton *et al.*[39] and our group have suggested that satiety is due to the additive effect of gastrointestinal hormones. In addition, our studies suggested that bombesin produced its satiety effects in the mouse both by releasing CCK and by an independent effect. In keeping with this theory, bombesin was slightly more potent in older than in younger mice.[37] In contrast, glucagon was equally effective in adult and old mice.

The major components of the central feeding system appear to be neuropeptide Y (NPY) which drives carbohydrate intake,[40] and the opioid system, which is predominantly responsible for fat intake.[41] Pharmacological studies could show no difference in the responsiveness of young and old mice to NPY as far as food intake was concerned.[42] However, Sahu *et al.*[43] did show a decrease in NPY release from the hypothalamus by 12 months of age, suggesting that decreased release and/or synthesis of NPY may occur with maturation.

TABLE 4. Factors Implicated in the Pathogenesis of the Anorexia of Aging

1. **Decreased Demand**
   Reduced metabolic rate
   Decreased physical activity

2. **Altered Appreciation of the Hedonic Qualities of Food**
   ↓ Taste
   ↓ Smell
   ↓ Vision

3. **Decreased Feeding Drive**
   Impaired opioid feeding drive
   Zinc deficiency

4. **Increased Satiety Factor Activity**
   ↑ Satiety effect of cholecystokinin
   ↑ Circulating levels of cholecystokinin

With advancing age, there is a decrease in both opioid receptor binding affinity and receptor concentrations.[44,45] In addition, a number of studies have found a decrease in opioid peptide concentrations in older animals.[46,47] Gosnell *et al.*[48] reported that older rats were 100 times less sensitive to the suppressive effects of naloxone than were younger rats. Older rats also increased their feeding poorly in response to an injection of the kappa opiate receptor agonist, butorphanol tartrate. Kavaliers and Hirst[49] reported that old mice had reduced feeding responsiveness to morphine and ketocyclazocine. As was the case with rats, the opioid antagonist, naloxone, does not decrease feeding in older mice. Overall, these data suggest that the opioid feeding system is attenuated with advancing age.

The elderly, as a whole, are in a state of precarious zinc balance.[50] Zinc deficiency produces anorexia.[52] Zinc-deficient animals are resistant to dynorphin-induced feeding, and dynorphin levels have been reported to be reduced in the hypothalamus of zinc-deficient animals.[52] It is possible that zinc deficiency may play a role in the anorexia of aging by reducing the activity of the opioid feeding system.

Corticotropin-releasing factor (CRF) is a potent anorectic agent when administered intracerebroventricularly to rodents.[53] The demonstration that a CRF antagonist can partially reverse stress-induced anorexia suggests that this may be a physiological action of CRF.[54] CRF administered intracerebroventricularly was equally effective at suppressing food intake in old (27-month) and mature (10-month) C57B1 male mice, suggesting that CRF does not play a major role in the pathogeneis of the anorexia of aging.

In summary, animal studies have suggested that the cause of the anorexia of aging may involve both an enhanced satiety effect of CCK and a decreased effectiveness of the opioid feeding system. Further studies are necessary to delineate the exact roles of these neuropeptides in the anorexia of aging. In particular, studies in older humans need to be carried out to determine whether similar alterations in neuropeptide responsiveness also occur in humans.

CONCLUSION

Anorexia is not an unusual occurrence with advancing age. While some of this anorexia can be explained by physical and psychiatric diseases that occur more commonly in the elderly, a substantial proportion of anorexia in older persons has no obvious cause. Depression represents an important, and often missed, cause of anorexia in older persons. Recognition is increasing that anorexia nervosa occurs in older subjects and results of the responses to the EAT-26 in underweight males over 70 years suggest that abnormal attitudes toward eating are not rare in this group. Animal studies have suggested that the anorexia of aging may be due to a decrease in the opioid feeding drive and an increase in the responsiveness to the satiety effect of CCK.

REFERENCES

1. MORLEY, J. E., A. J. SILVER, M. A. FIATARONE & A. D. MOORADIAN. 1986. J. Am. Geriatr. Soc. **34:** 2067–2077.
2. MITCHELL, C. O. & D. A. LIPSCHITZ. 1982. Am. J. Clin. Nutr. **36:** 396–406.
3. PINCHOFSKY-DEVIN, G. D. & M. V. KAMINSKI. 1986. J. Am. Geriatr. Soc. **34:** 435–440.
4. SILVER, A. J., J. E. MORLEY, L. S. STROME, D. JONES & L. VICKERS. 1988. J. Am. Geriatr. Soc. **36:** 487–491.
5. RUSSELL, R. M., N. R. SAHYOUN & R. WHINSTON-PERRY. 1986. Nutritional assessment. *In* The Practice of Geriatrics, 1st Ed. E. Calkins, P. J. Davis & A. B. Ford, Eds.: 135–148. W. B. Saunders. Philadelphia, PA.

6. AGARVAL, N., F. ACEVEDO, C. G. CAYTON & C. S. PITCHOMONI. 1986. Am. J. Clin. Nutr. **43:** 659.
7. ABRAHAM, S., M. D. CARROLL, C. M. DRESSER et al. 1977. Dietary intake of persons 1–74 years of age in the United States. Advance data from Vital and Health Statistics of the National Center for Health Statistics, No. 6. Health Resources Administrtion. Public Health Service. Rockville, MD.
8. McGANDY, R. B., C. H. BARROW & A. SPARIAS. 1966. J. Gerontol. **21:** 581–587.
9. MORLEY, J. E. & A. J. SILVER. 1988. Neurobiol. Aging **9:** 9–16.
10. MORTON, K. I., H. C. SOR & J. R. KRUPP. 1981. Ann. Int. Med. **95:** 568–572.
11. PENG, M. T., M. J. JIANG & H. K. KSIO. 1980. J. Gerontol. **35:** 339–347.
12. GARNER, D. M. & P. E. GARFINKEL. 1979. Psychol. Med. **9:** 273–279.
13. FOLSTEIN, M. J., S. E. FOLSTEIN & P. R. McHUGH. 1975. J. Psychiatr. Res. **12:** 189–198.
14. YESAVAGE, J. A., T. L. BRINK, T. L. ROSE, D. LUM, V. HUANG, M. ADEY & V. D. LEIRER. 1982–3. J. Psychiatr. Res. **17:** 37–62.
15. MASTER, A. M., R. P. LASER & G. BECKMAN. 1960. J. Am. Med. Assoc. **172:** 658–662.
16. GARNER, D. M., M. P. OLMSTED, Y. BOHR & P. E. GARFINKEL. 1982. Psychol. Med. **12:** 871–878.
17. BLAND, R. C., S. C. NEWMAN & H. ORN. 1988. Acta Psychiatry Scand. **77**(Suppl. 338): 57–63.
18. BLAZER, D., J. R. BUCHAR & D. C. HUGHES. 1987. J. Am. Geriatr. Soc. **35:** 427–432.
19. ZUNG, W. W. 1967. Psychosomatics **8:** 287–292.
20. KIVELA, S. L., A. NISSIN, J. TUOMILEHTO, J. PEKKANEN, S. PUNSAR, U. LAMMI & P. PUSKA. 1986. Acta Psychiatry Scand. **73:** 93–100.
21. NEMEROFF, C. B., G. BISSETTE & E. WIDERLOV. 1984. Science **226:** 1342–1343.
22. MORLEY, J. E. & J. E. BLUNDELL. 1988. Biol. Psychol. **23:** 53–78.
23. SANDMAN, P. O., R. ADOLFSSON, C. NYGREN, G. HALLMANS & B. WINBLAD. 1987. J. Am. Geriatr. Soc. **35:** 31–38.
24. FAIRBURN, C. G. & R. A. HOPE. 1988. Neurobiol. Aging **9:** 28–29.
25. GHAZIUDDIN, N. & C. McDONALD. 1985. Br. Med. J. **147:** 312–313.
26. RYLE, J. A. 1936. Lancet **2:** 893–894.
27. NAGARATNAM, N. & D. F. GHOUGASSIAN. 1988. Br. Med. J. **296:** 1443–1444.
28. BERNSTEIN, I. C. 1972. Minn. Med. **55:** 552–553.
29. LAUNER, M. A. 1978. Br. J. Med. Psychol. **51:** 375–377.
30. KELLETT, J., M. TRIMBLE & A. THORLEY. 1976. Br. J. Psychiatry **128:** 555–558.
31. PRICE, W. A., A. J. GIANNINI & J. COLELLA. 1985. J. Am. Geriatr. Soc. **33:** 213–215.
32. SOLOMON, D. H., H. L. JUDD, H. C. SIER, L. Z. RUBENSTEIN & J. E. MORLEY. 1988. Ann. Int. Med. **108:** 718–732.
33. STEINBROOK, R. & B. LO. 1988. N. Engl. J. Med. **318:** 286–290.
34. LEVINE, A. S., S. S. MURRAY, J. KNEIP, J. GRACE & J. E. MORLEY. 1982. Physiol. Behav. **28:** 23–25.
35. MORLEY, J. E. 1980. Life Sci. **27:** 355–368.
36. MORLEY, J. E. 1982. Life Sci. **30:** 479–493.
37. SILVER, A. J., J. F. FLOOD & J. E. MORLEY. 1988. Peptides **9:** 221–225.
38. KHALIL, T., J. P. WALKER, J. WEINER, C. J. FAGAN, C. M. TOWNSEND, JR., G. H. GREELEY, JR. & L. C. THOMPSON. 1985. Surgery **98:** 423–429.
39. HINTON, V., M. ROSOFSKY, J. GRANGER & N. GEARY. 1986. Brain Res. Bull. **17:** 615–619.
40. GRAY, T. S. & J. E. MORLEY.. 1986. Life Sci. **38:** 389–401.
41. MORLEY, J. E., A. S. LEVINE, G. K. YIM & M. T. LOWY. 1983. Neurosci. Biobehav. Rev. **7:** 281–305.
42. MORLEY, J. E., E. N. HERNANDEZ & J. F. FLOOD. 1987. Am. J. Physiol. **253:** R516-R522.
43. SAHU, A., P. S. KALRA, W. R. CROWLEY & S. P. KALRA. 1988. Endocrinology **122:** 2199–2203.
44. HESS, G. D., J. A. JOSEPH & G. S. ROTH. 1981. Neurobiol. Aging **2:** 49–55.
45. MESSING, R. B., B. J. VASQUEZ, B. SAMANIEGO, R. A. JENSEN, L. L. MARTINEZ & J. L. McGAUGH. 1981. J. Neurochem. **36:** 784–790.
46. DUPONT, A., P. SAVARD, Y. MERAND, F. LABRIE & J. R. BOISSIER. 1981. Life Sci. **29:** 2317–2322.
47. TANG, F., J. TANG, J. CHOU & E. COSTA. 1984. Life Sci. **35:** 1005–1014.
48. GOSNELL, B. A., A. S. LEVINE & J. E. MORLEY. 1983. Life Sci. **32:** 2793–2799.
49. KAVALIERS, M. & M. HIRST. 1985. Brain Res. **326:** 160–167.

50. MORLEY, J. E. 1986. Am. J. Med. **81:** 679–695.
51. ESSATARA, M'B., A. S. LEVINE, J. E. MORLEY & C. J. MCCLAIN. 1984. Physiol. Behav. **32:** 469–474.
52. ESSATARA, M'B., J. E. MORLEY, A. S. LEVINE, M. K. ELSON, R. B. SHAFER & C. J. MCCLAIN. 1984. Physiol. Behav. **32:** 475–478.
53. MORLEY, J. E. & A. S. LEVINE. 1982. Life Sci. **31:** 1459–1464.
54. KRAHN, D. D., B. A. GOSNELL, M. GRACE & A. S. LEVINE. 1986. Brain Res. Bull. **17:** 285–289.
55. PRICE, W. A., R. B. MASSOOD, M. S. TOREM & J. HILLSIDE. 1986. J. Clin. Psychiatry **8:** 144–151.
56. RUSSELL, J. D., J. BERG & J. R. LAWRENCE. 1988. Med. J. Aust. **148:** 199–201.

DISCUSSION

DR. B. ROLLS (*Johns Hopkins University, Baltimore, MD*): I'd like to comment on the issue of the elderly spitting the food out and not wanting to swallow it. My understanding, from talking to people at the swallowing center at Johns Hopkins, is that often it's because they have a true swallowing disorder that is often probably undetected and often probably the cause of death. There are estimates that up to 40% of the people in nursing homes might have swallowing disorders. I wonder if you or anyone else have done any studies to determine whether the elderly have a true loss of the ability to detect hunger the way we showed the elderly — this is the healthy elderly we're talking about — don't experience thirst.

DR. MORLEY (*Sepulveda VA Medical Center, Sepulveda, CA*): To take the second question first, we also used healthy elderly in our studies so we can't really answer that. The opiate defect appears to be there for the loss of thirst, but we haven't done the studies you're asking about on loss of hunger.

As for as the dysphagia versus psychiatric causes of keeping food in the mouth, there are two subgroups. One is clearly a group of medically debilitated patients, often malnourished, who have problems with swallowing and will have recurrent aspiration pneumonia. I agree wholeheartedly that we're not talking about that group when we talk about the apraxia. However, there is another group of people who take great delight in getting food, chewing it, and using it as a weapon. If you go into the psychodynamics, if you talk to the people dealing with them, this is a totally different thing. In some cases it's saying "Gee whiz, maybe I've got a passive suicide wish and I'm going to starve myself to death but I still want the taste of food." So there are a lot of things going on, and clearly what we're presenting here is provocative and certainly very preliminary data suggesting that maybe we should be spending more time looking at the elderly than looking at young girls because there are far more elderly people in this world. All of us will be the elderly in about 20 years' time, so these are important issues for all of us. We need to look at the elderly, and sort some of these data out. It's a very complex interaction, no simpler than anorexia nervosa, bulimia, and depression in young people. In fact, maybe even more complex because of some of the ethical issues involved.

DR. MADELYN FERNSTROM (*University of Pittsburgh, Pittsburgh, PA*): I have two different questions. One relates back to your interesting finding of the older men who were terrified about being overweight and gaining weight despite the fact that they were thin. I'm wondering if there was any recurrent medical illness that might account for this. For example, those who had had bypass surgery might have become Pritikin disciples and decided the thinner the better. That's the first issue.

The second relates to a question of natural history and whether as Barbara Rolls has demonstrated with the natural decline in metabolic rate that one sees with aging, if this might be related at all to body weight regulation as one ages. That is, a natural reduction in caloric intake might occur in the normal individual and be compensated for by an increased efficiency of the body.

Dr. Morley: Regarding the second question, there is a small reduction of intake as we get older related to decreased needs, due to decreased physical activity as well as the changes in metabolic rate. However, if you look at animals there are abnormalities. We've now had a number of older animals, this is anecdotal, who are losing weight and in some of these we're seen tremors. If you change them over from food that is difficult to consume, that is, the normal food pellet, to a liquid diet, they will actually put on weight and their tremors will disappear, so there are a lot of interactions going on even in animals. It's difficult to give you a clear answer on that question. In response to your first question, our study does not rule out medical illness. It was done as a pilot when we were looking at something else. We were interested in acute depression in the elderly and against everyone's advice I included the EAT-26, which is a questionnaire that the subjects answer themselves, that is, without an interviewer. This questionnaire was the source of the data on eating and weight-related attitudes.

Dr. Allan Levine (*Minneapolis VA Medical Center, Minneapolis, MN*): John, you had one slide that showed some individuals, it wasn't your work, who had a history of prior psychiatric illness. Also, there was the woman who had a daughter with anorexia. What do you think is the possibility of some reappearance in the elderly of early anorexia nervosa either because of environmental influences or some kind of manipulative behavior?

Dr. Morley: I think this is a possibility, and it's tough to get some of this history. Anorexia nervosa that a person survived many years before does not necessarily come out as a clear history in many of our older people, so there can be recurrence that is undetected. One or two of the case reports in the literature certainly report recurrences in older women. The male was someone who was in a Japanese concentration camp during the war. He developed symptoms of anorexia nervosa then and had recurrent episodes throughout his life, so he was a very difficult patient to figure out. The point I want to stress is that what we have seen is the tip of the iceberg. This needs to be properly studied, and it needs a number of different people to look at it from different viewpoints. Certainly I would welcome any psychiatric colleagues in the audience, and psychologists, to get into this area.

Summary: Part I

PAUL ROBINSON

Department of Psychological Medicine
King's College Hospital Medical School
London SE5 9RS, England

The contributors to this volume hail from numerous different disciplines including clinical and experimental psychology, psychiatry, general medicine, neuroscience, pharmacology, and ethology. The variety testifies to the complexity and breadth of the research problems facing workers in eating disorders today. It seems likely that insights derived from study of the molecular basis of behavior, and its genetic and environmental determinants, will inform discussion of the etiology of anorexia nervosa. While Professor Russell and his colleagues have demonstrated an important genetic element in the cause of anorexia nervosa,[1] the question remains concerning the nature of what is inherited. Enhanced secretion of endogenous opioids during fasting in predisposed individuals, leading to "starvation dependence,"[2] is one mechanism that could increase the likelihood of weight loss continuing once it has begun; a disorder of weight homeostasis, with failure to regain weight following weight loss induced by a precipitating illness is another. Gastric slowing, with enhanced satiety following the onset of food restriction,[3] is a third physiological change that might occur more readily in subjects with a greater genetic predisposition. Each of these hypotheses is potentially testable using genetic techniques, of which the most powerful is the twin study. It is also possible that genetic influences produce psychological changes that predispose a person to anorexia nervosa. Personality traits such as self-esteem, assertiveness, tendency to dysphoric moods, and interest in sexual activity may all be under genetic control.[4] A disturbance in such an attribute could contribute to a vulnerability which, when associated with environmental factors in family, social network, and in wider society, leads to the development of a clinical eating disorder. Professor McHugh seeks the ultimate and proximate causes of anorexia nervosa. This is a helpful dichotomy, and indicates for us the genetic and early environmental influences that may be of relevance and the influences of the more recent developmental maturations in the anorexic patient as well as changes in the system within which she lives. These changes often take the form of family life-cycle shifts, such as the younger generation moving toward independence, which often seem to determine the timing of the appearance of the disorder.[5]

Bulimia nervosa has, since its description in 1979,[6] shown an explosive increase in the number of cases referred while epidemiological studies suggest that anorexia nervosa is also on the increase.[7] Moreover, both eating disorders have now been described in many subjects from racial groups hitherto thought to be relatively immune.[8] Little information is available to indicate the forces behind these evolving epidemiological patterns, and the research most likely to yield useful explanations would appear to come from anthropological studies of the roles of young people of both sexes in a variety of cultural milieus. In this century, many communities throughout the world have cast off European rulers and have exchanged tribal traditions for centralized government, often with increasing adoption of Western values. A detailed study of the patients who present with eating disorders in such cultures, together with an examination of the changes occurring in wider society that might be relevant to the development of these disorders, would be likely to provide important insights into the socio-cultural determinants of eating disorders. Such a study would include investigation of changing family structure; patterns of adolescent development and individuation; ideal body image; economic and academic pressures, particularly on women; and changes in societal expectations of the woman's role. In Western contexts, it is very important that the changes responsible for the apparently increasing numbers of patients with eating disorders be identified. It would seem unlikely that physiological or genetic factors will provide the answers, and researchers will need to look at changes occurring in culturally determined patterns of behavior. There is little evidence that such studies are being performed, either in Western or in non-Western societies.

While it has been established that skilled nursing care is effective in producing short-term weight restoration in anorexia nervosa,[9] research in the efficacy of interventions intended to improve its long-term prognosis has produced little of satisfaction to the clinical pharmacologist or, indeed, to the behavior therapist. The main advance has been that family therapy has been shown to be the treatment of choice for young patients without chronic illness.[10] As with any disorder, it is helpful to know when the patient has recovered, and it is recognized that a number of patients continue to suffer disturbed eating, psychological distress, and social disruption even when weight and menstrual function have been restored.[11] The most reliable measure of clinical state apart from weight is menstruation, and this aspect of recovery can now be predicted using sequential ovarian ultrasound scans.[12] When the scan shows a dominant ovarian follicle, weight can be regarded as adequately restored. This technique should prove of great value for clinical management and for research investigations as it accurately indicates the point of weight recovery.

In bulimia nervosa, drugs have had a rather better record. Treatment with a variety of antidepressant drugs appears to reduce the occurrence of episodes of bulimia.[13] Transatlantic differences in definition of bulimic disorders have dogged research in the field, and there is a suspicion that many patients diagnosed as having "DSMIII bulimia"[14] would, in Europe, be regarded as having a primary affective disorder with overeating as part of the illness. Thus, the fact that antidepressants were effective antibulimic drugs in New but not in Old England[15] could be related to diagnostic differences. The new more restrictive DSMIII-R definition of bulimia nervosa[16] will do much to ease this sorry situation. The latest findings by Mitchell and coworkers suggest that antidepressant drugs, while effective, do not improve the results of cognitive–behavioral treatment,[17] and we must consider the ethical position. Drugs are relatively easy to provide and appear to reduce the symptoms effectively. However, they are potentially harmful and their long-term efficacy unknown, as is the degree to which improvement is maintained after stopping medication. Cognitive behavioral therapy is effective, and appears to lack adverse effects.[18] It requires, however, trained staff and intensive treatment. If the use of tricyclic antidepressants can be shown to produce lasting improvement in bulimia nervosa, without the need for long-term treatment, then they might reasonably form part of the range of therapeutic options. At present, however, the balance of evidence appears to be tipped in favor of psychological methods of treatment, although no one particular approach has been established as superior.

Contributors have, importantly, looked beyond the classical eating disorders to direct our attention to other settings in which disturbances of eating contribute significantly to morbidity. The overeating of seasonal affective disorder and the true anorexia associated with drug (especially digoxin) toxicity in the elderly are examples. The possibility of eating disorders occurring in elderly males has been suggested by Dr. Morley, but must at present be regarded as not proven. The weight loss associated with cancer and, sometimes, with nonmalignant disease is poorly understood, and it is at least possible that professionals with expertise in the investigation, diagnosis, and management of eating disorders will be able to pursue research and help patients whose weight loss is related to physical disease. Some of these patients may be suffering from the effects of agents such as cachectin or peptides such as cholecystokinin, which could result in weight loss. Others may be suffering from true anorexia as part of a depressive illness, while still others may have an atypical form of anorexia nervosa. Much needs to be done to clarify the nutritional disorder associated with physical illness, with great potential benefit to patients.

REFERENCES

1. HOLLAND, A. J., A. HALL, R. MURRAY, G. F. M. RUSSELL & A. H. CRISP. 1984. Anorexia nervosa: A study of 34 twin pairs and one set of triplets. Br. J. Psychiatry 145: 414–9.
2. SZMUCKLER, G. I. & D. TANTAM. 1984. Anorexia nervosa: Starvation dependence. Br. J. Med. Psychol 57: 303–310.
3. ROBINSON, P. H., J. BARRETT & M. CLARKE. 1988. Determinants of delayed gastric emptying in anorexia nervosa and bulimia nervosa. Gut 29: 458–464.
4. EAVES, L. & P. A. YOUNG. 1981. Genetical theory and personality differences. In Dimension in Personality. R. Lynn, Ed. Pergamon Press. New York.
5. MINUCHIN, S., B. L. ROSMAN & L. BAKER. 1978. Psychosomatic Families: Anorexia Nervosa in Context. Harvard University Press. Cambridge, MA.
6. RUSSELL, G. 1979. Bulimia nervosa: An ominous variant of anorexia nervosa. Psychol. Med. 9: 429–448.
7. SZMUKLER, G., C. McCANCE, L. McCRONE & D. HUNTER. 1986. Anorexia nervosa: A psychiatric case register study from Aberdeen. Psychol. Med. 16: 49–58.
8. HOLDEN, N. L. & P. H. ROBINSON. 1988. Anorexia and bulimia nervosa in British blacks. Br. J. Psychiatry 152: 544–549.
9. RUSSELL, G. F. M. 1983. Anorexia nervosa and bulimia nervosa. In Handbook of Psychiatry 4. Neuroses and Personality Disorders. G. F. M. Russell & L. A. Hersov. Eds.: 285–298. Cambridge University Press. Cambridge, England.
10. RUSSELL, G. F., G. I. SZMUKLER, C. DARE & I. EISLER. 1987. An evaluation of family therapy in anorexia nervosa and bulimia nervosa. Arch. Gen. Psychiatry 44: 1047–1056.
11. MORGAN, H. G. & G. F. M. RUSSELL. 1975. Value of family background and clinical features as predictors of long term outcome in anorexia nervosa: Four year follow-up study of 41 patients. Psychol. Med. 5: 355–71.
12. TREASURE, J. L., P. A. GORDON, E. A. KING, M. WHEELER & G. F. RUSSELL. 1985. Cystic ovaries: A phase of anorexia nervosa. Lancet 2: 1379–1382.
13. POPE, H. G., J. I. HUDSON, J. M. JONAS & D. YURGELUN-TODD. 1983. Bulimia treated with imipramine: A placebo-controlled, double-blind study. Am. J. Psychiatry 140: 554–558.
14. AMERICAN PSYCHIATRIC ASSOCIATION. 1980. Diagnostic and Statistical Manual of Mental Disorders, 3rd Edition: 69–71. American Psychiatric Association. Washington, D.C.
15. SABINE, E. J., A. YONACE, A. J. FARRINGTON, K. H. BARRATT & A. WAKELING. 1983. Bulimia nervosa: A placebo controlled double-blind therapeutic trial of mianserin. Br. J. Clin. Pharmacol. 15: 195s–202s.
16. AMERICAN PSYCHIATRIC ASSOCIATION. 1987. Diagnostic and Statistical Manual of Mental Disorders. 3rd Edition (revised). American Psychiatric Association. Washington, DC.
17. MITCHELL, J. E., R. L. PYLE, E. D. ECKERT, D. HATSUKAMI, C. POMEROY & R. ZIMMERMAN. 1988. Preliminary results of a comparison treatment trial of bulimia nervosa. In The Psychobiology of Bulimia Nervosa. K. M. Pirke, W. Vandereycken & D. Ploog, Eds. Springer-Verlag. Berlin/Heidelberg.
18. FAIRBURN, C. G. 1985. Cognitive-behavioral treatment for bulimia. In Handbook of Psychotherapy for Anorexia Nervosa and Bulimia. D. M. Garner & P. E. Garfinkel, Eds. Guilford Press. New York.

Animal Models of Human Eating Disorders[a]

GERARD P. SMITH

Department of Psychiatry
E. W. Bourne Behavioral Research Laboratory
New York Hospital-Cornell Medical Center
White Plains, New York 10605

Animal models have not been used much in the investigation of anorexia nervosa and bulimia nervosa. This is surprising, given the severity and increasing incidence of these clinical disorders and the usefulness of animal models in other psychiatric conditions.[1,2]

The failure to use animal models is the result of two factors:

First, clinicians have emphasized the complexity of the syndromes — especially the restrictive type of anorexia nervosa. They suggest that alterations in eating and body weight are symptomatic of, and secondary to, the pervasive psychological and psychosocial abnormalities present in many of these patients.

Second, confronted with this view, experimentalists have rejected animal preparations that are only relevant to parts of the clinical syndrome and, in the case of potential rodent models, have concluded that there is insufficient psychological complexity to model the human psychopathology.

These factors have erected a barrier to the development of animal models of human eating disorders. I believe this barrier should be breached because it is based on an unnecessarily restrictive view of a useful animal model and because it prevents experimental scrutiny of the presumed secondary position of the disorders of food intake and body weight in the hierarchy of psychopathology that characterizes these patients.

What is the unnecessarily restrictive criterion of an animal model that is so prevalent? It is that the animal model should mimic all the important aspects of the human syndromes. This is an example, I believe, of what Whitehead called "misplaced concreteness." But no animal model of other medical or psychiatric disorders fulfills this criterion. For example, in the closely related problems of eating and body weight in human obesity, animal models have been extensively investigated since 1939 when Hetherington and Ranson described the ventromedial hypothalamic syndrome.[3] In a recent review, Sclafani[4] listed 50 animal models of obesity produced by neurological damage, genetic mutation, dietary manipulations, and drug treatment. None of these models are considered replicas of the human problem, but all of them are considered useful for developing ideas and experimental techniques that can be applied to the investigation of human obesity. The fact that animal models with different etiologies (neurological, genetic, or dietary) produce a common syndrome of hyperphagia, hyperinsulinism, and increased storage of fat suggests that the human syndrome can have different causes. This emphasizes that the use of imperfect animal models leads to closer scrutiny of the clinical condition with the result that new clinical insights change

[a] This work was supported by Research Scientist Award MH00149.

the description of what needs to be modeled. At its best, animal modeling is dialectical.

So far, we have referred to two types of animal models: the etiologic and the isomorphic (TABLE 1). The etiologic model is based on the same cause, for example, genetic or dietary obesity; the isomorphic model is based on similar forms, for example, hyperphagia and increased storage of fat. The third type is mechanistic. Hyperinsulinism and increased lipoprotein lipase (LPL) activity are examples of mechanistic models of obesity. The fourth type of animal model is predictive. In obesity research, all of the models have been used to investigate the anorectic potency of drugs or putative, endogenous, satiating substances.[5] The predictive power of such models varies, but this kind of model generates new information. For example, Blundell and Hill[6] showed that d-fenfluramine was a more potent anorectic in the static phase of dietary-induced obesity than in the dynamic phase.

It is clear that intensive study of these various animal models has enriched the thinking about and guided the investigation of human obesity. Because problems of eating and body weight are common to obesity, anorexia nervosa, and bulimia nervosa, the successful use of animal models for the investigation of human obesity should encourage the development of animal models for the other two clinical syndromes. What animal preparations might be useful models of anorexia nervosa and bulimia nervosa?

MODELS OF ANOREXIA NERVOSA

Of the four types of animal models (TABLE 1), only the isomorphic and the predictive can be developed for the restrictive type of anorexia nervosa at this time because neither the cause nor the physiological mechanism(s) of anorexia nervosa are known. The aspects of the human syndrome that could be modeled isomorphically are female sex at puberty or in the adolescent period; decreased food intake; decreased body weight; increased activity; abnormal neuroendocrine function, particularly decreased gonadotrophin and sex hormone secretion; abnormal sleep; and acquired taste aversions. I will consider only potential rodent models because they are easier to obtain, less expensive, and more commonly used in research concerned with eating and body weight than other species.

It is now clear that restricting access to food so that rats lose significant amounts of weight reproduces the significant abnormalities of neuroendocrine function and sleep found in the emaciated anorectic. These results are consistent with recent human studies that had emphasized that most, if not all, of the neuroendocrine changes present in the emaciated anorectic patient are reversible when food intake increases so that sufficient body weight is regained to maintain adequate nutrition.[7]

A major weakness of this model is that food is restricted by the experimenter. But one of the crucial aspects of anorexia nervosa is that the patient restricts her/his intake. Is there an animal model that consists of voluntary food restriction interacting with hyperactivity so that body weight decreases to the extent that life is threatened? There is. If a rat is given access to unlimited amounts of food for 30–60 min each

TABLE 1. Types of Animal Models

1.	Etiologic
2.	Isomorphic
3.	Mechanistic
4.	Predictive

day, rats adapt to this situation and maintain body weight and apparently normal nutrition. If a running wheel is introduced and rats have access to it at all times except during the interval in which they eat, a major change occurs in their food intake and body weight.[8,9] As wheel running increases over days, body weight decreases because food intake does not increase sufficiently to compensate for the energy expenditure of wheel running. In fact, rats that run eat significantly *less* during the feeding interval than rats living in standard laboratory cages. The nutritional effects of the inadequate intake and decrease in body weight are lethal—all rats eventually die unless investigators intervene. Routtenberg and Kuznesof[8] called the reduction in food intake self-starvation to emphasize that the extent of wheel running, the amount of food eaten, and the resultant starvation were under the control of the rat.

Daily administration of chlorpromazine, but not pentobarbital, ameliorated that syndrome by decreasing wheel running, increasing food intake, and eliminating the difference in body weight between wheel-running rats and rats living in standard cages on the same restricted feeding schedule.[8,9] The authors noted that this ameliorative effect of chlorpromazine had its clinical parallel in the use of chlorpromazine in the treatment of anorexia nervosa, but they did not suggest this rat preparation as a model of anorexia nervosa and, in fact, used male rats. Recent work, however, has extended this phenomenon to female rats (Aravich *et al.* and Ogawa *et al.*, this volume) and obtained further evidence for this preparation as an isomorphic model of anorexia nervosa.

Self-starvation in the rat is important in that it models one of the perplexing aspects of the clinical syndrome, the ability of the patient to overwhelm homeostatic mechanisms for energy balance by a combination of restricted eating and excessive activity. Routtenberg's experiments were explicitly carried out to understand another form of self-starvation that he had previously produced when he gave rats a choice between eating food or pressing a lever to obtain positively reinforcing, electrical stimulation of the posterior hypothalamus. Rats chose brain stimulation reward to such an extent that unless the investigator intervened, they would starve to death.[10]

Thus, from an analysis of behavior and its response to available sources of reinforcing actions (eating, running, and brain stimulation), the fundamental problem of self-starvation in the rat is located in the relationship between maladaptive behavior (decreased eating despite weight loss) and positive incentive mechanisms (brain stimulation and wheel running).

Because this functional relationship also describes the anorexia and weight loss frequently associated with drug addiction, Marrazzi and Luby[11] suggested that endorphins could be mediating the addictive-like behavior of the patient with anorexia. The evidence for this idea is incomplete (see Marrazzi and Luby, this volume), but it is testable, and the fact that the wheel-running rat with restricted access to food has increased circulating β-endorphin (Doerries *et al.*, this volume) suggests that the problem can be pursued in this model.

Epling and Pierce[12] recently reviewed the relevant human data concerned with the interrelationships between activity and anorexia. The convergence of experimental interest in this problem in the laboratory and the clinic makes this a very promising area for the artful use of an animal model in the search for clinical answers.

In contrast to the infrequent discussion of the self-starvation phenomenon, there have been several recent reviews of the spontaneous anorexias that occur in various species during hibernation or reproduction. The value of these preparations as models are debatable—Mrosovsky[13] is skeptical; Beumont[14] is more optimistic. I think they will not be useful models because none of these anorexias are accompanied by hyperactivity, none are life-threatening, all are difficult to produce in the laboratory, some are expensive, and none of them has a data base concerning food intake and body weight that is equal to the rat's. Furthermore, patients with anorexia nervosa are not spontaneously anorectic.

There is an aversion to concentrated fat solutions in patients with anorexia nervosa.[15] This aversion is probably acquired rather than innate, but this issue has not been investigated. There is a large literature on acquired taste aversions in rats and other animals,[16] and it has recently been used to develop a model of anorexia nervosa in which estrogen serves as the unconditioned stimulus (Young et al., this volume).

Stricker and Andersen[17] rejected the rat with bilateral, lateral hypothalamic lesions as a useful model of anorexia nervosa because the deficits in that rat were more extensive than occurred in patients, for example, decreased water intake and severe sensorimotor disturbances. But it may be useful to reopen this possibility now that more controlled hypothalamic damage can be produced with local injections of excitotoxins or neurotoxins. For example, Leibowitz and her colleagues[18,19] used the neurotoxin 6-hydroxydopamine (6-OHDA) in their studies of the role of noradrenergic mechanisms in the paraventricular nucleus for increasing food intake. Although the observed reduction in food intake and body weight loss is small after 6-OHDA lesions that damage the noradrenergic innervation of the paraventricular nucleus, this rat preparation could be more vulnerable than normal to other experimental manipulations that produce anorexia. If this were true, then the noradrenergic-damaged rat might be used to investigate the observation of Kaye et al.[20] that cerebrospinal fluid norepinephrine was low in weight-recovered anorexia nervosa patients.

Review of these animal models of anorexia nervosa leads to the conclusion that the development of rat models that do not show evidence of the human syndrome when food is freely available, but develop some of the signs of the syndrome when food is restricted and/or activity is increased, should be used to model the problem of specific vulnerability that is operating in the human situation in which a very small number of the young people who are dieting go on to develop anorexia nervosa.

MODELS OF BULIMIA NERVOSA

Although bulimia or binge eating is a defining characteristic in bulimia nervosa, it also occurs in anorexia nervosa and in obesity. The first modern clinical descriptions of binge eating were provided by Binswanger[21] in 1944 and by Stunkard et al.[22] in 1955.

Dieting often precedes bulimia.[23,24] The motivation for dieting — a cultural imperative for women, a functional imperative for ballerinas and wrestlers, or an experimental constraint for conscientious objectors in World War II — is apparently not crucial; all of these types of dieting can lead to bulimia.

The case of the conscientious objectors is instructive: Keys and his colleagues[25,26] took a group of normal-weight men and persuaded them to restrict their food intake to the extent that they lost about 26% of their initial body weight. When food was no longer restricted, the men frequently took excessively large meals even after their weight had returned to normal. It is not known how long this bulimic tendency persisted. What is instructive here is that bulimia occurred in *men* after a diet imposed within experimental conditions. This suggests that the reason that most people with bulimia are women may be simply that dieting begins earlier and is much more frequent in women than in men.[27] This does not mean that the developmental, psychological, and cultural factors that may account for the differential dieting between women and men reviewed by Rodin and her colleagues[24,28] and by Polivy and Herman[23] are not important for understanding and treating patients, but it does suggest that the development of animal models of bulimia can proceed without waiting for current research to distill the important from the plausible among the many psychosocial factors that have been proposed.

The recent successful efforts to study bulimia under laboratory conditions has already produced information that is important for animal models. As reviewed by Walsh *et al.* (this volume), a binge meal is larger and has a higher percent of fat and a lower percent of protein than a nonbinge meal. The percent of carbohydrate does not necessarily change.

Given these results, recent experiments concerned with the effect of dieting on food intake and metabolism appear relevant. For example, Coscina and Dixon[29] took normal rats and deprived them of food for four days and then observed their response to refeeding. When the rats were given chow, they regained weight so that they caught up to the control group. When given a palatable, high-fat diet for four weeks, however, the previously deprived rats showed a significantly larger weight gain than control rats because they ate more — estimates of food utilization were not different for the deprived and control rats. Furthermore, when the palatable diet was replaced with chow, the deprived rats maintained their heavier body weights for seven weeks.

Coscina and Dixon[29] used total deprivation for four days. A better model of severe human dieting is the restriction of food intake for a period of weeks that leads to a loss of 20-30% body weight followed by refeeding. There are behavioral and metabolic effects of repeated cycles of such dieting. During refeeding, rats show a preference for fats[30] and a significant shift in hormonal and metabolic processes that facilitate the flux of absorbed nutrients into fat.[31] It is important to note, however, that excessively large meals that could be considered analogous to human binge meals have not been observed after such cycles of dieting. This is consistent with the fact that only a small number of dieters develop clinical bulimia and suggests that those who do have a vulnerability that is exposed by restricted eating.

Professor Hilda Bruch[32] was the first to suggest that this vulnerability was a defect in the normal mechanisms for satiation. She based this idea on her impression that patients with eating disorders have an abnormal developmental history that leads them to have distorted images not only of their body surface, but also of their visceral surfaces so that their perception of visceral sensations relevant to hunger and satiety are abnormal.

In 1974, Garfinkel[33] confirmed this insight concerning satiety, but not hunger, in patients with anorexia. This has now been extended to patients with bulimia. Even an experimental binge meal does not satiate bulimic patients as much as controls despite the fact that the binge meal of bulimics was almost twice as large as the "binge meal" of controls (see Walsh *et al.*, this volume).

Uncovering this defect in satiation in these patients coincided with considerable experimental interest in the analysis of satiation in animals.[34,35] Satiation begins during the ingestion of food and culminates in the termination of eating at the end of the meal. The unconditioned satiating potency of ingested food is determined primarily by its preabsorptive effects and is apparently stronger in the stomach and in the small intestine than in the mouth.[36] With experience these unconditioned satiating effects are amplified by conditioning.

Serotonin has been established as one of the mechanisms of satiation.[37] Cholecystokinin (CCK), pancreatic glucagon, and bombesin are candidate mechanisms in the periphery and GABA is a candidate mechanism in the brain. I emphasize the word *candidate*: None of these mechanisms has been established, but all of them have sufficient experimental support to be potentially interesting for the clinical investigation of the defect in satiation observed in bulimic patients.

For example, Robinson *et al.*[38] demonstrated that increasing central serotonergic activity by the administration of fenfluramine decreased food intake by bulimics in the laboratory. Geracioti and Liddle[39] reported that decreased subjective satiety ratings by bulimics after a test meal were correlated with a diminished release of CCK into the blood. Furthermore, after a period of treatment when the satiety ratings to the test meal increased, a more normal increase of plasma CCK was observed. When this interesting correlation is coupled with the failure of infused CCK to decrease meal size in bulimics despite using a dose that decreased meal size in normal and obese subjects,[40] further investigation of the apparent abnormal release of and response to CCK in bulimics seems warranted and will benefit from concurrent work on these issues in relevant animal models.

Whatever defect in satiation mechanisms bulimics have, those defects can be exaggerated by postprandial vomiting and purging or by chewing the food and then spitting it out. Although patients exhibit these behaviors in order to dissociate the orosensory and psychological pleasures of eating from the caloric value of the food, these behaviors also reduce the postingestive satiating effects of the food by preventing or diminishing the time of contact of the food with the mucosal surfaces of the stomach and small intestine where satiating mechanisms are activated. Van Vort[41] has suggested that the effects of these behaviors can be modeled in the sham-feeding rat.

The most common sham-feeding preparation is the chronic gastric fistula (GF) rat,[42] but other preparations, such as the rat with a chronic esophageal fistula (developed by Mook[43]) and the rat with a chronic gastric catheter (devised by Davis and Campbell[44]), have been used successfully.

Sham feeding occurs in the GF rat when the GF is open so that ingested liquid food drains out of the stomach. Drainage of the food out of the stomach minimizes contact of food with the gastric mucosa, prevents gastric distention, and eliminates or minimizes the entry of food into the small intestine. All of these effects of draining food out of the stomach markedly reduce the satiating effects of food. Thus, the sham-feeding rat is a good model of an acquired, reversible defect in satiation. If this defect in satiation is relevant to human bulimia, then when rats are sham feeding, they should eat abnormally large meals. This prediction has been confirmed. For example, when rats sham feed after three hours of food deprivation, an interval that is within the range of the normal intermeal interval of rats during the light phase, the first sham-fed meal is about twice as large as the normal meal, that is, the size of the meal of the same diet that rats eat when the GF is closed and ingested food accumulates in the gut.[45] In addition to producing a larger meal, sham feeding also shortens the interval until the next meal by about 60%.[45]

With repetition, the size of sham-fed meals increases.[44,46-48] Despite very large intakes during sham feeding, rats ultimately stop eating and enter the state of postprandial satiety. The evidence for this is that rats stopped eating for an interval of about 25 min,[45] and at the termination of sham feeding, they displayed the postprandial sequence of satiety.[49] Thus, ingested food elicits satiety when it is restricted to pregastric sites during sham feeding, but the potency of the satiating effect is weak so that meals are abnormally large and last longer, and the postprandial intermeal interval is abnormally short.

The increased size of sham-fed meals with repeated sham-feeding experience suggests that the rat is learning to eat more under these unusual conditions. Booth and Davis called this conditioned desatiation.[50]

Not only do repetitive episodes of sham feeding increase meal size during sham feeding, but repetitive episodes of sham feeding also affect meal size when real feeding is resumed. For example, when rats *really* fed a diet that they had sham fed in a number of tests, they ate abnormally large meals for two to three days.[51]

Thus, the sham feeding rat model of bulimia suggests that *repetition* of binge meals followed by vomiting or purging increases the size of those meals and tends to produce larger meals when the patient attempts to eat the same food in a more restrained and normal manner. If clinical investigation could confirm these phenomena in bulimic patients, it would reinforce the value of early treatment of bulimia.

The binge meals of the sham-feeding rat are not stereotyped; they are increased by deprivation[45,46] and affected by palatability of the diet.[52] Deprivation and palatability also affect the size of binge meals in patients.

Given that the rat does not get any caloric value from sham-fed meals (rats maintain nutritional balance by eating food outside of the sham-feeding test), why does the rat continue to sham feed day after day? It must be that the orosensory stimulation of sham feeding is sufficiently reinforcing to maintain sham feeding across repeated tests (see Schneider, this volume, for a discussion of sham feeding as oral self-stimulation). In fact, under one set of experimental conditions, rats showed *equal* preference for the flavors of two diets, when one of those diets was sham fed and the other was really fed and the volumes ingested under both conditions were equal.[53] Under these conditions, the onset of satiety and postabsorptive caloric effects of the food ingested during real feeding did not add to the reinforcing effect of the orosensory effects of the diet that was equivalent in the sham-fed and really fed meals.

This emphasizes that the major positive reinforcing effect of food occurs in the mouth of the rat. There is no evidence that humans differ from rats in this, and it raises the possibility that the positive feedback effect on eating produced by orosensory stimuli in bulimic patients is exaggerated either innately or, more likely, by previous bulimic experience. After all, exaggerated positive, reinforcing feedback could serve just as well to drive feeding during a binge meal as diminished negative, satiating feedback. (See Smith *et al.*[36] for a discussion of control of meal size by the interaction of positive and negative feedback effects of food stimuli.)

CONCLUSION

I conclude by making three points:

First, the occurrence of disordered satiety and the ingestion of abnormally large meals among normal weight, bulimic patients as well as in patients with anorexia nervosa provides a focus for the development of animal models of eating disorders.

Second, current animal models are isomorphic. Their strength lies in the analysis of the control of meal size within the experimental framework provided by the fact that the size and duration of a meal is controlled by the interaction between the positive and negative feedbacks provided by the ingested food.[36,54] Because the potency of these positive and negative feedback stimuli can be altered by such factors as time of day, the ease of access to food, prior episodes of fasting and body weight loss, prior eating experiences, and levels of circulating sex hormones, the framework is complex enough to model the disorders of human eating, but it is explicit enough to answer testable questions.

Third, isomorphic animal models have the advantage that they are neither etiologic nor exhaustive. That they are not etiologic is important because we do not know the cause of anorexia nervosa or bulimia nervosa. Thus, the models do not claim more than they can produce. By not being exhaustive, I mean that the models are concerned only with disordered eating and its relationships to restricted food intake, decreased body weight, and increased activity. Being able to model this part of these complex clinical syndromes will provide, at best, a partial answer to the perplexing questions raised by the psychopathology of these patients. In our current state of ignorance, however, partial answers are better than none.

One last word. My intellectual position on the use of animal models in the study of human eating disorders was described some time ago by the late Harry Harlow whose research on infant separation in monkeys has become a classic of animal modeling of psychiatric disorders. When asked to defend the use of animal models to investigate the twists and turns of human psychopathology, Harlow said, "You'd be crazy to use animal models, but you'd also be crazy not to use them."[55]

ACKNOWLEDGMENT

I thank Mrs. Jane Magnetti for processing this manuscript.

REFERENCES

1. BOND, N. W., Ed. 1984. Animal Models in Psychopathology. Academic Press. Sydney, Australia.
2. McKINNEY, W. T. 1988. Models of Mental Disorders. Plenum. New York.
3. HETHERINGTON, A. W. & S. W. RANSON. 1939. Experimental hypothalamic-hypophyseal obesity in the rat. Proc. Soc. Exp. Biol. Med. 41: 465–466.
4. SCLAFANI, A. 1984. Animal models of obesity: Classification and characterization. Int. J. Obesity 8: 491–508.
5. BLUNDELL, J. E. & P. L. THURLBY. 1987. Experimental manipulations of eating: Advances in animal models for studying anorectic agents. Pharm. Ther. 34: 349–401.
6. BLUNDELL, J. E. & A. J. HILL. 1985. Effect of dextrofenfluramine on feeding and body weight: Relationship with food composition and palatability. In Metabolic Complications of Human Obesities. J. Vague, B. Guy-Grand & P. Bjorntorp, Eds.: 199–206. Elsevier. Amsterdam.
7. RUSSELL, J. & P. J. V. BEUMONT. 1987. The endocrinology of anorexia nervosa. In Handbook of Eating Disorders. P. J. V. Beumont, G. D. Burrows & R. C. Casper, Eds.: 201–232. Elsevier. New York.
8. ROUTTENBERG, A. & A. W. KUZNESOF. 1967. Self-starvation of rats living in activity wheels on a restricted feeding schedule. J. Comp. Physiol. Psychol. 64: 414–421.
9. ROUTTENBERG, A. 1968. Self-starvation of rats living in activity wheels. J. Comp. Physiol. Psychol. 66: 234–238.
10. ROUTTENBERG, A. & J. LINDY. 1965. Effects of the availability of rewarding septal and hypothalamic stimulation on bar pressing for food under conditions of deprivation. J. Comp. Physiol. Psychol. 60: 158–161.
11. MARRAZZI, M. A. & E. D. LUBY. 1986. An auto-addiction opioid model of chronic anorexia nervosa. Int. J. Eating Disord. 5: 191–208.
12. EPLING, W. F. & W. D. PIERCE. 1988. Activity-based anorexia: A biobehavioral perspective. Int. J. Eating Disord. 7: 475–485.
13. MROSOVSKY, N. 1983. Animal anorexias, starvation and anorexia nervosa: Are animal models of anorexia nervosa possible? In Anorexia Nervosa: Recent Developments in Research. P. L. Darby, P. E. Garfinkel, D. M. Garner & D. V. Coscina, Eds.: 199–205. Alan R. Liss. New York.
14. BEUMONT, P. J. V. 1987. Anorexia nervosa and spontaneous hypophagias in animals. In Handbook of Eating Disorders. P. J. V. Beumont, G. D. Burrows & R. C. Casper, Eds.: 15–21. Elsevier. New York.
15. DREWNOWSKI, A., K. A. HALMI, B. PIERCE, J. GIBBS & G. P. SMITH. 1987. Taste and eating disorders. Am. J. Clin. Nutr. 46: 442–450.
16. BRAVEWMAN, N. S. & P. BRONSTEIN, Eds. 1985. Experimental Assessments and Clinical Applications of Conditioned Food Aversions. Ann. N.Y. Acad. Sci., Vol. 443. New York Academy of Sciences. New York.
17. STRICKER, E. M. & A. E. ANDERSEN. 1980. The lateral hypothalamic syndrome: Comparison with the syndrome of anorexia nervosa. Life Sci. 26: 1927–1934.

18. LEIBOWITZ, S. F. & L. L. BROWN. 1980. Histochemical and pharmacological analysis of noradrenergic projections to the paraventricular hypothalamus in relation to feeding stimulation. Brain Res. **201:** 289–314.
19. LEIBOWITZ, S. F., N. J. HAMMER & L. L. BROWN. 1980. Analyses of behavioral deficits produced by lesions in the dorsal and ventral midbrain tegmentum. Physiol. Behav. **25:** 829–843.
20. KAYE, W. H., M. H. EBERT, M. RALEIGH & C. R. LAKE. 1984. Abnormalities in CNS monoamine metabolism in anorexia nervosa. Arch. Gen. Psychiatry **41:** 350–355.
21. BINSWANGER, L. 1944. Der Fall Ellen West. Schweiz. Arch. Neurol. Psychol. **54:** 69–71.
22. STUNKARD, A. J., W. J. GRACE & H. G. WOLFF. 1955. The night-eating syndrome: A pattern of food intake among certain obese patients. Am. J. Med. **19:** 78–86.
23. POLIVY, J. & C. P. HERMAN. 1985. Dieting and binging. Am. Psychol. **40:** 193–201.
24. STRIEGEL-MOORE, R. H., L. R. SILBERSTEIN & J. RODIN. 1986. Toward an understanding of risk factors for bulimia. Am. Psychol. **41:** 246–263.
25. FRANKLIN, J. S., B. C. SCHIELE, J. BROZEK & A. KEYS. 1948. Observations on human behavior in experimental starvation and rehabilitation. J. Clin. Psychol. **4:** 28–45.
26. KEYS, A., J. BROZEK, A. HENSCHEL, O. MICKELSEN & H. L. TAYLOR. 1950. The Biology of Human Starvation. University of Minnesota Press. Minneapolis, MN.
27. HAWKINS, R. C. II, S. TURELL & L. J. JACKSON. 1983. Desirable and undesirable masculine and feminine traits in relation to students' dietary tendencies and body image dissatisfaction. Sex Roles **9:** 705–724.
28. RODIN, J., L. SILBERSTEIN & R. STRIEGEL-MOORE. 1985. Women and weight: A normative discontent. In Psychology and Gender. Nebraska Symposium on Motivation, 1984. T. B. Sonderegger, Ed.: 267–307. University of Nebraska Press. Lincoln, NB.
29. COSCINA, D. V. & L. M. DIXON. 1983. Body weight regulation in anorexia nervosa: Insights from an animal model. In Anorexia Nervosa: Recent Developments in Research. P. L. Darby, P. E. Garfinkel, D. M. Garner & D. V. Coscina, Eds.: 207–220. Alan R. Liss, Inc. New York.
30. REED, D., R. J. CONTRERAS, C. MAGGIO, M. R. C. GREENWOOD & J. RODIN. 1988. Cycling in female rats increases dietary fat selection and adiposity. Physiol. Behav. **42:** 389–395.
31. BROWNELL, K. D., E. STELLAR, M. R. C. GREENWOOD & E. E. SHRAGER. 1986. The effects of repeated cycles of weight loss and regain in rats. Physiol. Behav. **38:** 459–464.
32. BRUCH, H. 1973. Eating Disorders. Basic Books. New York.
33. GARFINKEL, P. E. 1974. Perception of hunger and satiety in anorexia nervosa. Psychol. Med. **4:** 309 315.
34. SMITH, G. P. & J. GIBBS. 1979. Postprandial satiety. In Progress in Psychobiology and Physiological Psychology. J. M. Sprague & A. N. Epstein, Eds. Vol. **8:** 179–242. Academic Press. New York.
35. GIBBS, J. & G. P. SMITH. 1986. Gut peptides and feeding behavior: The model of cholecystokinin. In Feeding Behavior: Neural and Humoral Controls. R. Ritter, S. Ritter & C. D. Barnes, Eds.: 329–352. Academic Press. Orlando, FL.
36. SMITH, G. P., D. GREENBERG, E. CORP & J. GIBBS. Afferent information in the control of eating. In Obesity: Towards a Molecular Approach. G. Bray, D. Ricquier & B. Spiegelman, Eds. In press. University of California Press. Los Angeles, CA.
37. BLUNDELL, J. E. 1987. Structure, process, and mechanism: Case studies in the psychopharmacology of feeding. In Handbook of Psychopharmacology. L. L. Iversen, S. D. Iversen & S. H. Snyder, Eds. Vol. **19:** 123–182. Plenum. New York.
38. ROBINSON, P. H., S. A. CHECKLEY & G. F. M. RUSSELL. 1985. Suppression of eating by fenfluramine in patients with bulimia nervosa. Br. J. Psychiatry. **146:** 169–176.
39. GERACIOTI, T. D. JR, & R. A. LIDDLE. 1988. Impaired cholecystokinin secretion in bulimia nervosa. N. Engl. J. Med. **319:** 683–688.
40. MITCHELL, J. E., D. E. LAINE, J. E. MORLEY & A. S. LEVINE. 1986. Naloxone but not CCK-8 may attenuate binge-eating behavior in patients with the bulimia syndrome. Biol. Psychiat. **21:** 1399–1406.
41. VAN VORT, W. B. 1988. Is sham feeding an animal model of bulimia? Int. J. Eating Disord. **7:** 797–806.
42. GIBBS, J., R. C. YOUNG & G. P. SMITH. 1973. Cholecystokinin elicits satiety in rats with open gastric fistulas. Nature **245:** 323–325.

43. Mook, D. G. 1963. Oral and postingestional determinants of the intake of various solutions in rats with esophageal fistulas. J. Comp. Physiol. Psychol. **56:** 645–659.
44. Davis, J. D. & C. S. Campbell. 1973. Peripheral control of meal size in the rat: Effect of sham feeding on meal size and drinking rate. J. Comp. Physiol. Psychol. **83:** 379–387.
45. Kraly, F. S., W. J. Carty & G. P. Smith. 1978. Effect of pregastric food stimuli on meal size and intermeal interval in the rat. Physiol. Behav. **20:** 779–784.
46. Young, R. C., J. Gibbs, J. Antin, J. Holt & G. P. Smith. 1974. Absence of satiety during sham feeding in the rat. J. Comp. Physiol. Psychol. **87:** 795–800.
47. Mook, D. G., R. Cuberson, R. J. Gelbart & K. McDonald. 1983. Oropharyngeal control of ingestion in rats: Acquisition of sham drinking patterns. Behav. Sci. **97:** 574–584.
48. Sclafani, A. & J. W. Nissenbaum. 1985. On the role of the mouth and gut in the control of saccharin and sugar intake: A reexamination of the sham-feeding preparation. Br. Res. Bull. **14:** 569–576.
49. Antin, J., J. Gibbs, J. Holt, R. C. Young & G. P. Smith. 1975. Choloecystokinin elicits the complete behavioral sequence of satiety in rats. J. Comp. Physiol. Psychol. **89:** 784–790.
50. Booth, D. A. & J. D. Davis. Gastrointestinal factors in the acquisition of oral sensory control of satiation. Physiol. Behav. **11:** 23–29.
51. Van Vort, W. & G. P. Smith. 1987. Sham feeding experience produces a conditioned increase of meal size. Appetite **9:** 21–29.
52. Weingarten, H. P. 1982. Diet palatability modulates sham feeding in VMH-lesion and normal rats: Implications for finickiness and evaluation of sham-feeding data. J. Comp. Physiol. Psychol. **96:** 223–233.
53. Van Vort, W. & G. P. Smith. 1983. The relationships between the positive reinforcing and satiating effects of a meal in the rat. Physiol. Behav. **30:** 279–284.
54. Smith, G. P. 1982. The physiology of the meal. *In* Drugs and Appetite. T. Silverstone, Ed.: 1–21. Academic Press. New York.
55. Harlow, H. *quoted in* C. Kornetsky. 1977. Animal models: promises and problems. *In* Animal Models in Psychiatry and Neurology. I. Hanin & E. Usdin, Eds.: 1. Pergamon Press. Elmsford, NY.

DISCUSSION

Dr. John Morley (*Sepulveda VA Medical Center, Sepulveda, CA*): I'd like to suggest that there are two other animal models. I think that CRF (corticotropin releasing factor), intraventricularly or into the paraventricular nucleus, is a good model for anorexia nervosa. There is some controversy about whether CRF given chronically will produce weight loss or not. George Bray and Gosnell and Chron's data seem to be conflicting at the moment, but certainly CRF also decreases in the LH (lateral hypothalamus) and therefore makes a very nice animal model for anorexia nervosa. Two groups now, Kaye's group and a Japanese group, have shown an increase in CRF in anorexia nervosa patients.

The other model is peptide YY (PYY) not NPY, for bulimia. Both Sarah Leibowitz and Glenn Stanley showed that NPY increased feeding chronically in rats. We showed peptide YY increased feeding chronically. Recently, in our studies the animals had huge distended stomachs at the same time, and very recently Walter Kaye has looked at CSF in bulimic patients and finds no alterations in NPY, but in his personal communication to me showed that, in fact, PYY was markedly altered in the bulimic patient, suggesting perhaps a role for PYY. So I think in both of these instances the animal modeling came ahead of the human modeling and suggested what should be measured in the CSF of human patients.

DR. GERARD P. SMITH (*New York Hospital–Cornell Medical Center, NY*): I agree.

DR. PAUL F. ARAVICH (*Veterans Administration Medical Center, Hampton, VA*): I disagree. I wonder if you might comment on the phenomenon of activity-based anorexia that we're reporting at these meetings. It's a phenomenon whereby normal rats, when exposed to simultaneous restricted feeding and exercise, starve themselves literally to death. The phenomenon traces back at least to Spear in 1962, so it's been around for 30 years and hasn't been explored.

The thing that appeals to me about this phenomenon is that it can be produced in normal animals by manipulating environmental contingencies, and the beauty of that particular treatment is reflected in the supermarket obesity phenomenon as well. This occurs when a normal animal, placed in a particular environment, is able to manifest a clinically relevant eating disorder. I wonder if you might comment on activity-based anorexia, because we're reporting that there are 2-DG deficits in that particular model that mimic the deficits that are being reported here. In anorexics it is reported that there are abnormalities in β-endorphin.

DR. SMITH: It's a perfectly reasonable model and the recent results that you just cited would make it even more interesting. I certainly didn't mean to exclude any of these, and I'm happy to have them brought up. I do think we ought to let a thousand flowers grow.

There was another point that I wanted to make, and I didn't have time to include it. The point you make about environmental manipulations is important. There's just no question that meal size can be dramatically influenced by environmental pressures. George Collier's work has been able to operationalize a lot of the issues that go on in foraging, and to read that work and then to read the clinical literature and the way in which people arrange environments when they want to binge, for example, suggests all kinds of things that I don't think have been nearly as exploited as they might be.

DR. BARRY KEATING (*Bureau of Applied Research, Washington, DC*): It seems to me there is another possibility for animal models. The criticism that ethologists often have of experimental psychologists and their animal models is that the psychologist depends too much on a very few species that are easily and traditionally raised, for instance, rats and mice. In the wild there's a great variety of animal models including a good number that fast for months; this is self-induced fasting and not because food is not available. The example that I recall is that of apparently the most common deer in New Jersey. The males of this type of deer fast for months before rut. So I would think that the mechanisms of voluntary fasting in animals that do have extensive fasting behaviors might well be very interesting in terms of these variables.

DR. SMITH: Yes, I agree, and there was a very nice review recently of that by Professor Beaumont on what he calls "spontaneous hypophagias" and their possible utility as animal models.

DR. BART HOEBEL (*Princeton University, Princeton, NJ*): You pointed out in your list of neurotransmitters that they were there primarily to show that they could help people think about what to look at in humans. I think that's correct and would like to emphasize that by pointing out that in the list of excitatory transmitters, that is, those that tend to induce feeding, you had norepinephrine and dopamine. One needs to be very careful because while it is correct that dopamine seems to be involved in initiating eating, for example, in the nucleus accumbens, it seems to have the opposite effect in the lateral hypothalamus. Research in my lab and Hernandez's lab shows that chronic blockade of dopamine in the lateral hypothalamus with the neuroleptic sulpiride produces in female rats another animal model of obesity. Similarly with norepinephrine, while it is of course essentially correct that norepinephrine can induce feeding as you demonstrated, again in the lateral hypothalamus it seems to have the opposite effect. Work in our laboratories has shown that depleting norepinephrine with 6-hydroxydopamine, where you're depleting the ventral noradrenergic pathways as opposed to the dorsal, produces again an animal model of obesity, not anorexia. So I think we need to be careful about putting those neurotransmitters in a column labeled "initiates feeding," because it depends on what part of the brain you're looking at. You can get opposite effects, even animal models of obesity, by blocking what you've labeled as feeding neurotransmitters.

DR. SMITH: I agree. I think location is everything.

DR. MORLEY: That point is very important and perhaps at the general discussion we could come back to that because there are a number of examples where treatments create their effect by the anatomical localization, a critical factor which is often ignored when we're thinking about animal modeling.

Nutrient Imbalances in Depressive Disorders

Possible Brain Mechanisms[a]

R. J. WURTMAN,[b] D. O'ROURKE,[c]
AND J. J. WURTMAN[b]

[b]Clinical Research Center and
Department of Brain and Cognitive Sciences
Massachusetts Institute of Technology
Cambridge, Massachusetts 02139

[c]Department of Psychiatry
Massachusetts General Hospital
Boston, Massachusetts 02114

Numerous disease states and disorders apparently share the propensity of causing both appetitive and affective symptoms. Patients usually exhibit carbohydrate craving (and the actual overconsumption of this macronutrient, as such or in foods that also contain fats) and signs of atypical depression (such as decreased subjective energy, fatigue, social withdrawal, anxiety, "muddleheadedness," and hypersomnia).[1] Sometimes they present themselves to their physicians complaining of their inability to lose weight, or to sustain weight loss, and only later are recognized as also suffering from affective symptoms. Other patients are initially seen for depression, but at that time also give a history of carbohydrate craving and weight gain, and yet others solicit medical assistance for their premenstrual syndrome ("late luteal-phase dysphoric disorder"), complaining about disturbances of both the mood and the appetite during the week or two before menstruation.

These diseases and disorders share a tendency to be cyclic:[1] Obese carbohydrate-cravers suffer their worst symptoms at a particular time of day (late afternoon–early evening); those with the premenstrual syndrome are, of course, afflicted only during the luteal phase of the menstrual cycle and are asymptomatic during the follicular phase; those with atypical depression plus carbohydrate craving most typically suffer from seasonal affective disorder (or "SAD"), becoming symptomatic when the daily period of daylight shortens in the fall, and remitting spontaneously as days lengthen in the spring (or, during fall or winter, when exposed to supplemental illumination). This tendency to cyclicity suggests a role for the pineal hormone melatonin in their pathogenesis.[1-3]

The diseases also often exhibit useful therapeutic responses to a drug, d-fenfluramine, which is thought, in the doses used (15 mg orally twice daily), to cause a selective increase in serotonin-mediated neurotransmission.[4] The responses of obese carbohydrate cravers to this drug have been described previously[5]; those of patients with SAD are the subject of this report.

[a] These studies were supported in part by National Institutes of Health GCRC Grant M-01-RR00088-24 to the Massachusetts Institute of Technology Clinical Research Center.

METHODS

Potential subjects were screened as outpatients at the MIT Clinical Research Center during the fall of 1986 by completing questionnaires about their psychiatric and weight histories and were interviewed by a psychiatrist and a clinical nutritionist. Twenty-three (19 women and 4 men) who satisfied the diagnostic criteria for seasonal affective disorder, described above,[1] participated in the study; three others chose not to do so. All of the subjects were free of other medical or psychiatric disorders, were not taking medications, and were 10–40% above their ideal body weight for height (Metropolitan Life Insurance Co. height and weight tables for men and women, 1983). A physical examination was conducted by a physician; blood samples for clinical measurements were obtained (CBC, thyroid indices, BPRO 20 blood profile, serum pregnancy test); and a urinalyis and EKG were performed. Psychometric testing, consisting of the Hamilton Depression Scale (HDS) and its SAD addendum (ADD),[6] was used to quantify depressive symptoms before and after each of the two treatment periods, and again during the month of June following the completion of the study. Only patients with HDS of 15 or more, or a combined HDS + ADD score of 21 or more, were included in the study. At each of these times, subjects also were weighed and interviewed by a psychiatrist and a clinical nutritionist. Each subject was also contacted weekly by telephone to ensure early detection of possible side effects of the treatment, or deterioration of clinical condition. Informed consent forms were signed by each subject, which included specific commitments not to travel to a southern latitude, nor to change eating or life-style patterns, nor to become pregnant while participating in the study.

Subjects received d-fenfluramine (15 mg p.o. twice daily) and its placebo in random order, using a double-blind crossover design, for four-week periods, separated by a two-week washout period. Only the nurse who controlled the drug knew the code; patients and researchers were all blind to it. The drug and its placebo were obtained from the Servier Co., Neuilly-sur-Seine, France. Its use in this study was based on an IND previously approved by the U. S. Food and Drug Administration.

Side effects were determined using a checklist; this was self-administered by the subjects, and then returned to an outpatient nurse (who was not a member of the research team). This nurse would have informed the study physician about significant side effects had they occurred, but this was not necessary for any of the subjects who completed the study. Patients did not report that side effects provided them with an indication of when they were receiving the drug. Some did attempt to determine when they were receiving the drug from their improvement in mood; however, a retrospective assessment indicated that this subjective improvement sometimes coincided with the drug period and sometimes with placebo.

Five women failed to complete the study. Two violated the study protocol by taking a vacation in southern California during the treatment phase (which resulted in their being exposed to summer levels of illumination); one became pregnant; one developed dysuria while receiving d-fenfluramine and was discharged from the study; and the fifth had to leave Massachusetts for personal reasons. Statistical analyses included data from the 18 subjects (14 women, 4 men) who completed the study. The null hypothesis of no change was tested for significance using analysis of variance with repeated measures, followed by Tukey's test for pairwise comparisons. The relationship between weight change and depression score was evaluated using Pearson's product-moment correlation.

A second uncontrolled study was conducted in 1987–1988, on nine of the subjects [1-4,7-9,11,13] (TABLE 1) who had responded to d-fenfluramine during the previous fall and winter, in order to determine whether the drug could be effective for more

TABLE 1. Effect of *d*-Fenfluramine on Body Weight in SAD Patients

Patient	Sex	Age	Pre-Drug	Post Drug	Diff.	Pre-Placebo	Post Placebo	Diff.
					Body Weight (Kg)			
1	F	35	68.3	66.9	−1.4	68.7	68.0	−0.7
2	F	44	83.1	80.8	−2.3	78.9	81.4	+2.5
3	F	36	68.0	67.3	−0.7	63.3	65.8	+2.5
4	M	30	79.0	76.8	−2.2	79.4	78.0	−1.4
5	F	35	118.1	117.8	−0.3	117.1	106.3	−10.8
6	M	45	84.1	81.7	−2.4	84.4	83.0	−1.4
7	F	43	140.0	135.3	−4.7	135.6	137.9	+2.3
8	F	52	69.0	66.6	−2.4	69.3	70.1	+0.8
9	F	32	132.9	129.7	−3.2	130.2	131.5	+1.3
10	F	41	71.1	71.5	+0.4	71.7	72.1	+0.4
11	F	54	59.0	56.6	−2.4	57.0	56.4	−0.6
12	F	41	75.3	75.4	+0.1	75.5	76.7	+1.2
13	F	55	63.5	62.0	−1.5	64.8	65.1	+0.3
14	M	48	76.9	80.2	+3.3	81.4	81.7	+0.3
15	M	42	90.2	85.5	−4.7	87.5	89.4	+1.9
16	F	31	65.3	63.9	−1.4	65.7	66.7	+1.0
17	F	29	96.7	98.7	+2.0	104.2	105.3	+1.1
18	F	35	81.8	84.4	+2.6	83.9	88.6	+4.7
Mean:		40.4	84.6	83.3	−1.2	84.3	84.6	+0.3
SEM:		1.9	5.5	5.3	0.5	5.3	5.3	0.7
p =					0.033			0.69

[a] Differs from pre-drug group, *p* < 0.033.

than a single treatment period, and whether it remained active in responders for the full duration of each year's period of symptoms. As described above, patients were seen by a psychiatrist and underwent psychometric testing by the Hamilton Depression Scale and its SAD addendum on November 20 and December 4, when treatment (*d*-fenfluramine, 15 mg, p.o., twice daily) was started. Treatment continued for twelve weeks; patients were evaluated at intervals while on treatment, and again on March 18, three weeks after the discontinuation of treatment.

RESULTS

Demographic data describing the 14 women and 4 men who completed the first year's study are summarized in TABLE 1. Their ages ranged from 29 to 55 years (mean ± SEM, 40.4 ± 1.9 years). Mean depression scores were identical before drug (20.9 ± 1.3, HDS; 13.3 ± 0.8, ADD) and placebo (21.4 ± 1.2, HDS; 13.2 ± 0.6, ADD) treatments (TABLE 2). Placebo treatment resulted in a small (22%) but significant mean decline in HDS scores (by 4.5 ± 1.6, *p* < 0.02), but no significant mean decline in ADD scores (by 1.2 ± 1.1, *p* > 0.2). Treatment with *d*-Fenfluramine reduced both scores by 71–73% (i.e., by 14.8 ± 1.2 for the HDS, and 9.7 ± 1.3 for the ADD; *p* < 0.0001). *d*-Fenfluramine also caused significant improvements in various ADD subscales (TABLE 3), including decreased energy (*p* < 0.0001), fatigue (*p* < 0.0001), social withdrawal (*p* < 0.0001), increased appetite (*p* < 0.0001), carbohydrate craving (*p* < 0.0001), and hypersomnia (*p* < 0.001). The placebo diminished subjective fatigue by 25%, (*p* < 0.05), compared with the 74% reduction seen with *d*-fenfluramine, and failed to affect any of the other subscales significantly.

TABLE 2. Effect of d-Fenfluramine on Depression Scores in SAD Patients[a]

| Patient | Fall | | | | Spring |
	Pre-Drug	Post Drug	Pre-Placebo	Post Placebo	
1	31/14	10/4	19/14	20/16	0/0
2	23/16	4/4	25/11	21/15	0/0
3	18/14	1/0	24/14	12/13	0/0
4	18/10	0/0	19/10	17/7	0/0
5	18/16	3/2	18/14	16/14	0/2
6	26/13	3/1	24/12	26/10	0/0
7	22/17	5/1	22/15	22/17	0/0
8	10/11	5/0	15/8	13/11	1/1
9	22/16	1/0	19/17	18/15	0/0
10	21/15	6/2	29/15	28/16	3/0
11	16/13	1/3	15/12	19/19	0/0
12	22/17	6/1	34/15	32/16	0/0
13	15/4	0/0	24/14	14/11	0/0
14	15/12	0/4	15/9	1/2	5/0
15	19/11	6/4	21/14	4/7	0/1
16	22/10	15/12	20/15	2/2	0/0
17	27/13	20/14	18/14	17/14	0/1
18	32/18	25/14	24/15	22/12	5/0
Mean:	21/13	$6^b/3.6^b$	21/13	17/12	$0.8^b/0.2^b$
SEM:	1.3/0.8	1.7/1.1	1.2/0.6	1.9/1.1	0.4/0.13

[a] Fall tests were conducted in November; spring tests were conducted in June. The number to the left of the slash represents the subject's score on the Hamilton Depression Scale; the number to the right of the slash represents the subject's score on the Addendum for Atypical Depression to the Hamilton Depression Scale (see text).
[b] Differs from pre-drug fall scores, $p < 0.001$.

Subjects who received d-fenfluramine before placebo ($n = 11$) exhibited significantly greater responses ($p < 0.05$; unpaired t-test) in mood scores than those initially receiving placebo ($n = 7$); however, the effects of the drug on HDS and ADD were highly significant ($p < 0.0001$) in both subgroups.

TABLE 3. Effect of d-Fenfluramine on Scores for Individual Symptoms in the Hamilton SAD Addendum Scale

Subscales	Pre-drug	Post drug	Mean Diff.	Pre-placebo	Post placebo	Mean Diff.
Decreased energy	2.1 ± 0.07	0.4 ± 0.18	$1.8 ± 0.2^a$	2.0 ± 0.08	1.6 ± 0.19	0.3 ± 0.2
Fatigue	2.7 ± 0.13	0.7 ± 0.26	$2.0 ± 0.3^a$	2.8 ± 0.14	2.1 ± 0.27	$0.7 ± 0.2^b$
Social withdrawal	2.5 ± 0.25	0.7 ± 0.28	$1.8 ± 0.3^a$	2.4 ± 0.24	2.2 ± 0.31	0.2 ± 0.3
Increased appetite	1.7 ± 0.10	0.3 ± 0.14	$1.4 ± 0.2^a$	1.5 ± 0.12	1.4 ± 0.14	0.1 ± 0.1
Carbohydrate craving	2.7 ± 0.13	0.5 ± 0.21	$2.2 ± 0.3^a$	2.7 ± 0.15	2.4 ± 0.20	0.3 ± 0.3
Hypersomnia	2.4 ± 0.25	0.9 ± 0.20	1.4 ± 0.3	1.9 ± 0.24	1.9 ± 0.29	−0.1 ± 0.2

NOTE: Data are presented as mean scores ± SEM.
[a] $p < 0.0001$ (pre–post) score vs. 0.
[b] $p < 0.05$ (pre–post) score vs. 0.

Thirteen of the 18 subjects (72%) demonstrated complete reversal of their SAD symptoms when taking d-fenfluramine. Of the remaining subjects, two responded to both drug and placebo; one responded to only placebo; and two failed to respond to either treatment. Abundant published evidence indicates that a 30% placebo response rate typifies studies on drugs for depression.

The majority of subjects lost weight while receiving d-fenfluramine (1.2 ± 0.5 kg; $p = 0.033$), but not on the placebo (0.3 ± 0.7 kg; $p = 0.69$), TABLE 1). No significant correlations were observed in mood score in either the placebo or the drug-treated group.

None of the 18 subjects showed evidence of depression, either clinically or by psychometric testing, when evaluated in June, three months after completion of the study (TABLE 2). Upon questioning, a majority of subjects reported frequent but not severe cases of dry mouth, as well as infrequent episodes of mild headache and diarrhea. The latter conditions were experienced by only a small number of patients. None of the subjects showed symptoms of depression or reduced energy on cessation of the drug.

Among the patients retested in 1987–1988, Hamilton and ADD Scores were abnormally elevated by November 20, and the Hamilton Score exhibited a further significant rise by December 4, when treatment was started (FIG. 1). Within two weeks, scores of both tests had fallen to their normal ranges (21.4 ± 0.9 HDS and 13.8 ± 0.8 ADD, to 4.1 ± 1.8 HDS and 2.2 ± 0.7 ADD); they remained normal during the subsequent ten weeks of treatment, and were also normal on March 18, three weeks after treatment had been discontinued. Moreover, each of the subscales described in TABLE 3 exhibited similar responses.

DISCUSSION

These data show that d-fenfluramine, a drug that selectively enhances serotonin-mediated neurotransmission without causing psychostimulant effects or enhancing catecholamine-mediated neurotransmission,[4] was effective in relieving both the depressive (TABLE 2) and appetitive (TABLE 1) symptoms of seasonal affective disorder, whereas placebo had only minor effects on the depressive symptoms, and none on the appetitive symptoms. Moreover, patients apparently retained their ability to respond to d-fenfluramine from year to year, and the drug remained effective throughout the annual three-month period when symptoms usually are worst (FIG. 1). Atypical depressive symptoms (TABLE 3) were also completely resolved by d-fenfluramine but unaffected by placebo (TABLE 3). This finding is particularly encouraging because these symptoms, also often encountered in depressed patients without SAD, can be refractory to, and even aggravated by, currently available antidepressants. In practice, some tricyclic antidepressants and monoamine oxidase inhibitors commonly cause weight gain associated with hyperphagia and carbohydrate craving.

A significant ($p < 0.05$) order effect was observed; patients who received d-fenfluramine before placebo exhibited a greater drug response (i.e., in mood scores) than those initially receiving placebo. However, in both subsets, the effect of the drug on HDS and ADD was very highly significant ($p < 0.001$). The order effect may reflect the fact that patients initially receiving placebo were probably sicker by the time they received d-fenfluramine than those receiving the drug first (FIG. 1).

Thirteen of the eighteen subjects who completed the 1986–1987 study lost weight on the drug, but only five of these thirteen also lost weight while on placebo. Moreover, only one subject (#5) lost more weight on placebo than on the drug; no subject lost

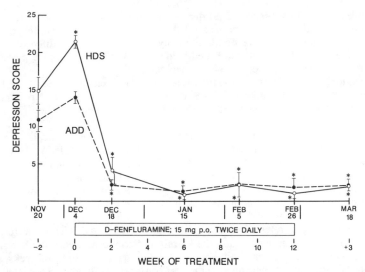

FIGURE 1. Effect of *d*-fenfluramine treatment on depression scores in patients with seasonal affective disorder. Nine patients who had previously exhibited a short-term (one month) therapeutic response to *d*-fenfluramine received the drug for twelve weeks, starting on December 4, 1987. Depressive symptoms were quantified, using the Hamilton Depression Scale (HDD) and its SAD addendum (ADD) at intervals before, during, and after drug treatment. *Differs from initial (November 20) score, $p < 0.05$.

weight only on the placebo, but two (numbers 14 and 17) gained less on placebo than on *d*-fenfluramine. Eleven of these thirteen subjects also experienced a significant decrease in affective symptoms while on the drug; however, the magnitude of weight loss (or gain) did not correlate with that of the anti-depressant response. *d*-Fenfluramine was also highly effective in ameliorating hyperphagia and carbohydrate craving within the patient population as a whole (TABLE 3), whereas placebo affected neither of these symptoms. All of our subjects had described a history of annual weight gain during the "winter depression months," and, indeed, thirteen of them gained weight while receiving placebo (TABLE 1). Our data suggest that the drug may also remain effective in SAD patients when administered for the three months per year when their symptoms usually are worst (FIG. 1).

The observed responses of SAD patients to *d*-fenfluramine, a drug known to enhance serotonin-mediated neurotransmission selectively,[4] are consistent with the known roles of serotoninergic neurons in the control of appetite and mood (*cf.* Young[7]). Transmitter release from these neurons is affected by food consumption, and, in turn, may influence subsequent food choice: Consumption of carbohydrate-rich, protein-poor foods can enhance serotonin synthesis via insulin-mediated changes in the plasma amino acid pattern[1,8] that facilitate the uptake of circulating tryptophan into the brain and thus increase the substrate-saturation of tryptophan hydroxylase and the production and release of serotonin. Conversely, the administration to normal rats of *dl*-fenfluramine, or of such other selectively serotoninergic drugs as fluoxetine, or MK-212 can (as discussed in 5) decrease their consumption of carbohydrates, while sparing that of protein-rich foods; nonserotoninergic anorectic agents like D-amphetamine lack these nutrient-specific effects.

Among obese subjects who professed to be carbohydrate cravers, and in whom this behavior was quantified in a clinical research center,[5] administration of *d*-fenfluramine also selectively diminished carbohydrate intake without significantly diminishing that of protein. Carbohydrate intake was also shown, in these patients, to have a positive effect on mood[9]; this improvement was not exhibited among obese individuals who did not snack on carbohydrate-rich foods (noncarbohydrate cravers). The present data on patients with SAD raise the possibility that serotoninergic drugs might also be useful in patients with other depressive disorders associated with hyperphagia and carbohydrate craving, for example, normal weight bulimia.[10] We have already obtained preliminary evidence of *d*-fenfluramine's efficacy in patients with the late luteal-phase disorder (unpublished observations).

SUMMARY

We examined the utility of *d*-fenfluramine, a serotonin-releasing drug previously shown to diminish carbohydrate craving and weight gain in obese people, in treating patients with seasonal affective disorder (SAD), a variant of depression that occurs each fall and winter and is usually associated with hyperphagia and carbohydrate craving. Eighteen patients participated in a double-blind, placebo-controlled study in 1986–1987, each receiving, in random order, *d*-fenfluramine (15 mg p.o. twice daily) or a placebo for four weeks, separated by a two-week washout period. Symptoms of SAD were assessed before and after each treatment period using clinical interviews by a psychiatrist, and the Hamilton Depression Rating Scale (HDS) with a special SAD addendum (ADD). Subjects were also weighed. Patients' depression scores (mean ± SEM) were identical before treatment with drug (20.9 ± 1.3, HDS: 13.3 ± 0.8 ADD) or placebo (21.4 ± 1.2, HDS; 13.2 ± 0.6 ADD). During placebo treatment, HDS scores declined by 22.6% ($p < 0.02$) and ADD scores by 9% ($p > 0.2$). During *d*-fenfluramine treatment, HDS scores fell by 71% ($p < 0.0001$) and ADD scores by 73% ($p < 0.0001$).

Thirteen of the subjects (72%) demonstrated complete reversal of their abnormal test scores on *d*-fenfluramine. In two others, test scores fell to normal levels with both the drug and its placebo; one subject responded only to placebo; and two failed to show therapeutic responses to either drug or placebo treatment. The group as a whole lost weight (1.2 kg) on *d*-fenfluramine ($p < 0.033$) but not on placebo. A subsequent study on nine of the responders showed that improvements persisted for the full three-month duration of the SAD season.

These results indicate that *d*-fenfluramine, a drug not previously identified as an antidepressant, may be useful in treating SAD. Moreover, since *d*-fenfluramine acts specifically to enhance serotonin-mediated neurotransmission, the data further suggest that serotonin is involved in both the affective and appetitive symptoms of SAD. Indeed, the carbohydrate craving of these patients may constitute a kind of substance abuse in which the nutrient is eaten precisely for its serotonin-mediated psychotropic effects.

REFERENCES

1. WURTMAN, R. J. 1989. Carbohydrates and depression. Sci. Am. January: 68–75.
2. BRZEZINSKI, A. & R. J. WURTMAN. 1988. The pineal gland: Its possible roles in human reproduction. Obstet. Gynaecol. Surv. 43(4): 197–207.
3. TERMAN, M., J. S. TERMAN, F. M. QUITKIN, T. B. COOPER, E. S. LO, J. M. GORMAN, J. W. STEWART & P. J. MCGRATH. 1988. Response of the melatonin cycle to phototherapy for seasonal affective disorder. J. Neural Transm. 72: 147–165.

4. GARATTINI, S., T. MENNINI & R. SAMININ. 1987. From fenfluramine racemate to *d*-fenfluramine: specificity and potency of the effects on the serotoninergic system and food intake. Ann. N. Y. Acad. Sci. **499:** 156–166.
5. WURTMAN, J. J., R. J. WURTMAN, S. MARK, R. TSAY & J. GROWDON. 1985. *d*-Fenfluramine selectively suppresses carbohydrate snacking in obese subjects. Int. J. Eating Disord. **4:** 89–99.
6. ROSENTHAL, N. & M. HEFFERNAN. 1986. Bulimia, carbohydrate craving and depression: A central connection? *In* Nutrition and the Brain. R. J. Wurtman & J. J. Wurtman, Eds. Vol. **7:** 139–166. Raven Press. New York.
7. YOUNG, S. N. 1986. The clinical psychopharmacology of tryptophan. *In* Nutrition and the Brain. R. J. Wurtman and J. J. Wurtman, Eds. Vol. **7:** 89–138. Raven Press. New York.
8. FERNSTROM, J. & R. J. WURTMAN. 1972. Brain serotonin content: Increase following ingestion of carbohydrate diet. Science **173:** 1023–1025.
9. LIEBERMAN, H., J. J. WURTMAN & B. CHEW. 1986. Changes in mood after carbohydrate consumption may influence snack choices of obese individuals. Am. J. Clin. Nutr. **44:** 772–778.
10. HUDSON, J., H. POPE, J. J. WURTMAN, D. YURGELUN-TODD, S. MARK & N. ROSENTHAL. 1988. Bulimia in obese individuals: Relationship to normal weight bulimia. J. Nerv. Ment. Dis. **176:** 144–152.

DISCUSSION

DR. JOHN E. MORLEY (*Sepulveda VA Hospital, Sepulveda, CA):* In your earlier slides, fat intake is at least as greatly influenced, or maybe even more influenced, than carbohydrate appetite. I heard your explanation just now that fat doesn't alter neurotransmitters. There are millions of neurotransmitters, so we haven't looked at enough to be sure. You were also talking about carbohydrate craving, which to me looks like palatable food craving. Can you respond to that?

DR. RICHARD J. WURTMAN (*Massachusetts Institute of Technology, Cambridge, MA*): Believe me, this is not a new question. We raised it before anybody else did. Was there any evidence for regulation of fat? I can affirm that we are not able to find a selective effect on fat intake. Now to be sure, we may bias the question out of existence because when we design our snacks we make them isofat; so there's no way that somebody can change the proportion of fat that they're taking whether they take one snack or *n* snacks. Prior to doing that we did other studies on rats and on humans to see whether we could detect an effect on fat intake by biasing them the other way. And we just can't do it. I would like to; I'm sorry that we can't. I think it would be nice if there were some evidence for regulation of fat intake. I would invite you to accept my challenge. Go back to your laboratory and see if you can find an effect of fat on brain composition and then let me know.

DR. ADAM DREWNOWSKY (*University of Michigan, Ann Arbor, MI*): Could you define the term "carbohydrate craving" for us? You've used the term repeatedly, but I'm still not sure I quite understand what is craving and whether these are carbohydrates.

DR. WURTMAN: There are two components to it. One is a description of behavior on the part of the subjects, that is, the NIMH group, and is based on what the patients tell them. The other description is an operational description. What do the people actually do? We use the term to refer to a situation in which a typical obese or SAD patient, in an afternoon or an evening, consumes what most people would consider ast quantities of high glycemic index carbohydrates independent of the coinjested fat content and independent of the taste of the carbohydrates. How's that?

DR. DREWNOWSKY: Okay. You mentioned high glycemic index carbohydrates. That really leaves us with simple sugars.

DR. WURTMAN: How about potato starch? It has the same glycemic index as simple sugars.

DR. DREWNOWSKY: But in most cases . . .

DR. WURTMAN: No, not in most cases.

DR. DREWNOWSKY: . . . it's simple sugars.

DR. WURTMAN: You have to look at the literature on diabetes in the last couple of years. It's been a surprise to most of us to discover that simple sugars are by no means more effective as a group in eliciting insulin secretion than many starches. It depends on the sugar, it depends on the amount of fiber that's with it, it depends on the starch.

DR. DREWNOWSKY: Yes, but the very same data you just quoted also show that Mars bars and Snickers bars effectively had a very low glycemic index, and these are the foods that you have in fact used.

DR. WURTMAN: We have measured CHO snacking patterns among obese subjects, women with severe premenstrual syndrome, and women who have gone through smoking cessation using very low-fat, high-carbohydrate snacks, such as breakfast cereals, which contain no fat, and pretzels, which contain very little fat. We have seen the same pattern of late afternoon and midevening snacking on high-carbohydrate foods as established earlier using foods that contained more fat. Thus, the pattern of consuming high-carbohydrate foods persists regardless of the fat content of the foods.

DR. DREWNOWSKY: Well in that case wouldn't it be fair in your talk to replace every word carbohydrate with either potato starch or sugar? If we're dealing with specifics we shouldn't really give it the global term carbohydrates because different things may occur with different carbohydrates.

DR. WURTMAN: The issue here is not glycemic index; after all, foods that are high in fiber but low in fat may also have a low glycemic inex. Whether a food is going to satisfy a CHO craver depends on whether the plasma tryptophan ratio goes up. This is easy to determine. All you have to do is give humans a snack and ask whether the plasma tryptophan ratio went up.

DR. DREWNOWSKY: Okay, thank you.

DR. KENNY J. SIMANSKY (*Medical College of Pennsylvania, Philadelphia, PA*): Assuming that changes in brain serotonin modulate macronutrient preference at any particular meal, that demands a rather abrupt change in behavior or detection by the rat or other mammal. What is the mechanism and what are the stimuli that permit the animal to make an adjustment so quickly?

DR. WURTMAN: There are two aspects to the question. One has to do with how tight the mechanism is. You eat 13 plus or minus 1% of your calories as protein. Now, are you eating 13% at every meal? Of course not, but over a long enough period of time this is the average that you're attaining. This is by no means the average that you would attain if you went to the supermarket and took one of everything. There's a real selection process occurring. In answer to the first part of the question, the mechanism does not work at every meal. What it does is to work over a long enough period of time, and the number, by the way, is changeable, for instance with estrus cycle in the rat.

Now the second question, I honestly don't have any way of answering. How does the rat or the human know? If you ask the patients who are craving carbohydrates during wintertime with seasonal depression why they are doing this, they're not going to say because they are or are not hungry. It's also not because they want something sweet. Anna Wirz-Justice did a nice paper showing that the majority of the SAD patients eat starches and not sweet carbohydrates. So what is it they're sensing that is the basis of their behavior?

What the question really comes down to is Are there automatic behaviors that are not associated with conscious sensations?

QUESTION: I'll just ask whether fats can alter prostaglandin synthesis in the brain.

DR. WURTMAN: No, there's no evidence that fats can alter prostaglandin synthesis. We have given animals very large amounts of fat, within the normal range, in order to determine whether or not the composition of the number two fatty acid on phosphatidylcholine was changed, so that when that was cleaved the likelihood of forming prostaglandins or thromboxanes would increase. We've never found a consistent significant effect.

DR. PAUL F. ARAVICH (Eastern Virginia Medical School, Hampton, VA): I'd like to take exception with that last comment. I think there's unequivocal evidence that prostaglandin composition, or at least fatty acid composition, within the brain can be altered through dietary intervention depending upon whether it's omega 6 or omega 3 fatty acids that are fit.

DR. WURTMAN: You're absolutely right about that, but that's not the question that I answered. Within the retina, for instance, approximately half of all the fatty acids in the outer segments are polyunsaturates, so 22.6 of them basically, and of course that's extremely dependent. But that's not the same as saying neurotransmission is affected by it.

DR. ARAVICH: If indeed you're altering the fatty acid composition of membranes, membrane phospholipids relate to everything from growth factors to neurotransmitters. It's inconceivable to me that fat-intake manipulations would not affect neurotransmitter efficacy, number one. Number two, there's unequivocal evidence that essential fatty acid deficiency causes changes in vasopressin content within the hypothalamus. Number three, we have evidence showing that diets high in fat and sucrose have very marked effects on the vasopressin content within the hypothalamus.

DR. SARAH LIEBOWITZ (The Rockefeller University, New York, NY): Do you have an explanation for the different results in the literature in terms of the effects of estrogen on macronutrient intake, the studies with pure macronutrients as well as with mixed diets in your own laboratory?

DR. WURTMAN: Judy Wurtman and Dr. Michael Baum found an increase in the proportion of the diet chosen as protein on the day of estrus. What they were able to show, using diets that were isocaloric but varied in protein or CHO, was that the expected estrus-associated calorie intake decreased, but protein intake remained constant. These findings fit nicely with earlier results by Dr. George Wade showing an increase in protein intake in pregnant rats.

DR. LIEBOWITZ: I meant the effects of ovariectomy and estrogen, in terms of effects that Geiselman observed in terms of the increase in carbohydrate versus the study of Judy's (Dr. Judith Wurtman).

DR. WURTMAN: You're asking me to do something that may not be polite so I won't.

DR. BENDER (Bayer AG, Wuppertal, F.R.G.): You said that a carbohydrate-rich diet has an insulin-positive effect on the serotonin concentration in the hypothalamus. Did you test perhaps an aracabose inhibitor like Acavose on the serotonin concentration?

DR. WURTMAN: No.

DR. MADELYN FERNSTROM (University of Pittsburgh, Pittsburgh, PA): Many of you know that it has been argued quite convincingly that carbohydrates are not regulated at all in a number of very elegant studies by both Peter Leathwood and Tom Castonguay. So I'd just like to interject the point that there is controversy in this area that carbohydrate intake is not at all regulated. Secondly, a number of investigators have not seen the macronutrient-specific effect of serotonergic compounds, though some have. The selective effect of carbohydrate suppression with serotonergie compounds, I think, is also highly controversial.

DR. WURTMAN: Have you done any experiments that have failed to demonstrate it?

DR. FERNSTROM: No, these are studies of other investigators, and I would just like to raise the point that there is controversy in this area, that there is some disagreement as to the specificity of the effect.

DR. WURTMAN: First, I would like to mention that carbohydrate regulation has been confirmed in the painstaking experiments of Dr. Sarah Liebowitz in rats, thus disputing the studies you mentioned of Leathwood and Castonguay. Moreover, carbohydrate craving is a diagnostic criterion for seasonal affective disorder and one of the characteristics defining premenstrual syndrome. The ubiquity of this type of eating disorder has generated, in part, the development of new drugs to be used specifically for its treatment. As of last week, when I collected the numbers, 150 million dollars worth of drugs have been sold this past year to treat the excessive consumption of carbohydrates. So I imagine we will have many opportunities to characterize the utility of serotoninergic agents in treating this set of diseases in humans.

DR. MORLEY: We should all realize that new drugs often only are considered specific while they have not been extensively tested. Certainly something as old as reserpine now is known to deplete neuropeptide Y as well as catecholamines, and this gives a totally different viewpoint on how to interpret those data.

Metabolic Rate and Feeding Behavior[a]

STYLIANOS NICOLAIDIS[b] AND PATRICK EVEN

Neurobiologie des Régulations
CNRS URA 637,
College de France,
75231 Paris, France

INTRODUCTION

The physiological purpose of feeding behavior is to insure the maintenance of normal energy metabolism. Yet, feeding has seldom been explored in relation with its metabolic correlates for reasons that will be analyzed below.

Theoretically, food intake is susceptible to affecting metabolic rate, and, conversely, metabolic rate may, in turn, affect feeding. From these two effects the most obvious and the most explored was the former, that is, the increase of thermogenesis in response to feeding.[1-3]

The second effect was explored more recently, because, according to the ischymetric hypothesis, hunger was proposed to be under the control of the actual metabolic rate. [4-6]

This article will deal with the causal relation between the fluctuations of hunger and those of the background metabolic rate. As shown below background metabolic rate is that part of the metabolic rate that is free from the extra cost owing to locomotor activity and to other extra "services."

Understanding the notion of background metabolism is the prerequisite for understanding the entire problem of the control of feeding by the metabolism and vice versa. The total metabolic rate that all devices measure is meaningless because the amount of locomotor activity required by the search and ingestion of food completely obscures the locomotion-free metabolism, that is, the only metabolic rate that reflects the nutritional state of the organism and, therefore, could serve as a signal of depletion/repletion.

Only recently was the technology for the instantaneous discrimination between the various components of metabolism in the freely moving, freely feeding animal made possible. This is why the assessment of the mutual effects between background metabolism and feeding, without interference of noise-inducing locomotion, is now possible.

[a] This work was partially supported by grants from Le Ministère de la Recherche et de la Technologie (88G0523), Fondation pour la Recherche Medicale and l'INSERM (857009).
[b] Address for correspondence: S. Nicolaidis, Neurobiologie des Régulations, CNRS URA637, Collège de France, 11 place Marcelin Berthelot, 75231 Paris CEDEX 05, France.

CONCEPTUAL AND TECHNICAL INNOVATIONS: MEASUREMENT OF RESTING METABOLISM IN MOVING ANIMALS AND THE NOTION OF BACKGROUND METABOLISM OR *"MÉTABOLISME DE FOND"*

All of the classic notions, such as basal and resting metabolism or cost of loco-motor activity and of feeding, were established by early investigators using closed-circuit techniques with animals confined for various time intervals.[1,2,7]

The main inconvenience in these techniques was the inertia of detection of metabolic changes in relation to the confinement. Studying non–steady-state changes of metabolism such as those related to spontaneous feeding was incompatible with closed-circuit techniques.

Dynamic measurement of shifts of metabolism together with the concomitant behaviors was made possible when accurate and stable gas analyzers were made available.[8,9] Today's open-circuit calorimeters are able to monitor metabolic changes with reasonably short inertia. But despite this progress, the problem of discriminating the portion of the total metabolic rate that has been consumed for the locomotor effort was unresolved in the open-circuit devices using freely moving, freely feeding animals. It is obvious that, when the animal makes a movement, the related increased gas exchanges are detected by the analyzers of oxygen and of carbon dioxide after a delay and with some deformation depending on the configuraton and the volume of both the metabolic chamber and the tubing connecting the chamber to the monitors. As a result, a long time after a movement was accomplished, the overall metabolic rate remained elevated even though the animal had returned to its resting state. Resting metabolism can be measured only after a more or less prolonged period of resting, the length of which depends mainly on the degree of the previous locomotor effort. In the rat, particularly during darkness, sufficiently long resting episodes are rather unusual. As a result, monitoring total metabolism during a given interval of immobilization does not necessarily reflect the resting metabolic rate.

In this type of feeding study, other problems make simple measurements impossible to interpret. An increased metabolic rate during a locomotor episode may not reflect the simple addition of the resting metabolic rate and the extra energy cost of the muscular effort. The activity-related metabolic enhancement may hide a possible parallel increase of the nonmotor metabolism due, for example, to feeding.

From these remarks it appears that in both the resting and the active periods, it is necessary to evaluate quantitatively the fraction of energy expenditure produced by the locomotor effort in order to factor out this fraction from the total metabolic rate and so compute the locomotion-free metabolic rate. This figure is very close but not identical to what could be qualified as resting metabolism in a moving animal. However, this expression could be misleading because metabolism of the cells unrelated to the locomotor effort may differ between resting and active periods. Indeed, muscular effort, particularly when it is sustained, induces a complete upset of circulating metabolites that may affect the metabolic status of "resting" cells of the body.

Because the nonlocomotive metabolic rate is susceptible to change in response to either locomotion or nutritional states, it was necessary to use a neutral expression to designate the overall metabolic rate that isn't produced for the purpose of locomotion or other services such as thermoregulation, hyperosmolar urine production, and so forth. We used the expression *métabolisme de fond* [5,10]; in English its best equivalent is "background metabolism."

Needless to say, the theoretically variable background metabolism is also different from the theoretically stable basal metabolism. The latter is reached only when various conditions, such as long immobility, thermal neutrality, and food deprivation, are met although the former underlies all states. Note, however, that background metabolism is meant to reach the level of basal metabolism under basal conditions.

Our interest in background metabolism results from the idea that the intensities of the ongoing background metabolism can perhaps be sensed and so determine the degree of hunger/satiety as proposed by the ischymetric hypothesis.[4]

DEVICE DEVELOPED FOR THE MEASUREMENT OF BACKGROUND METABOLISM IN RELATION TO FEEDING

In order to test the ischymetric mechanism of the control of feeding, it was necessary to develop a system capable of monitoring rapid changes of various parameters of metabolism, as well as the pattern of food intake and intensity of locomotor activity on free-moving animals housed in conditions of thermal comfort.

To reach these conditions, an open-circuit calorimeter was developed using a relatively small-volume cage (9 liters) to minimize dead space (FIG. 1). The animal's platform rested on three piezo-resistive strain gauges so that the work produced on the platform by the animal was measured. The food cup was independently weighed and temperature was closely controlled by a powerful system of thermoregulation.

The data made available by the analyzers and monitors, that is, oxygen consumption, carbon dioxide release (CO_2), air flow, food intake, locomotor activity, and temperature, were recorded at 10-second intervals, then treated on line by a computer (FIG. 2). Thus, respiratory quotient ($RQ = CO_2/O_2$) and *métabolisme de fond* could be further computed from the original data.

Computation of the *métabolisme de fond*, particularly within a small interval (10 seconds) needs precise and quantitative measurement of the rate of locomotor effort, the estimation of the corresponding cost and the subtraction of this cost from the total metabolism. The first difficulty comes from the fact that the ergometric strain gauges monitor activity instantly, whereas respiratory changes follow a complex and necessarily delayed path before being monitored. Therefore, these two desynchronized magnitudes have to be matched.

To match delayed and nondelayed parameters, we used various procedures. They all consisted of modeling the deformation induced by the aerodynamics of the system measuring the animal's gas exchanges and in matching the outcome of the model with the instantaneously monitored locomotor profile. If the model of computation was correct, the *métabolisme de fond* would remain stable whether the animal was immobile or moderately moving, provided there were no concurrent events that might modify the *métabolisme de fond* (e.g., stress, feeding, injection of metabolically active drugs or hormones).

The best results were obtained by adjusting the equation of diffusion of O_2 and CO_2 in the calorimeter and by correcting for this diffusion by using the process of numerical filtering of the data which was developed by Kalman (see Meyer & Guillot[11]). FIGURE 3 shows the transformation of the initial total metabolic changes as diffused in the chamber and transferred to the oxygen and carbon dioxide analyzers, into *métabolisme de fond* and energy cost of locomotor activity. Both parameters were modeled as if they were analyzed at the level of the nostrils of the rat.

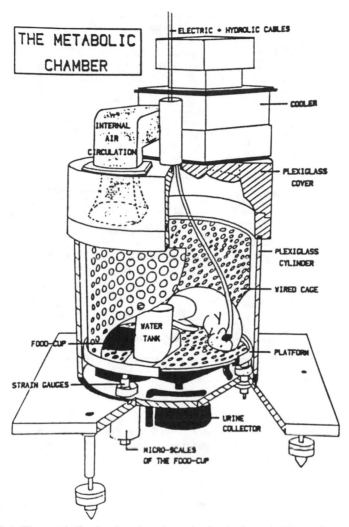

FIGURE 1. The metabolic chamber. Its schematic view is shown in FIGURE 2.

PHYSIOLOGICAL CONTROL OF FEEDING: ISCHYMETRIC AND OTHER HYPOTHESES

The Ischymetric Control of Feeding among the Other Hypotheses

We do not think there is much to say about central versus peripheral mechanisms in the control of feeding. There are numerous peripheral messages, but they only add information to the central mechanism and modulate, particularly during ingestion, its activity. They are not peripheral mechanisms but signals. We shall deal only with

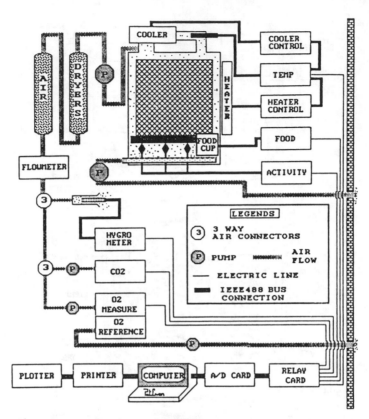

FIGURE 2. Overall schematic view of the circuitry and devices of the system based on an open-circuit, indirect calorimetry. Monitors of air flow, respiratory exchanges (O_2, CO_2, and RQ), quantitative evaluation of locomotor activity, feeding and drinking patterns, temperature and its regulatory system, and hygrometry are shown. The size of the cage allows the rat unrestrained behavior. If necessary the rat bears indwelling catheters and/or electrodes connected to the outside apparatuses for the purpose of i.v. or i.c.v. infusions and for electrophysiological recordings. All of the monitors are connected to the computer, which processess on line the responses and calculates the respiratory quotient, the *métabolisme de fond*, and the locomotor work and cost.

the mechanisms that have been proposed to signal the degree of substrate depletion to the brain and thus to promote the corrective response of feeding. The main mechanism proposed by J. Mayer was his historic glucostatic theory.[12] According to Mayer's final position, feeding is controlled by the level of cellular availability and utilization of glucose. He recognized that the degree of utilization of glucose is not dependent only on its availability. Hormonal co-availability interferes with that of the substrate. This notion is important and is present also in the ischymetric hypothesis. Soon after this theory was advanced, Kennedy[13] and Mellinkoff *et al.*[14] involved the metabolism of lipids and amino acids, respectively, in the control of feeding. They did not really question the fact that glucose utilization was the major factor. Mayer also admitted that lipid metabolism certainly had an influence in the long-term control

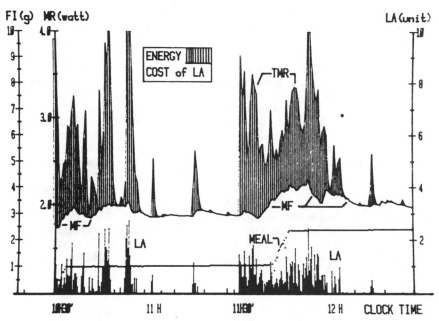

FIGURE 3. Total metabolic rate (MR) in watts, one-minute histograms of locomotor activity (LA), meal pattern (MEAL), and total metabolic rate (TMR). Energy cost of LA and *métabolisme de fond* (MF) were calculated using the Kalman's filtering method. FI: Food intake in grams (g). Recording during the 10:30 to 12:30 A.M. period. Note that MF remained unchanged during LA but was modified in relation to feeding.

of feeding. As early as 1956, it was clear that the control of feeding was dependent upon at least the three main substrates supplying energy to the cells. Later on, various catabolites of the three families of macronutrients and particularly those located at branch points of biochemical cycles (such as pyruvate and glycerol) were proposed to influence feeding. In addition to control by metabolite availability, it was also suggested that feeding was controlled by metabolic hormones such as insulin, glucagon, thyroxine, and adrenaline. As a result moleculo-static or hormono-static hypotheses taking into account molecules or hormones became highly complex. One of the problems was that the regulatory system had to assay each of the proposed molecules by means of some accurate apparatus in order to quantify their concentration or their yield. Even when Mayer proposed that the rate of glucose utilization was the main signal of control of feeding, the computation of this utilization was believed to result from two instead of one dosing apparatus (arterial glucose minus venous glucose or delta glucose). A molecule-dosing system was not inconceivable, particularly for glucose.[15] After all, during the fifties and the sixties, many substances were found to be quantitatively measured by hypothalamic sensors (sex steroids, thyroid hormones, glucose itself). More recently Campfield and Smith[16] proposed that a slight decrease followed by restoration of (V-shaped) blood glucose level is necessary and sufficient to trigger the onset of a meal. Whatever the difficulties in the validation of this interesting hypothesis, the problem of the cause and the detection of this V-shaped preprandial glycemia curve remains to be determined.

Two remarks should be made concerning all the above hypotheses: (a) On the one hand, numerous experimental data partially contradict every one of these hypotheses. To mention only the glycostatic hypothesis as an example: i.v. glucose or glucose plus insulin infusions are unable to affect the occurrence of a spontaneous meal.[17] (b) On the other hand, each of the previous hypotheses is more or less convincingly supported by one or several experimental findings. Therefore, the question is Can they all be right? Is it possible to reconcile the various moleculostatic hypotheses? Obviously, it was necessary to find a signal of depletion able to integrate all the metabolic consequences of the molecules and/or hormones. A global estimation of utilization of macronutrients was proposed first by Ugolef and Kassil[18] in the sixties and by Booth in 1972 who hypothesized some sort of measure of the "yield" of macronutrients that produce energy.[19,20] The question still was, how? There was no suggestion about the way the yield of macronutrients could be sensed and integrated. Interestingly, as early as 1948, Brobeck[21,22] perceived the close relationship that existed between hypothalamic temperature and feeding and pointed out indirectly that there certainly was some link between the rate of metabolism and feeding.[23]

At that point the ischymetric model was proposed as an integrated signal, proportional to the rate of energy production (power, i.e. E/t), and as a biochemical event susceptible to becoming a biologically meaningful signal. The mechanism of such a transduction will be reviewed in the next section.

The Central Receptor Transducing Metabolic Intensity into a Meaningful Biological Signal

One of the findings that supported the glucostatic theory was the presence of neurons in the hypothalamus sensitive to glucose utilization, although evidence that these neurons were directly involved in the control of feeding and not in glucoregulation or something else has never been definitely established. In 1981, Davis et al.[24] showed that ketone bodies were able to decrease feeding following their intracerebroventricular infusion. In 1986 S. Nicolaïdis, S. Miyahara, and M. J. Meile reported that some neurons were also able to modify their electrical activity in the same direction in response to iontopheretic application of either glucose or ketone bodies,[25] reinforcing the idea that several substrates act together to provide an integrated response. The neuron that is capable of performing such an integration could serve as an elementary model of a biological ischymeter. One example of this type of neuron from the lower limit of the dorsomedial nucleus of the hypothalamus is presented in FIGURE 4. Unlike the glucoreceptive and glucosensitive neurons reported by the school of Oomura,[15] these neurons respond in the same direction to the iontophoretic application of both glucose and ketone bodies. The delayed and prolonged way iontophoretically applied metabolites affect neuronal activity in the present example (see FIGURE 4) suggests that these substances may act via their intracellular supply of the pump turnover, which supports the neuronal discharges. More work is needed to verify that neurons in this area have their spike frequency increased in proportion to the availability of other utilizable (other than glucose or ketone bodies) substrates and are also dependent on the presence of hormones such as insulin.

To summarize the proposed mechanism of ischymetry, the increase of metabolic substrates and of humoral factors of their cellular utilization at the level of specialized neurons enhances intracellular power production. The increment of power production supplies the ATP/ADP machinery of spike production and enhances spike frequency. As a result, repletion of macronutrients is transduced into spike acceleration and per-

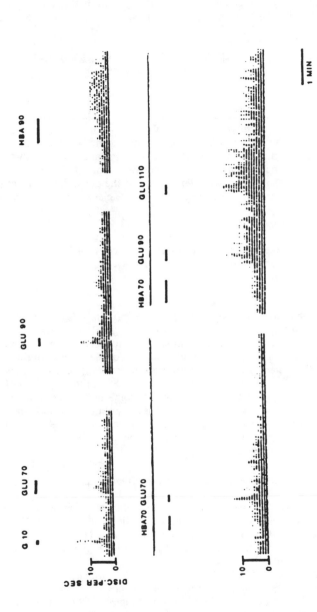

FIGURE 4. Integrated discharges per second from a single neuron located within the lower aspect of the dorsomedial nucleus of the hypothalamus. Frequency increased in a dose-dependent way in response to iontophoretic application on the neuron's membrane (as indicated by horizontal bars with negative current, the numbers corresponding to nanoampères) of either glucose (GLU) or hydroxybutyric acid (HBA). The response of HBA was more progressive. Efficacy of glutamate (G) indicates that the discharges originate from a soma.

haps, ultimately, into a synaptic enhancement of neurotransmitter. The so-generated neuronal response becomes thereafter a biologically meaningful message of satiety.

This model could apply to the classic glucostatic hypothesis if glucose were the only metabolite susceptible to be used by the neurons.

EXPERIMENTS ON METABOLISM AND FEEDING: RESULTS AND DISCUSSION

In these experiments the various parameters of metabolism were monitored together with feeding pattern in the undisturbed, free-feeding albino male rat. Because a concomitant decrease of *métabolisme de fond* and of the onset of a spontaneous meal was insufficient to show that the metabolic events induced the behavioral response, new experiments were designed. In these experiments the metabolic changes were induced experimentally and their consequence on feeding was examined. The same strategy was followed in the attempt to assess whether the end of the meal, that is, meal size, was also a correlate, and possibly the consequence, of the elevation of *métabolisme de fond*.

Decrease of Métabolisme de Fond as a Correlate and as a Determinant of the Onset of a Meal

Spontaneous Feeding[6,27]

The relationship between spontaneous feeding and *métabolisme de fond* was studied during 22 hours of recording sessions on 10 rats that ate a total of 81 meals. Plotting the data in relation to the onset of the 81 meals showed the *métabolisme de fond* decreased spontaneously during the 5 to 10 minutes that preceded the onset of the meals (FIGS. 3 and 5). On the other hand, the respiratory quotient (RQ) did not show any significant changes during the interval between meals. The fact that the *métabolisme de fond* decreased in the preprandial period without concomitant changes in RQ points out that the hypometabolic state was due to a decrease in both glucide and lipid utilization. In particular, no RQ decrease was revealed, as would have been the case if glucose utilization had dropped before the onset of the meals (FIG. 5).

Changes in Feeding Behavior Induced by Metabolic Treatments

Several experiments have been performed in which feeding was stimulated. Feeding-promoting challenges were either 2DG injections or insulin infusions.[10,27,28] In all circumstances, both *métabolisme de fond* and RQ were investigated to challenge whether it was a moleculostatic (change in RQ) or an ischymetric (change in *métabolisme de fond*) mechanism that controlled feeding.

In all cases, changes induced in feeding (increase or decrease) could be accounted for by changes in *métabolisme de fond* (respectively, decrease or increase) induced by the treatments (FIG. 6). In contrast, small or no changes of RQ were observed in relation to the experimentally induced meals. There was no particular trend toward a preprandial drop of RQ, which would have indicated that a decrease in the use of glucose could initiate the meal, as the glucostatic hypothesis would predict. As a result of all these experiments, it was concluded that *métabolisme de fond* and not RQ changes

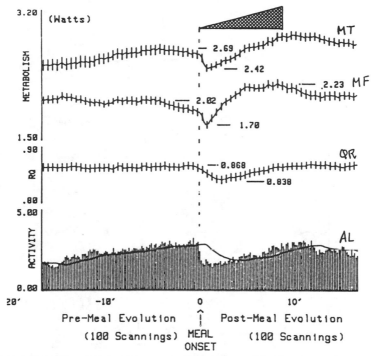

FIGURE 5. General evolution of the metabolic correlates of feeding. From the upper to the lower part of the figure: means and SD of total metabolism (TM), *métabolisme de fond* (MF), respiratory quotient (QR) and locomotor activity (AL) in relation to the onset of 81 spontaneous meals, ranging from 0.3 to 10.3 g, which occurred during both the light and dark periods. Mean size 1.84 g (1.38 SD) and mean duration 10 min (6 SD) of the meals are symbolized by the upper triangle.

controlled feeding, and thus that a ischymetric rather than a moleculostatic mechanism could be proposed as exerting a control on feeding behavior.

Although the above experiments were mainly aimed at challenging the ischymetric hypothesis, the experimental design, in fact, also altered the metabolism of glucose. As a result, it could be argued that the changes in *métabolisme de fond* are closely related to the changes in glucose metabolism. In order to answer this question, we studied the control of feeding under other experimental conditions in which both lipid and glucid metabolism was modified and the consequences on feeding were assessed. The enhancement of feeding was obtained by the simultaneous inhibition of glucose and free fatty acid utilization by means of a combined treatment with both 2DG and nicotinic acid.

Stimulation of Feeding by Simultaneous Treatment with 2DG and Nicotinic Acid[28]

Recent data [29-31] shows that in the rat, feeding can be enhanced by the inhibition of lipid utilization if the treatment is given during the period when current metabolic

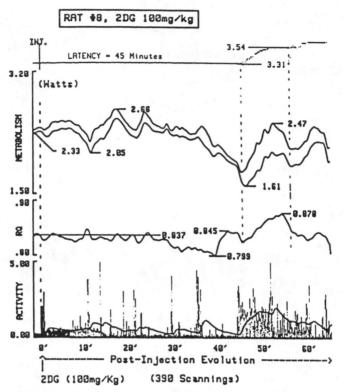

FIGURE 6. Effect on feeding pattern (top), total (higher), and background (lower) metabolism, respiratory quotient (RQ), and activity of an injection at time zero minute of 100 ng/kg of 2-deoxy-D-glucose (2DG). The one-minute histograms of activity were integrated and modified (superimposed smooth trace), taking into account the algebraic functions of both the delay and the deformation that the respiratory exchanges undergo before reaching the gas analyzers. As a result the instantaneous signals that originated from the activity strain gauges coincide with the delayed signals that originated from the gas analyzers. Note the preprandial decrease of background metabolism and its prandial elevation. RQ showed a preprandial V-shaped decrease–increase and a prandial rebound.

requirements are met by lipid substrates. On the basis of these data, we studied the effects of 2DG and nicotinic acid (NIC) injections on *métabolisme de fond* and RQ of rats fed a medium-fat diet. Rats fed this fat diet *ad libitum* were deprived of food for two hours before they were given the treatment, which was followed by another three-hour period before the food was made available again. The purpose of this experiment was to investigate whether the blockade of utilization of both glucose and lipids was able to decrease the *métabolisme de fond* and to what extent the drop of *métabolisme de fond* would predict the amount eaten when food was restored.

Both 2DG and NIC as well as the simultaneous 2DG+NIC treatments induced a decrease in *métabolisme de fond*. The injection of both 2DG and NIC induced a decrease in *métabolisme de fond* that was almost the sum of the individual effect of either substance (FIG. 7). When access to feeding was restored, the consumption that

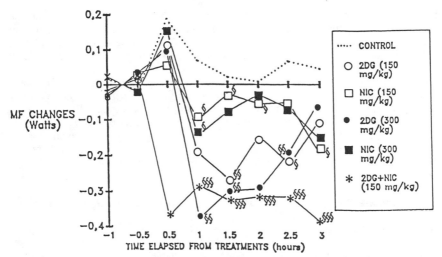

FIGURE 7. Changes in *métabolisme de fond* (MF), relative to pretreatment values, induced by treatments with 2-deoxy-D-glucose (2DG) and nicotinic acid (NIC) (period 2). (§ $p < 0.05$. §§ $p < 0.01$. §§§ $p < 0.001$ vs. saline-treated group (analysis of variance).

followed during the next hour was increased as a function of the decrease in *métabolisme de fond*, whatever the treatment.

As for the RQ changes, all treatments induced its increase, including the treatments with 2DG, which is supposed to block glucose utilization (FIG. 8). In fact, 2DG treatment did induce a transient (less than half an hour) decrease in RQ, but it was followed

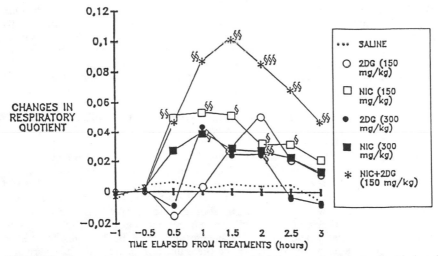

FIGURE 8. Changes in respiratory quotient (expressed relative to pretreatment values) induced by treatments with 2-deoxy-D-glucose (2DG) and nicotinic acid (NIC) (period 2). § $p < 0.05$. §§ $p < 0.01$. §§§ $p < 0.001$ vs. saline-treated group (analysis of variance).

by a long-lasting and more dramatic increase in RQ that lasted 30 to 60 minutes, (i.e., precisely when feeding is usually observed after i.p. 2DG treatment). These results con firm our previous observations on rats fed a standard diet where 2DG induced an increase of feeding that was proportional to the decrease in *métabolisme de fond*, rather than to the decrease in RQ.[27]

It is remarkable that whatever the treatment, there was no systematic RQ change that could have supported the idea that glucose utilization per se accounted for the size of the feeding response. In many instances RQ increased before the initiation of the meal. This observation, taken together with data from Campfield *et al.*,[16] suggests that the preprandial locomotor activity, which consumes glucose, may account for both the preprandial slight decrease of blood glucose and in the concomitant increase in RQ, which is indicative of an increased rate in utilization of glucose.

Enhancement of Métabolisme de Fond *as a Correlate and Signal of Satiety*

Spontaneous Feeding

Similarly to the idea that a decrease of *métabolisme de fond* could be transduced into a signal of hunger and so facilitate the onset of a meal, the ischymetric hypothesis predicts a symmetrical phenomenon for the occurrence of satiety. To test this idea, it was necessary to show first its feasibility, which requires at least some correlation between the enhancement of *métabolisme de fond* and the actual termination of the ongoing spontaneous meal.

FIGURE 9 shows indeed that the metabolic rebound reaches its zenith around the end of the meal as previously observed.[8] This coincidence does not tell us whether the metabolic enhancement is the cause or the effect of the termination of the behavior or a simple correlate of it.

The next step was to see to what extent changes of metabolic events occurring early in the meal could be predictive of the size of the meal. As shown in TABLE 1, the size of meals was negatively correlated with the slope of rebound of *métabolisme de fond*; that is, the more the metabolic rate returned rapidly to higher levels the more rapidly satiety occurred. It was as if a certain level of metabolic rate was necessary for satiety to occur, and that level could be reached either rapidly, so inducing a small meal, or slowly, so inducing a large meal. Further work is necessary before proposing that the slope of the prandial enhancement of *métabolisme de fond* determines the offset of feeding.

Satiety Induced by Pharmacological Manipulation of Métabolisme de Fond: *Effect of Dexfenfluramine*

Dexfenfluramine is a molecule widely used as an inhibitor of feeding in the treatment of obesity. Inhibition of feeding was shown to be in part the consequence of fenfluramine's property of promoting the utilization of endogenous lipids [26,28,32] and also increasing glucose uptake by the muscles.[33] Fenfluramine's effects are complex and involve lipid as well as glucose metabolism into complex interactive mechanisms.[26,28,32,33] The time course of feeding and metabolic changes that follow dexfenfluramine administration shows the following profile. During the first hours that follow the treatment, the release of fat stores and the utilization of free fatty acids are dramatically enhanced. This enhanced lipo-utilization is expressed by a drop in RQ together with an increase in *métabolisme de fond*. Thus, food intake may be considered

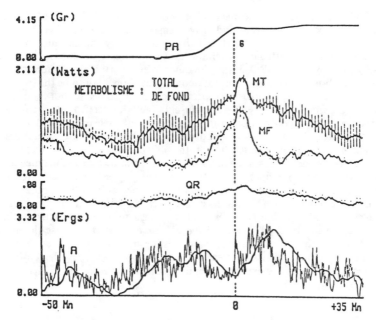

FIGURE 9. Means and SD of total metabolism (MT), *métabolisme de fond* (MT: in watts), respiratory quotient (QR), and locomotor activity (A in ergs) 50 minutes before and 40 minutes after the termination of six meals (PA). The locomotor activity signal was treated by a program as in FIGURE 6. Gr = grams.

TABLE 1. Correlations between Various Parameters Recorded: Day and Night Values Pooled[a]

	DM[b]	RI	MS	PDMF	SPIMF
DM	—	—	—	—	—
RI	−0.4043	—	—	—	—
	0.0001				
MS	0.7885	0.3025	—	—	—
	0.0000	0.7625			
PDMF	0.1028	0.0677	0.0677	—	—
	0.3377	0.5286	0.5287		
SPIMF	−0.3550	0.2139	−0.3997	−0.1350	—
	0.0006	0.0442	0.0001	0.2073	
TIMF	0.3969	−0.0024	0.4607	−0.2252	0.3322
	0.0001	0.9821	0.0000	0.0338	0.0015

[a] Upper figures: correlation coefficients; lower figures: probabilities.
[b] DM: duration of meal; RI: rate of ingestion; MS: meal size; PDMF: preprandial decreases of *métabolisme de fond*; SPIMF: slope of prandial increase of *métabolisme de fond*; TIMF: Total increase (from nadir to zenith) of *métabolisme de fond*; n = 89.

to be inhibited by an ischymetric mechanism promoted by the accelerated metabolism of endogenous free fatty acids abundantly released, as after forced feeding. Another phenomenon takes place later on. This is increased energy expenditure during muscular effort in parallel with a concomitant transient increase of glucose utilization as shown by the elevation of RQ during locomotor events (FIG. 10). Interestingly, the increased metabolism during locomotor activity was shown not to be the result of the increase of the energetic cost of the muscular contraction per se, but to an increase in *métabolisme de fond* induced by the muscular activity itself. In dexfenfluramine-treated rats, muscular contraction results in excessive glucose uptake and in recycling of the catabolites of this excessive glucose uptake. The so-generated metabolites are released in the circulation and, as a result, the *métabolisme de fond* increases. Therefore, dexfenfluramine increases the *métabolisme de fond* by two distinct mechanisms: (a) one independent from muscular contraction, owing to enhancement of release and utilization of endogenous fat reserves from the adipocytes, and (b) another initiated by the muscular contraction via the excessive glucose uptake and the recycling of the nonutilized metabolites. This is one example where the term "extrapolated resting metabolism" could not be used instead of *métabolisme de fond*, because the muscular activity changes what would have been the resting metabolism.

Whatever the mechanism of increase of *métabolisme de fond* by dexfenfluramine, this increase is made at the expense of endogenous reserves and is sufficient to promote anorexia.

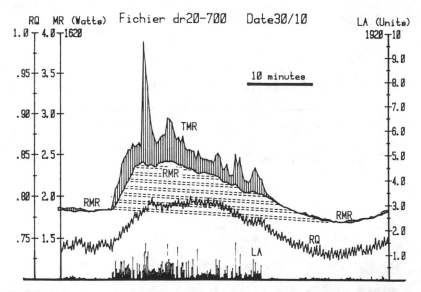

FIGURE 10. Evaluation of the energy cost of locomotor activity (area with vertical shading) and of *métabolisme de fond* (RMR) obtained by using treatment of the data according to the method of Kalman. Dexfenfluramine induced an increased energy expenditure in the present case mainly due to the elevation of RMR, related to substrate recycling. There was a parallel elevation of RQ during the locomotor activity (LA).

GENERAL DISCUSSION

The subtle action that the metabolic rate exerts on feeding wasn't easy to investigate until technological achievements allowed the instantaneous measurement of *métabolisme de fond* in freely moving animals.

The data available today strongly support the idea that the ultimate event that informs the brain about the nutritional depletion to be corrected by feeding is indeed ischymetric. This is shown by the observation that spontaneous as well as experimentally imposed hypo-ischymetric states are sufficient and almost necessary to induce hunger.

The parallel monitoring of respiratory quotient reliably indicates the level of utilization of carbohydrates versus lipids. Using parallel assessment of *métabolisme de fond* and of respiratory quotient, the onset of feeding is currently better predicted ischymetrically than glucostatically. It is thus possible to reappraise the role of glucose utilization as an exclusive signal of depletion/repletion. However, because carbohydrates are the main source for energy production in the rat, changes in glucose utilization very closely reflect changes of *métabolisme de fond*. This is why the intuition by Jean Mayer was so valuable and close to the ischymetric truth. If the only macronutrient to be used by the animal was a carbohydrate, the levels of "glucose utilization" would be identical to the levels of *métabolisme de fond*. However, when other macronutrients contribute to the *métabolisme de fond* they all participate in the generation of the signal of hunger as much as they are utilized. In other words, the metabolic signal is the result of the integration of the level of utilization of carbohydrates, lipids, and amino acids. Thus the ischymetric mechanism reconciles the moleculostatic hypotheses and also provides a potential mechanism for the transduction of the metabolic event into a biologically meaningful message at the neuronal level.

If necessary, these data would also confirm that, whatever the physiological signal of hunger and satiety, the final decision to initiate the behavior of feeding or to terminate it depends on many other concurrent factors which either facilitate or suppress the efficiency of the physiological signal. This is why every hypo-ischymetric signal does not necessarily induce a meal, and every meal is not necessarily triggered by a hypo-ischymetric signal. This holds for the rat and even more for humans. However, whatever the number and the relative importance of the modulatory signals, they act upon the only physiological signal in order to adapt this signal to the current circumstances.

The main difficulty of all hypotheses is to propose and to show how the hypothesized signal may become an effective message at the neuronal level. So far, the strength of the glucostatic hypothesis depended on the findings on the glucoresponsive hypothalamic neurons.[15] However, previous electrophysiological findings did not fit with the idea of the glucostatic hypothesis, which proposes that the message comes not from the level but from the rate of utilization of glucose. These electrophysiological data favored the idea that neurons respond to concentration rather than to rate of utilization of glucose. The electrophysiological data presented in this article demonstrate the opposite. In spite of their preliminary nature, they show that neurons respond to both carbohydrate and lipid substrates. In addition, the pattern of these neuronal responses suggests a process linked with a post membrane utilization of the stimulating substances rather than a response to the amount of these substances when applied on the surface of the neuronal membrane. Therefore, transduction in the hypothalamus of the ischymetric signal seems to be possible.

In this article the effect of feeding on *métabolisme de fond* was not dealt with. Yet, thanks to a technique that eliminates the noise of locomotor energy expenditure, new findings in this classic field of the specific dynamic action (SDA) of foods are emerging. Since the early description of SDA, a number of authors have reported new characteristics and often new names such as "luxuskonsomption" or, more recently, "diet-induced thermogenesis" or "thermic effect of feeding."[34-37] These new names somehow expressed the discrepancy of findings, and this discrepancy was partly due to the lack of separate evaluation of the cost of locomotion, which varied from one experiment to another. The new, yet unreported findings concern the feeding-associated changes of the *métabolisme de fond* itself. Feeding induces an elevation of *métabolisme de fond*. This elevation shows several components. The perprandial and early post-prandial thermic effect is followed by a more sustained metabolic enhancement that exceeds the duration of the SDA. Thus, *métabolisme de fond* is elevated during satiation and satiety and drops when hunger occurs. This is a very simple scheme of a negative feedback mechanism of regulation and may be too simple to describe the real-life event. Obviously, in the short term, numerous internal as well as environmental factors alter the efficiency of the physiological signal of hunger, and feeding can be either inhibited or enhanced. However, in the long term, the so-induced deficits or surfeits are integrated into the physiological signal via their metabolic consequences. This is why, in the long term, the physiological signal cumulates the corrective needs and so sets the appropriate feeding response.

SUMMARY

According to the ischymetric hypothesis, hunger is induced by the decrease of overall metabolic rate. In order to assess such a mechanism, it was necessary to monitor the muscular contraction-free metabolic rate designated *"métabolisme de fond"* (MF) in rats that were either resting or moving. MF was then examined in relation to either spontaneous or induced feeding patterns. A computerized open-circuit gas analysis system allowed us to monitor MF and behavior and to show that the onset of a spontaneous meal was preceded by a decrease of MF and its termination is preceded by a rebound of MF. Pharmacological blockade of utilization of both glucose and lipids enhanced feeding only to the extent that it reduced MF. These findings apply to pharmacotherapy because the anorexigenic effect of dexfenfluramine results from the enhancement of MF induced by the capacity of this drug to mobilize endogenous fat reserves and to so provide an endogenous meal that inhibits the exogenous meal. The ischymetric mechanism of hunger does not exclude important modulatory input from hormonal, circadian, and environmental factors in the control of feeding.

ACKNOWLEDGMENTS

The authors thank Simon N. Thornton for correcting the English wording.

REFERENCES

1. NEUMANN, R. O. 1902. Experimentelle Beitrage zur Lehre von dem taglichen Nahrungs-bedarf des Menschen unter besonderer Berucksichtigung der notwendigen Eiweissmenge. Achi. Hyg. Bakterio. **45:** 1–87.
2. RUBNER, N. 1902. Die Gesetze des Energieverbrauchs bei der Ernahrung. Franz Dauticke. Leipzig and Vienna.

3. GULICK, A. 1922. A study of weight regulation in the adult human body during overnutrition. Am. J. Physiol. **60**: 371–395.
4. NICOLAIDIS, S. 1974. Short term and long term regulation of energy balance. Proceedings of the XXVI International Union of Physiological Sciences (IUPS). pp. 122–123.
5. EVEN, P. & S. NICOLAIDIS. 1984. Le metabolisme de fond. Definition et dispositif de mesure. C. R. Acad. Sci. (Paris) **298(9)**: 261–266.
6. NICOLAIDIS, S. & P. EVEN. 1984. Mesure du mètabolisme de fond en relation avec la prise alimentaire: Hypothese ischymetrique. C. R. Acad. Sci. (Paris) **298(9)**: 295–300.
7. BENEDICT, F. G. & G. McLEOD. 1928. The heat production of the albino rat I. Technique, activity control, and the influence of fasting. J. Nutr. **1**: 343–366.
8. NICOLAIDIS, S. 1969. The prandial calorigenic effect. Exerpta Med. Int. Congr. Ser. No. 213: 63–69.
9. EVEN, P. & S. NICOLAIDIS. 1982. Effet orexigenique ou anorexigenique de l'insuline; mecanisme ischymetrique? J. Physiol. (Paris) **78(1)**: 4A.
10. NICOLAIDIS, S. & P. EVEN. 1985. Physiological determinant of hunger, satiation and satiety. Am. J. Clin. Nutr. **422**: 1083–1092.
11. MEYER, J. A. & A. GUILLOT. 1986. The energetic cost of various behaviors in the laboratory mouse. Comp. Biochem. Physiol. **3**: 533–538.
12. MAYER, J. 1955. Rugulation of energy intake and the body weight: The glucostatic theory and the lipostatic hypothesis. Ann. N.Y. Acad. Sci. **63**: 15–42.
13. KENNEDY, J. C. 1953. The role of a depot fat in the hypothalamic control of food intake in the rat. Proc. R. Soc. (London) ScrB **140**: 578–592.
14. MELLINKOFF, S. M., M. FRANKLAND, D. BOYLE & M. GRIEPEL. 1956. Relationship between serum amino-acid concentration and fluctuation in appetite. J. Applied Physiol **8**: 535–538.
15. OOMURA, Y. 1976. Significance of glucose, insulin and free fatty acid on the hypothalamic feeding and satiety neurons. *In* Hunger: Basic Mechanisms and Clinical Implications. D. Novin, W. Wyrwicka & G. A. Bray, Eds.: 145–157. Raven Press. New York.
16. CAMPFIELD, L. A., P. BRANDON & F. J. SMITH. 1985. On-line continuous measurement of blood glucose and meal pattern in free feeding rats: The role of glucose in meal initiation. Br. Res. Bull. **14**: 605–616.
17. EVEN, P. & S. NICOLAIDIS. 1986. Short term control of feeding: Limitation of the glucostatic theory. Br. Res. Bull. **17(5)**: 621–626.
18. UGOLEF, A. M. & V. G. KASSIL. 1961. Physiology of Appetite. Usp. Sovrem. Biol. **51(3)**: 352–368.
19. BOOTH, D. A. 1972. Post absorbtive induced suppression of appetite and the energostatic control of feeding. Physiol. Behav. **9(2)**: 199–202.
20. TOATES, F. M. & D. A. BOOTH. 1974. Control of food intake by energy supply. Nature **251(5477)**: 710–711.
21. BROBECK, J. R. 1948. Food intake as a mechanism of temperature regulation. Yale J. Biol Med. **20**: 545–599.
22. BROBECK, J. R. 1957. Neural control of hunger, appetite and satiety. Yale J. Biol. Med. **29**: 565–574.
23. BROBECK, J. R. 1960. Hormone and metabolism: Food and temperature. *In* Recent Progress in Hormone Research. Volume **XVI**: 439–459. Academic Press. New York.
24. DAVIS, J. D., D. WIRSHAFTER, K. E. ASIN & D. BRIEF. 1981. Sustained intracerebroventricular infusion of brain fuels reduces body weight and food intake in rats. Science **212**: 81–83.
25. NICOLAIDIS, S. 1987. What determines food intake? The ischymetric theory. NIPS **2**: 104–107.
26. MOORE, R. E. & D. SAN-YI. 1971. The effect of fenfluramine on heat production in rats S. Afr. Med. J. **45(Suppl. 21)**: 18.
27. EVEN, P. & S. NICOLAIDIS. 1985. Spontaneous and 2DG induced metabolic changes and feeding: The ischymetric hypothesis. Br. Res. Bull. **15**: 429–435.
28. EVEN, P. & S. NICOLAIDIS. 1986. Metabolic mechanism of the anorectic and leptogenic effects of the serotonin agonist fenfluramine. Appetite **7(Suppl)**: 141–163.
29. FRIEDMAN, M. I., M. G. TORDOFF & I. RAMIREZ. 1986. Integrated metabolic control of food intake. Br. Res. Bull. **17(6)**: 855–859.
30. LANGHANS, W. & E. SCHARRER. 1985. Regulation of food intake by hepatic oxydation of fatty acids. Proceedings of the XIII International Congress of Nutrition.

31. RAMIREZ, I. & M. I. FRIEDMAN. 1983. Metabolic concomitants of hypophagia during recovery from insulin-induced obesity in rats. Am. J. Physiol **245**: E211–E219.
32. CHANDLER, P. T., W. N. DANNENBURG, C. E. POLAN & N. R. THOMSON. 1970. Effect of fenfluramine on appetite and lipid metabolism of the young ruminant. J. Dairy Sci. **53**: 1747.
33. FRAYN, K. N., A. HEDGES & M. J. KIRBY. 1974. Stimulation by fenfluramine of glucose uptake into skeletal muscle. Horm. Metab. Res. **6(1)**: 86.
34. ROTHWELL, N. J. & M. J. STOCK. 1982. Energy expenditure of cafeteria-fed rats determined from measurements of energy balance and indirect calorimetry. J. Physiol. London **328**: 371–377.
35. LEVITSKY, D. A., J. A. SCHUSTER, D. D. STALLONE & B. J. STRUPP. 1986. Modulation of the thermogenic effect of nutrients by fenfluramine. Int. J. Obesity.
36. NEWSHOLMES, E. A. & C. START. 1973. Regulation in metabolism. Wiley. London and New York.
37. HERVEY, G. R. & G. TOBIN. 1982. The part played by the variation of energy expenditure in the regulation of energy balance. Proc. Nutr. Soc. **41**: 147–153.

DISCUSSION

DR. JOHN E. MORLEY (*Sepulveda A V Medical Center, Sepulveda, CA*): Stylianos, thank you very much for bringing us back to the reality that we cannot look at eating by itself, but have to look at what we're doing at the same time.

DR. KARL M. PIRKE (*Max-Planck-Institut, Munich*): In eating disorders, in anorexia nervosa and in bulimia, as well as in dieting, we observe a decrease of resting metabolism. On the other hand, under the starvation condition you mobilize fat and muscle, and you have described the effect of these on the basic metabolism. It would be extremely interesting here to see what happens with regard to hunger regulation under conditions of chronically reduced resting metabolism. Did you do any experiment to test that?

DR. STYLIANOS NICOLAIDIS (*College de France, Paris*): Yes, we did. Actually, we spent a lot of time looking at the metabolisms that fall under starvation. We were unable to find the classic drop of metabolic rate in emaciated rats and neither were other participants of the NASO meeting at Banff last month. Starvation induces a drop of the overall metabolic rate but not of metabolism per unit of weight. This was surprising to all of us. Whether starvation reduces *metabolism de fond* to below basal level or just at basal level, it is accompanied by an increase of hunger.

Anorexia nervosa may decrease metabolic rate, but none of the signals of depletion results in feeding response because of pathological interference. As for the case of fenfluramine treatment, this therapy increases metabolism, and as a consequence of this increase, hunger and food intake decrease.

PROF. SILVIO GARATTINI (*Instituto de Richerche Farmacologiche Mario Negri, Milan*): There is not necessarily a contradiction between what you have observed and your emphasis on the effect on the utilization of fatty acids and the position of other groups, such as ours, which have emphasized the importance of changes in the central nervous system as mediating the action of D-fenfluramine. This is the case for two reasons. One is that which you just alluded to that we don't understand very well and which could be the relation between what happens in the central nervous system and what happens in the periphery. The second reason is that we are working with doses that are quite different. In the case of serotonin, the doses that we used are around 1.5 milligrams per kilogram.

DR. NICOLAIDIS: Our last experiments were done with 2 mg/kg.

PROF. GARATTINI: Was it not 7 mg/kg?

DR. NICOLAIDIS: No, using 2 mg/kg the phenomenon is even better.

PROF. GARATTINI: That gives me the opportunity to remind people that by using different doses of fenfluramine the difference is much more than it appears because there is a dose-dependent kinetics. If you increase the dose from 1 to 5 mg/kg, you actually increase by 10 times the concentration in the body.

DR. NICOLAIDIS: We discussed our first experiments where we used high doses; when we reduced the doses the effect was even clearer. Actually, nobody can explain this huge metabolic phenomenon by some peripheral action, particularly considering that researchers in Nice have shown that fenfluramine in tissue culture is not lipolytic. The brain has to be there; if you remove the brain there is no lipolytic effect anymore. That means that serotonin, or serotonergic drugs like fenfluramine, act upon some system which, among other things, brings about glycolysis.

The Microstructure of Ingestive Behavior

JOHN D. DAVIS

Department of Psychology
University of Illinois, Chicago
Chicago, Illinois 60680

INTRODUCTION

The most commonly used method for assessing the effects of experimental manipulations designed to influence hunger and satiety is to measure the total amount of a food that is ingested following the experimental manipulation. While this measure provides some information about the effectiveness of the treatment, interpretation of the result is difficult. If the treatment resulted in an increase in intake, was it because appetite was stimulated or satiety decreased? If the effect is a reduction in intake, was it due to a decrease in appetite or an increase in satiety? With volumetric intake as the only datum, it is impossible to distinguish between these two equally valid interpretations. The result is conflicting interpretations of experimental outcomes obtained by different investigators and an inability to specify or speculate, with some degree of accuracy, on the central nervous system mechanisms controlling ingestive behavior that were affected by the experimental treatment. It is widely recognized that ingestive behavior is under the control of a multitude of variables, many of them interacting continuously before and during a bout of ingestive behavior and that many different components of the central nervous system are involved in determining the amount of a diet that an animal will eat in any fixed period of time. If the only dependent variable we have at our disposal to evaluate the effect of lesions, drug treatments, variations in palatability, and manipulations of deprivation is the amount of the diet the animal eats in a fixed period of time, we are not going to be able to make much progress in understanding the complex sensory motor control system that controls ingestive behavior. Fortunately this situation has been changing.

During the past 20 years some investigators have been describing in detail the alterations in specific components of the behavior of rats that are involved in the ingestion of solid food and liquid diets. These studies are beginning to show that examining only the amount ingested obscures important differences in ingestive behavior induced by experimental manipulations designed to affect hunger, appetite, and satiety. The analysis of the structure of the behavioral components involved in ingestion reveals a much richer effect of a variety of experimental manipulations that are hidden when only the weight of food or volume of fluid ingested are measured.

RATE ANALYSIS

One approach to the study of the structure of ingestive behavior has been to measure the rate of ingestion during the ingestion interval.[1,2] When the rate of ingestion is measured, two parameters describing the animal's behavior can be obtained by standard curve-fitting techniques, the initial rate of ingestion, and the rate of decline of ingestive behavior during the ingestion interval. Davis and Levine[1] have shown that the initial rate of ingestion reflects the stimulating effectiveness of the substance being consumed, that is, the excitatory influence on the ingestive mechanism, and that the rate of decline of ingestion is a measure of the effectiveness of a negative feedback inhibitory signal on ingestive behavior. This interpretation has received support from other studies.[2,3] The value of this approach is illustrated in FIGURE 1, which shows the results of a study designed to compare the effects of Na-saccharin (0.006 M) and sucrose (0.4 M) on the ingestive behavior of rats. The left panel shows that the amount ingested of both fluids during a 30-minute period was virtually the same, about 8 ml. The right panel, which displays these same data plotted as rate of ingestion at successive three-minute intervals during the session, reveals that although the same volume of these two fluids was ingested, the way in which they were ingested was very different. The initial rate of ingestion of the sucrose solution was much greater than that of the saccharin solution, but the decline in the rate of ingesting the former was much more rapid than the decline when the rats were ingesting the sucrose solution. Nevertheless, because the area under each of these two curves is approximately the same, the volume ingested of the two solutions was approximately the same.

This is not a unique or unusual result. Because the so-called "preference–aversion" function for carbohydrate solutions has an inverted V shape, it is possible to find an unlimited number of pairs of solutions, one on each side of the peak, that are ingested

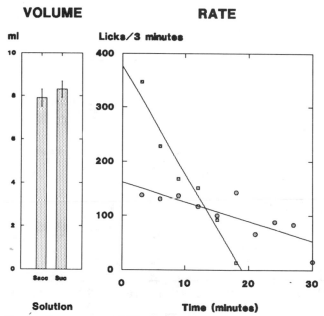

FIGURE 1. The panel on the left displays the volume intakes by the same group of rats ingesting, under non-food-deprived conditions, a 0.4 M sucrose and a 0.006 M Na-saccharin solution. On the right these same data are plotted as rate of ingestion (number of licks) at successive three-minute periods during the test session.

in equal volumes. The solution on the left of the peak is always less concentrated than the one on the right, a good indication that they will affect the ingestive behavior of the animal differently. The palatabilities will be different and the postingestive effects on the viscera will be different. FIGURE 2 shows that this is indeed the case. These results, from an experiment done in collaboration with G. P. Smith,[3] show the rate functions for a pair of sucrose solutions on either side of the peak of the preference–aversion function. The volumes ingested were statistically the same for both concentrations (0.05 M = 10.3 ml, SE = 1.03, 0.8 M = 11.5 ml, SE = 0.9), but it is clear that the behavior is very different. The initial rate of the more concentrated solution is greater than that of the less concentrated solution, but the rate of decline is steeper. Clearly, measuring volume alone obscures important differences in the behavior of rats ingesting these two different solutions.

BOUT ANALYSIS

One of the characteristics of the behavior of animals ingesting both dry and liquid foods is that the ingestive behavior tends to occur in bouts or bursts separated by intervals of varying duration. Wiepkema[4,5] was first to analyze the bouts of eating displayed by rats eating dry food. He found that, following a period of food deprivation, the number of bouts was the same when compared to the nondeprived condition, but the duration of the bouts was increased and the intervals between them decreased. He also found large differences in the duration of the bouts and interbout intervals, depending upon whether the animals were tested in their home cage or in a novel environment.

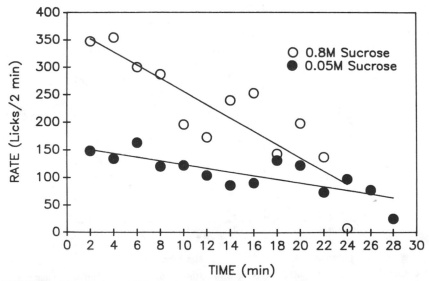

FIGURE 2. The number of licks during each two-minute interval in a 30-minute test session by the same group of non-food-deprived rats. The lines through the data points are the least-squares regression lines for the respective data.

Machlis[9] has performed an extremely detailed and exhaustive analysis of the pecking behavior of chicks pecking at colored objects using the technique of log-survivor analysis of the intervals between successive pecks. She reported that pecking is organized into bursts of pecks separated by very short intervals between pecks and clusters of bursts separated by somewhat longer range of intervals. It is well known the licking behavior of rats ingesting liquids is characterized by bursts of licking at a high rate (6–7 per second) separated by intervals of varying duration.[6–8] What is less well known is that bursts of licking in rats tends to be organized into clusters in a way that is remarkably similar to the clustering of bursts that Machlis[9] has described as characterizing the pecking behavior of chicks. FIGURE 3, which displays a log-survivor plot of the inter-lick intervals of licking by a rat ingesting a 0.4 M sucrose solution, shows the same pattern reported by Machlis[9] for the pecking behavior of chicks. The plot shows a steep initial linear descent, a transition zone followed by a long, relatively flat tail. FIGURE 4 shows the transition zone in more detail. Here it can be seen that the entire function is composed of three regions, an initial steep slope defining the bursts, an intermediate region defining the intervals between bursts that are clustered together, and a long, flat tail that describes the intervals between clusters. This pattern can be seen in another way by plotting a frequency distribution of the interlick intervals as shown in FIGURE 5. Here it can be seen that a vast majority of the interlick intervals (90% or more is typical) falls in the range of 0 to 0.2 second. This range describes the distribution of ILIs within a burst. It typically has an average of about 0.16 second with a SD of about 0.01 second. To the right of this distribution there is another, much smaller, mode in the ILI range of 0.2 to 0.4 second. This mode describes the clustering of bursts. It typically has an average of about a quarter of a second and a SD of about 0.04 second. Beyond about 0.5 second, the distribution is extremely skewed, with a clustering of relatively short ILIs and a long extended tail to the right.

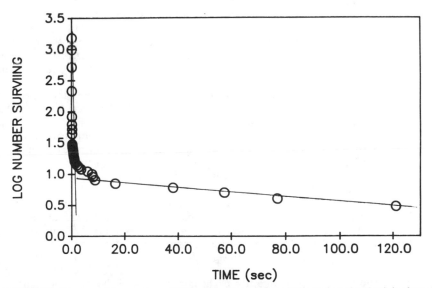

FIGURE 3. The log of the number of ILIs greater than the one indicated on the X axis is plotted against the ordered list of all the recorded ILIs in the test session.

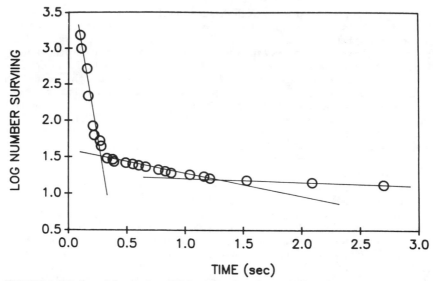

FIGURE 4. The log of the number of ILIs greater than the one indicated on the X axis is plotted against the ordered list of the recorded ILIs in the test session from the minimum ILI (0.01 sec) to an ILI equal to three seconds. The truncation was done to provide a clearer picture of the transition zone between 0.2 second and one second, which is obscured in FIGURE 3.

Machlis[9] reported that clusters of bursts tended to be larger when chicks were pecking at preferred colors. Recently, in collaboration with G. P. Smith,[10] I have found that the same appears to be true of rats ingesting carbohydrate solutions. In a number of studies we have measured the size of bursts (SB, runs of licks with ILIs less than 0.2 sec), the size of clusters (SC, runs of licks with ILIs less than 0.5 sec), the length of the intervals between clusters (ICI). We have been interested in the effects of variations in the concentration of some carbohydrate solutions and the effects of sham feeding on these parameters.

FIGURE 6 shows the effects of the concentration of sucrose and maltose on the size of clusters (a run of ILIs less than 0.5 sec) in rats deprived of food but not water for 4 hours before testing. For both the sucrose and maltose solutions, the size of the clusters increases significantly with increasing concentrations of both carbohydrates ($F = 14.63$; df $=1, 9$; $p < 0.005$; $F = 5.22$, df $= 1, 9$; $p < 0.05$, sucrose and maltose, respectively). Thus with increasing concentration of either of these two palatable solutions, bursts tend to be clustered more with the higher than the lower concentrations of these two carbohydrates.

When rats sham feed, most of the effects of the accumulation of food in the gastrointestinal tract are eliminated and the volume ingested increases dramatically.[11-13] In an experiment, carried out in collaboration with G. P. Smith,[10] I examined the effects of sham feeding on the microstructural parameters of ingestive behavior. In this experiment rats were tested for 30 minutes with three different concentrations of maltose (0.2 M, 0.4 M, and 0.8 M) following a four-hour period of food deprivation under both real and sham feeding conditions. The microstructural changes that occur as a result of the sham feeding conditions are shown in FIGURE 7. The left panel summarizes the effects of concentration and real versus sham feeding conditions on the size

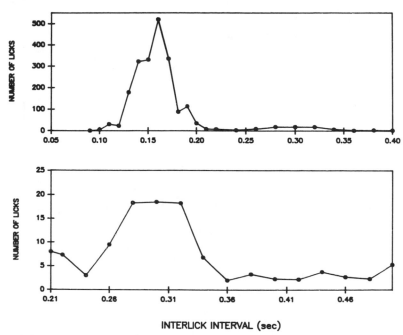

FIGURE 5. The frequency distribution of all of the ILIs in a test session in which the rat was ingesting 0.4 *M* sucrose. The top panel shows this distribution over the range of 0.1 second to 4 seconds. The bottom panel shows the distribution over the range of 0.2 to 0.5 second.

of the clusters. It is clear that increasing the concentration increases the size of the clusters, but that sham feeding does not affect this parameter. The right-hand panel shows the effect of concentration and sham versus real feeding conditions on the average length of the intercluster intervals. Under real feeding conditions the intercluster interval increases with concentration, but under sham feeding conditions this trend is no longer present, and for each concentration the average intercluster interval is much shorter under sham than under real feeding conditions. The effect of the accumulation of food in the stomach during real feeding has no effect on clustering of bursts, but it increases the average interval between clusters.

It should be pointed out that the variations in the microstructural patterns induced by variations in the test diets in our experiments with rats is remarkably similar to those reported by France Bellisle (this volume) in humans. In those cases where the same microstructural elements were measured by her and by us, the results and conclusions are virtually identical. Microstructural analysis thus seems to provide a common ground for assessing the effects of palatability variations in humans and rats.

BRAIN LESION

The microstructural analysis of ingestive behavior can provide information about the nature of the alterations in behavior caused by some experimental manipulation

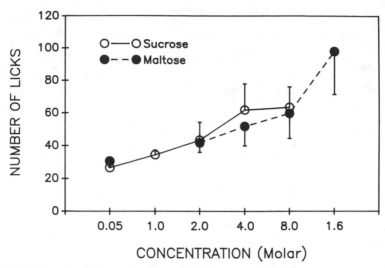

FIGURE 6. The size of clusters (number of ILIs in a run with ILIs < 0.45 sec) as a function of the concentration of the test solution. The data are from the same group of rats tested for 30 minutes under non-food-deprived conditions on sucrose and maltose solutions.

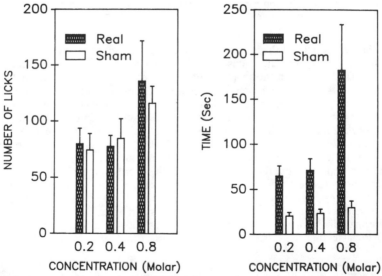

FIGURE 7. The panel on the left displays the mean size of the clusters of ILIs for three different concentrations of maltose when non-food-deprived rats ingest them under real and sham feeding conditions. The panel on the right displays the mean intercluster intervals observed under the same testing conditions and in the same group of rats.

that results in an alteration in volumetric intake. For example, Asin and Wirtshafter have reported that electrolytic lesions of the median raphe nuclei alter the feeding behavior of rats by increasing the amount of spillage without affecting the total amount eaten.[14]

In collaboration with Dave Wirtshafter, I have studied the effects of midbrain raphe lesions on the microstructure of ingestive behavior of non-food-deprived rats ingesting a 0.4 M sucrose solution. The lesioned animals, which showed about a 70% reduction in hippocampal and striatal serotonin levels, ingested about 63% of the volume ingested by sham-operated control animals (18.7 ml vs. 11.8 ml). The duration of ingestion, however, was only reduced to about 90% of the control value (24.3 min vs. 21.8 min), indicating that the reduction in intake was only partially caused by early termination of the meal. Furthermore, the reduction in intake was not due to motor impairment because the average rate of licking within a burst of licking was the same in both the lesioned (6.27 licks/sec, SE = 0.16) and control animals (6.39 licks/sec, SE = 0.13). Rather the lesion produced a restructuring of behavior that can be seen clearly when the size of the bursts and clusters are measured. FIGURE 8 compares the size of the clusters in the control and lesioned group for a variety of different cluster criteria ranging from 0.2 seconds to 3.4 seconds. The criteria define the minimum ILI included within a cluster. Thus, for example, a one-second criterion defines a cluster as a run if ILIs are less than one second. Because increasing the criterion will include more ILIs within a cluster, the cluster size will increase with the criterion. This is readily apparent in FIGURE 8, and it is also clear that at any selected criterion the size of the cluster for the lesioned animals is always significantly less than that for the sham-operated control animals. The reason for this is shown in FIGURE 9, which is a frequency distribution of the percentage of all of the ILIs in the range of 0.1 second to 0.4 second. The top half of the figure shows this for the range 0.1 to 0.2 second, and the bottom half shows it for the range 0.2 to 0.4 second. Microstructural analysis of the ingestive behavior indicates that the raphe lesion causes a reduction in the intake because it reduces the amount of time the animal engages in sustained periods of licking. The licking behavior has become more fragmented, which results in a reduction in the volume ingested even though the length of the ingestion interval is only slightly reduced in the lesioned as compared to the sham-operated control animals.

DRUG STUDIES

This type of microstructural analysis of licking behavior in rats has been used increasingly to study the effects of drugs on ingestive behavior since Blundell and his colleagues[15,16] demonstrated its effectiveness in analyzing the actions of a variety of anorectic drugs on feeding behavior. Blundell and Latham[15] compared the effects of fenfluramine, (a sertonergic drug) with amphetamine, whose action is mediated by catecholaminergic mechanisms, on the microstructure of ingestive behavior. Although both of these drugs suppress intake in a dose-dependent manner, their effects on the microstructure of ingestive behavior is different. Amphetamine increased the latency to eat but once begun ingestion rate was increased above normal. Fenfluramine, on the other hand, slowed the rate of eating.

Using a similar method, Cooper & Sweeny[17] have shown that the dopamine D-2 receptor blocker spiperone reduces intake by reducing the rate of feeding but not the duration of the meal, whereas amphetamine, a dopamine agonist, reduces intake by increasing the latency to eat and reducing the duration of the meal, effects that can be blocked by spiperone. Willner and Towell[18] have analyzed the effects of d-am-

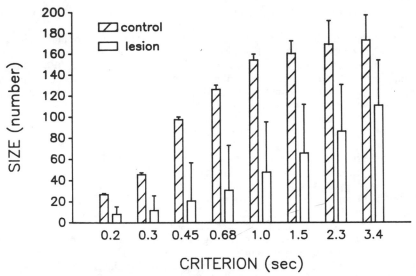

FIGURE 8. The size of the clusters of ILIs as a function of the cluster criterion for a group of rats with lesions in the median raphe nucleus and a group of rats with sham lesions (control).

phetamine and propranolol on the size of bouts of feeding and the intervals between them. They have reported that d-amphetamine reduced feeding time and increased the lengths between the bouts while propranolol increased eating time and bout length. They also reported that propranolol blocked the anorectic effect of amphetamine by increasing eating rate sufficiently to compensate for reduced eating time and bout size. The effects of apomorphine on total intake, eating rate, and eating time have been studied by Muscat, Willner, and Towell[19] who report that apomorphine decreases intake by reducing eating time and eating rate, effects that can all be blocked by the dopamine D-2 receptor blockers pimozide and sulpiride.

In one of the first studies on the microstructure of water drinking in the rat, Knowler and Ukena[20] reported that the drugs pentobarbital, chlordiazepoxide, and d-amphetamine, all of which, at sufficiently high doses, are capable of reducing water intake in water-deprived rats, had very different effects on a variety of measures of the microstructure of licking. With the exception of amphetamine the drugs increased the interlick interval (ILI) distribution in the range of 0 to 220 msec, which includes about 95% of all of the ILIs and characterizes a burst of licking. Amphetamine, on the other hand, decreased the mean ILI in this range in doses up to 0.75 mg/kg and increased it at doses higher than that. Amphetamine decreased the time spent in bursts of licking, in a dose-related manner, whereas pentobarbital and chlordiazepoxide increased this parameter in a dose-related manner. Thus each of these three drugs that are capable of reducing water intake do it in quite different ways. A microstructural analysis reveals subtle but important differences that clearly indicate that the adipsia caused by these drugs is quite different when the details of the specific components of the ingestive behavior of the animal is studied.

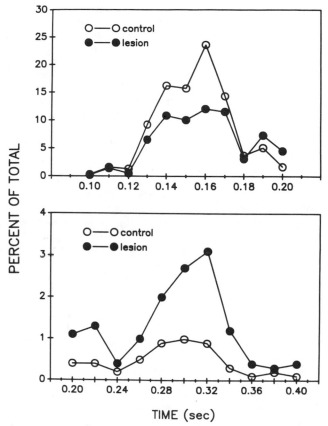

FIGURE 9. Top panel shows the distribution of ILIs in the range of 0.1 to 0.2 seconds for a group of rats with lesions in the median raphe nucleus compared to a control group. The bottom panel makes the same comparison over the restricted ILI range of 0.2 to 0.5 seconds.

Recently Snodgrass and Allen[21] have reported that apomorphine and haloperidol affected the temporal patterning of licking by water-deprived rats ingesting water. At the higher doses (0.15 and 0.7 mg/kg) apomorphine suppressed drinking at the beginning of the session with the degree of recovery being inversely related to dose. Haloperidol did not affect drinking during the first minute of the session; however with higher doses (0.2 and 0.3 mg/kg), the rate of drinking dropped rapidly from the second minute on.

A similar type of analysis has been used to investigate the effects of dopamine antagonists and agonists on the microstructure of licking. Gramling, Fowler, and Collins[22] have studied the effects of the dopamine D-2 receptor blocker pimozide on the microstructure of the licking behavior of rats ingesting a 32% sucrose solution. They reported that pimozide (0.5 and 1 mg/kg) decreased the rate of licking within the burst by a small but significant amount and increased the interlick intervals in the range outside the burst (ILIs greater than 200 msec). Gramling and Fowler[23] reported that haloperidol, chlorpromazine, and clozapine all decreased the average lick rate and tended to increase the lick duration in a dose-related manner.

In collaboration with Linda Schneider[24] and John Kebabian,[25] I have been investigating the effects of dopamine receptor stimulation and antagonism on the licking behavior of rats tested under sham and real feeding conditions. These studies have shown that the pattern of anorexia that occurs following the systemic administration of dopamine D-1 and D-2 receptor antagonists and agonists have very different effects on the ingestive behavior of rats.[24,25]

Linda Schneider and I[24] studied the effects of the D-2 antagonist raclopride on the microstructure of the ingestive behavior of rats sham feeding a 10% sucrose solution. The doses of raclopride selected (100–300 mcg/kg) were individualized for each subject to produce about a 50% reduction in intake. The animals were tested on the 10% sucrose solution following both raclopride and vehicle pretreatment and on a 5% sucrose solution following only the control vehicle pretreatment. The results were that raclopride pretreatment had the same effects on volume intake, cluster size, and intercluster interval as diluting the test solution. Volume intake and the average size of the clusters were both reduced by equivalent amounts and the intercluster intervals were increased by equivalent amounts by raclopride and by dilution of the test solution to 5%. (See Schneider, this volume, for more details on this experiment.) These results are consistent with the view that dopamine D-2 receptor antagonism causes a reduction in the intake of palatable solutions by reducing the hedonic rewarding effect of the solution.[26] Furthermore, because there was no effect on the rate of licking within a burst in those animals treated with raclopride, it would appear that the reduction in intake was not due to motor impairment, at least at the level of the motor system controlling lick rate.

In collaboration with John W. Kebabian and Christina Vasillatos,[25] I have studied the effects on the microstructure of ingestive behavior of two other dopamine D-2 receptor antagonists piquindone and metoclopramide, the D-1 receptor antagonist SCH-23390, the D-1 receptor agonist SRF-38393 and the D-2 receptor agonist quinpirole. In all cases the animals were tested after 2 hours of food deprivation under real feeding conditions with a 0.006 M Na-saccharin + 0.1 M maltose test solution, a mixture that stimulates relatively high volumetric intake.

The dopamine D-2 receptor antagonists metoclopramide and piquindone reduce the cluster size in rats real feeding a saccharin–maltose mixture in the same way that raclopride reduces cluster size in rats sham feeding a 10% sucrose solution.[25] Thus three different compounds, all of which block the dopamine D-2 receptor, reduce cluster size in both sham and real feeding rats. Because reduction of the concentration of palatable test solutions has the same effect on cluster size, these results support the view[26] that the dopamine D-2 receptor is involved in the hedonics of reward.

Antagonism of the dopamine D-1 receptor by SCH-23390 and stimulation of both the dopamine D-1 and D-2 receptors by SKF-38393 and quinpirole, respectively, has quite different effects on the microstructure of ingestive behavior. FIGURE 10 summarizes these results. The bars represent the percentage change from the baseline values of four microstructural parameters induced by doses of the four drugs selected to produce about a 50% reduction in intake (SCH-23390, 0.013 mg/kg; piquindone, 0.05 mg/kg; SKF-38393, 0.75 mg/kg; quinpirole, 0.012 mg/kg; all doses s.q.). It is clear that antagonism of the dopamine D-1 and D-2 receptors has very different effects on all but one of these parameters. The exception is the rate of licking within the burst, which is reduced by a small amount by both compounds. The pattern generated by

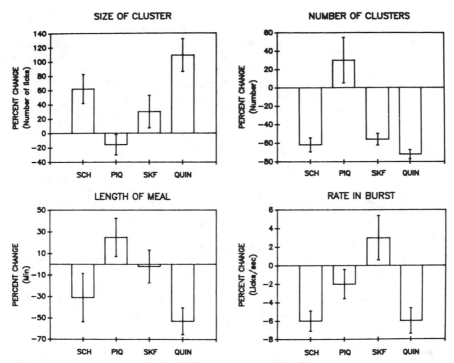

FIGURE 10. Percent change from saline control baseline values in the size of cluster, number of clusters, length of meal, and the rate of licking within a burst induced by a concentration of SCH-23390, piquindone, SKF-38393, and quinpirole adjusted to produce about a 50% reduction in volume intake.

stimulation of the D-1 and D-2 receptors is different. Both compounds increase cluster size and decrease the number of clusters. The D-1 agonist SKF-38393 has no effect on the length of the meal, but the D-2 agonist quinpirole decreases it by about 50%. The only compound that increases the lick rate within a burst is the D-1 agonist SKF-38393. It is interesting to note that Knowler and Ukena[20] reported that among the various drugs they studied only amphetamine increased this microstructural parameter. Because amphetamine is a classical dopamine receptor agonist, it may be that their effect was due to stimulation by dopamine of D-1 receptors induced by amphetamine-stimulated release of dopamine from presynaptic vesicles rather than stimulation of the D-2 receptor, because quinpirole, a D-2 agonist, at the dose producing an equivalent effect on volume intake, produced a significant decrease in this parameter.

Here again it is clear that examining the microstructure of ingestion yields valuable information that, when more is known about the variables influencing these various parameters, may be able to provide clearer insight into the mechanisms underlying the anorexias that can be so easily induced by a great variety of methods. The patterns displayed in FIGURE 10 are different for each of the compounds, yet the "anorexia" as measured by volumetric intake for each is similar, about a 50% reduction in intake. Examining only volumetric intake obscures all of these adjustments in the ingestive behavior of the animal receiving the "anorectic" drug.

Microstructural analysis of ingestive behavior has also been applied to the effects of cholecystokinin (CCK) and bombesin (BBS) on the structure of milk ingestion in rats by Hsiao and Spencer.[27] They found clear differences in the microstructure of licking following administration of these two "satiety" peptides. CCK decreased the duration of contact by the tongue with the drinking tube and increased interlick interval, whereas, although BBS reduced intake as expected, it did not produce these two changes in the microstructure of ingestion. Although Hsiao and Spencer concluded that CCK did not produce a "satiety" pattern in the microstructure of the behavior, it is interesting to note that Allison and Castelan[28] have reported that lick duration decreases toward the end of a meal and that Davis and Smith[3] have reported that satiety is characterized by increasing interlick interval. These studies tend to support the view that CCK does produce a satiety-like microstructural pattern. Regardless of this though, their study shows clearly that analysis of the microstructure of ingestion reveals important differences in the anorectic effects of two different peptides capable of producing "satiety."

Grill and his colleagues[29,30] have developed a somewhat different approach to the study of the microstructure of ingestion. It is, however, complimentary to those discussed above and should prove to be very important in developing an interpretation of variations in burst size, interburst intervals, cluster size, and intercluster interval that are obtained when licking rate is measured. This approach involves the detailed analysis of the motor acts that constitute the ingestive sequence of rats by high-speed video recording of their oral motor responses under a variety of experimental conditions. Recently they have applied this method to the study of conditioned taste aversions with very informative results. Pelchat, et al.[32] have shown that although pairing foot shock, lithium chloride (LiCl), or lactose intolerance with sucrose ingestion produced equivalent conditioned taste aversions (CAT) as measured by volume intake, taste reactivity following conditioning with these three UCSs is different. Conditioning with LiCl as the UCS produced a pattern of oral motor rejection similar to that produced by quinine, whereas conditioning with either of the other two UCSs did not. Thus although the intake tests did not discriminate between the three UCSs, the taste reactivity test revealed that LiCl appeared to change the palatability of sucrose, whereas conditioning with the other two UCSs did not. This type of microstructural analysis of the ingestive behavior of rats thus reveals major differences in the taste aversions established by different UCSs that could not be and have not been detected by the traditional method of measuring volumetric intake. This type of analysis can only help to provide a better understanding of some of the many mysteries of taste aversion learning and other phenomena as well.

It should be clear from this brief review of some of the literature on the microstructure of ingestive behavior that much can be learned from a study of ingestion at this level of analysis. In particular it is abundantly clear that manipulations, such as drug treatments, that produce equivalent reductions in intake can do it in very different ways. When the microstructure of ingestion is studied, it becomes clear that that there are a variety of anorexias. Reduction in intake can be achieved by decreasing the size of the bouts or the rate of ingestion within them, increasing the interbout interval or any combination of these. As more is learned about these microstructural changes in ingestion, it may be possible to classify the multiple anorexias that apparently exist and thus achieve a better understanding of the mechanisms of these various anorexias. The studies that have examined the microstructure indicate that this is a profitable line of research that should greatly expand our understanding of the structure of ingestive behavior.

ACKNOWLEDGMENTS

The author is indebted to his collaborators on the research summarized here. They are John W. Kebabian, Linda H. Schneider, Gerard P. Smith, Christina Vasillatos, Chris A. Watson, and David Wirtschafter. I would also like to acknowledge the value of a continuing dialogue with James Gibbs, Gerard P. Smith, and David Wirtschafter on the issues discussed in this paper. I won't hold them responsible for any errors that may be discovered in the manuscript, but I must thank them for the inspiration, exchange of ideas, and encouragement that they have given me in the development of the ideas presented here.

REFERENCES

1. DAVIS, J. D. & M. LEVINE. 1977. Psychol. Rev. **84**: 379–412.
2. KISSILEFF, H. R., J. THORNTON & E. BECKER. 1982. Appetite **3**: 255–272.
3. DAVIS, J. D. & G. P. SMITH. 1987. Soc. Neurosci. Abstr.
4. WIEPKEMA, P. R. 1971. Behaviour **39**: 266–273.
5. WIEPKEMA, P. R. 1971. Proc. Nutr. Soc. **30**: 141–149.
6. DAVIS, J. D. 1973. Physiol. Behav. **22**: 39–45.
7. DAVIS, J. D. & J. D. KEEHN. 1959. Science **130**: 269–271.
8. STELLAR, E. & J. H. HILL. 1957. J. Comp. Physiol. Psychol. **45**:
9. MACHLIS, L. 1977. Behaviour **LXIII**: 1–70.
10. DAVIS, J. D. & G. P. SMITH. 1978. Abstr. Soc. Neurosci. Sattelite. San Antonio, TX.
11. YOUNG, R. C., J. GIBBS, J. ANTIN, J. HOLT & G. P. SMITH. 1974. J. Comp. Physiol. Psychol. **87**: 795–800.
12. DAVIS, J. D. & C. S. CAMPBELL. 1973. J. Comp. Physiol. Psychol. **83**: 379–387.
13. MOOK, D. G. 1963. J. Comp. Physiol. Psychol. **56**: 645–659.
14. ASIN, K. E. & D. WIRTSHAFTER. 1982. Physiol. Behav. **28**: 89–93.
15. BLUNDELL, J. E. & C. J. LATHAM. 1980. Pharmacol. Biochem. Behav. **12**: 717–722.
16. BLUNDELL, J. E. 1986. Serotonin manipulations and the structure of feeding behavior. Appetite **7**: 39–56.
17. COOPER, S. J. & K. F. SWEENEY. 1980. Neuropharmacol. **19**: 997–1003.
18. WILLNER, P. & A. TOWELL. 1982. Pharmacol. Biochem. Behav. **17**: 255–262.
19. MUSCAT, R., R. WILLNER & A. TROWELL. 1986. Eur. J. Pharmacol. **123**: 123–131.
20. KNOWLER, W. & T. UKENA. 1973. J. Pharmacol. Exp. Ther. **184**: 385–397.
21. SNODGRASS, S. H. & J. D. ALLEN. 1987. Pharmacol. Biochem. Behav. **27**: 463–475.
22. GRAMLING, S. E., S. C. FOWLER & K. R. COLLINS. 1984. Pharmacol. Biochem. Behav. **21**: 617–624.
23. GRAMLING, S. E. & S. C. FOWLER. 1986. Pharmacol. Biochem. Behav. **25**: 219–222.
24. SCHNEIDER, L. H., J. D. DAVIS & G. P. SMITH. 1987. Soc. Neurosci. Abstr.
25. DAVIS, J. D., J. W. KEBABIAN & C. VASILATOS. 1988. Soc. Neurosci. Abstr.
26. WISE, R., J. SPINDLER, H. deWITT & G. J. GERBER. 1978. Science **201**: 262–264.
27. HISAO, S. & R. SPENCER. 1983. Behav. Neurosci. **97**: 234–246.
28. ALLISON, J. & N. J. CASTELLAN, JR. 1970. J. Comp. Physiol. Psychol. **70**: 116–125.
29. GRILL, H. J. & R. NORGREN. 1978. Brain Res. **143**: 263–269.
30. PELCHAT, M. L., H. J. GRILL, P. ROZIN & J. JACOBS. 1983. *Rattus norvegicus*. J. Comp. Psychol. **87**: 140–153.

DISCUSSION

DR. ANTHONY SCLAFANI (*Brooklyn College, CUNY, Brooklyn, NY*): Your microstructure analysis is a significant innovation in the study of ingestive behavior, but I would just like to insert one additional caution, and that is if you only look at the rate of feeding or ingestion it may not completely describe the animal's response to the food. I'm reminded of that by the data that you show with maltose and sucrose in which the two curves were completely overlapping. And yet if you give the animal a choice, at least in our laboratory, at low concentrations they actually prefer maltose to sucrose and at high concentrations the reverse is true. So simply looking at the rate of ingestion, no matter how fine you look at it, may not predict what the animals' preference might be.

DR. JOHN D. DAVIS (*University of Illinois, Chicago, IL*): I quite agree with you, Tony. In fact I was rather startled to see that overlap because if you look at three-minute lick rates you find that there's a big difference between maltose and sucrose at the same concentrations as well. I don't think we should rely on a single measure. What we need is a large variety of different kinds of measures that together will be able to give us a much clearer picture of what's going on when we do things like vary palatability, the nature of the food molecule, or the deprivation period, or administer drug treatments, and so forth.

DR. HARRY KISSILEFF (*St. Luke's–Roosevelt Hospital, New York, NY*): Can you discriminate between the hypotheses that the raclopride, the dopamine D-2 antagonist, is changing the animal's perception of the fluid, which you call palatability, or reducing the animal's drive, or what we might call hunger, a kind of internal state change.

DR. DAVIS: Let me point out something which I may not have mentioned. The animals in that study were deprived of food for four hours, so I wouldn't say they were hungry. What we can say at this point is that if you give them raclopride you produce a profile that's indistinguishable from diluting the solution by 50%. For me, that's pretty good evidence that one of the things you've done is to change the palatability.

DR. KISSILEFF: What if you deprived the animal for a few more hours? Would you also produce a pattern with the lower concentration that would be indistinguishable so that you would argue that you just made the animal hungrier?

DR. DAVIS: I can't answer your question because one of the things on the agenda is to look at the effects of deprivation on these various parameters. One of the things that Wiepkema reported was that deprivation, at least with dry food, didn't change the burst size. What it did change was the intervals between the clusters. So I suspect that deprivation is going to do something, I'd be very surprised if it didn't, to one or more of these parameters. Of course then it would be interesting to compare that effect to the data we have with raclopride.

DR. KISSILEFF: It probably would be important to look at a few more sugar concentrations too.

PROFESSOR ELLIOT STELLAR (*University of Pennsylvania, Philadelphia, PA*): Jack, that's a very interesting analysis you made on the rat. I just want to point out that a similar analysis has been made in human eating behavior in mealtaking. Hudel with liquid diets and we in our laboratory with solid diets have shown that obese subjects have a different pattern throughout the meal even though they may wind up eating close to the same amount as lean subjects. The lean subjects start out at the high rate and fall off rapidly like your sucrose function. The obese subjects start out often at a lower rate and remain at a fairly steady rate, falling off much less. It's a very valuable analysis. We're pursuing this further.

DR. DAVIS: Have you done cluster analysis?

PROF. STELLAR: No we haven't. I'm very interested in that, and I think we want to talk to you more about this.

DR. MORLEY: We did some studies with neuropeptide Y, and in mice it turns out that instead of increasing drinking, neuropeptide Y actually inhibits drinking while increasing feeding. We found that in those studies we ran into problems. When we gave a sucrose solution up to 36%, we could no longer get the feeding effect of NPY. When you do this sort of study using a liquid diet, how do you tease out whether you're affecting drinking or feeding versus palatability? This becomes very difficult, I think. With a liquid diet, drinking clearly has a different hierarchical organization of neurotransmitter control than feeding.

DR. DAVIS: I'm not sure I can answer your question. Clearly the mechanisms are different. There's an oscillator that's controlling the tongue; when the animal drinks, that oscillator turns on and turns off. As far as dry food is concerned I don't think anybody has proposed anything like that. They do drink in bursts and these bursts tend to be clustered. I'm not surprised that you get different effects with fluids and with different sugar concentrations than you do with dry food.

PROF. STELLAR: In our laboratory, Joel Kaplan has been looking at dry food by measuring electromyographically chews and swallows in the rat, and Terry Spiegel and I are now beginning to do this in humans. The import of the results that we're getting is they look very much like the lick data.

DR. DAVIS: On your question about palatability. We won't be able to rely on just a single measure, because licking in sham-feeding animals doesn't give you the predicted two-bottle test that you would expect to get.

Mood- and Nutrient-Conditioned Appetites

Cultural and Physiological Bases for Eating Disorders

D. A. BOOTH

School of Psychology
University of Birmingham
Birmingham, England

ORIGINS, MANAGEMENT, AND PREVENTION OF DISORDERED EATING

The case presented in this paper is that what we know about normal psychobiology and the effects of social culture on individual development can explain eating disorders and also provide pointers toward more successful treatment.

More broadly, it is argued that research into the psychobiology of eating and the remedying of disordered eating cannot make definite progress without introducing causal analysis, that is, the measurement of the effects of the experimental or clinical interventions on defined mechanisms.

Psychobiologically Normal Bases

The psychopathological syndromes diagnosed as anorexia nervosa or bulimia (nervosa) can be explained as the outcome of a process of cultural inveiglement of the sufferer into self-reinforcing extreme operation of the mechanisms that establish normal appetite for food.[1]

That is, the cause of these syndromes does not necessarily involve anything organically or functionally wrong in the hypothalamus, the limbic system, the gastrointestinal tract, or any other part of the brain or body involved in the physiology of appetite, the emotions, or endocrine control. On this account, any biologically normal person may be susceptible to developing disordered eating behavior and abnormal attitudes to foods and to the body.

Treatment Support of Self-Management

The proposal is that success in managing and indeed in preventing disordered eating will depend on the use of normal physiological, psychological, and social capacities to adapt the sufferer back to more orderly psychobiosocial performance.

Drug treatment in particular, if used at all, should be directed at assisting psychophysiological reintegration,[1] not at the correction of some presumed underlying abnormality of the brain mechanisms of appetite, mood control, or neurovisceral control.

A PHYSIOLOGICAL AND COGNITIVE THEORY OF NORMAL APPETITE

A holistic theory of the mechanisms controlling normal eating behavior was developed nearly 20 years ago.[2-4] It is a psychological framework for the cultural anthropology of eating habits.[5,6] It also provided what is still the only integrated quantitative basis for a central and peripheral physiology of appetite.[7,8]

No concepts were included in this theory except those required by the evidence. Thus, for example, the limited regulation of body weight actually observable was achieved without set points.[7] Behavior processes that integrate sensory and visceral signals and form a basis for cognitive aspects of appetite and satiety were analyzed out, rather than burying the issues by postulating unspecified mechanisms within hypothalamic centers.[8] Appetite and its hungers, satieties, palatabilities, cravings, likings, and distastes are not boxes or arrows within the working diagram: They are abstracted aspects of the overall performance of the system organizing influences on eating.[6]

This simple and operationalized theory[5,7-10] has not been widely used in the design and interpretation of animal or human experimental models or of investigations in the field or the clinic. Yet when we have been able to tackle a research issue with it, the behavioral physiology has proved to be powerfully explanatory and predictive[11-13] as well as diagnostic of muddled thinking.[6-10,14] Also, the cognitive postulate [4,6,15] that eating is a set of learned reactions to sensori-somato-social *Gestalten* provided the basis for fundamental methodological advance in the scientific analysis, in the form of linear causal analysis, of the influences on appetite in the single individual, for example from sensory characteristics of the diet[16,17] and their integration with its perceived bodily effects[18] or socioeconomic attributes.[19] These general methodological implications for research on eating and its disorders (and indeed for all psychobiology and social psychology) are addressed at the end of this article.

CULTURAL BASES OF EATING DISORDER

There seems no cogent reason to doubt that we and our culture are entirely based on physical reality. This faith, however, in no way commits us to treating the organization of behavior (mentation)—let alone the organization of our culture, social institutions, and economy—as biologically determinate or reducible.

These cultural processes operate over and above the actions and reactions of persons toward one another. Also, a person's (and a rat's or a computer program's) conscious and nonconscious mental world works according to its own laws, which it is the historic mission of experimental psychology to identify. The biological processes (and the laws of physics) merely constrain and influence the psychological and social processes. The slimming culture, an individual's weight control, and the physiology of fat deposition are each real (and interlinked) causal networks, but they all have to operate within the first law of thermodynamics, that is, energy balance across the skin.

Thus, any realistic scientific approach to the eating disorders will regard people as integral psychobiosocial systems.[1,5,6,9]

The Religion of Leanness

The fashion mannequin has become the representative of an institution or ideology or the priest of a religion whose gods are slimness and youth. Her "dry" bones come to life all too impressively when dressed in fine clothing.

Devotion to scrawniness is sociologically comprehensible during widespread affluence. While plumpness can be functional and gross obesity can be prestigious when most people barely get enough to eat, such shapes become repellant when food is generally abundant because then fatness can be taken as a sign of weakness and not strength, and perhaps as a biological signal of infertility more than of reproductive nurturance.

In such a culture, the normal female distribution of subcutaneous fat (or of either sex's musculature) can become like possession with a demon, to be exorcised by suitable rituals,[1] practices widely known as "going on a diet." They include exercising, fasts, taboos on "danger" foods, self-denial of palatability and satiety, and the consumption of "diet" or "slimming" foods, beverages, potions, and pills. Dietary restraint is thus not a personal trait.[6]

Given the normal human capacity for ideological or religious commitment and given particularly the fervor of adolescent identity seeking and conflict resolution, it is hardly surprising that many young people (and especially the sex sculpted to maturity by adipose tissue) become converted to this specialized form of asceticism. Normal enthusiasm, coupled with ecological gains, such as an alternative to social competition and an escape from sexual predation, could carry the acolyte to the extreme of a complete and unremitting fast. Genuinely theological or political motivation can produce a not totally dissimilar disruption of eating in presumably psychobiologically normal adults.

The demonology already implicated in the religion of leanness, however, provides a ready justification for such ultimate devotion to the dieting rituals, expressed as a loathing for even normal rounding or fleshiness.[1,6] This specific type of fasting can then be diagnosed as anorexia nervosa. Self-starvation of this or any other sort might be made easier by physiological adaptations such as reduction of gastric capacity or emptying rate.[20]

From Cyclic Dieting to Bulimia

Some recovering anorexics or ordinary dieters may, in contrast, exercise a more intermittent affiliation, with phases of ritual observance. Such cyclic dieting carries the risk of developing into compulsive food abuse. Again, this is not necessarily because of any biological abnormality. It could be just a perversion of the normal mechanisms by which appetite develops and adapts to which we now turn.

APPETITE IS ENTIRELY LEARNED

The key to this theory of eating disorder is evidence that your regular, ordinary, orderly appetite is an addiction to the usual circumstances of eating, not just to the foods themselves but also to states of the body and to times of day, emotional states, and interpersonal situations.

Even our smooth-brained commensal, the rat, provides evidence for this proposition. Indeed, the first evidence for the conditioning of appetites or satieties jointly cued by diet and viscera was from rats.[4,15] More recent work in human subjects[21] has confirmed that eating motivation is under learned control by food stimuli in configuration with contexts, such as internal cues to the need to eat or to stop eating.

This appetite *Gestalt* does not depend on any particular learning mechanism. The combination of cues that most motivates ingestive activity may have been formed by mere habituation. An appetite or a satiety could be respondent elicitation by a conditioned configural stimulus, operant emission occasioned by reinforcement-discriminative stimulus, or deliberate action ruled by reasoned objectives. These theoretical issues will not be further addressed here. What matters is the evidence that palatability, satiety, and eating habits, including bingeing, are all learned responses of some sort. However, the nature of the appetite-conditioning reinforcers will be considered, because this brings out their ubiquity.

As soon as controlled naturalistic designs were used instead of extremes of toxicity or nutritional deprivation and of aversiveness and chemical purity of the test diets, it became clear from animal and human experiments that dietary energy and essential amino acids were strong reinforcers of dietary preferences.[22] Such nutritional conditioning would be sufficient to explain the emergence of bulimia from cyclic dieting. Nevertheless, sometimes socio-affective conditioning and sheer familiarization may also be operative.

AFFECTIVELY REINFORCED EATING

Use of a food as a reward[23] and the sight of one's peers eating a food[24] increases that food's attractiveness to the preschool child. Either of these situations could be providing social or emotional associations that condition preference to the food.

It has also been proposed that the association of emotional gains with eating could contribute to cravings for snack foods in obese or depressed people and even to the tendency to binge or indeed to refuse food in the eating disorders. Attempts to assess moods and their changes around the time of a binge have not clearly supported this hypothesis. Often, unless vomiting occurs (or even when it does), distress increases after a binge.

Nevertheless, the timing and sensitivity of the mood assessments to date may not have been adequate to pick up slight and transient elevations of mood during the binge itself. In theory, a transient but prompt change can be a strong reinforcer. Thus, it could become increasingly tempting to eat and to keep eating certain foods in certain circumstances after they had been paired with sensual pleasure, distraction from distress, or sheer sedation.

We have now demonstrated that relief of mild anxiety induced in normal schoolchildren, after a single pairing with a distinctive drink flavor, increases the liking rating for that flavor in a majority of the girls and boys tested. Thus, no special susceptibility would appear to be necessary for repeated affective gains to create food cravings.

This experiment provided no evidence that the relief-conditioned preference depends on the presence of anxiety. However, considerable variation in the design of the experiment would be necessary before one could conclude that contextualization of emotionally conditioned preferences does not occur, and that therefore this mechanism for the development of emotional overeating does not apply.

Mere Exposure

Possibly, there exists in addition a mechanism of acquiring likings for foods or contextualized eating habits that does not depend on caloric or affective associates.

Repeated exposure to the unreinforced stimulus at least habituates neophobia and may induce some hedonic qualities.

Many sorts of stimuli are rated as more pleasant after they have been experienced without obvious consequences. Familiarization-induced food preferences have been extensively studied in animals and must be controlled for in caloric conditioning experiments.[25,26] There is evidence that familarity increases food preference in preschool children[27] and in adults.[28] However, both these experiments confounded mere exposure with slight caloric and affective reinforcement. The test foods or drinks were caloric and, even though the amounts were small, a few calories can condition a preference.[29] Also, there is an implicitly hospitable gesture in any offer of food or drink, and other potential for positive affective associations. The food preference steadily increased up to 20 presentations,[27,28] and so the limit remains to be defined.

LEARNING FROM PROTEIN AMINO ACIDS

The essential amino acids were first identified by the reduction of food intake when one was omitted from the diet. However, as soon as the idea was tested, it became evident that the balanced mixture of essential amino acids provided by good-quality proteins helps to establish the normal strong likings for distinctive sensory characteristics of protein-containing foods.[30] The omission of no more than one or two normal mealtime intakes of protein was sufficient to make amino acid balance preference-reinforcing.[31]

Postingestional Conditioning of Odor Preferences

Protein eaten in a flavored diet[31] or a balanced amino acid mixture intubated in association with an odorized diet[30] conditioned a strong preference (unlike the weak preferences conditioned by partial recovery from illness) for the purely olfactory stimulus (not just to tastes).

Furthermore, food preferences were fully acquired in one or at most two experiences with bland diets under mild food deprivation. Finally, the learning was strong enough to occur over delays between sensory cue and postingestional consequence up to a maximum of about 30 minutes.[32] This interval would be appropriate for metabolic needs, although longer delays would be adaptive for slow-acting poisons.

Healthy adult rats,[31] fast-growing adolescent rats,[30] and rat pups who were just beginning to sample solid foods independently of the dam[33] all showed the rapid acquisition of ingestive motivation for protein-associated dietary qualities.

We now also have evidence in human subjects that, after a low-protein breakfast, protein disguised in a lunch makes that menu more palatable subsequently.[34] Protein-conditioned preferences are not easy to see, however, because they are easily buried in food likings from other sources. Clearly, nonetheless, this mechanism is likely to contribute to the attractions of any cuisine, for virtually all traditional food mixtures are adequate in amino acid balance.

Somatic Contextualization of Food Preferences

As pointed out above, acquired eating motivation is not always attached only to sensory characteristics of the diet. The dietary preference reinforced by effects of protein in adult rats is not expressed unless there has been no protein intake for four to six hours.[12] Our human experiments have also provided some evidence for protein preference only during the incipient protein need that was present along with the distinctive diet during conditioning.[34] That is, the repleting protein conditioned ingestion to a combination of dietary and physiological cues. In principle, external environmental cues might also be recruited to the *Gestalt* if, for example, protein needs were greater at certain times of day.

LEARNING FROM CALORIES

It is usually assumed that ordinary hunger subserves energy intake and that other needs (except perhaps water) are usually met automatically from the nutrients in energy-containing foods. Yet few psychobiologists have considered how it is that aversive or, much more commonly, neutral sensory characteristics of foods become so highly palatable in later life, especially some hours after a meal. Theorists have been distracted by the ingestive power of sweetness and indeed of fluidity from birth in both rat and man[35] and by the experimentally convenient toxic conditioning of flavors.[22]

Caloric Conditioning of Sweetness Preference

Caloric conditioning of flavor preferences was first demonstrated over 15 years ago in rats.[29] Up to virtually 100% preference for a tastant was acquired and yet the myth has persisted that only conditioned taste aversions can be so strong. Indeed, the effect was so powerful that it reversed the innate preference for greater sweetness.

We have now demonstrated psychophysically that the liking for sweetness in familiar drinks and foods is entirely acquired in human adults. As part of the hedonic *Gestalt*, a food's sweetness becomes no different from its creaminess, crispness, color, and whatever. Thus, causal analysis of reactions to common types of food or beverage shows that the congenitally greater preference for strong sweetness is overwhelmed by an aversion to too much sweetness, which is no less strong than the aversion to too little sweetness.[36]

Hepatic Oxidation Reinforcer

The sweetness preference conditioning in rats was obtained with hypotonic sugars or any solution of maltodextrin.[29] Gastric intubation data[29] and our subsequent gastric and intravenous[37] infusion data demonstrated that this was not only postingestional conditioning, as has now been shown with gastric maltodextrin infusion,[38] but that it was specifically parenteral conditioning, as has recently been confirmed with intravenous glucose infusions.[39]

Similar infusions or injections suppress appetite for food in freely fed rats by supplying energy to hepatic oxidation.[3,39-42] This energy-supply satiety mechanism was in fact the second postulate of our original cognitive and physiological theory of appetite.[3,40] A privileged position for hepatic glucose sparing[7,40] was subsequently discounted by others.[43] "Cytodynamometric" satiety from the energy flux into intermediary metabolism[3-5,7-9] also has to be distinguished from some manner of sensing the energy exchange across the skin (less physical activity),[44] variations in which will reflect absorption, for example, via dietary thermogenesis and lipogenesis.

In sum then, readily assimilated food calories of any sort probably both satiate transiently and also reinforce a subsequent increase in the propensity to eat in the perceived circumstances.

This interpretation is rather neatly supported by observations that alcoholic drinks both satiate rats[40] and people[45] and condition dietary odor preferences in rats.[46,47] Such caloric conditioning could well play an important role in the development of alcohol abuse and of bulimia involving alcohol, alongside the psychoactive effects usually attributed to ethanol.

Somatic Contextualization

It is not only the dietary stimuli that are conditioned by calories. Somatic[4,15,21,25,26] and external environmental[8] stimuli can be combined with the taste, aroma, texture, and appearance of food in the learned stimulus complex for an appetite or a satiety.[6]

The hunger and stress induced by dieting are therefore likely to become conditioned with the characteristics of convenience foods if the dieter lapses by eating such items. More direly, their energy (and protein) contents acting on metabolic lack could condition craving for such foods even when the stomach has been filled by the snack. Such food preferences depending on a full gut were seen in the rat[4,26,48,49] and in people.[21] These appetites cued by a full gut might be dubbed "belly bulimia," to distinguish them from the emotion-dependent eating of doom, gloom, or "boom!" (anger) bulimia.[1]

Emesis-Conditioned Loss of Meal-Size Control

A mechanism for further loss of control and increase in size of binges is suggested by the fact that the main effect evident from rat and human data on the learning of dietary–somatic satiation *Gestalten* was the conditioning of desatiation, that is, enlargement of the meal caused by a conditioned increase in liking for a food when already full. Such a preference after considerable ingestion could be conditioned by the small amount of calories getting into the intestine and being absorbed. The same mechanism could explain the further increase in meal size observed with repeated withdrawal[50] or drainage[51] of some of the ingested food from the stomach. (The stomach is a pump, not a passive globe, and we have found that variable proportions of radioisotope in a liquid diet drunk with a gastric fistula open rapidly get into liver and brain via absorption.)

Learning of reduced or at least sustained moderate sizes of meals seems likely to be reinforced by duodenal bloat following some initial dumping of undigested calorically rich liquid diet.[48] Dilute diets[4,48] or removal of much of the diet from the stomach[50,51] will not generate this bloat and so the underlying potential for caloric preference conditioning is not countered. Delay of a calorically rich diet by a mere five minutes into the training meal prevented the conditioning of satiety,[48] as did intravenous infusion of glucose at the rate it is absorbed from the rich diet.[37] Carbohydrate-rich entree conditions dessert satiety but dumping from dessert comes too late.[52]

Emesis after a large meal could be another way to reduce or even prevent this bloat. Thus, vomiting after a binge would condition desatiation to the foods eaten toward the end of the binge, making them all the more attractive even when the next binge has gotten well under way. This mechanism could provide powerful unconscious underpinning for the subjectively obvious physical, emotional, and rational relief at getting rid of much of the food binged on.

TREATMENT IMPLICATIONS

On this theory, the bulimic's binge and the anorexic's refusal to eat are largely acquired involuntary reactions to complex situations comprised of available foods and bodily and socio-affective states, coupled with propositional thoughts about foods and their use to change bodily shape.

The characteristic loathing for quite normal roundness of the body could be more a way of making sense of this mysterious compulsion than an immediate source of its strength. This personal stance is second nature. Our culture links food use to shape control in ways that children learn long before puberty. The individual may well have been deeply involved before succumbing to the eating disorder.

Counter-Conditioning

Of course, if the traps opened up by dieting and relapsing are to be avoided in the longer term, the sufferer must become disentangled from the worst of this web of intolerant attitudes to foods and the body. The present theory, nevertheless, is that the immediate problem is the abnormal control of the behavior toward food that has been acquired by the food stimuli and the emotional and somatic states to which the foods may have been contextualized.

Exposure to negative or neutral associates for the binge- or fast-eliciting stimulus complexes needs to be managed. Positive associations need to be found for alternative situations that do not evoke disordered eating. Advice on sensible eating, as included in cognitive–behavioral therapy and counseling, might succeed in directing the patient to the appropriate contingencies, but more specific advice that suited the person's own daily habits could be more effective.

Allowing a binge but preventing vomiting would restore satiety-conditioning contingencies to the bulimic. It remains to be ascertained whether the usefulness response prevention therapy may have in bulimia[53] rests mainly on this eating-specific mechanism or on more general processes.

Drug Treatment

According to the above-stated theory, there is no reason to expect there to be a bulimia or anorexia "button" in the head, perhaps with its own transmitter receptor subtype. A drug cannot act on satiety or bingeing as such[54]; it can only act on a pathway in a mechanism contributing to the tendency to stop eating or to binge. Attempts to hit broader systems such as pleasure pathways or addiction mechanisms are likely to have too many side effects. A drug might in principle reduce the potency of reinforcers of the disordered eating, but it is not clear that this would help the necessary relearning of orderly eating.

Appetite suppressants or mood-altering drugs might reduce the strength of instigators of the disordered eating. That, however, would not weaken acquired stimulus control in the absence of the drug. At best, a drug would suppress the disordered behavior while some even more urgent task was tackled.

Unintended effects of existing pharmaceutical management of bulimia[54] may well provide an opportunity for integration with dietary and cognitive–behavioral therapy.[1] The hepatic energy-supply satiety postulate of the cognitive and physiological theory of appetite implicates rate of gastric emptying as the most powerful modulator of physiological controls of appetite.[5,7-9] The slowing of the emptying and absorption of a meal should therefore delay the rise of learned and unlearned somatic hunger cues and so reduce the temptations to binge. This aspect of appetite-suppressant action has been pointed out many times[8,35,55-57] and is supported by mechanistic data[58] but continues to be ignored in favor of unanalytical research designs.[59] Benefits that antidepressants have been suggested to have in the treatment of bulimia[54] may in fact also arise from slowing of gastric emptying. These drugs are anticholinergic or have peripheral monoaminergic effects that contribute to reduced and reversed gastrointestinal motility. Thus they should prolong the satiating effect of the previous meal and so reduce the instigation of binges — reducing their frequency,[54] not their size, as might be predicted for a "satiety drug."

Also, antidepressants sometimes reduce and sometimes increase appetite or food cravings. In part, this could be because gastrointestinal stasis induces nausea (and constipation) while a less extreme slowing of transit and absorption induces hunger and stronger caloric conditioning.

Changes in gastric emptying or capacity in adaptation to starvation[20] or to habitual vomiting may contribute to abnormal learned and unlearned cues in anorexia or bulimia nervosa. If so, readaption to normal gastric function will be an important contribution of a normalization of the ingestion and retention of food early in treatment.

RESEARCH STRATEGY

Science is the identification of causal processes. A disorder in an otherwise functioning system can only be understood and thus systematically rectified in terms of development and change in the relationships among normal coordination mechanisms.

Intake Testing or Appetite Analysis?

Basic research on animal and human eating behavior has neglected the scientific task of elucidating the causal processes of appetite. The usual tests of intake and its temporal patterns are underspecified and therefore not mechanistically interpretable. Even when adequately controlled designs have been run, incorrect comparisons have sometimes been made.

A striking example is the analysis of satiety mechanisms. Meal sizes, intermeal intervals, and various verbal scores (e.g. fullness), undissociated from other effects, have been "defined" as satiety or palatability, and yet these effects are likely all to be measures of the tendency to eat. Only observations of the inhibition or facilitation of the eating tendency by a distinct cause would constitute measurement of a satiating or appetizing influence.

Appropriate analyses for influences on satiety were used in the initial experiments on energy flow[3] and on learning.[4] These measures were the sensitivity of group differences in meal size, intermeal interval, ingestion rate, or choice to differences in some unambiguously dissociated input, whether sensory, visceral, or environmental. The engineers' classic measure of sensitivity is the proportion of the range of output variation that is under the control of variation in input. Instead, quite fallaciously, proportion of the control meal's size has been used as a measure of strength of a satiating influence.[60] Also, comparisons confounded by differences in dietary dilution have been selected from the data[60] or falsely attributed to the experimental design.[61]

Such departures from scientific principles of data interpretation have fostered reiteration of unfounded claims that sensory factors have a negligible role in satiation[60] or in the effects of serotoninergic drugs on carbohydrate intake.[14] When unconfounded comparisons of purely sensory or purely postingestional factors are made in the original data on learned satiety[4] and in its replications and extensions in rats[25,26,48] and in human subjects,[21,22,52] the evidence shows that from half to virtually all of the control of differences in meal size is vested in the dietary stimuli *and*, at the same time, as much control is exerted by the internal stimuli (for they are both necessary to the appetite *Gestalt*). Those who misdescribe these data have themselves obtained evidence of the same dual control by mouth and gut simultaneously.[51,61] The key dissociation of relative preference at the start of the meal and greater satiation toward its end, originally postulated[4] and observed,[48] has furthermore been replicated recently in gastric fistula experiments.[51]

Such a satiety-learning process accounts for food-specific "oral metering."[4,15,25,35] Once the mechanism is properly specified, there is no need to invoke extra complexities such as criterion-setting mechanisms[62] or differential memories.[61]

Animal and Human Models and Clinical Description

This analytical approach to ingestive behavior, the eating disorders, and their treatment puts in question any assumption that animal models of disorders of human behavior are essential to scientific advance. Animal models of eating disorders, self-starvation, hyperphagia, or indeed obesity[63] are helpful only to the extent that they provide mechanisms likely to be important in the human syndrome. Models of overeating, studied regardless of causation, will not help us to develop treatments of real bulimia, whether by drugs or diets or by any other means.

Even the continued observation of symptoms, course, origins, and treatment outcome in clinical patients will not by itself advance our scientific understanding or therapeutic effectiveness. We need to analyze causation.

Causal Analysis

The only way to establish viable explanations and cures for disordered eating is to analyze results from experimental studies or controlled observations that have been adequately designed to demonstrate the processes operative in the individual (FIG. 1).[16-19] In addition, for mental,[18,64] psychobiological,[7-9,65] psychosocial,[66] and psychobiosocial systems,[67,68] as in engineering, such single-mechanism experiments have to be complemented by holistic causal network analysis. This, then, is the fully scientific approach to research into the organization of behavior.

It is crucial to extend such causally analytic research designs to sufferers from eating disorder. The innovative approaches in the last four papers of this conference[20,69-71] need extending to fully disconfounded input–output designs (FIG. 1).[5,14,16-19,72] Food intake has the limitation as an output measure of being the cumulative result of much behavior and hence is at best an indirect index of causal output; more direct output measures are momentary eating rates, food choosings, and ratings of the disposition to eat. Yet then it is logically fallacious[10,72] and contrary to the evidence[6] to assume that somatic influences on eating behavior are reliably identified by ratings of sensations of hunger and satiety, or dietary factors by the pleasantness of foodstuffs or of their sensory characteristics. Despite their verbal distinctions (no doubt expressing genuine experience), these ratings are in fact all highly correlated with the tendency to eat.[6,52] Hence, each is no more than another measure of overall appetite.

We must therefore measure actual causal inputs to eating. Furthermore, the identification of mediating causative processes requires the double dissociation of responses to those inputs (FIG. 1), be they gastric wall tension, gustatory stimulation, tactile sensing of skinfold or muscle thickness, or whatever. Then the quantitation of identified causal influences on orderly or disordered eating would require in addition unconfounded and unbiased psychophysical (dose–response) analyses: only two levels of a factor cannot establish linearity (FIG. 1).

Yet the ethical and technical limits to research on patients are severe. Therefore, we must complement such studies by elucidating in behaviorally normal human beings (and indeed in sufficiently related animals) those specific mechanisms that can be shown to be relevant to human eating disorders or to their remediation or prevention. So far, very little experimental work on normal human or animal food intake and choice meets this criterion, even for study of one discrete mechanism, let alone for identifying the actually operative network of mechanisms.

The research strategy of studying mechanisms rather than models would be clearly vindicated in the case of eating disorders if some form of the theory presented here

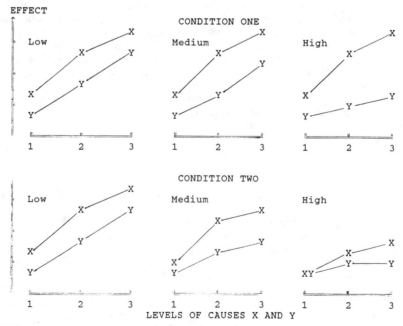

FIGURE 1. Identification of the differential effect of a condition (such as two forms of eating disorder or two drugs with distinct receptor specificities) on an identified and measured causal process. The causal effect (the ordinate in each panel) could be a measure of eating behavior, contrasted with other behavior. The causal influences (X or Y, each tested here at three levels) could be dietary sugar and salt, gastric distension and hepatic oxidation, or nearness to mealtime and work-break time.[72] The strength of a mechanism is measured by the slope and precision of its linear effect.[17–19,72] The specificity of the effect of the condition on one mechanism rather than on the other is shown by differential effects on slope or intercept with increasing intensity of condition (i.e., severity of disorder or dose of drug). Here, Condition One weakens the effect of Y specifically, whereas Condition Two disrupts the category of X and Y generally.

proves viable, because this theory is based on evidence from a quartercentury of human and animal research into discrete mechanisms of normal appetite, directed according to an inclusive theoretical framework.

REFERENCES

1. BOOTH, D. A. 1988. Culturally corralled into food abuse: The eating disorders as physiologically reinforced excessive appetites. *In* The Psychobiology of Bulimia Nervosa. K. M. Pirke, W. Vandereycken & D. Ploog, Eds.: 18–32. Springer-Verlag. Heidelberg.
2. BOOTH, D. A. 1969. Food preferences and nutritional control in rats and people. Annual Meeting of the British Association for the Advancement of Science (Exeter, U.K.): 90.
3. BOOTH, D. A. 1972. Satiety and behavioral caloric compensation following intragastric glucose loads in the rat. J. Comp. Physiol. Psychol. **78:** 412–432.
4. BOOTH, D. A. 1972. Conditioned satiety in the rat. J. Comp. Physiol. Psychol. **81:** 457–471.
5. BOOTH, D. A. & P. MATHER. 1978. Prototype model of human feeding, growth and obesity. *In* Hunger Models. D. A. Booth, Ed.: 279–322. Academic Press. London.
6. BOOTH, D. A. 1987. Cognitive experimental psychology of appetite. *In* Eating Habits. R. A. Boakes, M. J. Burton & D. A. Popplewell, Eds.: 17–209. Wiley. Chichester, England.
7. BOOTH, D. A., F. M. TOATES & S. V. PLATT. 1976. Control system for hunger and its implications in animals and man. *In* Hunger: Basic Mechanisms and Clinical Implications. D. Novin, W. Wyrwicka & G. A. Bray, Eds.: 127–142. Raven Press. New York.
8. BOOTH, D. A. 1978. Prediction of feeding behavior from energy flows in the rat. *In* Hunger Models. D. A. Booth, Ed.: 227–278. Academic Press. London.
9. BOOTH, D. A. 1980. Acquired behavior controlling energy intake and output. *In* Obesity. A. J. Stunkard, Ed.: 101–143. W. B. Saunders, Philadelphia.
10. BOOTH, D. A. 1981. How should questions about satiation be asked? Appetite **2:** 237–244.
11. DUGGAN, J. P. & D. A. BOOTH. 1986. Obesity, overeating and rapid gastric emptying in rats with ventromedial hypothalamic lesions. Science **231:** 609–611.
12. BAKER, B. J., D. A. BOOTH, J. P. DUGGAN & E. L. GIBSON. 1987. Protein appetite demonstrated: Learned specificity of protein-cue preference to protein need in adult rats. Nutr. Res. **7:** 481–487.
13. MATTHEWS, J. W., E. L. GIBSON & D. A. BOOTH. 1985. Norepinephrine-facilitated eating: Reduction in saccharin preference and conditioned flavor preferences with increase in quinine aversion. Pharmacol. Biochem. Behav. **22:** 1045–1052.
14. BOOTH, D. A. 1987. Central dietary "feedback onto nutrient selection": Not even a scientific hypothesis. Appetite **8:** 195–201.
15. BOOTH, D. A. 1977. Satiety and appetite are conditioned reactions. Psychosom. Med. **39:** 76–81.
16. BOOTH, D. A., A. L. THOMPSON & B. SHAHEDIAN. 1983. A robust, brief measure of an individual's most preferred level of salt in an ordinary foodstuff. Appetite **4:** 301–312.
17. CONNER, M. T., D. A. BOOTH, V. J. CLIFTON & R. P. GRIFFITHS. 1988. Individualized optimization of the salt content of white bread for acceptability. J. Food Sci. **53:** 549–554.
18. BOOTH, D. A. & A. J. BLAIR. 1988. Objective factors in the appeal of a brand during use by the individual consumer. *In* Food Acceptability. D. M. H. Thomson, Ed.: 329–346. Elsevier Applied Science. London.
19. BOOTH, D. 1987. Individualized objective measurement of sensory and image factors in product acceptance. Chem. Ind. (London) **13:** 441–446.
20. ROBINSON, P. 1989. Ann. N.Y. Acad. Sci. This volume.
21. BOOTH, D. A. & A. -M. TOASE. 1983. Conditioning of hunger/satiety signals as well as flavour cues in dieters. Appetite **4:** 235–236.
22. BOOTH, D. A. 1985. Food-conditioned eating preferences and aversions with interoceptive elements: Learned appetites and satieties. Ann. N.Y. Acad. Sci. **443:** 22–37.
23. BIRCH, L. L., S. ZIMMERMAN & H. HIND. 1980. The influence of social affective context on preschool children's food preferences. Child Div. **51:** 856–861.
24. BIRCH, L. L. 1980. Effects of peer models' food choices and eating behaviors on preschoolers' food preferences. Child Dev. **51:** 489–496.

25. BOOTH, D. A. 1977. Appetite and satiety as metabolic expectancies. *In* Food Intake and Chemical Senses. Y. Katsuki, M. Sato, S. F. Takagi & Y. Oomura, Eds.: 317–330. University of Tokyo Press. Tokyo.

26. GIBSON, E. L. & D. A. BOOTH. 1989. Dependence of carbohydrate-conditioned flavor preference on internal state in rats. Learn. Motiv. **20**: 36–47.

27. BIRCH, L. L. & D. W. MARLIN. 1982. I don't like it; I never tried it: Effects of exposure on two-year-old children's food preferences. Appetite **3**: 353–360.

28. PLINER, P. 1982. The effect of mere exposure on liking for edible substances. Appetite **3**: 283–290.

29. BOOTH, D. A., D. LOVETT & G. M. McSHERRY. 1972. Postingestive modulation of the sweetness preference gradient in the rat. J. Comp. Physiol. Psychol. **78**: 485–512.

30. BOOTH, D. A. & P. C. SIMSON. 1971. Food preferences acquired by association with variations in amino acid nutrition. Q. J. Exp. Psychol. **23**: 135–145.

31. BOOTH, D. A. 1974. Acquired sensory preferences for protein in diabetic and normal rats. Physiol. Psychol. **28**: 344–348.

32. SIMSON, P.C. & D. A. BOOTH. 1973. Effect of CS-US interval on the conditioning of odour preferences by amino acid loads. Physiol. Behav. **11**: 801–808.

33. BOOTH, D. A., R. STOLOFF & J. NICHOLLS. 1974. Dietary flavor acceptance in infant rats established by association with effects of nutrient composition. Physiol. Psychol. **2**: 313–319.

34. BOOTH, D. A. & E. L. GIBSON. 1988. Control of eating behaviour by amino acid supply. *In* Amino Acid Availability and Brain Function in Health and Disease. G. Heuther, Ed.: 259–266. Springer-Verlag. Berlin.

35. BOOTH, D. A. 1976. Approaches to feeding control. *In* Appetite and Food Intake. T. Silverstone, Ed.: 417–478. Abakon Verlagsgesellschaft/Dahlem Konferenzen. Berlin.

36. CONNER, M. T., A. V. HADDON, E. S. PICKERING & D. A. BOOTH. 1988. Sweet tooth demonstrated: Individual differences in preference for both sweet foods and foods highly sweetened. J. Appl. Psychol. **73**: 275–280.

37. MATHER, P., S. NICOLAIDIS & D. A. BOOTH. 1978. Compensatory and conditioned feeding responses to scheduled glucose infusions in the rat. Nature **273**: 461–463.

38. SCLAFANI, A. 1989. Ann. N.Y. Acad. Sci. This volume.

39. TORDOFF, M. G. & M. I. FRIEDMAN. 1986. Hepatic portal glucose infusions decrease food intake and increase food preference. Am. J. Physiol. **251**: R192–R196.

40. BOOTH, D. A. 1972. Postabsorptively induced suppression of appetite and the energostatic control of feedings. Physiol. Behav. **9**: 199–202.

41. BOOTH, D. A. & S. P. JARMAN. 1976. Inhibition of food intake in the rat following complete absorption of glucose delivered into the stomach, intestine or liver. J. Physiol. (London) **259**: 501–522.

42. LANGHANS, W., F. WIESENRIETER & E. SCHARRER. 1983. Different effects of subcutaneous D,L-3-hydroxybutyrate and acetoactetate on food intake in rats. Physiol. Behav. **31**: 483–486.

43. FRIEDMAN. M. I. & E. M. STRICKER. 1976. The physiological psychology of hunger: A physiological perspective. Psychol. Rev. **83**: 409–431.

44. NICOLAIDIS, S. 1989. Metabolic rate and feeding behavior. Ann. N.Y. Acad. Sci. This volume.

45. BOOTH, D. A. 1981. The physiology of appetite. Br. Med. Bull. **37**: 135–140.

46. SHERMAN, J. E., C. F. HICKIS, A. G. RICE, K.W. RUSINIAK & J. GARCIA. 1983. Preferences and aversions for stimuli paired with ethanol. Anim. Learn. Behav. **11**: 101–106.

47. MEHIEL, R. & R. C. BOLLES. 1984. Learned flavor preferences based on caloric outcome. Anim. Learn. Behav. **12**: 421–427.

48. BOOTH, D. A. & J. D. DAVIS. 1973. Gastrointestinal factors in the acquisition of oral sensory control of satiation. Physiol. Behav. **11**: 23–29.

49. BOOTH, D. A. 1980. Conditioned reactions in motivation. *In* Analysis of Motivational Processes. F. M. Toates & T. R. Halliday, Eds.: 77–102. Academic Press. London.

50. DAVIS, J. D. & C. S. CAMPBELL. 1973. Peripheral control of meal size in the rat: Effect of sham feeding on meal size and drinking rate. J. Comp. Physiol. Psychol. **83**: 379–387.

51. VAN VORT, W. & G. P. SMITH. 1987. Sham feeding experience produces a conditioned increase of meal size. Appetite **9**: 21–29.

52. BOOTH, D. A., P. MATHER & J. FULLER. 1982. Starch content of ordinary foods associa-

tively conditions human appetite and satiation, indexed by intake and eating pleasantness of starch-paired flavours. Appetite **3**: 163–184.

53. WILSON, G. T. 1988. Cognitive-behavioral treatments of bulimia nervosa: The role of exposure. *In* The Psychobiology of Bulimia Nervosa. K. M. Pirke, W. Vandereycken & D. Ploog, Eds.: 137–145. Springer-Verlag. Heidelberg.

54. BLOUIN, A. G., *et al.* 1988. Treatment of bulimia with fenfluramine and desipramine. J. Clin. Psychopharm. **8**: 261–269.

55. BOOTH, D. A. & D. STRIBLING. 1978. Neurochemistry of appetite mechanisms. Proc. Nutr. Soc. (London) **37**: 181–191.

56. BOOTH, D. A. 1985. Holding weight down: Physiological and psychological considerations. Medicographia **7(3)**: 22–25 & 52.

57. BOOTH, D. A., E. L. GIBSON & B. J. BAKER. 1986. Gastromotor mechanism of fenfluramine anorexia. *In* Serotoninergic System, Feeding and Body Weight Regulation. S. Nicolaidis, Ed.: 57–69. Acadmic Press. London.

58. BAKER, B. J., J. P. DUGGAN, D. J. BARBER & D. A. BOOTH. 1988. Effects of *dl*-fenfluramine and xylamidine on gastric emptying of maintenance diet in freely feeding rats. Eur. J. Pharmacol. **150**: 137–142.

59. APFELBAUM, M., Ed. 1988. Brain and nutrition: Dexfenfluramine weight control and regulation of eating patterns. Clin. Neuropharmacol. **11(Suppl. 1)**: 1–222.

60. SMITH, G. P. & J. GIBBS. 1979. Postprandial satiety. Prog. Psychobiol. Physiol. Psychol. **10**: 179–242.

61. DEUTSCH, J.A. 1983. Dietary control and the stomach. Prog. Neurobiol. **20**: 313–332.

62. MOOK, D. G. 1989. Oral factors in appetite and satiety. Ann. N.Y. Acad. Sci. This volume.

63. BOOTH, D. A. 1988. Mechanisms from models — actual effects from real life: The zero-calorie drink-break option. *In* Sweeteners, Appetite and Obesity. D. A. Booth, J. Rodin & G. L. Blackburn, Eds.: 94–102. Academic Press. London.

64. NEWELL, A. You can't play 20 questions with nature and win. *In* Visual Information Processing. W. G. Chase, Ed.: 283–310. Academic Press. New York.

65. RUMELHART, D., *et al.* 1986. Parallel Distributed Processing. MIT Press. Cambridge, MA.

66. BENTLER, P. M. 1980. Structural modeling with latent variables. Ann. Psychol. Rev. **31**: 419–456.

67. LEWIS, V. J. & D. A. BOOTH. 1986. Causal influences within an individual's dieting thoughts, feelings and behaviour. *In* Measurement and Determinants of Food Habits and Food Preferences. J. M. Diehl & C. Leitzmann, Eds.: 187–208. University Department of Human Nutrition. Wageningen.

68. BOOTH, D. A. 1988. A simulation model of psychobiosocial theory of human food-intake controls. Int. J. Vit. Nutr. Res. **58**: 55–69.

69. DREWNOWSKI, A. 1989. Ann. N.Y. Acad. Sci. This volume.

70. WALSH, B. T. & H. R. KISSILEFF. 1989. Ann. N.Y. Acad. Sci. This volume.

71. HALMI, K. 1989. Ann. N.Y. Acad. Sci. This volume.

72. BOOTH, D. A. 1987. Objective measurement of determinants of food acceptance: Sensory, physiological and psychosocial. *In* Food Acceptance and Nutrition. J. Solms, D. A. Booth, R. M. Pangborn & O. Raunhardt, Eds.: 1–27. Academic Press. London.

The Economics of Hunger, Thirst, Satiety, and Regulation[a]

GEORGE COLLIER

Department of Psychology
Rutgers University
New Brunswick, New Jersey 08903

The biological baggage carried by the human primate has hardly begun to be inspected. In their current habitats, humans are generalist omnivores who consume a wide spectrum of foods, ranging from fruit and nuts to meat and predigested (cooked) vegetation. In the world of primates, humans have a short, simple gut of moderate efficiency with almost no capacity to digest complex plant carbohydrates. They retain few of the digestive skills of their herbivorous ancestors.[1-4] That this primate has moved in an evolutionary instant from the small-group, hunter-gatherer niche that it occupied for hundreds of thousands of years to its present status is a tribute to its adaptability.

Human morphology, physiology, neurology, and neurochemistry are well studied, but little is known about the selection pressures that guided human evolution.[1,5,6] Even less is known about the economic (that is, cost/benefit) principles that were programed into human feeding behavior. Recent animal studies have demonstrated that both the choices among food sources and the pattern of meals — their frequency, size, distribution, and regulated total intake — are functions of the costs and benefits of gaining access to and consuming food. Because we cannot recover the past behavioral histories of human primates in any detail (with the possible exception of the few remaining hunter-gatherer societies), and because we cannot explore the human feeding repertoire by constructing test environments different from the ones currently occupied, we must rely on the development of animal models in our attempts to uncover our behavioral inheritance.

The leap from animal behavior to human behavior is a difficult one, particularly because "the wisdom of the culture" may supersede "the wisdom of the body." However, one can assume that human animals share their biological roots with their other animal contemporaries. It is our hope that by examining the specifics of animal feeding behavior, we can gain some insights into human feeding behavior. While we are not yet prepared to take a large leap or even a small jump, we can outline some of the more important economic variables in animal feeding behavior that may have implications for human feeding behavior. The basic questions in feeding (that is, in meal initiation and meal termination) are what, when, where, which, how often, how much, and how fast to eat. We have been hampered in our attempts to answer these questions by our long-time commitment to the study of feeding mechanisms, that is, its proximate causation, and by our neglect of the evolutionary origin of feeding, that is, its ultimate causation.[7-9] Two concepts, homeostasis and regulation, have dominated our thinking. The modern viewpoint rests on Bernard's brilliant insight that the condition

[a] This research was supported by AM 31016.

for adaptation to different environments is the constancy of the internal milieu. Cannon,[10] in his concept of homeostasis, added behavior to the list of mechanisms defending this constancy. The argument is that deficiencies initiate eating and drinking, surfeits terminate eating and drinking, and together, deficiencies and surfeits determine the pattern of meals. These facts have been modeled with feedback loops in which deviations from setpoints produce signals that modulate intake (for reviews see References 11–13). The latency to initiate feeding and the avidity of ingestion are proportional to the degree of deviation from setpoint[14–16]: A cumulative signal anticipating repletion leads to termination of ingestion. These feedback loops hunt around setpoints. Thus, feeding patterns are regarded as expressions of cycles of physiological depletion and repletion that are interpreted as cycles of hunger and satiety.

A second concept that has played a major role is that of regulation. Observed over a longer time scale, body weight (or growth rate) and body composition are constant.[17–19] The implication is that there is some target for these values—a genetic potential for size and composition—that controls total intake on a long-term basis.

A third concept that has directed our thinking is that, in experiments, all variables except those of immediate interest should be eliminated or controlled. The resulting experimental paradigm, the refinement paradigm, was derived from physics. Much of the conventional wisdom about feeding behavior, however, is an artifact of attempts to simplify and restrict the stimulus environment, response complexity, and the options of the animal.[9,16,20,21] This approach fails to differentiate between a rock and an animal. For the former, its history is irrelevant; only its current locus in the CGS system and its composition are important. For the latter, its behavior is a conjoint function of its current state, its current habitat, and the niche within which it evolved. For an animal to display its wares, options must be available in an experimental environment that simulates crucial features of the structure of its niche.

I wish to argue that this classic viewpoint neglects major aspects of species' adaptations to their feeding niche—in particular, adaptations to the economic structure of their niche. In stable, resource-adequate habitats, animals anticipate their requirements and buffer the vagaries of environmental fluctuations and seasonal changes by storage (e.g., caches, crops, stomachs, adipose tissue) and regulatory shifts in, for example, activity, body temperature, level of activity, and efficiency of absorption and utilization. Animals normally do not undergo substantive physiological depletion. Feeding patterns are determined not by momentary states but by the cost/benefit structure of the niche and of the current habitat. Regulation reflects not only genetic potential, but also economic structure in such terms as seasonal resource density, current weather, inter- and intraspecies competition, allocation of time and effort to other biologically significant activities (e.g., reproduction, territorial defense, predation), and, in the case of humans, cultural imperatives. Intrameal and intra-feeding-cycle periods are buffered by various physiological and behavioral mechanisms. I will attempt to detail below some of the experimental evidence that supports these conclusions.

In a simple experimental situation in which a rat is required to earn access to food by bar-pressing (or some other instrumental activity like wheel-running, chain-pulling, or key-pecking), the frequency of initiating meals declines as the cost of access increases, and the size of meals taken increases compensatorily, conserving total intake and body weight (FIG. 1). This is a revolutionary finding in that it indicates that the frequency and size of meals are controlled by factors other than the momentary physiological state, and it suggests a major revision of what is meant by hunger and satiety. That is, hunger and satiety do not reflect the current physiological state but, rather, are signals generated by the animal's response to the current economics of its habitat, probably in conjunction with its circadian and ultradian clocks,[22] which aid the animal to optimize its intake.

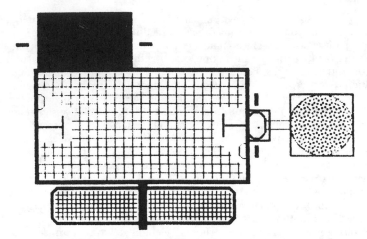

FIGURE 1. Top view of apparatus in which animal lives 24 hours per day and obtains all of its own food whenever it "wishes" (a closed economy). Either the cost of procurement (cost of initial access to the feeder) or the cost of consumption (cost per pellet within a meal) or both is manipulated by varying the operant requirement.

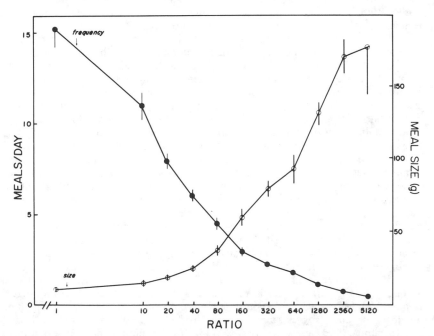

FIGURE 2. Meal frequency and meal size as a function of procurement (meal access) cost for eight chickens. Costs ranged from 1 to 5120 key-pecks per meal. Total intake was conserved except at the highest costs.

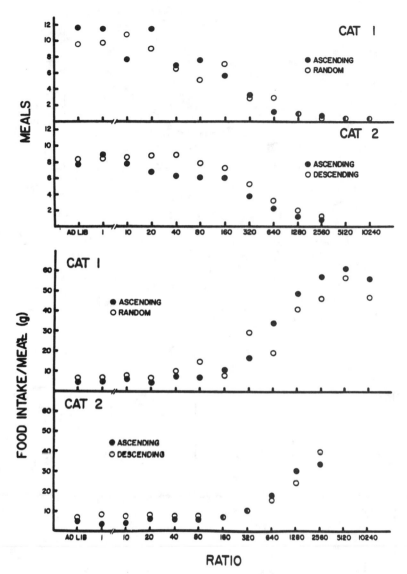

FIGURE 3. Meal frequency and meal size as a function of procurement cost for two cats. Costs ranged from 1 to 10,240 bar-presses per meal. Total intake was conserved.

These results were obtained in a nondepleting, closed-economy paradigm in which the animal lives continuously in the experimental apparatus (FIG. 1) and earns all of its food there.[8,23-25] The initiation and termination of a meal are under the animal's control rather than the experimenter's. Thus, the animal rather than the experimenter determines the bout (session) frequency, size, and interbout (intersession) interval.

We have tested a number of species in the access-cost or procurement-cost paradigm. All show the same form of the relationship between cost of access to a com-

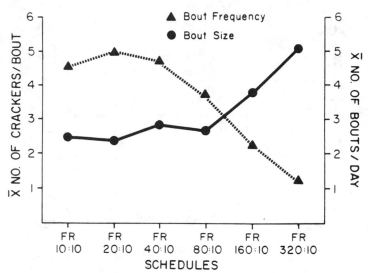

FIGURE 4. Meal frequency and meal size as a function of procurement cost for eight bonnet macaques. Total intake was conserved.

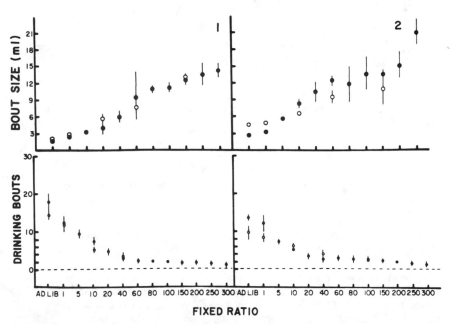

FIGURE 5. Drinking bout frequency and bout size as a function of procurement cost for two rats. Total water intake was conserved. Meal frequency and size were unaffected by changes in drinking patterns.

modity and the frequency and size of bouts, but the slope and intercept of the meal-frequency function differ. FIGURES 2, 3, and 4 present data from chickens, cats, and bonnet macaques, respectively, foraging for access to food.[26-28] Numerous other studies have shown the same results.[8] FIGURE 5 shows rats foraging for access to water.[29]

To what extent is the form of these functions determined by physiological depletion, that is, by the long intermeal intervals that are seen at higher access costs? I have argued extensively against interpreting these functions in terms of deprivation effects[8,20] and will only present the argument briefly here.

Classic drive theory[14] is based on the well-demonstrated fact that rates of spontaneous, instrumental, and consummatory responding are increasing functions of deprivation (best measured as percent body weight loss[15]). In the closed, free-feeding economy, described above, rates of responding do not vary consistently with intermeal interval, even when intermeal intervals increase as a function of access cost.[24] This suggests that no substantial physiological deprivation occurs in this paradigm.

Another cherished view is that large meals follow periods of deprivation,[16] and it might be argued that the large meals that follow long intermeal intervals produced by high access costs are the result of deprivation. However, the preprandial correlations between the length of the intermeal interval and the size of the following meal are neither strong nor significant at any access cost. In fact, we have never obtained the prandial correlations that have formed the backbone of theorizing about meal patterns. We believe that these correlations only occur in small, stimulus-poor, restricted environments.[26,27]

The lack of any relation between these measures and intermeal interval is in part due to the fact that in the free-feeding or closed economy, the animal does not lose a substantial amount of *ad lib* body weight (> 10%), and in part due to the fact that intermeal intervals in a closed economy are buffered by stored food in caches, mouth pouches, crops, stomachs, or adipose tissue. This is visually apparent in chickens when access cost is high. Using the same mechanism with which they buffer their obligatory overnight fast, they store large amounts of food in their crop preceding a long intermeal interval.[27] Another example is the ability of passarines to store fat rapidly each day during cold weather, buffering their obligatory overnight fast and their multiple-day fasts when inclement weather prevents foraging.[30]

It might be argued, on the other hand, that an animal that just expended a large amount of time and/or effort gaining access to a meal would be expected to take a large meal. We tested this possibility by using a variable ratio schedule that presented the subjects with a random mixture of different costs of access to a meal. If the "large effort, large meal" hypothesis were correct, then large meals would be expected to follow large ratios, and small meals, small ratios. This was not the case, however. For a given group of costs, meal size fluctuated around an average value appropriate to the average cost but was not related to the just-paid cost.[31]

What does this strategy of reducing meal frequency and compensatorily increasing meal size as a function of access cost do for an animal? As access cost increases, there are, at least, three possible strategies of feeding an animal can employ while defending its total intake: holding daily meal frequency and size constant, holding daily bar press effort constant while eating larger and larger meals as access cost increases, and allowing meal frequency and size to vary compensatorily. The upper curve in FIGURE 6 shows that the number of bar presses an animal would have to make would increase exponentially as access cost increased, if an animal continued to eat its usual daily number of meals. The second strategy (not shown in FIG. 6) of maintaining the same average bar press cost per day would result in less frequent meals as cost increased. For example, a price of one bar press for access to each meal for 10 meals/day would

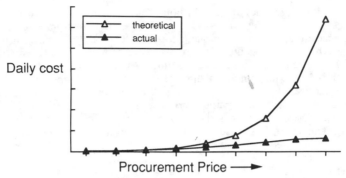

FIGURE 6. Possible strategies in response to rising procurement costs: (1) maintain a fixed number of meals per day, which leads to an exponential increase in the cost of feeding (top curve); (2) maintain a fixed number of bar presses per day (constant effort), which leads to an exponential decline in meal frequency (not plotted); (3) reduce meal frequency as a function of cost with a compensatory increase in meal size (bottom curve). The latter strategy is a compromise that conserves both meal frequency and total effort. The decline in meal frequency is, typically, a linear function of log cost.

require 10 bar presses per day. To maintain the total cost at 10 bar presses per day when the access price was 10 bar presses, only one meal per day would be taken. An access price of 20 bar presses would result in one meal every other day, a price of 40 bar presses would result in one meal every four days, and so on. The cat would very rapidly reach its maximum intermeal interval. The lower curve shows a third possible strategy, a compromise: decreasing meal frequency with compensatory increases in meal sizes as access cost increased, resulting in moderate increases in the number of bar presses while conserving average daily total intake. Thus, by eating less-frequent, larger meals and conserving total intake, an animal can reduce the time and effort expended gaining access to food. A fascinating, unanswered question arising from these results is, How does the animal monitor total caloric intake so accurately during such differing patterns of intake?

Another variable that influences meal size is the rate of depletion of resources as they are used. An animal may leave a depleted patch to forage for another, more profitable patch to complete its intake. This problem has been modeled in a patch-leaving rule, the marginal value theorem, which states that the consumer should leave the patch when the rate of return falls below the average rate for the habitat.[32-34]

Once a predator has searched for and procured prey, it may consume it. Consumption occurs in bouts and has associated costs and benefits. We have modeled the cost of consumption by placing an instrumental requirement on each portion (e.g., bites or licks) taken with a bout of feeding or drinking.[20,23,29,35] Raising the instrumental cost of consumption has three, not necessarily independent, major consequences: (1) it slows the rate of intake within a meal, (2) it extends the duration of each bout of feeding, and (3) it increases the total cost of food or water, both within a meal and over total intake. The animal has the potential to compensate for these effects by increasing both the rate of instrumental and consummatory responding, decreasing the size of meals, and/or reducing total intake. Thus, increases in the unit price (BP/calorie) of consuming food within a meal results in a decrease in meal size, an increase in meal frequency, increases in rates of instrumental and consummatory responding, and a decrease in total intake at higher costs (FIG. 7).[23,25,35,36] Even though both instrumental and consummatory rates increase where possible, the increase is not suffi-

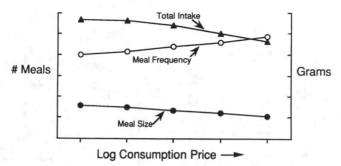

FIGURE 7. Meal frequency and meal size as a function of consumption cost (cost per portion within a meal). Meal size decreases and meal frequency increases but not sufficiently to maintain total daily intake. This figure is a composite of results from several different experiments on several different species.

cient to prevent a fall in the rate of intake. Total daily intake falls owing to this decrease in meal size and the noncompensatory increase in meal frequency. No one of these tactics alone is completely compensatory.

Other variables influencing consumption cost are portion size, for example, pellet size or duration of feeder presentation[23]; caloric density[37,38]; and competition within a meal between conspecifics.[1] It should be noted that the effects of cost on consumption are the opposite of the effects of cost on access in terms of meal frequency, meal size, and rate of instrumental and consummatory responding. The decline in total intake seen with increasing unit price has been interpreted as an example of the demand law of economics, and the rate of decline in intake, as a measure of elasticity of demand.[25,39,40]

These results differ from those obtained with the techniques of classic operant psychology, which are based on the study of consumption in experimenter-determined sessions with deprived animals (open economies). Most resources are not distributed continuously but spatially and temporally in patches that vary in size and resource quality and density. This poses an additional problem to that of discovering and harvesting the resource, that is, the problem of choosing among patches. MacArthur and Pianka[42] first posed this problem in terms of what items or patches an optimal forager should include in its diet. We have simulated this problem in a number of experiments.

FIGURE 8 illustrates one of our simulations of a patchy environment. It consists of a search bar, the single bar on the left. This bar is active during the intermeal interval, and search can be initiated at any time during this interval. Completion of the search requirement results in the search cue-light going off, and one of two other cue lights (determined randomly) being illuminated, indicating that the opportunity to procure a meal has been encountered. The animal can either "accept" this meal opportunity or "reject" it and return to search again. Rejection can be either passive (for example, by waiting 30 sec) or active (for example, by making three responses on the search bar). Acceptance of the meal opportunity by completing a bar press access cost requirement turns on the feeder. During the meal, a consumption cost (e.g., n bar presses/pellet) may also be imposed. Thus, a foraging bout consists of searching for feeding opportunities, perhaps rejecting some number of opportunities and returning to search until an acceptable opportunity is encountered, and then procuring and consuming a meal.

Choice between patches differing in procurement cost is shown in FIGURE 9 in terms of the percentage of opportunities accepted.[41] Two possible strategies, to take only

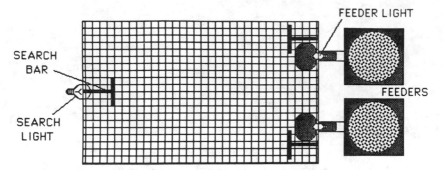

FIGURE 8. Top view of an apparatus used to study choice between patches differing in either cost of access to the patch or cost of consumption within a patch. Completion of the bar-press requirement on the single search bar on the left will cause one of the two patch lights on the right to be illuminated in a random sequence, indicating that a meal is available at that patch by bar-pressing. The animal can accept the opportunity to gain access to and consume the resources in the patch, or he can reject it and search again.

low-cost meal opportunities and to take both high- and low-cost opportunities, are diagramed in FIGURE 10. The take-both strategy yields the lowest response expenditure up to the point at which its total cost (search + procurement) exceeds the take-only-low strategy. At this point, if it is to minimize total cost, the animal should shift to an exclusive take-only-low strategy.[24,33,42] Both strategies predict that low-cost opportunities should always be taken and, with few exceptions, this did occur. However, acceptance of high-cost opportunities was not all-or-none; rather, the rats showed partial preferences, accepting high-cost opportunities in proportion to the *relative* differences in high and low costs. Meal frequencies were a function of the average cost produced by the choices. Meal sizes did *not* differ between patches but were appropriate to the daily meal frequencies: Total intake was defended. Increasing search costs result in an increased frequency of accepting the high-cost opportunities — the animals became less finicky. This paradigm has been tested with a number of species (rats,

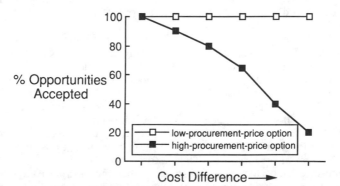

FIGURE 9. Percent acceptance of opportunities for access to either high- or low-cost patches as a function of the cost of access to the expensive patch. This figure is a composite of the results from several different experiments on several different species.

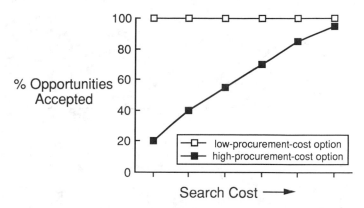

FIGURE 10. Percent acceptance of opportunities for access to either high- or low-cost patches as a function of the cost of search. This figure is a composite of results from several different experiments on different species.

cats, chickens, blue jays, and ferrets), and similar results have been obtained — same problem, same solution.[24]

Another version of this patch-choice paradigm is to vary the cost of consumption other than the cost of access between patches. That is, the pellet cost, caloric density, size of pellet, or rate of delivery may be greater in one patch than the other. The variables measured in this paradigm are total intake and relative total intake, relative acceptance of feeding opportunities, relative meal sizes, and relative rates of responding in the patches. As would be expected, rats prefer the patch with the lowest per calorie cost (BP/calorie). See the first points (10;10) in FIGURE 11. Unlike the case in which access cost was varied, when consumption cost within a meal is varied, meal size becomes the major strategy for dealing with the different patch costs. The functions obtained are independent of the experimental manipulation that generates the cost difference: Rats prefer the patch with the cheapest pellets, the largest pellets, the highest caloric-density pellets, or fastest rate of pellet delivery.

Now, if two factors are manipulated simultaneously, that is, if the per pellet cost of the larger pellets or of the higher calorie pellets is raised, the rats come to prefer the smaller or lower calorie pellets (FIG. 10). FIGURE 12 shows that these shifts in preference can be predicted from the relative profitability within the patches (calories/min).

Similar results have been obtained in patchy paradigms where the choice is among the macronutrients, protein, fat, and carbohydrate.[43] As the cost of access to a nutrient is raised, access is sought less often and larger meals are taken. Fat and carbohydrate are substitutable, but the relative intake of protein is defended as protein becomes more expensive.

A second interesting feature of these data is the time window within which the economic variables act on the pattern of meals. Historically, meals have been viewed as individual events whose initiation and termination are determined by the momentary state of the animal's physiology. The data presented here indicate, however, that meal patterns reflect an integration of costs and benefits over several meals. For the rat, this time frame appears to be on the order of 24 hours. For cats[26] and chickens,[27] it is on the order of days. Animals anticipate their requirements and, like all good accountants, balance their books. There are other regulatory time windows, ranging

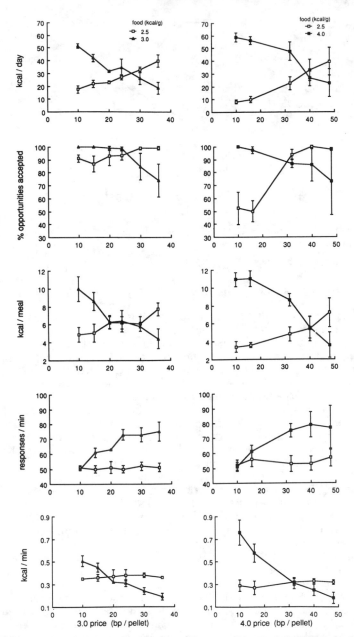

FIGURE 11. Total intake, percent acceptance of opportunities, and size of meals, taken from two patches differing in the cost of consumption within the patch (caloric density or pellet size) as a function of pellet cost within the least expensive patch.

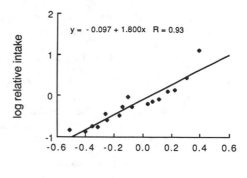

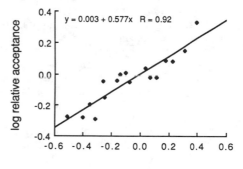

FIGURE 12. Log relative total intake, percent opportunities accepted, and meal size as a function of the log relative profitability (calories/min) within patches.

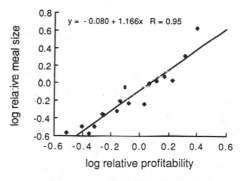

from the diurnal or nocturnal fasts in some niches to seasonal variations in resource density that require physiological or physical stockpiling of resources in others. For example, chickens anticipate their obligatory nocturnal fast by storing food in the crop during a pretwilight intensification of feeding and then metering out that food overnight.[27,44] Other avian species anticipate this nocturnal fast by the daily storage and nightly use of fat.[30] Hibernators depend upon fat storage to buffer periods of low resource density. Circadian and ultradian rhythms appear to play major roles in these anticipatory patterns of feeding.[22] Thus long-term regulation reflects not only the genetic potential for size and composition, but also the economic structure of the niche and the current habitat in such terms as diurnal and seasonal resource density, current weather, inter- and intraspecies competition and predation, and allocation of time and effort to other biologically significant activities (for example, reproduction, territorial defense, predation).

How can these findings be placed in the context of current views of the controls of feeding and drinking derived from Cannon's hypothesis that the constancy of the internal milieu is defended by behavior as well as physiological mechanisms? In this view, eating and drinking are instigated by perturbations in the internal milieu. There is no question that the constancy of the internal milieu is defended. The physiological mechanisms by which this is accomplished are a central topic in physiology. At issue is whether animals exploit information about the structure of their environment acquired phylogenetically or ontogenetically to alleviate or to anticipate deficits and surfeits? Our view of this issue is illustrated by a metaphor based on a job analysis (FIG. 13). First, we assign to the resident physiologist (RP) the task of defending the internal milieu *with whatever resources are provided*. He/she is in charge of utilization of inputs varying in quality, quantity, and temporal distribution and coping with changing metabolic demands. Second, we assign to the house economist (HE) the tasks of anticipating requirements, shopping for the cheapest resources, making economic (cost/benefit) decisions about when, where, what, which, how much, how often, how fast to eat, allocating time to different activities, and balancing the books. Third, we assign to the cuisinier (C) the task of classifying (taste, smell, nutritive value) the incoming items. Presumably, the occupation of each of these individuals was shaped by the feeding niche in which their host (species) evolved. The primary question that arises from this analysis is, How do these jobs interact? What is the dialogue among them? Our assumption is that the HE, in normal environmental circumstances, supplies to the RP food items, in sufficient amounts and of adequate quality, on an appropriate schedule for the RP to perform his job without any necessity for communication between them. One must assume that the RP has sufficient latitude, shaped by his phylogenetic history, to manage his job with a variable input depending upon the HE's reactions to the normally variable market. On the other hand, HE's choices and economic rules are also shaped by selection — "grass not rabbits," "medium-sized ones are cheaper than big or small ones," "this patch has a relatively higher rate of energy flow than the average one" — and learning. The HE's learning is most likely mediated, in part, by communications between C and RP about the associations of stimulus properties (both proximal and distal) of food items with their nutrient or noxious consequences.[45,46] Such a mechanism would be most useful to an omnivore with a wide diet breadth. Two major points are contained in this metaphor: (1) The feeding patterns of a species cannot be understood without considering the economic structure of its environment, and (2) hunger and satiety are functions of the HE not the RP. That is, if hunger and satiety are defined in terms of the tendency to eat or drink, these tendencies are governed by economics rather than physiological depletion or repletion.

Perhaps the most important message of this analysis is the flexibility or adaptability of animals in their patterns of feeding. From examining a single, simple, restricted, refined experimental situation, it is impossible to comprehend either the variety or possible patterns or the variables controlling them for even a single species, since the economic context is the major determinant. Further, it is not likely that the study of physiological mechanisms will by itself elucidate the repertoire of feeding patterns stored in a species.

Returning to humans, we would expect that feeding strategies similar to those described above would be embedded in their current feeding patterns. The history of hominoid evolution is controversial, but certain general features are known. Primates are basically herbivorous. Herbivory enjoys the advantage of the general abundance and relative ease of procuring food. On the other hand, the ratio of protein to energy

FIGURE 13. A metaphor describing the variables involved in meal patterns. The house economist is portrayed in the upper left, the resident physiologist at the bottom, and the cuisinier at the upper right.

in the diet is low, and the amino acid ratios vary greatly among plant species and differ from those in animals. This presents a problem because animals are unable to synthesize essential amino acids. Moreover, caloric density is low because of obstructive, indigestible plant carbohydrates (plant cell walls), and often plants contain toxic secondary compounds that deter consumption. These features require that a herbivore extract an adequate amount of protein from a diet that usually contains an excess of energy, and then to improve its quality. Herbivores have evolved two basic strategies, emphasizing either digestion or selection, to meet these problems.

One digestive strategy, seen in ruminants, depends upon mechanical degradation and fermentation by microorganisms in the rumen. These microorganisms produce volatile fats and sugars, and, because of their capacity to synthesize most of the essential amino acids required by their host, are themselves a source of balanced protein. In effect, this strategy makes good food out of bad by chemistry and uses plant food efficiently. In a second version of this digestive strategy, used by monogastric herbivores, the volume of food consumed is increased and useful nutrients are extracted as the ingestant passes through the gut. Fermentation and absorption of its products take place in the lower gut or cecum. This latter, digestive strategy is used by long-gutted primates. The price paid for these digestive strategies are the volume of material that must be consumed, the time spent consuming it, and the time spent processing it. The benefits are the minimal foraging costs and the efficiency of utilization.[47,48]

The selective strategy is characteristic of short-gutted, monogastric, herbivorous primates.[2-4] These animals compose a balanced and calorically sufficient diet by choosing among food items, such as plant parts (flowers, fruits, seeds, nuts, new leaves, shoots, etc.) that have higher ratios of protein to carbohydrate, higher caloric density, and lower levels of obstructive carbohydrates. These foods are digested without the (major) intervention of fermentation. The price paid for this strategy is greater foraging time and effort, both to locate food items and to choose among them to compose a balanced diet. The benefits are (1) the smaller volume of food required, (2) the simplified digestive chemistry, and (3) the more rapid processing of the consumed items.

The foraging component of this strategy requires the ability to identify sources of macronutrients, recognize their relative quality, and to assess and remember their abundance and seasonal availability within the habitat. This foraging niche provides strong selection pressure for the processing and storage of information about the habitat and an ability to process and act upon a knowledge of the relative costs and benefits of the food items.

The shifting of the task of composing a balanced diet from gut chemistry to selection requires that the animal consume the appropriate proportions of macro- and micronutrients within a limited time frame. Whether this is accomplished by feedback or foreknowledge (or both) remains an open question. This strategy places a premium on expanding diet breadth to reduce foraging costs by increasing the number of items that can be searched for. Clearly, however, expanding the diet introduces higher costs in terms of decreased digestibility and added competition for the resources than are incurred with greater specialization.

The hominoid line apparently arose from the latter primate strategy. One of the most characteristic features of this evolutionary line is diet breadth. This may have made possible the initial move of our hominoid ancestors from the forest to the savannah and the subsequent evolution of their successive feeding strategies: herbivory, gathering, scavenging, hunting, and finally agriculture.[49,50] The inclusion of meat in the diet provided a source of high-quality, easily digestible protein but enormously increased foraging costs. Particularly affected were the costs of search, procurement, and handling because prey animals were relatively low in abundance and highly reluctant to become prey. An additional cost was coping with the boom-and-bust economy entailed by hunting. Because both the probability of encountering game during a hunt and the probability of capturing it once encountered were variable and often low, the resulting capricious success rate entailed an irregular pattern of feeding with unpredictable and often long intermeal intervals. The development of the ability to store large amounts of energy rapidly in the adipose tissue permitted early hunting humanoids to buffer the consequences of these variable intermeal intervals.[1] Humanoids also countered part of the costs of hunting by socializing it. Socialization entailed the unusual strategies of hunting and gathering in anticipation of need, postponing consumption, and sharing. The socialization of hunting also made possible the storage of information in the culture about the temporal and geographical location of prey and the techniques of capture. These strategies led to the eventual development of the capability of storing food by means other than depositing it in the adipose tissue. The wide diet breadth meant that hominoid feeding was less menu-driven. Humanoids became the ultimate generalist omnivores, imposing an enormous burden on their ability to diet-select, that is, to compose a diet providing a balance of nutrients and sufficient calories within a "short" time. The problems of variable abundance and availability (but not distribution) were eventually solved by the development of agriculture. This resulted in a more predictable source of food and stable meal patterns but again imposed the cost of dealing with plant food of poor quality in terms of protein-to-energy and amino acid ratios. The agricultural period occupies only a brief instant of hominoid history.

The strategies evolved during the hunting-gathering fraction of hominoid history are the source of the diagnostic human features: eusociality, language, and intelligence (for reviews see,[1,51-53]). It is this repertoire of strategies and tactics, developed over the course of evolution, that fills the shelves of the human feeding behavior library. This library contains both "biological wisdom" and "cultural wisdom," the results of very different selection pressures. It is clearly difficult to parcel out the biological and cultural determinants of human behavior. The fact that cultural wisdom is based on group selection rather than individual selection may account in part for the accumulation of unadaptive cultural feeding patterns.

Returning to the first portion of this paper, it is clear that animals have developed flexible feeding strategies that are sensitive to the economic structure of their environment. These can be elucidated experimentally by constructing environments within which the animal is able to display its talents — the solutions that evolved in the different habitats encountered in its niche. It seems probable that humans have a similar repertoire of strategies. Considering meal frequency and size, for example, there are the variable meals of hunters, the frequent daily meals of farmers, the less frequent daily meals of people living in industrial societies, and so forth. Attempts to understand human feeding are based primarily on studies of mechanism or on survey-type studies of anthropologists. There have been few attempts to discover the essential and pervasive economic features of the human feeding environment, the cost/benefit rules that humans bring to their different habitats. Because experiments must be retrospective, perhaps our best approach to gain an insight into the economics of human feeding patterns is to ask what major problems were faced in hominoid evolution. Three are obvious: First is the problem of *diet selection* arising from the diet breadth that humans evolved during their travel from herbivory to omnivory through carnivory. Second is the problem of *social foraging*. Third is the problem of *postponed consumption*, delaying the interval between capture or harvest to ingestion, which is one pillar of human sociality.

The required proportions of macro- and micronutrients and the time window over which these must be achieved are approximately the same for all animals, but the methods of meeting this balance vary widely. There are possible animal models for diet selection among omnivores, but few have the catholic taste of humans, with, perhaps, the exception of our compatriot, the rat. The problems of diet selection involve both the cost and benefits of foods and the difficult problem of recognition. This latter problem can be met by a fixed menu that meets requirements or by a capricious menu based, for example, on encounter rate, in which the consequences are evaluated and the diet, adjusted. Recognition of the required items can occur at the level of taste; at the level of feedback for the resident physiologist; or, in the case of humans, at the level of culture (mothers, ethnic prescriptions and restrictions, cookbooks, health-food advertisements, the Tufts Newsletter, etc.). The problem with the culture is that the relation between the consequences of intake and the development of the rules for feeding is attenuated.

There are also possible animal models of social foraging, but few, outside of the social insects, display the complexity and division of labor seen in humans. One could almost view human society as having evolved out of the requirements of social foraging. Of interest here, though, is how the constraints imposed by social foraging have "fed back" on the patterns of human intake.

Finally, there may be animal models of postponed consumption among the central-place foragers. For most animals, successful foraging expeditions are followed immediately by consumption. Most of our extant theories of motivation are based on this immediacy. For humans, however, foraging and consumption are independent activities, with the exception of meal preparation. The solution to our understanding of human feeding patterns may lie in the recognition that the patterns of feeding are determined by the economic context within which they occur, that is, in a study of its ultimate rather than, exclusively, its proximate causation.

ACKNOWLEDGMENTS

The author gratefully acknowledges the collaboration of Dr. Deanne Johnson and the criticism and editing of Dr. Carolyn Rovee-Collier.

REFERENCES

1. GEIST, V. 1978. Life Strategies, Human Evolution, Environmental Design. Springer-Verlag. New York.
2. MILTON, K. 1980. The Foraging Strategy of Howler Monkeys. Columbia University Press. New York.
3. MILTON, K. 1981. Food choice and digestive strategies of two sympatric primate species. Am. Nat. 117: 496–505.
4. MILTON, K. & M. W. DEMMENT. 1988. Digestion and passage kinetics of Chimpanzees fed high and low fiber diets and comparison with human data. J. Nutr. 118: 1082–1088.
5. CLARK, J. D. 1968. Studies of hunter-gatherers as an aid to the interpretation of prehistoric societies. In Man the Hunter. R. B. Lee & I. DeVore, Eds.: 276–289. Aldine-Atherton. Chicago.
6. HARDING, R. S. & G. TELEKI. 1981. Omnivorous Primates. Columbia University Press. New York.
7. COLLIER, G. 1986. The dialogue between the House Economist and the Resident Physiologist. Nutr. Behav. 3: 9–26.
8. COLLIER, G. 1987. Operant methodologies for studying feeding and drinking. In Feeding and Drinking. F. Toates & N. Rowland, Eds.: 37–76. Elsevier. Amsterdam.
9. MAYR, E. 1982. The Growth of Biological Thought. Harvard University Press. Cambridge, MA.
10. CANNON, W. B. 1932. The Wisdom of the Body. Norton. New York.
11. BOOTH, D. A., Ed. 1978. Hunger Models: Computable Theory of Feeding Control. Academic Press. London.
12. KISSILEFF, H. R. & T. B. VAN ITALLIE. 1982. Physiology of the control of food intake. Ann. Rev. Nutr. 2: 371–418.
13. TOATES, F. M. 1979. Homeostasis and drinking. Behav. Brain Sci. 2: 95–139.
14. BOLLES, R. C. 1967. Theory of Motivation. Harper & Row. New York.
15. COLLIER, G. H. 1969. Body weight loss as a measure of motivation in hunger and thirst. Ann. N.Y. Acad. Sci. 157: 594–609.

16. LE MAGNEN, J. 1985. Hunger. Cambridge. New York.
17. ADOLPH, E. F. 1947. Urges to eat and drink in rats. Am. J. Physiol. **178:** 110–125.
18. KEESEY, R. E. & T. L. POWLEY. 1986. The regulation of body weight. Ann. Rev. Psychol. **37:** 109–133.
19. MAYER, J. 1955. Regulation of energy intake and body weight: The glucostatic theory and the lipostatic hypothesis. Ann. N.Y. Acad. Sci. **63:** 15–43.
20. COLLIER, G. H. 1982. Determinants of choice. *In* Nebraska Symposium on Motivation: Response Structure and Organization. D. Bernstein, Ed. University of Nebraska Press. Lincoln, NE.
21. SKINNER, B. F. 1938. The Behavior of Organisms. Appleton-Century-Crofts. New York.
22. ARMSTRONG, S. A. 1980. A chronometric approach to the study of feeding behavior. Neurosci. Biobehav. Rev. **4:** 27–53.
23. COLLIER, G. H., D. F. JOHNSON, W. HILL & L. W. KAUFMAN. 1986. The economics of the law of effect. J. Exp. Anal. Behav. **46:** 113–136.
24. COLLIER, G. & C. K. ROVEE-COLLIER. 1981. A comparative analysis of optimal foraging behavior: Laboratory simulations. *In* Foraging Behavior: Ecological, Ethological & Psychological Approaches. A. C. Kamil & T. D. Sargent, Eds.: 39–76. Garland Press. New York.
25. HURSH, S. R. 1984. Behavioral economics. J. Exp. Anal. Behav. **42:** 435–452.
26. KANAREK, R. B. 1975. Availability and caloric density of the diet as determinants of meal patterns in cats. Physiol. Behav. **15:** 611–618.
27. KAUFMAN, L. & G. COLLIER. 1983. Meal-taking by domestic chicks (*Gallus gallus*). Anim. Behav. **31:** 397–403.
28. PAULEY, G. 1984. Feeding strategies in individual and group living Bonnet Macaques. Unpublished Doctoral Dissertation. Downstate Medical Center. Brooklyn, NY.
29. MARWINE, A. G. & G. H. COLLIER. 1979. The rat at the waterhole. J. Comp. Physiol. Psychol. **93:** 391–402
30. DAWSON, W. R., R. L. MARSH & M. E. YACOE. 1983. Metabolic adjustments of small passerine birds for migration and cold. Am J. Physiol. **14:** R755–R767.
31. MAHANEY, A., D. F. JOHNSON & G. COLLIER. 1985. Variable food access cost and meal patterns in rats. Presented at The Eastern Psychological Association. Boston, MA.
32. CHARNOV, E. L. 1976. Optimal foraging: The marginal value theorem. Theor. Popul. Biol. **2:** 129–136.
33. KREBS, J. R. 1984. Optimization in behavioral ecology. *In* Behavioural Ecology. 2nd edit. J. R. Krebs & N. B. Davies, Eds.: 91–121. Sinauer. Sunderland, U.K.
34. JOHNSON, F. & C. A. MORGAN. 1989. Satiety in foraging rats: Effects of patch access cost and patch depletion rate. Animal Behavior Society. Northern Kentucky University.
35. COLLIER, G., E. HIRSCH & R. KANAREK. 1977. The operant revisited. *In* Handbook of Operant Behavior. W. K. Honig & J. E. R. Staddon, Eds.: 28–52. Prentice Hall. Englewood Cliffs, NJ.
36. RASHOTTE, M. E., J. M. O'CONNELL & V. J. DJURIC. 1987. Mechanisms of signal-controlled foraging behavior. *In* M. L. Commons, A. Kacelnik & S. J. Shettleworth, Eds.: 153–179. Erlbaum. Hillsdale, NJ.
37. JOHNSON, D. F., K. M. ACKROFF, G. H. COLLIER & L. PLESCIA. 1984. Effects of dietary nutrients and foraging costs on meal patterns in rats. Physiol. Behav. **33:** 465–470.
38. JOHNSON, D. F. & G. COLLIER. 1987. Caloric regulation and food choice in a patch environment: The value and cost of alternative foods. Physiol Behav. **39:** 351–359.
39. LEA, S. E. G. 1978. The psychology and economics of demand. Psychol. Bull. **85:** 441–466.
40. RACHLIN, H. 1982. Absolute and relative consumption space. *In* Nebraska Symposium on Motivation: Response Structure and Organization. D. J. Bernstein, Ed.: 129–167. University of Nebraska Press. Lincoln, NE.
41. KAUFMAN, L. W. 1979. Foraging strategy: Laboratory simulations. Unpublished Doctoral Dissertation. Rutgers University. New Brunswick, NJ.
42. MACARTHUR, R. H. & E. R. PIANKA. 1966. On the optimal use of a patchy environment. Am. Nat. **100:** 603–610.
43. ACKROFF, K. M. 1987. Foraging for macronutrients: Effects of variation in the availability and abundance of the protein source. Unpublished Doctoral Dissertation. Rutgers University. New Brunswick, NJ.

44. ROVEE-COLLIER, C., B. A. CLAPP & G. H. COLLIER. 1982. The economics of food choice in chicks. Physiol. Behav. **28:** 1097–1102.
45. GARCIA, J. & R. A. KOELLING. 1966. The relation of cue to consequence in avoidance learning. Psychonom. Sci. **4:** 123–124.
46. SCLAFANI, A. 1989. Nutrient-base learning flavor preference in rats. *In* Taste Experience and Feeding. APA. In press.
47. BELL, R. H. V. 1971. A grazing ecosystem in the Serengeti. Sci. Am. **225:** 86–93.
48. BELOVSKY, G. E. 1978. Diet optimization in a generalist herbivore. Theor. Pop. Biol. **14:** 105–134.
49. ISAAC, G. LL. & D. C. CRADER. 1981. To what extent were early hominoids carnivorous? An archaeological perspective. *In* Omnivorous Primates: Gathering and Hunting in Human Evolution. R. S. O. Harding & G. Teleki, Eds. Columbia University Press. New York.
50. MANN, A. E. 1981. Diet and human evolution. *In* Omnivorous Primates: Gathering and Hunting in Human Evolution. R. S. O. Harding & G. Teleki, Eds. Columbia University Press. New York.
51. DART, R. A. 1953. The predatory transition from ape to man. Int. Anthropol. Linguist. Rev. **1:** 201–217.
52. LEE, R. B. & I. DEVORE. 1968. Man the Hunter. Aldine-Atherton. Chicago.
53. WILSON, E. O. 1975. Sociobiology. Harvard University Press. Cambridge, MA.

Summary: Part II

ARTHUR CAMPFIELD

Hoffmann-La Roche Inc.
Nutley, New Jersey 07110

This afternoon's session has provided a good overview of the status of feeding research and some of the attempts to apply it to the problem of clinical eating disorders. From this discussion of the clinical entity, it's quite clear that the challenges for all of us are great. Those of us working on the animal physiology side need the answer to a couple of simple questions. Is binging just a big meal or are there components, behavioral components, to binging that are unique and different? The assumption that big meals are binges has been argued by at least two speakers. Similarly, is anorexia nervosa just voluntary fasting? Again, we need a behavioral answer and we need metabolic answers.

The papers presented in this session were beautiful examples of attempts to simplify a fundamentally very complicated problem. We must understand food intake regulation in a clear situation where it's eating and intake that are disordered, as in anorexia and bulimia, as opposed to obesity. Many have argued about the relative contribution of hyperphagia to obesity. There's no question here that it's the behavorial issue that we need to address.

So this is a complicated problem, and we have heard some very simplified analyses, which are perfectly appropriate at the beginning of a search. Somewhere along the line, however, we have to analyze more complex problems than one neurotransmitter or one particular disease and move away from the notion that drugs are "clean." Believe me, I have learned in two years that drugs are not clean. The perfect example of this is *d*-fenfluramine, a centrally acting anorectic that has powerful effects on basal metabolism measured in animals and in humans. John Morley pointed out, quite correctly, the naiveté of some of us regarding the actions of D2 agonists.

As I see it, there are four basic questions. One is the search for mechanisms. Gerry Smith sent us out on this road; David Booth brought us back to this road; and I think this is absolutely the fundamental issue of the enterprise we've embarked upon. What are the mechanisms of these eating disorders, and how can we tease them out in animal models? The question here immediately becomes, in Gerry Smith's demarcation, Do we create etiological or isomorphic models? I would argue that we may have to settle for distributed and lumped models. A lumped model of anorexia nervosa would be an animal that exhibits all of the characteristics of the average human patient. I doubt if we'll find that. I think what we are going to find is various aspects of an eating disorder (large meal size, avidity to bar pressing, etc.) distributed among many different kinds of feeding situations. What we must do as animal researchers is to define for the clinician what he or she should look for and measure to test the hypotheses about the organization of feeding control.

The second issue is what is the driving force for research in this field? Is it the questions about how is eating regulated and how can it be disordered? Is it the search for a tool, a CCK antagonist? Or is it relevance, that is, are third parties interested enough to provide funding? I think some of us have to decide that this problem, with its dramatic manifestations in the clinic, deserves a full frontal attack. This can't be a side interest; it has got to be a major focus for research.

Going back to lumped models, can we take animal models and shape them to resemble clinical eating disorders? In order to accomplish this we need help from the clinicians. We need to know the time course of changes, behavioral and metabolic, in each of these disorders. We need to know about recovered anorectics and recovered bulimics. What about their behavior is abnormal; what is abnormal metabolically. If we succeed in bringing an anorectic to normal weight, what have we achieved? In rats we don't have to consider the motivational or the "I'm afraid to be fat" aspects. We are going to be able to easily tell you what is body weight dependent as far as the response to altered conditions. We need to know what part of the brain is involved, what signals to measure, and so forth.

We need adjuncts for psychotherapy. Here we need what Gerry Smith called a predictive model. We need animals that display part of the syndrome that we can use in testing pharmacological and other means of treatment. This is the role of the pharmaceutical industry. We need an animal model; but we must proceed carefully, because this is where animal models get used and abused a lot. Probably we are not going to be able to find one model for either bulimia or anorexia. We are going to have to look carefully over a range of animal models to find drugs or other adjuncts to therapy that will truly be effective.

I would like to make an analogy to another area of research where animal models have been well established, many meetings have been held, and many books have been published: experimental hyperglycemia. You will note I did not call it diabetes. I had the privilege to do a post-doctorate under the tutelage of Albert Reynolt, who more or less invented the field of animal models of diabetes. The problem developed as researchers found diabetes or glucosuria or hyperglycemia and went off and studied it in the animal model, and they had to be pulled back to the clinical problem. So perhaps the fact that we are in the early stage in the animal models for these diseases is lucky, because we can ask questions that are always conditioned on the clinical entity. So clinicians need to keep explaining to those of us in basic research what it is they are faced with, and we need to be able to produce an animal model and say, in effect, "Here's a rat that will do this if I probe him this way. Is this interesting to you?" Then we can deal with models of altered eating behavior or ingestive behavior that will relate to clinical eating disorders. Animal models are never the same thing as the disease; investigators who confuse the two don't make much progress.

In closing, I believe that we have begun to discuss the problem very well, but I think we need to separate these disorders into subtypes very soon. For this reason I do not believe we can fully explain these diseases as examples of serotonin dysregulation. We need to do some redefining and approach these problems from several different angles in order to obtain a satisfying rate of progress.

General Discussion: Part II

JOHN E. MORLEY, *Chair*

DR. HARRY KISSILEFF (*St. Luke's-Roosevelt Hospital, New York, NY*): I'd like to ask David Booth if he would clarify what he means by a mechanism as opposed to a description. Also, perhaps Dr. Campfield would comment on Dr. Booth's answer to that.

DR. DAVID A. BOOTH (*University of Birmingham, Birmingham, U.K.*): I would like to make two points. I think that simplifying the phenomena of anorexia nervosa or bulimia or bulimia nervosa according to the terminology that you are asking about would be to oversimplify. Attempting to pick out the main major causal processes is the classic approach of experimental and theoretical science, and it generates testable hypotheses, although of course it's very easy to slide into oversimplifying the complexity. One has to start somewhere to develop a theory, however, and that should not be called oversimplification if it can be shunted into being testable, picking out what's really happening out there.

More precisely, you asked if it is big meals that we are talking about. That again, in my terminology Harry, is to talk about the phenomenon, and in bulimia it isn't necessarily big meals. There's a clinical argument that it's just the sense of being out of control. It can be a normal-sized meal, but it's still a binge by this definition if the individual feels out of control at the meal. So I think the answer to your question, are we really talking about big meals, should be no. That's a superficial, oversimplified view of the phenomenon I'm trying to explain and find causal mechansims for, which is something like involuntarily motivated ingestion.

DR. CAMPFIELD (*Hoffmann–La Roche, Inc., Nutley, NJ*): I don't think we disagree. I think as far as the phenomenon is concerned, it's clear and it's robust. If you've seen it or heard it presented today, it was mostly in tables and data, but even in anecdotal reports it's powerful. I think the search for basic mechanisms is essential, that's what we're about. The problem comes when we focus on one and only one mechanism, or when an individual laboratory has one mechanism under study and they find it is effective, such as tricyclic antidepressants. That immediately becomes the mechanism by which these drugs help patients. I think we have to be more sophisticated than that; I think we don't disagree.

I have a question for Dr. Collier. I'm wondering what you think might happen if you not only limit access by requiring a high cost for gaining access to food, but put a high cost on meal size. Would you have a tradeoff between access and meal size and might you induce feeding behavior that would look "out of control"?

DR. COLLIER: We've looked at consumption of a meal under those conditions. Once access has been gained to the meal and a price is put on eating it, you would expect to see a reduction in intake. That is not the case until you get to a very extreme level. If you start at 10 barpresses and increase to 100 barpresses per pellet, you start seeing evidence of what the economists call the demand law or fall of intake in order to conserve total expenditure. But even with a fairly substantial cost placed on consuming the meal, the rat, or other animal, tends to eat the same size of meal.

I would like to take this opportunity to make another point which might be relevant to what you're saying. The typical way of describing meal patterns is in terms of hunger and satiety. I think the distinction that comes out of our research is that if you want to call initiating a meal and terminating a meal hunger and satiety, then hunger and satiety do not refer to physiological processes in the way we've used these terms in the past. They're economic processes, and you have to make a very clear distinction between an animal that is physiologically deprived and one that is able to manage its own affairs and eat in such a way that it can take into account these economic factors.

PROFESSOR STYLIANOS NICOLAIDIS (*College de France CNRS, Paris*): I have some comments for George Collier. George, I'm sure that there is no difference between us, but you should make clear that there is no contradiction between the regulatory feeding that responds to maturation, physiological maturation, and your beautiful findings that we all admire. What is more remarkable is not that the animals stop eating five times a day because they have to work for it, what is remarkable is that they still eat after being obliged to barpress 5000 times to get that food. The persistence of feeding despite the difficulties shows how powerful the regulatory motivated feeding behavior is.

DR. ELIOTT BLASS (*Johns Hopkins University, Baltimore, MD*): I want to say something that seems so apparent that everybody will agree with it, and I think in this colloquy between Stylio and George, we saw an example of it. We are all agreed that in some fashion our behavior is determined by internal factors and in another fashion by cognitive factors that George has been calling to our attention over the recent past. To the extent that we've embarked on the idea of establishing animal models to account for various pathologies of feeding, then I feel compelled to make the following comment: Can we assess how much of the phenomenon of feeding, both in short term and in long term, we might be able to account for by these so-called physiological models, either in isolation or in some form of combination. I mention this from a biographical perspective. Those of you who are familiar with my earlier work know that it concerned mechanisms of thirst and drinking but more particularly drinking in response to physiological challenges. Quite a few people about 15 to 20 years ago were investing a tremendous amount of effort in identifying the physiology of thirst, and quite a bit of progress was made in that regard.

One of my reasons for leaving this area was that I felt that a lot of progress had been made in understanding mechanisms of drinking in regard to body fluid dehydration. We were assuming at the outset that we were accounting for drinking, and given the various sources of fluid availability to mammals, 70% of the food that's eaten in the wild is water, and given our habits of drinking I felt that we were accounting for very, very little of the phenomenon of water intake or fluid intake. I'm wondering how much we're coming up against that now as we focus on this or that metabolic or physiological control, and now as we take the next step and look to apply these ideas towards a model for anorexia or bulimia. It might be premature to undertake this type of an enterprise. I want to illustrate with something from my own therapeutic experiences.

A number of years ago Paul McHugh was kind enough to let me take residency in psychiatry, and as part of my training I spent about four or five months on the ward run by Bob Robinson for the treatment of feeding disorders. I had the occasion to treat two bulimic patients. So what I'm about to say is derived from a very small sample size, but came through the eyes of somebody who had expected to see something very different from what was actually seen.

To me, there were two striking things about these bulimic patients. One was that bulimia was a very exaggerated and spectacular behavorial syndrome, but it was the least of these patients' problems. The very least. I have wanted to make that public, at least my own experience, because from the clinicians with whom I've spoken I have not heard anything enormously to the contrary.

DR. CAMPFIELD: I'd like to comment a little bit on what you said, Elliot. Your points are very well taken. I think, as Gerry Smith pointed out in his presentation, that the areas in feeding research in which we've gotten down to a specific hypothesis, be it CCK or be it small changes in blood glucose, come now more from the rat studies than the clinic. The clinicians can make this measurement, as we saw in the data presented from the measurements of CCK in bulimia. So where we have specific hyptotheses, I think it's not premature to take them and see if they are informative in all sorts of feeding, normal feeding as well as in clinical situations.

In your second comment based on your clinical experience, you raised a major issue. It's hard to know how much of what we're seeing as eating disorders is secondary to other things. This is, again, an area where we need further definition in the clinic of the primacy of the eating disorder to the other manifestations. I think that complicated Professor Russell's historical analysis. This is a complicated problem, but it's not premature, when we have a specific notion, to test it. That's why I've asked people who advocate various mechanisms in feeding to be specific, what can the clinician measure to test the fatty acid oxidation theory, to measure metabolism and define. They need to know what to do to test these ideas. Certainly gastic emptying, from Dr. Booth's work, is a good example of such an idea.

DR. KATHERINE HALMI (New York Hospital–Cornell Medical Center, White Plains, NY): I do appreciate Dr. Blass's comments, but I would like to point out that Professor Russell did implicate all the other serious problems that we cope with in both anorexia and bulimia. The reason why Russell and I and others in the field are interested in pursuing and looking at eating disorders, the eating behaviors in these disorders, is because it virtually hasn't been done except for in clinical descriptions. We have spent a great deal of time historically trying to analyze the psychodynamics, trying to analyze other behaviors in these patients, looking at family histories of other psychiatric illnesses, and trying a variety of different psychotherapeutic approaches, and we still have no answers. I don't believe the answer results in what we specifically find out about the eating behavior, but it is an area that has been virtually ignored in serious systematic scientific research. I do think that we can learn something from it to add to all the other things we're studying. Professor Russell and myself and other clinical researchers not only do endocrine research in these disorders, we do family interactive studies. In a way, we're jacks-of-all-trades and expert in none because of the complexity of these disorders. Somebody made the point earlier in the conference that the important thing is to look at the interactions, and that is what we're trying to do.

DR. JOHN E. MORLEY (Sepulveda VA Medical Center, Sepulveda, CA): I'd just like to add to Kathy's remarks in that anecdotal medicine is perhaps the biggest problem we can all get into. Any of us who deal with patients on a daily basis understand that we all remember the one case that it suited us to remember. One is always surprised when things are studied properly as opposed to written down as anecdotes. That's a very important point for us to remember. We should be looking at collective series where patients have been carefully studied, not at an "n" of one or two, where we can get ouselves into real trouble with the magnificent case which doesn't bear any relationship to reality.

DR. PAUL ROZIN (University of Pennsylvania, Phildelphia, PA): I just have two comments related to Dr. Collier's talk. One has to do with the function/mechanism issue. I think the issue here is that function and mechansim are not tightly linked. Let me illustrate this one or twice. They are related, of course, but a selection pressure for any particular behavior may or may not tell you anything about the mechanism through which it is brought about. So that, for example, it is clear that energy is regulated in some sense or other and that may well be what was selected for through evolution, but it doesn't mean that the mechanism through which it's regulated provides, in fact, the measurement for energy. It would seem energy is regulated without paying much attention to energy *per se*. If you eat a constant density food you can meet your need and handle energy regulation that way. So the point I want to make is that it's a very complex and interesting relationship between the kind of data that George presents and the mechanisms that are involved. It's certainly a function that is suggestive of mechanism and sometimes dictates mechanism but other times it doesn't.

George showed that different aspects within the food domain can affect animal behavior. Of course, animals do other things besides eat. Animals, whenever they eat, are choosing to not do something else, and in the typical laboratory situation they have basically nothing else to do. This effects enormously how much eating they do or their pattern of eating. I think the clearest example in the laboratory is Dr. Nicolaidis's study, which shows that if you give rats a place to sleep a little, the number of meals and the meal pattern change substantially simply because they have another alternative. Now in the case of humans, I'm sure how much humans eat and the patterns in which they eat depend very much on the alternatives available to them, including social activities and hobbies and so forth. It's all right to study this in isolation, but as we try to understand real world behavior, we have to consider perdition risks, other activities, sexual behavior, and so on. So I just want to mention that as George expands the context of the food world to other alternatives, we also have yet to put that into the bigger context of all the opportunities that an animal has.

DR. MORLEY: Paul, please forgive me for this one comment, but do you mean that the rest of the animals in this audience, other than George, are totally unaware that they do anything else but eat? George, do you want to make a response?

DR. COLLIER: I'd like to support Paul's point. All you have to do is to change the cage size and you change the number of meals. A long time ago there was a psychologist named Kurt Richter who put together a multiple activity environment. Unfortunately it was too big for Johns Hopkins, and he didn't continue the research, but what he found was that all these activities interact with each other. As one activity changed in frequency of occurrence or duration all the others were influenced. It's clear that animals have time and energy budgets, and the true problem of feeding is not feeding *per se* but the question of optimal allocation between all different activities. And that extremely difficult problem is one that we're all probably going to forego probably because it takes an incredible amount of work.

In the case of thirst, with respect to Elliott's [Dr. Blass] comments, you have to ask what problem is the animal trying to solve. If you're a camel sitting out in the desert eating very dry food or maybe a little contained water, you have the problem of going to the water hole occasionally and picking up water. Now the further you have to go the less often you want to go. What happens is that the camel, if he's very close to the water hole, will drink quite frequently. When he's far away he drinks very infrequently, and he can consume 30% of his body weight in a single 15- or 20-minute bout. That brings up a couple of physiological mechanisms. What is the camel doing when he's out there not drinking? What he's doing is concentrating his urine, a physiologic mechanism we don't generally look at. What is he doing when he drinks 30% of his body weight? He should be inebriated with water, but he manages by some mechanism to take care of that problem.

DR. KARL M. PIRKE (*Max-Planck-Institute, Munich, F.R.G.*): I would like to make a suggestion with regard to animal experiments. Peter Brook already has observed that in patients with eating disorders, especially in anorexia nervosa, a lot of symptoms and the behavior you can observe were secondary to one kind of behavior: starvation. What you can do, and what should direct our animal experiments, is to analyze the behavior of these patients. Then you can easily see that starvation is dominating anorexia nervosa. For instance, in bulimia you have intermittent dieting, and in both of these eating disorders you can have hyperactivity, and it is very easy to perceive animal models where you can study the effects of this pathological behavior. We have followed this path in an effort to try to explain the many neuroendocrine abnormalities in eating disorders because these have been considered to be the consequence of neurotransmitter abnormalities. When you follow the method I suggest here, then you at least will not make the wrong assumption when you find some abnormality with regard, say, to norepinephrine in patients. That is the cause, but it may even be the consequence, and by this strategy you really can't find out.

DR. JOHN E. BLUNDELL (*University of Leeds, Leeds, U.K.*): I won't delay people very long: I want to make a couple of comments about animal models. It seems to me that animals left to their own devices do things pretty well. Their physiology functions fine, their behavior functions fine, and they're fairly successful. It is our job as research scientists to devise situations and to design experiments to allow animals to tell us how it is they do what they do very well. And at the moment I think we're not clever enough to do that. We understand less than perfectly what animals do very well indeed.

When it comes to eating disorders, what we have to do is to model behavior which is not rational but which is chaotic and irrational, and which to ourselves is a mystery. In humans we are mystified by what goes on, and yet we want to develop an animal model that will reflect this chaotic behavior. At the same time, it is perhaps a misnomer to call an animal that uses a bar press on a schedule that the experimenter devises an animal that is allowed to pick and choose when and how much food he wants to take. It might be instructive to put the animal in a situation where it could, in fact, determine which bar it wanted to work on to get a meal. I know you've done two bars, but if you had an animal in a situation where it had a choice of working on various fixed-ratio schedules, I think it would be interesting to know whether the animal would choose to take its meals more frequently or less frequently and which bar it would choose. Then you could say that the animal was truly determining how much it wanted to deprive itself as opposed to the experimenter determining how much it is going to deprive itself.

DR. MICHEL CABANAC (*Université Laval, Quebec, Canada*): We have replicated Dr. Collier's experiments with a completely different experimental situation where the rats have to go outside their warm nests to forage at a distance in an extremely cold environment which kills them if they stay there. We confirmed his results exactly, and we replicate his conclusions totally.

DR. PAUL H. ROBINSON (*Kings College Hospital School of Medicine, London*): Just one comment about what Dr. Morley said about individual case studies. I think an individual case study performed properly and in depth can be useful to us. We must maintain some link to the natural underlying physiological pursuit of normal behaior. And on top of that we want a model that is economic enough and brief enough to allow us to use it in all of our labs. Now it seems to me that's an almost impossible objective, to try and develop a model of some things we call chaos. We might be able to do it with a computer system, but at the moment it seems to me that we're being too simple. We're not prepared to be adventurous enough to develop models of complex behavior, and in fact I don't think it can be done in the laboratory. It might be possible on a computer.

What we can do, as Professor Pirke, I think, was suggesting, is that we can model fragments of eating behavior, behavioral fragments, certain aspects, certain factors of the syndrome. We can't model the entire syndrome, and I think we should forget about the possibility of trying to do that with an animal model.

DR. MORLEY: I think we'd all agree that breaking the syndrome down into its specific parts and using multiple animal models is more likely to be a resonable approach than looking for the single ultimate animal model.

DR. KISSILEFF: Regarding George Collier's work, it is important to recognize that when you place an animal in a situation where it has to perform can in fact yield very useful information. If you look at a herd of elephants from 10 miles away you just see gray, but if you go up close you can really describe what an elephant looks like.

I also have a question which arises from Dr. Campfield's comment about describing and subdividing the eating disorders further. We've subdivided them into anorexia nervosa, bulimia nervosa, and something indefinable in between. I just wonder if perhaps Professor Russell would like to comment about the advisability or the feasibility of further subdividing in the field.

DR. MORLEY: While you're preparing to respond, Professor Russell, I didn't mean a well-studied case, of which, I hope, I've published a few in the literature, is not useful. I think the problem is clinical anecdote, which is very different from the well-studied case. It involves a patient you saw in the ward, and you sort of vaguely remember, but you never did all the studies that were appropriate.

DR. G. F. M. RUSSELL (*The Institute of Psychiatry, London*): It's a difficult question. I think there may be a slight hidden catch in it, but to take it at face value I think it would be useful to become more specific, certainly for those syndromes where it is clear that there is much overlap and much uncertainty about intermediate conditions which makes replication very difficult and very problematical.

Let me give an example of that. In the American Psychiatric Association Classification of DSM III, the criteria that were put forward for the classification of bulimia did result in all sorts of energetic and interesting studies looking at the prevalence of behavior defined in that way. When DSM III R came along with greater refinement and showed that you should be more constricted and more refined in your classifications, then the results, for example, of prevalence of bulimic behavior as defined in the new way, became much closer among different nations. So that clarity of definition and circumscribing different syndromes has a lot of potential value in it.

On the other hand, if you look at an illness that has been well established for a long time and try and dissect out little fragments of its behavior, there is a danger that you might lose sight of the totality of it. So there is no easy answer. It will depend enormously on the question you are asking yourself and on the kind of answer that you want.

Impact of Nutrition on the Pharmacology of Appetite

Some Conceptual Issues

JOHN E. BLUNDELL

BioPsychology Group
Psychology Department
University of Leeds
Leeds, LS2 9JT, United Kingdom

BACKGROUND

A good deal of research involving pharmacological agents and appetite has been predicated on the idea that drugs will influence some general controller of food consumption. This state of affairs has arisen in part because the dominant central theories of appetite control postulated mechanisms for the quantitative adjustment in intake via a single critical zone or a key set of linked components. Consequently, much data has accumulated on the capacity of drugs to augment or inhibit food intake (mainly the latter). Although there has long been a tradition in feeding research that investigated qualitative features of ingestion, this approach has not been greatly favored by researchers. However, in the last decade there has been renewed interest in a number of related issues concerning qualitative aspects of food consumption. These include both the sensory and nutritional dimensions of food. Concerning nutrition, a number of enquiries have been made into the relationship between available nutrients and obesity, the possible separate regulation of carbohydrate and protein intake (and the possible lack of regulation of fat), and the effect of drugs and neurochemical manipulations on dietary or nutrient selection. All of these issues are relevant for research on the pharmacology of appetite, embracing both theoretical and practical matters. In theory, construction drugs can be used as tools to throw light on the mechanisms of nutrient regulation and on the mechanisms relating nutrient intake and body weight regulation. From a practical point of view, research could move toward developing drugs for the selective adjustments of nutrients in appetite or weight disorders. These developments represent some consequences of the recognition of the relevance of nutritional factors in appetite control and indicate some outcomes of the impact of nutrition on pharmacological research.

NUTRITION, APPETITE, AND OBESITY

A good deal of interest in the pharmacology of appetite is generated by the drive to develop drugs for the treatment of obesity. If there exists a coherent relationship between nutritional factors and fatness, then this has implications for the capacity of a drug to inhibit intake of the commodities provoking hyperphagia and weight gain. A number of animal models have been developed and these have been the subject of fairly recent reviews.[1-3] These reviews indicate that dietary manipulations in animals can promote the ingestion of excessive calories and lead to increases in body weight. If this intake of excess calories is regarded as an expression of appetite, then it is clear that nutritional manipulations alone can induce appetite and overconsumption. This enhanced appetite can be induced by carbohydrate (presented in the appropriate fashion), high-fat food, or by a variety of highly palatable foods presented simultaneously or sequentially. This latter technique may depend upon an elevated intake of fat or of fluid for the induction of weight gain. There is evidence that the nature of the appetite response and the resulting gain in adipose tissue differ among these three treatments (see Faust[4] for comment).

Concerning pharmacological approaches to appetite, these animal models of nutrition-induced weight gain have both theoretical and practical significance. Do drugs have different effects upon total intake and weight gain according to the nutritional regime employed? It is difficult to find truly comparative studies, but at least one serotoninergic drug — dexfenfluramine — suppresses energy intake and weight gain in all three animal models. When administered continually for five weeks during the dynamic or plateau phases of cafeteria-induced obesity, the drug reduced weight in both phases but was much more effective in the plateau stage.[5] In addition the drug is equally effective in the long term with both carbohydrate- and fat-supplemented weight-increasing diets[6] and is also effective against the weight gain induced by a highly palatable fat-containing, low-density diet.[7] Consequently, if d-fenfluramine is representative of serotoninergic anorectic agents, then this class of compounds appears to inhibit all of the major nutrition-induced weight gain syndromes. It has also been reported that at least one thermogenic drug (BRL 26830A) effectively reduces body weight in all types of nutrition-induced obesity.[8] Other compounds, such as those with specific metabolic activity on pancreatic lipase, for example,[9] would be expected to be more effective with high-fat, weight-increasing diets. Because quite different classes of drugs, such as dopamine (D2) antagonists, suppress feeding by blunting the response to sweet taste,[10] it becomes theoretically possible to design drugs that could be effective against specific types of nutrition-induced overconsumption. In view of these findings, it is no longer possible to consider automatically that drugs will be effective against "food in general." Foods with different nutritional profiles can exert different effects on appetite and body weight and may generate different responses to pharmacological treatments.

What is the significance of these studies on animals for the expression of appetite and its suppression by drugs in humans? Do humans display hyperphagia and weight gain in response to particular nutritional commodities? For carbohydrate it has been proposed that a certain class of individuals display a high demand for carbohydrate because of its ultimate action on brain neurotransmitter metabolism. These people have been referred to as "carbohydrate cravers."[11] For fat, no group of individuals has been identified specifically as "fat cravers," but it is of course well known that fat provides a very acceptable texture for foods that improves palatability. Owing to the high caloric density of fatty foods, it appears rather easy to consume a large number of calories for a minimal volume of food product. Moreover, it has been discovered[12] that in taste tests on cream varying in sugar (sweetness) and fat (greasiness) content, lean and obese people display different preferences. The obese sample preferred a high-fat, low-sugar combination. Consequently, although these obese individuals cannot be said to crave fat, they do express a liking for fatty foods and many therefore generally choose such foods in preference to foods with a different taste and texture profile. Their fatty preference may be said to constitute a deviant of appetite and would certainly predispose these persons to weight gain and the maintenance of overweight.

Interestingly, a number of studies have indicated that altering dietary fat intake can lead to a substantial loss of body weight. For example, the time–energy displacement approach to weight control[13] has demonstrated substantial weight loss on a low energy density diet compared to high energy density foods.[14] The major differences between the high and low energy density diets were fat and fiber content. Therefore, if the appetite for fat can be overcome (in this case by an obligatory dietary maneuver), then weight loss can occur. A similar investigation has tested the effects of three diets in which either 15–20%, 30–35%, or 45–50% of the energy was derived from fat.[15] Relating to their energy consumption on the medium-fat diet, subjects spontaneously consumed an 11.3% deficit on the low-fat diet and a 15.4% surfeit on the high-fat diet. In keeping with other studies,[16] these studies indicate that a high-fat diet tends to be a hyperphagic diet. In addition it appears that high-fat diets give rise to less intense satiety than high-carbohydrate diets of equal caloric value.[17] In other words, after eating a high-fat meal, subjects are left with a higher level of hunger than after lower energy-dense foods.

It follows that there may be specific groups of persons — of unknown numerical size — who are particularly vulnerable to the appetite-enhancing effect of carbohydrate or fat. Such persons would therefore presumably benefit from treatment with drugs with an action targeted on these nutrients. Consequently, nutritional aspects of the pharmacological treatment of human obesity are not trivial.

PHARMACOLOGY AND THE SATIETY CASCADE

One way to conceptualize the short-term relationship between pharmacological agents and nutritional factors is to consider the satiating efficiency of foods (e.g., Kissileff[18] and Blundell et al.[19]). This term refers to the power of foods to depress perceived hunger and to inhibit subsequent eating. Foods may vary greatly in their satiating power.[20] For example, protein appears to have a greater satiating capacity than carbohydrate (e.g., Hill & Blundell[21]), and, as noted above, fat may be less satiating than carbohydrate. Other nutritional factors, such as the presence of fiber[22] or sweetness,[23] influence the impact of food upon the time course or intensity of satiety.

Some of the major mediating processes that induce satiation or maintain satiety are set out in FIGURE 1. These mediated processes — sensory, cognitive, postingestive, and postabsorptive — are in turn expressed through particular physiological, metabolic, or neurochemical mechanisms. Consequently, foods varying in nutritional composition not only have differing satiating powers, but they recruit different biological events in the mediation of this power. Such events may include the activation of amino acid receptors in the gastrointestinal tract[24]; the induction of cephalic phase responses[25]; the release or prolonged activation of gut hormones, such as cholecystokinin[26] or insulin[27]; alteration of plasma amino acid profiles[28]; adjustment of oxidative metabolism in the liver[29]; and the modulation of brain aminergic[30] or peptidergic[31] neurotransmitters. Because pharmacological agents also exert particular effects upon these biological events, there exists a clear physiological basis for the interaction between the effects of particular nutrients and the action of drugs. The ultimate effect of this interaction would be to modify satiating efficiency.

This proposition has certain implications for the treatment of obesity by using drugs that suppress appetite. First, it is worth noting that the reduction by a drug in food consumed will actually decrease the commodity (food) that confers satiating power. This would naturally make it more difficult for the drug to continue to exert an effect. This, of course, is not at all different from the situation encountered in dieting or any other strategy that seeks to reduce caloric intake; the ultimate effect is to reduce the material that produces satiety and serves to inhibit intake. Recognition of this suggests

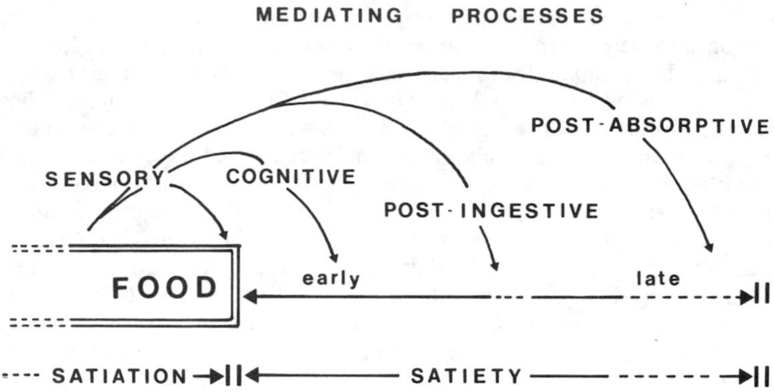

MEDIATING　PROCESSES

FIGURE 1. Conceptualization of the satiety cascade indicating the likely contributions of sensory, cognitive, postingestive, and postabsorptive processes to the intensity and time course of satiety.

a slightly different way of approaching the control of appetite by drugs. Instead of searching for compounds that inhibit food intake, an alternative strategy would be to consider compounds that intensify the satiating power of foods. In other words, drugs would not work to directly block intake but would work synergistically or additively with food itself to create an enhanced satiating efficiency. Obviously the ultimate goal would be identical in both cases—a reduction in caloric consumption—but the means of achieving this end should lead to different lines of investigation and different tactics for screening potential antiobesity agents. The mechanisms that underlie the satiety cascade (FIG. 1) provide a common basis for understanding the effects of nutrients and drugs upon food intake and further serve to bring together the fields of nutrition and pharmacology in appetite research.

PSYCHOPHARMACOLOGY AND FOOD SELECTION

One further area of research in which nutritional concerns have an impact on pharmacology involves the effect of drug or neurochemical treatments upon the selection of foods. Theoretically, animals or humans could change the pattern of food choice without any alteration in the consumption of calories, but in practice some adjustment of energy intake is likely to be observed. This field of study is little more than a decade old and was initially primed by proposals that the neurotransmitter serotonin was implicated in the long-term control of protein intake[32] or in short-term protein sparing[33] or carbohydrate suppression.[34] These propositions prompted a number of investigations in which the effects of various drugs upon the intake of fat, protein, or carbohydrate have been examined. Compounds including serotoninergic agents, such as fenfluramine and fluoxetine, opiate antagonists (naloxone and naltrexone), and noradrenergic compounds, have all exhibited varying degrees of selectivity when administered to animals allowed to choose between two or more dietary commodities. Reviews have drawn attention to methodological problems in food selection studies and to the dependence of the drug's action upon experimental circumstances (e.g., Blundell[35]). Consistent patterns of nutrient selection can apparently be achieved by using nondeprived animals tested under strictly controlled photoperiods. It seems that a strong preference for carbohydrate is shown during the early part of the dark phase of the cycle and that this can be enhanced by noradrenergic stimulation of the paraventricular nucleus or inhibited by serotoninergic activation.[36] At other times during the light–dark cycle, carbohydrate consumption may be relatively insensitive to drug administration.

Nutrient-selection research has therefore revealed a further important interaction, namely, between drugs, nutrients, and biological rhythms. In the case cited above the interaction is exemplified by noradrenergic/serotoninergic compounds, carbohydrate–protein intake, and the circadian rhythm entrained by the light–dark zeitgeber. Recognition of these interrelated influences may help us to understand the numerous negative or ambiguous results that have arisen in studies on the effects of drugs upon food selection (e.g., Blundell[35]).

In human studies much interest in this issue has been generated by the claim that antidepressant drugs could both promote weight gain and cause carbohydrate craving.[37] Antidepressant drugs clearly do lead to an increase in body weight in treated patients,[38] but the effect certainly depends upon the neurochemical profile of the drug. Whereas broad-spectrum uptake blockers often cause weight gain, antidepressant drugs with a more specific blockade of serotonin uptake appear to have the opposite effect. There is some debate about whether the effects on appetite are due to the nutrient composition of foods or to some other characteristic of the food, such as the interaction between taste profile and nutrient content. In any case it is clear that in this domain a casual approach to nutrition will not be helpful. In order to elucidate the relationship between psychotropic medication and dietary intake, a disciplined approach to nutrition is essential. This is an area of research in which nutritionists can play an important role in collaboration with pharmacologists. Interestingly, because there is also evidence that food selection is influenced by the menstrual cycle,[39] human research must also take account of a three-cornered relationship between nutrition, pharmacology, and biological rhythms.

OVERVIEW

This essay has drawn attention to domains of research in which nutritional issues influence the outcome of studies of drugs or other neurochemical manipulations upon appetite, food intake, or body weight changes. In many investigations in which outcomes are expressed in terms of the weight of food consumed or energy values, increased understanding could be generated by an explicit statement about the nutritional composition of the test food. A different outcome may have been obtained with an alternative test diet, and this could have implications for the interpretation of the experimental result. The various issues noted above suggest the need for expert nutritional control in studies of appetite, particularly those involving pharmacological manipulations. These issues are of theoretical and practical significance and are equally important in animal and human research. The full impact of nutrition upon the pharmacology of appetite research has not yet been felt. The interrelationships are likely to become more fully appreciated during the last decade of this century.

REFERENCES

1. KANAREK, R. B. & E. HIRSCH. 1977. Dietary-induced overeating in experimental animals. Fed. Proc. **36:** 154–158.
2. SCLAFANI, A. 1984. Animal models of obesity: Classification and Characterisation. Int. J. Obesity **8:** 491–508.

3. BLUNDELL, J. E. 1987. Nutritional manipulations for altering food intake: Towards a causal model of experimental obesity. Ann. N.Y. Acad. Sci. **499:** 144–155.
4. FAUST, I. M. 1980. Nutrition and the fat cell. Int. J. Obesity **4:** 314–321.
5. BLUNDELL, J. E., A. J. HILL & T. C. KIRKHAM. 1987. Dextrofenfluramine and eating behaviour in animals: Action on food selection, motivation and body weight. *In* Human Body Weight. A. Bender & L. J. Brookes, Eds.: 233–239. Pitman Publishing. London.
6. BLUNDELL, J. E. & A. J. HILL. 1989. Do serotoninergic drugs decrease energy intake by reducing fat or carbohydrate intake? Effect of *d*-fenfluramine with supplemented weight-increasing diets. Pharmacol. Biochem. Behav. **31:** 773–778.
7. McCORMACK, J. G., J. G. DEAN, G. J. JENNINGS & J. E. BLUNDELL. 1989. Chronic effects of low doses of *d*-fenfluramine on weight gain and calorie intake, brain neurotransmitter content, and brown adipose tissue thermogenic parameters in rats fed chow or palatable diets. Int. J. Obesity, in press.
8. ARCH, J. R. S. 1989. Thermogenic drugs and weight loss. Meeting of the Society for Drug Research. School of Pharmacy, London.
9. SULLIVAN, A. C., S. HOGAN & J. TRISCARI. 1987. New developments in pharmacological treatments for obesity. Ann. N.Y. Acad. Sci. **499:** 269–276.
10. SCHNEIDER, L. H., J. GIBBS & G. P. SMITH. 1986. D-2 selective receptor antagonists suppress sucrose sham feeding in the rat. Brain Res. Bull. **17:** 605–611.
11. WURTMAN, R. J. 1987. Dietary treatments that affect brain neurotransmitters. Effects on calorie and nutrient intake. Ann. N.Y. Acad. Sci. **499:** 179–190.
12. DREWNOWSKI, A. & M. R. C. GREENWOOD. 1983. Cream and sugar: Human preferences for high-fat foods. Physiol. Behav. **30:** 629–633.
13. WEINSIER, R. L., M. H. JOHNSTON, D. M. DOLEYS & J. A. BACON. 1982. Dietary management of obesity: Evaluation of the time–energy displacement diet in terms of its efficacy and nutritional adequacy for long-term weight control. Br. J. Nutr. **47:** 367–379.
14. DUNCAN, K. H., J. A. BACON & R. L. WEINSIER. 1983. The effect of high and low energy density diets on satiety, energy intake, and eating time of obese and nonobese subjects. Ann. J. Clin. Nutr. **37:** 763–767.
15. LISSNER, L., D. A. LEVITSKY, B. J. STRUPP, H. KACKWARF & D. A. ROE. 1987. Dietary fat and the regulation of energy intake in human subjects. Am. J. Clin. Nutr. **46:** 886–892.
16. TREMBLAY, A., G. PLOURDE, J-P. DESPRES & C. BOUCHARD. 1989. Impact of dietary fat content and fat oxidation on energy intake in humans. Am. J. Clin. Nutr. In press.
17. VAN AMELSVOORT, J. M. M., P. VAN STRATUM, J. H. KRAALE, R. N. LUSSENBURG & U. M. T. HOUTSMULLER. 1989. Effects of varying the carbohydrate : fat ratio in a hot lunch on postprandial variables in male volunteers. Br. J. Nutr. **61:** 267–283.
18. KISSILEFF, H. R. 1984. Satiating efficiency and a strategy for conducting food loading experiments. Neurosci. & Biobehav. Rev. **8:** 129–135.
19. BLUNDELL, J. E., P. J. ROGERS & A. J. HILL. 1988. Hunger and the satiety cascade – their importance for food acceptance in the late 20th century. *In* Food Acceptability. D. M. H. Thompson, Ed.: 233–250. Elsevier. Amsterdam.
20. BLUNDELL, J. E., P. J. ROGERS & A. J. HILL. 1987. Evaluating the satiating power of foods: Implications for acceptance and consumption. *In* Chemical Composition and Sensory Properties of Food and Their Influence on Nutrition. J. Solms, Ed.: 205–219. Academic Press. London.
21. HILL, A. J. & J. E. BLUNDELL. 1986. Macronutrients and satiety: The effects of a high protein or a high carbohydrate meal on subjective motivation to eat and food preference. Nutr. Behav. **3:** 133–144.
22. BLUNDELL, J. E. & V. J. BURLEY. 1987. Satiation, satiety and the action of fibre on food intake. Int. J. Obesity. **11(Suppl. 1):** 9–25.
23. BLUNDELL, J. E., P. J. ROGERS & A. J. HILL. 1988. Uncoupling sweetness and calories: Methodological aspects of laboratory studies on appetite control. Appetite **11:** 54–61.
24. MEI, N. 1985. Intestinal Chemosensitivity. Physiol. Rev. **65:** 211–237.
25. POWLEY, T. L. & H-R. BERTHOLD. 1985. Diet and cephalic phase insulin responses. Am. J. Clin. Nutr. **42:** 991–1002.
26. SMITH, G. P. & J. GIBBS. 1976. Cholecystokinin and satiety: Theoretic and therapeutic implications. *In* Hunger: Basic Mechanisms and Clinical Implications. D. Novin, W. Wyr-

wicka & G. Bray, Eds.: 249–355. Raven Press. New York.

27. STEFFENS, A. B., J. VAN DER GUGTEN, J. GODEKE, P. G. M. LUIPEN & J. H. STRUBBE. 1986. Meal-induced increases in parasympathetic and sympathetic activity elicit simultaneous rises in plasma insulin and free-fatty acids. Physiol. Behav. **37:** 119–122.

28. FERNSTROM, J. D. & R. J. WURTMAN. 1973. Control of brain 5-HT content by dietary carbohydrates. *In* Serotonin and Behaviour. J. Barchas & E. Usdin, Eds.: 121–128. Academic Press. New York.

29. FRIEDMAN, M. I., M. G. TORDOFF & I. RAMIREZ. 1986. Integrated metabolic control of food intake. Brain Res. Bull. **17:** 855–859.

30. HOEBEL, B. G. & S. F. LEIBOWITZ. 1981. Brain monoamines in the modulation of self-stimulation, feeding and body weight. *In* Brain, Behaviour & Bodily Disease. H. A. Weiner, M. A. Hofer & A. J. Stunkard, Eds.: 103–142. Raven Press. New York.

31. MORLEY, J. E. & A. A. LEVINE. 1985. The pharmacology of eating behaviour. Ann. Rev. Pharmacol. Toxicol. **25:** 127–146.

32. ANDERSON, G. H. 1977. Regulation of protein intake by plasma amino acids. Adv. Nutr. Res. **1:** 145–166.

33. WURTMAN, J. J. & R. J. WURTMAN. 1977. Fenfluramine and fluoxetine spare protein consumption while suppressing caloric intake by rats. Science **198:** 1178–1180.

34. WURTMAN, J. J. & R. J. WURTMAN. 1979. Drugs that enhance central serotoninergic transmission diminish elective carbohydrate consumption by rats. Life Sci. **24:** 895–904.

35. BLUNDELL, J. E. 1983. Problems and processes underlying the control of food selection and nutrient intake. *In* Nutrition and the Brain. R. J. Wurtman & J. J. Wurtman, Eds. Vol. **6:** 163–222. Raven Press. New York.

36. LEIBOWITZ, S. F. & G. SHOR-POSNER. 1986. Brain serotonin and eating behaviour. Appetite **7:** 1–14.

37. PAYKEL, E. S., P. S. MUELLER, P. S. & P. M. DE LA VERGNE. 1973. Amitriptyline, weight gains and carbohydrate craving: A side effect. Br. J. Psychiatry **123:** 501–507.

38. STEIN, E. M., S. STEIN & M. W. LINN. 1985. Geriatric sweet tooth—a problem with tricyclics. J. Am. Gerontol. Soc. **33:** 687–692.

39. BANCROFT, J., A. COOK & L. WILLIAMSON. 1988. Food craving, mood and the menstrual cycle. Psychol. Med. **18:** 855–860.

DISCUSSION

DR. HARRY KISSELEFF (*St. Luke's-Roosevelt Hospital, New York, NY*): John, I want to ask you about how you deal with the problem of statistical analysis when you have a system where you've got literally thousands of variables collected from the subject. It would seem to me that in order to really insure that you're not just getting random effects you would have to have tens of thousands of experimental subjects to do this work on.

DR. JOHN E. BLUNDELL (*University of Leeds, Leeds, U.K.*): We try to keep the experimental system sufficiently simple that the animals or the humans are not faced with unsolvable problems, and we keep the data output under control so that we are able to manage that. Also, we use conventional statistics.

DR. L. ARTHUR CAMPFIELD (*Hoffmann-LaRoche, Nutley, NY*): I enjoyed the presentation very much, I have a lot of sympathy with this sort of approach. I have, however, a comment and then a question.

I think your statement that drug effects and neurotransmitter effects are conditioned by lots of other external factors is quite correct. I would just like to point out the fact that changes in peripheral metabolic signals have been shown, by the work of Liebowitz and others, to strongly condition the response of the neurotransmitters in brain areas. So I think not only are changes in the external world going to affect the way drugs may act, but reliable changes in the internal world may also produce an effect.

Your dissection of the analysis of drug effects in rats has been very powerful and I think helped a lot of us understand experimental approaches to undertake. My question is, In your experience has this work been directly translatable to human studies, or do we have to do a lot of different pioneering work in humans?

DR. BLUNDELL: Well I certainly still believe in the ideology that if you have a structure of behavior and a structure of subjective experiences then you have a powerful tool for examining what the underlying processes are, and if the parameter that you're dealing with is very simple and crude, then you have a less sensitive device. So it seems to me that although one doesn't want to say human feeding is the same as rat feeding, that would be absurd, the same philosophy can apply with certain provisions.

DR. ANTHONY SCLAFANI (*Brooklyn College, Brooklyn, NY*): John, I have one question concerning structure and the microstructural approach. I think you've done a great service in pointing out the details involved, but I still think that in just looking at the microstructure we may, perhaps, miss something important. For example, when we looked at a very gross example of a change in behavior such as the overeating seen in the hyperphagic rat, the DMH dorsomedial hypothalamic lesioned rat, it was discovered that these rats took very large meals. This finding led to a lot of satiety hypotheses. However, if you intervene, prevent the animal from taking his large meals, they still overeat but now they shift to taking multiple meals. So the change in structure doesn't necessarily directly tell you what the underlying mechanism might be.

DR. BLUNDELL: I agree in the sense that the topographical expression of behavior is, in my view, in animals and humans an attempt to resolve problems posed by change in the internal environment and in the external environment, and it reflects both. If you intervene in one or the other, the animal will show adaptive behavior, and as you just pointed out if you prevent the animal from displaying behavior which it presumably deems to be appropriate, it will adopt another strategy. So it's clear that looking at the structure of behavior doesn't give invariant information about underlying processes. It simply reflects the animal's capacity to manage the problems that we impose upon it.

One other thing to mention is that the structure of behavior is certainly not dissociated from metabolism. When we impose physiological or environmental demands upon animals, give them problems to solve, they can solve them behaviorally or metabolically, and it seems to me that they do both simultaneously. The work that is now beginning to emerge on neurotransmitters shows that neurotransmitters which are involved in the expression of feeding are equally involved in metabolism.

Microdialysis Studies of Brain Norepinephrine, Serotonin, and Dopamine Release During Ingestive Behavior

Theoretical and Clinical Implications[a]

B. G. HOEBEL, L. HERNANDEZ, D. H. SCHWARTZ, G. P. MARK, AND G. A. HUNTER

Department of Psychology
Princeton University
Princeton, New Jersey 08544-1010

INTRODUCTION: MONOAMINES AND FEEDING

To help understand the neurochemical basis of behavior reinforcement, we have perfected the technique of *in vivo* microdialysis for studying brain functions in behaving animals. Monoamines and their main metabolites were sampled in the extracellular space of the hypothalamus or nucleus accumbens in rats given food, water, salt, anorectic drugs, conditioned taste aversion, or addictive psychomotor stimulants. This has contributed to the view that in the paraventricular nucleus (PVN) norepinephrine facilitates feeding and serotonin inhibits it; in the perifornical lateral hypothalamus (PFH), the monoamines contribute to inhibition of feeding; and in the nucleus accumbens (NAC), dopamine facilitates positive reinforcement. Microdialysis results are summarized in the last paragraph. To put the new results in the context of eating disorders, we begin with a review of earlier monoamine depletion and injection studies.

Monoamine Depletion Studies

When pathways for dopamine (DA), norepinephrine (NE), and serotonin (5-HT) were discovered by histofluoresence techniques, researchers noted that the ascending paths coursed through the hypothalamic regions involved in feeding. Ungerstedt[99] suggested that lateral hypothalamic (LH) lesions that cause aphagia and weight loss can damage the ascending DA paths. It was demonstrated that 6-hydroxydopamine (6-OHDA) lesions that depleted DA pathways were enough to cause sensory neglect, akinesia, and aphagia,[96,98,99] but this did not rule out a role for LH cells in feeding,

[a] The microdialysis studies of food and salt were supported by Campbell Soup Company and the New Jersey Commission on Science and Technology. Drug abuse research was supported by the United States Public Health Service Grant DA-03597. Fenfluramine and self-stimulation research was supported by Servier Amerique and MH-08493. Tryptophan research was supported by Weight Watchers, Inc.

especially if they acted indirectly by way of a DA system.[39–42] It has since been shown that there are important differences between the mesoaccumbens and mesocortical pathways[13,99] that will influence future research on feeding reward.

We found that midbrain 6-OHDA lesions that spared DA cells, but damaged ascending *ventral* norepinephrine and epinephrine fibers, caused hyperphagia and weight gain. Animals with this type of obesity were depleted of NE in many regions including the LH and were refractory to amphetamine anorexia.[1,2] It was concluded that the ventral noradrenergic bundle (VNAB) normally contributes to the inhibition of food intake and the regulation of body weight. This was confirmed when it was found that hyperphagia and obesity were prevented by uptake blockers that protected NE from the destructive action of 6-OHDA.[32] Hyperphagia after 6-OHDA was also confirmed by Leibowitz and Brown,[55] who suggested that feeding was inhibited not only by the ventral noradrenergic bundle but also by a subset of dopamine neurons that were also necessary for amphetamine anorexia in the LH. Part of the ventral bundle projects to the PVN where it influences the neuroendocrine system,[97] but the role of that NE branch in feeding behavior is not known. Noradrenergic input in the *dorsal* bundle, on the other hand, projects to the medial and paraventricular hypothalamic regions to induce feeding, and depletion of the dorsal NE bundle can lower body weight.[53,57]

The effects of overall serotonin depletion have become clear. We reported hyperphagia and weight gain with intraventricular parachlorophenylalanine methylester (PCPA) that has as one of its effects the temporary inhibition of serotonin synthesis.[11] Serotonin depletion with 5,7-DHT also caused weight gain under certain conditions,[84,103] but lesions of raphe serotonin cell regions did not cause obesity.[18] Recently 8-hydroxy-DPAT has provided a selective means to turn off serotonin cells by activating inhibitory autoreceptors on serotonin cell bodies. This drug causes hyperphagia and obesity as an unambiguous correlate of diminished serotonin output.[21] The above findings are summarized in TABLE 1, column C.

Monoamine Injection Studies and Microdialysis Rationale

The traditional way to determine the behavioral effect of local changes in monoamine release is to inject monoamines and their releasers or receptor agonists and antagonists directly into the terminal region in a freely moving animal to cause observable changes in behavior with a local change in transmitter balance.

TABLE 1, column D, shows some results of direct monoamine injections and summarizes some of the effects of monoamines on feeding as we presently understand them. This information also provides the rationale for the present microdialysis experiments (column E). As shown in line 1, the dorsal noradrenergic bundle is a substrate necessary for some of the effects that can be obtained by injecting exogenous NE in the paraventricular nucleus (PVN) and medial hypothalamic (MH) regions.[57] NE or one of its cotransmitters injected in the PVN-MH is sufficient to induce feeding[54,57]; therefore microdialysis was used to measure the circadian rhythm of PVN extracellular NE.[94] Line 2 indicates that the VNAB is necessary for some aspect of adrenergic inhibition of feeding,[2,32] which can be studied by injecting NE or epinephrine (EPI) in the LH.[57] NE or amphetamine injected in the LH inhibited feeding, so we used microdialysis to see if LH amphetamine (AMPH) releases NE and other monoamines there. Line 3 presents evidence that serotonin facilitates satiety in the PVN-MH. Serotonin inhibits NE-induced feeding,[58,106] thereby disinhibiting the classic MH satiety system.[43] Microdialysis evidence will be presented showing that a meal releases 5-HT in the MH. In line 4 we suggest that serotonin in the LH also inhibits feeding

TABLE 1. Monoamines in Feeding and Arousal

A Cell Body Region	B Pathway	C Result of Suppressing the Pathway	D Result of Microinjections at Terminal	E Results of Microdialysis and Infusion
1. A7 (NE) and A6 (NE, locus coeruleus)	Dorsal NE bundle	6-OH-DA hypophagia & weight loss	PVN-MH NE feeding, i.e., inhibit satiety, induce carbohydrate intake	PVN NE release in early dark
2. A1 (NE), C1 (EP1)	Ventral NE bundle	6-OH-DA hyperphagia & weight gain, hyper self-stimulation	LH NE or EPI satiety, inhibit feeding	AMPH releases LH NE
3. Raphe (5-HT)	Ascending 5-HT paths	PCPA, 5,7-DHT 8-OH-DPAT hyperphagia	PVN-MH 5HT inhibits NE feeding and carbohydrate intake. LH 5HT inhibits feeding reward	Feeding & FEN releases PVN-MH and LH 5HT, AMPH releases LH 5HT
4. A8 (DA)	Ascending DA	6-OH-DA hyperphagia	LH DA inhibits feeding & drinking	AMPH releases LH DA
5. A9 Sub.Nigra (DA)	Nigrostriatal DA	6-OH-DA aphagia & weight loss	STR DA facilitates stereotyped response arousal, activation	LH Self-stimulation releases STR DA
6. A10, VTA (DA)	Mesolimbic DA: Mesoaccumbens path	6-OH-DA aphagia & weight loss	NAC DA facilitates locomotion, feeding drinking, and operant behavior, self-administration	Feeding, drinking, salt & self-stimulation release NAC DA
7. A10, VTA (DA)	Mesocortical DA	6-OH-DA aphagia & weight loss		Feeding releases PFC DA

reward.[87,90] We tested the hypothesis that anorectic drugs or a meal would increase extracellular 5-HT in the LH. Line 5 refers to a DA system arising in A8 that projects, in part, to the LH and could be one source of the DA that inhibits feeding[55] and drinking[77] by activating D_2-type receptors.[3,77] For this article it is important to remember that dopaminergic activation of the LH inhibits feeding, because the effects of DA are very different in the striatum (STR), nucleus accumbens (NAC), and prefrontal cortex (PFC). For example, DA receptor blockers can induce feeding by an action in the LH,[77] but they can also block feeding by actions in other DA terminal regions.[16,92,110,112]

As summarized in line 7 of TABLE 1, it has been found that certain neurotransmitters that activate the mesolimbic cell bodies in the ventral tegmental area (VTA, A10) or otherwise increase DA release in the NAC can have at least three effects: locomotion, feeding, and behavior reinforcement.[9,40,110] Injection of low doses of opiates in the VTA stimulate DA cells and thereby induce locomotion, feeding,[5,9,14,48] and the reward of local self-injection[8,9] and conditioned place preference.[24,26,41] Similarly, VTA iontophoresis of the peptide neurotensin activated DA cells in anesthetized rats, and when applied through a cannula in awake rats caused locomotion[48,72] and supported local self-injection.[27] Theoretically neurotensin would also induce feeding in the VTA, but this has not been tested. Cholecystokinin (CCK) also stimulates some DA cells, which would predict locomotion and self-injection; but CCK can also potentiate DA inhibition[12]; and high doses cause excess depolarization, known as depolarization inactivation, which renders the cells unresponsive.[13] In the NAC, dopaminergic agonists such as amphetamine facilitate locomotion,[19] self-stimulation,[16,112] and feeding[112] and will reinforce local self-injection.[44] DA itself is a reinforcer there.[28]

A Dopamine and Serotonin Hypothesis

We used microdialysis to determine which monoamines were released in the NAC by amphetamine and other psychomotor stimulants, then tested self-stimulation, feeding, drinking, and salt intake. DA was released by all of these stimuli. With present microdialysis techniques, we are having difficulties distinguishing between DA as a general system for psychomotor activation and reward versus a fine-tuned set of specific subsystems for behaviors such as feeding, drinking, and salt intake. An exciting recent result shows that DA in the NAC is decreased by conditioned taste aversion, as described further on. Therefore we currently hypothesize that the function of DA is to facilitate or reinforce synapses that are active at the site of DA release during approach behavior to positive, not negative, primary and secondary reinforcing stimuli. In the NAC these synapses may involve circuits that reinforce self-administration. In other forebrain regions DA may facilitate or reinforce other functions, such as multimodal stimulus combinations (amygdala), place memory (hippocampus), and learning criteria (prefrontal cortex), all of which are involved in feeding.[41,42] Depletion of extracellular serotonin by 8-OH-DPAT prevented the expression of a conditioned taste aversion[46] as well as diminishing normal satiety such that rats became obese.[21] We will also present an experiment in which serotonin was released before rats started their meal. These findings suggest to us that serotonin is necessary for some aspect of the negative reinforcing properties in conditioned cessation of feeding. Thus our working hypothesis is that serotonin somewhere in the brain, including the hypothalamus, inhibits positive reinforcement, at least for food stimuli and responses.[42]

Monoamines and Anorexia

To the extent that monoamines might be a factor in some types of anorexia, we can follow down TABLE 1 and hypothesize that a *loss* of appetite could result from any of the following: (1) anorexia from diminished NE in the PVN,[51] (2) excess NE in the LH,[39] (3) excesses of 5-HT functions in the PVN,[43,53] or excess 5-HT in the LH,[107] (4) excess DA in the LH,[53] or (5,6,7) anorexia from a lack of monoaminergic reinforcement of feeding in the accumbens and related telencephalic sites.[33,110] We would expect CCK and neurotensin could also be involved as cotransmitters with DA,[72,104] and NPY and galanin could be involved as cotransmitters with norepinephrine and serotonin.[54]

The reinforcement circuits may involve many other transmitters. For example, opioid peptides in NAC interneurons are thought to be involved.[9,49,111] The primary sensory input to the accumbens arrives over neurons that release glutamate as an excitatory neurotransmitter. The primary NAC outputs are GABA neurons containing substance P and neurotensin as peptide cotransmitters. Thus, it is impossible to say that the monoamines that modulate reinforcement circuits are the single cause of any feeding disorder.

On the other hand, it is well known that monoamines play a central role in several movement disorders. For example, a dopamine deficit is the single most important neural element of Parkinson's disease, and dopaminergic excess is probably involved in psychosis.[82] If an augmented source of dopamine can cure Parkinson's disease, and dopaminergic reduction can treat psychosis, why not feeding disorders? Most people with anorexia are hyperkinetic, which is suggestive of elevated dopaminergic function in the accumbens, which, if anything, should facilitate eating if it ever got started, but elevated dopaminergic function in the LH would tend to inhibit eating. Indeed, hyperkinesis and anorexia happen to fit the model of excess DA function in the NAC and LH, respectively. In this hypothetical example, one way to help an anorectic person eat would be to reduce DA function in the LH selectively, but there is no known way to do that because both NAC and LH functions involve the D_2-type-receptor.[19,77,92] A reduction in serotonergic satiety would also make sense for appropriate anorectic patients if it could be achieved.

Monoamines and Obesity

It has been said many times that there are several kinds of obesity.[39] Obesity is not a simple, single syndrome; therefore it may require different treatments in different cases, a treatment to fit the cause. But what if there is a common element in many forms of obesity? Then it would be possible to treat that common element, if not the particular cause. TABLE 1 reminds us that excess appetite and obesity can be induced in the following ways: (1) PVN or MH lesions[10,43,91] or excess NE or copeptide,[57] (2) depletion of NE and epinephrine in the LH,[1,2,32] (3) loss of 5-HT input to the hypothalamus by a neurotoxic action in the MH[103] of females or by turning off the serotonin cell bodies with an agonist for their inhibitory autoreceptors,[21] or abnormality of 5-HT function in the LH,[87,107] (4) depletion of DA in the LH by destruction of A8 DA cell bodies without too much damage to A9 or A10,[55] chronic D_2 blockade with a neuroleptic,[77] abnormally low DA function in the LH for any reason, or (5,6,7) addiction to DA release in the STR, NAC, and PFC achieved through eating.[34,110] Given this plethora of findings, it would be helpful to find a common feature of these animal models of obesity that might help us understand the role of monoamines in hyperphagia.

Hypothalamic Reinforcement System: Is It a Neural Basis
for Feeding Disorders?

Our studies have shown that three forms of hyperphagia mentioned above involve an increase in self-stimulation: MH hyperphagia, VNAB hyperphagia, and taste-induced appetite all can increase LH self-stimulation rate.[35,39,41] Increased food intake resulting from deprivation is another instance in which some studies find a correlation between the increased tendency to eat and to self-stimulate.[32]

We hypothesize that an alteration in the LH feeding–reinforcement system is a common element of underfeeding, overfeeding, and feeding disorders that place the animal at variance with a stable body weight. This change in the LH reinforcement system helps alter the animal's voluntary food intake in a manner which brings body weight to a stable level. Note that LH self-stimulation increased in four situations that make rats gain weight. Two could be described as "organic disorders": MH lesions and VNAB norepinephrine depletion. The other two are responses to "environmental disorders": constant sucrose availability and food scarcity. All four can increase feeding and self-stimulation.

In rats that weigh less than their preferred weight plateau, there is an increase in feeding on standard chow and self-stimulation. In rats at a normal bodyweight, LH self-stimulation is analogous to eating without calories and thus resembles bulimia with regurgitation in humans, or sham eating through a gastric fistula, or intake of saccharin or aspartame; these are all cases of working for food rewards without nutrition. Thus, self-stimulation is an animal model of bulimia. If the animal cannot avoid the calories, then self-stimulation-induced eating, bulimia, or palatable foods can lead to increased body weight. In sum, certain physiological-brain disorders that cause obesity increase hypothalamic reward until the animal gets fat. Similarly, certain "environmental disorders" also cause hypothalamic reward to increase with the result that the animal gains weight. LH reinforcement is pushed by good food and pulled by physiological correlates of body weight.

By studying the neural effects of LH self-stimulation, it may be possible to find the neural circuits and neurotransmitters that provide the reinforcement of feeding behavior. Then it will be possible to manipulate those circuits and transmitters through organic or environmental means to enhance pleasure without sacrificing health and longevity. So far we have found that LH self-stimulation was selectively inhibited by anorectic doses of food, glucose, hypertonic saline, insulin, phenylpropanolamine, and *d*-fenfluramine. Nonspecific behavioral stimulants, such as amphetamine, and depressants, such as *d,l*-fenfluramine, did not have selective effects on self-stimulation when compared to another operant behavior, stimulation-escape.[38]

HYPOTHALAMIC MICRODIALYSIS EXPERIMENTS

In this new series of experiments, instead of injecting neurotransmitters into a region of nerve terminals to cause changes in behavior, we sample from the terminal region and assay it for monoamines to correlate release with ongoing behavior.[71,108] The combination of these two techniques, local injection and local sampling, provide a powerful scientific tool for determining cause, effect, timing, and context in neurochemical mediation of behavior.

For behavioral experiments with microdialysis, we adapted the removable cannula techniques of the physiological psychologist to the *in vivo* sampling technique of Delgado,[29] Ungerstedt,[100] and Hernandez.[36] Guide shafts were implanted in the brain so a microdialysis probe could be inserted at later times after recovery from anesthesia.[37] Dialysis probes were constructed of 36-ga tubing inside of 26-ga hypodermic needle tubing. The outer tube was fitted to a 0.2-mm diameter semipermeable cellulose tube that was 2, 3, or 4 mm long and occluded with epoxy at the tip. Ringer's solution was pumped through PE 20 polyethylene tubing and a swivel joint leading to the probe inlet. The Ringer's circulated inside the probe tip, then up and out through PE 10 tubing to a 400 µl vial clipped to the rat's headpiece. The probe was inserted into the guideshaft where it was taped or cemented in place and left to equilibrate with the extracellular fluid for 2–12 hrs while the rat moved without restriction in a standard Skinner box. Perfusates were collected in 20–30-min samples and assayed for monoamines by high-pressure liquid chromatography with electrochemical detection (HPLC-EC) as described in the referenced articles below.

Circadian Norepinephrine Release in the Paraventricular Nucleus Correlates with Feeding Time If Food Is Available

It is well documented that NE induces feeding in the PVN and push–pull studies have already shown there are measurable changes in hypothalamic NE release associated with food intake.[56] Therefore our first microdialysis test in the hypothalamus was a collaboration between the Hoebel and Leibowitz laboratories to measure NE with Luis Hernandez from Venezuela providing the microdialysis expertise and the experiments performed by Glenn Stanley and David Schwartz. The goal was to find out when NE was released naturally.

Male rats were accustomed to a microdialysis cage and a 12 : 12 light/dark circadian cycle with Purina pellets *ad libitum*. Extracellular levels of NE in a 20-mm sample were taken every 2 hours using a 2-mm-tip probe in the PVN. Results showed that NE varied in a similar manner on two successive days ($n = 11$; $r = +0.67$). Analyses of variance (ANOVA) showed a main effect for the time of day. NE increased during the first hour after onset of the dark cycle.[94] Food deprivation on the third day led to an irregular, gradual increase in extracellular NE. This gradual increase reversed the decreasing trend caused by gliosis that accumulates around a probe. Refeeding after the 24-hour deprivation diminished NE for a few hours. Histology showed the probes' tips passed through the PVN in most rats.

This study showed that microdialysis can be used to monitor a neurochemical in the extracellular fluid around the clock for three days. It revealed both a transient NE increase that occurred during the hour after lights went off during *ad libitum* feeding the first two days and a gradual increase caused by food deprivation during the third day. The increase in NE in the early dark correlates with the burst of feeding that rats exhibit at that time. This is also the time when the PVN is most sensitive for NE-induced feeding, most sensitive to α-2-adrenergic receptor binding, and when circulating corticosterone levels needed for NE-induced feeding are highest.[54,57] Thus microdialysis suggests that a surge of NE is released into the PVN just when the region is most sensitive to NE. This is when the animals have the strongest tendency to eat. The day of deprivation when NE levels increased only gradually suggests that the surge depends to some degree on feedback from food. Without food the surge was not detected, but instead NE rose gradually and sporadically, then decreased after a big meal. Apparently food may be needed to trigger maximal release, and ingestion may be needed to turn off release. Clearly there are several cause-and-effect relations to be established that are only hinted at by this correlative study. In summary, this study suggests that NE in the PVN correlates with feeding time during the beginning of the animal's active cycle and may also increase gradually during food deprivation.

Extracellular 5-Hydroxyindoleacetic Acid in the Paraventricular Nucleus Increases During Feeding

Extracellular serotonin in the circadian paradigm was not measured, but its metabolite, 5-hydroxyindoleacetic acid (5-HIAA), which reflects intracellular metabolism of serotonin varied as follows: Each day for two days 5-HIAA increased at lights out when the animals were eating, then failed to increase during the day of food deprivation and surged during refeeding. This pattern is consistent with a role for serotonin turnover in the satiety processes that occurred during the hour of intense eating. This contrasts with NE, which gradually rose during deprivation and fell after refeeding.[95]

Lateral Hypothalamic Amphetamine Anorexia May Involve All Three Monoamines

When we turned our attention to the LH, Luis Hernandez and his colleague Marco Parada were able to observe neurochemical effects of anorectic doses of AMPH[7,50,76] infused directly in the microdialysis site.[78] It was known that the LH is the most sensitive site for AMPH-induced anorexia[50] and that ventral bundle NE depletion reduced systemic[1,2] and local[55] AMPH anorexia while reducing NE fluorescent varicosities in the LH.[1] This strongly suggested a role for NE in amphetamine's LH effects. In addition to NE, DA had been implicated by a loss of AMPH anorexia after A8 DA lesions[55] and by a strong correlation between the degree of AMPH anorexia and the anorexia caused by 5-HT or DA in the LH.[76] Furthermore, local AMPH anorexia was largely blocked by DA antagonists[50] as well as by NE antagonists.[7] Our task was to see if local AMPH increased extracellular DA and NE in the LH. Fortunately 5-HT was measured at the same time.

Eight male rats had guide shafts aimed to place microdialysis probes with 3-mm tips ending in the perifornical LH. Samples collected every 20 min were assayed for three monoamines and three metabolites. This meant that 5-HT eluted late and was often undetectable during baseline conditions. After a stable baseline of DA and NE was achieved, AMPH was infused by "reverse dialysis" by passing a concentration of $10 \mu g/\mu l$ through the probe for 20 min. Judging by *in vivo* calibration studies in which monoamines and metabolites diffused through the cellulose tip with a relative recovery of 5–10%,[37,108] AMPH probably diffused out of the probe at about the same rate. If so, an estimated 20 μg of AMPH reached the extracellular compartment as if it were coming out of a blood vessel over the course of 20 min. This is a dose which, if injected locally in the usual way, would cause anorexia.[7,50,76]

The result of AMPH infusion was a significant increase in extracellular DA and NE as predicted. The baseline of a few picograms per sample increased to more than 10 pg/sample for 1–2 hrs. AMPH increased 5-HT as well. Serotonin levels rose from the noise level to 140 pg. The metabolites DOPAC and 5-HIAA decreased, which helps to explain the large increase in DA and 5-HT; not only were monoamines released, but also their breakdown was impaired.

Fenfluramine Affects Synaptic Serotonin and DOPAC in the Lateral Hypothalamus as Well as the Medial Hypothalamus

This strong 5-HT presence in the LH raised our curiosity about its function. A major 5-HT satiety effect is known to exist in the PVN-MH region.[58] Lesion data suggested the intact LH was unnecessary; LH lesions can even augment systemic *dl*-fenfluramine anorexia.[6] Given that LH lesions themselves produce anorexia, and that *d*-fenfluramine directly or indirectly affects catecholamines, acetylcholine, and GABA as well as 5-HT,[25] the overall role of serotonin in the LH was a total mystery.

David Schwartz has used microdialysis to study the pharmacology of LH serotonin. He has tested the effects of systemic and local *d*-fenfluramine (*d*-FEN) in high doses to release 5-HT, local fluoxetine to block 5-HT reuptake, systemic tryptophan as a serotonin precursor to increase 5-HT synthesis and 8-OH-DPAT to stop 5-HT cells from generating action potentials.

In 53 male rats with LH guide shafts and dialysis probes with 3-mm tips, 5-HT, DOPAC, 5-HIAA and HVA were assayed while *d*-FEN was administered three ways. Groups of 4–6 rats received 0, 3, or 10 mg/kg *d*-FEN i.p., or 0, 0.1, 1.0, and 10 μg injected in the LH by removing the microdialysis probe for a few minutes to insert a 33-ga injector, or 10 μg/μl introduced in the perfusate for 20 min for infusion by reverse dialysis.

The result of i.p. administration of 10 mg/kg *d*-FEN was an increase in extracellular 5-HT in the LH in the first post-injection sample and return to baseline an hour later. 5-HIAA gradually decreased. DOPAC and HVA increased significantly with a long, slow time course. Local injection of 1 μg and 10 μg *d*-FEN again increased 5-HT and decreased 5-HIAA as with i.p. injections, but the DA metabolites were notably different. DOPAC and HVA decreased after local *d*-FEN. Local infusion by reverse dialysis confirmed this result.[88]

The finding that systemic *d*-FEN increased extracellular 5-HT was expected for a 5-HT releaser. The concomitant decrease in 5-HIAA confirms that *d*-FEN can also retard 5-HT metabolism, probably by acting as a 5-HT reuptake blocker. High doses in the 3–30 mg/kg range were reported to cause a persistent reduction in 5-HT reuptake sites,[17,102] but doses as low as 0.1 mg/kg were sufficient for anorexia.[58] The increase in DA metabolites, DOPAC and HVA, after systemic *d*-FEN suggests an intriguing interaction between serotonin and dopamine systems. This interaction with the DA system evidently took place outside the LH, because local LH infusion of *d*-FEN had the opposite effect on DOPAC and HVA. Perhaps systemic *d*-FEN directly or indirectly excites DA cells that project to the LH. These results illustrate the value of microdialysis in comparing the effects of systemic administration with local application of a drug. Systemic *d*-FEN also acts in many other ways including increased free fatty acid release and increased basal metabolic rate.[73] The net result of systemic *d*-FEN measured in the LH was increased extracellular 5-HT and increased turnover of DA. This suggests that both serotonergic and dopaminergic function could contribute to inhibition of feeding in the LH. The local application of *d*-FEN proves that it can increase extracellular 5-HT by its actions at the terminals. Both systemic and local *d*-FEN increased measurable 5-HT in the LH, but the effects on metabolites did not match. This suggests that a major part of the systemic effect of the drug was exerted outside the LH and then manifested within the hypothalamus.

Peripheral Tryptophan Loading Increases Lateral Hypothalamic Extracellular Serotonin

The science of nutrition and brain is an exciting field built on the premise that certain neurotransmitter precursors in the diet can influence neurochemical function in the brain.[113] It is known that the 5-HT precursor, tryptophan, injected systemically can augment 5-HT levels in dissected chunks of brain tissue. Microdialysis made it possible to test the effect of i.p. tryptophan on extracellular 5-HT in the hypothalamus where it could have a functional role in tryptophan-induced satiety.

Starting with 19 male rats with microdialysis probes in the LH, subgroups received saline vehicle or 100 mg/kg tryptophan methyl ester when fed *ad libitum* or when deprived of food for 48 hours to clear the bloodstream of competing amino acids. Peripheral tryptophan loading increased extracellular 5-HT and 5-HIAA in the LH of the deprived rats.[89]

This tryptophan dose, which increased extracellular 5-HT, is known to cause anorexia. It is impossible to know from this experiment alone if elevated synaptic 5-HT in the LH contributes to the anorexia. We note that similar increases in 5-HT were produced by tryptophan, by *d*-fenfluramine (described above) and by the events surrounding a meal (described below). A major difference was an increase in 5-HIAA only in the experiment with tryptophan. Apparently tryptophan loading led to intraneuronal 5-HT loading through augmented synthesis; then some of the extra 5-HT was metabolized intracellularly to 5-HIAA, and both 5-HT and the 5-HIAA were extruded into the extracellular space where they diffused to the dialysis probe.

Food Releases Serotonin in the Lateral Hypothalamus and the Medial Hypothalamus Even before the Meal Starts

On the theory that eating a meal would release LH serotonin, eight male rats were prepared with dialysis probes in the perifornical LH region. They were accustomed to the dialysis environment, deprived routinely for 14–16 hrs and then tested with food to smell and then to eat after a stable 5-HT baseline of 30-min samples was obtained. In a second experiment 13 rats had both LH and MH probes for comparison, and 10 μM fluoxetine was added to the perfusate to block 5-HT reuptake and improve 5-HT detectability.

In the experiment with no fluoxetine, the stable baseline level of extracellular 5-HT in the LH increased only during the 30 min of vigorous eating.[90] In the second experiment with fluoxetine to prevent 5-HT reuptake, a significant increase in 5-HT also occurred during 60 min when the rats could see and smell the food before eating it. Some animals showed a larger effect in the LH and some in the MH; the mean increase averaged across rats was about the same at both sites.[87] Extracellular serotonin was highest during the 30 min of actual eating when the animals consumed 15 g of sweet mash.

These tests show that extracellular 5-HT can increase during feeding and also when the hungry rats are aroused by the smell of food. This is the period of appetite whetting, or cephalic phase responses, which occurs before a meal. Surprisingly, in the period after the meal when the animals were too satiated to eat, detectable 5-HT returned to normal. The MH, rather than providing a control, mimicked the LH. If 5-HT in the hypothalamus is involved in normal satiety, then either it has synaptic effects longer than we can detect, or its effects are transient and intermeal satiety depends on other neurotransmitters such as NE and DA in the LH[78] or CCK[86] and neurotensin in the PVN.[40,41,93]

Serotonin release during the appetite-whetting period when the animal smelled food was detected only in the second experiment using fluoxetine to boost basal levels of extracellular 5-HT. This suggests that in the first experiment the 5-HT that was released by the smell of food was taken back into the terminals before it could spill over into the extracellular compartment surrounding the microdialysis probe. The lack of increase in 5-HIAA in either experiment suggests that released 5-HT was taken back into the terminals and stored in vesicles without detectable breakdown to 5-HIAA.

We do not know if release of 5-HT before and during a meal is due to presynaptic inputs to the hypothalamic 5-HT terminals or increased firing of serotonin cells. A third possibility is increased serotonin synthesis resulting from increased tryptophan uptake following cephalic-phase insulin release, which tends to clear competing amino acids from the bloodstream.[23,113] Tryptophan in the food was probably not a factor because an increase in 5-HT occurred even before eating, and because rat chow contains protein that yields competing amino acids that diminish tryptophan uptake.[23] We surmise that the 5-HT release we observed before feeding was either a raphe "arousal" effect and/or was due to specific odor or conditional food-related effects mediated via a subset of raphe 5-HT cells or presynaptic inputs to the hypothalamic 5-HT terminals. Perhaps 5-HT released in anticipation of eating does nothing until local circuits become active during the meal. Then it depotentiates them, leading to circuit-specific inhibition. Behaviorally this could be manifested as sensory-specific satiety or commodity-specific satiety.[66]

Oomura's group[47] reports that 5-HT iontophoresed onto LH glucose-sensitive neurons inhibits them in the majority of cases. Presumably those are neurons that facilitate feeding. They further propose, on the basis of recording studies in monkeys, that LH glucose-sensitive neurons, which are inhibited by glucose plus insulin, are involved in internal metabolic regulation and thus fit the serotonin satiety model. They suggest, on the other hand, that LH neurons that are not the glucose-sensitive type respond to external feeding stimuli and are excited by iontophoretic 5-HT. This could be a feeding arousal function for the 5-HT that was released in anticipation of a meal.[87] LH cells have been described that respond during one or more of the following phases of feeding: looking at food, food acquisition, and food taste.[74,75] Rolls describes LH neurons that respond to self-stimulation and some that respond to sweet taste when hungry for sugar but not when satiated on sugar. This led Rolls[81] to agree with the proposition that self-stimulation at an LH feeding site could be augmented by external palatable tastes and inhibited by internal metabolic factors.

NUCLEUS ACCUMBENS MICRODIALYSIS EXPERIMENTS

Lateral Hypothalamic Self-Stimulation Releases Accumbens and Striatal DA

As documented in the introduction, everything that produces locomotion or feeding by an action in the mesolimbic system seems to be reinforcing too. LH stimulation might fall into this category; it activates a rat to search, eat, and self-stimulate.

Rats with both STR and NAC guide shafts were trained to self-stimulate in the perifornical LH. Next, microdialysis probes were inserted in one site or the other, basal DA was measured, and then the rat self-stimulated for 1 hr. The result was an increase in extracellular DA in both the NAC and STR.[45]

Self-stimulation could have activated neurons that directly or indirectly stimulated dopamine cells in the midbrain. These, in turn, may have released DA in the NAC and STR.[79] This is the most likely explanation based on evidence for an LH-to-VTA-NAC circuit.[111] We have not ruled out the possibility of direct stimulation of DA axons passing near the self-stimulation electrode, but this is unlikely with perifornical electrodes. An ascending route from the LH to the DA terminals is also a possibility, not to mention round-about routes through the limbic system, including LH–nucleus tractus solitarius (NTS), LH–amygdala, or LH–pre-frontal cortex connections that could project to the mesolimbic system to release DA.[24,65,67,69,75] Like self-stimulation, tail-pinch stress induces feeding and releases accumbens DA (Abercrombie & Zigmond, personal communication). Therefore our working hypothesis is that both stress and self-stimulation activate some parts of the mesolimbic DA system, and that this is sufficient to facilitate feeding, but a major difference between stress and LH self-stimulation is that periformical LH stimulation activates a path to NTS taste cells which could generate a food-like sensation more directly and reliably than nonspecific stress.[69] Stress-induced release of DA may facilitate circuits in the NAC and other forebrain sites that process feeding stimuli and responses; periformical LH self-stimulation not only releases DA, but also directly activates some of these feeding processes.

Earlier research from this laboratory showed that hypothalamic stimulation could induce not only feeding, but also drinking, copulation, running, and killing.[38] The animal switches from one to another depending on prior experience, environmental stimuli, electrode site, and state of deprivation.[38,101] Valenstein's group[101] has emphasized a nonspecific role of DA along with individual differences and experiential factors in these electrically induced behaviors in the rat. Researchers using other animals emphasized separate, specific hypothalamic circuitry for feeding and its fractional behavior and components.[29] New evidence suggests that a major group of cell bodies contributing to LH self-stimulation lies in the dorsal medial hypothalamus.[114] Our present working hypothesis is that hypothalamic output circuits such as those descending to the NTS[69] potentiate specific behavior reflexes, and that connections to the VTA activate cells, which release DA in the forebrain for the reinforcement of sensory–motor circuits that are active at the time.

Involuntary Lateral Hypothalamus Stimulation Releases Dopamine Preferentially in the Accumbens

Compared to self-stimulation, involuntary stimulation of the LH involves relatively little motor activity on the part of the animal. Luis Hernandez prepared rats with periformical LH electrodes and guide shafts in the NAC or STR for microdialysis, then selected five animals that would hold a food pellet in the forepaws and quietly eat during 10 sec of LH stimulation. LH stimulation for 20 min induced 2 g of food intake and caused ipsilateral, extracellular DA to increase significantly in just the NAC for 40 min, DOPAC for 60 min, and homovanillic acid (HVA) for 80 min. The same neurochemical pattern emerged during LH stimulation when food was absent.[33]

This experiment, and the self-stimulation experiment before it, suggest that LH stimulation induces DA release in the NAC whether the rat eats or not. It was surprising that extracellular DA remained elevated for about 20 min after stimulation ceased. Phillips reported the same prolonged effect with accumbens voltammetry electrodes in rats self-stimulating the VTA; DA release was proportional to self-stimulation rate. Thus our LH self-stimulation had a neural effect similar to their VTA self-stimulation. It leads one to wonder what DA is doing in the NAC so long after self-stimulation stops. It could be involved in reinforcing stimulus events associated with the environmental setting; it could simply reflect residual arousal, or it could be nonfunctional in the absence of activity in other circuits or in the absence of other transmitters. Microdialysis reveals the phenomenon of residual DA, but does not tell us what it means.

Feeding Can Release Dopamine in the Accumbens without a Detectable Change in the Striatum

Next we induced feeding by natural means with loss of body weight or with 24-hr deprivation. Five male rats with NAC microdialysis probes were fed about 17 g/day of chow to maintain them at 80% body weight. Nineteen others with both NAC and contralateral STR guide shafts were deprived, but at normal weight, and were trained to bar press for 45-mg pellets during a 20-min period when a signal light came on. Groups of four to seven rats were tested to determine the effects of continuous reinforcement and extinction reinforcement schedules.

Free feeding at 80% body weight increased NAC extracellular DA, DOPAC, and HVA. These effects outlasted the feeding period. Operant responding for food reward had the same effects in the NAC. No effect was detectable with the striatal placements, and no effect was seen in the NAC when the cue light was present during response extinction without food.[33,34] DA was detected in the NAC when the animals ate a meal at the accustomed time, but not before.

In summary, the effect of natural eating on DA turnover in the NAC was similar to the effect of LH stimulation in the prior experiment. Striatal DA did not increase detectably during bar pressing for food or involuntary LH stimulation, but it did increase during self-stimulation in most rats. The results together show that both LH stimulation and feeding can activate the mesolimbic dopamine system. Dopamine in the extracellular space outlasted the consummatory act, which suggests it is involved in various aspects of arousal or reinforcement beyond those accompanying the sensations of tasting food and LH stimulation. The increase in DA turnover during feeding confirms an earlier report based on *postmortem* assays[31] and raises questions about other ingestive behaviors.

Water and Salt Intake Can Increase Dopamine Release Too

To find out if the above feeding effects on DA were unique to food, we deprived rats of salt with a diuretic (furosemide 30 mg/kg) plus a salt-free diet until they developed a strong salt appetite as judged by avidity for an 0.9% saline solution. Extracellular DA increased significantly to 200% of baseline during saline drinking.[15]

The next group was deprived of water for 20 hours. During subsequent drinking extracellular DA increased 40% above baseline. The effect lasted for at least one hour after drinking stopped.[15]

Next, one group was tested with intracerebroventricular (ICV) angiotensin or saline, and another group was given ICV angiotensin along with water to drink for 20 min. Angiotensin alone caused a small but statistically reliable 25% increase in extracellular DA, and this effect dissipated 40 min post-injection. In contrast, water to drink for 20 min in addition to the ICV angiotensin caused NAC dopamine to increase 70% above baseline, reaching a peak after 40 min. DA remained elevated in these subjects for an additional 40 min. These results implicate dopaminergic involvement in several reward-related behaviors and suggest that DA may be released differentially in the accumbens depending on whether an animal is under the influence of angiotensin alone or angiotensin plus water consumption.[4,60]

The Taste of Saccharin Alone Can Increase Dopamine Release; Conditioned Taste Aversion Reverses It

All the above experiments support the suggestion that accumbens DA release is related to the reward value of a stimulus. If so, aversive stimuli might have the opposite effect. To test this hypothesis, we used the well-known conditioned taste aversion paradigm, which pairs a neutral or good taste with illness. This procedure has been shown to switch the NTS electrophysiological across-fiber response from a sweet-type pattern to the bitter type.[62,85] In the present experiment the question was whether or not the forebrain dopamine response would switch too.

The first taste of intraoral saccharin increased accumbens DA by 26% with a 20-min delay. After this taste was impaired with LiCl-induced malaise, the same dose of oral saccharin by itself caused a rapid 50% decrease in accumbens DA. Thus DA increased when the taste signaled a good thing and decreased when the taste signaled a bad thing. The effect did not occur in pseudo-conditioning control groups.[60,61]

Psychomotor Stimulants Increase Synaptic DA; Weight Loss Decreases It

Stimulant drugs are not the topic of this conference, so I will just summarize their effects, which are fascinating because they are so much like palatable food, water, and salt. In brief, amphetamine, phenylpropanolamine (PPA), cocaine (COC), phencyclidine and nicotine released DA when applied directly to the mesolimbic terminal region where amphetamine can generate stimulus properties and behavior reinforcement.[34,42,64] Rats reduced to 80% of normal body weight had lower basal DA levels and i.p. amphetamine had a reduced DA effect.[80] The implication of this series of experiments is that psychomotor stimulants are a substitute for some of food's effects, and food is like a psychomotor stimulant. Mesolimbic DA seems to be intimately involved in addiction to drugs, because so many drugs of abuse increase extracellular DA in the NAC when given systemically or locally. To the extent that mesolimbic DA is involved in addiction to drugs, this DA system may also be involved in addiction to food.[34] We have confirmed what Hebb[34] and Wise[110] proposed, addictive drugs act on brain circuits that evolved with one of their functions being the reinforcement of survival behavior such as feeding, drinking, and salt intake.

We propose that drugs that are both anorectics and psychostimulants generate their reward properties in part via the mesolimbic DA system and their anorectic properties in part by inhibiting the LH feeding system. Under normal conditions food, water, and salt probably stimulate the appropriate LH system, thereby facilitating taste and ingestive reflexes in the hindbrain and reinforcing DA-gaited circuits for ongoing cognition and behavior in the forebrain. Satiety signals or anorectic drugs such as AMPH, PPA, FEN, and fluoxetine inhibit these effects in part through 5-HT in the PVN and all the monoamines in the LH. Thus a drug or a behavior that increases extracellular DA in the NAC and PFC is likely to be reinforcing and addictive, for example, AMPH, COC, and feeding. A drug or behavior that increases extracellular 5-HT in the hypothalamus is likely to cause satiety, for example, AMPH, FEN, and feeding. Therefore feeding reinforcement is self-limiting. We have shown that AMPH and COC can act directly in the NAC; therefore their hypothalamic satiety effects are largely bypassed during drug self-administration. Bulimia with vomiting may be a similar addiction to reward that by-passes satiety; food without absorption, dopamine without calories.

THE THEORETICAL TREATMENT OF BULIMIA

Many experiments remain to be done, but the above analysis does suggest a route to therapy. Given the evidence that MH-lesion hyperphagia and VNAB, 6-OH-DA hyperphagia are reflected in LH hyper-self-stimulation, and the finding that LH self-stimulation releases NAC dopamine which reinforces behavior, we can surmise that an effective treatment for hyperphagic behavior would inhibit the LH self-stimulation system ("feeding-reward system") and thereby limit dopamine release. We cannot use dopaminergic drugs like amphetamine because they are counterproductive by being addictive in the NAC. We cannot use noradrenergic drugs because they are also counterproductive by inducing feeding in the PVN. That leaves serotonergic drugs, their dietary precursors, and perhaps their copeptides or synergists such as CCK. The serotonergic drug *d*-FEN does inhibit LH self-stimulation,[63] as does CCK,[3,22] although there is a question of specificity, and both have been tested for the treatment of obesity or bulimia.[5,52,58,70,83] Perhaps new approaches can be found based on the criteria that they increase release or mimic serotonin and CCK in the hypothalamus without releasing DA in the accumbens or cortex. An effective treatment may be recognizable in an initial screening by selective inhibition of self-stimulation at stimulation-bound feeding sites in the hypothalamus. An alternative is to let the person or animal enjoy the food intake, and enjoy the mesolimbic dopamine, by using food that lacks calories or means to block the absorption of calories. Unfortunately, these approaches may be addictive because they lack the negative feedback that normally inhibits intake. Modern antidepressants are largely serotonergic, which suggests that depressed patients benefit from serotonin. A natural way to release serotonin may be to eat real food. What is needed then is a procedure that provides dopamine for reward without addiction and provides cognitive enhancement without psychosis and provides dopamine, norepinephrine, and serotonin or their cotransmitters for satiety and antidepression without excessive calories. The new demonstrations that monoamine release can be altered by body weight,[80] dietary precursors,[89] and conditioning[62] may help point the way to dietary and behavioral therapies to augment or replace the monoaminergic drugs.

SUMMARY

This minireview deals with the possible roles of monoamines in feeding and feeding disorders. The introduction sketches the results of earlier studies with local drug injections and selective neurotoxins which provided pharmacological evidence that monoamines can influence food intake and body weight. A table summarizing this evidence is used to list monoamine changes that could underlie anorexia or hyperphagia. It is apparent that abnormalities in the monoamines, along with their cotransmitters, could cause many forms of feeding disorder. It is proposed as a working hypothesis that several varieties of hyperphagia leading to obesity have a common element. This common factor is a change in excitability of a lateral hypothalamic reinforcement system as manifested in self-stimulation at a stimulation-bound feeding site. Understanding this feeding reward–aversion system helps us understand hyperphagia and anorexia. The neurochemistry of reward and aversion involves the monoamines. This paper focuses on dopamine and serotonin. The data support the hypothesis that dopamine systems projecting to the nucleus accumbens and other forebrain areas from the midbrain ventral tegmental area (VTA) are important for approach and positive reinforcement in ingestive behavior and self-stimulation. Serotonin is hypothesized to facilitate satiety and inhibition of feeding reward in the hypothalamus.

The next section abstracts our recent experiments that measured pharmacological and physiological release of the monoamines in the hypothalamus and nucleus accumbens during ingestive behavior and self-stimulation. *In vivo* microdialysis in freely moving rats suggested the following: (1) Norepinephrine was released in the paraventricular nucleus during the active, feeding period of the circadian cycle. (2) The serotonin metabolite 5-HIAA also increased in the PVN at the same time if there was food to eat. (3) Amphetamine infused into the lateral hypothalamus (LH) by reverse dialysis increased synaptic dopamine, norepinephrine, and serotonin. (4) The anorectic drug d-fenfluramine increased synaptic serotonin in the LH and also increased the dopamine metabolite DOPAC, suggesting that serotonin and dopamine in the LH might contribute to fenfluramine-induced satiety. Local d-fenfluramine injection into the LH or local infusion by reverse dialysis again increased serotonin and decreased 5-HIAA and interfered with local dopamine metabolism as reflected in decreased DOPAC and HVA. (5) Tryptophan, a serotonin precursor, given systemically at an anorectic dose, increased extracellular serotonin in the LH, but this effect was only detectable in food-deprived rats. (6) The sight and smell of food increased LH serotonin release; this effect was detectable when local fluoxetine was used to block serotonin reuptake. Eating a meal released LH serotonin for about 20 min with or without fluoxetine. (7) d-Fenfluramine i.p. inhibited LH self-stimulation, and (8) LH self-stimulation released dopamine in the nucleus accumbens (NAC) and striatum. Stimulation-bound feeding, free feeding, or bar-pressing for pellets in food-deprived rats released dopamine in the NAC more than the striatum, but (9) this release was not specific to feeding because angiotensin-induced drinking or deprivation-induced salt intake also released NAC dopamine. (10) Dopamine was released by the taste of saccharin, and this was reversed by conditioned taste aversion. This suggests that increased release of dopamine potentiates accumbens circuits for approach and positive reinforcement when activated by a taste when it tastes like a safe food, and that decreased release of dopamine depotentiates these circuits when activated by tastes associated with nausea. (11) Psychomotor stimulants, such as amphetamine, cocaine, phencyclidine, and nicotine, increased extracellular DA in the NAC, supporting the view that addictive stimulants act in part by way of the mesolimbic dopamine system that evolved to arouse or reinforce ingestive behavior. Food addiction and self-stimulation may therefore have a neurochemical relation to drug addiction.

ACKNOWLEDGMENTS

The author's acknowledge Kathleen McGeady and Dawn Davidson, who provided expert assistance.

REFERENCES

1. AHLSKOG, J. E. 1974. Food intake and amphetamine anorexia after selective forebrain norepinephrine loss. Brain Res. **82:** 211–240.
2. AHLSKOG, J. E., P. K. RANDALL, L. HERNANDEZ & B. G. HOEBEL. 1984. Diminished amphetamine anorexia and enhanced fenfluramine anorexia after midbrain 6-hydroxydopamine. Psychopharmacology **82:** 118–121.
3. BAPTISTA, T., M. PARADA & L. HERNANDEZ. 1987. Long-term administration of some antipsychotic drugs increases body weight and feeding in rats. Are D_2 dopamine receptors involved? Pharmacol. Biochem. Behav. **27:** 399–405.
4. BLANDER, D. S., G. P. MARK, L. HERNANDEZ & B. G. HOEBEL. 1988. Angiotensin and drinking induce dopamine release in the nucleus accumbens. Soc. Neurosci. Abstr. **14:** 527.
5. BLOUIN, A. G., J. H. BLOUIN, E. L. PEREZ, T. BUSHNIK, C. ZURO & E. MULDER. 1988. Treatment of bulimia in fenfluramine and desipramine. J. Clin. Psychopharm. **8:** 261.
6. BLUNDELL, J. E. 1984. Serotonin and appetite. Neuropharm. **23:** 1537–1551.
7. BOOTH, D. A. 1968. Amphetamine anorexia by direct action on the adrenergic feeding system of the rat hypothalamus. Nature **217:** 869–970.
8. BOZARTH, M.A. 1983. Opiate reward mechanisms mapped by intracranial self-adminis-

tration. *In* The Neurobiology of Opiate Reward Processes. J. E. Smith & J. D. Lane, Eds.: 331–359. Elsevier Biomedical. New York.

9. BOZARTH, M.A. 1987. Ventral tegmental reward system. *In* Brain Reward Systems and Abuse. J. Engel & L. Oreland *et al.*, Eds.: 1–17. Raven Press. New York.

10. BRAY, G. 1987. Factors leading to obesity: Physical (including metabolic) factors and disease states. *In* Body Weight Control. A. E. Bender & L. J. Brookes, Eds. Churchill Livingston. New York.

11. BREISCH, S. T., F. P. ZEMLAN & B. G. HOEBEL. 1976. Hyperphagia and obesity following serotonin depletion with intraventricular parachlorophenylalanine. Science **192**: 383–385.

12. BRODIE, M. S. & T. V. DUNWIDDIE. 1987. Cholecystokinin potentiates dopamine inhibition of mesencephalic dopamine neurons *in vitro*. Brain Res. **425**: 106–113.

13. BUNNEY, B. S. 1984. June. Antipsychotic drug effects on the electrical activity of dopaminergic neurons. Trends Neurosci. **7**: 212–215.

14. CADOR, M., A. E. KELLEY, M. LE MOAL & L. STINUS. 1986. Ventral tegmental area infusion of Substance P, neurotension and enkephalin: Differential effects on feeding behavior. Neuroscience **18**: 659–669.

15. CHANG, V. C., G. P. MARK, L. HERNANDEZ & B. G. HOEBEL. 1988. Extracellular dopamine increases in the nucleus accumbens following rehydration or sodium repletion in rats. Soc. Neurosci. Abstr. **14**: 527.

16. COLLE, L. M. & R. A. WISE. 1988. Effects of nucleus accumbens amphetamine on lateral hypothalamic brain stimulation reward. Brain Res. **459**: 361–368.

17. CONTRERA, J. F., G. BATTAGLIA, R. ZACZEK & E. B. DE SOUZA. 1988. Fenfluramine neurotoxicity: Selective degeneration and recovery of brain serotonin neurons. Soc. Neurosci. Abstr. **14**: 556.

18. COSCINA, D. V. 1978. Effects of central 5,7-dihydroxytryptamine on the medial hypothalamic syndrome in rats. *In* Serotonin Neurotoxins. J. H. Jacoby & L. D. Lytle, Eds. Vol. **305**: 627–644. Ann. N. Y. Acad. Sci. New York.

19. CREESE, I., Ed. 1983. Stimulants: Neurochemical, Behavioral, and Clinical Perspective. Raven Press. New York.

20. DELGADO, J. M. R., F. V. DeFEUDIS, R. H. ROTH, D. K. RYUGO & B. M. MITRUKA. 1972. Dialytrode for long term intracerebral perfusion in awake monkeys. Arch. Int. Pharmacodyn. **198**: 9–21.

21. DOURISH, C. T., P. H. HUTSON & G. CURZON. 1985. Characteristics of feeding induced by the serotonergic agonist 8-hydroxy-2-(di-n-propylamine) tetralin (8-OH-DPAT). Brain Res. Bull. **15**: 377–384.

22. ETTENBERG, A. & G. F. KOOB. 1984. Different effects on cholecystokinin and satiety on lateral hypothalamic self-stimulation. Physiol. Behav. **32**: 127–130.

23. FERNSTROM, J. D. 1986. Acute and chronic effects of protein and carbohydrate ingestion on brain tryptophan levels and serotonin synthesis. Nutr. Rev. **44(Suppl.)**: 25–36.

24. FIBIGER, H. C. & A. G. PHILLIPS. 1986. Reward, motivation, cognition: Psychobiology of mesotelencephalic dopamine systems. Handbook of Physiology, Section 1: The Nervous System. V. B. Mountcastle, Ed. Intrinsic Regulatory Systems of the Brain. F. E. Bloom, Ed. Vol. **IV**: 647–675.

25. GARATTINI, S., T. MENNINI, C. BENDOTTI, R. INVERNIZZI & R. SAMANIN. 1986. Neurochemical mechanism of action of drugs which modify feeding via the serotonergic system. *In* Serotoninergic System, Feeding and Body Weight Regulation. S. Nicolaidis, Ed.: 15–38. Academic Press. New York.

26. GLIMCHER, P. G., A. A. GIOVINO, D. H. MARGOLIN & B. G. HOEBEL. 1984. Endogenous opiate reward induced by an enkephalinase inhibitor, thiorphan, injected into the ventral midbrain. Behav. Neurosci. **98**: 262–268.

27. GLIMCHER, P. G., A. A. GIOVINO & B. G. HOEBEL. 1987. Neurotensin self-injection in the ventral tegmental area. Brain Res. **403**: 147–150.

28. GUERIN, G. F., N. E. GOEDERS, S. U. DWORKIN & J. E. SMITH. 1984. Intracranial self-administration of dopamine into the nucleus accumbens. Soc. Neurosci. Abstr. **10**: 1072.

29. HALLONQUIST, J. D. & N. MROSOVSKY. 1986. Electrically induced behavior and neural specificity in ground squirrels and dormice. Physiol. Behav. **38**: 387–397.

30. HAMILTON, M. E. & M. A. BOZARTH. 1986. Feeding elicited by opioid microinjection into the ventral tegmental area. Soc. Neurosci. Abstr. **12:** 412.
31. HEFFNER, T., J. A. HARTMAN & L. S. SEIDEN. 1980. Feeding increases dopamine metabolism in the rat brain. Science **208:** 1168–1170.
32. HERNANDEZ, L. & B. G. HOEBEL. 1982. Overeating after midbrain 6-hydroxydopamine: Prevention by central injection of selective reuptake blockers. Brain Res. **245:** 333–343.
33. HERNANDEZ, L. & B. G. HOEBEL. 1988. Feeding and hypothalamic stimulation increase dopamine turnover in the accumbens. Physiol. Behav. **44:** 599–606.
34. HERNANDEZ, L. & B. G. HOEBEL. 1988. Food reward and cocaine increase extracellular dopamine in the nucleus accumbens as measured by microdialysis. Life Sci. **42:** 1705–1712.
35. HERNANDEZ, L. & B. G. HOEBEL. 1989. Food intake and lateral hypothalamic self-stimulation covary after medial hypothalamic lesions or ventral midbrain 6-hydroxydopamine injections that cause obesity. Behav. Neurosci. **103:** 412–422.
36. HERNANDEZ, L., A. PAEZ & C. HAMLIN. 1983. Neurotransmitter extraction by local intracerebral dialysis in anesthetized rats. Pharmacol. Biochem. Behav. **18:** 159–162.
37. HERNANDEZ, L., B. G. STANLEY & B. G. HOEBEL. 1986. A small, removable microdialysis probe. Life Sci. **39:** 2629–2637.
38. HOEBEL, B. G. 1976. Brain-Stimulation reward and aversion in relation to behavior. *In* Brain-stimulation Reward. A. Wauquier & E. T. Rolls, Eds.: 335–372. Elsevier. Amsterdam.
39. HOEBEL, B. G. 1984. Neurotransmitters in the control of feeding and its rewards: Monoamines, opiates and brain-gut peptides. *In* Eating and Its Disorders. A. J. Stunkard & E. Stellar, Eds.: 15–38. Association for Research in Nervous and Mental Disease. Raven Press. New York.
40. HOEBEL, B. G. 1985. Brain neurotransmitters in food and drug reward. Am. J. Clin. Nutr. **42:** 1133–1150.
41. HOEBEL, B. G. 1988. Neuroscience and motivation: Pathways and peptides that define motivational systems. *In* Stevens' Handbook of Experimental Psychology. 2nd Ed. R. C. Atkinson, R. J. Herrnstein, G. Lindzey & R. D. Luce, Eds.: 547–625. John Wiley & Sons, New York.
42. HOEBEL, B. G., L. HERNANDEZ & G. MARK. Neuropharmacology of appetite and reinforcement. *In* Neuropharmacology of Appetite. S. J. Cooper & J. M. Liebman, Eds. In preparation.
43. HOEBEL, B. G. & S. F. LEIBOWITZ. 1981. Brain monoamines in the modulation of self-stimulation, feeding, and body weight. *In* Brain, Behavior and Bodily Disease. H. Weiner, M. A. Hofer & A. J. Stunkard, Eds. Vol. **59:** 103–142. Association for Research in Nervous and Mental Disease. Raven Press. New York.
44. HOEBEL, B. G., A. P. MONACO, L. HERNANDEZ, E. F. AULISI, B. G. STANLEY & L. LENARD. 1983. Self-injection of amphetamine directly into the brain. Psychopharmacology **81:** 158–163.
45. HUNTER, G. A., L. HERNANDEZ & B. G. HOEBEL. 1988. Microdialysis shows increased dopamine turnover in the nucleus accumbens during lateral hypothalamic self-stimulation. Soc. Neurosci. Abstr. **14:** 1100.
46. HUNTER, G. A., G. P. MARK & B. G. HOEBEL. 1989. The 5-HT$_{1A}$ agonist, 8-OH-DPAT, prevents the expression but not the development of a conditioned taste aversion. Soc. Neurosci. Abstr. **15:** 773.
47. KAI, Y., Y. OOMURA & N. SHIMIZU. 1988. Responses of rat lateral hypothalamic neuron activity to dorsal raphe nuclei stimulation. J. Neurophysiol. **60:** 524–535.
48. KALIVAS, P., C. B. NEMEROFF & A. J. PRANGE. 1982. Neuroanatomical sites of action of neurotensin. *In* Neurotensin, A Brain and Gastrointestinal Peptide. C. B. Nemeroff & A. J. Prange, Eds. **400:** 307–315. Ann. N.Y. Acad. Sci. New York.
49. KOOB, G. F. & F. E. BLOOM. 1988. Cellular and molecular mechanisms of drug dependence. Science **242:** 715–723.
50. LEIBOWITZ, S. F. 1975. Catecholaminergic mechanisms of the lateral hypothalamus: Their role in the mediation of amphetamine anorexia. Brain Res. **98:** 529–545.
51. LEIBOWITZ, S. F. 1984. Noradrenergic function in the medial hypothalamus: Potential relation to anorexia nervosa and bulimia. *In* The Psychobiology of Anorexia Nervosa. K. M. Pirke & D. Ploog. Eds.: 35–45. Springer-Verlag. Berlin.

52. LEIBOWITZ, S. F. 1984. Brain monoamine projections and receptor systems in relation to food intake, diet preference, meal patterns, and body weight. *In* Neuroendocrinology of Psychiatric Disorder. G. M. Brown, S. H. Koslow & S. Reichlin, Eds.: 383–399. Raven Press. New York.

53. LEIBOWITZ, S. F. 1988. Brain neurotransmitters and drug effects on food intake and appetite: Implications for eating disorders. *In* Eating Behavior in Eating Disorders. B. T. Walsh, Eds.: 19–35. American Psychiatric Press. Washington, D.C.

54. LEIBOWITZ, S. F. 1989. Hypothalamic neuropeptide Y and galanin: Function studies of coexistence with monoamines. *In* Nobel Conference on Neuropeptide. Y. V. Mutt, Ed. Raven Press. New York.

55. LEIBOWITZ, S. F. & L. L. BROWN. 1980. Histochemical and pharmacological analysis of catecholaminergic projections to the perifornical hypothalamus in relation to feeding inhibition. Brain Res. **201:** 289–314.

56. LEIBOWITZ, S. F. & R. D. MYERS. 1987. The neurochemistry of ingestion: Chemical stimulation of the brain and *in vivo* measurement of transmitter release. *In* Feeding and Drinking. Techniques in the Behavioral and Neural Sciences. F. Toates & N. E. Rowland, Eds. Vol. **1:** 271–315. Elsevier Science. Amsterdam.

57. LEIBOWITZ, S. F. & B. G. STANLEY. 1986. Brain peptides and the control of eating behavior. *In* Neural and Endocrine Peptides and Receptors. T. W. Moody, Ed.: 333–352. Plenum Press. New York.

58. LEIBOWITZ, S. F., G. F. WEISS & G. SHOR POSNER. 1988. Hypothalamic serotonin: Pharmacological, biochemical and behavioral analyses of its feeding-suppressive action. Clin. Neuropharm. **11**(Suppl. 1): S51-S71.

59. LOUILET, A., M. LE MOAL & H. SIMON. 1989. Opposite influences of dopaminergic pathways to the prefrontal cortex or the septum on the dopaminergic transmission in the nucleus accumbens. An *in vivo* voltammetric study. Neuroscience **29:** 45–56.

60. MARK, G. P., D. S. BLANDER & B. G. HOEBEL. 1989. Effects of salt intake, rehydration and conditioned taste aversion development on dopamine output in the rat nucleus accumbens. Proc. X[th] Intl. Conf. Physiology of Food and Fluid Intake, Paris, France. In press.

61. MARK, G. P., D. S. BLANDER & B. G. HOEBEL. 1989. Conditioned taste aversion reverses dopamine release in the nucleus accumbens. Soc. Neurosci. Abstr. **15:** In press.

62. MARK, G. P. & T. R. SCOTT. 1988. Conditioned taste aversions affect gustatory-evoked activity in the NTS of chronic decerebrate rats. Soc. Neurosci. Abstr. **14:** 1185.

63. MCCLELLAND, R. C., T. SARFATY, L. HERNANDEZ & B. G. HOEBEL. 1989. The appetite suppressant, *d*-fenfluramine, decreases self-stimulation at a feeding site in the lateral hypothalamus. Pharmacol. Biochem. Behav. **32:** 411–414.

64. MIFSUD, J. C., L. HERNANDEZ & B. G. HOEBEL. 1989. Nicotine infused into the nucleus accumbens increases synaptic dopamine as measured by *in vivo* microdialysis. Brain Res. **478:** 365–367.

65. MOGENSON, G. J. 1987. Limbic-motor integration. Prog. Psychobiol. Physiol. Psychol. **12:** 117–170.

66. MOOK, D. G. 1988. On the organization of satiety. Appetite **11:** 27–39.

67. MORGANE, P. J. & J. PANKSEPP. 1979. Handbook of the Hypothalamus, Vol. 1, Anatomy of the Hypothalamus. Marcel Dekker, Inc. New York.

68. MUCHA, R. F. & S. D. IVERSEN. 1986. Increased food intake after opioid microinjection into nucleus accumbens and ventral tegmental area of rat. Brain Res. **397:** 214–224.

69. MURZI, E., L. HERNANDEZ & T. BAPTISTA. 1986. Lateral hypothalamic sites eliciting eating affect medullary taste neurons in rats. Physiol. Behav. **36:** 829–834.

70. MUURAHAINEN, N., H. R. KISSILEFF, A. J. DEROGATIS & F. X. PI-SUNYER. 1988. Effects of cholecystokinin-octapeptide (CCK-8) on food intake and gastric emptying in man. Physiol. Behav. **44:** 645–649.

71. MYERS, R. D. & P. J. KNOTT, Eds. 1986. Neurochemical Analysis of the Conscious Brain: Voltammetry and Push-Pull Perfusion. Vol. 473. Annals of the New York Academy of Sciences. New York.

72. NEMEROFF, C. F. & A. J. PRANGE, JR., Eds. 1982. Neurotensin, A Brain and Gastrointestinal Peptide. Vol. 400. Annals of the New York Academy of Sciences. New York.

73. NICOLAIDIS, S. & P. EVEN. 1986. Metabolic action of leptogenic (anorexigenic) agents on feeding and body weight. *In* Pharmacology of Eating Disorders: Theoretical and Clinical Developments. M. O. Carruba & J. E. Blundell, Eds.: 117–131. Raven Press. New York.

74. NISHINO, H., Y. OOMURA, Z. KARADI, S. AOU, L. LENARD, Y. KAI, A. FUKUDA, C. ITO, B. I. MIN & C. P. SALAMAN. 1988. Internal and external information processing by lateral hypothalamic glucose-sensitive and insensitive neurons during bar press feeding in the monkey. Brain Res. Bull. **20:** 839–845.

75. OOMURA, Y., H. NISHINO, S. AUO & L. LENARD. 1986. Opiate mechanism in reward-related neuronal responses during operant feeding behavior of the monkey. Brain Res. **365:** 335–339.

76. PARADA, M. A. & L. HERNANDEZ. 1982. Correlacion significativa entre la anorexia por anfetamina, serotonina y dopamine intrahipotalamicas. XXXII Convencion anual de ASOVAC, Caracas, Venezuela.

77. PARADA, M. A., L. HERNANDEZ & B. G. HOEBEL. 1988. Sulpiride injections in the lateral hypothalamus induce feeding and drinking in rats. Pharmacol. Biochem. Behav. **30:** 917–923.

78. PARADA, M. A., L. HERNANDEZ, D. SCHWARTZ & B. G. HOEBEL. 1988. Hypothalamic infusion of amphetamine increases serotonin, dopamine and norepinephrine. Physiol. Behav. **44:** 607–610.

79. PHILLIPS, A. G. 1988. Neurochemical correlates of brain-stimulation reward measured by *in vivo* and *ex vivo* analyses. Neurobiol. Biobehav. Rev. **13:** In press.

80. POTHOS, E., G. P. MARK & B. G. HOEBEL. 1989. *In vivo* dialysis measurements of dopamine and serotonin release in the nucleus accumbens as a function of body weight. Proc. Xth Intl. Conf. Physiology of Food and Fluid Intake, Paris, France. In press.

81. ROLLS, E. T. 1975. The Brain and Reward. Pergamon Press. Oxford.

82. ROTH, R. H. 1983. Neuroleptics: Functional neurochemistry. *In* Neuroleptics, Neurochemical, Behavioral, and Clinical Perspectives. J. T. Coyle & S. J. Enna, Eds.: 119–156. Raven Press. New York.

83. RUSSELL, G. F. M., S. A. CHECKLEY & P. H. ROBINSON. 1986. The limited role of drugs in the treatment of anorexia and bulimia nervosa. *In* Pharmacology of Eating Disorders: Theoretical and Clinical Developments. M. O. Carruba & J. E. Blundell, Eds.: 151–167. Raven Press. New York.

84. SALLER, C. F. & E. M. STRICKER. 1976. Hyperphagia and increased growth in rats after intraventricular injection of 5,7-dihydroxytryptamine. Science **192:** 385–397.

85. SCOTT, T. R. & G. P. MARK. 1986. Hedonics and taste: Modulation of gustatory afferent activity by learning and need state in the rat. *In* Neuronal and Endogenous Chemical Control of Mechanisms on Emotional Behavior. Y. Oomura, Ed.: 117–126. Springer-Verlag. Berlin.

86. SCHWARTZ, D. H., D. B. DORFMAN, L. HERNANDEZ & B. G. HOEBEL. 1988. Cholecystokinin: 1. CCK antagonists in the PVN induce feeding, 2. Effects of CCK in the nucleus accumbens on extracellular dopamine turnover. *In* Neurology and Neurobiology, Cholecystokinin Antagonists. R. Y. Wang & R. Schoenfeld, Eds. Vol. **47:** 285–305. Alan R. Liss. New York.

87. Schwartz, D. H., L. Hernandez & B. G. HOEBEL. 1989. Serotonin release in the medial and lateral hypothalamus during feeding and its anticipation. Soc. Neurosci. Abstr. **15:** 225.

88. SCHWARTZ, D., L. HERNANDEZ & B. G. HOEBEL. 1989. Fenfluramine administered systemically or locally increases extracellular serotonin in the lateral hypothalamus as measured by microdialysis. Brain Res. **482:** 261–270.

89. SCHWARTZ, D. H., S. McCLANE, L. HERNANDEZ & B. G. HOEBEL. 1988. Tryptophan and food increase extracellular serotonin in the lateral hypothalamus as measured by microdialysis in rat. Soc. Neurosci. Abstr. **14:** 25.

90. SCHWARTZ, D. H., S. McCLANE, L. HERNANDEZ & B. G. HOEBEL. 1989. Feeding increases extracellular serotonin in the lateral hypothalamus of the rat as measured by microdialysis. Brain Res. **479:** 349–354.

91. SCLAFANI, A & A. KIRCHGESSNER. 1986. The role of the medial hypothalamus in the control of food intake: An update. *In* Feeding Behavior, Neural and Humoral Controls. R. C. Ritter, S. Ritter & C. D. Barnes, Eds.: 27–66. Academic Press. New York.

92. SMITH, G. P. & L. H. SCHNEIDER. 1988. Relationships between mesolimbic dopamine function and eating behavior. Ann. New York Acad. Sci. **535:** 254–261.
93. STANLEY, B. G., S. F. LEIBOWITZ, N. EPPEL, S. ST-PIERRE & B. G. HOEBEL. 1985. Suppression of norepinephrine-elicited feeding by neurotensin: Evidence for behavioral, anatomical and pharmacological specificity. Brain Res. **343:** 297–304.
94. STANLEY, B. G., D. H. SCHWARTZ, L. HERNANDEZ, B. G. HOEBEL & S. F. LEIBOWITZ. 1989. Patterns of extracellular norepinephrine in the paraventricular hypothalamus: Relationship to circadian rhythm and deprivation-induced eating behavior. Life Sci. **45:** 275–282.
95. STANLEY, B. G., D. H. SCHWARTZ, L. HERNANDEZ, S. F. LEIBOWITZ & B. G. HOEBEL. 1989. Patterns of extracellular 5-hydroxyindoleacetic acid (5-HIAA) in the paraventricular hypothalamus (PVN): Relation to circadian rhythm and deprivation-induced eating behavior. Pharmacol. Biochem. Behav. **33:** 257–260.
96. STRICKER, E. M. 1983. Brain neurochemistry and the control of food intake. *In* Handbook of Behavioral Neurobiology. E. Satinoff & P. Teitelbaum, Eds. Vol. 6: 329–326.
97. SWANSON, L. W. & P. P. SAWCHENKO. 1983. Hypothalamic integration: Organization of the paraventricular and supraoptic nuclei. Ann. Rev. Neurosci. **6:** 269–324.
98. TEITELBAUM, P. 1982. What is the "zero condition" for motivated behavior? *In* The Neural Basis of Feeding and Reward. B. G. Hoebel & D. Novin, Eds.: 7–23. Haer Institute, Brunswick, ME.
99. UNGERSTEDT, U. 1971. Adipsia and aphagia after 6-hydroxydopamine induced degeneration of the nigrostriatal dopamine system. Acta Physiol. Scand. Suppl. **367:** 95–122.
100. UNGERSTEDT, U. 1984. Measurement of neurotransmitter release by intracranial dialysis. *In* Measurement of Neurotransmitter Release *In Vivo*. C. A. Marsden, Ed.: 81–105. John Wiley & Sons. New York.
101. VALENSTEIN, E. S. 1964. Problems of measurement and interpretation with reinforcing brain stimulation. Psychol. Rev. **71:** 415–437.
102. WAGNER, J. A. & S. J. PEROUTKA. 1988. Comparative neurotoxicity of fenfluramine and 3,4-methylenedioxymethamphetamine (MDMA). Soc. Neurosci. Abstr. **14:** 327.
103. WALDBILLIG, R. J., T. J. BARTNESS & B. G. STANLEY. 1981. Increased food intake, body weight, and adiposity in rats after regional neurochemical depletion of serotonin. J. Comp. Physiol. Psychol. **95:** 391–405.
104. WANG, R. Y. & R. SCHOENFELD, Eds. 1988. Neurology and Neurobiology. Vol. 47, Cholecystokinin Antagonists. Alan R. Liss, Inc. New York.
105. WAYNER, M. J. & Y. OOMURA, Eds. 1975. Central Neural Control of Eating and Obesity. Pharmacol. Biochem. Behav. **3:** Suppl. 1.
106. WEISS, G. F., P. PAPADAKOS, K. KNUDSON & S. F. LEIBOWITZ. 1986. Medial hypothalamic serotonin: Effects of deprivation and norepinephrine-induced eating. Pharmacol. Biochem. Behav. **25:** 1223–1230.
107. WEST, H. L., D. H. SCHWARTZ & B. G. HOEBEL. 1989. Local injection of serotonin into the lateral hypothalamus suppresses food intake. Soc. Neurosci. Abstr. **15:** 1281.
108. WESTERINK, B. H. C., G. DAMSMA, H. ROLLEMA, J. B. DE VRIES & A. S. HORN. 1987. Scope and limitations of *in vivo* brain dialysis: A comparison of its application of various neurotransmitter systems. Life Sci. **41:** 1763–1776.
109. WHITE, F. J. & R. Y. WANG. 1984. Interactions of cholecystokinin octapeptide and dopamine on nucleus accumbens neurons. Brain Res. **300:** 161–166.
110. WISE, R. A. 1982. Common neural basis of brain stimulation reward, drug reward, and food reward. *In* The Neural Basis of Feeding and Reward. B. G. Hoebel & D. Novin, Eds.: 445–454. Haer Institute. Brunswick, ME.
111. WISE, R. A. 1983. Brain neuronal systems mediating reward processes. *In* The Neurobiology of Opiate Reward Processes. J. E. Smith & J. D. Lane, Eds.: 405–437. Elsevier Biomedical. New York.
112. WISE, R. A. & P.-P. ROMPRE. 1989. Brain dopamine and reward. Ann. Rev. Psychol. **40:** 191–225.
113. WURTMAN, R. J. 1988. Effects of their nutrient precursors on the synthesis and release of serotonin, the catecholamines, and acetylcholine: Implications for behavioral disorders. Clinical Neuropharm. **11:** (Suppl. 1): S187–S193.
114. GLIMCHER, P. G. 1989. Ph.D. thesis, University of Pennsylvania, Philadelphia, PA.

DISCUSSION

DR. IAN ACWORTH (*Massachusetts Institute of Technology, Cambridge, MA*): The basal concentration of the monoamines, as you've shown, are very, very low, and physiologically they change by 30% or so. I just wondered what manipulations you've used, both pharmacologically and on your HPLC system, to show the purity of those basal peaks of serotonin and dopamine, and what manipulations are designed to lower their concentration. Second, I wonder if you have any problems with 5-HT measurements from platelets when they burst through with serotonin.

DR. BARTLEY G. HOEBEL (*Princeton University, Princeton, NJ*): That is an excellent technical question, and I did gloss over that. Briefly, with regard to dopamine, it turns out that dopamine is blocked by TTX which stops the firing of the cells, so it's probably coming from neurons. Low-calcium media will do the same thing.[b] Serotonin is an even bigger problem in that respect because if, as you say, it comes from blood platelets, from mast cells, from endothelial cells, then you wonder whether the serotonin is really coming out of neurons from the raphe. The answer seems to be that it is neuronal serotonin, because Sid Auerbach, formerly at Princeton and now at Rutgers, has shown that 8-hydroxy-DPAT, which acts on autoreceptors in the raphe, turns off serotonin cells and makes that serotonin peak go away in the hypothalamus. To make sure that the serotonin peak really is serotonin, we now do feeding studies in which we measure serotonin using a dual potentiostat so that we oxidize the serotonin at two different potentials and make sure that the ratio of those two potentials is the same as the ratio for a standard of pure serotonin. I agree with you that there are problems; we're being very careful.

DR. LINDA SCHNEIDER (*New York Hospital–Cornell Medical Center, White Plains, NY*): I am interested in your observation that the tryptophan increased serotonin only if the animals were food deprived. Was that true?

DR. HOEBEL: That's right.

DR. SCHNEIDER: I think we all need to be very careful with our food deprivation conditions in understanding the results obtained by pharmacological treatment with agonists, antagonists, precursors, and so forth. For example, it's very difficult to show an increase in food intake with cholecystokinin antagonists when animals are food deprived, while positive results are coming through in nondeprived situations.

DR. HOEBEL: Yes, you're right, and it brings up a point of Bob Myer's, who is a past master of push–pull techniques; he has shown that some of these effects can even reverse at different times of day. What I've been showing you are the times of day when performing these experiments works. As we do more experiments, I'm sure we're going to find that there are times of day when some of these don't work. We're going to have to do circadian studies for all of these monoamines.[94,95]

When I asked John Fernstrom for his opinion on our results with tryptophan, he felt that the reason that we did not get a tryptophan effect in the nondeprived animals is that there were more competing amino acids in the bloodstream. That fits the Wurtman and Fernstrom view of how that sort of thing works. In deprived animals, one can suppose that the competing amino acids have been taken out of the bloodstream, making

---

[b] We have shown that extracellular DA is increased by local cocaine but by equimolar lidocaine, which controls for neural anesthetic effects. Inadvertently, we have also used a Ringer's perfusate with high calcium, which may have facilitated neuronal dopamine release [*note added in proof*].

it easier for the big injection of tryptophan to swamp the carrier that transports tryptophan into the brain. We suspect that that is why tryptophan loading worked best in deprived animals.

DR. DAVID SANDBERG (*North Shore University Hospital, Manhasset, NY*): You've demonstrated, very nicely, that both feeding and drugs of abuse can lead to increases in dopamine in the nucleus accumbens. I'm wondering if you know of any work that's looked at the conditioning of environmental stimuli to feeding. Are they adequate to increase dopamine levels in the accumbens?

DR. HOEBEL: We are starting to do that now in two ways. One way would be to give the rat a palatable food, show the dopamine release, then train a conditioned aversion to that food, and ask does that food still release dopamine. We'd like to do the same thing with positive conditioned stimuli.

The only thing we've done just like that so far has been with a light cue. The light alone was a discriminative stimulus signaling the availability of food, but our technique was not sensitive enough to pick up dopamine in response to that light.[33] Phillips and Fibiger are using *in vivo* voltammetry, which is much more rapid, and I would recommend voltammetry to you for the kinds of experiments that require a rapid time course. If you want to see a change to a light signal, you had better use something faster than our 20-minute measurements. But, in something like learned aversion, microdialysis should be perfect, and we will have to do that soon.[c]

DR. SILVIO GARATTINI (*Instituto di Ricerche Farmacologiche "Mario Negri," Milan, Italy*): I'd like to comment on the effect of amphetamine on serotonin. This effect is related to the inhibition of uptake of serotonin, which occurs when amphetamine is given at a relatively high concentration. I suppose that this effect occurs only at concentrations which exceed by several times the anorectic effect of amphetamine.

DR. HOEBEL: You're the expert. I take that as a good point of advice. We have not tried to run dose–response curves for all of these drugs because it is so much work with microdialysis, and we wanted to move on to feeding. We started out using these drugs because we could get a big effect back in the days when the HPLCs were not so sensitive. Now that the HPLCs are more sensitive, we've moved on to measuring natural releasers of dopamine. In the process I'm afraid we have failed to go back and do careful dose–response curves with these drugs. I think you're absolutely correct. Those were high doses of amphetamine, and as you say, lower doses that are sufficient to produce anorexia would have less effect.

[c] The experiment was successful; see Mark *et al.*[61] [*note added in proof*].

Serotonin and the Pharmacology of Eating Disorders

ROSARIO SAMANIN AND SILVIO GARATTINI

Istituto di Ricerche Farmacologiche "Mario Negri"
via Eritrea 62
20157 Milan, Italy

INTRODUCTION

Important aspects of feeding in animals have been found to be controlled by changes in serotonin (5-HT) activity that have relatively little effect on other behaviors.[1-5] The importance of 5-HT in the control of feeding in man derives essentially from the fact that fenfluramine (F), and particularly its dextro isomer, *d*-fenfluramine (DF), two agents that enhance the release of 5-HT from nerve terminals and inhibit its reuptake,[6-10] reduce the desire for food in human subjects by a mechanism that seems to involve enhanced serotonergic transmission.[11] Moreover, nutrient selection appears to be similarly affected by F and DF in animals and man,[12,13] although this is still a matter of some controversy[14] (see various contributions to June 1987 issue of *Appetite*). In animals it is difficult in some instances to establish whether a substance causes changes in feeding by acting on mechanisms specifically controlling hunger and satiety or by altering arousal or causing malaise. However, methods involving sophisticated descriptions and quantitation of feeding behavior make it likely that "true anorectic" effects of F and DF are identified when appropriate doses of these agents are used in animals.[5]

Inhibitors of neuronal uptake have been known for many years as antidepressant drugs, and recently selective inhibitors of 5-HT neuronal uptake have been proposed as potentially useful agents in the treatment of clinical obesity.[15-17] Although it appears reasonable to expect that increased 5-HT availability following uptake inhibition should result in reduction of food intake, it is not yet clear to what extent blockade of 5-HT uptake is an adequate mechanism for reducing food intake in animals and man.[18,19] Knowledge of the exact mechanism by which drugs modify serotonergic transmission is therefore a prerequisite for interpreting their effects on feeding and, more generally, to establish the extent to which findings in animals can be applied to humans.

Recent progress in the pharmacology of 5-HT has made available new tools, particularly specific agonists and antagonists at 5-HT receptor types and subtypes, enabling the role of 5-HT in feeding control to be explored in more detail in animals and man.

This review is a progress report of current research on effects of drugs that modify feeding by acting on various serotonergic mechanisms. The following classes will be discussed:

(a) 5-HT releasers and uptake blockers such as F and DF;
(b) 5-HT uptake blockers;
(c) direct agonists at postsynaptic 5-HT receptor types and subtypes; and
(d) agents reducing 5-HT transmission by blocking postsynaptic receptors or stimulating autoreceptors.

5-HT RELEASE VERSUS UPTAKE INHIBITION

As stated above, F is the prototype of drugs affecting 5-HT release and uptake. In animals and humans treated with fenfluramine, the D and L stereoisomers and their respective nor-metabolites have different biochemical and functional effects. DF and D-norfenfluramine (DNF) have more potent effects than the L-isomers on *in vitro* 5-HT neuronal uptake and 5-HT metabolism and synthesis in rat brain[8] while L-fenfluramine preferentially affects catecholamines[20] and may have antidopaminergic properties through a mechanism not involving direct blockade of dopaminergic receptors.[20,21] Various recent reviews on the neurochemical and behavioral effects of F and DF are available[9,10,14,22]; only the most recent studies will be discussed in some detail here.

In vitro studies have shown that DF potently and specifically inhibits the neuronal uptake of 5-HT and, to a lesser degree, enhances the release of 5-HT from a granular (reserpine-sensitive) pool.[23,24] In reserpinized animals, in which the effect of DF on 5-HT release is completely abolished, DF is still very active in inhibiting 5-HT uptake into brain synaptosomes[24] suggesting that the effect on uptake is not influenced by the effect on release. DNF instead is more potent as a 5-HT releaser than as an uptake inhibitor, and, unlike DF, it releases 5-HT particularly from an extragranular (reserpine-insensitive) pool.[22,23,25]

The ability of relatively low doses of DF (close to those causing significant effects on feeding) to enhance serotonergic transmission in intact animals is presumably the result of the fact that DF and DNF, respectively, inhibit 5-HT neuronal uptake and enhance its release from an extragranular pool. At higher doses DF causes a marked and long-lasting reduction of brain 5-HT whose mechanism is not completely clear.[9]

At doses and times close to those causing a marked reduction of food intake in starved rats (2.5 mg/kg, 1 hr after injection) DF specifically reduces the synthesis of 5-HT in the hypothalamus and brainstem, two areas particularly important for DF anorexia, whereas at higher doses the effect on brain 5-HT synthesis is more diffuse.[20] These findings suggest that the role of brain 5-HT in the anorectic activity of DF might be more specifically examined using relatively low doses of DF. At higher doses it could prove difficult to separate the anorectic effect of DF from effects on sensorimotor performance, such as reduced locomotion and sedation.

The decrease in 5-HT synthesis has been attributed to a feedback mechanism consequent to presynaptic rather than postsynaptic 5-HT receptor stimulation, because metergoline, an antagonist at postsynaptic with little effect on presynaptic receptors, did not change the effect of DF on 5-HT synthesis.[20] That the decrease in 5-HT synthesis is related to increased 5-HT availability in the synaptic cleft is also suggested by the fact that the anorectic effect of 2.5 mg/kg DF is completely antagonized by metergoline.[26]

Studies using *in vivo* dialysis or voltammetric techniques have shown effects of DF on extracellular 5-HT or 5-hydroxyindoleacetic acid (5-HIAA), the main metabolite of brain 5-HT, only at doses much higher than those causing anorexia. Using microdialysis in freely moving rats, intraperitoneal injections of 10 mg/kg, but not 3 mg/kg, significantly increased extracellular 5-HT in the perifornical lateral hypothalamus within one hour of injection while 5-HIAA concentrations were decreased, reaching statistical significance one hour and later after injection.[27] Similar results were recently obtained by measuring 5-HIAA voltammetrically in the nucleus accumbens of freely moving rats treated with 10 mg/kg DF.[28] In the hippocampus, even 25 mg/kg DF did not significantly reduce 5-HIAA concentrations, confirming that there are differences in regional sensitivity of 5-HT neurons to DF in rat brain. In the same study, 10 mg/kg DNF significantly raised extracellular 5-HIAA within one hour of injection, probably related to the metabolite's ability to preferentially stimulate 5-HT release. A similar, but insignificant, tendency was found with 25 mg/kg DF. It seems therefore that currently available neurochemical techniques *in vivo* are unable to identify minute amounts of 5-HT released by DF in the synaptic cleft, with the possible exception of a reduction in 5-HT synthesis, probably consequent to activation of presynaptic 5-HT receptors. See TABLE 1 for a summary of these findings.

Unfortunately, these limitations in method mean we cannot separate the contributions of enhanced release and uptake inhibition to the effects of DF and DNF in intact animals, because specific 5-HT uptake inhibitors also reduce 5-HT synthesis and metabolism.[29,30] It has been recently reported by Fuller *et al.*[31] that DF, unlike fluoxetine (a putative specific 5-HT uptake inhibitor) did not block the depletion of brain 5-HT caused by *p*-chloroamphetamine (PCA) over a wide dose range. In the same study 5 mg/kg DF and fluoxetine, respectively, raised or reduced the 5-HIAA/5-HT ratio one hour after injection. While these differences may be due to DF (or more likely DNF) and fluoxetine acting preferentially on 5-HT release and uptake, they provide no information on the extent to which uptake inhibition contributes to the effects of DF in intact animals, because the synergism between DF and PCA on 5-HT release may completely mask DF's effect on 5-HT inhibition.

The question of the relative involvement of enhanced release and uptake inhibition in the anorectic effect of drugs acting on 5-HT nerve terminals is important, because various specific 5-HT uptake inhibitors such as fluoxetine and sertraline have recently been proposed as potential anorectic agents.[15,16,17] It is not yet clear to what extent an action on 5-HT release by active metabolites is involved in the effect of these agents in intact animals. For instance, after fluoxetine administration to rats, brain levels of norfluoxetine exceed by several times the levels of the parent drug (Caccia, unpublished results). Considering that both norfluoxetine and fluoxetine enhance 5-HT re-

TABLE 1. Effect of Systemically Administered *d*-Fenfluramine on 5-HT Biochemical Indices in Rat Brain

5-HT Indices	Dose DF (mg/kg)	Effects and Comment	References
5-HT, 5-HIAA levels[a]	1.25 p.o.	No effect	9
5-HT, 5-HIAA levels	2.5 p.o.	Decrease or no effect	9, 20
5-HT synthesis[b]	1.25 p.o.	No effect in various brain areas	20
5-HT synthesis	2.5 p.o.	Decrease in hypothalamus and brainstem	20
5-HT synthesis	5.0 p.o.	Decrease in various brain areas	20
5-HIAA/5-HT ratio[b]	5.0 i.p.	Increase in the whole brain	81
5-HT release	3.0 i.p.	No effect in paraventricular hypothalamus (assessed by *in vivo* dialysis)	27
5-HT release	10.0 i.p.	Increase in paraventricular hypothalamus	27
Extracellular 5-HIAA	2.5 i.p.	No effect in the nucleus accumbens (assessed by voltammetry)	28
Extracellular 5-HIAA	10.0 i.p.	Decrease in the nucleus accumbens (starting 1 hr after injection)	28
Extracellular 5-HIAA	10–25 i.p.	Tendency to increase (within 1 hr of injection)	28
Extracellular 5-HIAA	25.0 i.p.	No effect in the hippocampus	28

NOTE: Anorectic activity of DF (ID_{50}) in the rat is around 1 mg/kg or less depending on the test used.

[a] Four hours after injection. DF's effects on brain 5-HT and 5-HIAA levels are better seen 4–8 hrs after injection.

[b] One hour after injection.

lease with a potency similar to that of DF and NDF,[25] the possibility exists that brain levels of norfluoxetine after doses of fluoxetine causing reduction of food intake may well be adequate to release significant amounts of 5-HT from nerve terminals. The same goes for norsertraline, which is formed after sertraline administration and whose effects on 5-HT release are not known.

We have found that indalpine (LM 5008), a very potent and selective inhibitor of 5-HT uptake with no effect on 5-HT release,[32] did not reduce food intake at doses 27 times the ED_{50} for inhibiting 5-HT uptake *in vivo*.[18] By contrast, Angel *et al.*[16] recently reported a similar ED_{50} of indalpine for causing anorexia and inhibiting 5-HT uptake *in vivo*.

In the same study, a good correlation was obtained between doses of various drugs inhibiting *in vivo* 5-HT uptake and food intake by 50%. The method used to measure 5-HT uptake *in vivo* may be crucial, because an ED_{50} of 0.4–0.6 mg/kg indalpine was necessary for inhibiting the depletion of brain 5-HT caused by H 75/12 or fenfluramine,[18,33] while doses approximately ten times higher were needed to antagonize the 5-HT-depleting effect of *p*-chloroamphetamine.[33]

Sertraline inhibited the effect of *p*-chloroamphetamine on brain 5-HT with an ED_{50} of 0.69 µmol/kg,[34] whereas doses between 7 and 32 µmol/kg significantly reduced ingestive behavior in rats.[17] These findings are summarized in TABLE 2. On the basis of studies on *ex vivo* uptake in striatal synaptosomes using [³H]5-HT, an ED_{50} of about 10 µmol/kg sertraline was needed for inhibiting 5-HT uptake.[34] A dissociation between 5-HT uptake inhibition and anorexia was found with the *cis* and *trans* isomers of RU 25591, a selective 5-HT uptake inhibitor.[19]

Although the role of active metabolites of fluoxetine and sertraline on 5-HT release remains to be established, the possibility of increased 5-HT availability in the synaptic cleft following uptake inhibition causing anorectic effects in certain conditions cannot be excluded with certainty. Various factors, such as the time during which food is measured after drug treatment, the animals' nutritional status, and the quality of the food, may all influence the effect of 5-HT uptake blockers on food intake.

DIRECT 5-HT AGONISTS

In line with the hypothesis that increased availability of 5-HT in the synapse causes anorectic activity, direct 5-HT postsynaptic receptor agonists such as quipazine and *m*-chlorophenylpiperazine (mCPP) were reported to reduce food intake in animals.[18,35,36]

Of the various 5-HT receptor types and subtypes described,[37-39] the 5-HT₁ receptors, particularly the 5-HT$_{1B}$ subtype, seem to cause anorexia in rats when activated, because RU-24969, a specific agonist at 5-HT$_{1A}$ and 5-HT$_{1B}$ receptors, caused a dose–de-

TABLE 2. Effects of Drugs on *in Vivo* 5-HT Uptake and Food Intake in Rats

Compound	5-HT Uptake[a] ID_{50} µmol/kg	Food Intake ID_{50} µmol/kg	References
Fluoxetine	25.9	About 32.4	87, 88
Indalpine[b]	3.2	>87.0	18
Indalpine	25.4	25.4	16
Sertraline	0.69	5.8–29.2	17, 34

NOTE: ID_{50} is the dose inhibiting 5-HT uptake or food intake by 50%.
[a] Ability to prevent brain 5-HT depletion of parachloroamphetamine.
[b] Fenfluramine instead of parachloroamphetamine was used as 5-HT depletor.

pendent reduction of food intake that was attenuated by metergoline, a nonselective 5-HT receptor antagonist, and (−)-pindolol, an antagonist with affinity for 5-HT_1 receptors.[40,41] A role of 5-HT_{1A} receptors in anorexia seems to be excluded by the fact that low doses of a specific 5-HT_{1A} receptor agonist were found to increase food intake, whereas higher doses reduced it, besides inducing motor disturbances in the animals.[20,42,43]

On the basis of studies in which various antagonists at various receptor types and subtypes were used, it has been recently suggested that 5-HT_{1C} receptors mediate the anorexic effect of mCPP.[44] Although this is compatible with the particularly high affinity of mCPP for these receptors,[45] the role of 5-HT_{1C} receptors in 5-HT-dependent anorexia is not firmly established, because mCCP has affinity for various 5-HT receptors,[10,25,45] and mesulergine, a potent 5-HT_{1C} and 5-HT_2 receptor antagonist, did not reduce the anorectic effect of mCPP.[44] Antagonists with affinity for 5-HT_3 and 5-HT_{1B} receptors also failed to antagonize the effect of mCPP while nonselective 5-HT receptor antagonists were effective.[36,44] These findings suggest that more 5-HT receptors (5-HT_{1B} and 5-HT_{1C} types?) are involved and blockade of one type may not be enough to modify the effect of mCPP on food intake. TABLE 3 shows the relative affinity of some compounds for 5-HT receptor types and subtypes and their effects on food intake.

A potent and selective agonist at 5-HT 2 receptors, 1-(2,5-dimethoxy-4-iodophenyl)-2-aminopropane (DOI), has been reported to cause a dose-related inhibition of feeding in rats adapted to a schedule in which a milk diet was presented for six hours daily.[46] The effect was antagonized by ketanserin, a 5-HT_2 receptor antagonist, but not by xylamidine, which blocks these receptors only in the periphery, so it was suggested that central 5-HT_2 receptors were involved. A role of 5-HT_2 receptors was also indicated by findings that the effects of fenfluramine and quipazine on food intake were antagonized by 5-HT_2 receptor antagonists.[47,48] Investigation of the role of central 5-HT_2 receptors in feeding is complicated by the fact that their activation is known to result in associational disturbances that could interfere with various behaviors including feeding. One study compared different doses of metergoline, a nonselective 5-HT_2 receptor antagonist, and ritanserin, a selective 5-HT_2 receptor antagonist, for their ability to antagonize the anorectic effect of DF, to occupy central 5-HT_2 receptors, and to affect brain concentrations of DF and DNF. It was found that, unlike metergoline, ritanserin significantly antagonized the effect of DF only at doses that lowered DNF brain levels.[49] Associational disturbances of 5-HT_2 agonists and interference with drug distribution and metabolism by 5-HT_2 antagonists should therefore be considered in studies exploring the role of central 5-HT_2 receptors in feeding.

TABLE 3. Direct 5-HT Agonists: Affinity for 5-HT Receptor Types and Subtypes and Effect on Food Intake

Compound	Affinity to 5-HT Receptors	Effect on Food Intake	References[a]
mCPP	5-HT_{1C}>5-HT_{1B}>5-HT_2>5-HT_{1A}	Decrease, antagonized by metergoline	18
Quipazine	5-HT_{1C}>5-HT_{1B}>5-HT_2>5-HT_{1A}	Decrease, antagonized by metergoline, ritanserin	35, 89
RU-24969	5-HT_{1B}>5-HT_{1A}>>>5-HT_{1C}>5-HT_2	Decrease, antagonized by metergoline, (−)-pindolol	40, 41
8-OH-DPAT	5-HT_{1A}>>>5-HT_{1C}>5-HT_2>$5HT_{1B}$	Increase, antagonized by 5-HT neuron lesions	55
Buspirone	5-HT_{1A}>>>5-HT_2>>5-HT_{1C}>5-HT_{1B}	Increase	10, 45

[a] See References 45, 90, and 91 for affinity to 5-HT receptors.

Evidence exists that 5-HT in the periphery may use 5-HT_2 receptors to control feeding behavior[56] and 5-HT_2 receptor antagonists have been reported to enhance food intake in sated rats.[44,50]

Whatever the role of 5-HT_2 receptors in feeding, it seems that they are not used by indirect 5-HT agonists such as DF and sertraline. In fact, at doses occupying about 50% of central 5-HT_2 receptors, metergoline, but not ritanserin, antagonized the effect of DF[22,49], and metergoline, but not ketanserin, antagonized the effect of sertraline.[17] TABLE 4 summarizes the effects of various 5-HT receptor antagonists on anorexia by DF and sertraline.

CENTRAL VERSUS PERIPHERAL 5-HT:
EFFECTS OF F AND DF

Various authors who have injected 5-HT intracerebrally into animals found no consistent changes in food intake.[4,5,51] Some studies using injections of 5-HT in various hypothalamic areas have provided more convincing evidence of its role in feeding regulation. The hypothalamic paraventricular nucleus (PVN) is particularly sensitive to direct serotonergic stimulation. Dose-related inhibition of food intake was seen in hungry rats given doses of 5-HT (1–10 µg) into the PVN that had no apparent effect on sensorimotor performance.[1]

5-HT injected in the PVN of freely feeding rats reduced the size and duration of the first meal with no effect on meal initiation. A significantly larger interval occurred between the first and second meal in 5-HT-injected animals.[52] On the basis of these findings, it was suggested that 5-HT in the PVN induces a satiety state with no effect on hunger (defined as meal initiation).

In experiments on selection of carbohydrate or protein intake, 5-HT in the PVN showed selective suppression of the carbohydrate-rich diet. A selective effect on carbohydrate intake was also found on injecting 5-HT into the PVN of freely feeding rats given three pure macronutrient diets—protein, carbohydrate, and fat—during the early phase (1 hr) of the nocturnal period.[53] These findings suggest that in the PVN 5-HT acts by controlling specific aspects of meal patterns and macronutrient selection. It is of interest that 5-HT particularly inhibits the effect of noradrenaline, which has opposite effects from 5-HT in the PVN.[54]

TABLE 4. Effect of Various 5-HT Receptor Antagonists on Anorexia by Indirect 5-HT Agonists in Deprived Rats

Antagonist (mg/kg)	Characteristic	Indirect Agonist (mg/kg)	Effect	References
Metergoline (1)	Nonselective	DF (2.5)	Antagonism	26
Ritanserin (0.5)	5-HT_2	DF (2.5)	No change	49
Odanserin (1)	5-HT_3	DF (2.5)	No change	10
Xylamidine (2)	Peripheral	DF (2.5)	No change	26
Xylamidine (1.5)	Peripheral	DF (2.5)	No change	63
Xylamidine (3)	Peripheral	F (2.5–5)	No change	62
Xylamidine (3)	Peripheral	F (2.5)	Antagonism	64
Ketanserin (1–2.5)	5-HT_2	F (3)	Antagonism	47
Metergoline (2)	Nonselective	Sertraline (10)	Antagonism	17
Ketanserin (3.3)	5-HT_2	Sertraline (10)	No change	17
Xylamidine (2.5)	Peripheral	Sertraline (10)	No change	17

Although much interest has been focused on hypothalamic 5-HT, the nucleus accumbens was recently found to be sensitive to the inhibitory effect of 5-HT on a particular type of overeating associated with behavioral activation, that is, eating caused by muscimol injected in the nucleus raphe dorsalis.[55] Interestingly, doses of 5-HT (2.2–8.8 µg) that caused dose-related inhibition of muscimol-induced eating had no effect on food intake of deprived rats.[55] Thus, particular types of overeating not associated with nutritional deficits may be under the control of 5-HT mechanisms different from those regulating physiological satiety.

Peripherally administered 5-HT appears to reduce food intake without interfering with sensorimotor performance or causing malaise.[2,3] 5-HT$_2$ receptors may be involved in this effect since ritanserin, a selective antagonist of these receptors, prevented the effect of 5-HT on food intake.[56] Using the technique of microstructural analysis in food-deprived rats, Fletcher and Burton[57] found that 1–4 mg/kg 5-HT reduced bout size and duration with no effect on other parameters such as both frequency, mean eating rate, and median inter-pellet interval. In the authors' opinion these data suggested, but did not prove, that 5-HT was involved in the control of satiety. Further support for this hypothesis derives from one study in which peripherally administered 5-HT accelerated the development of satiation in a runway with no effect on feeding initiation.[58] Peripherally administered 5-HT delays gastric emptying,[3] an effect that, according to Moran and McHugh,[59] may reduce meal size. However, no causal relationship has yet been established between slowing gastric emptying and reduction of food intake. In one study methysergide reversed anorexia but not the slowing of gastric emptying induced by 5-HT (1 and 2 mg/kg, respectively) in food-deprived rats.[3] Because 5-HT in the brain and periphery may enhance satiation, it is of interest to examine the possibility that drugs enhancing 5-HT transmission, particularly F and DF, use 5-HT in one region or both to cause anorexia when administered systemically.

The first evidence that F uses brain 5-HT to cause anorexia was the finding that electrolytic lesions of the nucleus raphe medianus, where some of the 5-HT neurons innervating the forebrain originate, blocked fenfluramine's lowering of food intake of food-deprived rats.[60] Subsequent studies with intracerebral injections of a neurotoxin for 5-HT neurons confirmed these findings.[61] The strength of the phenomenon has been questioned by some authors who found that electrolytic lesions and intracerebral injections of 5-HT neurotoxins failed to modify fenfluramine's anorexia. (The reasons for these discrepancies have been discussed elsewhere.[4,5]) Further support for the hypothesis that DF reduces food intake of rats by interacting with brain 5-HT came from studies in which the anorectic activity of 2.5 mg/kg DF and 1.25 mg/kg DNF in food-deprived rats was completely prevented by metergoline, a potent central 5-HT antagonist, but was not affected by xylamidine, a 5-HT antagonist that penetrates the brain very poorly, at a dose (2 mg/kg p.o.) well above the level reported to have peripheral antiserotoninergic effect.[26] These findings have been confirmed[62,63] except in one study[64] in which 3 mg/kg i.p. xylamidine was administered to rats deprived of food for 3.5 hours.

Besides the possibility that xylamidine at higher doses may interfere with F metabolism and distribution, the nutritional status of the animals may be relevant, because the anorectic effect of fenfluramine on freely feeding rats, unlike that in food-deprived animals, was not affected by lesions of central 5-HT neurons.[65] In this study it was suggested that part of the suppression of feeding by F in nonstarved rats was due to its ability to slow gastric emptying, because the drug potency apparently decreased in relation to the time needed for gastric emptying. Although other factors, such as changes in hormone release, nutrient utilization, or rats' arousal at different times after the first meal, might contribute to the results with F, these findings do suggest that the interval between two large meals may be prolonged by administering F immediately after the first meal but provide no information on the mechanism by which F slows eating and reduces meal size. It should be stressed that these are the main effects of F and DF in starved and freely feeding rats.[5,66] Xylamidine, unlike metergoline, does not modify the effect of DF on the behavior of deprived rats in a food-rewarded runway behavior,[67] suggesting that DF's effects on various aspects of feeding in food-deprived rats are mediated by central 5-HT mechanisms.

Cholecystokinin, a proposed short-term satiety factor in the periphery, has been found to affect feeding by fasted rhesus monkeys only when the stomach was filled with saline; this effect was correlated with the hormone's ability to delay gastric emptying.[59] On the basis of correlative findings, slowing of gastric emptying has been suggested as one mechanism by which fenfluramine reduces meal size in fasted rhesus monkeys.[68]

That some gastric replenishment is necessary for F or DF to affect feeding is apparently disproved by several studies showing that F delays the onset of feeding in animals and man.[69-71] Peripheral administration of F or NF produces effects on meal patterns and choice between two diets containing different proportions of carbohydrate and protein similar to those of 5-HT in the PVN.[12,52] No information is available on the effect of peripherally administered 5-HT on nutrient selection. In conclusion, it remains to be proved whether F or DF use peripheral 5-HT to affect some aspects of feeding not easily revealed by measuring food intake in deprived rats.

BEHAVIORAL SPECIFICITY OF FENFLURAMINE AND ITS EFFECTS ON HYPERPHAGIAS

Development of drugs selectively using peripheral 5-HT to reduce feeding is certainly an attractive prospect in view of the fact that brain transmitters, including 5-HT, affect so many functions and behaviors that drugs enhancing central 5-HT transmission are hardly likely to have specific effects on satiety and hunger. Besides the fact that large doses of F cause motor impairment, it has been discussed that the reduction of meal size and rate by 2.5 mg/kg F may be due to the animal being unable to generate high response rates.[72] Lower doses of F may even affect forms of motivated behavior other than feeding. For instance, 1.5 mg/kg DF reportedly blocks hypermotility induced by d-amphetamine, an effect commonly attributed to the ability of this drug to enhance dopamine release in the nucleus accumbens.[73]

However, the fact that relatively low doses of F or DF attenuate dopamine-dependent behaviors in the brain is not incompatible with its specificity on feeding behavior, because various conditions that have in common the ability to provoke nonspecific motivational excitement enhance ingestive behavior by a mechanism apparently involving enhanced dopamine transmission.[49] It is of interest that F and DF are particularly effective in reducing eating caused by tail-pinch, a model of overeating associated with behavioral excitement and dopamine hyperfunction.[74,75] TABLE 5 summarizes the effects of DF in various feeding paradigms. Incidentally the doses of DF active in these conditions (0.6 mg/kg) are very similar to those used in the treatment of clinical obesity. Models of overeating associated with behavioral excitement may be more predictive than normal feeding of the effects of F and DF in human overeating, particularly when associated with emotional disorders such as the so-called "reactive obesity," "the night eating syndrome," and perhaps even bulimia nervosa.[76]

Another form of overeating that is particularly sensitive to the effect of DF is that caused by injection of neuropeptide Y in the PVN.[77] This endogenous peptide potently stimulates feeding when administered in various hypothalamic areas,[78] a finding

TABLE 5. Effective Doses of *d*-Fenfluramine in Various Feeding Paradigms

Paradigm	Approximate ID_{50}[a] (mg/kg)	References
Laboratory chow by starved rats	1.29	8
Sucrose by sated rats	1.25	92
Runway performance	1.25	67, 69
Insulin	0.75	63
2-deoxy-*d*-glucose	0.75	63
Muscimol in the dorsal raphe	1.25	93
Tail pinch	0.6	75
Neuropeptide Y in paraventricular hypothalamus	0.6	77
Norepinephrine in paraventricular hypothalamus	0.2–0.5	1
Carbohydrate intake (early night)	0.13–0.25	53

[a] ID_{50} is the dose causing 50% reduction of feeding parameters.

that suggests that neuropeptide Y may play a role in the pathogenesis of clinical hyperphagias, including bulimia.[79]

APPETITE STIMULATION BY DRUGS THAT REDUCE 5-HT TRANSMISSION

If 5-HT acts by inhibiting feeding, one would expect reduced transmission to enhance food intake. Until recently, this has been only occasionally reported in animals subjected to lesions of central 5-HT neurons or treated with 5-HT receptor antagonist.[4,5,51] One major reason for the apparent ineffectiveness of these treatments seems to be that food-deprived rats were used in most studies. In agreement with previous findings with methysergide,[51] various 5-HT receptor antagonists, including selective 5-HT$_2$ receptor antagonists, enhanced food intake in rats satiated immediately before drug treatment, but not in hungry animals.[50] The site of action of 5-HT receptor antagonists is not known, but peripheral 5-HT$_2$ receptors may be involved.

Enhancement of feeding by satiated, but not starved, rats has also been reported with 8-hydroxy-2-(di-*n*-propylamino)tetralin (8-OH-DPAT), a selective 5-HT$_{1A}$ receptor agonist.[43] The effect of 8-OH-DPAT appears to be centrally mediated because it was prevented by intraventricular injection of a 5-HT neurotoxin.[42] Further evidence that a reduction in central 5-HT transmission may facilitate feeding is provided by the finding that injection of 8-OH-DPAT in midbrain raphe nuclei, where most 5-HT neurons innervating the forebrain originate, significantly increased eating by free-feeding rats.[42,80] This effect was attributed to 8-OH-DPAT's ability to stimulate autoreceptors located in serotonergic cell bodies in the midbrain raphe region.

It has been argued that 8-OH-DPAT causes animals to eat solid foods by inducing gnawing, because a reduction rather than an increase in glucose consumption was found with 60–120 µg/kg in nondeprived rats.[58,81] Besides the fact that subsequent studies have shown that 8-OH-DPAT also increased consumption of palatable wet mash and liquid diets by the rat,[82,83] no gnawing response was elicited by 8-OH-DPAT injected in the midbrain raphe nuclei.[40] Other 5-HT$_{1A}$ receptor agonists, such as buspirone, gepirone, and isapirone, that cause no gnawing enhance food intake in nonfasted rats.[25,54–86] A significant interaction has been found between 5-HT$_{1A}$ receptor agonists and $F^{83,85}$ or DF.[25] These findings suggest that activation of 5-HT_{1A} receptors specifically stimulates feeding, probably by reducing 5-HT transmission in the rat brain.

CONCLUSIONS

Evidence is increasing that important aspects of feeding may be controlled by 5-HT in the brain and periphery. Drugs enhancing transmitter release from nerve terminals and/or inhibiting neuronal uptake reduce food intake by enhancing 5-HT availability at central 5-HT_1 receptors. Studies with direct 5-HT receptor agonists suggest that activation of central 5-HT_{1B} and possibly 5-HT_{1C} receptors inhibits food intake, whereas the opposite effect is obtained by activating central 5-HT_{1A} receptors. Activation of central 5-HT_2 receptors have been reported to reduce food intake, but the specificity of this effect needs to be further elucidated. Peripheral 5-HT_2 receptors may be involved in the control of feeding and partly also in the effect of indirect 5-HT agonists. No role of 5-HT_3 receptors has been found in studies using the appropriate selective antagonists.

The encouraging clinical results with indirect 5-HT agonists such as F, DF, and fluoxetine suggest that some new findings in animals can be applied to humans. This could provide a basis for better understanding the role of 5-HT in human feeding behavior and for developing new drugs with more potent and specific effects on ingestive behavior.

REFERENCES

1. WEISS, G. F., P. PAPADAKOS, K. KNUDSON & S. F. LEIBOWITZ. 1986. Medial hypothalamic serotonin: Effects on deprivation and norepinephrine-induced eating. Pharmacol. Biochem. Behav. **25:** 1223–1230.
2. Fletcher, P. J. & M. J. BURTON. 1984. Effects of manipulations of peripheral serotonin on feeding and drinking in the rat. Pharmacol. Biochem. Behav. **20:** 835–840.
3. FLETCHER, P. J. & M. J. BURTON. 1985. The anorectic action of peripherally administered 5-HT is enhanced by vagotomy. Physiol. Behav. **34:** 861–866.
4. SAMANIN, R. 1983. Drugs affecting serotonin and feeding. In Biochemical Pharmacology of Obesity. P. B. Curtis-Prior, Ed.: 339–356. Elsevier. Amsterdam.
5. BLUNDELL, J. E. 1984. Serotonin and appetite. Neuropharmacology **23:** 1537–1551.
6. GARATTINI, S., W. BUCZKO, A. JORI & R. SAMANIN. 1975. The mechanism of action of fenfluramine. Postgrad. Med. J. **51**(Suppl. 1): 27–35.
7. GARATTINI, S. & R. SAMANIN. 1976. Anorectic drugs and brain neurotransmitters. In Appetite and Food Intake. T. Silverstone, Ed.: 83–108. Dahlem Konferenzen. Berlin.
8. GARATTINI, S., S. CACCIA, T. MENNINI, R. SAMANIN, S. CONSOLO & H. LADINSKY. 1979. Biochemical pharmacology of the anorectic drug fenfluramine: A review. Curr. Med. Res. Opin. **6**(Suppl. 1): 15–27.
9. GARATTINI, S., T. MENNINI, C. BENDOTTI, R. INVERNIZZI & R. SAMANIN. 1986. Neurochemical mechanism of action of drugs which modify feeding via the serotoninergic system. Appetite **7(Suppl.):** 15–38.
10. GARATTINI, S., A. BIZZI, S. CACCIA, T. MENNINI & R. SAMANIN. Progress in assessing the role of serotonin in the control of food intake. Clin. Neuropharmacol. In press.
11. SILVERSTONE, T. & E. GOODALL. 1986. Recent studies on the clinical pharmacology of anorectic drugs. In 5th International Congress on Obesity. Jerusalem, Israel. Sept. 14–19, 1986. 47. Abstracts book.
12. WURTMAN, J. J. & R. J. WURTMAN. 1977. Fenfluramine and fluoxetine spare protein consumption while suppressing caloric intake by rats. Science **198:** 1178–1180.
13. WURTMAN, J. J. & R. J. WURTMAN. 1984. d-Fenfluramine selectively decreases carbohy-

drate but not protein intake in obese subjects. Int. J. Obes. **8(Suppl. 1):** 79–84.

14. SAMANIN R. Serotonin and feeding. *In* Behavioral Pharmacology of 5-HT. T. Archer, P. Bevan & L. Cools, Eds. Lawrence Erlbaum. In press.

15. YEN, T. T., D. T. WONG & K. G. BEMIS. 1987. Reduction of food consumption and body weight of normal and obese mice by chronic treatment with fluoxetine: A serotonin reuptake inhibitor. Drug Dev. Res. **10:** 37–45.

16. ANGEL, L., M. A. TARANGER, Y. CLAUSTRE, B. SCATTON & S. Z. LANGER. Anorectic activities of serotonin uptake inhibitors: Correlation with their potencies at inhibiting serotonin uptake in vivo and ³H-maxindol binding in vitro. Life Sci. In press.

17. LUCKI, I., M. S. KREIDER & K. J. SIMANSKY. 1988. Reduction of feeding behavior by the serotonin uptake inhibitor sertraline. Psychopharmacology **96:** 289–295.

18. SAMANIN, R., S. CACCIA, C. BENDOTTI, F. BORSINI, E. BORRONI, R. INVERNIZZI, R. PATACCINI & T. MENNINI. 1980. Further studies on the mechanism of serotonin-dependent anorexia in rats. Psychopharmacology **68:** 99–104.

19. DUMONT, C., J. LAURENT, A. GRANDADAM & J. R. BOISSIER. 1981. Anorectic properties of a new long acting serotonin uptake inhibitor. Life Sci. **28:** 1939–1945.

20. INVERNIZZI, R., C. BERETTERA, S. GARATTINI & R. SAMANIN. 1986. D- and L-isomers of fenfluramine differ markedly in their interaction with brain serotonin and catecholamines in the rat. Eur. J. Pharmacol. **120:** 9–15.

21. BETTINI, E., A. CECI, R. SPINELLI & R. SAMANIN. 1987. Neuroleptic-like effects of the L-isomer of fenfluramine on striatal dopamine release in freely moving rats. Biochem. Pharmacol. **36:** 2387–2391.

22. GARATTINI, S., T. MENNINI & R. SAMANIN. 1987. From fenfluramine racemate to *d*-fenfluramine: Specificity and potency of the effects on the serotoninergic system and food intake. Ann. N.Y. Acad. Sci. **409:** 156–166.

23. MENNINI, T., E. BORRONI, R. SAMANIN & S. GARATTINI. 1981. Evidence of the existence of two different intraneuronal pools from which pharmacological agents can release serotonin. Neurochem. Int. **3:** 289–294.

24. BORRONI, E., A. CECI, S. GARATTINI & T. MENNINI. 1983. Differences between *d*-fenfluramine and *d*-norfenfluramine in serotonin presynaptic mechanisms. J. Neurochem. **40:** 891–893.

25. GARATTINI, S., T. MENNINI & R. SAMANIN. 1989. Experimental treatments involving brain serotonin that reduce food intake. Br. J. Psychiatry, in press.

26. BORSINI, F., C. BENDOTTI, A. ALEOTTI, R. SAMANIN & S. GARATTINI. 1982. *d*-Fenfluramine and *d*-norfenfluramine reduce food intake by acting on different serotonin mechanisms in the rat brain. Pharmacol. Res. Commun. **14:** 671–678.

27. SCHWARTZ, D., L. HERNANDEZ & B. G. HOEBEL. 1989. Fenfluramine administered systemically or locally increases extracellular serotonin in the lateral hypothalamus as measured by microdialysis. Brain Res. **482:** 261–270.

28. DE SIMONI, M. G., Z. JURASZCZYK, F. FODRITTO, A. DE LUIGI & S. GARATTINI. 1988. Different effects of fenfluramine isomers and metabolites on extracellular 5-HIAA in nucleus accumbens and hippocampus of freely moving rats. Eur. J. Pharmacol. **153:** 295–299.

29. CORRODI, H. & K. FUXE. 1969. Decreased turnover in central 5-HT nerve terminals induced by antidepressant drugs of the imipramine type. Eur. J. Pharmacol. **7:** 56–59.

30. SCATTON, B., Y. CLAUSTRE, D. GRAHAM, T. DENNIS, A. SERRANO, S. ARBILLA, C. PIMOULE, H. SCHOEMAKER, D. BIGG & S. Z. LANGER. 1988. SL 81.0385: A novel selective and potent serotonin uptake inhibitor. Drug Devel. Res. **12:** 29–40.

31. FULLER, R. W., H. D. SNODDY & D. W. ROBERTSON. 1988. Mechanisms of effects of *d*-fenfluramine on brain serotonin metabolism in rats: Uptake inhibition versus release. Pharmacol. Biochem. Behav. **30:** 715–721.

32. LE FUR, G. & A. UZAN. 1977. Effects of 4-(3-indolyl-alkyl)piperidine derivatives on uptake and release of noradrenaline, dopamine and 5-hydroxytryptamine in rat brain synaptosomes, rat heart and human blood platelets. Biochem. Pharmacol. **26:** 497–503.

33. LE FUR, G., N. MITRANI & A. UZAN. 1977. Effects of 4-(3-indolyl-alkyl) piperidine derivatives on brain 5-hydroxytryptamine turnover and on cardiac and brain noradrenaline or 5-hydroxytryptamine depletion induced by 6-hydroxydopamine, H 75/12 and 4-chloroamphetamine. Biochem. Pharmacol. **26:** 505–509.

34. KOE, B. K., A. WEISSMAN, W. M. WELCH & R. G. BROWNE. 1983. Sertraline, 1*S*,4*S*-*N*-

methyl-4-(3,4-dichlorophenyl)-1,2,3,4-tetrahydro-1-naphthylamine, a new uptake inhibitor with selectivity for serotonin. J. Pharmacol. Exp. Ther. **226:** 686–700.

35. SAMANIN, R., C. BENDOTTI, G. CANDELARESI & S. GARATTINI. 1977. Specificity of serotoninergic involvement in the decrease of food intake induced by quipazine in the rat. Life Sci. **21:** 1259–1266.

37. PEROUTKA, S. J. & S. H. SNYDER. 1979. Multiple serotonin receptors: Differential binding of [³H]5-hydroxytryptamine, [³H]lysergic acid diethylamide and [³H]spiroperidol. Mol. Pharmacol. **16:** 687–699.

38. PEDIGO, N. W., H. I. YAMAMURA & D. L. NELSON. 1981. Discrimination of multiple [³H]5-hydroxytryptamine binding sites by the neuroleptic spiperone in rat brain. J. Neurochem. **36:** 220–226.

39. PAZOS, A., D. HOYER & J. M. PALACIOS. 1984. The binding of serotonergic ligands to the porcine choroid plexus: Characterization of a new type of serotonin recognition site. Eur. J. Pharmacol. **106:** 539–546.

40. BENDOTTI, C. & R. SAMANIN. 1987. The role of putative 5-HT$_{1A}$ and 5-HT$_{1B}$ receptors in the control of feeding in rats. Life Sci. **41:** 635–642.

41. KENNETT, G. A., C. T. DOURISH & G. CURZON. 1987. 5-HT$_{1B}$ agonists induce anorexia at a postsynaptic site. Eur. J. Pharmacol. **141:** 429–435.

42. BENDOTTI, C. & R. SAMANIN. 1986. 8-Hydroxy-2-(di-*n*-propylamino)tetralin (8-OH-DPAT) elicits eating in free-feeding rats by acting on central serotonin neurons. Eur. J. Pharmacol. **121:** 147–150.

43. DOURISH, C. T., P. H. HUTSON, & G. CURZON. 1985. Low doses of the putative serotonin agonist 8-hydroxy-2-(di-*n*-propylamino) tetralin (8-OH-DPAT) elicit feeding in the rat. Psychopharmacology **86:** 197–204.

44. KENNETT, G. A. & G. CURZON. 1988. Evidence that mCPP may have behavioural effects mediated by central 5-HT$_{1C}$ receptors. Br. J. Pharmacol. **94:** 137–147.

45. HOYER, D. 1988. Functional correlates of serotonin 5-HT$_1$ recognition sites. J. Recept. Res. **8:** 59–81.

46. SCHECHTER, L. E. & K. J. SIMANSKY. 1988. 1-(2,5-dimethoxy-4-iodophenyl)-2-aminopropane (DOI) exerts an anorexic action that is blocked by 5-HT$_2$ antagonists in rats. Psychopharmacology **94:** 342–346.

47. HEWSON, G., G. E. LEIGHTON, R. G. HILL & J. HUGHES. 1988. Ketanserin antagonises the anorectic effect of DL-fenfluramine in the rat. Eur. J. Pharmacol. **145:** 227–230.

48. HEWSON, G., G. E. LEIGHTON, R. G. HILL & J. HUGHES. 1988. Quizapine reduces food intake in the rat by activation of 5-HT$_2$-receptors. Br. J. Pharmacol. **95:** 598–604.

49. SAMANIN, R., T. MENNINI, C. BENDOTTI, D. BARONE, S. CACCIA & S. GARATTINI. Evidence that central 5-HT$_2$ receptors do not play an important role in the anorectic activity of D-fenfluramine in the rat. Neuropharmacology, in press.

50. FLETCHER, P. J. 1988. Increased food intake in satiated rats induced by the 5-HT antagonists methysergide, metergoline and ritanserin. Psychopharmacology **96:** 237–242.

51. BLUNDELL, J. E. 1977. Is there a role for serotonin (5-hydroxytryptamine) in feeding? Int. J. Obes. **1:** 15–42.

52. SHOR-POSNER, G., J. A. GRINKER, C. MARINESCU, O. BROWN & S. F. LEIBOWITZ. 1986. Hypothalamic serotonin in the control of meal patterns and macronutrient selection. Brain Res. Bull. **17:** 663–671.

53. WEISS, G. F. & S. LEIBOWITZ. 1988. The impact of serotonergic agonists on nocturnal patterns of macronutrient selection. *In* Society for Neuroscience. Abstracts. V. **14** (part I): 613.

54. LEIBOWITZ, S. F., G. F. WEISS & G. SHOR-POSNER. 1988. Hypothalamic serotonin: Pharmacological, biochemical, and behavioral analyses of its feeding-suppressive action. Clin. Neuropharmacol. **11(Suppl. 1):** S51–S71.

55. BENDOTTI, C., S. GARATTINI & R. SAMANIN. 1986. Hyperphagia caused by muscimol injection in the nucleus raphe dorsalis of rats: Its control by 5-hydroxytryptamine in the nucleus accumbens. J. Pharm. Pharmacol. **38:** 541–543.

56. MASSI, M. & S. MARINI. 1987. Effect of the 5-HT$_2$ antagonist ritanserin on food intake and on 5-HT-induced anorexia in the rat. Pharmacol. Biochem. Behav. **26:** 333–340.

57. FLETCHER, P. J. & M. J. BURTON. 1986. Microstructural analysis of the anorectic action of peripherally administered 5-HT. Pharmacol. Biochem. Behav. **24:** 1133–1136.

58. FLETCHER, P. J. 1987. 8-OH-DPAT elicits gnawing, and eating of solid but not liquid foods. Psychopharmacology **92:** 192–195.

59. MORAN, T. H. & P. R. MCHUGH. 1982. Cholecystokinin suppresses food intake by inhibiting gastric emptying. Am. J. Physiol. **242:** R491-R497.

60. SAMANIN, R., D. GHEZZI, L. VALZELLI & S. GARATTINI. 1972. The effects of selective lesioning of brain serotonin or catecholamine containing neurons on the anorectic activity of fenfluramine and amphetamine. Eur. J. Pharmacol. **19:** 318–322.

61. CLINESCHMIDT, B. V. 1973. 5,6-Dihydroxytryptamine: Suppression of the anorexigenic action of fenfluramine. Eur. J. Pharmacol. **24:** 405–409.

62. FLETCHER, P. J. & M. J. BURTON. 1986. Dissociation of the anorectic actions of 5-HTP and fenfluramine. Psychopharmacology **89:** 216–220.

63. CARRUBA, M. O., P. MANTEGAZZA, M. MEMO, C. MISSALE, M. PIZZI & P. F. SPANO. 1986. Peripheral and central mechanisms of action of serotoninergic anorectic drugs. Appetite **7**(Suppl.): 105–113.

64. BAKER, B. J., J. P. DUGGAN, D. J. BARBER & D. A. BOOTH. 1988. Effects of *dl*-fenfluramine and xylamidine on gastric emptying of maintenance diet in freely feeding rats. Eur. J. Pharmacol. **150:** 137–142.

65. DAVIES, R. F., J. ROSSI III, J. PANKSEPP, N. J. BEAN & A. J. ZOLOVICK. 1983. Fenfluramine anorexia: A peripheral locus of action. Physiol. Behav. **30:** 723–730.

66. BLUNDELL, J. E., C. J. LATHAM & M. B. LESHEM. 1976. Differences between the anorexic actions of amphetamine and fenfluramine: Possible effects on hunger and satiety. J. Pharm. Pharmacol. **28:** 471–477.

67. THURLBY, P. L., S. GARATTINI & R. SAMANIN. 1985. Effects of serotonin antagonists of the performance of a simple food acquisition task in rats treated with fenfluramine isomers. Pharmacol. Res. Commun. **17:** 1129–1138.

68. ROBINSON, P. H., T. H. MORAN & P. R. MCHUGH. 1986. Inhibition of gastric emptying and feeding of fenfluramine. Am. J. Physiol. **250:** R764–R769.

69. THURLBY, P. L., V. E. GRIMM & R. SAMANIN. 1983. Feeding and satiation observed in the runway: The effects of d-amphetamine and *d*-fenfluramine compared. Pharmacol. Biochem. Behav. **18:** 841–846.

70. KIRKHAM, T. C. & J. E. BLUNDELL. 1986. Effect of naloxone and naltrexone on the development of satiation measured in the runway: Comparisons with *d*-amphetamine and d-fenfluramine. Pharmacol. Biochem. Behav. **25:** 123–128.

71. KYRIAKIDES, M. & T. SILVERSTONE. 1979. Comparison of the effects of *d*-amphetamine and fenfluramine on hunger and food intake in man. Neuropharmacology **18:** 1007–1008.

72. BURTON, M. J., S. J. COOPER & D. A. POPPLEWELL. 1981. The effect of fenfluramine on the microstructure of feeding and drinking in the rat. Br. J. Pharmacol. **72:** 621–633.

73. BENDOTTI, C., F. BORSINI, M. G. ZANINI, R. SAMANIN & S. GARATTINI. 1980. Effect of fenfluramine and norfenfluramine stereoisomers on stimulant effects of *d*-amphetamine and apomorphine in the rat. Pharmacol. Res. Commun. **12:** 567–574.

74. ANTELMAN, S. A., A. R. CAGGUILA, A. J. EICHLER & R. R. LUCIK. 1979. The importance of stress in assessing the effects of anorectic drugs. Curr. Med. Res. Opin. **6:** 73–82.

75. GARATTINI, S. 1987. Mechanisms of the anorectic activity of dextrofenfluramine. *In* Body Weight Control. The Physiology, Clinical Treatment and Prevention of Obesity. A. E. Bender & L. J. Brookes, Eds.: 261–270. Churchill Livingstone. Edinburgh.

76. ROBINSON, P. H., S. A. CHECKLEY & G. F. M. RUSSELL. 1985. Suppression of eating by fenfluramine in patients with bulimia nervosa. Br. J. Psychiatry **146:** 169–176.

77. BENDOTTI, C., S. GARATTINI & S. SAMANIN. 1987. Eating caused by neuropeptide-Y injection in the paraventricular hypothalamus: Response to (+)-fenfluramine and (+)-amphetamine in rats. J. Pharm. Pharmacol. **39:** 900–903.

78. STANLEY, B. G., A. S. CHIN & S. F. LEIBOWITZ. 1985. Feeding and drinking elicited by central injection of neuropeptide Y: Evidence for a hypothalamic site(s) of action. Brain Res. Bull. **14:** 521–524.

79. SAMANIN, R. & S. GARATTINI. 1988. Neurotransmitters and pharmacology of obesity. *In* Handbook of Eating Disorders. Part 2: Obesity. G. D. Burrows, P. J. V. Beumont & R. C. Casper, Eds.: 129–144. Elsevier. Amsterdam.

80. HUTSON, P. H., C. T. DOURISH & G. CURZON. 1986. Neurochemical and behavioural evidence for mediation of the hyperphagic action of 8-OH-DPAT by 5-HT cell body autoreceptors. Eur. J. Pharmacol. **129:** 347–352.

81. MONTGOMERY, A. M. J., P. WILLNER & R. MUSCAT. 1988. Behavioural specificity of 8-OH-DPAT-induced feeding. Psychopharmacology **94:** 110–114.

82. DOURISH, C. T., M. L. CLARCK & S. D. IVERSON. 1988. 8-OH-DPAT elicits feeding and not chewing: Evidence from liquid diet studies and a diet choice test. Psychopharmacology **95:** 185–188.

83. DOURISH, C. T., S. J. COOPER, F. GILBERT, J. COUGHLAN & S. D. IVERSEN. 1988. The 5-HT$_{1A}$ agonist 8-OH-DPAT increases consumption of palatable wet mash and liquid diets in the rat. Psychopharmacology **94:** 58–63.

84. DOURISH, C. T., P. H. HUTSON, G. A. KENNETT & G. CURZON. 1986. 8-OH-DPAT-induced hyperphagia: Its neural basis and possible therapeutic relevance. Appetite **7(Suppl.):** 127–140.

85. DOURISH, C. T. & F. GILBERT. 1987. Interactions between 5-HT$_{1A}$ agonists on food intake in rats. Br. J. Pharmacol. **91:** 425P.

86. WONG, D. T. & L. R. REID. 1987. Fenfluramine antagonizes the stimulation of food intake induced by the putative 5-hydroxytryptamine$_{1A}$ agonist, isapirone, in non-fasted rats. J. Pharm. Pharmacol. **39:** 570–571.

87. WONG, D. T., F. P. BYMASTER, L. R. REID, R. W. FULLER & K. W. PERRY. 1985. Inhibition of serotonin uptake by optical isomers of fluoxetine. Drug Devel. Res. **6:** 397–403.

88. ANTELMAN, S. M., N. ROWLAND & D. KOCAN. 1981. Anorectics: Lack of cross tolerance among serotonergic drugs and sensitization of amphetamine's effect. In Anorectic Agents: Mechanisms of Action and Tolerance. S. Garattini & R. Saminin, Eds.: 45–62. Raven Press. New York.

89. SAMANIN, R., C. BENDOTTI, F. MIRANDA & S. GARATTINI. 1977. Decrease of food intake by quipazine in the rat: Relation to serotoninergic receptor stimulation. J. Pharm. Pharmacol. **29:** 53–54.

90. ENGEL, G., M. GOTHERT, D. HOYER, E. SCHLICKER & K. HILLENBRAND. 1986. Identity of inhibitory presynaptic 5-hydroxytryptamine (5-HT) autoreceptors in the rat brain cortex with 5-HT$_{1B}$ binding sites. Naunyn-Schmiedebergs Arch. Pharmacol. **332:** 1–7.

91. GLENNON, R. A. 1987. Central serotonin receptors as targets for drug research. J. Med. Chem. **30:** 1–12.

92. BORSINI, F., C. BENDOTTI & R. SAMANIN. 1985. Salbutamol, d-amphetamine and d-fenfluramine reduce sucrose intake in freely fed rats by acting on different neurochemical mechanisms. Int. J. Obes. **9:** 277–283.

93. BORSINI, F., C. BENDOTTI, B. PRZEWLOCKA & R. SAMANIN. 1983. Monoamine involvement in the overeating caused by muscimol injection in the rat nucleus raphe dorsalis and the effects of d-fenfluramine and d-amphetamine. Eur. J. Pharmacol. **94:** 109–115.

DISCUSSION

DR. PAUL ROBINSON (*Kings College Hospital School of Medicine, London*): Professor Garattini, could I draw your attention to the work of Davies and Panksepp, who have shown that the action of the racemic fenfluramine on rats that have raphe lesions suggests that fenfluramine doesn't inhibit food intake in the starved state, but it does in the free-feeding state. The suggestion in their paper and in other subsequent papers is that a substantial part of fenfluramine's anorectic action is by inhibiting gastric emptying. Could I ask what is your view about the relevance of that pharmacological action on the anorectic effect of fenfluramine?

DR. SILVIO GARATTINI (*Instituto di Ricerche Farmacologiche "Mario Negri," Milan*): It depends very much on the type of test that one is using. What I'm saying is valid only for this particular model. It can not be extrapolated to all the other models. We believe that the gastric emptying effect does not have much importance. But under other conditions, it may well have importance. It was shown definitely that *d*-fenfluramine decreases gastric emptying.

DR. KENNETH SIMANSKY (*Medical College of Pennsylvania, Philadelphia, PA*): Dr. Garattini, you mentioned that metergoline would not block the anorectic effect of DPAT and concluded that it is therefore not a serotonergic process. But it's also been shown that DPAT induced stereotypy, which is presumably mediated by the postsynaptic 5-HT$_{1A}$ receptors, is also not blocked by metergoline, but it is blocked by methiothepine, pindolol, and propranolol. I wonder if you'd care to expand on your statement.

DR. GARATTINI: Yes, the anorectic effect that you can show with 5-HT$_{1A}$ drugs, in fact given by systemic route, is an effect which occurs in conjunction with a number of other behavioral activities. So that may be the reason for the decrease of food intake. When 5-HT$_{1A}$ drugs and DPAT are injected directly into the dorsal raphe, they produce instead an increase in food intake, which is considered to be related to a blockade of the transmission of serotonin. That this effect in the doral raphe is related to serotonin is shown by the fact that by giving 5–7DHT in the same area one can inhibit completely the effect of DPAT.

DR. SIMANSKY: I have one other question. Your ritanserin data showed a decreased pharmacokinetic interaction with *d*-fenfluramine in the cortex and hypothalamus. You use those data to suggest that there is no pharmacodynamic action of the 5-HT$_2$ antagonists on the anorexia. However, do you measure the concentration of *d*-fenfluramine in those areas? Do you know that it is dose related to the anorexia? Is that amount that you now measure less than the dose required for anorexia?

DR. GARATTINI: There is certainly a dose–effect relationship in the sense that by increasing the dose you increase the prime concentrations of *d*-fenfluramine and d-norfenfluramine. The decrease that we have observed may explain the decrease in the anorectic effect of *d*-fenfluramine.

DR. GRAEME HEWSON (*Parke Davis Research Unit, Cambridge, U.K.*): I wonder if you would like to comment on the possibility that several groups have found that 5-HT$_2$ receptors appear to be involved in the anorectic effects of drugs in nondeprived animals. Do you think there's differential involvement in 5-HT receptor subtypes depending on the deprivation state?

DR. GARATTINI: Yes, it may well be that under conditions where you have food available that the major contribution to the decrease of food intake is represented by a decrease of the gastric emptying, and that may be related to 5-HT$_2$ rather than to 5-HT$_1$. We don't have direct data for that, but I know that Dr. Booth has shown it, at least under some experimental conditions.

Opioids

Are They Regulators of Feeding?[a]

ALLEN S. LEVINE[b] AND CHARLES J. BILLINGTON

Neuroendocrine Research Laboratory
VA Medical Center and Departments of Food Science and
Nutrition, Medicine, Psychiatry, and Surgery
University of Minnesota
St. Paul–Minneapolis, Minnesota 55417

By now most persons conducting research in the area of food intake believe that opioids have something to do with feeding. This is based on findings that opioids stimulate short-term feeding, and that antagonists of the opioid receptor decrease the amount of food ingested by an organism.[1-6] Also there are a variety of studies that indicate that levels of opioid peptides change during periods of feeding or food deprivation. In spite of an overwhelming amount of data supporting a role for opioids in the regulation of food intake, there is still a great deal of confusion on the specific mechanisms. It is the purpose of this review to briefly summarize the data concerning the effect of opioids on food intake in animals and humans, emphasizing some of the inconsistencies and problems that are present in the literature.

The most consistent data indicating the involvement of opioids in feeding behavior comes from those studies using opioid antagonists. There is a relatively long history demonstrating that antagonism of the opioid receptor(s) results in decreased feeding. In 1974 Holtzman demonstrated that naloxone, an opioid antagonist, decreased food and water intake in rats.[7] Since this initial study, investigators have shown that naloxone decreases short-term food intake in chicks, cockroaches, mice, monkeys, sheep, guinea pigs, cats, rabbits, tigers, wolves, ground squirrels, woodchucks, deer, dogs, and humans.[4,8-10] Naloxone decreases feeding in rats and/or mice following injection of norepinephrine, muscimol, 2-deoxyglucose, neuropeptide Y, benzodiazepines, and after food deprivation, stress, electrical stimulation of the brain, and social conflict.[1,6] Other opioid antagonists, such as naltrexone, diprenorphine, WIN-44,441–3, nalmefene, ICI 154,129, ICI 174,864, β-chlornaltrexamine (β-CNA), MR2266, and naloxonazine, also decrease feeding, though they have not been studied as extensively as naloxone.[1,6,11] Most of these studies examined meal feeding and few have asked whether blockade of the opioid receptor chronically results in the continued decrease in eating, with a resultant alteration in body weight.

Anytime one observes a decrease in feeding, the question of specificity comes to mind. Does naloxone or any other antagonist of the opioid receptor decrease feeding due to illness, change in motor activity, lack of motivation, or other events that seem to be unrelated to consummatory behavior? It is difficult to ask a rat whether it feels

[a] This work supported by grants from the Veterans Administration and the National Institute of Drug Abuse (Grant # RO1-DA03999).

[b] Address for correspondence: Allen S. Levine, Ph.D., VA Medical Center, Research Service (151), One Veterans Drive, Minneapolis, MN 55417.

sick after one injects it with a substance. However, behavioral scientists have come up with several clever ways to test illness in a laboratory animal. Using techniques known as conditioned place aversion and conditioned taste aversion, investigators have found that naloxone may have a slightly aversive effect. Naloxone, when paired to the presence of a fluid or place a rat prefers, results in avoidance of either that fluid or the place.[12-14] Lesham[15] suggested that the aversive effects of naloxone administration could not totally account for the decrease in food intake due to naloxone. Naloxone does not seem to alter locomotor activity or operant responding at levels that decrease feeding. Because the latency to feeding is not increased following administration of naloxone, it seems unlikely that this opioid antagonist results in decreased motor ability.[16]

A second source of evidence for the opioid–feeding connection involves studies with opioid agonists. About 60 years ago Flowers and colleagues noted that during morphine withdrawal, food intake increases in rats.[17] In 1963 Martin *et al.* reported that morphine-addicted rats ate large amounts of food after the daily injection of morphine.[18] Grandison and Guidotti noted that injection of β-endorphin into the ventromedial region of the hypothalamus increased feeding in rats.[19] This trend has continued for the past 20 years and virtually all ligands of every opioid receptor have been found to increase food intake, albeit only for a relatively short period of time. The increase in feeding noted after injection of opioids or opiates is not only short acting in its effect, but generally is fairly mild relative to the increase in feeding seen after injection of norepinephrine or neuropeptide Y.

In addition to injections of exogenous opioids or antagonists of the opioid receptor, measurements of changes in opioid levels have been supportive of an opioid–feeding relationship. For example, the pituitaries dissected from genetically obese mice contain more leu-enkephalin and dynorphin than their lean littermates.[20] Elevated β-endorphin levels have been found in the pituitaries of genetically obese rats and mice and increased feeding was accompanied by increased plasma levels of β-endorphin.[21] Others also reported increased levels of β-endorphin in the pituitaries of obese rats; however, the increase was not noted until the obesity developed.[22-25] McLaughlin *et al.* noted that in Zucker obese rats levels of hypothalamic (VMH) β-endorphin was decreased compared to lean rats.[26] Levels of β-endorphin have also been measured in obese and lean humans. In 1980, Givens and colleagues reported elevated levels of β-endorphin in obese women who had oligoamenorrhea.[27] Others have shown that both plasma and cerebrospinal fluid (CSF) β-endorphin are increased in obese patients. Genazzani *et al.* reported that obese children and adolescents had fasting levels of β-endorphin that were about twice the concentration of nonobese controls.[28] Anorexic patients appear to have reduced cerebrospinal fluid levels of immunoreactive proopioimelanocortin-related peptides.[29] Steele *et al.* reported that there was a nocturnal depletion of hypothalamic dynorphin in anorexic Walker-256 tumor-bearing rats.[30] Levels of opioids appear to change with circadian rhythm. Met-enkephalin concentrations have been shown to increase in the hypothalamus during the night, the time at which rats ingest most of their food. McLaughlin *et al.* also showed that met-enkephalin levels in the PVN and VMH were higher in rats during the dark cycle compared to the light cycle.[31] Takahashi and colleagues have reported influences of feeding and drinking on circadian rhythms of opioid peptides in hypothalamus, pituitary, and plasma of rats.[32] Reid and colleagues reported that dynorphin levels were higher in the hypothalamus during nocturnal feeding.[33] Changes in feeding behavior also produce changes in levels of opioids. Majeed *et al.* found that food deprivation or drug-induced decreases in food intake (following fenfluramine administration) increased β-endorphin, but not dynorphin levels, in the hypothalamus.[34] McLaughlin *et al.* demonstrated that β-endorphin levels increased in satiated animals compared to hungry ones in the VMH and decreased in the supraoptic nucleus.[26] Dynorphin levels have been shown to decrease in the hypothalamus and striatum after four days of food deprivation in male rats.[35] Met-enkephalin levels decreased in the striatum, hippocampus, and cortex on the fourth day of food deprivation. In contrast, β-endorphin levels increased in the striatum following food deprivation. When food-deprived rats were fed, the levels returned to normal. We demonstrated that tail-pinch-induced feeding and insulin-hypoglycemia-induced feeding alter dynorphin levels in the CNS.[6] On the basis of such data, it is difficult to build a consistent story. The experiments use different species, extract opioids from different parts of the animal, and measure different peptides. It does, however, appear that under conditions that result in increased feeding behavior, there is an increase in brain and serum levels of some opioids. Work with regulation of gene expression for the various opioid peptides may eventually help our understanding of the relationship between eating and opioids.

Since the initial studies with naloxone and morphine, our understanding of opioid chemistry has increased dramatically. Using biochemical, pharmacological, behavioral, bioassay, and molecular techniques, we now know there are three families of opioid peptides, and most agree that there are at least three receptor types (see Akil *et al.*[36] for a review). This has resulted in a virtual avalanche of studies in which agonists or antagonists of various opioid receptors are injected into various parts of the brains and consummatory behavior evaluated. Two questions have emerged from this effort: Which opioid receptor regulates food intake, and where is the site of action for this effect?

Ligands of all receptor types have been shown to increase short-term eating, with unequal degrees of reliability or vigor. β-Endorphin (an epsilon receptor agonist) stimulates feeding when infused into the ventromedial hypothalamus, lateral ventricle, and paraventricular hypothalamus.[19,37,38] The effect of β-endorphin on feeding can be decreased by administration of the α-adrenergic antagonist phentolamine.[38] These data suggest that opioids may work via an adrenergic mechanism. It has been reported that autoimmunization of rats against β-endorphin increases food intake and body weight. Antibodies to β-endorphin significantly reduced feeding and drinking when injected into the periventricular nucleus of the hypothalamus.[39] Gonzalez *et al.* found that intraventricular administration of antibodies to β-endorphin antagonized diazepam-induced feeding in rats.[40]

Morphine, a mu receptor agonist, stimulates feeding in rats when injected peripherally, and this effect is enhanced when morphine is injected repeatedly.[41,42] We have found that the highly selective mu receptor agonist, Try-D-Ala-Gly-(Me)Phe-Gly-ol (DAGO) also stimulates food intake.[43] However, we found that morphiceptin, another selective mu agonist, had no effect on intake when administered centrally.[44] The discrepancy between DAGO and morphiceptin may be related to the lower affinity of morphiceptin (relative to DAGO) for mu receptors. A subtype of the mu receptor known as the mu-1 receptor has been reported to affect feeding.[45] The mu-1 antagonist naloxonazine decreases morphine-induced feeding at low doses, but not ethylketocyclazocine, d-ala^2, d-leu^5-enkephalin, or dynorphin-induced feeding.[46]

Delta opioid receptor agonists also increase feeding in laboratory animals. Tepperman and Hirst demonstrated that D-ala^2-D-met^5-enkephalin (DADLE) increased food intake when injected into the VMH[47] and D-ala^2-D-met^5-enkephalinamide stimulated intake when injected into the PVN.[48] Also, we found that the specific delta agonist, D-ser^2-leu^5-enkephalin-thr (DSLET), enhanced feeding when injected intracerebroventricularly (ICV).[43] The nigrostriatal dopaminergic tract is thought to play a role in the regulation of food intake. Consistent with this idea is that DADLE was found to decrease the firing rate of neurons in the zona reticulata of the substantia nigra, which in turn inhibit dopaminergic neurons of the zona compacta.[49] Additionally, DADLE increases dopamine metabolism in the rat striatum.[50]

The sigma receptor agonist, N-allynormetazocine (NANM), also increases food intake, albeit only by a small amount.[51] This effect is naloxone-reversible and does increase with repeated injections. Herling and Shannon[52] showed that the 1-isomer of NANM produces some ethylketocyclazocine-appropriate responding (EKC is a kappa agonist) in drug-discrimination trials. In support of this finding, we found that repeated injections of NANM potentiate the feeding response of the kappa agonist ketocyclazocine, but did not potentiate the feeding response of morphine.[51]

Several lines of evidence indicate that the kappa opioid receptor may be of importance in the regulation of food intake. Ketocyclazocine, tifluadom, butorphanol tartrate, U-50,488H, bremazocine and dynorphin, all of which show some specificity for the kappa receptor, stimulate feeding more potently than other opioid agonists.[42,53–56] Unilateral microinjections of antibodies to α-neo-endorphin (part of the pre-pro-dynorphin parent compound) into the VMH inhibited both food and water intake.[39] Also, antibodies to dynorphin (1–13) given intraventricularly elevate the threshold for electrical brain stimulation-induced feeding.[57] Antibodies to dynorphin produced similar effects, but the effect was less pronounced.[39] Steele et al. recently reported that anorectic Walker-256 tumor-bearing rats have very low levels of dynorphin in the hypothalamus during the lights-off cycle, suggesting that dynorphin is involved in stimulated feeding.[30] Another kappa agonist, bremazocine, increases feeding more effectively after repeated injection. However, this effect is not seen when bremazocine is injected following repeated injections of morphine, indicating that morphine and bremazocine effects on feeding appear to be at different receptors.[56] Injections of dynorphin into specific regions of the brain demonstrates that the PVN and VMH are areas of the brain involved in dynorphin-stimulated feeding.[58] However, knife cuts lateral to the PVN failed to alter the effectiveness of butorphanol tartrate, a kappa agonist known to increase feeding.[59] Recent data from our laboratory indicates that use of a specific kappa opioid antagonist, norbinaltorphimine (nor-BNI), results in a decrease in kappa opioid-induced feeding as well as starvation-induced feeding.[60] The effect of nor-BNI appears to be dependent on the site of injection. Bak et al. suggest, based on studies with nor-BNI, that kappa opioid activity in the rostral periventricular structures may facilitate feeding while kappa activity in the caudal periventricular structures may inhibit feeding.[61]

β-Chlornaltrexamine (β-CNA) is a nonequilibrium opioid receptor antagonist that alkylates and inactivates opioid receptors.[62] We examined the effects of intraventricular injections of β-CNA on food intake and body weight of male rats.[11] Treatment with this compound caused a two- to four-day reduction in daily food intake and concomitant reduction in body weight. An additional study indicated that the weight loss after β-CNA treatment could be completely accounted for by the reduction in intake. β-CNA also attenuated or abolished feeding following administration of DAGO, DSLET, or dynorphin, even when these peptides were tested 26 hours after β-CNA administration.

We can see that a variety of opioid ligands and antagonists can alter feeding behavior. In addition to this, there are a variety of sites where such effects can occur.[63] Lynch demonstrated that very high kappa-receptor densities reside within feeding sites such as the nucleus of the solitary tract, parabrachial nuclei, ventral posterior, and medial portions of the thalamus, medial hypothalamus, medial nuclei of the amygdala, and bed nucleus of the stria terminalis.[64] Naloxone reduces food intake and/or water intake after microinjection into the lateral hypothalamus, paraventricular nucleus, ventromedial hypothalamic nuclei, globus pallidus, preoptic area, and zona incerta, but not in the striatum.[65,66] Several groups have shown that opioid agonists can stimulate feeding in satiated rats after injection into the VMH, PVN, LH, nucleus accumbens, ventral tegmental area, and the amygdala.[19,38,47,48,67,68] Dynorphin appears to be more effective when injected into the PVN than DADLE or β-endorphin.[57] However, dynorphin is not always the most potent agonist when injected into other regions of the brain. For example, Gosnell recently noted that DAGO was more effective than injections of dynorphin or DSLET in the amygdala.[69] Lesions of the hippocampus,[70] pineal, optic nerve, or superior cervical ganglionectomy[71] failed to alter responses to naloxone or butorphanol tartrate (a kappa agonist that potently enhances feeding). King et al. found that ventromedial hypothalamic lesions did not alter feeding responses to naloxone.[72] Also, parasagittal hypothalamic knife-cuts did not alter the feeding responses of rats to naloxone and butorphanol tartrate.[59] Lesions of the striatum, globus pallidus, or PVN have been reported to attenuate the effect of various opioid agonists.[73]

Opioids not only increase feeding, but also alter taste and nutrient selection. Morphine injections increase the ingestion of sweet solutions,[74,75] and naloxone reduces the preference for solutions containing saccharin or glucose.[76-78] Naloxone has been reported to reduce the perceived pleasantness of glucose solutions and food odors in humans.[79] Lynch[75] reported that pretest injections of naloxone blocked the acquisition of saccharin preference, suggesting that opioids are involved in a hedonic response to sweet solutions. Cooper and Gilbert demonstrated that naloxone also reduced the ingestion of hypotonic salt solutions in a two-bottle test.[77] Apfelbaum and Mandenoff demonstrated that naltrexone reduced food intake in cafeteria-fed rats, but not in the control group.[80] As well as increasing intake of sweet and salty solutions, opioids alter macronutrient selection. Several investigators have found that opioid ligands result in a preference for high-fat diets and that naloxone suppresses feeding of a high-fat diet to a greater degree than a high-carbohydrate diet.[81,82] Shor-Posner et al.[83] found that morphine increased protein intake in rats that were food deprived.

We recently found that chronic sucrose ingestion alters naloxone's ability to suppress food. One group of rats was forced to ingest a 10% sucrose solution (no water available) for 61 days, and the other group had water ad libitum. Baseline glucose levels were unaffected by this regimen, but the rats were slightly glucose intolerant. Animals were then stimulated to eat by 24-hour food deprivation (no sucrose, but ad libitum water). At the time of the experiment only laboratory chow was available. We injected the rats with 5, 1, and 0.5 mg/kg naloxone subcutaneously and measured food intake at 30, 60, and 120 minutes. There was a main effect of sucrose exposure on naloxone-induced suppression of feeding (FIG. 1), with naloxone being more effective in decreasing food in those rats that drank the sucrose solution for the 61-day period (5 mg/kg naloxone suppressed feeding by 74% in the sucrose group at 120 minutes and by only 45% in the control group). Sucrose feeding has been reported to increase the binding affinity to opioid receptors, which may explain why naloxone is more potent in the sucrose-fed animals. Also, chronic imbibition of saccharin solutions results in rats being tolerant to morphine. Thus, opioids can influence the ingestion of sweet solutions and sweet solutions can alter the way opioids function.

With the abundance of animal data, one might expect that investigators would be interested in using opioid antagonists to decrease feeding in humans and perhaps decrease body weight. Atkinson found that intravenous injection of naloxone (2 mg) had no effect on a meal given 30 minutes later, whereas 15 mg of naloxone (5 mg i.v. bolus followed by a 5 mg/hr infusion) decreased food intake by 29% in obese subjects compared with a saline infusion.[84] This effect was not seen in lean subjects. Wolkowitz and colleagues[85] found that obese subjects decreased food intake about three and eight hours after infusion of 0.5 mg/kg of naloxone. Trenchard and Silverstone[86] found that 1.6 mg of naloxone decreased food intake by about 25%, two hours after administration to nonobese subjects. Cohen et al.[87] found that 2 mg/kg of naloxone decreased feeding in normal-weight persons. In the latter two studies and in a study by O'Brien

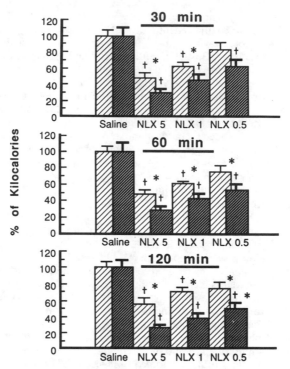

FIGURE 1. Effect of naloxone (5, 1, 0.5 mg/kg) on 24-hour food deprivation-induced food intake in rats that were chronically exposed to a 10% sucrose solution or water *ad libitum*. † p < 0.05 compared to saline; * p < 0.05 sucrose versus water. Baseline kcal intake: Sucrose group 30 min = 20.7 kcal; 60 min = 27.0 kcal; 120 min = 31.7 kcal. Control group 30 min = 24.3 kcal; 60 min = 35 kcal; 120 min = 36.7 kcal. Sucrose main effect: $F(1,64) = 6.98$, $p = 0.01$ (30 min); $F(1,64) = 9.77$, $p = 0.002$ (60 min); $F(1,64) = 22.68$, $p = 0.0002$ (120 min). Naloxone main effect: $F(3,64) = 25.07$, $p = 0.0001$ (30 min); $F(3,64) = 30.58$, $p = 0.0001$ (60 min); $F(3,64) = 30.98$, $p = 0.0001$ (120 min).

et al.,[88] naloxone doses did not alter hunger. Mitchell and colleagues[89] reported that intravenous administration of naloxone (6 mg i.v. bolus followed by 0.1 mg/min; maximum 12 mg over 120 minutes) decreased binge eating episodes in five subjects by about 23%. Recently, Jonas and Gold[90] reported that high-dose naltrexone (200–300 mg daily) reduces both bingeing and purging. Aside from decreasing food by blockade of the opioid receptor, our laboratory demonstrated that butorphanol administration increases feeding in humans over a six-hour period.[91]

Such promising data resulted in a series of trials using the long-acting antagonist naltrexone, which can be administered orally. In uncontrolled studies it appeared that naltrexone might decrease body weight. But when double-blind studies were conducted, no effects were noted with doses as high as 300 mg daily for periods up to eight weeks.[92-95] Thus, opioid blockade is not an effective means of long-term weight management.

From the above discussion it seems reasonable to believe that opioids may be involved in the regulation of food intake; however, there are also reasons to believe that they are not very important regulators of food intake. We know that opioid antagonists decrease feeding and agonists increase feeding. Unfortunately, agonists of the opioid receptors are not always consistent in their effects on feeding. We and others have found that one needs to administer opioid agonists more than once for reliable feeding to occur. Furthermore, if the control group eats very much food, it is difficult to observe a statistically significant increase in food intake above baseline. The fact that naloxone decreases virtually all types of feeding makes one think this effect may be nonspecific. For example, naloxone decreases NPY-induced feeding, a peptide that stimulates feeding better than most opioids. How is it possible that opioid receptor blockade decreases feeding that was induced by a compound that stimulates feeding better than any opioids? If NPY is dependent on the opioid receptor for activity, then it must do so by a different mechanism than opioid agonists. Also, most of the effects of opioids on feeding have been observed during short-term studies. The results from the limited number of chronic experiments are not supportive of an important role for opioids in feeding. Many more questions need to be answered before we can clearly state that opioids play a major role in regulating consummatory behaviors.

REFERENCES

1. COOPER, S. J., A. JACKSON, T. C. KIRKHAM & S. TURKISH. 1988. Endorphins, opiates and food intake. *In* Endorphins, Opiates and Behavioural Processes. R. J. Rodgers & S. J. Cooper, Eds.: 143–186. John Wiley. New York.
2. BAILE, C. A., C. L. MCLAUGHLIN & M. A. DELLA-FERA. 1986. Role of cholecystokinin and opioid peptides in control of food intake. Physiol. Rev. **66:** 172–234.
3. LEVINE, A. S., J. E. MORLEY, B. A. GOSNELL, C. J. BILLINGTON & T. J. BARTNESS. 1985. Opioids and consummatory behavior. Brain Res. Bull. **14:** 663–672.
4. REID, L. D. 1985. Endogenous opioid peptides and regulation of drinking and feeding. Am. J. Clin. Nutr. **42:** 1099–1132.
5. SANGER, D. J. 1981. Endorphinergic mechanisms in the control of food and water intake. Appetite **2:** 193–208.
6. MORLEY, J. E., A. S. LEVINE, G. K. YIM & M. T. LOWY. 1983. Opioid modulation of appetite. Neurosci. Biobehav. Rev. **7:** 281–305.
7. HOLTZMAN, S. G. 1974. Behavioral effects of separate and combined administration of naloxone and *d*-amphetamine. J. Pharmacol. Exp. Ther. **189:** 51–60.
8. LEVINE, A. S., J. E. MORLEY, S. E. NIZIELSKI, E. D. PLOTKA, B. A. GOSNELL, C. J. BILLINGTON & U. S. SEAL. 1985. Species diversity in opioid feeding systems. *In* Recent Advances in Obesity Research: IV. J. Hirsch & T. van Itallie, Eds.: 65–70. John Libbey.
9. STEINMAN, J. L., D. G. FUJIKAWA, C. G. WASTERLAIN, A. CHERKIN & J. E. MORLEY. 1987. The effects of adrenergic and pancreatic polypeptidergic compounds on feeding and other behaviors in neonatal leghorn chicks. Peptides **8:** 585–592.
10. KAVALIERS, M. & M. HIRST. 1987. Slugs and snails and opiate tales: Opioids and feeding behavior in invertebrates. Fed. Proc. **46:** 168–172.
11. GOSNELL, B. A., M. GRACE & A. S. LEVINE. 1987. Effects of beta-chlornaltrexamine on food intake, body weight and opioid-induced feeding. Life Sci. **40:** 1459–1467.
12. WU, M-F., S. E. CRUZ-MORALES, J. R. QUINAN, J. M. STAPLETON & L. D. REID. 1979. Naloxone reduces fluid consumption: relationships of this effect to conditioned taste aversion and morphine dependence. Bull. Psychol. Soc. **14:** 323–325.
13. FRENK, H. & G. H. ROGERS. 1979. Suppressant effects of naloxone on food and water intake in the rat. Behav. Neural. Biol. **26:** 23–40.
14. STOLERMAN, I. P. & G. D. D'MELLO. 1978. Aversive properties of narcotic antagonists in rats. Life Sci. **22:** 1755–1762.
15. LESHEM, M. 1984. Suppression of feeding by naloxone in rat: A dose–response comparison of anorexia and conditioned taste aversion suggesting a specific anorexic effect. Psychopharmacology **82:** 127–130.
16. KIRKHAM, T. C. & J. E. BLUNDELL. 1984. Dual action of naloxone on feeding revealed by behavioural analysis: separate effects on initiation and termination of eating. Appetite **5:** 45–52.
17. FLOWERS, S. H., E. S. DUNHAM & H. G. BARBOUR. 1929. Addiction edema and withdrawal

edema in morphinized rats. Proc. Soc. Exp. Biol. Med. **26:** 572–574.

18. MARTIN, W. R., A. WIKLER, C. G. EADES & F. T. PESCOR. 1963. Tolerance to and physical dependence on morphine in rats. Psychopharmacologia **4:** 247–260.

19. GRANDISON, L. & A. GUIDOTTI. 1977. Stimulation of food intake by muscimol and beta-endorphin. Neuropharmacology **16:** 533–536.

20. FERGUSON-SEGALL, M., J. J. FLYNN, J. WALKER & D. L. MARGULES. 1982. Increased immunoreactive dynorphin and leu-enkephalin in posterior pituitary of obese mice (ob/ob) and super-sensitivity to drugs that act at kappa receptors. Life Sci. **31:** 2233–2236.

21. MARGULES, D. L., B. MOISSET, M. J. LEWIS, H. SHIBUYA & C. B. PERT. 1978. β-Endorphin is associated with overeating in genetically obese mice (ob/ob) and rats (fa/fa). Science **202:** 988–991.

22. GIBSON, M. J., A. S. LIOTTA & D. T. KRIEGER. 1981. The Zucker fa/fa rat: Absent circadian corticosterone periodicity and elevated β-endorphin concentration in brain and neurointermediate pituitary. Neuropeptides **1:** 349–362.

23. GOVONI, S. & H.-Y. T. YANG. 1981. Sex differences in the content of β-endorphin and enkephalin-like peptides in the pituitary of obese (ob/ob) mice. J. Neurochem. **36:** 1829–1833.

24. GUNION, M. W. & R. H. PETERS. 1981. Pituitary β-endorphin, naloxone, and feeding in several experimental obesities. Am. J. Physiol. **241:** R173–R184.

25. ROSSIER, J., J. ROGERS, T. SHIBASAKI, R. GUILLEMAN & F. E. BLOOM. 1979. Opioid peptides and alpha-melanocyte-stimulating hormone in genetically obese (ob/ob) mice during development. Proc. Natl. Acad. Sci. USA **76:** 2077–2080.

26. MCLAUGHLIN, C. L., C. A. BAILE & M. A. DELLA-FERA. 1985. Meal-stimulated increased concentrations of β-endorphin in the hypothalamus of Zucker obese and lean rats. Physiol. Behav. **35:** 891–896.

27. GIVENS, J. R., E. WIEDEMANN, R. N. ANDERSEN & A. E. KITABACHI. 1980. β-endorphin and β-lipotropin plasma levels in hirsute women: Correlation with body weight. J. Clin. Endocrinol. Metab. **50:** 975–976.

28. GENAZZANI, A. R., F. FACCHINETTI, F. PETRAGLIA, C. PINTOR & R. CORDA. 1986. Hyperendorphinemia in obese children and adolescents. J. Clin. Endocrinol. Metab. **62:** 36–40.

29. KAYE, W. H., W. H. BERRETTINI, H. E. GWIRTSMAN, M. CHRETIEN, P. W. GOLD, D. T. GEORGE, D. C. JIMERSON & M. H. EBERT. 1987. Reduced cerebrospinal fluid levels of immunoreactive proopiomelanocortin related peptides (including beta-endorphin) in anorexia nervosa. Life Sci. **41:** 2147–2155.

30. STEELE, T. D., H. U. BRYANT, P. V. MALVEN & G. K. YIM. 1988. Nocturnal depletion of hypothalamic dynorphin in anorexic Walker-256 tumor-bearing rats. Pharmacol. Biochem. Behav. **29:** 541–545.

31. MCLAUGHLIN, C. L., C. A. BAILE & M. A. DELLA-FERA. 1987. Circadian rhythm of feeding induced changes in hypothalamic met-enkephalin concentrations. Physiol. Behav. **41:** 465–469.

32. TAKAHASHI, H., T. MOTOMATSU, H. NAWATA, K. KATO, H. IBAYASHI & M. NOBUNAGA. 1986. Influences of feeding and drinking on circadian rhythms of opioid peptides in plasma, hypothalamus and pituitary gland in rats. Physiol. Behav. **37:** 609–614.

33. REID, L. D., A. M. KONECKA, R. PREZEWLOCKI, M. H. MILLAN, M. J. MILLAN & A. HERZ. 1982. Endogenous opioids, circadian rhythms, nutrient deprivation, eating and drinking. Life Sci. **31:** 1829–1832.

34. MAJEED, N. H., W. LASON, B. PRZEWLOCKA & R. PRZEWLOCKI. 1986. Brain and peripheral opioid peptides after changes in ingestive behavior. Neuroendocrinology **42:** 267–272.

35. VASWANI, K. K. & G. A. TEJWANI. 1986. Food deprivation-induced changes in the level of opioid peptides in the pituitary and brain of rat. Life Sci. **38:** 197–201.

36. AKIL, H., S. J. WATSON, E. YOUNG, M. E. LEWIS, H. KHACHATURIAN & J. M. WALKER. 1984. Endogenous opioids: Biology and function. Annu. Rev. Neurosci. **7:** 223–255.

37. MCKAY, L. D., N. J. KENNEY, N. K. EDENS, R. H. WILLIAMS & S. C. WOODS. 1981. Intracerebroventricular beta-endorphin increases food intake of rats. Life Sci. **29:** 1429–1434.

38. LEIBOWITZ, S. F. & L. HOR. 1982. Endorphinergic and alpha-noradrenergic systems in the paraventricular nucleus: Effects on eating behavior. Peptides **3:** 421–428.

39. SCHULZ, R., A. WILHELM & G. DIRLICH. 1984. Intracerebral injection of different antibodies

against endogenous opioids suggested alpha-neo-endorphin participation in control of feeding behavior. Naunyn Schmiedebergs Arch. Pharmacol. **326:** 222–226.

40. GONZALEZ, Y., M. P. FERNANDEZ-TOME, F. SANCHEZ-FRANCO & J. DEL RIO. 1984. Antagonism of diazepam-induced feeding in rats by antisera to opioid peptides. Life Sci. **35:** 1423–1429.

41. MORLEY, J. E., A. S. LEVINE, M. GRACE & J. KNEIP. 1982. An investigation of the role of kappa opiate receptors in the initiation of feeding. Life Sci. **31:** 2617–2626.

42. THORNHILL, J. A. & W. S. SAUNDERS. 1983. Acute stimulation of feeding with repeated injections of morphine sulfate to non-obese and fatty Zucker rats. Prog. Neuropsychopharmacol. **7:** 477–485.

43. GOSNELL, B. A., A. S. LEVINE & J. E. MORLEY. 1986. The stimulation of food intake by selective agonists of mu, kappa and delta opioid receptors. Life Sci. **38:** 1081–1088.

44. MORLEY, J. E., A. S. LEVINE, B. A. GOSNELL & C. J. BILLINGTON. 1984. Which opioid receptor mechanism modulates feeding? Appetite **5:** 61–68.

45. SIMONE, D. A., R. J. BODNAR, E. J. GOLDMAN & G. W. PASTERNAK. 1985. Involvement of opioid receptor subtypes in rat feeding behavior. Life Sci. **36:** 829–833.

46. MANN, P. E., D. ARJUNE, M. T. ROMERO, G. W. PASTERNAK, E. F. HAHN & R. J. BODNAR. 1988. Differential sensitivity of opioid-induced feeding to naloxone and naloxonazine. Psychopharmacology **94:** 336–341.

47. TEPPERMAN, F. S. & M. HIRST. 1983. Effects of intrahypothalamic injection of D-ala², D-Leu⁵-enkephalin on feeding and temperature in the rat. Eur. J. Pharmacol. **96:** 243–249.

48. MCLEAN, S. & B. G. HOEBEL. 1983. Feeding induced by opiates injected into the paraventricular hypothalamus. Peptides **4:** 287–292.

49. HOMMER, D. W. & A. PERT. 1983. The actions of opiates in the rat substantia nigra: An electrophysiological analysis. Peptides **4:** 603–608.

50. WOOD, P. L. 1983. Opioid regulation of CNS dopaminergic pathways: A review of methodology, receptor types, regional variations and species differences. Peptides **4:** 595–601.

51. GOSNELL, B. A., J. E. MORLEY & A. S. LEVINE. 1983. N-allylnormetazocine (SKF-10,047): The induction of feeding by a putative sigma agonist. Pharmacol. Biochem. Behav. **19:** 737–742.

52. HERLING, S. & H. E. HANNON. 1982. Discriminative effects of ethylketocyclazocine in the rat: Stereospecificity and antagonism by naloxone. Life Sci. **31:** 2371–2374.

53. LOWY, M. T. & G. K. W. YIM. 1983. Stimulation of food intake following opiate agonists in rats but not hamsters. Psychopharmacology (Berlin) **81:** 28–32.

54. JACKSON, A. & S. J. COOPER. 1986. An observational analysis of the effect of the selective kappa opioid agonist U-50,488H, on feeding and related behaviours in the rat. Psychopharmacology **90:** 217–221.

55. MORLEY, J. E., A. S. LEVINE, M. GRACE, J. KNEIP & H. ZEUGNER. 1983. The effect of the opioid-benzodiazepine, tifluadom, on ingestive behaviors. Eur. J. Pharmacol. **93:** 265–269.

56. MORLEY, J. E., A. S. LEVINE, J. KNEIP, M. GRACE, H. ZEUGNER & G. T. SHEARMAN. 1985. The kappa opioid receptor and food intake. Eur. J. Pharmacol. **112:** 17–25.

57. CARR, K. D., T. H. BAK, T. L. GIOANNINI & E. J. SIMON. 1987. Antibodies to dynorphin A(1–13) but not beta-endorphin inhibit electrically elicited feeding in the rat. Brain Res. **422:** 384–388.

58. GOSNELL, B. A., J. E. MORLEY & A. S. LEVINE. 1986. Opioid-induced feeding: Localization of sensitive brain sites. Brain Res. **369:** 177–184.

59. GOSNELL, B. A., D. R. ROMSOS, J. E. MORLEY & A. S. LEVINE. 1985. Opiates and medial hypothalamic knife-cuts cause hyperphagia through different mechanisms. Behav. Neurosci. **99:** 1181–1191.

60. LEVINE, A. S., M. GRACE, W. WELCH, C. J. BILLINGTON & P. S. PORTOGHESE. 1988. The kappa opioid antagonist, nor-binaltorphimine, decreases starvation- and opioid-induced feeding. Soc. Neurosci. Abstr. **14:** 761.

61. BAK, T., K. D. CARR, E. J. SIMON & P. S. PORTOGHESE. 1988. Opposite effects of rostral and caudal ventricular infusion of nor-binaltorphimine on stimulation-induced feeding. Soc. Neurosci. Abstr. **14:** 1107.

62. PORTOGHESE, P. S., D. L. LARSON, J. B. JIANG, T. P. CARUSO & A. E. TAKEMORI. 1979.

Synthesis and pharmacological characterization of an alkylating analogue (chlornaltrexamine) of naltrexone with ultra long-lasting narcotic antagonist properties. J. Med. Chem. **22:** 168–173.

63. GOSNELL, B. A. 1987. Central structures involved in opioid-induced feeding. Fed. Proc. **46:** 163–167.

64. LYNCH, W. C., J. WATT, S. KRALL & C. M. PADEN. 1985. Autoradiographic localization of kappa opiate receptors in CNS taste and feeding areas. Pharmacol. Biochem. Behav. **22:** 699–705.

65. SIVIY, S. M., F. BERMUDEZ-RATTONI, G. A. ROCKWOOD, C. DARGIE & L. REID. 1981. Intracerebral administration of naloxone and drinking in water-deprived rats. Pharmacol. Biochem. Behav. **15:** 257–262.

66. THORNHILL, J. A. & W. SAUNDERS. 1984. Ventromedial and lateral hypothalamic injections of naloxone or naltrexone suppress the acute food intake of food-deprived rats. Appetite **5:** 25–30.

67. TEPPERMAN, F. S. & M. HIRST. 1982. Concerning the specificity of the hypothalamic opiate receptor responsible for food intake in the rat. Pharmacol. Biochem. Behav. **17:** 1141–1144.

68. STANLEY, B. G., D. LANTHIER & S. F. LEIBOWITZ. 1984. Feeding elicited by the opiate peptide D-ala-2-met enkephalinamide: Sites of action in the brain. Soc. Neurosci. Abstr. **10:** 1103.

69. GOSNELL, B. A. 1988. Involvement of μ opioid receptors in the amygdala in the control of feeding. Neuropharmacology **27:** 319–326.

70. GOSNELL, B. A., J. E. MORLEY, A. S. LEVINE, J. KNEIP, M. FRICK & R. P. ELDE. 1984. Opiate induced feeding is not dependent on the hippocampus. Physiol. Behav. **33:** 27–30.

71. GOSNELL, B. A., D. W. WAGGONER, J. E. MORLEY & A. S. LEVINE. 1985. The pineal gland and opiate-induced feeding. Physiol. Behav. **34:** 1–6.

72. KING, B. M., F. X. CASTELLANOS, A. J. KASTIN, M. C. BERZAS, M. D. MAUK, G. A. OLSON & R. D. OLSON. 1979. Naloxone-induced suppression of food intake in normal and hypothalamic obese rats. Pharmacol. Biochem. Behav. **11:** 729–732.

73. GOSNELL, B. A. J. E. MORLEY & A. S. LEVINE. 1984. Lesions of the globus pallidus and striatum attenuate ketocyclazocine-induced feeding. Physiol. Behav. **33:** 349–355.

74. CALCAGNETTI, D. J. & L. D. REID. 1983. Morphine and acceptability of putative reinforcers. Pharmacol. Biochem. Behav. **18:** 567–569.

75. LYNCH, W. C. & L. LIBBY. 1983. Naloxone suppresses intake of highly preferred saccharin solutions in food deprived and sated rats. Life Sci. **33:** 1909–1914.

76. COOPER, S. J. 1983. Effects of opiate agonists and antagonists on fluid intake and saccharin choice in the rat. Neuropharmacology **22:** 323–328.

77. COOPER, S. J. & D. B. GILBERT. 1984. Naloxone suppresses fluid consumption in tests of choice between sodium chloride solutions and water in male and female water-deprived rats. Psychopharmacology **84:** 362–367.

78. SIVIY, S. M., & L. D. REID. 1983. Endorphinergic modulation of acceptability of putative reinforcers. Appetite **4:** 249–257.

79. LYNCH, W. C. 1986. Opiate blockade inhibits saccharin intake and blocks normal preference acquisition. Pharmacol. Biochem. Behav. **24:** 833–836.

80. APFELBAUM, M. & A. MANDENOFF. 1981. Naltrexone suppresses hyperphagia induced in the rat by a highly palatable diet. Pharmacol. Biochem. Behav. **15:** 89–91.

81. MARKS-KAUFMAN, R. & R. B. KANAREK. 1981. Modifications of nutrient selection induced by naloxone in rats. Psychopharmacology **74:** 321–324.

82. ROMSOS, D. R., B. A. GOSNELL, J. E. MORLEY & A. S. LEVINE, 1987. Effects of kappa opiate agonists, cholecystokinin and bombesin on intake of diets varying in carbohydrate-to-fat ratio in rats. J. Nutr. **117:** 976–985.

83. SHOR-POSNER, G., A. P. AYAR, R. FILART, D. TEMPEL & S. F. LEIBOWITZ. 1986. Morphine-stimulated feeding: analysis of macronutrient selection and paraventricular nucleus lesions. Pharmacol. Biochem. Behav. **24:** 931–939.

84. ATKINSON, R. L. 1982. Naloxone decreases food intake in obese humans. J. Clin. Endocrinol. Metab. **55:** 196–198.

85. WOLKOWITZ, O. M., A. R. DORAN, M. R. COHEN, R. M. COHEN, T. N. WISE & D. PICKAR. 1985. Effect of naloxone on food consumption in obesity. N. Engl. J. Med. **313:** 327.

86. TRENCHARD, E. & T. SILVERSTONE. 1983. Naloxone reduces the food intake of normal volunteers. Appetite **4:** 43–50.
87. COHEN, M. R., R. M. COHEN, D. PICKAR & D. L. MURPHY. 1985. Naloxone reduces food intake in humans. Psychosom. Med. **47:** 132–138.
88. O'BRIEN, C. P., A. J. STUNKARD & J. TERNES. 1982. Absence of naloxone sensitivity in obese humans. Psychosom. Med. **44:** 215–218.
89. MITCHELL, J. E., D. E. LAINE, J. E. MORLEY & A. S. LEVINE. 1986. Naloxone but not CCK-8 may attenuate binge-eating behavior in patients with the bulimia syndrome. Biol. Psychiatry **21:** 1399–1406.
90. JONAS, J. M. & M. S. GOLD. 1988. The use of opiate antagonists in treating bulimia: A study of low-dose versus high-dose naltrexone. Psychiatr. Res. **24:** 195–199.
91. MORLEY, J. E., S. PARKER & A. S. LEVINE. 1985. The effect of butorphanol tartrate on food and water consumption in humans. Am. J. Clin. Nutr. **42:** 1175–1178.
92. ATKINSON, R. L., L. K. BERKE. C. R. DRAKE, M. L. BIBBS, F. L. WILLIAMS & D. L. KAISER. 1985. Effects of long-term therapy with naltrexone on body weight in obesity. Clin. Pharmacol. Ther. **38:** 419–422.
93. MALCOLM, R., P. M. O'NEIL, J. D. SEXAUER, F. E. RIDDLE, H. S. CURREY & C. COUNTS. 1985. A controlled trial of naltrexone in obese humans. Int. J. Obesity **9:** 347–353.
94. MITCHELL, J. E., J. E. MORLEY, A. S. LEVINE, D. HATSUKAMI, M. GANNON & D. PFOHL. 1987. High-dose naltrexone therapy and dietary counseling for obesity. Biol. Psychiatry **22:** 35–42.
95. MAGGIO, C. A., E. PRESTA, E. P. BRACCO, J. R. VASSELLI, H. R. KISSILEFF & S. A. HASHIM. 1984. Naltrexone and human feeding behavior: A dose-ranging inpatient trial in moderately obese men. *In* Neural and Metabolic Bases of Feeding, 68. University of California. Davis, CA.

DISCUSSION

DR. PAUL ARAVICH (*Veterans Administration Medical Center, Hampton, VA*): I wonder if you could provide an interpretation for the paradoxical effect that naloxone has on food-deprived mice, in that it stimulates food intake in the food-deprived mouse.

DR. ALLEN S. LEVINE (*University of Minnesota, Minneapolis, MN*): I don't have an explanation. The kind of explanation I might come up with is that opioids, in fact, are not necessary stimulators of feeding long-term and only affect short-term food intake. The naloxone effect may actually be reversing the other effect at low doses. So, just as I showed for the adenosine agonists that could either suppress or increase with opioids, that's probably the case with naloxone as well. We have to do a lot more work with chronic studies to get any handle on that.

DR. STYLIANOS NICOLAIDIS (*College de France CNRS, Paris*): Inhibition of feeding is not very interesting to study because you never know what's happening. But an *increase* of feeding is interesting. I would like you to comment on side effects or collateral effects obtained during these increases of feeding, for example, aggressiveness, or other behaviors that you have been able to observe in animals or that have been reported by human beings during an increase in food intake.

DR. LEVINE: We have done a series of behavioral studies comparing opiates to various other stimulators of feeding, such as muscimol, norepinephrine, and neuropeptide Y. I would say with many of the opioid agonists there is such a long period of sedation that it does not look in any way similar behaviorally to feeding that occurs after food deprivation, for example, whereas neuropeptide Y looks much closer. However, when you give very low doses of naloxone into the ventricles, as low as 10 micrograms, you can suppress neuropeptide-Y-induced feeding. So again, that adds a little bit of confusion by showing that we can change the effect with an antagonist of the opioid of something that isn't opioid related.

Hypothalamic Neuropeptide Y, Galanin, and Amines

Concepts of Coexistence in Relation to Feeding Behavior[a]

SARAH FRYER LEIBOWITZ

The Rockefeller University
New York, New York 10021

Brain monoamines have been extensively studied with respect to their effects on food intake, meal patterns, and appetite for specific nutrients.[1,2] It is now evident, however, that certain peptides coexist with the monoamines in neurons of the brain,[3] and investigators have attempted to determine the nature of the interaction between these neuropeptides and the classical neurotransmitters, as well as their receptors. The peptides may act directly via their own peptidergic receptors and independently of the monoamines; they may also act in a dependent fashion, either presynaptically through modulating the release of the monoamines or postsynaptically through modulation of the monoaminergic effector response or through a direct receptor–receptor interaction. There is evidence for each of these possibilities, and the specific role, relative importance, and mode of interaction of the different coexisting messengers in the overall effector response appears to vary with the geometry of innervation and the receptor characteristics of the specific tissue under investigation.

This review will focus on two peptides, namely, neuropeptide Y (NPY) and galanin (GAL), which, like the monoamines, are found to have dramatic effects on ingestive behavior and endocrine processes. These peptides are known to have particularly high concentrations within the hypothalamus where they coexist, in certain neurons, with the classical aminergic neurotransmitters. Recent findings[4] suggest that these hypothalamic neurocircuits may provide excellent model systems for examining, in localized brain areas, the precise nature of the peptide–amine interactions in the brain and their physiological function in controlling ingestive behavior and related endocrine and metabolic processes.

The monoamines are found to have potent and varied effects on eating behavior, in the rat as well as in a variety of other species.[1,5,6] This review will concentrate on two monoaminergic systems identified in the medial hypothalamus, namely, the α_2-noradrenergic and serotonergic systems, and then examine their relation to the neuropeptides, NPY and GAL.

MONOAMINES AND FEEDING BEHAVIOR

α_2-Noradrenergic System

Hypothalamic stimulation with norepinephrine (NE) or epinephrine (EPI) has long

[a] This work was supported by Public Health Service Grants MH 22879 and MH 43422.

been known to elicit feeding in satiated animals.[1,2] Studies in rats demonstrate that this phenomenon has a rapid onset ($<$ 1 min) and a short duration ($<$ 15 min); it is anatomically localized, predominantly to the hypothalamic paraventricular nucleus (PVN), and it is mediated via α_2-, rather than α_1-, type receptors located on the postsynaptic membrane.[7-9] Destruction of the PVN, as opposed to other brain sites, disturbs the animal's ability to respond to NE[2,5] and to regulate normally circadian patterns of carbohydrate and protein intake.[10]

The primary effect of NE, or the α_2-receptor agonist clonidine, is to cause a preferential increase in the animal's appetite for carbohydrate, generally at the expense of protein intake.[5,11] In addition, NE or EPI injection into the PVN increases circulating levels of the adrenal hormone, corticosterone (CORT), as well as vasopressin and glucose,[12] hormones that synergize with NE to potentiate feeding and carbohydrate intake.[5]

The activity of this α_2-noradrenergic system in the PVN is closely linked to the light/dark cycle. That is, at the start of the active period (nocturnal cycle for the rat), the α_2-noradrenergic system exhibits a sharp, unimodal peak in activity.[5] This is reflected in: (1) microinjection studies of the animal's sensitivity to NE; (2) microdialysis studies of endogenous PVN NE levels; and (3) radioligand binding studies of PVN α_2-receptor density. It is important to note that this peak in α_2-noradrenergic activity occurs in association with a *natural* rise in circulating levels of CORT, as well as in the animal's preference for carbohydrate.[5,13]

Serotonergic System

In contrast to NE or EPI, hypothalamic administration of serotonin (5-HT) has a suppressive effect on food intake in freely feeding or food-deprived animals.[6,14-17] This effect occurs with both peripheral and central administration of serotonergic drugs that are believed to act through the release of endogenous 5-HT. Cannula mapping and lesion studies indicate that this phenomenon is anatomically localized to the medial hypothalamus, specifically the PVN, ventromedial and suprachiasmatic nuclei. Pharmacological tests suggest that it is mediated by postsynaptic 5-HT$_{1B}$ receptor sites.

The serotonergic system, similar to the α_2-noradrenergic system, has a selective effect on macronutrient intake.[5,6,14-16] Serotonin in the PVN dose dependently suppresses carbohydrate intake, while sometimes enhancing appetite for protein. Similar effects can be observed with PVN injection of the serotonergic compounds, *d*-norfenfluramine and fluoxetine, as well as with peripheral injection of these or related compounds at low doses. As indicated for NE, the activity of the PVN serotonergic system shifts across the light/dark cycle, exhibiting a peak at the onset of the active period. This is reflected in microdialysis analyses of PVN 5-HT metabolism,[18] as well as in pharmacological experiments showing hypothalamic injections of 5-HT or the serotonergic drugs to be effective in suppressing carbohydrate intake predominantly at the start of the natural feeding cycle.[6,16]

On the basis of this and related evidence, it has been proposed[2,6] that NE and 5-HT in the medial hypothalamus interact antagonistically to control carbohydrate and protein ingestion, specifically at the beginning of the animal's active cycle. Norepinephrine stimulates the first meal of the nocturnal period, which behavioral studies in the rat indicate is generally rich in carbohydrate.[13] As a consequence of this meal, there occurs a surge in serotonergic activity. This monoamine, through activation of satiety mechanisms, first helps to terminate the carbohydrate meal initiated by NE; it then switches the animal's preference toward protein, the macronutrient of choice for the second meal of the natural feeding cycle.[13]

PEPTIDES AND FEEDING BEHAVIOR

Neuropeptide Y, a 36 amino acid peptide, is among the most abundant peptides in neurons of the peripheral and central nervous system.[19] This peptide has been shown to coexist with the classical neurotransmitters, in particular, NE, EPI, and 5-HT. Galanin, a 29 amino acid peptide, is another neuropeptide known to coexist with NE, as well as 5-HT, in peripheral and central neurons.[20] Both peptides are believed to have a variety of physiological and endocrine functions, although considerably fewer studies have been conducted with GAL.[19,21,22]

Neuropeptide Y

In addition to containing NPY receptor binding sites,[23] the hypothalamus, and in particular the PVN, is known to receive a rich innervation of NPY-immunoreactive nerve endings, either from EPI-containing neurons in the medulla (C1 and C2), NE-containing neurons in the medulla (A1) and dorsal pons (A6), or non-catecholaminergic neurons in the arcuate nucleus.[21] When injected directly into the PVN, a primary site of action for NE and EPI,[8] the eating response induced by NPY, as well as by the related substance peptide YY (PYY), is dose dependent, within the range of 0.02 to 1.0 nmole.[24] The maximal feeding response induced by an optimal dose of NPY or PYY (0.25 nmol) in satiated rats is 15 g in 1 hour, which is approximately 50% of the rat's normal daily intake.

With measurements taken during the first hour after injection, the maximal feeding responses elicited by NE and NPY in the PVN are comparable in magnitude.[12,25] However, the latency of these two responses differs considerably, with NE acting within <1 min[8] and NPY after 10 min.[26] Moreover, their response duration also differs, <30 min for NE and >4 hrs for NPY, which allows NPY to yield a more potent, long-term effect.[26] This difference in duration of action has similarly been detected in studies of the inhibitory effect of PVN NE and NPY on gastric acid secretion,[27] as well as in studies of peripheral autonomic function.[28,29]

The behavioral responses elicited by NPY and NE in the PVN have several similarities. In addition to producing a small increase in drinking behavior, both substances increase food intake by potentiating the rate of eating, as well as the duration of the eating response.[30-32] They also stimulate preferentially the rat's intake of carbohydrate, while having little or no effect on protein or fat ingestion.[11,24,33] Moreover, both substances produce their largest response at the onset of the nocturnal (active) cycle, as compared to a relatively weak response at the end of the nocturnal period.[4,34] Similar to NE and EPI, NPY in the PVN stimulates the release of CORT and vasopressin,[12] and the feeding response elicited by NPY, as with NE,[5] is dependent upon circulating CORT levels which naturally peak at dark onset.[37]

Galanin

Studies with direct hypothalamic injection of GAL have found this peptide, similar to NE and NPY, to have a stimulatory effect on food intake in satiated rats.[35] As with NPY, GAL injection into the PVN of the rat elicits a feeding response, at doses of 0.03 to 3.0 nmol. This response in satiated animals is almost comparable in magnitude to that observed with NPY and NE.[4,25,35] Moreover, the response elicited by GAL is positively correlated with that induced by NE.[25,36] The latency of the GAL effect is approximately 5.0 min; this is somewhat shorter than that with NPY (10 min) but still longer than that of NE (1.0 min). The duration of the GAL-induced feeding response, generally 15–30 min, is similar to that of NE and notably shorter than that of NPY (>4 hrs). Galanin fails to alter water intake, as well as other behaviors such as grooming, rearing, general activity, and sleeping.[35]

PHARMACOLOGICAL STUDIES OF PEPTIDE/MONOAMINE INTERACTIONS

This evidence, revealing considerable similarities between the behavioral/endocrine effects of NE, EPI, NPY, and GAL in the hypothalamus, suggests that these peptides and amines function, to some extent, via common neural mechanisms to control eating behavior and associated endocrine and metabolic processes.[4] From pharmacological, anatomical, and biochemical studies, however, it appears that NPY and GAL act differently in this process, in terms of their interaction with the catecholamines. In particular, the evidence indicates that NPY functions largely independently of the amines, whereas GAL acts, at least in part, through the release of endogenous NE and its subsequent activation of α_2 receptors in the PVN.

Pharmacological evidence, obtained in a variety of peripheral and central systems, has generally indicated that NPY, while mimicking the action of NE or EPI, acts via its own peptide receptor and independently of the postsynaptic α-noradrenergic receptor site.[28,29,38,39] This also appears to be the case with the feeding-stimulatory effect of NPY in the PVN. This eating response is unaffected by local administration of general α-noradrenergic or selective α_2-noradrenergic receptor antagonists,[26,40–42] which abolish eating elicited by NE.[7] It may in fact be potentiated by peripheral administration of an α_2-receptor antagonist.[40]

In addition to their independent action on the postsynaptic membrane, other evidence indicates that NPY elicits feeding independently of presynaptic stores of NE, consistent with findings obtained in other systems.[3,28,29,38] Specifically, the feeding stimulatory effect of NPY remains intact and may in fact be significantly potentiated, after local PVN administration of catecholamine synthesis inhibitors,[4,43] as well as after brainstem knife cuts which reduce hypothalamic NE and EPI levels.[40] These manipulations, which damage adrenergic afferents to the PVN, are both effective in antagonizing the behavioral effects of catecholamine-releasing drugs in this nucleus.[1,9,44]

Tests with receptor antagonists and NE synthesis inhibitors indicate that GAL, unlike NPY, is dependent upon intact α_2-adrenergic receptor sites, as well as presynaptic stores of NE. Feeding elicited by PVN administration of GAL, similar to NE, is antagonized by general α-adrenergic as well as selective α_2-receptor blockers; it is unaffected, however, by α_1-receptor blockers.[4,7,41] Moreover, the eating response to GAL, unlike NPY, is attenuated by prior PVN administration of NE synthesis inhibitors.[43] These drugs are similarly effective in blocking the action of compounds that act through the release of endogenous NE; in contrast, they leave intact or even potentiate the postsynaptic action of injected NE.[44] These findings, consistent with reports of a presynaptic excitatory interaction between GAL and NE in peripheral sympathetic nerves,[22] support the hypothesis that GAL, in modulating food intake, may require the functional release of NE from presynaptic nerve endings in the PVN.

NEUROANATOMICAL STUDIES

Additional evidence dissociating the action of NPY and NE derives from experiments that tested the sensitivity of multiple brain sites to NPY injection. These studies have demonstrated that, while NE acts in a localized fashion within the area of the PVN to stimulate food intake,[8] the eating response produced by NPY administration can be observed throughout multiple hypothalamic sites, although generally not in extra-hypothalamic areas.[33,45] Until the extent of NPY spread from the injection site is determined and controlled, conclusions drawn from these results must remain tentative.

While NPY may act through multiple hypothalamic areas, the available evidence suggests that the PVN is at least one of this peptide's sites of action. The PVN receives a particularly dense innervation of NPY-containing neurons, both from adrenergic and noradrenergic cells in the lower brainstem and from non-catecholaminergic cells in the arcuate nucleus.[19,21] The importance of these projections in feeding is reflected in the finding that electrolytic lesions of the PVN significantly attenuate the feeding response elicited by intraventricular NPY injection,[46] similar to their effect on NE's action.[5] Moreover, NPY content[47] or NPY-positive innervation,[48] specifically in the PVN, is increased by food deprivation (3–4 days) and reversed by refeeding. The PVN is likely to be critical in the stimulatory effect of NPY on CORT release[12] and in the feedback action of CORT on local α_2 and possibly NPY receptor sites.[4,5,37]

While GAL exists throughout the brain, anatomical studies have revealed a prominent focus of GAL neurons and fibers in the hypothalamus, and in particular the PVN,[49–51] where [^{125}I]GAL binding sites have also been detected.[52] Cannula mapping studies similarly focus on the PVN as a primary site of action for GAL and its interaction with NE in controlling eating behavior.[35,36]

While the three substances, GAL, NPY, and NE, are each found to produce a strong feeding response when administered into the PVN, GAL is distinguished as having a localized site of action, similar to that of NE.[8,35,36] In contrast to NPY, which is found to be effective in multiple areas of the hypothalamus, GAL is relatively or totally ineffective in hypothalamic areas outside the PVN, as well as in extra-hypothalamic sites. Further analyses within the PVN itself have identified the medial parvicellular region of the PVN as the critical site for GAL's action, similar to that observed with NE.[8] This is consistent with the finding of a particularly dense GAL innervation to · this subdivision of the PVN.[49]

Additional anatomical evidence supports the proposal that this GAL projection to the PVN originates in part from the A1 and A6 cell groups in the lower brainstem.[49] These noradrenergic neurons, which co-store GAL, send fiber projections toward the PVN along a similar course previously described for the PVN noradrenergic feeding system.[9] Moreover, this ascending pathway innervates predominantly the periventricular region, where both GAL and NE are believed to be most active. With regard to the efferent projection of this neurocircuit, it is noteworthy that a dense population of GAL-containing cells in the adjoining magnocellular division of the PVN descends toward the midbrain periventricular grey,[53] along a course similar to that identified for the efferent projection of the noradrenergic feeding-stimulatory system.[54]

BIOCHEMICAL STUDIES

Results of biochemical studies further support the proposal that NPY, while mimicking the action of exogenous NE, acts independently of presynaptic release of endogenous NE. Generally, in the periphery as well as the brain, NPY fails to enhance the turnover of NE and may, in fact, depress its release.[28,29,38,55] At low doses, NPY injection into the ventricles reduces NE utilization in the hypothalamus and specifically in the PVN.[56,57] Moreover, in freely moving animals with a microdialysis probe in the PVN, local injection of NPY fails to increase, and may tend to reduce, extracellular concentration of PVN NE.[58]

In contrast to NPY, biochemical results support a cooperative interaction between GAL and NE by revealing a stimulatory effect of GAL on noradrenergic function.

This has been demonstrated in peripheral sympathetic nerve fibers,[59] as well as in the median eminence where GAL causes a selective reduction of catecholamine stores.[52] Furthermore, studies of endogenous PVN NE, using the microdialysis/HPLC technique in freely moving rats, have revealed a dramatic increase in extracellular NE levels in the PVN after local injection of GAL.[58] This stimulatory effect of GAL on NE utilization in the hypothalamus contrasts with this peptide's presynaptic, inhibitory effect on other classical neurotransmitter systems in the brain.[60–63]

NATURAL PATTERNS OF EATING BEHAVIOR

In understanding the physiological function of the peptides and amines, it is important first to characterize, as precisely as possible, the different components of the natural behavior under investigation. Recent computer-assisted analyses of feeding behavior during the nocturnal cycle of freely feeding rats have revealed that patterns of macronutrient intake differ dramatically at different points of the daily cycle.[13,64] In particular, rats eat their first meal of the night within approximately 10 min after lights go out. In over 80% of the animals, this meal is rich in carbohydrate; it lasts approximately 12 min and is then followed within an hour by the second meal, which is richer in protein. This early pattern changes toward the end of the nocturnal cycle, when preference for carbohydrate is low and protein or fat intake predominate.

Function of Norepinephrine and Serotonin

On the basis of a variety of behavioral, pharmacological, and biochemical studies (see above), it has been proposed that the α_2-noradrenergic system in the PVN exhibits peak activity specifically at the start of the dark (active) cycle, and that endogenous PVN NE (or EPI) is physiologically active in stimulating the first carbohydrate meal normally exhibited at this time.[5] Additional studies suggest that the serotonergic innervation to the medial hypothalamus also becomes activated at this time, possibly in response to ingestion of the initial carbohydrate meal.[6,16] This monoamine first terminates this carbohydrate meal, possibly by antagonizing NE's action and inducing satiety for this nutrient. It then switches the animal's preference toward protein, which is generally preferred in the second meal of the natural feeding cycle.[13,64]

Cooperative Interaction between Neuropeptide Y and Norepinephrine

The question is, Does hypothalamic NPY play a physiological role in the control of food intake and appetite, and if so, to what extent does it interact with or depend upon the monoamines? Evidence indicates that the relative importance of NPY as a cotransmitter increases with the frequency of the nerve impulses. That is, NPY coexists with NE primarily in large dense-cored vesicles, and intense, high-frequency stimulation favors exocytosis of NPY from these large vesicles.[28,29,39] This suggests that NPY may exert its effect on food intake specifically under conditions that evoke high-frequency stimulation, such as when energy stores are most depleted by an extended period of little eating.

It is proposed that NPY, in conjunction with NE or EPI, is activated specifically at the onset of the active feeding cycle to potentiate carbohydrate intake. The strongest evidence in support of this idea[4,34] is the finding that PVN injection of NPY, like NE, is most effective in producing this response at this time, when the density of PVN α_2 receptors has been shown to peak[5,65]; in contrast, it is weakest later in the nocturnal period, when there is a decline both in the α_2 receptors and in the rat's natural preference for carbohydrate.[13,65] This is consistent with the report that NPY-elicited feeding is stronger in the dark cycle, as compared to the light cycle.[30] Furthermore, NPY injected into the PVN causes the release of CORT,[12] which is normally known to rise toward the onset of the dark cycle,[5,65] and the stimulatory action of this peptide on feeding is dependent upon high levels of circulating CORT.[4,37]

A state of energy depletion, and a consequent NPY release in response to intense neural stimulation, may similarly occur after environmentally imposed periods of deprivation. It is known that food deprivation stimulates carbohydrate intake as well as fat ingestion.[10] Deprivation, in addition to potentiating NE turnover and decreasing α_2-receptor sites specifically in the PVN,[66,67] has been shown to cause an increase in PVN NPY-positive innervation,[48] as well as a rise in NPY content that is reversed by refeeding.[47] A particular importance of NPY, relative to NE, in potentiating energy intake under such conditions may be suggested by its greater potency and longer duration of action.[26] This potency is particularly evident under conditions of *chronic* NPY stimulation of the PVN, which causes a marked increase in carbohydrate as well as fat ingestion, in association with a substantial rise in body weight.[68]

Thus, NPY appears to have an important direct function as an auxiliary mediator of carbohydrate appetite at a time of greatest energy depletion. While NPY may exhibit this effect in the absence of presynaptic NE release, cooperativity between NPY and NE may be further exhibited on the postsynaptic membrane in the form of a receptor–receptor interaction. This interaction between closely coupled receptors has been demonstrated in the lower brainstem, where NPY stimulation modulates the α_2-receptor binding sites and where a reciprocal interaction occurs between α_2-adrenergic stimulation and the NPY receptor sites.[38]

Antagonistic Interaction between Neuropeptide Y and Norepinephrine

While NPY and NE may initiate feeding via separate receptors on the postsynaptic membrane, there is additional evidence for a reciprocal antagonistic interaction between NPY and the α_2 receptors at the presynaptic terminal. This is reflected in the finding that NPY, via its own receptors, acts similarly to α_2 receptors in controlling the release of NE from noradrenergic nerve terminals (see above). In particular, NPY reduces NE utilization in the hypothalamus[57] and PVN,[56,58] and it has been shown to potentiate the presynaptic action of the α_2-receptor agonist clonidine in the brainstem.[69] A reciprocal release-modulating mechanism between the cotransmitters may also be operative, whereby NE, via its presynaptic α_2 receptors, controls the release of NPY, as well as the density of its receptors. This has been demonstrated by the finding that α_2-receptor antagonists, as well as NE or EPI synthesis inhibitors, enhance the release of NPY and potentiate its receptor action in the periphery and brain.[28,38,70,71]

Such an antagonistic interaction between NPY and NE specifically in the PVN may explain the finding that NPY is more effective in eliciting feeding when α_2 receptors are blocked and when endogenous NE stores are reduced or depleted. This result has been detected after PVN administration of NE synthesis inhibitors,[4,43] peripheral injection of α_2-receptor antagonists,[40] and brainstem knife cuts that damage NE or EPI fibers projecting to the PVN.[40]

In light of these diverse actions of NPY, it has been proposed that this peptide and NE may have a biphasic mode of interaction.[29] With specific reference to their physiological function in the PVN, it is suggested that NPY and NE have a initial cooperative, postsynaptic role in reinforcing the signal for carbohydrate ingestion at dark onset; subsequently, however, these cotransmitters interact presynaptically to antagonize the secretory mechanism of hyperactive nerve terminals and thus help to terminate the carbohydrate meal and thereby allow for ingestion of other macronutrients, such as protein. A shift of this nature, between carbohydrate and protein intake, has been found to occur naturally in freely feeding rats.[13,64]

Cooperative Interaction between Galanin and Norepinephrine

There is some evidence to suggest that GAL, similar to NE as well as NPY (see above), may become activated specifically at the beginning of the active feeding period to control carbohydrate intake. Studies of macronutrient intake indicate that GAL, like NE, has a stimulatory effect on carbohydrate intake, while producing no change in protein consumption.[25] Furthermore, this effect of GAL is positively correlated with that produced by NE. It occurs predominantly at dark onset, when NE is believed to be most active,[5] and it is absent at the end of the dark period.[34] Thus, together with the pharmacological and biochemical evidence described above, this finding suggests that GAL acts to release endogenous NE in the PVN and thereby has a stimulatory influence on the first carbohydrate meal that occurs naturally at the start of the active cycle.[5]

Interaction between Peptides and Other Monoamines

It is likely that NPY and GAL, in addition to their close link to NE or EPI in the hypothalamus, may exert their effects on eating behavior via interactions with other monoaminergic systems. One such system may involve the monoamine 5-HT, which is believed to act specifically at the onset of the dark cycle, first to inhibit carbohydrate intake and then to switch the animal's preference toward protein.[6,14] Neuropeptide Y and GAL are colocalized with 5-HT in dorsal raphe neurons known to innervate the hypothalamus and, in particular, the PVN.[20,72,73] Moreover, both peptides are found to reduce 5-HT metabolism in the brain,[57,61,62] possibly via impact on presynaptic 5-HT$_{1A}$ receptors,[63] and an antagonistic interaction between serotonergic stimulation and NPY-elicited feeding has been demonstrated.[74] Thus, NPY and GAL may potentiate ingestion of carbohydrate, in part, by controlling 5-HT release presynaptically and thereby disinhibiting the eating response.

In addition to its role in controlling carbohydrate intake, GAL is also found to have a stimulatory influence on fat ingestion, and the magnitude of this effect, relative to GAL's potentiation of carbohydrate intake, varies at different times of the light/dark cycle.[4,25,34] The increase in fat intake is particularly strong at the end of the nocturnal cycle, when GAL is ineffective in stimulating carbohydrate consumption; a smaller effect, however, is also apparent early in the dark period, when GAL is most active in potentiating carbohydrate intake.

While this GAL-induced increase in fat consumption may be related to a smaller and more variable response observed with NE,[11] it more likely reflects an action of this peptide on a non-noradrenergic system in the hypothalamus. The dopaminergic system is one possibility, because GAL is known to coexist with DA in the hypothalamus and inhibit its release.[60] Studies with amphetamine, which is believed to act in part via hypothalamic DA,[1] reveal an inhibitory effect of this agent on fat ingestion, as well as on protein intake.[75,76] Because fat and protein are the naturally preferred macronutrients at the end of the nocturnal cycle[13,64] and GAL is most potent in stimulating fat consumption at this time,[34] it is possible that this effect of GAL may in part involve the inhibition of hypothalamic DA.

FUNCTION OF PEPTIDES IN CLINICAL EATING DISORDERS

Several studies implicate NPY in the development of abnormal eating patterns. For example, chronic PVN injection of NPY in rats produces severe overeating, particularly of carbohydrate and fat, that leads to the development of obesity.[68,77] Moreover, NPY is found to be differentially effective in stimulating eating behavior in genetically obese rats, as compared to their littermates.[78]

Studies of the pathophysiology of clinical eating disorders have detected disturbances in CSF content of NPY, or its related pancreatic polypeptide PYY, in anorexic or bulimic patients.[79] In particular, a dramatic increase in CSF PYY was detected in bulimics who had abstained from bingeing. This finding led to the proposal that bulimics, when they initiate a binge, may be responding to heightened levels of PYY.

There is further evidence suggesting a relationship between hypothalamic NPY, the onset of puberty, and the transition toward development of adult eating patterns in young females. A recent report indicates that, in rats, immunoreactive NPY content in the hypothalamus rises steadily from birth to the onset of puberty.[80] Moreover, a sharp rise in hypophysial-portal levels of NPY occurs only in female rats on the day of puberty onset, immediately before the prepubertal surge in luteinizing hormone (LH) secretion. Studies of feeding behavior in pubescent rats indicate that female rats exhibit a natural rise in preference for carbohydrate at this time, in contrast to the preference for protein exhibited by male rats.[81] It is possible that these simultaneous behavioral and endocrine events are related, because central injection of NPY induces LH secretion[82] and preferentially stimulates carbohydrate ingestion.[24] Furthermore, food deprivation increases NPY content within the PVN,[47,48] while producing a strong increase in preference for carbohydrate and fat.[10]

It is of interest that anorexia nervosa, a disturbance in appetite for energy-rich foods, occurs predominantly in females, most often around the time of puberty and as a consequence of malnutrition.[83] It is possible[79] that abnormal peptide activity in anorexia nervosa may provide the link between disturbed appetite and menstrual function, as well as contribute to the vicious cycle characteristic of this eating disorder. In view of the link established between hypothalamic NPY and circulating CORT[37] or glucose,[84] any disturbances in such hormones or nutrients in the blood may be expected to alter peptide activity in the brain and consequently alter eating patterns.

While fewer studies have been conducted on GAL in relation to clinical eating disorders, there is one recent report[85] that describes an increase in GAL innervation within the brains of Alzheimer patients known to exhibit abnormal eating patterns.[86] This disturbance in brain GAL, however, can not be detected with CSF analysis, which failed to reveal changes in patients with either Alzheimer's, anorexia, or bulimia.[87] Studies of pituitary GAL immunoreactivity have demonstrated dramatic changes in peptide content in association with fluctuations in circulating estrogen.[88] Moreover, GAL is known to potentiate growth hormone secretion,[89] possibly through activation of growth hormone-releasing factor, a hypothalamic peptide active in stimulating feeding behavior.[90] It is possible that, as described for NPY, shifts in macronutrient preference that occur around the time of puberty, as well as across the menstrual cycle, may be attributed to these hormone-linked changes in endogenous GAL activity.

CONCLUSIONS

It is clear from the available evidence that hypothalamic NPY and GAL, along with the amines, NE and 5-HT, have distinct effects on patterns of eating behavior and macronutrient intake, as well as related endocrine processes. Additional pharmacological and biochemical evidence suggests that these effects may reflect a role of these neurotransmitters under physiological conditions. In this process, NPY and GAL appear to operate through somewhat different synaptic mechanisms, in terms of their interaction with the classical neurotransmitters, and the control they exert on carbohydrate and fat intake appears to be influenced by circulating hormones, which themselves affect the metabolism of carbohydrate and fat. Behavioral studies demonstrate natural shifts in the animal's preference for the macronutrients over the course of the active feeding cycle, as well as from meal to meal. Evidence indicates that NPY, GAL, and the amines interact in the hypothalamus, and in particular the PVN, to produce these shifts in macronutrient intake and possibly associated changes in metabolism. This control may involve a single projection system, from neurons containing both peptides as well as NE,[91] or it may involve multiple inputs, such as from adrenergic neurons in the medulla and pons, as well as from non-noradrenergic neurons within the hypothalamus itself.

It has been speculated that peptides represent a phylogenetically older group of chemical messengers, playing a prominent role as hormones, in contrast to the biogenic amines, which evolved more recently to serve the function as neurotransmitters.[92] In support of this hypothesis is the finding that certain neuropeptides occur abundantly in embryonic and neonatal brain regions, but they disappear at a later stage in development. It is possible, therefore, that neuropeptides coexisting with the classical aminergic neurotransmitters may be rudimentary phenomena of limited functional significance.

An alternative suggestion[93] is that neurons involved in fast communication have developed the small synaptic vesicle, to store and release classical transmitters for rapid transfer of information at synapses. With the synaptic transmission process performed by the small-molecule amines, the coexisting peptides may be available to serve as modulators and/or to perform alternative functions such as being involved in long-term, perhaps trophic, events. Thus, the peptides may have a wide range of effects and functions of varying significance, depending upon the system under investigation. The versatility of the chemical message, transmitted by neurons costoring classical neurotransmitters and peptides, is further enhanced by the link that exists between the frequency of stimulation of a neuron and the stoichiometrical proportion of the neurochemicals being released.

Clearly, the existence of multiple transmitters and modulators in the same synapse not only allows for modulation of a main transmission line, but also provides the mechanism for multiple transmission lines and complex patterns of postsynaptic responses. In this context, we may propose that the neuropeptides perform a broader function in control of eating behavior and endocrine processes; this is in contrast to the amines which, with their rapid action, mediate functions of a more refined nature.

REFERENCES

1. LEIBOWITZ, S. F. 1980. *In* Handbook of the Hypothalamus. P. J. Morgane & J. Panksepp, Eds. Vol **3**: 299–437. Marcel Dekker. New York.
2. Leibowitz, S. F. 1986. Fed. Proc. **45**: 1396–1403.
3. HOKFELT, T., V. R. HOLETS, W. STAINES, B. MEISTER, T. MELANDER, M. SCHALLING, M. SCHULTZBERG, J. FREEDMAN, H. BJORKLUND, L. OLSON, B. LINDH, L.-G. ELFVIN, J. M. LUNDBERG, J. A. LINDGREN, B. SAMUELSSON, B. PERNOW, L. TERENIUS, C. POST, B. EVERITT & M. GOLDSTEIN. 1986. Prog. Brain Res. **68**: 33–70.
4. LEIBOWITZ, S. F. 1988. *In* Progress in Catecholamine Research, Part B: Central Aspects. M. Sandler, A. Dahlstrom & R. H. Belmaker, Eds.: 245–250. Alan R. Liss. New York.
5. LEIBOWITZ, S. F. 1988. Neurosci. Biobehav. Rev. **12**: 101–109.
6. LEIBOWITZ, S. F., G. F. WEISS & G. SHOR-POSNER. 1988. Clin. Neuropharmacol. **2(Suppl. 1)**: S51-S71.
7. GOLDMAN, C. K., L. MARINO & S. F. LEIBOWITZ. 1985. Eur. J. Pharmacol. **115**: 11–19.
8. LEIBOWITZ, S. F. 1978. Pharmacol. Biochem. Behav. **8**: 163–175.
9. LEIBOWITZ, S. F. & L. L. BROWN. 1980. Brain Res. **201**: 289–314.
10. SHOR-POSNER, G., A. P. AZAR, S. INSINGA & S. F. LEIBOWITZ 1985. Physiol. Behav. **35**: 883–890.
11. LEIBOWITZ, S. F., G. F. WEISS, F. YEE & J. B. TRETTER. 1985. Brain Res. Bull. **14**: 561–567.
12. Leibowitz, S. F., C. Sladek, L. Spencer & D. TEMPEL. 1988. Brain Res. Bull. **21**: 905–912.
13. TEMPEL, D. L., G. SHOR-POSNER, D. DWYER & S. F. LEIBOWITZ. 1989. Am. J. Physiol. **256**: R541-R548.
14. LEIBOWITZ, S. F. 1989. *In* Serotonin: From Cell Biology to Pharmacology and Therapeutics. R. Paoletti & P. M. Vanhoutte, Eds.: In press. Kluwer Academic Publishers. The Netherlands.
15. SHOR-POSNER, G., J. A. GRINKER, C. MARINESCU, O. BROWN & S. F. LEIBOWITZ. 1986. Brain Res. Bull. **17**: 663–671.
16. WEISS, G. F. & S. F. LEIBOWITZ. 1988. Soc. Neurosci. Abstr. **14**: 613.
17. WEISS, G. F., P. PAPADAKOS, K. KNUDSON & S. F. LEIBOWITZ. 1986. Pharmacol. Biochem. Behav. **25**: 1223–1230.
18. STANLEY, B. G., D. H. SCHWARTZ, L. HERNANDEZ, S. F. LEIBOWITZ & B. G. HOEBEL. 1989. Pharmacol. Biochem. Behav. **33**: 257–260.
19. O'DONOHUE, T. L., B. M. CHRONWALL, R. M. PRUSS, E. MEZEY, J. Z. KISS, L. E. EIDEN, V. J. MASSARI, R. E. TESSEL, V. M. PICKEL, D. A. DIMAGGIO, A. J. HOTCHKISS, W. R. CROWLEY & Z. ZUKOWSKA-GROJEC. 1985. Peptides **6**: 755–768.
20. MELANDER, T., T. HOKFELT, A. ROKAEUS, A. C. CUELLO, W. H. OERTEL, A. VERHOFSTAD & M. GOLDSTEIN. 1986. J. Neurosci. **6**: 3640–3654.
21. McDONALD, J. K. 1988. Crit. Rev. Neurobiol. **4**: 97–135.
22. ROKAEUS, A. 1987. TINS **10**: 158–164.
23. MARTEL, J.-C., S. ST. PIERRE & R. QUIRION. 1986. Peptides **7**: 55–60.
24. STANLEY, B. G., D. R. DANIEL, A. S. CHIN & S. F. LEIBOWITZ. 1985. Peptides **6**: 1205–1211.
25. TEMPEL, D. L., K. J. LEIBOWITZ & S. F. LEIBOWITZ. 1988. Peptides **9**: 309–314.
26. STANLEY, B. G. & S. F. LEIBOWITZ. 1985. Proc. Natl. Acad. Sci. USA **82**: 3940–3943.
27. HUMPHREYS, G. A., J. S. DAVISON & W. L. VEALE. 1988. Brain Res. **456**: 241–248.
28. PERNOW, J. 1988. Acta Physiol. Scand. (Suppl. 568) **133**: 1–56.
29. STJARNE, L., J. M. LUNDBERG & P. ASTRAND. 1986. Neuroscience **18**: 151–166.
30. CLARK, J. T., P. S. KALRA & S. P. KALRA. 1985. Endocrinology **117**: 2435–2441.
31. SHOR-POSNER, G., J. A. GRINKER, C. MARINESCU & S. F. LEIBOWITZ. 1985. Physiol. Behav. **35**: 209–214.
32. STANLEY, B. G. & S. F. LEIBOWITZ. 1984. Life Sci. **35**: 2635–2642.
33. MORLEY, J. E., A. S. LEVINE, B. A. GOSNELL, J KNEIP & M. GRACE. 1987. Am. J. Physiol. **252**: R599-R609.
34. TEMPEL, D., L. NICHOLAS & S. F. LEIBOWITZ. 1988. Proc. Eastern Psychol. Assoc. **59**: 55.
35. KYRKOULI, S. E., B. G. STANLEY & S. F. LEIBOWITZ. 1986. Eur. J. Pharmacol. **122**: 159–160.
36. KRYKOULI, S. E., R. D. SEIRAFI, B. G. STANLEY & S. F. LEIBOWITZ. 1988. Proc. Eastern Psychol. Assoc. **59**: 54.

37. STANLEY, B. G., D. LANTHIER, A. S. CHIN & S. F. LEIBOWITZ. 1989. Brain Res. In press.
38. FUXE, K., L. AGNATI, A. HARFSTRAND, A. M. JANSON, A. NEUMEYER, K. ANDERSSON, M. RUGGERI & M. GOLDSTEIN. 1986. Prog. Brain Res. 68: 303–320.
39. LUNDBERG, J. M. & T. HOKFELT. 1986. Prog. Brain Res. 68: 241–262.
40. KALRA, S. P., J. T. CLARK, A. SAHU, M. G. DUBE & P. S. KALRA. 1988. Synapse 2: 254–257.
41. KYRKOULI, S. E., B. G. STANLEY, R. HUTCHINSON & S. F. LEIBOWITZ. 1987. Proc. Eastern Psychol. Assoc. 58: 17.
42. LEVINE, A. J & J. E. MORLEY. 1984. Peptides 5: 1025–1030.
43. HUCHINSON, R., S. E. KYRKOULI, B. G. STANLEY & S. F. LEIBOWITZ. 1987. Proc. Eastern Psychol. Assoc. 58: 13.
44. LEIBOWITZ, S. F., A. ARCOMANO & N. J. HAMMER. 1978. Prog. Neuropsychopharmacol 2: 349–358.
45. STANLEY, B. G., A. S. CHIN & S. F. LEIBOWITZ. 1985. Brain Res. Bull. 14: 521–524.
46. KYRKOULI, S. E., R. D. SEIRAFI, B. G. STANLEY & S. F. LEIBOWITZ. 1989. Proc. Eastern Psychol. Assoc. 60: 24.
47. SAHU, A., P. S. KALRA & S. P. KALRA. 1988. Peptides 9: 83–86.
48. BATTISTINI, N., L. GIARDINO, V. MONTANINI, M. TIENGO & L. CALZA. 1987. Neuroscience 22(Suppl.): S140.
49. LEVIN, M. C., P. E. SAWCHENKO, P. R. C. HOWE, S. R. BLOOM & J. M. POLAK. 1987. J. Comp. Neurol. 261: 562–582.
50. MELANDER, T. T. HOKFELT & A. ROKAEUS. 1986. J. Comp. Neurol. 248: 475–517.
51. SKOFITSCH, G. & D. M. JACOBOWITZ. 1985. Peptides 6: 509–546.
52. MELANDER, T., K. FUXE, A. HARFSTRAND, P. ENEROTH & T. HOKFELT. 1987. Acta Physiol. Scand. 131: 25–32.
53. GRAY, T. S. & D. J. MAGNUSON. 1987. Neurosci. Lett. 83: 264–268.
54. WEISS, G. F. & S. F. LEIBOWITZ. 1985. Brain Res. 347: 225–238.
55. WESTFALL, T. C., J. MARTIN, X. CHEN, A. CIARLEGLIO, S. CARPENTIER, K. HENDERSON, M. KNUEPFER, M. BEINFELD & L. NAES. 1988. Synapse 2: 299–307.
56. HARFSTRAND, A., K. FUXE, L. AGNATI, P. ENEROTH, I. ZINI, M. ZOLI, K. ANDERSSON, G. VON EULER, L. TERENIUS, V. MUTT & M. GOLDSTEIN. 1986. Neurochem. Int. 8: 355–376.
57. VALLEJO, M., D. A. CARTER, S. BISWAS & S. L. LIGHTMAN. 1987. Neurosci. Lett. 73: 155–160.
58. KYRKOULI, S. E., B. G. STANLEY & S. F. LEIBOWITZ. 1988. Soc. Neurosci. Abstr. 14: 614.
59. OHHASHI, T. & D. M. JACOBOWITZ. 1985. Reg. Peptides 12: 163–171.
60. NORDSTROM, O., T. MELANDER, T. HOKFELT, T. BARTFAI & M. GOLDSTEIN. 1987. Neurosci. Lett. 73: 21–26.
61. FUXE, K., S.-O. OGREN, A. JANSSON, A. CINTRA, A. HARFSTRAND & L. F. AGNATI. 1988. Acta Physiol. Scand. 133: 579–581.
62. SUNDSTROM, E. & T. MELANDER. 1988. Eur. J. Pharmacol. 146: 327–329.
63. FUXE, K., G. VON EULER, L. F. AGNATI & S.-O. OGREN. 1988. Neurosci. Lett. 85: 153–167.
64. SHOR-POSNER, G., C. IAN, C. GUERRA & S. F. LEIBOWITZ. 1987. Soc. Neurosci. Abstr. 13: 464.
65. JHANWAR-UNIYAL, M., C. R. ROLAND & S. F. LEIBOWITZ. 1986. Life. Sci. 38: 473–482.
66. JHANWAR-UNIYAL, M., M. DARISH, B. E. LEVIN & S. F. LEIBOWITZ. 1987. Pharmacol. Biochem. Behav. 26: 271–275.
67. JHANWAR-UNIYAL, M. & S. F. LEIBOWITZ. 1986. Brain Res. Bull. 17: 889–896.
68. STANLEY, B. G., K. C. ANDERSON, M. H. GRAYSON & S. F. LEIBOWITZ. 1989. Physiol. Behav. 46: In press..
69. MARTIRE, M., K. FUXE, G. PISTRITTO, P. PREZIOSI & L. F. AGNATI. 1986. J. Neural. Transm. 67: 113–124.
70. GOLDSTEIN, M., N. KUSANO, C. ADLER & E. MELLER. 1986. Prog. Brain Res. 68: 331–335.
71. SCHOUPS, A. A., V. K. SAXENA, K. TOMBEUR & W. P. DE POTTER. 1988. Life Sci. 42: 517–523.
72. BLESSING, W. W., P. R. C. HOWE, T. H. JOH, J. R. OLIVER & J. O. WILLOUGHBY. 1986. J. Comp. Neurol. 248: 285–300.
73. SAWCHENKO, P. E., L. W. SWANSON, H. W. M. STEINBUSCH & A. A. J. VERHOFSTED. 1983. Brain Res. 277: 355–360.
74. BENDOTTI, C., S. GARATTINI & R. SAMANIN. 1987. J. Pharm. Pharmacol. 39: 900–903.
75. KANAREK, R. B., L. HO & R. G. MEADE. 1981. Pharmacol. Biochem. Behav. 14: 539–542.
76. LEIBOWITZ, S. F., G. SHOR-POSNER, C. MACLOW & J. A. GRINKER. 1986. Brain Res. Bull. 17: 681–689.

77. STANLEY, B. G., S. E. KYRKOULI, S. LAMPERT & S. F. LEIBOWITZ. 1986. Peptides **7**: 1189–1192.
78. BRIEF, D. J., A. J. SIPOLS & S. C. WOODS. 1989. Physiol. Behav. In press.
79. BERRETTINI, W. H., W. H. KAYE, H. GWIRTSMAN & A. ALBRIGHT. 1988. Neuropsycholobiology **19**: 121–124.
80. SUTTON, S. W., N. MITSÚGI, P. M. PLOTSKY & D. K. SARKAR. 1988. Endocrinology **123**: 2152–2154.
81. SHOR-POSNER, G., G. BRENNAN, R. JASAITIS, C. IAN, B. LEIBOWITZ & S. F. LEIBOWITZ. 1989. Ann. N. Y. Acad. Sci. This volume.
82. KALRA, S. P. & W. R. CROWLEY. 1984. Life Sci. **35**: 1173–1176.
83. SILVERMAN, J. A. 1983. Int. J. Eating Disorders **2**: 159–166.
84. ROWLAND, N. E. 1988. Peptides **9**: 989–992.
85. CHAN-PALAY, V. 1988. Neurosci. Abstr. **14**: 1222.
86. MORLEY, J. E. & A. J. SILVER. 1988. Neurobiol. Aging **9**: 9–16.
87. BERRETTINI, W. H., W. H. KAYE, T. SUNDERLAND, C. MAY, H. E. GWIRTSMAN, A. MELLOW & A. ALBRIGHT. 1988. Neuropsychobiology **19**: 64–68.
88. KAPLAN, L. M., S. M. GABRIEL, J. I. KOENIG, M. E. SUNDAY, E. R. SPINDEL, J. B. MARTIN & W. W. CHIN. 1988. Proc. Natl. Acad. Sci. **85**: 7408–7412.
89. OTTLECZ, A., W. K. SAMSON & S. M. MCCANN. 1986. Peptides **7**: 51–53.
90. VACCARINO, F. J., F. E. BLOOM, J. RIVIER, W. VALE, & G. F. KOOB. 1985. Nature **314**: 167–168.
91. HOLETS, V. R., T. HOKFELT & A. ROKAEUS. 1988. Neuroscience **24**: 893–906.
92. CARLSSON, A. 1987. Ann. Rev. Neurosci. **10**: 19–40.
93. HOKFELT, T., B. MEISTER, T. MELANDER & B. EVERITT. 1987. *In* Hypothalamic Dysfunction in Neuropsychiatric Disorders. D. Nerozzi, F. K. Goodwin & E. Costa, Eds.: 21–34. Raven Press. New York.

DISCUSSION

DR. ALLEN S. LEVINE (*VA Medical Center, Minneapolis, MN*): Because we know that carbohydrate preference could be related to taste, I was wondering about your source of carbohydrate. Was it sweet, or was it a polysaccharide? Also, were you expressing your carbohydrate, fat, and protein as percent of total weight or as percent of total calories?

DR. SARAH F. LEIBOWITZ (*The Rockefeller University, New York*): The source is a mixture of sucrose, corn starch and dextrose. As to whether it's sweet versus nonsweet, we find that neuropeptide Y as well as norepinephrine do not seem to be stimulating a sweet preference because they stimulate intake of a nonsweet carbohydrate and they do not affect consumption of saccharine. We feel that it is not a taste phenomenon, but that's always a question that we're going to have to address. When we talk about the percent of the diet, we calculate the percent of total kilocalories.

DR. PAUL F. ARAVICH (*VA Medical Center, Hampton, VA*): I wonder if you could clarify your point on vasopressin with respect to food intake. As you know, vasopressin abnormalities have been reported in anorectics, although I think those data are very difficult to interpret. Also, we've published the hypothesis that vasopressin may play a very specific role in bulimia nervosa and that's based on data related to evidence in the rat suggesting a role of vasopressin in stress-induced feeding, and a role of vasopressin in carbohydrate appetite. That was published 1986, in Brain Research.

DR. LEIBOWITZ: I'm well aware of your paper, and I think it's a definitive study. We are looking at vasopressin, and I do believe it has a very important role in feeding. I believe it's a stimulatory role, so our work is developing along those lines and is very consistent with your ideas.

DR. RICHARD J. WURTMAN (*Massachusetts Institute of Technology, Cambridge, MA*): I want to congratulate Dr. Leibowitz again on an elegant paper. I think your perception of the complexity of feeding, your early decision to look around the clock, sets an example for all of us.

In terms of the effects of estrogen and progesterone, etcetera, on feeding, I think we can learn something from talking to clinicians, gynecologic endocrinologists, who see a lot of women who complain about having severe carbohydrate craving during the few days of the month when they stop the pill, as opposed to another set who have severe carbohydrate craving when they start the pill. My impression is that both complaints are real and are probably related to the fact that the results of early studies by Bank, Meyerson, and others on the effects of steroid hormones on serotonin neurons were also very complex. One could demonstrate excitatory and inhibitory effects of progesterone based simply on how much estrogen was around. I think that one consequence of your studies is that perhaps now neuroscientists will go back and better characterize the effects of estrogen and progesterone on serotonergic function.

DR. LEIBOWITZ: We have a lot to discuss in terms of the effects of the steroids. One question is whether the pattern at puberty is different from an established pattern in an adult animal.

DR. DAVID BOOTH (*University of Binghamton, Binghamton, England*): Sarah, you're very carefully talking about stimulation of carbohydrate intake, fat intake, so forth. Not talking about carbohydrate appetites, cravings, or whatever.

DR. LEIBOWITZ: You've taught me to do that.

DR. BOOTH: As you know, with norepinephrine-induced feeding, the only effect we can find on intake is a blockade of the carbohydrate-conditioned satiety. There's no evidence, as yet anyway, that the carbohydrate-conditioned satiety is carbohydrate need related. I was very interested by this division amongst the types of rats to notice that the high carbohydrate eaters were small meal eaters and the fat-eating ones ate large and infrequent meals. I wonder if what you got here is not nutrient-specific behavior but something to do with the physiological effects of these different nutrients, the starch being liable to produce an aversive effect and limit the size of the meals, and the fat producing a long-delayed satiety effect in spacing out the meals.

DR. LEIBOWITZ: I don't think we have any sense of aversion in the carbohydrate case. In terms of fat, we don't feel that fat necessarily produces a long intermeal interval. May I just reflect, perhaps, off that topic to say that we find, consistent with John Blundell's work and others, that the intermeal interval after protein intake is long. That is, we get a long intermeal interval after the protein meal in the beginning of a dark cycle, but we don't regularly get long intermeal intervals after a carbohydrate meal or a fat meal.

DR. SILVIO GARATTINI (*Istituto di Richerche Farmacologic "Mario Negri" Milan, Italy*): Have you any data on the effect of α_2 inhibitors injected directly into the PVN? My second question is, Since galanin is associated with release of acetylcholine, at least in certain parts of the hippocampus, is there any role for acetylcholine in the PVN?

DR. LEIBOWITZ: Cholinergic action, perhaps there, yes. Now your first question: The α_2-receptor antagonists injected into the paraventricular nucleus suppressed feeding at doses that were phenomenally low. We're very encouraged by that. They suppressed carbohydrate intake.

In terms of a cholinergic mechanism, indeed that's been illusive and I really have no speculation.

DR. GARATTINI: *In vivo* you don't see much effect with the α_2 inhibitors when they are injected systemically.

DR. LEIBOWITZ: I have not done it systemically.

Dr. GARATTINI: We have done it, and systemically there is no effect.

Dr. LEIBOWITZ: Which antagonist did you use?

Dr. GARATTINI: Dexacen.

Dr. LEIBOWITZ: Okay. We get a very strong effect when the antagonist is injected locally.

The Regulation of Food Intake by Peptides[a]

STEPHEN C. WOODS[b]

Department of Psychology
University of Washington
Seattle, Washington 98195

JAMES GIBBS

Department of Psychiatry
Cornell University Medical College
New York Hospital-Cornell Medical Center
White Plains, New York 10605

For much of this century, scientists investigating the physiological mechanisms regulating food intake concentrated their efforts upon potential metabolic signals. The rationale for this approach is clear and compelling. Eating is an essential behavior that provides all of the energy needs of the body. Its control should, therefore, at least in part, be under the influence of the energy-using machinery of the body. Hence, major hypotheses concerning the control of food intake focused on the utilization of carbohydrates; on the mass, mobilization, and/or use of adipose stores; and various parameters related to protein and amino acid metabolism as potential signals which could initiate or stop meals. Among the best known examples of this conceptual approach are Mayer's glucostatic hypothesis[1] and Kennedy's lipostatic theory.[2] All such hypotheses critically linked the control of ingestive behavior with changes of cellular energy metabolism in one or more target organs.

A conceptually different approach to the physiological control of food intake began to emerge around fifteen years ago. It coincided with the availability of relatively pure peptide hormones for experimentation, followed by the advent of new techniques for measuring these substances and their receptors in various tissues. Briefly stated, this approach ties the control of feeding and adiposity to intercellular messengers (mainly peptides, which presumably interact with receptors on the surface of specialized target cells) rather than to changes of metabolic activity within cells. This newer approach is the subject of this brief review. It should be stated at the outset that we do not wish to suggest that the two strategies — metabolic and peptidergic — are mutually exclusive, nor to imply that there are not ardent adherents to the more metabolically oriented position.

[a] Preparation of this review was supported by National Institutes of Health Grants DK 17844 (to SCW) and DK 33248 (to JG).

[b] Address for correspondence: Dr. Stephen C. Woods, Department of Psychology, NI-25, University of Washington, Seattle, WA 98195.

236

PEPTIDE SIGNALS FOR THE CONTROL OF MEAL SIZE

In 1973, Gibbs, Young, and Smith reported that the exogenous administration of either partially purified cholecystokinin (CCK) or synthetic CCK to hungry rats caused them to eat smaller meals.[3] This paper, based in part upon earlier work of Davis[4] which had demonstrated the existence of a circulating satiety factor in the blood of rats that had just eaten, was the first demonstration that a peptide could produce chemically and behaviorally specific reductions of meal size, and it initiated a research effort into the area of peptides and feeding. This area has expanded rapidly over the intervening 16 years; there are several current reviews of this now quite large literature (e.g., Gibbs[5] and Morley et al.[6]).

The hypothesis is simple. As a meal is consumed, the ingested food interacts with an extensive array of receptors along the gastrointestinal tract. These critical events enable the gut to adjust the entire digestive process to the particular meal being eaten, and the mediators of the control process are peptides, acting either as hormones or as local intercellular messengers. Each meal presumably results in an appropriate blend of these peptide hormones being released into the blood from cells lining the gut and sampling the ingested meal. The peptides in turn control not only the motility and secretions of the various segments of the gut, but more distant digestive organs such as the exocrine pancreas and liver as well.

The hypothesis is that some of these same peptides also provide information to the brain, such that the meal can be terminated when sufficient food is consumed. The peptides might circulate to interact directly with the brain, or they could trigger activity initially at peripheral sites, with the satiety messages then being relayed to the brain. Alternatively, or in addition, peptides might act initially within the gut, in a paracrine or neurocrine fashion, rather than via the circulation. Evidence consistent with each of these possibilities exists for particular peptides.

Although the vast majority of published experiments have focussed on one or another individual peptide, it is generally believed that when a meal is being eaten, a number of different peptides are secreted into the blood, are released locally in the gastrointestinal tract, or are released from nerve endings containing the peptide; as these accumulate in the blood or critical receptor areas, sufficient signals are generated to terminate the meal. TABLE 1 lists several of the peptides that reduce meal size. It is noteworthy that most of these have been localized within the brain as well as in the gut.

Physiological Relevance of Satiety Peptides

As the list of peptides that are capable of reducing meal size after exogenous administration lengthens, it becomes increasingly clear that criteria will have to be devised to determine which endogenous peptides play a normal, or physiological, role in the day-to-day control of meal size, and which peptides are capable of reducing food intake when administered at some dose, but do not ordinarily function as satiety signals at meals. The recent and increasing availability of potent and selective antagonists of the different peptides should provide crucial help in this regard. For example, it has recently been shown that administration of a highly potent and highly selective CCK antagonist *increases* feeding in rats[7,8]—the effect that would be predicted if endogenous CCK plays a significant role in the normal limitation of food intake.

If circulating, rather than local, levels of a peptide are the critical feedback signal, it should be the case that the blood levels required to produce the satiety effect after

TABLE 1. Peptides Reported to Decrease Food Intake

Bombesin
Calcitonin
Calcitonin Gene-Related Peptide
Cholecystokinin
Corticotropin Releasing Factor
Glucagon
Neurotensin
Somatostatin
Thyrotropin Releasing Hormone

exogenous administration should be comparable to the levels that occur naturally after a meal. For CCK, there are conflicting data on this point. In one recent experiment on baboons, the amount of CCK-like activity in the blood following a normal meal was found to be essentially the same as seen when exogenous CCK is given to reduce gastric emptying and/or meal size.[9] This suggests that the levels of CCK achieved in the blood following its exogenous administration are in fact within the physiological range.

Satiety Peptides and Eating Disorders

Another consideration is the possibility that the chronic or continued administration of satiety agents might alter adiposity. It does not necessarily follow that a compound that reduces the size of individual meals should lead to weight loss. There is a somewhat confused literature in this area, based largely upon different techniques for the chronic administration of one or another compound. In some experiments, for example, CCK was given as a continuous slow infusion for several days. However, physiological secretion of CCK is thought to be mainly episodic, in response to meals, rather than continuous. In a more convincing test, West et al.[10] interfaced free-feeding rats with a computer-controlled system that would automatically administer CCK whenever a spontaneous meal was initiated. Under these conditions, CCK significantly reduced the size of every meal over a six-day interval, but the rats compensated by eating more meals such that body weight remained relatively stable.[10] It therefore appears as if CCK remains efficacious over long intervals for reducing meal size, but that, used alone, it might not be an effective weight-reducing agent.

The demonstration that the administration of exogenous peptide hormones alters meal size has obvious significance as a potential therapeutic tool in eating disorders and obesity. Such an extrapolation requires that several other conditions be met. For one thing, a factor that reduces meal size could work nonspecifically (for example, by making animals sick) rather than through the normal mechanisms regulating meal-size. Although this possibility has been largely discarded for many putative satiety hormones, the important controls have not been done for many others. A second obvious presumption is that what has been demonstrated in experimental animals should exist in humans. It has been reported that both CCK[11] and bombesin,[12] two of the best documented satiety hormones, effectively reduce meal size in humans at doses that do not appear to produce signs of malaise. However, it should be noted that the effects in humans, while statistically reliable, are not as robust as has been observed in animals and often require complex experimental designs and analyses. This may reflect in part an inability to control as many factors in human as in animal experiments.

Whether pathological alterations in CCK may underlie eating disorders is also a question under active investigation. Recently, Geracioti and Liddle found abnormally low circulating levels of endogenous CCK in response to a standardized test meal in patients with bulimia nervosa; following successful treatment of the bulimia, CCK responses to the same test meal returned toward normal.[13] Although the relationship of the abnormality in CCK to the illness is unclear from these results, they strongly encourage further work to determine whether the relationship may be a causal one.

In summary, considerable support has accumulated for the hypothesis that peptide signals secreted as a meal is being consumed act to limit the size of that meal. The potential use of such agents for the treatment of obesity has not been established; there is evidence suggesting that, even if they prove useful, they will not be sufficient. Finally, recent evidence suggests that altered satiety hormone levels may be implicated in the pathogenesis of bulimia.

Orexigenic Peptides

Whereas most peptides studied to date have a satiety effect (i.e., they reduce the size of individual meals), some actually increase meal size. This is true of the opioid peptides and peptides of the pancreatic polypeptide family.[6] The latter includes neuropeptide Y (NPY) and peptide YY (PYY) as well as pancreatic polypeptide (PP). All of these compounds that increase meal size must be administered centrally (directly into the central nervous system), whereas many meal-size-reducing peptides are efficacious when given peripherally. It might therefore be that the appetite-stimulating compounds work in a fundamentally different manner from the appetite-suppressing compounds, rather than the two categories of peptides merely adding together at a final common site. It also suggests that multiple controllers over meals have diverse points of entry into the calculus of the control system.

PEPTIDE SIGNALS OF ADIPOSITY

Evidence exists for an additional group of signals that influence food intake but that are postulated to be proportional to the size of the adipose mass. It is generally agreed that robust mechanisms exist to maintain adiposity at some constant level (presumably highly genetically influenced). This concept has been reviewed adequately elsewhere[14] and is based upon the following observations:

(1) In the free-feeding condition, adult persons and animals tend to maintain a relatively constant body weight (and size of adipose mass) over time, and they resist externally induced attempts to change their weight.

(2) While body weight can be changed via forced food restriction or forced feeding, once the period of forced intake is over, weight tends to revert to its pre-perturbation level, and the predominant mechanism of this return is altered food intake. Thus, individuals who have dieted and lost weight tend to eat more food and regain their lost weight over time; and individual humans or animals who gain weight via forced consumption of excess food eat less and lose the weight when the experiment is finished.

(3) Direct changes in the size of the adipose mass result in changes of food intake and restoration of adiposity stores. For example, following lipectomy, animals given an adequate diet eat more food and replace precisely the amount of fat lost.[15]

There is evidence that this robust defense and maintenance of a particular adipose mass is mediated via circulating signals. One demonstration of this derives from experiments on parabiotic animals. These animals are joined at the skin such that some vascular, but no neural, connections develop between the two. Such animals typically maintain their individual, pre-surgical weights. However, if an obese animal is parabiotically connected to a lean one, appetite is altered. The obese animal often eats slightly more food, but the dramatic effect occurs with the lean partner. The lean member eats very little food and may die of starvation unless the experiment is discontinued. These findings are generally interpreted to indicate that a signal related to the size of the adipose mass crosses between the two animals, such that the lean animal now perceives itself to be fatter than it is, and it responds by eating less and losing weight.

A circulating adiposity signal could be a nutrient (or metabolite) or a hormone. Woods and Porte and their colleagues have focused their research efforts in the last fifteen years upon the possibility that the pancreatic hormone, insulin, is one such signal. This belief developed from work showing a direct correlation between adiposity and plasma insulin levels,[16] and from other work demonstrating a reciprocally interactive association between insulin and the central nervous system.[17]

The hypothesis is that insulin provides information to the brain concerning the degree of adiposity in the body. Because insulin secretion is known to increase with increasing body adiposity, the fatter an individual is, the higher the plasma insulin levels and the greater the magnitude of the signal that reaches the brain. Conversely, when an individual diets and loses weight, insulin secretion is suppressed, and a smaller signal would reach the brain. The effect of the change of insulin on the brain appears to result from an interaction with the multitude of other factors that influence food intake, including satiety factors determining single meal size, nutrient and energy me-

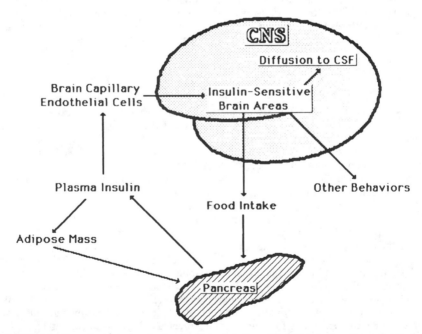

FIGURE 1. Hypothetical organization for the regulation of food intake by adipose tissue mass, with insulin as the mediating peptide signal.

tabolism, and hedonic factors. The net result is that if a person is overweight relative to the level at which weight is regulated, he or she will tend to eat smaller meals until the two are better aligned. On the other hand, the dieter will experience a reduction of the brain insulin signal once weight loss has occurred, and thus have an additional factor tending to increase the size of each meal until weight is restored to its regulated level. The hypothesized feedback mechanism is depicted in FIGURE 1.

Insulin in the Brain

One obvious assumption of this hypothesis is that insulin in the blood be able to gain access to the brain. Several groups initially found insulin within the cerebrospinal fluid (CSF) of dogs, and that as plasma insulin increased, insulin levels in the CSF did also.[18] More recently, insulin has been found within the CSF of a number of species, including humans,[19] and in every species tested, changes of plasma insulin are reflected in changes of CSF insulin. However, in every instance, the levels within the CSF are considerably lower than those in the plasma, and there is always a lag between peak changes in the plasma and in the CSF.

Insulin has also been localized within the brain itself. When segments of brain are individually analyzed, a highly reliable regional localization of insulin can be demonstrated. Of interest is that areas of the brain known to be important in the control of food intake and body weight have somewhat higher levels of insulin. These areas include specific hypothalamic nuclei and the olfactory bulbs (see Woods et al.[14]).

Insulin Receptors in the Brain

Specific insulin binding sites have also been found in regionally localized brain areas. Binding sites tend to exist in the same areas as insulin itself, suggesting that much of the insulin that can be detected within the brain may actually be bound to receptors and/or internalized into the intracellular compartment of brain tissue. This is consistent with a lack of identified insulin secretory granules or proinsulin, or insulin messenger RNA, in brain tissue, and with the location of insulin on the outer cell surface by electron microscopy (see review, Baskin et al.[20]).

Therefore, two fundamental assumptions of the hypothesis have been met. Insulin can gain access to the brain from the plasma, and the brain contains specific insulin binding sites in areas important in the control of food intake and body weight.

Influence of Insulin upon Food Intake

If insulin in fact provides a signal related to adiposity to the brain, changes of insulin locally within the brain should result in changes of food intake; and if these changes persist, they should result in changes of body weight. An increase of insulin in the brain should be interpreted by the brain as an increase of adiposity and cause the individual to reduce food intake. The opposite should be the case if brain insulin concentrations were suddenly suppressed, as in starvation of insulin-deficient diabetes mellitus.

In a test of the hypothesis, baboons were given infusions of small amounts of insulin directly into their CSF for two- to three-week intervals. As the dose of insulin was increased to 10 or 100 μU/kg/day, the animals ate significantly less food and lost weight.[21] This occurred in the absence of an increase of plasma insulin, and the infusion of the same amount of glucagon had no effect, suggesting that the effect is specific to insulin. The same basic phenomenon has since been found in rats.[22] Therefore, when a small amount of insulin is infused chronically into the CSF, animals eat less food per day and either fail to gain or actually lose weight. The converse phenomenon, that of lowering brain insulin, has not been as easy to accomplish. Strubbe and Mein[23] administered insulin antibodies directly into hypothalamic tissue and observed an increase of the size of the subsequent meal. They did not continue the experiment chronically.

Therefore, there is compelling evidence that insulin provides an adiposity-related signal to the brain. The fatty Zucker rat is an animal with reduced insulin receptors at capillaries where insulin enters the brain, as well as within the brain itself (see Baskin et al.[20]). Predictably, these rats do not reduce food intake nor body weight when insulin is infused into their CSF whereas their lean controls do.[24] Future research should concentrate on the factors that control the rate of insulin uptake or transport into brain.

Interaction of Insulin with Single-Meal Satiety Factors

In both baboons and rats (see review in Woods et al.[14]), the addition of a very small amount of insulin into the CSF caused no change of food intake in and of itself. However, when these animals were given peripheral CCK, they were more sensitive to its satiating properties in the presence of the insulin. This suggests that insulin might work by changing the gain to other, meal-generated signals, thus incorporating the degree of adiposity into other influences determining how much food is eaten during a meal. When an animal is underweight, a reduction of brain insulin will diminish the perception of or response to meal-generated satiety signals, and the animals will tend to eat larger meals; when an animal is overweight, a greater signal will reach the brain and average meal size will be reduced. Such a model also accounts for the well-known hyperphagia of insulin-deficient diabetes mellitus. These individuals have considerably increased food intake in spite of hyperglycemia. They also would be expected to have reduced plasma insulin or insulin activity and presumably reduced brain insulin as well.

SUMMARY

Historically, nutrients and related metabolic signals were considered to control the onset and offset of meals. Recent research has focused upon the roles of peptides found in the gastrointestinal tract and brain as alternate controllers of these processes. During a meal, the gut secretes a variety of peptides as part of the digestive process. Some of these substances, acting as hormonal or as local signals, may also provide information which is relayed to the central nervous system, causing eating to stop and producing the sense of satiety. When administered to animals or people before a meal, exogenous cholecystokinin (CCK), the most studied of the putative satiety peptides, reduces food intake in a dose-dependent manner. Recent findings support the concept that endogenous CCK acts during meals to limit meal size, and evidence is reviewed suggesting a possible pathophysiological role for CCK in bulimia. Adiposity is also regulated via peptide hormones, especially insulin. Insulin is secreted in direct proportion to adiposity, and blood-borne insulin gains access to brain areas important in the regulation of feeding. The administration of insulin into the brain causes reduced eating and weight loss.

REFERENCES

1. MAYER, J. 1955. Ann. N.Y. Acad. Sci. **63:** 15–43.
2. KENNEDY, G. C. 1953. Proc. Roy. Soc. Lond. (Biol.) **140:** 579–592.
3. GIBBS, J., R. C. YOUNG & G. P. SMITH. 1973. J. Comp. Physiol. Psychol. **84:** 488–495.
4. DAVIS, J. D., R. J. GALLAGHER, R. F. LADOVE & A. J. TURANSKY. 1969. J. Comp. Physiol. Psychol. **67:** 407–417.
5. GIBBS, J. 1988. *In* The Eating Disorders. B. J. Blinder, B. F. Chaitin & R. Goldstein, Eds.: 57–62. PMA Publishing Corp. New York.
6. MORLEY, J. E., T. J. BARTNESS, B. A. GOSNELL & A. S. LEVINE. 1985. Intl. Rev. Neurobiol. **27:** 207–298.
7. REIDELBERGER, R. D., M. F. O'ROURKE & T. E. SOLOMON. 1988. Soc. Neurosci. Abstr. **14:** 1196.
8. WATSON, C. A., L. H. SCHNEIDER, E. S. CORP, S. C. WEATHERFORD, R. SHINDLEDECKER, R. B. MURPHY, G. P. SMITH & J. GIBBS. 1988. Soc. Neurosci. Abstr. **14:** 1196.
9. FIGLEWICZ, D. P., A. J. SIPOLS, D. PORTE, JR., S. C. WOODS & R. A. LIDDLE. 1989. Am. J. Physiol. **256:** R1313–R1317.
10. WEST, D. B., D. FEY & S. C. WOODS. 1984. Am. J. Physiol. **246:** R776–R787.
11. KISSILEFF, H. R., F. X. PI-SUNYER, J. THORNTON & G. P. SMITH. 1981. Am. J. Clin. Nutr. **34:** 154–160.
12. MUURAHAINEN, N. E., H. R. KISSILEFF, J. THORNTON & F. X. PI-SUNYER. 1983. Soc. Neurosci. Abstr. **9:** 183.
13. GERACIOTI, T. D., JR. & R. A. LIDDLE. 1988. N. Engl. J. Med. **319:** 683–688.
14. WOODS, S. C., D. PORTE, JR., J. H. STRUBBE & A. B. STEFFENS. 1986. *In* Feeding Behavior: Neural and Humoral Controls. R. C. Ritter, S. Ritter & C. D. Barnes, Eds.: 315–327. Academic Press. New York.
15. FAUST, I. M., P. R. JOHNSON & J. HIRSCH. 1977. Science **197:** 391–393.
16. WOODS, S. C., E. DECKE & J. R. VASSELLI. 1974. Psychol. Rev. **81:** 26–43.
17. WOODS, S. C. & D. PORTE, JR. 1974. Physiol. Rev. **54:** 596–619.
18. WOODS, S. C. & D. PORTE, JR. 1977. Am. J. Physiol. **233:** E331–E334.
19. WALLUM, B. J., G. J. TABORSKY, D. PORTE, JR., D. P. FIGLEWICZ, L. JACOBSEN, J. C. BEARD, W. K. WARD & D. M. DORSA. 1986. J. Clin. Endocrinol. Metab. **64:** 190–193.
20. BASKIN, D. G., D. P. FIGLEWICZ, S. C. WOODS, D. PORTE, JR. & D. M. DORSA. 1987. Ann. Rev. Physiol. **49:** 335–347.
21. WOODS, S. C., E. C. LOTTER, L. D. McKAY & D. PORTE, JR. 1979. Nature **282:** 503–505.
22. BRIEF, D. J. & J. D. DAVIS. 1984. Brain Res. Bull. **12:** 571–575.
23. STRUBBE, J. H. & C. G. MEIN. 1977. Physiol. Behav. **19:** 309–313.
24. IKEDA, H., D. B. WEST, J. J. PUSTEK, D. P. FIGLEWICZ, M. R. C. GREENWOOD, D. PORTE, JR. & S. C. WOODS. 1986. Appetite **7:** 381–386.

Summary: Part III

JAMES GIBBS

Department of Psychiatry
Cornell University Medical College
E. W. Bourne Behavioral Research Laboratory
White Plains, New York 10605

Several years ago, Professor Gerald Russell, who spoke yesterday about the history and diagnosis of anorexia nervosa and of bulimia nervosa, pointed out that one reason we are unable to identify biological abnormalities in these disorders may be that we know so little about how *normal* food intake is regulated. Thus, there is little physiological ground on which to base a pathophysiological understanding of the illness. Our session today has outlined some of the most promising work that is trying to expand this physiological ground. There are two themes I would like to emphasize.

The first theme is the apparent complexity of relationships among the many factors involved in determining when eating begins or ends. This is the same point Professor Blundell referred to as the required integration among the various "fluxes" or levels of organization controlling feeding behavior, and which Dr. Leibowitz touched on in referring to how an amine (norepinephrine) and a peptide (NPY) might relate in the initiation of a meal. Stallone, Nicolaïdis, and I have recently published findings[2] indicating a similar relationship between an amine (in this case, serotonin) and a peptide (cholecystokinin) in the regulation of the termination of a meal. We were able to show that the inhibitory action of peripherally administered cholecystokinin on food intake could be substantially attenuated by the prior administration of metergoline, an antagonist that blocks the action of serotonin at several different subtypes of receptors. Thus, the results indicate that the satiety action of cholecystokinin depends upon intact functioning of the serotonin system. Further studies, now in progress, should tell us the anatomical site(s) and the identity of the serotonin receptor subtype(s) involved in this interaction between two systems thought to be involved in satiety — one aminergic, the other peptidergic.

The second point that I would like to draw your attention to in the presentations today has perhaps been more of an undercurrent than a theme. It is the crucial and difficult issue of how we are going to find out what all of these effects have to do with *normal* food intake. It is quite clear that investigators have identified a variety of factors — opioids, NPY, other peptides, monoamines, indoleamines — which can influence food intake when they are administered centrally or peripherally. But which of these substances plays a necessary role? Professor Garattini has drawn our attention to a powerful class of tools to answer this question: the growing number of potent and specific antagonists for the various putative physiological agents. In our own work, we have recently taken advantage of the availability of such an antagonist for cholecystokinin. Following the design of the elegant initial work of Dr. Roger Reidelberger,[3] Dr. Linda Schneider in our laboratory has recently shown that the specific cholecystokinin antagonist L-364,718 produces a significant *increase* in food intake when it is administered before food availability, both acutely and chronically.[4] These findings constitute strong evidence that endogenous cholecystokinin plays a physiological role in the normal inhibition of feeding behavior. Again, further work should clarify the anatomical site and the cholecystokinin receptor subtype that must be blocked to produce this effect.

This is but one of several recent examples one could choose. Given the careful use of antagonists, which can be shown to be both specific and potent, investigators should be in a position to decide which of the naturally occurring substances they have tested are normally involved in controlling feeding behavior. Then, we will surely be in a better position to identify and effectively treat the pathological mechanisms underlying eating disorders.

REFERENCES

1. RUSSELL, G. F. M. 1968. *In* Studies in Psychiatry. M. Shepherd & D. L. Davies, Eds.: 240. Oxford University Press. London.
2. STALLONE, D., S. NICOLAÏDIS & J. GIBBS. 1989. Cholecystokinin-induced anorexia depends on serotoninergic function. Am. J. Physiol. **256:** R1138-R1141.
3. REIDELBERGER R. D. & M. R. O'ROURKE. 1987. Comparative effects of the CCK receptor antagonist L-364,718 on food intake and pancreatic secretion in rats. Symposium on Appetite, Thirst, and Related Disorders. San Antonio, TX.
4. WATSON, C. A., L. H. SCHNEIDER, E. S. CORP, S. C. WEATHERFORD, R. SHINDLEDECKER, R. B. MURPHY, G. P. SMITH & J. GIBBS. 1988. The effects of chronic and acute treatment with the potent peripheral cholecystokinin antagonist L-364,718 on food and water intake in the rat. Soc. Neurosci. Abstr. **14:** 1196.

Taste Responses from the Entire Gustatory Apparatus[a]

RALPH NORGREN AND HISAO NISHIJO

Department of Behavioral Science
College of Medicine
The Pennsylvania State University
Hershey, Pennsylvania 17033

SUSAN P. TRAVERS

Department of Oral Biology
College of Dentistry
The Ohio State University
Columbus, Ohio 43210

INTRODUCTION

The primary biological function of the gustatory system is to evaluate foods and fluids passing though the oral cavity. Within the brain, then, taste should interact with the neural systems that control feeding and drinking behavior. Taste is an anatomically distinct sense, and thus it should be possible to follow the gustatory system, synapse by synapse, into the CNS and use it to probe neural mechanisms involved in the maintenance of energy, water, and electrolyte balance. To paraphrase Freud, taste is the royal road to the neural mechanisms of feeding. This simple logic has guided much of the research in our laboratory and often is implicit in other experiments in the field.

The road may be royal, but Dr. Freud neglected to add that it is neither straight nor paved. The logic may be sound, but some of the supporting facts and assumptions need work. First, the neural control of feeding behavior is true, but not pure. Control of ingestion is distributed throughout the brain and gut, and the same neural systems contribute to more than one function. The activity of hypothalamic neurons has been correlated with ingestion, gastric motility, blood pressure, and sudomotor response to name only a few. The function correlated with hypothalamic neural activity often has as much to do with the interests of the investigator as with the biology of the preparation. Similarly, the central gustatory system distributes widely within the brain, but in the process, somatic and visceral afferent neurons converge with the taste neurons to an extent that blurs the distinction of a dedicated chemosensory line.[1]

Even assuming that it plays a unique role in feeding, the import of taste as a physiological probe remains limited by our relatively poor understanding of its sensory characteristics. Taste buds are organized into subpopulations within the oral cavity based upon location and innervation (TABLE 1). Data on chemosensory responsiveness still

[a] The authors' research summarized here was supported by grants from the National Institutes of Health (NS 20397 and NS 24884) and the National Institute of Mental Health (MH 43787). Dr. Norgren is the recipient of a Research Scientist Development Award, Level II, also from the National Institute of Mental Health (MH 00653).

246

TABLE 1. Gustatory Receptor Subpopulations in the Rat: Innervation and Relative Distribution[a]

Receptor Subpopulation	Number	Percentage[b]	Innervation[c]
Anterior tongue			
Fungiform papillae	185	13.7	CT
Posterior tongue			
Foliate papillae	460	34.2	IX
Circumvallate papilla	350	26.0	IX
Anterior (hard) palate			
Nasoincisor ducts	67	5.0	GSP
Posterior (soft) palate			
Geshmacksstrieffen	66	4.9	GSP
Posterior palatal field	88	6.5	GSP
Buccal wall	46	3.4	CT
Sublingal organ	34	2.5	CT
Epiglottis	50	3.7	SLN

[a] Travers, Travers & Norgren. 1987. Gustatory neural processing in the hindbrain. Ann. Rev. Neurosci. **10**: 595–632.

[b] Refers to the percentage of the total taste receptor population.

[c] Abbreviations as follows: Chorda tympani branch of the facial nerve (CT), glossopharyngeal nerve (IX), greater superficial petrosal branch of the facial nerve (GSP), superior laryngeal branch of the vagus nerve (SLN).

derive primarily from the taste buds on the anterior tongue, which comprise only 15% of the total receptor population.[2] Compared with other sensory systems, experiments involving the other gustatory receptor subpopulations are recent, rare, and restricted usually to the peripheral sensory neurons of one or two species. Another, perhaps more serious, limitation of gustatory neurophysiology stems from the effects of anesthesia. Anesthesia affects the relationship between taste and feeding in at least two ways. First, within the central nervous system, sedation reduces neural responsiveness to sapid stimuli. Second, ingestive behavior introduces taste stimuli into the oral cavity. The stimulation techniques required under anesthesia are inherently artificial. Until recently, virtually all taste afferent data were collected in anesthetized preparations.[3]

These few paragraphs sketch some of the limitations in using taste as a sensory probe for evaluating the neural control of feeding behavior. The wide distribution and functional overlap in feeding systems, the relatively meager description of gustatory sensory neurons, and the dissociation imposed by anesthesia between afferent activity and behavior are empirical hobbles rather than theoretical disabilities. After a brief refresher on the central organization of the gustatory system, the remainder of this paper will summarize our initial attempts to reduce these impediments and thus pick up the pace of exploring the gustatory road to the control of feeding behavior.

THE CENTRAL GUSTATORY SYSTEM

Data on the central gustatory system may be relatively scarce, but reviewing that meager literature has become something of a cottage industry.[3-6] The neuroanatomy of the system has been covered from fish to humans and need only be outlined for reference here (FIG. 1).[7-9] Gustatory afferent axons reach the medulla over four branches of three cranial nerves. These nerve branches, the chorda tympani and greater superficial petrosal of VII, the lingual-tonsilar of IX, and the superior laryngeal of X, terminate in both the spinal trigeminal nucleus (SpV) and the nucleus of the solitary tract (NST). Each nerve branch contains both somatosensory and gustatory fibers, but so far as is known the taste axons synapse only in the nucleus of the solitary tract. Somatosensory axons, however, end in both the SpV and the NST.[7-9] Within the NST, the three cranial nerves end in rostrocaudal order, but functionally the organization may be more complex. Second-order gustatory neurons that respond to sapid stimulation of the tongue and palate are located in the anterior third of the NST; somatosensory neurons for the same surfaces appear to be caudal to taste. Laryngeal afferent axons terminate still further caudally, but somatosensory and sapid functions may intermix.[11-15] Pulmonary, cardiovascular, and gastrointestinal afferent fibers from the cervical vagus fill the caudal third of the nucleus.[16-18] When both the gustatory and visceral afferent systems are considered, in general, the anatomic evidence supports somatotopic arrangement within the NST, while the electrophysiological data indicate some functional convergence from separate receptor fields.[1,19,20]

From the caudal, visceral afferent end of the nucleus of the solitary tract, neurons project into the spinal cord, specifically to the vicinity of the phrenic motoneurons and into the intermediolateral cell column, as well as to areas within the pontine and medullary reticular formation functionally identified with respiratory and cardiovascular regulation. Axons from NST neurons also penetrate rostrally into the ventral forebrain. All these projections, however, arise from relatively circumscribed areas within the NST. In rodents, only the pontine parabrachial nuclei (PBN) receive substantial projections from all levels of the nucleus of the solitary tract, including those involved with gustatory and oral somatosensory functions. In general gustatory neurons, which are rostral in the NST, terminate medially in the PBN; visceral afferent cells, which are caudal in the NST, end further laterally.[21,22] Although electrophysiology supports this rough organization, more detailed anatomical data indicate a patchwork of overlapping or interdigitating NST terminal zones in and near the parabrachial nuclei.[23]

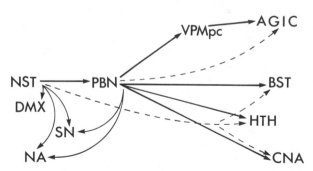

FIGURE 1. Schematic representation in the sagittal plane of the central projections of the gustatory system in the rat. Rostral is right, dorsal is up. Heavy lines indicate major pathways to the forebrain; thin lines, local connections; dashed lines, related pathways without documented gustatory function. Abbreviations: AGIC, agranular insular (gustatory) cortex; BST, bed nucleus of the stria terminalis; CNA, central nucleus of the amygdala; DMX, dorsal motor nucleus of the vagus; HTH, hypothalamus including paraventricular nucleus; NA, nucleus ambiguus; NST, nucleus of the solitary tract; PBN, parabrachial nuclei; SN, salivatory nuclei; VPMpc, parvicellular division of the ventral posteromedial nucleus (thalamic gustatory relay). (From R. Norgren. 1985. Taste and the autonomic nervous system. Chemical Senses **10**: 143–161. Reprinted with permission.)

The nucleus of the solitary tract and the parabrachial nuclei clearly function as sensory relays for gustatory and visceral afferent activity ascending to the forebrain. They must also serve other functions, however, because both relays receive substantial axonal projections from the somatosensory system and from the reticular formation.[24-27] Indeed, in an early horseradish peroxidase investigation of projections to the PBN, the cells in the NST represented only a minor concentration on the dorsal edge of a sea of retrogradely labeled reticular neurons.[28] In addition to these anatomical complexities, immunohistochemical analysis has documented an impressive heterogeneity of neurotransmitters and other peptides within the somata and axonal ramifications of both the NST and PBN. At present this neurochemical plethora increases, rather than reduces, the functional dilemma. Nevertheless, one generalization can be made that presumably has relevance for understanding the gustatory control of ingestive behaviors. The neurochemical diversity exists primarily within the visceral afferent sectors of both the NST and PBN. By comparison, the gustatory areas are neurochemically bland.[29]

From the parabrachial nuclei axons ascend in two systems, one through a thalamic relay to the cortex, the other dispersed widely within the limbic system. Once again, aside from the fact that they serve to convey gustatory and visceral afferent activity,[30-32] remarkably little is known about the functions of either system. Combining the data that do exist with what is known otherwise about cortical and limbic systems does provide a basis for inferring some division of labor within the central gustatory projections. To some extent, the thalamocortical projections appear to preserve the anatomical and electrophysiological order present on the periphery. Gustatory nerves that innervate the anterior tongue are represented on the cortex rostrally to those that innervate the caudal tongue, and the vagal–visceral afferent projection appears to be still further caudally.[33-37] In general, the response properties of cortical gustatory neurons differ little from those of taste cells at other levels of the CNS or on the periphery.[38,39] Finally, lesions of the cortical gustatory area produce categories of learning and performance deficits that resemble those observed after lesions in other cortical sensory systems.[40] The implication is that gustatory cortex functions as do the other sensory representations in providing the neural basis for the finest discriminations and perhaps for the initial stages of acquired skill based upon those discriminations.

Less is known about the gustatory projections to the ventral forebrain, but a few general points can be made. From the PBN, the thalamocortical projections contain more gustatory axons and the ventral forebrain systems, more visceral afferent axons.[41] Unlike the thalamic and cortical gustatory areas, which are quite circumscribed, the ventral forebrain projections disperse through a number of structures, including the hypothalamus, amygdala, and bed nucleus of the stria terminalis, without any obvious sensory organization.[42,43] Based upon retrograde labeling studies, some anatomical organization does exist — neurons that project to the central nucleus of the amygdala concentrate in specific areas of the PBN — but, as yet, no functional relevance can be attached to these patterns.[44] Parabrachial gustatory axons reach the hypothalamus and the amygdala, and neurons in both areas respond to sapid stimulation.[30,42,45-49] The percentage of neurons encountered that respond to taste varies, but usually is quite low (<10%), and, when tested, most of these cells also respond to other sensory stimuli.[47,48,50] In other words, in the ventral forebrain, neurons that respond to taste stimuli have sensory properties that are more reminiscent of the reticular formation than of the gustatory relay nuclei. Although the logic of the limbic system remains uncertain, these characteristics imply that gustatory afferent activity is not necessarily further refined by the ventral forebrain, but rather informs the integration of endocrine, autonomic, and behavioral processes taking place there.

This hypothetical division of labor between the thalamocortical and ventral forebrain gustatory systems was proposed shortly after the projections from the parabrachial nuclei were first described.[51] Indeed, the original formulation was more robust than the one presented here and was based almost entirely on the functions attributed to the neocortex and limbic system rather than on the nature of the gustatory afferent activity that reach them. Evidence to support or refute this hypothesis has been slow to accumulate. This returns us to the problems encountered in using the gustatory system as a royal road to investigations of ingestive behavior. As mentioned in the introduction, two major problems involve assessing the nature of taste afferent activity generated from the entire gustatory apparatus, rather than just those receptors on the anterior tongue, and determining whether or not that sensory activity changes significantly in an awake, behaving animal.

TASTE BUD SUBPOPULATIONS

In the rat, taste buds occur in nine subpopulations that are distinguished by their location within the oral cavity, their innervation, and their associated epithelial structures (TABLE I). Based upon the responses of peripheral axons, the chemical sensitivity of taste buds varies considerably both across subpopulations and across species.[2] The number of investigations and the number of chemical stimuli used also varies depending upon the nerve, with the chorda tympani having the largest by far, and the greater superficial petrosal nerve, the smallest. With the exception of the chorda tympani studies, the receptor subpopulation being stimulated seldom was specified. For the central gustatory system, only a handful of experiments attempted to stimulate anything other than the anterior tongue. Halpern and Nelson[52] separated the anterior tongue from the remainder of the oral cavity and recorded multiunit responses in the NST. Using the same technique, Norgren and Pfaffmann[53] examined both multiunit and single-unit responses in the PBN. In both cases, the assumption was made that the chemical stimuli were being applied to either the fungiform papillae on the anterior tongue or to the foliate and circumvallate papillae on the posterior tongue. No reference was made to the other receptor subpopulations, all of which potentially were exposed to the posterior tongue stimulation. More recently, Chang and Scott[54] introduced an irrigation tube designed to stimulate the entire oral cavity, but the effectiveness of this technique in reaching all of the receptor subpopulations has yet to be examined.

We devised a technique for independently applying sapid chemicals on as many as eight of the nine gustatory receptor subpopulations. This involved using a headbolt to stabilize an anesthetized rat, thus eliminating the need for either the earbars or the bitebar of the stereotaxic instrument. Removing the bitebar allowed us to view the oral cavity through an operating microscope (FIG. 2). This visual control, in turn, permitted stimulation of individual receptor subpopulations by using fluid-soaked paintbrushes of an appropriate size. Admittedly, the technique compounds the tediousness of gustatory neurophysiology and diminishes some aspects of stimulus control. Compared with other sensory modalities, sapid stimuli must be applied slowly and with long intertrial intervals. When these stimuli are applied to four or five separate locations, the time required to test an individual neuron is multiplied accordingly. Nevertheless, this approach already has yielded important new insight into functional properties of the gustatory system.

In the first set of experiments using this novel stimulating technique, we documented several new characteristics of the central gustatory system.[55] One enduring conundrum of the rat gustatory system was an avid acceptance of stimuli that taste sweet to humans

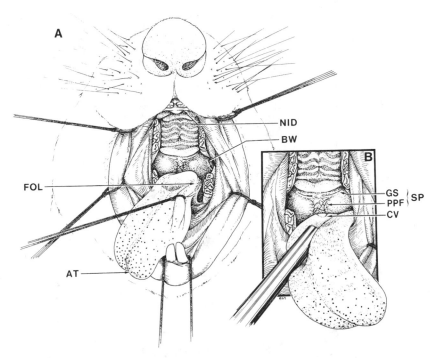

FIGURE 2. The view of the rat oral cavity needed for independent stimulation of the individual subpopulations of taste buds. Abbreviations: AT, anterior tongue (fungiform papillae); BW, buccal wall; CV, circumvallate papilla; FOL, foliate papillae; GS, geschmacksstreifen; NID, nasoincisor ducts; PPF, posterior palatal field of taste buds; SP, soft palate.

coupled with an unimpressive response of the peripheral taste nerves to the same chemicals. This problem turned out to be an instance of searching for a lost quarter under the wrong streetlight. As with previous investigations, when the fluids were applied to the anterior tongue, many neurons in the anterior NST responded well to NaCl, but poorly if at all to sucrose. When these stimuli were applied to the small population of taste buds concentrated in the nasoincisor ducts on the hard palate, however, many of the same NST neurons responded vigorously to sucrose and barely at all to NaCl (FIG. 3). About half the neurons tested thoroughly ($n = 29$) responded better to sucrose applied on the nasoincisor ducts, but better to NaCl on the anterior tongue. The remainder responded only to anterior tongue stimulation, with NaCl or HCl as the most effective stimulus. At our standard testing concentrations (1.0 *M* sucrose and 0.3 *M* NaCl), sucrose on the hard palate drove NST neurons about four times as fast as the same stimulus applied to the anterior tongue. For NaCl, the ratio was similar, but reversed — the anterior tongue was more effective than the palate (FIG. 4). These data supported two conclusions — first, that the gustatory receptors on the nasoincisor ducts were peculiarly sensitive to sweet stimuli and, second, that the neural activity from the receptor subpopulations on the anterior tongue and the nasoincisor ducts converged onto the same neurons within the NST.

Subsequent analysis of these data and a separate study devoted to chemicals preferred by rats have further documented the importance of the nasoincisor duct taste buds and the technique used to investigate separate receptor subpopulations. For most elec-

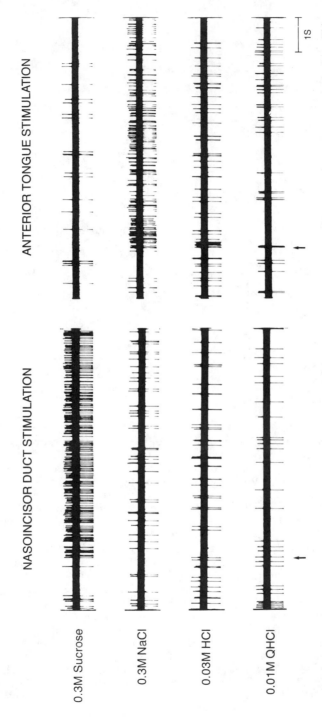

FIGURE 3. Oscillographic records of action potentials recorded from a single neuron in the nucleus of the solitary tract in an anesthetized rat. This cell responded to sucrose applied to the nasoincisor ducts and to NaCl applied to the anterior tongue, but not vice-versa. It responded weakly or not at all to HCL or quinine applied to either field. The arrows below the bottom panel mark the onset of stimulation.

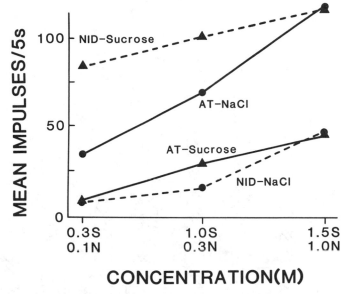

FIGURE 4. Mean responses of five NST neurons tested with a concentration series of both NaCl (N) and sucrose (S) applied to both the anterior tongue (AT) and the nasoincisor ducts (NID). (From Travers, Pfaffmann & Norgren.[55] By permission of *Brain Research*.)

trolytes, the typical gustatory neural response consists of a transient burst of activity that peaks in about 1.0 sec, followed by an exponential decrease to a slowly declining steady state. Responses to sweeteners fail to exhibit this characteristic; activity usually increases slowly over 3.0 or 4.0 sec to achieve a low steady state. In our sample of NST cells, NaCl applied to either the anterior tongue or the nasoincisor ducts elicited typical fast-onset bursts of activity. Sucrose on the anterior tongue resulted in characteristically sluggish responses that took an average of more than 4.0 sec to reach a sustained level. When applied to the nasoincisor ducts, however, sucrose produced responses that mimicked those elicited by NaCl with a risetime of 1.0–1.5 sec.[56] This observation and several other lines of evidence argue that a slow initial transient response is not an inherent characteristic of sweet receptors as previously thought, but probably results from the relatively low density of such receptors on the anterior tongue of the rat.

The apparent concentration of sweet receptors in the nasoincisor ducts led us to forestall further investigation of the other gustatory receptor subpopulations in order to examine one other peculiarity of sweet responsiveness in rats—relative preference. As with humans, rats demonstrate a reliable preference order for sweet-tasting chemicals. At least in the chorda tympani nerve, however, the magnitude of the electrophysiological response to these same stimuli fails to correspond to the observed preference order. We tested the responsiveness of NST neurons with a battery of normally preferred sapid stimuli applied independently to either the anterior tongue or to the nasoincisor ducts. As predicted, the activity elicited from the anterior tongue was relatively low in magnitude and unrelated to preference. When the stimuli were applied to the nasoincisor ducts, the same neurons produced larger responses, and the order of stimulus effectiveness closely matched the preference order (FIG. 5).[57] The only exceptions to

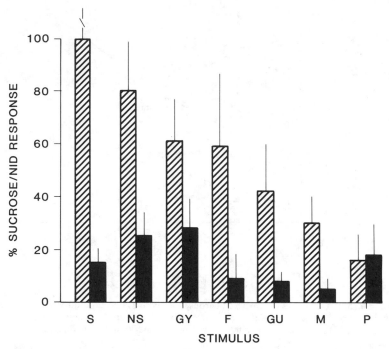

FIGURE 5. Mean response (+SE) of NST neurons to 0.3 *M* sucrose (S), 0.002 *M* Na-saccharin (NS), 0.3 *M* glycine (GY), 0.3 *M* fructose (F), 0.3 *M* glucose (G), 0.3 *M* maltose (M), and 0.1 *M* polycose (P) when applied to either the nasocisor ducts (hatched bars) or the anterior tongue (solid bars). The stimuli are ranked in order of their effectiveness when applied to the nasoincisor ducts. The responses are expressed as a percentage of the mean response to sucrose applied to the nasoincisor ducts. (From Travers & Norgren.[57] Used by permission.)

this match came from maltose and polycose. These two stimuli are highly preferred by rats but, based upon generalization gradients, probably do not taste sweet to them.[58]

Our initial investigations have emphasized the contrasts between only two of the taste receptor subpopulations in the oral cavity, but already have demonstrated the importance of examining the entire gustatory apparatus. Other laboratories that used a similar approach have produced complementary results.[59,60] Another obvious means for stimulating gustatory receptors is to let the rat ingest the fluids itself. This has the advantage of being entirely natural, and the disadvantage of losing some control over stimulus application.

CHRONIC RECORDING

We have developed a preparation for chronic recording in the rat CNS that permits near-natural ingestion while providing for some stimulus control. Rats were first trained to ingest water while in a modified plastic restraining cage. After a few days, the animals were anesthetized and an acrylic appliance fitted to their skulls that permitted their heads to be held painlessly in the stereotaxic plane. During the same procedure intraoral cannulae[61] and EMG electrodes also were implanted. After recovering from the surgery, intake training was reinstituted using both a standard drinking spout or fluid introduced via the intraoral cannulae. Once well-trained, the rats remained calmly in the apparatus for 3–4 hours when presented with periodic drafts of water or sapid fluids. This provided ample opportunity to isolate and test at least one neuron per session.

We have recorded from more than 190 parabrachial gustatory neurons in three separate experiments. Each neuron was tested with at least one trial of sucrose (0.3 M), NaCl (0.1 M), citric acid (0.003 or 0.01 M), and quinine HCl (0.0001 M) as well as with water; subsets of cells were tested with a concentration series of these chemicals or the standards plus an array of other sapid stimuli. Normally, the stimuli were delivered through the intraoral cannulae as a 0.05-ml infusion at room temperature. In one experiment, many cells were tested with infusions and while the rat licked drops of the same stimuli from a spatula (FIG. 6). Although we have only recorded from one of the central gustatory relays, the technique has proven to be reliable, flexible, and efficient. This approach does not guarantee stimulation of all the gustatory receptors, but it does approximate natural ingestion.

The results of these first three studies are still being summarized for publication, so only the major points will be touched on here. For several reasons, intraoral infusions are convenient for administering sapid stimuli, but do not represent entirely natural ingestion. In this laboratory, Dr. Joseph Travers has demonstrated that the electromyographic signatures of muscles active during ingestion were indistinguishable regardless of whether the fluid came from intraoral infusions and during active licking.[62]

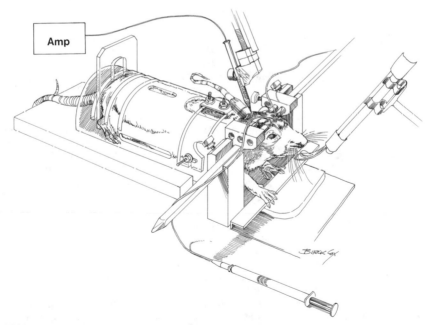

FIGURE 6. A line drawing of a rat in the chronic recording apparatus. Its head is held firmly by the cranioplastic acrylic, but its front paws are free to move. When given fluids periodically, either from the spatula held in front of its mouth or via the intraoral cannulae fed out through the acrylic, the animal will remain calmly in this apparatus for 3–4 hours.

Nevertheless, we felt it necessary to compare neural responsiveness during both forms of sapid stimulation. The activity of 35 parabrachial gustatory neurons was tested during infusions and licking of each of our four standard stimuli. On most measures, the responses did not vary greatly. The mean spontaneous rates were almost identical, 11.1 and 10.8 spikes/sec. The mean Pearson correlation coefficient for the individual neural responses elicited with the two stimulus delivery methods was >0.95. Similarly, regardless of the stimulation procedure, the best-stimulus category for each neuron remained the same.

The primary difference in activity engendered by licking or infusions appeared in the secondary or sideband responses. This characteristic was illustrated by the specificity of the neural responses, that is, how many of the standard stimuli elicited significant responses. Of the 35 cells tested, 12 responded to only one chemical during one form of stimulation, but to two or more during the other; nine were specific during licking only, three during infusions.[63] Based upon this preliminary analysis, the dominant responsiveness of a central gustatory neuron might be relatively insensitive to the stimulus delivery procedure. Other characteristics, particularly those that rely upon arbitrary statistical criteria, may change as a function of intake. In the present form (infusions vs. licking), this point may be arcane. When expanded to include fluid and solid forms of the same stimuli, however, this comparison might have real significance for understanding the neural mechanisms of sensory evaluation.

Although possibly of theoretical value, we investigated the gustatory differences between licking and infusions for practical reasons. Originally we had the rats licking from a typical drinking spout, but found that they tended to struggle when the spout was removed between trials. The animals were water-deprived overnight, and when it was moved away, they tried to reach the spout with either their front paws or their tongues. This reduced the period of useful electrophysiological isolation. Infusions alleviated this problem. Although the rats avidly accepted infused fluids, they remained calm between trials. (Eventually, using a spatula with drops of fluid on it proved to be an acceptable compromise; the rats actively licked up the stimuli without becoming excessively active.) Our first set of data relied completely on infused stimuli. The similarities and differences between these data from awake, behaving preparations and those reported for anesthetized animals were among the factors that prompted concern about the method of stimulation.

In our first sample of 70 PBN neurons, 59 responded to sapid stimuli. Nine other cells responded significantly only to water, that is, sapid fluids elicited activity similar to that of water (FIG. 7).[64] Of the taste neurons, 10 also responded to water, but gustatory stimuli induced an additional, significant increase in activity. None of the cells, neither those activated by water nor those that were not, exhibited significant inhibition during taste stimulation. Of the four standard stimuli, the most effective was 0.1 M NaCl; 71% of the cells responded best to this chemical, 24% responded best to sucrose. Only three neurons responded best to acid (2) or quinine (1). A subsample of these cells was tested with a full or a partial concentration series of the four stimuli. When tested with a concentration series of their best stimulus, all cells produced monotonically increasing response functions. Of the five Na-specific cells tested, three responded only to NaCl at all concentrations of all stimuli (FIG. 8A); in addition to NaCl, the remaining two responded weakly to the highest concentration of one other chemical. When tested with an effective stimulus rather than their best stimulus, half the cells had a monotonically increasing response function, but half exhibited more or less stable levels of activity (FIG. 8B).

In anesthetized preparations, parabrachial gustatory neurons generally are sensitive to sapid NaCl and acid, and insensitive to sucrose and quinine HCl. In our sample of PBN neurons in awake, behaving rats, NaCl remained the most effective stimulus

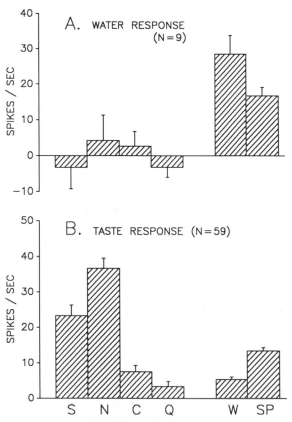

FIGURE 7. Mean response profiles (±SE) of (**A**) nine water-responsive neurons and (**B**) 59 taste-responsive neurons. Responses to sapid stimuli were corrected for water response; water responses, for spontaneous rate. Abbreviations: C, 0.003 or 0.01 *M* citric acid; N, 0.1 *M* NaCl; S, 0.3 *M* sucrose; SP, spontaneous rate; Q, 0.0001 *M* quinine HCl; W, distilled water. (From Nishijo & Norgren.[64])

and quinine, the least. Unlike in the anesthetized animal, however, sucrose affected many neurons and acid, few. In addition to these gustatory characteristics, PBN cells in the awake rat responded to water more often and had higher spontaneous rates of activity than the same type of neurons isolated from anesthetized preparations. Most of these similarities and differences are interpretable, but at least one presents a puzzle.

The difference in spontaneous rates, roughly a factor of 2.5, presumably can be attributed to either the direct or indirect effects of general anesthetics. Similarly, in awake rats the increased number of neurons that responded to intraoral water may reflect the added somatosensory stimulation introduced by the animal's behavioral response to the fluid. The increased efficacy of sucrose in awake animals also probably results from the animal's behavioral response — tongue movements bring the sucrose solution into contact with the taste buds of the nasoincisor ducts. Given these tongue movements, the lack of response to quinine seems peculiar. The usual rationale for poor quinine sensitivity assumes that, because the receptors most responsive to

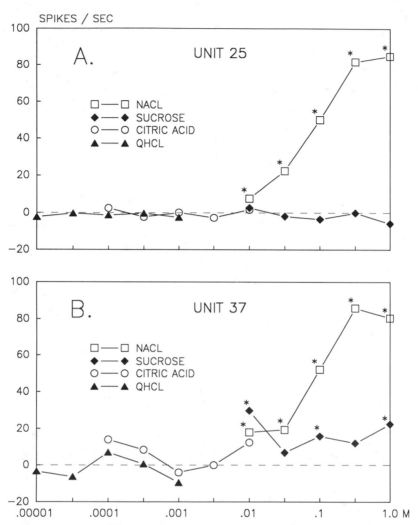

FIGURE 8. Intensity-response functions for two neurons recorded in the parabrachial nuclei of awake, behaving rats using a concentration series of sapid chemicals. The taste responses were corrected for water responses (dashed line). Asterisks indicate significant taste responses. (Adapted from Nishijo & Norgren.[64])

bitter stimuli are concentrated in the crypts of the foliate and, particularly, the circum-vallate papillae, they are relatively inaccessible to fluid on an immobile tongue. A moving tongue should solve that problem, but in our case it did not. Several explanations come to mind; none are supported by more than anecdotal evidence.

First, the rationale might be incorrect, but when pipettes are introduced into or near the crypts of the papillae, robust responses to bitter chemicals can be obtained from the glossopharyngeal nerve.[65–67] Second, neurons that respond to bitter may exist in the pons, but our recording did not sample that population. Anatomical and some electrophysiological data indicate that the gustatory neurons in the PBN occur in a single compact zone.[30,53] We have made more than 500 penetrations into and near the PBN and tested multiple loci in each penetration with sapid stimuli. Third, the animals are overtrained and learn to avoid letting bitter fluids reach the crypts of these papillae. With the glossopharyngeal nerve cut bilaterally, rats still emit early aversive responses to quinine, but fail to sustain them.[68] Thus rats can detect quinine quickly and might have time to avoid the aversive sensory consequences of stimulating more sensitive receptors. Indeed, the gaping induced by some sapid solutions functions to remove the fluid from the oral cavity.[69] Finally, the volume of fluid used in these experiments (0.05 ml) might be too small to stimulate these protected receptors, at least within our standard observation period of 5.0 sec. In several instances, when we examined records beyond 5.0 sec, an infusion of quinine was followed by a gradual increase in activity over a period of 10.0–15.0 sec. Subsequent water rinses produced a equally gradual return to baseline.

In awake rats, the relative lack of quinine responsiveness from the PBN neurons was unexpected, but at least several plausible hypotheses exist in lieu of an empirical answer. The lack of acid responses in the same neural population was both unexpected and inexplicable. In the chorda tympani nerve, about half of the axons that respond well to NaCl also respond well to acids.[70,71] In most reports from acute preparations, neurons recorded in either the NST or the PBN exhibit a similar distribution of response properties (see Nishijo & Norgren[64] for a discussion). An obvious explanation for the relatively poor acid responses in the chronic preparations, such as a weak stimulus, was refuted by the concentration series data. Conceivably, a sampling bias could produce such results, but the percentage of Na-sensitive cells was about equal in both chronic and acute preparations. Only the associated acid responsiveness was absent. One final possibility requires consideration. Responses to water were more frequent in the chronic preparations and, in some acute studies, responses to cold water have been associated with acid sensitivity.[72,73] In a chronic preparation, room temperature fluids might be functionally cooler because, when the mouth is closed, the temperature of the oral cavity would be higher. In our analysis, the water response was subtracted from the taste activity and, if an association existed, the number of statistically significant acid responses might be reduced.

CONCLUSION

In theory, the gustatory system should be an ideal sensory probe for examining the neural controls of energy, water, and electrolyte balance. In practice, fluids are used frequently in behavioral investigations of these systems, if for no other reason because they facilitate automatic measurement. This paper has examined some of the obstacles that have precluded using taste to its full advantage in deciphering these complex regulatory processes. A probe can simplify the process of investigation, but it does not simplify the object of the investigation. The neuroanatomy of the gustatory system does lead to areas in the forebrain known to be involved in the regulation of energy, water, and electrolyte balance. At present, these sensory ramifications confirm, but do not illuminate the complexity of the regulatory system. For a probe to be maximally useful, the instrument itself must be understood. Understanding of the neural coding of chemical sensory stimuli remains in its infancy. Entire subpopulations of taste buds await investigation. Even the distribution of stimuli to these receptors during normal behavior needs to be documented. Once within the CNS, gustatory afferent activity from different receptor subpopulations converges onto the same neurons, further muddling any simple notions of spatial coding. These issues need to be addressed in order to tranform the gustatory system from a sensory pointer into an analytic instrument. Taste may be a royal road to feeding behavior, but will be more useful after it becomes a traveled way.

ACKNOWLEDGMENTS

Mrs. Joan Bernardo assisted with the bibliography and typing. Mr. Maurice Sherrard and Mr. Birck Cox drew the sketches for FIGURES 2 and 6, respectively. They each have our thanks.

REFERENCES

1. NORGREN, R. 1983. Afferent interactions of cranial nerves involved in ingestion. J. Autonom. Nerv. Sys. **9:** 67–77.
2. TRAVERS, J. B., S. P. TRAVERS & R. NORGREN. 1987. Gustatory neural processing in the hindbrain. Ann. Rev. Neurosci. **10:** 565–632.
3. NORGREN, R. 1984. Central neural mechanisms of taste. *In* Handbook of Physiology—The Nervous System III, Sensory Processes. J. Brookhart, I. Darien-Smith & V. Mountcastle, Eds: 1087–1128. American Physiological Society. Washington, DC.
4. FINGER, T. E. & W. L. SILVER, Eds. 1987. The Neurobiology of Taste and Smell. John Wiley & Sons. New York.
5. SCOTT, T. R. & F.-C. T. CHANG. 1984. The state of gustatory neural coding. Chem. Senses **8:** 297–314.
6. YAMAMOTO, T. 1985. Taste responses of cortical neurons. Prog. Neurobiol. **23:** 273–315.
7. ARENDS, J. J. A., J. M. WILD & H. P. ZEIGLER. 1988. Projections of the nucleus of the solitary tract in the pigeon (*Columbia livia*). J. Comp. Neurol. **278:** 405–429.
8. KANWAL, J. S., T. E. FINGER & J. CAPRIO. 1988. Forebrain connections of the gustatory system in Ictalurid catfishes. J. Comp. Neurol. **278:** 358–376.
9. NORGREN, R. 1990. Gustatory system. *In* The Human Nervous System. G. Paxinos, Ed. Academic Press. San Diego. In press.
10. NORGREN, R. 1981. The central organization of the gustatory and visceral afferent systems in the nucleus of the solitary tract. *In* Brain Mechanisms of Sensation. Y. Katsuki, R. Norgren & M. Sato, Eds. John Wiley & Sons. New York.
11. HAMILTON, R. & R. NORGREN. 1984. Central projections of gustatory nerves in the rat. J. Comp. Neurol. **222:** 560–577.
12. HANAMORI, T. & D. V. SMITH. 1989. Gustatory innervation in the rabbit: Central distribution of sensory and motor components of the chorda tympani, glossopharyngeal, and superior laryngeal nerves. J. Comp. Neurol. **282:** 1–14.
13. OGAWA, H., T. HAYAMA & Y. YAMASHITA. 1988. Thermal sensitivity of neurons in a rostral part of the rat nucleus of the solitary tract. Brain Res. **454:** 321–331.
14. SWEAZEY, R. D. & R. M. BRADLEY. 1986. Central connections of the lingual-tonsilar branch of the glossopharyngeal nerve and the superior laryngeal nerve in the lamb. J. Comp. Neurol. **245:** 471–482.
15. TRAVERS, S. P. & R. NORGREN. 1988. Oral sensory responses in the nucleus of the solitary tract. Soc. Neurosci. Absts. **14:** 1185.
16. LESLIE, R. A., D. G. GWYN & D. A. HOPKINS. 1982. The central distribution of the cervical vagus nerve and gastric afferent and efferent projections in the rat. Brain Res. Bull. **8:** 37–43.
17. KALIA, M. & M. M. MESULAM. 1980. Brain stem projections of sensory and motor components of the vagus complex in the cat: II. Laryngral, tracheobronchial, pulmonary, cardiac, and gastrointestinal branches. J. Comp. Neurol. **193:** 467–508.
18. NORGREN, R. & G. P. SMITH. 1988. Central distribution of subdiaphragmatic vagal branches in the rat. J. Comp. Neurol. **273:** 207–223.

19. ALTSCHULER, S., X. BAO, D. BIEGER, D. A. HOPKINS & R. R. MISELIS. 1989. Viscerotopic representation of the upper alimentary tract in the rat: Sensory ganglia and nuclei of the solitary and spinal trigeminal tracts. J. Comp. Neurol. **283:** 248–268.
20. NORGREN, R. 1989. Brainstem integration of gustatory and gut afferent activity. *In* Nerves and the Gastrointestinal Tract. M. V. Singer & H. Goebell, Eds.: 447–462. MTP Press. Lancaster, England.
21. NORGREN, R. 1978. Projections from the nucleus of the solitary tract in the rat. Neuroscience **3:** 207–218.
22. TRAVERS, J. B. 1988. Efferent projections from the anterior nucleus of the solitary tract of the hamster. Brain Res. **457:** 1–11.
23. HERBERT, H., M. M. MOGA & C. B. SAPER. 1987. Peptidergic projections from the nucleus of the solitary tract to the parabrachial nucleus. Soc. Neurosci. Abstr. **13:** 728.
24. BLOMQVIST, A., W. MA & K. J. BERKLEY. 1989 Spinal input to the parabrachial nucleus in the cat. Brain Res. **480:** 29–36.
25. CECHETTO, D., D. STANDERT & C. SAPER. 1985. Spinal and trigeminal dorsal horn projections to the parabrachial nucleus in the rat. J. Comp. Neurol. **240:** 153–160.
26. MENETREY, D. & A. I. BASBAUM. Spinal and trigeminal projections to the nucleus of the solitary tract: A possible substrate for somatovisceral and viscerovisceral reflex activation. J. Comp. Neurol. **255:** 439–450.
27. PANNETON, W. M. & H. BURTON. 1985. Projections of the paratrigeminal nucleus and the medullary and spinal dorsal horn to the peribrachial area in the cat. Neuroscience **15:** 779–797.
28. KING, G. W. 1980. Topology of ascending brainstem projections to nucleus parabrachialis in the cat. J. Comp. Neurol. **191:** 615–638.
29. MANTYH, P. W. & S. P. HUNT. 1984. Neuropeptides are present in the projection neurons at all levels of the visceral and taste pathways: From periphery to sensory cortex. Brain Res. **299:** 297–311.
30. DELL, R. & R. OLSEN. 1951. Projections thalamiques, corticales et cerebelleuses des afferences viscerale vagales. Soc. Biol. Comp. Ren. **145:** 1084–1088.
31. NORGREN, R. 1974. Gustatory afferents to ventral forebrain. Brain Res. **81:** 285–295.
32. O'BRIEN, J. H., A. PIMPANEAU & D. ALBE-FESSARD. 1971. Evoked cortical responses to vagal, laryngeal, and facial afferents in monkeys under chloralose anesthesia. Electroenceph. Clin. Neurophysiol. **31:** 7–20.
33. BENJAMIN, R. M. & H. BURTON. 1968. Projection of taste nerve afferents to anterior opercular-insular cortex in squirrel monkey (*Saimiri sciureus*). Brain Res. **7:** 221–231.
34. CECHETTO, D. F. & C. B. SAPER. 1987. Evidence for a viscerotopic sensory representation in the cortex and thalamus in the rat. J. Comp. Neurol. **262:** 27–45.
35. KOSAR, E. M., H. J. GRILL & R. NORGREN. 1986. Gustatory cortex in the rat. I. Physiological properties and cytoarchitecture. Brain Res. **379:** 329–341.
36. KOSAR, E. M., H. J. GRILL & R. NORGREN. 1986. Gustatory cortex in the rat. II. Thalamocortical connections. Brain Res. **379:** 342–352.
37. OGAWA, H., S. ITO & T. NOMURA. 1985. Two distinct projection areas from tongue nerves in the frontal operculum of macaque monkeys as revealed with evoked potential mapping. Neurosci. Res. **2:** 447–459.
38. SCOTT, T. R., S. YAXLEY, Z. SIENKIEWICZ & E. T. ROLLS. 1986. Gustatory responses in the frontal opercular cortex of the alert Cynomolgus monkey. J. Neurophysiol. **56:** 876–890.
39. YAMAMOTO, T. 1987. Cortical organization in gustatory perception. Ann. N.Y. Acad. Sci. **510:** 49–54.
40. BRAUN, J. J., P. S. LASITER & S. W. KIEFER. 1982. The gustatory neocortex of the rat. Physiol. Psych. **10:** 13–45.
41. NOMURA, S., N. MIZUNO, K. ITOH, K. MATSUDA, T. SUGIMOTO & Y. NAKAMURA. 1979. Localization of parabrachial nucleus neurons projecting to the thalamus or the amygdala in the cat using horseradish peroxidase. Exp. Neurol. **64:** 375–385.
42. SAPER, C. B. & A. D. LOEWY. 1980. Efferent connections of the parabrachial nucleus in the rat. Brain Res. **197:** 291–317.

43. NORGREN, R. 1976. Taste pathways to hypothalamus and amygdala. J. Comp. Neurol. **166:** 12–30.
44. FULWILER, C. E. & C. B. SAPER. 1984. Subnuclear organization of the efferent connections of the parabrachial nucleus in the rat. Brain Res. Rev. **7:** 229–259.
45. AZUMA, S., T. YAMAMOTO & Y. KAWAMURA. 1984. Studies on gustatory responses of amygdaloid neurons in rats. Exp. Brain Res. **56:** 12–22.
46. MOGENSON, G. J. & M. WU. 1982. Electrophysiological and behavioral evidence of interaction of dopaminergic and gustatory afferents in the amygdala. Brain Res. Bul. **8:** 685–691.
47. NISHIJO, H., T. ONO & H. NISHINO. 1988. Topographic distribution of modality-specific amygdalar neurons in alert monkey. J. Neurosci. **8:** 3556–3569.
48. NISHIJO, H., T. ONO & H. NISHINO. 1988. Single neuron responses in amygdala of alert monkey during complex sensory stimulation with affective significance. J. Neurosci. **8:** 3570–3583.
49. SCHWARTZBAUM, J. S. & C. H. BLOCK. 1981. Interrelations between parabrachial pons and ventral forebrain of rabbits in taste-mediated functions. *In* The Amygdaloid Complex. Y. Ben-Ari, Ed.: 367–382. Elsevier/North-Holland. New York.
50. NORGREN, R. 1970. Gustatory responses in the hypothalamus. Brain Res. **21:** 63–71.
51. PFAFFMANN, C., R. NORGREN & H. J. GRILL. 1977. Sensory affect and motivation. Ann. N.Y. Acad. Sci. **290:** 18–34.
52. HALPERN, B. P. & L. M. NELSON. 1965. Bulbar gustatory responses to anterior and to posterior tongue stimulation in the rat. Am. J. Physiol. **209:** 105–110.
53. NORGREN, R. & C. PFAFFMANN. 1975. The pontine taste area in the rat. Brain Res. **91:** 99–117.
54. CHANG, F.-C. T. & T. R. SCOTT. 1984. A technique for gustatory stimulus delivery in the rodent. Chem. Senses **9:** 91–96.
55. TRAVERS, S. P., C. PFAFFMANN & R. NORGREN. 1986. Convergence of lingual and palatal gustatory neural activity in the nucleus of the solitary tract. Brain Res. **365:** 305–320.
56. TRAVERS, S. P. & R. NORGREN. 1989. The time course of solitary nucleus gustatory responses: Influence of stimulus and site of application. Chem. Senses **14:** 55–74.
57. TRAVERS, S. P. & R. NORGREN. 1987. Responses of neurons in the nucleus of the solitary tract to lingual and palatal stimulation with preferred chemicals. Ann. N.Y. Acad. Sci. **510:** 673–676.
58. NISSENBAUM, J. W. & A. SCLAFANI. 1987. Qualitative differences in polysaccharide and sugar tastes in the rat: A two-carbohydrate taste model. Neurosci. Biobehav. Rev. **11:** 187–196.
59. NEJAD, M. S. 1986. The neural activities of the greater superficial petrosal nerve of the rat in response to chemical stimulation of the palate. Chem. Senses **11:** 283–293.
60. OGAWA, H., T. HAYAMA & S. ITO. 1982. Convergence of input from tongue and palate to the parabrachial nucleus neurons of rats. Neurosci. Lett. **28:** 9–14.
61. GRILL, H. J. & R. NORGREN. 1978. The taste reactivity test. I. Mimetic responses to gustatory stimuli in neurologically normal rats. Brain Res. **143:** 263–279.
62. TRAVERS, J. B. & R. NORGREN. 1986. An electromyographic analysis of the ingestion and rejection of sapid stimuli in the rat. Behav. Neurosci. **100:** 544–555.
63. NISHIJO, H. & R. NORGREN. 1989. Parabrachial neural activity during licking of sapid stimuli by rats. Soc. Neurosci. Abstr. **15:** 930.
64. NISHIJO, H. & R. NORGREN. Gustatory neural activity in the parabrachial nuclei of awake rats. Submitted.
65. BOUDREAU, J. C., L. T. DO, L. SIVAKUMAR, J. ORAVEC & C. A. RODRIGUEZ. 1987. Taste responses of the petrosal ganglion of the rat glossopharyngeal nerve. Chem. Senses **12:** 437–458.
66. FRANK, M. 1968. Single-fiber responses in the glossopharyngeal nerve of the rat to chemical, thermal, and mechanical stimulation of the posterior tongue. Doctoral dissertation, Brown University, Providence, RI.
67. HANAMORI, T., I. J. MILLER, JR. & D. V. SMITH. 1988. Gustatory responsiveness of fibers in the hamster glossopharyngeal nerve. J. Neurophysiol. **60:** 478–498.
68. TRAVERS, J. B., H. J. GRILL & R. NORGREN. 1987. The effects of glossopharyngeal and chorda tympani nerve cuts on the ingestion and rejection of sapid stimuli: An electromyographic analysis in the rat. Behav. Brain Res. **25:** 233–246.

69. NORGREN, R. & H. J. GRILL. 1982. Brain stem control of ingestive behavior. *In* Physiological Mechanisms of Motivation. D. W. Pfaff, Ed.: 99–131. Springer-Verlag. New York.
70. FRANK, M. E., S. L. BEIBER & D. V. SMITH. 1988. The organization of taste sensibilities in hamster chorda tympani nerve fibers. J. Gen. Physiol. **91:** 861–896.
71. FRANK, M. E., R. J. CONTRERAS & T. P. HETTINGER. 1983. Nerve fibers sensitive to ionic taste stimuli in the chorda tympani of the rat. J. Neurophysiol. **50:** 941–960.
72. OGAWA, H., M. SATO & S. YAMASHITA. 1968. Multiple sensitivity of chorda tympani fibres of the rat and hamster to gustatory and thermal stimuli. J. Physiol. **199:** 223–240.
73. TRAVERS, S. P. & D. V. SMITH. 1984. Responsiveness of neurons in the hamster parabrachial nuclei to taste mixtures. J. Gen. Physiol. **84:** 221–250.

DISCUSSION

DR. PAUL ARAVICH (*VA Medical Center, Hampton, VA*): I would like to make a clarification and ask a question, if I could. You mentioned briefly that the decerebrate animal is capable of eating and therefore that obviously implies that the hypothalamus is not necessary for food ingestion. I just want to make the point that the decerebrate animal that has been examined is an animal that has been decerebrated with a cut that goes between the forebrain and the hindbrain. That still leaves intact all of the neuroendocrine regulation systems that we can think of, and so, whereas it rules out a neural, if you will, necessity for forebrain mechanisms, it does not rule out a neuroendocrine role in forebrain regulation of feeding.

My question concerns a more intimate issue in the case of anorexia nervosa, and that is the impact that metabolic factors have on gustatory responsiveness and the changes that have been reported in anorexia nervosa and other instances. It is a fascinating issue and one tends to think of those changes in gustatory responsiveness as orally mediated, that is to say, coming from the tongue projections to the nucleus of the solitary tract (NTS) and a neurological system. My question concerns the data that Palkovitz has reported indicating that at least a component of the NST is outside the blood–brain barrier, which would raise the possibility, at least, of circulating metabolic factors as well as gustatory metabolic factors interacting directly in the NTS to modify taste perception. Do you have any information on that?

DR. RALPH NORGREN (*The Pennsylvania State University College of Medicine, Hershey, PA*): In December at another meeting at the Monell Institute, Tom Scott will summarize what has now become a fairly extensive body of data that he has gathered on various manipulations that are related to feeding and drinking behavior, and the effects that they have on gustatory responses in the NST of anesthetized animals. It is a fairly complicated story, but suffice it to say that there *are* some effects, and some of them make sense while some of them don't. The answer to your first question is that the area you are speaking of is the area postrema, and the areas immediately around it. The area postrema has no blood–brain barrier; it has very intimate connections with the NST. Indeed, if you consider a nucleus an area that receives common projections and has common projections, you can actually think of the area postrema as a part of the NST, because it receives primary afferent projections from the vagus nerve and it has efferent projections to the parabrachial nucleus.

DR. ARAVICH: Palkovitz's data, however, does not address the area postrema. He shows blood–brain barrier, fenestrated capillaries in the NTS, not in the area postrema.

DR. NORGREN: I don't know specifically what work you're referring to, but it doesn't surprise me, because in fact the border between the area postrema and the NTS is really a matter of definition. Some animals, such as rats, have a solid, single area postrema. However, in animals that have a bilateral area postrema, you can simply draw a line, but there is in fact no ependymal layer between the area postrema and the cells of the NTS. So what you call one and the other becomes a matter, probably, of the relative ratio of neurons to non-neural tissue.

DR. STYLIANOS NICOLAIDIS (*College de France CNRS, Paris*): Is the synergy between the fourth ventricle and its ependyma with this area significant or is it indifferent or does it have something to do with sensing of neuroendocrine factors coming from upstream?

DR. NORGREN: Do you mean the ependymal layer between the fourth ventricle and the area postrema?

DR. NICOLAIDIS: No, the fact that the NTS is so close to the fourth ventricle . . .

DR. NORGREN: Well, part of it is. The caudal half of it lines the fourth ventricle.

DR. NICOLAIDIS: What about experiments showing effects of peptide applications into the fourth ventricle? Are there motivating effects involving the NTS?

DR. NORGREN: I think there is a general assumption that if you put things in at the fourth ventricle they may act via the NTS, particularly when they have effects on the cardiovascular system. There isn't, I don't think, any direct proof of that.

DR. JOHN K. YOUNG (*Howard University, Washington D.C.*): I have one question regarding your data on the taste receptors and the nasoincisor duct. Why do you suppose they are so sensitive to sugars? Do you think more receptors for sugars are present on these taste receptor cells?

DR. NORGREN: I assume that the relative density of receptors on those taste buds must be much greater. That is the only explanation for it. Why that separation exists in rats is simply a matter of conjecture. In fact it is not the case in other rodents. Hamsters have very good sweet receptor responses on the anterior tongue. So it is perhaps a peculiarity of rats. No other nasoincisor duct has ever been stimulated, although there are gustatory receptors in other creatures on the nasoincisor ducts, but nobody knows anything about them.

DR. YOUNG: Is there any difference in the anatomy of these things? Has anyone ever looked?

DR. NORGREN: No, as far as I know the histological work that has been done on taste buds and gustatory receptors indicates that they are all histologically identical.

Oral Factors in Appetite and Satiety[a]

DOUGLAS G. MOOK

Department of Psychology
University of Virginia
Charlottesville, Virginia 22903

A discussion of oral factors must begin by introducing a complication. How we think about these factors depends upon how we think about the whole system.

The conventional approach to feeding behavior treats it as a negative-feedback loop (FIG. 1). Internal states or signals mobilize food search and, when food is found, ingestion. Ingestion activates internal inhibitory signals that shut ingestion down.

Within this framework, external food-related stimuli have three roles to play. First, of course, they are permissive; you cannot eat food if there is none. Second, they are excitatory on ingestion in their own right; and so a very potent food stimulus may embarrass the regulatory system, leading to such phenomena as taste-evoked drinking[1] and dietary obesity.[2] Third, while contributing to the excitation of feeding, they also may contribute to its inhibition (omitted from the figure for simplicity). Thus many writers see satiety as arising from a synergy between oral and systemic signals.[3]

For reasons that will become clear, however, I doubt that the oral–systemic interaction is one of synergy. I think it is a switching or gating operation—and that changes matters. To see what is meant by "gating," let us look at food-related stimuli from a different perspective.

OROSENSORY GATING OF INTERNAL SIGNALS

Deficit Signals

Consider a rat that is food- but not water-deprived. Offered water, it rejects it. Offered a saccharin solution, however, it ingests it with avidity. More importantly, the more severely food-deprived the rat is, the larger the ingestive bout will be[4,5]; if it were drinking water, this would not be so.[6] Presumably the rats are treating the solution as food, "eating" it by lapping as they would eat a liquid diet. The sweet taste, therefore, "can switch the rat's behavior from control by one . . . system, concerned with water balance, to control by another concerned with energy balance."[7] Or, saying it another way, the sweet taste gates the animal's response to signals correlated with severity of food deprivation. If the fluid tastes sweet, ingestion is responsive to such signals; if not, not.

[a] Much of this research was supported by National Science Foundation Grant No. BNS-8612653.

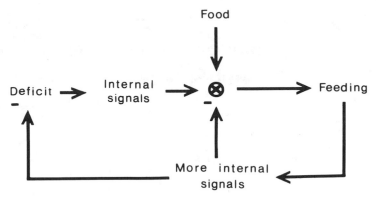

FIGURE 1. The conventional view of feeding as a negative-feedback system.

Postingestive Signals

As orosensory cues gate responsiveness to internal signals that are present when the meal begins, so they gate the animal's responsiveness to the internal signals that accrue during the meal, as consequences of ingestion. The operative principle is: *The oral stimulus determines what the necessary internal conditions for satiety will be.*[8] This principle, though it follows directly from familiar findings, has not been much discussed and requires some explanation.

Think again about a rat drinking saccharin as opposed to water. If the rat is drinking water, then, if we augment the systemic effects of the water (as by intragastric infusions of water concurrent with the drinking), spontaneous water intake is correspondingly reduced. If the rat is drinking saccharin, then the infusions do not affect spontaneous intake in the least.[9] The rat drinks the same amount by mouth, whether the infusions are given or not. Here the oral stimulus gates the animal's responsiveness to the systemic hydrational consequences of its drinking. Tasting water, it responds to these; tasting saccharin, it does not.

As another example, consider a severely salt-deficient rat. In such a rat, contact with the salt taste triggers avid ingestion, but it does something else as well: It sets up a new internal criterion for the "satiety" that will end ingestion. This was elegantly shown by Epstein and Stellar[10]: If some of the ingested sodium is picked up by an ion-exchange resin in the gut so that it is not absorbed, then the bout size is increased correspondingly. Some correlate or consequence of sodium absorption has now become a necessary condition, or "criterion," for the inhibition of ingestion. Why is that criterion now operative? It is because the rat is now tasting salt. The oral stimulus determines the necessary internal conditions for satiety.

In our recent work, we have found ourselves applying this principle not only to the differences among food, water, and salt, but also to various commodities within the food domain. It has taken us to a conception of the system's organization that is quite different from the one in FIGURE 1.

POSTINGESTIVE SATIETY

For many commodities, the size of an ingestive bout — a "meal" — is under postingestive control. This can be shown directly by eliminating postingestive events — that is, by sham-feeding or sham-drinking experiments. When this is done, the amount ingested (at least in experienced sham-drinkers) is greatly in excess of normal.[11,12] This is true of food intake in the dog,[13] water intake in the rat,[14] and liquid-food intake in the rat; this includes both complex liquid diets[15] and simpler ones, such as carbohydrate solutions.[16]

The experiments to be reported here began with the search for satiety mechanisms, using simple "model foods" — glucose or sucrose at high concentrations. These experiments were conducted by offering fasted rats a food, and measuring the amount ingested at a single meal. In some experiments, we also looked at the "satiety sequence"[3] that accompanies the cessation of ingestion: After a rat stops eating, it turns to grooming and exploring for a while. Then it rests, often immobile with head tucked under as if asleep. Such a sequence, accompanying the end of a "meal" of glucose solution, is shown in the left-hand portion of FIGURE 2.

Resetting Satiety?

It was these observations that told us something strange was going on.[17] These rats were maintained on a cyclic food-deprivation schedule. At the end of the drinking session, laboratory pellets were scattered in their cages, to be withdrawn again at the end of the afternoon. We noticed that when the pellets were offered, the "satiated" rats would rouse themselves, seize a pellet, and begin to eat vigorously. They would then go through the satiety sequence all over again, as shown in the right half of FIGURE 2. It is as if we had reset the sequence by offering pellets.

This was not because hunger had returned by that time. If, instead of offering pellets,

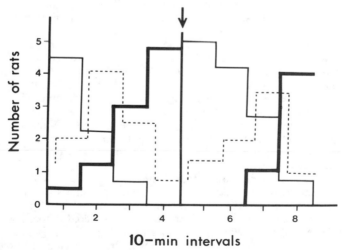

FIGURE 2. Frequencies of target behaviors over the course of a session: ingestion (light line); grooming or exploring (dashed line, displaced to the right for clarity); resting (heavy line). These behaviors were tallied over one-minute intervals and then averaged over five-minute intervals for clarity; that is why some frequencies have fractional values. The diet was changed at the arrow. (Data from Mook, Brane, Kushner, and Whitt.[17])

we simply left the solution in place (or removed and replaced it), negligible further ingestion took place over the second half of the session (not shown). The rats remained satiated — for the glucose solution. Offered pellets, they showed avid hunger. Were they hungry or satiated? They were both! They were satiated for *this*, but hungry for *that*.

Substituting Satieties: "Desatiation"

Similar effects have been observed when we substitute other commodities for glucose — for example, milk,[18] an oil-in-water suspension (unpublished data), or carbohydrate powder that does not change the nutrient at all.[8,18,19] I have recently discussed some of the ramifications of this "desatiation" phenomenon,[20] so here let us look at just a few instructive cases.

When glucose-satiated rats were offered a milk-based liquid diet, a substantial meal was consumed.[17] Not only that, but when the milk was diluted to half-strength with water, the size of the milk meal doubled — still in the glucose-sated rat.

That last finding is particularly informative. First, it is one line of evidence that intake of the second commodity is not driven by its palatability. Diluting the milk diet decreases its palatability as determined by choice tests. If milk were simply more palatable than $2\,M$ glucose, so that a postingestive inhibitory signal had to be stronger in order to balance it, then reducing its palatability should have reduced the strength of the signal so required and intake should have decreased. It increased instead.

Second, an increase in intake with caloric dilution is traditionally considered to be evidence that caloric intake, or its correlate, is being regulated. If so, then we have satiated rats regulating their caloric intakes! Rats that (a) have stopped ingesting, (b) would stay stopped if nothing else were offered, and (c) have gone through the behavioral "satiety sequence," not only resume feeding but adjust their volume intakes to caloric density when offered a different commodity.

Consider what that implies. If intake rises with dilution, we assume that it is because the onset of postingestive inhibition is delayed. It is as if the rat were following the rule, "Continue ingestion until Postingestive State X obtains." Then if the diet is diluted, more intake is required before State X will obtain and so meal size increases.

But in the present case, if the rat is waiting for State X to accrue before it stops drinking milk, it must be *ignoring the fact that another state Y, sufficient to shut down glucose intake altogether, has already been attained*. And if that is so, then which systemic signals are attended to, and which ignored, must depend upon what is offered to the mouth. Different satiety mechanisms (X and Y) can be "switched in" or "switched out," depending upon the food we offer. This of course is our guiding principle: The commodity determines the necessary conditions for satiety. Change the diet from glucose to milk, and we change the necessary conditions for satiety, from Y to X — whatever Y and X may turn out to be.

What about the converse case? Suppose the glucose solution is offered after the rat has eaten another commodity to "satiety"? FIGURE 3 shows another instructive finding.[21] Here, rats at varying deprivation levels were offered a $2\,M$ glucose solution (rising bars). On some occasions, the glucose session was preceded by access to laboratory chow (descending bars). When the chow was offered first, it was ingested in amounts sufficient to suppress the further intake of chow itself, as determined by control observations (not shown).

The rising bars represent size of the glucose meal, and we see at once that neither deprivation level, nor the preceding chow meal, affected it at all. (The small difference in the right-hand panel is not reliable and was actually reversed in some replications.)

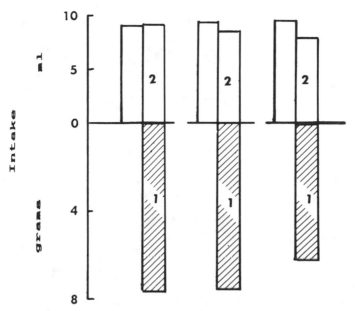

FIGURE 3. Intake of 2 *M* glucose (rising bars), with or without a prior meal of laboratory chow (descending bars). The data were taken at varying degrees of body-weight reduction: left to right, 5%, 8%, and 14%. (From Mook *et al.*[21] Reprinted with permission from *Physiology and Behavior.*)

When offered glucose after a "satiating" meal of chow, the rats drank just as much as if the meal of chow had never occurred, at all deprivation levels. (Control observations showed that the glucose drinking was not a matter of thirst evoked by the chow.)

In other words, the systemic effects of a full meal of laboratory chow made no contact at all with the mechanisms that limit glucose intake, thus determining size of the glucose meal. Here is a case, then, in which meal size for a second commodity simply takes no account of the inhibitory signals that have already been generated by the first one. Yet we know that intake of concentrated glucose is also under postingestive control.[22] Therefore, when the glucose is offered, the initial inhibitory process triggered by the chow must be disengaged or ignored, and a different one heeded instead. We see again our principle: The diet determines which postingestive signals the system will respond to. The stimulus properties of a commodity can switch specific satiety signals into, or out of, the controlling system.

Some Objections

Before going on, we should consider some obvious artifacts that might attend these findings. First, there is palatability. If a rat is satiated for commodity A, but willing to ingest commodity B, our first thought is that B may simply be more palatable than A. Clearly, however, our findings do not depend on an increment in palatability. First, rats sated for glucose will accept laboratory chow—a less palatable commodity, by any measure we choose. Second, we recall that diluting the milk diet, which decreased its palatability, actually increased the size of the meal — all in the rat that was "satiated" for glucose even before the milk was offered.

Second, various commentators have suggested that sensory-specific satiety[23,24] can account for our findings. It cannot. We tested it by administering an intragastric load of 2 M glucose, by-passing the oral cavity. Like a self-administered oral load, such a gastric load leaves the rat unwilling to drink any more glucose, but willing to take a substantial meal of powdered carbohydrate or of chow.[25] The specificity is postingestive, not orosensory.

An Alternative Model

The findings we have discussed — and our recurring principle that the internal conditions for satiety are diet-dependent — imply a conception quite different from the one in FIGURE 1. In FIGURE 4, we show a different way of looking at the system, one that seems to us to fit the facts better.

The diet, as stimulus, may drive ingestive behavior (but see below). However, it also sets up a specification of what the internal conditions for satiety are to be. Ingestion continues until the present internal state, P, matches the specified state, S.

The specification is variable. It may involve a correlate or consequence of salt absorption, *if* the rat is tasting salt — but only then. If the rat is eating chow, the system may specify one set of postingestive events as necessary to end the bout. If the rat is drinking glucose, it may specify a quite different set of postingestive events — ones to which the meal of chow, just completed, makes no contribution. That could explain the fact that a full meal of chow does not at all reduce the size of a subsequent meal of glucose solution.

The figure does not assign a role to internal excitatory signals, simply because their role is unclear. We know that for some foods (but not others[19]), meal size depends on degree of prior deprivation, so signals correlated with deprivation must be doing something — sometimes. They might affect the rat's internal state P. They might cooperate with some foods (but not others) to set the specification S; later we will see some evidence that this can happen. They might modulate the gain of the feedback loop. There are other possibilities, too; but we just do not yet know.

Most important, we notice that the figure does not assign any fixed, noncontingent role to internal inhibitory signals. A given internal signal may be heeded when the rat is eating one food; but the same signal may be quite ignored by the same rat moments later, when another food is offered instead. Postingestive signals, in other words, are not inhibitory per se. Their effects are gated by the oral stimulus.

We show the oral stimulus in FIGURE 4, then, as "gating" the effects of postingestive signals, by setting a specification with which they are compared. We also show it as encouraging feeding in its own right, as in FIGURE 1. But looking at the rest of the figure, we are led to wonder: Do we need that arrow? (And so we break the arrow with a question mark in the figure.) Might the effect of oral factors on ingestion be accounted for by the specification process only, and not by a direct effect of the stimulus on ingestive behavior? In the next section, we show that this can happen.

SHAM DRINKING: EVIDENCE FOR SPECIFICATION

The model in FIGURE 4 is compatible with the data. But can we test it? Is there direct experimental evidence that the system is organized in such a way? For some commodities, there is.

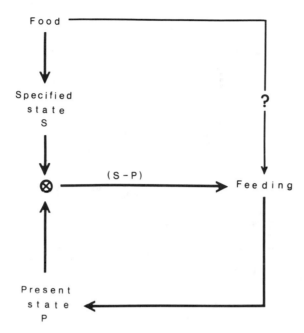

FIGURE 4. A modified view of feeding. (For explanation see text.)

Systemic Effects on Sham Drinking

In the experiments next to be described, the rats were sham-drinking through chronic esophageal fistulas so that material swallowed escaped through an opening in the throat. (We prefer this to the gastric-fistula preparation, for reasons discussed elsewhere.[26]) The rats were also prepared with chronic gastric cannulas to permit nutritional and hydrational maintenance, and also the experimental introduction of fluid into the stomach. Such intragastric infusions were given without disturbing the animal, through flexible tubing by which the rat was tethered to a remote syringe. All experiments were conducted in the morning, following overnight food and water deprivation in rats maintained at about 80% body weight. Each day the rat was offered fluid (the composition of which might vary from day to day) and was permitted to sham drink. Over the rest of the day, the rats were fed a milk-based liquid diet intragastrically by an automatic pumping system.

FIGURE 5 (filled circles) shows the quantities sham-drunk when the rats were offered water, or a low or a high glucose concentration, on different sessions after food and water deprivation.[27] Sham intake is very much higher than normal intake throughout. (These are asymptotic values for each fluid, observed after a transitional period during which the function gradually assumes its final form.[11,27])

In these studies, the rats were both food- and water-deprived, that is, both hungry and thirsty. In a further experiment, we isolated hunger as a controlling system by inhibiting thirst. Gastric preloads of water were administered before the drinking bout. Volume was adjusted individually, so that for each rat it sufficed to inhibit spontaneous water intake altogether (and for convenience, we will speak of this simply as "inhibiting thirst").

In nonthirsty rats the function looks quite different, as the open circles in FIGURE

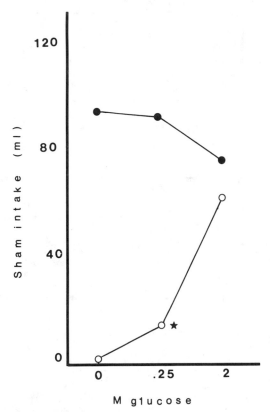

FIGURE 5. Sham-drinking of water or glucose solution in food- and water-deprived rats (filled circles) and in rats food-deprived but hydrated (open circles). (Data from Mook and Wagner.[27])

5 show. Sham-drinking at high concentrations is only slightly lower than in nonhydrated rats; but at the low concentration it is much reduced. In fact it hardly exceeds normal intake. Again these points represent asymptotic performance and are stable over repeated sessions. Observations with intermediate points (not shown) show a monotonic increasing function across the concentration range.[12,27,28] Therefore, hydrating the animal before the session not only inhibits water sham-drinking, but also depresses responsiveness to glucose solutions at low concentrations.

Stimulus Potency or Specification?

Now let us focus on the sham-drinking response to a low glucose concentration, 0.25 *M* (an approximately isotonic solution), shown by the star in the figure. Sham intake, as we see, is low but not negligible at that concentration in nonthirsty rats.

The low sham intake reflects a sustained, though small, bout of ingestion at the beginning of the session, then cessation of drinking. This cessation is not a delayed effect of the water preload, because if we *introduce* a delay between preload and test, the course of the sham-drinking bout remains the same. (Nor is it a nonspecific effect of the preload, for preloads of isotonic saline rather than water do not reduce sham intake nearly as much [not shown].)

Therefore, the early cessation of sham-drinking must reflect some suppressant effect of early lapping on later lapping—in other words, a purely oral satiety. And the difference between the two functions in FIGURE 5 shows that the rapidity of onset of this oral satiety is moduated in turn by hydrational status. But how, and why, does systemic hydration lead to this early cessation of drinking? The hydrated rate sham-drinks a modest amount, and then stops. Why does it stop so soon, or at all?

We see two possibilities.

1. Systemic hydration might set the potency of the oral stimulus for eliciting and maintaining ingestion. It might, for instance, affect the palatability of the solution.[29] A rat that is both hungry and thirsty might find even a dilute glucose solution very palatable indeed, and so drink copiously. After systemic hydration, the rat might find the solution only moderately palatable, and so sham-drink only a little before quitting. That account, of course, sees ingestion as driven by the oral stimulus itself.
2. Systemic hydration might set a specification. As sham-drinking progresses, orosensory feedback accumulates. Perhaps the accumulating feedback is compared with a reference value, or specification, that determines how much feedback is necessary to end the bout.

Notice that if there is such a specification, then its value must be set jointly by stimulus intensity and internal state. This follows from the data in FIGURE 5. If the taste is weak *and* the rat is hydrated, sham intake is quite low. However, if the taste is intense *or* if the rat is thirsty, sham intake is much higher. If sham intake reflects in turn the setting of a reference value, then that value itself must be responsive both to taste and hydrational status. If so, we have another model case of our principle: The oral stimulus (in conjunction with internal status) sets the necessary conditions for cessation of the bout.

Possibilities (1) and (2) are quite different. The first possibility is concerned with how potent the oral stimulus is now, and hence how much drinking the rat will do in response to it. The second—the specification idea—says that the system keeps track of how much drinking the rat has done. It then compares accumulated orosensory feedback with a reference value, asking "Has enough feedback accrued?" and ends ingestion when it has.

The two possibilities can be separated by the following three-stage procedure. Suppose that (1) a hungry-and-thirsty rat is allowed to sham-drink a moderate quantity of glucose before receiving its systemic water load. Then (2) the water load is administered, and (3) sham-drinking is allowed to continue. The control condition simply omits the first of these stages, and so we ask: What is the effect of the initial sham-drinking, done before the water load is given, on sham-drinking after it is given?

Now the two ideas make different predictions. Suppose the potency (e.g., the palatability) of the oral stimulus is decremented by the water load. Now it is only a moderately potent stimulus and will support only a modest ingestive bout. But such a bout, modest though it may be, should still occur. Sham intake after the load should be unaffected by sham-drinking that occurred before it. (We ignore for now the possible effects of adaptation, habituation, and the like. We will address these later.)

The reference-value account makes a different prediction. The controlling system has already received a substantial amount of oral feedback from the initial sham-drinking bout. Now suppose that the water load adjusts the system so that only a small accumulation of feedback signal is needed to shut off ingestion. If that amount of signal has already accumulated, then intake should cease immediately after the water load is delivered.

And that is what happens (FIG. 6). This time individual data are presented, to show that the conclusion holds for every rat without exception.

Look first at the open rising bars (the control condition). Here the intragastric water load was given before any sham-drinking was permitted. The rats then sham-drank moderate amounts, just as they did under the same conditions in FIGURE 5 above.

However, matters were different if the rats had already sham-drunk the solution in appreciable quantities (descending bars) before the water load was administered. Then, after the water load was delivered, further sham intake was negligible in every rat but one, and greatly reduced in that one (shaded rising bars).

These data suggest that the effect of the water load was to decrease the total amount of orosensory feedback that was required to bring sham-drinking to an end. Certainly the load did not just affect the potency of the oral stimulus itself. If it did only that, then the gastric load should bring the solution down to a fixed level of potency and the rat should sham-drink the same volume after the load, whether it has already done some sham drinking or not.

But that is not what happens. After intragastric hydration, the rat sham-drinks its moderate amount and then stops — *unless* an appreciable amount of sham drinking has already occurred. If it has, then the rat drinks no more after being hydrated. Clearly, then, the rat must not only consider its present state and the present stimulus, but

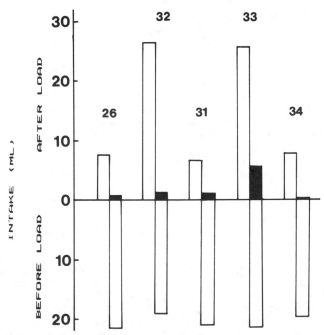

FIGURE 6. Sham intake of glucose after an intragastric water load (ascending bars), with or without a period of glucose sham drinking before the load (descending bars). (From Mook, Wagner, and Schwartz.[30] Reprinted by permission of *Appetite*.)

must also take account of the sham drinking it has already done when those circumstances are imposed.

Finally, notice that such a system has exactly the properties required by our revised model in FIGURE 4. It sees ingestion as driven, not by the oral stimulus per se, but by a mismatch between an existing state and a specification or reference value, which the oral stimulus helps to set.

Orosensory Feedback – The Response, Not the Taste

What then is the oral feedback signal? Is it an accumulation of gustatory input? No. FIGURE 7 shows a replication, with one variation, of the three-stage procedure: (1) sham-drinking permitted, (2) an intragastric water load, and (3) more sham-drinking permitted. The results are the same as those just described. Under the control condition (which simply omits stage 1 as before), the usual modest amount of glucose sham-drinking occurs (open rising bars). But if the rat has already sham-drunk before the gastric load is given (descending bars), then glucose sham-drinking after the load is virtually abolished (shaded rising bars). The difference is that in this case, the *initial* sham-drinking (descending bars) was of plain water, with no sweet taste at all.[30]

How can this be? A period of sham-drinking water does not by itself make rats unresponsive to glucose (not shown). And a systemic water load by itself obviously does not, as shown by the control condition. But if the water load comes *after* a period of sham-drinking (even without the sweet taste), then the sweet solution, when offered

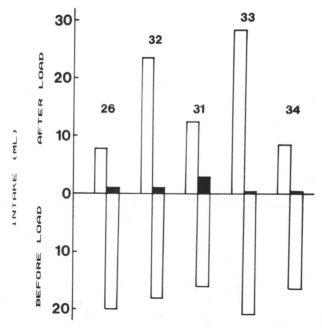

FIGURE 7. Sham intake of glucose after an intragastric water load (ascending bars), with or without a period of water sham drinking before the load (descending bars). (From Mook, Wagner, and Schwartz.[30] Reprinted by permission of *Appetite*.)

for the first time in the session, is refused. The rat approaches the cylinder, takes a few laps — and walks away.

We see only one possible interpretation: (1) The intragastric water load decrements the total amount of oral feedback required to end the bout, so that only a modest amount of oral feedback is needed to shut ingestion off. (2) The sham-drinking the rat has already done, before the load is given, contributes to that oral feedback signal. (3) Lapping water can provide all the oral feedback necessary. (This also rules out possible effects of habituation, adaptation, and the like in the previous experiment.) As a result, a rat that is severely food deprived can be made behaviorally satiated for a palatable food by the administration of nothing but water.

This finding is confusing, and a metaphor might help make it clear. Even a well-hydrated rat will sham-drink modest amounts (20 ml or so) of dilute glucose, *unless* it has already sham-drunk that modest amount when it receives hydration. In the latter case, it is as if the rat said, "I am well hydrated now, so I should only do a modest amount (X) of drinking in response to this sweet fluid. But I've already done X amount of drinking. True, I was drinking water, not glucose, but I'm not considering that. I have done the *amount of drinking* that is appropriate and am entitled to stop."

If the feedback signal is not gustatory, what is it? We do not yet know. Clearly the system is responsive to some consequence of the act of lapping. That consequence might be proprioceptive; it might depend on nonspecific tactile and/or thermal input from the tongue, or it might reflect a tally of motor commands. But it does not require the sweet taste or, indeed, any taste at all. Therefore, taste does not drive the ingestive response directly, at least in this case. It affects it only indirectly, in that taste, together with hydrational status, sets the amount of oral feedback that is "specified" as adequate to end the bout.

SUMMARY AND SPECULATION

We have looked at two sets of experiments. One dealt with the postingestive conditions for satiety. The other looked at the conditions for the "oral satiety" that can make sham-drinking self-limited.

What ties these two lines of research together is the notion of a "specification," or reference value, with which the existing state of affairs is compared. And in both contexts, we find that the reference value is taste-dependent. In other words, oral stimuli determine what that reference value will be. They determine what it is that has to happen before ingestion shuts down. Oral stimuli specify what the adequate systemic conditions for satiety will be, in normal feeding, drinking, or salt-solution intake. Similarly, oral and hydrational factors jointly specify the amount of *oral* feedback required to end a bout of glucose sham-drinking. We are back to the principle we began with: The oral stimulus specifies the adequate conditions for cessation of the bout.

If this suggested organization is at all close to the mark, we may have to rethink some cherished assumptions. First, it will no longer make sense to look for "the mechanisms of satiety" in the abstract. The fact is that an animal may be satiated for *this* and ravenously hungry for *that*, at the same time.

Second, the adequate conditions for satiety are diet-dependent. This suggests another role for the oral stimulus, in addition to — or instead of — the ones we listed at the outset: It sets the necessary conditions for satiety. Rather than seeking a fixed set of satiety signals — where they originate, what triggers them, how they get to the brain, and what they do there — we need to know how the food specifies the conditions for satiety, how the specification is compared with the present state, and how a mismatch between them takes hold of the feeding response.

Third, a virtual axiom in this literature is that sweet-solution drinking is driven by taste. But if we are right, glucose sham-drinking is not driven by the sweet taste at all (however transformed), but by a mismatch between the amount of orosensory feedback obtained and the amount required to end ingestion. Taste plays a role, and an important one, but not the ones conventionally assigned to it, at least in the cases we have considered here.

Finally, let us end on a speculative but also optimistic note. Many times in this discussion we have spoken of the system as "gating" the response to internal cues, switching them into or out of the controlling system, telling our rats which such signals to heed and which to ignore. We have emphasized that those gates are controlled by oral cues, but they could be controlled by other factors as well, environmental or cognitive ones, for instance.

As one example, consider the work of Collier and his colleagues.[31] A rat may take a meal of enormous size if the cost of an ingestive bout is very high. To do that, the rat must ignore systemic signals that would end the bout much earlier if the environmental constraints were less stringent. A system like that of FIGURE 4, which allows systemic signals to be heeded or ignored, seems to be the kind of system that Collier's compelling demonstrations require.

As another example, consider a rat encountering an unfamiliar food. It nibbles, taking a small amount and then stopping, whereas, if eating a familiar food, it might take in much more. Presumably the rat is monitoring something — so many bites or laps, or so much gastric fullness, or whatever — and stopping ingestion when whatever it is that is monitored reaches a criterial value. And the criterial value is set low, whatever the animal's internal state may be; the absence or weakness of internal "satiety signals" is ignored. Why? Because the food is unfamiliar — a cognitive control.

Finally, the human "restrained eater"[32] is presumably doing the same sort of thing. The criterial value is set low, not by oral factors, but by a deliberate decision ("This is all I'm allowed"), and again, internal signals are ignored.

The fact is that students of human feeding disorders are quite familiar with the concept of heeding, or ignoring, internal signals. They too speak of these signals as "gated," not by orosensory cues but by (for example) conscious decision. If we psychobiologists recognize that we too are studying gating systems, perhaps we will find new points of contact between our laboratories, the cognitive and sociopsychological laboratories, and the clinic.

ACKNOWLEDGMENTS

I thank Sue Wagner and Lisbeth Schwartz for assistance and colleagueship, and Emilie Rissman for her comments on a draft of the manuscript.

REFERENCES

1. ERNITS, T. & J. CORBIT. 1973. Taste as a dipsogenic stimulus. J. Comp. Physiol. Psychol. **83:** 27–31.
2. SCLAFANI, A. J. 1980. Dietary obesity. *In* Obesity. A. J. Stunkard, Ed. Saunders. Philadelphia.
3. SMITH, G. P. & J. GIBBS. 1979. Postprandial satiety. *In* Progress in Psychobiology and Physiological Psychology. J. M. Sprague & A. N. Epstein, Eds.: 179–242. Academic Press. New York.

4. TEITELBAUM, P. & A. N. EPSTEIN. 1962. The lateral recovery syndrome: Recovery of feeding and drinking after lateral hypothalamic lesions. Psychol. Rev. **69:** 74–90.
5. MOOK, D. G. & C. L. CSEH. 1981. Release of feeding by the sweet taste in rats: The influence of body weight. Appetite **2:** 15–34.
6. ADOLPH, E. F. 1947. Urges to eat and drink in rats. Am. J. Physiol. **151:** 110–125.
7. MOOK, D. G. & N. J. KENNEY. 1977. Taste modulation of fluid intake. *In* Drinking Behavior. Plenum Press. New York.
8. MOOK, D. G., J. A. BRANE & J. A. WHITT. 1983. "De-satiation": Reinstatement of feeding in glucose-satiated rats. Appetite **4:** 125–136.
9. MOOK, D. G., C. A. BRYNER, L. D. RAINEY & C. L. WALL. 1980. Release of feeding by the sweet taste in rats: Oropharyngeal satiety. Appetite **1:** 299–315.
10. EPSTEIN, A. N. & E. STELLAR. 1955. The control of salt preference in the adrenalectomized rat. J. Comp. Physiol. Psychol. **48:** 167–172.
11. MOOK, D. G., R. CULBERSON, R. J. GELBART & K. McDONALD. 1983. Oropharyngeal control of ingestion in rats: Acquisition of sham-drinking patterns. Behav. Neurosci. **97:** 574–584.
12. GEARY, N. & G. P. SMITH. 1985. Pimozide decreases the positive reinforcing effect of sham fed sucrose in the rat. Pharmacol. Biochem. Behav. **22:** 787–790.
13. JANOWITZ, H. D. & M. I. GROSSMAN. 1949. Some factors affecting the food intake of normal dogs and dogs with esophagostomy and gastric fistula. Am. J. Physiol. **159:** 143–148.
14. BLASS, E. M. & W. G. HALL. 1976. Drinking termination: Interactions among hydrational, orogastric, and behavioral controls in rats. Psychol. Rev. **83:** 356–374.
15. YOUNG, R. C., J. GIBBS, J. ANTIN, J. HOLT & G. P. SMITH. 1974. Absence of satiety during sham feeding in the rat. J. Comp. Physiol. Psychol. **87:** 795–800.
16. MOOK, D. G. 1963. Oral and postingestive determinants of the intake of various solutions in rats with esophageal fistulas. J. Comp. Physiol. Psychol. **56:** 645–659.
17. MOOK, D. G., J. A. BRANE, L. R. KUSHNER & J. A. WHITT. 1983. Glucose solution intake in the rat: The specificity of postingestive satiety. Appetite **4:** 1–9.
18. MOOK, D. G., L. GONDER-FREDERICK, P. H. KEATS & R. L. MANGIONE. 1984. "De-satiation" produced by liquid diet in rats satiated for glucose solution. Physiol. Behav. **32:** 875–877.
19. MOOK, D. G., J. A. BRANE & J. A. WHITT. 1983. Effects of food deprivation on intake of solid and liquid sugars in the rat. Appetite **4:** 259–268.
20. MOOK, D. G. 1988. On the organization of satiety. Appetite **11:** 27–39.
21. MOOK, D. G., J. A. BRANE, L. GONDER-FREDERICK & J. A. WHITT. 1986. Satieties and cross-satieties for three diets in the rat. Physiol. Behav. **36:** 887–895.
22. McCLEARY, R. A. 1953. Taste and postingestion factors in specific-hunger behavior. J. Comp. Physiol. Psychol. **46:** 411–421.
23. ROLLS, B. J. 1979. How variety and palatability can stimulate appetite. Nutr. Bull. **5:** 78–86.
24. ROLLS, B. J., E. A. ROWE & E. T. ROLLS. 1982. How sensory properties of food affect human feeding behavior. Physiol. Behav. **29:** 409–417.
25. MOOK, D. G., S. DREIFUSS & P. H. KEATS. 1976. Satiety for glucose in rat: The specificity is postingestive. Physiol. Behav. **36:** 897–901.
26. MOOK, D. G. & S. WAGNER. 1987. Preparation and maintenance of rats with chronic esophagostomy and gastric cannula. Physiol. Behav. **39:** 417–420.
27. MOOK, D. G. & S. WAGNER. 1988. Sham drinking of glucose solutions in rats: Some effects of hydration. Appetite **10:** 71–87.
28. WEINGARTEN, H. P. & S. D. WATSON. 1982. Sham-feeding as a procedure for assessing the influence of diet palatability on food intake. Physiol. Behav. **28:** 401–407.
29. CABANAC, M. 1971. Physiological role of pleasure. Science **173:** 1103–1107.
30. MOOK, D. G., S. WAGNER & L. A. SCHWARTZ. 1988. Glucose sham drinking in the rat: Satiety for the sweet taste without the sweet taste. Appetite **10:** 89–102.
31. KANAREK, R. & G. COLLIER. 1979. Pattern of eating as a function of the cost of the meal. Physiol. Behav. **23:** 141–145.
32. HERMAN, C. P. & J. POLIVY. 1980. Restrained eating. *In* Obesity. A. J. Stunkard, Ed. Saunders. Philadelphia.

DISCUSSION

PROFESSOR ELIOT STELLAR (*University of Pennsylvania, Philadelphia, PA*): Doug, that's just splendid work and it's going to turn us all upside down. One question: In the case where you prehydrated the animal and it's not drinking glucose solutions that it might be drinking under other circumstances, have you asked yourself whether it would still find those solutions rewarding, as in the case of running rapidly for them in a runway for one tiny lick or working on a high-ratio operant schedule, cases in which ingestion is really minimal or not at stake?

DR. MOOK (*University of Virginia, Charlottesville, VA*): It's an excellent question, Eliot. We're doing those experiments now; I don't have enough data to be able to say anything.

DR. DAVID BOOTH (*University of Birmingham, Birmingham, U.K.*): You're illustrating beautifully, it seems to me, the problems we have with humble scientists dealing with the concept of joint necessity. Magicians don't have any problem, mathematicians don't, even engineers don't, but we're trained to think of one cause, one effect. My conditions have blown that out of the water. Now you're blowing it out of the water with other phenomena that might involve the same mechanism. I suggest your diagram can be even more simplified than removing the direct stimulation from the food to feeding by removing the intermediate specified state in your other channel, from the food to the summing point. I suggest that needs to be replaced by an integration point like the neurophysiologists' notion of a neuron that only fires when it gets two inputs, two inputs of different sorts; when you have both these conditions met, then you get the output from the neuron, this integrator with a threshold. What I'm suggesting, therefore, is that your various examples may be reflecting the joint necessity for the behavior of a particular sensory input and a particular postingestional input which may have been learned, or as with the salt appetite case, may be unlearned. There is a joint necessity for stimulation with a simple stimulus from both sources and perhaps no more complicated a thing than state specification.

DR. MOOK: I quite agree that we're talking about joint necessity, but I think what we have to remember is not to confuse joint necessity with synergy. That's why I don't like the idea of a summing point. Now, I may be misusing an engineering convention here. I had intended my little circle with the cross through it simply to indicate some point where data come together and something is done, but I see it not as addition, which would imply synergy, but as subtraction, which would imply comparison. To have that going, I think you do need the specified state as well as the present state. What I'm suggesting is that an animal, as it eats, asks Have I done enough eating? What it means by enough eating may depend on a number of things: diet and deprivation conditions among them. But what I see driving ingestion now is a difference and not a sum.

DR. PAUL ROZIN (*University of Pennsylvania, Philadelphia, PA*): As this model was taking shape, I was wondering why nature would have done it that way. One of the appeals of the simple homeostatic model is that energy regulation is the bottom line in some sense. Why would such a system develop; why would a system this complex have been selected for? Why not select for a system that focuses basically on the issue of monitoring energy and controlling intake, which is the model in the minds of most people here. Could you speculate on the advantage that this system might have over the more commonly accepted one?

DR. MOOK: I think it is a myth, first of all, that energy intake is regulated, or even that energy balance is. Even if it is, it has to be regulated by the same effector system and the same orifice, if you will, that is also called into the service of regulating all kinds of other things, intake of various nutrients, for instance. One reason the system might have evolved this way—just as sensory-specific satiety could have evolved and could help serve that same purpose—is simply to insure that an omnivore, like the rat, that needs a number of dietary commodities has a reasonable shot at getting them all.

I think, even more than that, that an animal should be able to meet acute but specific nutritional emergencies, and again it's the example of salt appetite that comes to mind. An animal that needs salt ought not to eat indiscriminately. It ought to find salt, and it ought to have a way of setting the regulatory system so that adequate intake, when it does find salt, is assured. I guess my short speculation is that this might be an easier way of designing an animal than designing a whole battery of separate specific hungers in parallel.

DR. ARTHUR CAMPFIELD (*Hoffmann-La Roche Inc., Nutley, NJ*): I think you've set the stage for the one slide I didn't see. That is, the animal is doing his sham-drinking of water, and you deliver an intragastric load of differing sizes at different times, and you can terminate the behavior to the glucose as opposed to a second trial. The hypothesis is that the number of licks are being counted, and the check on having licked enough is made when the glucose solution is encountered. So, it seems as if you could apply your intragastric load to rehydrate your animal during sham-drinking, and before you get to the 200 licks he'll lick just 100 more times and stop. That would be a prediction of your theory. I think it would be convincing to see that as you arrange the volume of intragastric load.

DR. MOOK: We are doing those sorts of experiments now. The reason that I didn't emphasize experiments that look like that is that, again, it becomes very easy to mistake the findings for a synergy between oral and stomach factors, whereas I think what we're seeing is something quite different.

DR. CAMPFIELD: If you have animals sham-drinking solutions and then you administer glucose, you don't have much of an effect. However, if you let them sham-drink for a while and then apply CCK or glucose or other supposed satiety signals, these signals have a rather robust effect in terminating sham-drinking. That's another set of data you need to think about in terms of your model. It may not just be taste, it may be the postingestional effects coming back to modify this behavior.

Dietary-Induced Overeating[a]

ANTHONY SCLAFANI

Department of Psychology
Brooklyn College of the City University of New York
Brooklyn, New York 11210

The role of the diet in promoting overeating and obesity has been the subject of con-siderable interest. The degree to which dietary factors stimulate overeating in humans is difficult to establish with certainty because of the many factors that influence human food intake. Research with laboratory animals, however, clearly demonstrates that certain diets induce overeating and obesity. These diets include: high-carbohydrate diets, high-fat diets, and mixed diets containing a variety of fat- and sugar-rich foods, that is, the "supermarket" or "cafeteria" diet. As reviewed in several publications,[1-3] the effects of these dietary regimes on food intake, body weight, and body fat depend on a number of variables, including the strain, age, and sex of animals studied. This paper will focus on new findings concerning the orosensory and physicochemical properties of food that promote overeating in laboratory rats and the role of diet palatability in this effect. Note that the emphasis here is on overeating rather than obesity; dietary manipulations that produce obesity in the absence of overt hyperphagia will not be discussed.

DIET PALATABILITY

Diet-induced overeating is often attributed to the palatability of the food. According to one view, animals are very attracted to the taste, odor, and/or texture of certain nutrients (i.e., sugar and fat) and this causes them to overeat foods containing these nutrients. Until recently this view has not been critically evaluated, nor has the palat-ability concept been rigorously assessed.

Palatability, which literally means "pleasing to the palate or taste," is now thought by many investigators to be determined not only by the orosensory properties of food but also by the food's postingestive actions and the physiological state of the animal.[4-6] In particular, the pleasantness of a food is not an invariant property of the food's flavor but can change as the animal associates the flavor with the postingestive effects of the food. Conditioned taste aversion studies illustrate how palatability can be conditioned in a negative direction by postingestive events. For example, the rat's innate preference for sweet taste is turned into an aversion if the taste is paired with an experimentally induced nausea.[7] More relevant to the present discussion are conditioned increases in food palatability produced by the postingestive nutrient effects of foods. It is now well documented[8,9] that pairing a flavor with the intragastric or intravenous infusion of a nutrient can condition a robust preference for that flavor (see below).

[a] The preparation of this paper was supported by grants from the National Institute of Dia-betes and Digestive and Kidney Diseases (DK-31135) and the Faculty Research Award Program of the City University of New York.

In light of these considerations, the degree to which the palatability of carbohydrates and fats is due to an unconditioned response to their orosensory properties or to a learned response based on their postingestive nutritive effects is open to question. A more fundamental issue concerns the overall impact of diet palatability on food intake. Is it the case that increasing diet palatability stimulates hyperphagia? Conversely, are diets that promote hyperphagia necessarily palatable to animals? To answer these latter questions, it is necessary to independently measure food intake and palatability. As described in detail elsewhere,[6,10] a number of techniques have been developed to measure the hedonic response of animals to food stimuli. One simple procedure for assessing the relative palatability of different foods is the two-choice preference test. Although there may be exceptions,[11] in general if food A is preferred to food B than it can be assumed that A is more palatable to the animal than B.

HIGH-CARBOHYDRATE DIETS

The influence of dietary carbohydrates on food intake and body weight has been extensively investigated. In these studies the carbohydrate content of the diet has been manipulated in one of two ways. In the "composite diet" method, animals are fed a single, nutritionally complete food that varies in carbohydrate type and/or amount. In the "diet option" method, animals are given a choice between a pure carbohydrate source and a nutritionally complete diet. Previous research using these dietary regimes has focused almost exclusively on sugars, especially sucrose.[12] Recent work, however, demonstrates that sugars are not the only carbohydrates to promote overeating, and that the physical form of the carbohydrate is as important as its type in determining food intake.

Carbohydrate Type and Form

The feeding response to high-sugar diets depends in large part on whether the diet is in a hydrated or dry form. For example, rats fed a 32% sucrose or glucose solution, in addition to chow and water, typically consume 60% of their calories as sugar and increase their total caloric intake by about 25%.[13] When fed the same sugar in powdered form, on the other hand, rats eat less sugar and display little or no overeating.[13] Similarly, rats fed a high-sucrose composite diet rarely increase their caloric intake when the diet is in a dry form,[10,12] but are hyperphagic when the diet is presented as a liquid or wet mash.[14]

Comparable effects have been obtained with other carbohydrates. Rats given a solution of hydrolyzed starch (e.g., 32% Polycose) as an option to a chow diet increase their caloric intake as much or more as rats given a sucrose or glucose solution.[13] Polycose also stimulates overeating when it is presented in a hydrated form as a semisolid gel but not when it is presented as a dry powder.[13] These latter findings demonstrate that it is the water content, not liquid form *per se*, that is the important determinant of the hyperphagic response to carbohydrates.

Even pure starch can promote overeating if it is presented in a hydrated form. In one study rats fed chow and a separate source of corn starch as a 32% starch gel consumed more starch and total calories than did rats fed the corn starch as a dry powder.[15] Similarly, rats fed a high-starch composite food in semiliquid form consumed about 20% more calories and gained more weight than rats fed the same food in dry form.[14,16,17] In addition to hydration, the feeding response to starch is affected by the type of starch (raw versus pregelatinized) and method of cooking and mixing used.[16,17]

This may be related to the fact that the digestion of starch is influenced by cooking and gelatinization.[18]

Although hyperphagia and obesity can be obtained with hydrated starch diets the effects are not as pronounced as those obtained with sugar and Polycose diets. For example, compared to rats fed a Polycose gel, rats fed a starch gel consumed less carbohydrate (57.4 vs. 76.0 kcal/day), fewer total calories (82.5 vs. 95.9 kcal/day), and gained less weight (38.0 vs. 69.4 g/30 days).[15] Thus, food intake is influenced by both the type and form of carbohydrate included in the diet: sugars and hydrolyzed starch increase food intake more than raw starch, and hydrated carbohydrate diets increase food intake more than dry diets. An important consequence of the latter effect is that a hydrated starch diet may produce as much or more hyperphagia as a dry sugar diet.

Carbohydrate Taste and Palatability

The hyperphagia obtained with high-sugar diets has often been attributed to the sweet taste of sugar. The finding that Polycose solutions, which are minimally sweet to humans, produce as much overeating in rats as do sugar solutions initially suggested that taste was *not* an important factor in carbohydrate-induced hyperphagia.[19] Subsequent studies, however, revealed that rats, unlike humans, can taste starch-derived polysaccharides and find the taste very palatable.[10] It is possible, then, that the overeating produced by sugar and polysaccharide solutions is "driven" by the palatable sweet and "starchy" tastes, respectively, of these solutions. Alternatively, it may be the postingestive consequences of polysaccharides and sugars that are primarily responsible for the hyperphagia.[20]

In order to distinguish between the influence of taste and postingestive factors in carbohydrate-induced hyperphagia, it is necessary to experimentally dissociate these factors. One way this has been accomplished is by using an "electronic esophagus" preparation. In this preparation, rats are fitted with chronic intragastric catheters, and as they eat or drink normally by mouth a nutrient is automatically infused into their stomach. In this manner, rats can consume a sugar or Polycose solution without tasting the solution. In an initial experiment using this technique, rats were given 23 hr/day access to chow and flavored water.[9] On alternate days, as the rats drank water of one flavor (CS− flavor; e.g., grape-water), a 16% Polycose solution was infused intragastrically, and as they drank a different flavored water (CS− flavor; e.g., cherry-water) water was intragastrically infused. When subsequently given the choice between the two flavors the rats displayed an overwhelming preference (96%) for the CS+ flavor paired with the IG Polycose infusions. They also strongly preferred (89%) the CS+ flavor to plain water, which is notable because naive rats prefer plain water to the flavored water. Furthermore, the rats continued to display a near-total preference for the CS+ flavor during extinction tests when both the CS+ and CS− flavors were associated with water infusions. These findings, which were replicated using IG infusions of 32% Polycose,[21] clearly demonstrate that the postingestive effects of carbohydrate solutions can condition robust flavor preferences in rats.

In addition to conditioning a flavor preference, the intragastric Polycose infusions also increased total daily caloric intake. That is, the rats consumed 16% more calories when the CS+ flavor (and IG Polycose) was available compared to the baseline condition when only plain water and chow were available.[21] This finding demonstrates that in the absence of a sugary or starchy taste the postingestive consequences of carbohydrate solutions are sufficient to produce overeating. However, a much greater hyperphagic response was observed when the CS+ flavor was sweetened with saccharin. The addition of saccharin to the CS+ flavored water caused the rats to nearly double their CS+ intake (and consequently their IG Polycose intake) and to increase their total caloric intake from 16% to 37% above the baseline condition. Note that when rats orally consume a 32% Polycose solution, the addition of saccharin to the solution does not increase caloric intake; apparently the palatable taste of the Polycose is sufficient to generate a maximal hyperphagia response.[13] Taken together, these results indicate that the postingestive actions of carbohydrates can condition a strong flavor preference and induce overeating and that the presence of a sweet or starchy taste significantly enhances the flavor preference and hyperphagic response.

Carbohydrate Form and Palatability

As reviewed above, carbohydrates are most effective in promoting hyperphagia when they are presented in a hydrated rather than a dry form. This may occur because the addition of water to carbohydrate improves its palatability by enhancing its taste or texture. Alternatively, hydration may increase caloric intake because it facilitates carbohydrate digestion.

Adding water to carbohydrates does enhance its flavor, because rats show an immediate preference for hydrated forms over dry forms in short-term choice tests.[22,23] Improved flavor, however, cannot be the only reason that rats overconsume hydrated diets. This is indicated by the results of studies in which rats were given the choice (24 hr/day) between hydrated and dry carbohydrates in which the palatability of the hydrated form was decreased by the bitter adulterant sucrose octaacetate (SOA). In one experiment, rats initially preferred a dry sucrose powder to a 32% Polycose solution containing 0.05% SOA.[22] However, over the course of several days the rats switched their preference and consumed more calories as SOA-Polycose solution than as sucrose powder. This did not occur because the animals habituated to the bitter taste of the SOA.[22] Rather, it appears that the rats learned to prefer the SOA-Polycose solution based on its postingestive effects.

In related experiments conducted with high-starch composite diets, rats preferred the hydrated form of the diet to the dry form in two-choice tests. However, when given the choice of the dry diet and a hydrated diet adulterated with a high concentration (0.5%) of SOA, the rats show a persistent preference for the dry diet.[14,24] Yet, when only one diet was available, rats fed the SOA-adulterated, hydrated diet consumed more calories (≈8%) and gained more weight than did rats fed the dry diet. These data indicate that diet-induced overeating can occur even with an unpreferred food. It may be that adding water to the high-starch diet facilitates digestion and thereby reduces the duration of postprandial satiety. Thus, although not attracted to its bitter taste, rats may eat more of the SOA-hydrated diet than of the dry diet because of the diet's reduced satiating effect. Note that these results do not refute the idea that palatability can enhance the hyperphagic response to food. In particular, the overeating effect obtained with the SOA-adulterated, hydrated diet was rather small and less than that obtained in another experiment with a unadulterated hydrated diet (≈8% vs. 20%).[14,24]

HIGH-FAT DIETS

It is well documented that high-fat composite diets produce obesity in laboratory animals.[1-3] Such diets have inconsistent effects on caloric intake, however; that is, whereas in many experiments high-fat diets increased caloric intake by 10–20%, in other studies caloric intake remained unchanged even though the rats became obese.[25-28] Why high-fat diets produce hyperphagia in some studies but not in others remains uncertain, although differences in diet composition, and the strain, age, and sex of animal used may be contributing factors.

Fat Type and Form

The influence of the type and form of dietary fat on food intake is demonstrated by the results obtained in a recent study in which rats were fed a fat option diet, that is, chow plus a separate source of fat.[29,30] Rats given vegetable shortening as the fat option consumed more fat and total calories than did rats fed corn oil, and only the shortening-fed rats were hyperphagic relative to chow-fed controls (18% increase in caloric intake). Even greater hyperphagia was observed in a group of rats given vegetable shortening that was enriched with vitamins and minerals. These rats consumed 27% more calories than did chow-fed controls. The addition of the vitamins and minerals to the shortening may have permitted the rats to eat more fat because it provided them with micronutrients that were otherwise available only in the chow diet.

The importance of physical form on fat-induced hyperphagia is demonstrated by results obtained with fat emulsions.[29] Rats given a fat option in the form of a corn oil emulsion (35% oil in water) consumed significantly more fat and total calories than did rats fed pure corn oil. The rats fed oil emulsion also consumed more calories (23%), relative to chow-fed controls, than did the rats fed pure oil (10%). In contrast, rats fed vegetable shortening in an emulsified form (35% shortening in water) consumed slightly less fat and total calories than did rats fed pure vegetable shortening. Consequently, although pure vegetable shortening produced greater overeating than pure corn oil, when the two fats were in an emulsified form they produced similar hyperphagic effects.

In another recent study the effect of adding water to a high-fat composite diet was investigated; the fat was a mixture of corn oil and vegetable shortening.[14] Compared to a low-fat diet, the dry form of the high-fat diet produced overeating and obesity. The addition of water to the high-fat diet did not further increase caloric intake or weight gain. However, the rats fed the hydrated high-fat diet accumulated significantly more body fat than did the rats fed the dry high-fat diet. These results suggest that hydration of the high-fat diet improved the feed efficiency of the animal.

The above findings indicate that hydration has variable effects on the feeding response to high-fat foods. In some cases caloric intake is increased (i.e., with corn oil) and in other cases it is unchanged (i.e., vegetable shortening, composite diet). Of interest is the fact that adding water to high-fat foods, which decreases the caloric density of the foods, does not block the hyperphagia response. This argues against the idea that the hyperphagia and obesity produced by fat-rich diets is related to the high caloric density of these diets.

Fat Palatability

In addition to caloric density, the palatability of high-fat diets has been implicated as a cause of overeating. In early studies rats were found to prefer high-fat to low-fat foods in two-choice tests.[31,32] This preference is due in part to the texture of the high-fat foods, because rats also prefer chow diets made greasy or oily with the addition of noncaloric petrolatum or mineral oil. Yet, rats do not overeat diets adulterated with petrolatum or mineral oil, which indicates that texture alone does not account for the hyperphagia produced by high-fat diets.[31,32] Furthermore, when given the choice between a 30% fat (lard) diet and 30% petrolatum diet rats initially consumed comparable amounts of the two diets, but over the course of several days developed a strong preference for the high-fat diet.[32] This finding suggests that postingestive factors contribute to the animal's preference for high-fat diets. Direct evidence for the postingestive modulation of fat appetite is provided by recent experiments using the electronic esophagus preparation.[33] Rats that received intragastric infusions of a corn-oil emulsion as they drank flavored water developed a significant preference for that flavor over another flavor that was paired with IG water infusions.

Postingestive factors also appear to be largely responsible for the differential hyperphagic responses produced by different fat sources. As noted above, rats fed a corn-oil emulsion consumed more fat and total calories than did rats fed pure corn oil. Yet, when given the choice (24 hr/day) between the corn oil emulsion and pure corn oil, the rats initially consumed more calories as pure oil than as oil emulsion.[29] Over days the rats reduced their pure oil intake and increased their oil emulsion intake, but they never consumed more oil emulsion than pure oil (in calories). Other rats given the choice between pure corn oil and vegetable shortening initially displayed a slight preference for the oil but with repeated testing switched their preference and consumed more shortening than oil. Thus, in both cases the rats' initial preference, which was presumably based on the orosensory qualities of the fat sources, did not reflect their intake in long-term tests. This suggests that postingestive factors are more important than orosensory factors in determining the intake of different types and forms of dietary fat.

CAFETERIA DIETS

The supermarket or cafeteria diet is the most effective means of inducing hyperphagia and obesity in laboratory animals. In this dietary regime rats are fed a variety of commercially prepared foods (cookies, chocolate, cheese, condensed milk, etc.) in addition to chow. The cafeteria diet can produce as much as a 50–100% increase in caloric intake, which is considerably greater than the 15–30% increases observed with high-carbohydrate and high-fat laboratory diets.[34-36] Several factors may be responsible for the effectiveness of the cafeteria diet in promoting hyperphagia. Many of the foods included in the diet are high in fat and/or sugar and have a relatively high water content. In addition, the foods vary in their flavor and nutrient composition.

The importance of variety in promoting hyperphagia was suggested in the original cafeteria diet study[37] and has been confirmed in subsequent experiments.[34-36] These latter studies demonstrate that rats given simultaneous access to two or three cafeteria foods (e.g., bread, chocolate, crackers), in addition to chow, consumed more calories and gained more weight than did rats fed only one such food. Hyperphagia has also been produced by feeding rats a variety of lab chows that differ in their flavor and nutrient composition.[36] The hyperphagia effect obtained with the lab chows, however, is less than that produced by the cafeteria foods.[36]

Variety in the diet may enhance food consumption in different ways. Individual rats have specific food preferences and increasing the number of food items in the diet would improve the chance that all rats had a preferred food available.[34] The availability of different foods is also thought to promote overeating by counteracting the effect of monotony or "sensory-specific" satiety. Rats, like humans, consume more food in a meal when offered different tasting foods than when offered only a single food.[38] However, the importance of flavor variation *per se* in promoting overeating in long-term tests has been questioned. In one recent study rats were fed three diets that differed in flavor (taste, odor, texture) but not in nutritional composition, and a variety effect on food intake was not observed.[39] Because palatability is determined by both orosensory and postingestive factors, it may be that foods that differ only in flavor are not sufficiently different in palatability to obtain a variety effect.

Variety, while it contributes to the hyperphagia effect obtained with the cafeteria diet, is not the only factor involved. Two studies report that rats fed chow and only one cafeteria food (chocolate, cookies, crackers, or bread) consumed 50 to 70% more calories than did the chow-only control group.[34,35] In contrast, rats fed a chow plus pure fat (oil, vegetable shortening) or pure carbohydrate (sugar, Polycose, starch) option overeat by only 15 to 30% compared to controls.[13,15,29,30] To what degree it is the flavor or the nutritional composition of commercially prepared foods that promotes the greater hyperphagia effect remains to be determined.

A MULTIFACTOR MODEL

The findings reviewed above indicate that changes in both the nutrient composition and the physical form of the diet can influence caloric intake. As illustrated by the multifactor model in FIGURE 1, this influence can occur via a number of different paths. In this model the composition and form of the diet determines its orosensory properties, that is, its flavor (paths 1a and 1b in FIGURE 1). Flavor, in turn, determines the initial palatability of the diet (path 2). Palatability is then modulated by the postingestive actions of the diet (paths 3a and 3b). Thus, a food that is not particularly good tasting at first may become highly preferred as the animal associates its flavor with its nutritive effects. Relatively little is known about the physiological process involved in the postingestive conditioning of flavor preferences, but it appears to involve both preabsorptive and postabsorptive mechanisms.[8]

Food palatability, as determined by orosensory and postingestive factors, can promote overeating (path 4). This is illustrated by the finding that saccharin added to flavored water paired with intragastric Polycose infusions caused rats to significantly increase their caloric intake. Some overeating may occur, however, even with diets that are not very palatable, as in the case of the SOA-adulterated, high-starch diet.[24] In such cases, variations in diet composition or form may promote hyperphagia by facilitating the postingestive digestion and metabolism of food (paths 5a and 5b).

Hyperphagia will lead to the accumulation of body fat (path 6). As discussed elsewhere, the degree of obesity produced by a given amount of overeating may vary depending upon the animal's thermogenic response to the diet.[40] That is animals, partic-

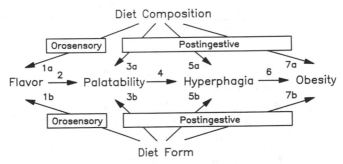

FIGURE 1. A multifactor model of diet-induced hyperphagia and obesity. See text for details.

ularly younger animals, may "waste" some of their excess caloric intake in the form of heat and thereby reduce the amount of energy stored as body fat. On the other hand, in some cases animals may improve rather then decrease their metabolic efficiency such that obesity develops in the absence of overt hyperphagia (path 7a and 7b). As noted previously, animals fed high-fat diets often become obese even though their caloric intake is not elevated.

Although this multifactor model of dietary-induced hyperphagia is based on results obtained with laboratory animals, many if not all of its features may be applicable to humans. In particular, food intake in humans may be affected by variations in both the physical form and the nutrient composition of foods. Thus, the total carbohydrate and fat content of foods may be less important than the specific type of carbohydrate and fat, and the form of the nutrient used in the diet. Some forms of starch, for example, may promote as much overeating as some forms of sugar or fat. Also food palatability in humans, like that in rats, may be a function of both the flavor and the postingestive effects of foods. In order to more completely understand normal and abnormal food preferences in humans, therefore, much more needs to be known about the processes involved in the postingestive conditioning of flavor preferences.

ACKNOWLEDGMENTS

The author thanks Dr. Francois Lucas for his helpful comments on this paper.

REFERENCES

1. KANAREK, R. B. & E. HIRSCH. 1977. Dietary-induced overeating in experimental animals. Fed Proc. **36:** 154–158.
2. SCLAFANI, A. 1980. Dietary obesity. *In* Obesity. A. J. Stunkard, Ed.: 166–181. Saunders. Philadelphia.
3. BLUNDELL, J. E. 1987. Nutritional manipulations for altering food intake: Towards a causal model of experimental obesity. Ann N.Y. Acad. Sci. **449:** 144–155.
4. SCLAFANI, A. 1990. The hedonics of sugar and starch. *In* The Hedonics of Taste. R. C. Bolles, Ed., Erlbaum Associates. Hillsdale, N.J. In press.
5. LEMAGNEN, J. 1987. Palatability: Concept, terminology, and mechanisms. *In* Eating Habits. R. A. Boakes, D. A. Popplewell & M. J. Burton, Eds.: 131–154. John Wiley & Sons. Chichester, England.
6. GRILL, H. J. & K. C. BERRIDGE. 1985. Taste reactivity as a measure of the neural control of palatability. *In* Progress in Psychobiology and Physiological Psychology. J. M. Sprague & A. N. Epstein, Eds.: 1–61. Academic Press. New York.
7. PELCHAT, M. L., H. J. GRILL, P. ROZIN & J. JACOBS. 1983. Quality of acquired responses to tastes by *Rattus norvegicus* depends on type of associated discomfort. J. Comp. Psychol. **97:** 140–153.
8. BOOTH, D. A. 1985. Food-conditioned eating preferences and aversions with interoceptive elements: Conditioned appetites and satieties. Ann N.Y. Acad. Sci. **443:** 22–41.
9. SCLAFANI, A. & J. W. NISSENBAUM. 1988. Robust conditioned flavor preference produced by intragastric starch infusions in rats. Am. J. Physiol. **255:** R672–R675.
10. SCLAFANI, A. 1987. Carbohydrate taste, appetite, and obesity: An overview. Neurosci. Biobehav. Rev. **11:** 131–153.
11. ROZIN, P. & D. ZELLNER. 1985. The role of Pavlovian conditioning in the acquisition of food likes and dislikes. Ann. N.Y. Acad. Sci. **443:** 189–202.
12. RAMIREZ, I. 1987. When does sucrose increase appetite and adiposity? Appetite **9:** 1–19.
13. SCLAFANI, A. 1987. Carbohydrate-induced hyperphagia and obesity in the rat: Effects of saccharide type, form, and taste. Neurosci. Biobehav. Rev. **11:** 155–162.

14. RAMIREZ, I. 1987. Feeding a liquid diet increases energy intake, weight gain, and body fat in rats. J. Nutr. 117: 2127–2134.
15. SCLAFANI, A., M. VIGORITO & C. L. PFEIFFER. 1988. Starch-induced overeating and overweight in rats: Influence of starch type and form. Physiol. Behav. 42: 409–415.
16. RAMIREZ, I. 1987. Diet texture, moisture and starch type in dietary obesity. Physiol. Behav. 41: 149–154.
17. RAMIREZ, I. 1987. Practical liquid diets for rats: Effects on growth. Physiol. Behav. 39: 527–530.
18. HOLM, J., I. LUNDQUIST, I. BJORCK, A-C. ELIASSON & N-G. ASP. 1988. Degree of starch gelatinization, digestion rate of starch in vitro, and metabolic response in rats. Am. J. Clin. Nutr. 47: 1010–1016.
19. SCLAFANI, A. & S. XENAKIS. 1984. Sucrose and polysaccharide induced obesity in the rat. Physiol. Behav. 32: 169–174.
20. GEISELMAN, P. J. & D. NOVIN. 1982. The role of carbohydrates in appetite, hunger and obesity. Appetite 3: 203–223.
21. ELIZALDE, G. & A. SCLAFANI. 1989. Flavor preferences conditioned by intragastric Polycose: A detailed analysis using an electronic esophagus preparation. Physiol. Behav. In press.
22. SCLAFANI, A. & M. VIGORITO. 1987. Effects of SOA and saccharin adulteration on Polycose preference in rats. Neurosci. Biobehav. Rev. 11: 163–168.
23. SCLAFANI, A., J. W. NISSENBAUM & M. VIGORITO. 1987. Starch preference in rats. Neurosci. Biobehav. Rev. 11: 253–262.
24. RAMIREZ, I. 1988. Overeating, overweight and obesity induced by an unpreferred diet. Physiol. Behav. 43: 501–506.
25. SCHEMMEL, R., O. MICKELSEN & J. L. GILL. 1970. Dietary obesity in rats: Body weight and body fat accretion in seven strains of rats. J. Nutr. 100: 1041–1048.
26. MALLER, O. 1964. The effect of hypothalamic and dietary obesity on taste preference in rats. Life Sci. 3: 1281–1291.
27. JEN, C. K. -L. 1988. Effects of diet composition on food intake and carcass composition in rats. Physiol. Behav. 42: 551–556.
28. OSCAI, L. B., M. M. BROWN & W. C. MILLER. 1984. Effect of dietary fat on food intake, growth and body composition in rats. Growth 48: 415–424.
29. LUCAS, F., K. ACKROFF & A. SCLAFANI. 1989. Dietary fat induced hyperphagia in rats as a function of fat type and physical form. Physiol. Behav. 45: 937–946.
30. ACKROFF, K., F. LUCAS & A. SCLAFANI. 1988. Dietary-fat induced overeating: Influence of fat composition. Ann. N.Y. Acad. Sci. This volume.
31. CARLISLE, H. J. & E. STELLAR. 1969. Caloric regulation and food preference in normal, hyperphagic, and aphagic rats. J. Comp. Physiol. Psychol. 69: 107–114.
32. HAMILTON, C. L. 1964. Rats' preference for high fat diets. J. Comp. Physiol. Psychol. 58: 459–460.
33. LUCAS, F. & A. SCLAFANI. 1989. Intragastric fat infusions condition flavor preferences in rats. Physiol. Behav. In press.
34. ROGERS, P. J. & J. E. BLUNDELL. 1984. Meal patterns and food selection during the development of obesity in rats fed a cafeteria diet. Neurosci. Biobehav. Rev. 8: 441–453.
35. ROLLS, B. J., P. M. VAN DUIJVENVOORDE & E. A. ROWE. 1983. Variety in the diet enhances intake in a meal and contributes to the development of obesity in the rat. Physiol. Behav. 31: 21–27.
36. LOUIS-SYLVESTRE, J., I. GIACHETTI & J. LE MAGNEN. 1984. Sensory versus dietary factors in cafeteria-induced overweight. Physiol. Behav. 32: 901–905.
37. SCLAFANI, A. & D. SPRINGER. 1976. Dietary obesity in adult rats: Similarities to hypothalamic and human obesity syndromes. Physiol. Behav. 17: 461–471.
38. ROLLS, B. J. 1979. How variety and palatability can stimulate appetite. Nutr. Bull. 5: 78–86.
39. NAIM, M., J. C. BRAND, M. R. KARE & R. G. CARPENTER. 1985. Energy intake, weight gain and fat deposition in rats fed flavored, nutritionally controlled diets in a multichoice ("cafeteria") design. J. Nutr. 115: 1447–1458.
40. ROTHWELL, N. J. & M. J. STOCK. 1982. Energy expenditure of 'cafeteria'-fed rats determined from measurements of energy balance and indirect calorimetry. J. Physiol. (London) 328: 371–377.

DISCUSSION

DR. JOHN DAVIS (*University of Illinois, Champaign-Urbana, IL*): I want to ask you a question about the hydrational effect. The impression I got was that you thought it was a texture effect. It occurred to me that by adding water you might make the molecules more accessible to the gustatory receptors, and in fact you're really stimulating them more effectively than you were before.

DR. ANTHONY SCLAFANI (*Brooklyn College, CUNY, Brooklyn, NY*): Certainly adding water to sugar or to Polycose enhances the gustatory effect and also enhances the texture effect. I'm less certain that it would affect the taste of the starch. It might be more of a textural effect. Adding water to all of these foods, we believe, increases the rate of digestion. In fact, we have evidence that you get a bigger plasma glucose response to the hydrated diet than you get to the dehydrated diet. So the postingestive conditioning effect is related to the rate of digestion, and adding water not only changes the orosensory qualities, but also the digestion of the food.

DR. ALLAN GELIEBTER (*St. Luke's–Roosevelt Hospital, New York*): Do you think there's a possibility that liquefying the diet enhances gastric emptying rate? If it does, you have an emptier stomach faster, and that could make the animal eat more.

DR. SCLAFANI: I think that there are a number of changes that occur when you add water and change the form of the diet. One change might be enhanced gastric emptying, another change is in the rate of digestion. There are gastric factors, intestinal factors, and postabsorptive factors involved. If we simply slow down the rate of absorption by adding acarbose, which is not supposed to affect gastric emptying, then we have a drastic effect on blocking conditioned preferences and decreasing intake. So, gastric emptying, I think, is important, but it's not the only element.

DR. GELIEBTER: Yes, I think you have an opportunity with your beautiful set-up to look at gastric emptying correctly.

DR. JOHN YOUNG (*Howard University, Washington, D.C.*): I want to ask you about the sex of your rats. My question relates to an old study of mine in which we gave rats powdered chow mixed with either Crisco or dextrose. We found that, sure enough, male rats would overeat and get fat on those diets, but females wouldn't.

DR. SCLAFANI: These are all female rats. I tend to use female rats, because we get stronger overeating effects with females than with males. I think there is a significant sex effect, and I think there's a sex–diet interaction. The effects are obtainable with both sexes, but we have used the sex that gives us the greatest effect.

DR. PAUL ARAVICH (*VA Medical Center, Hampton, VA*): How does this relate to anorexia nervosa? For example, instead of treating desperately low-weight anorectics parenterally with i.v.-infused fluids, would your hypothesis predict that intragastric intubations paired with particular foods or distinctive flavors might promote a conditioned appetite for those flavors or foods?

DR. SCLAFANI: Our prediction is that people would respond in the same way and that you could produce conditioned preferences in humans as well. David Booth presented data several years ago with intravenous infusions of nutrients, so it doesn't necessarily have to be intragastric. From an experimental point of view, I think the intragastric is the most convenient and the most readily manipulated because the stomach is acting as a reservoir. I should add, that it took us a long time to get conditioned preferences. If you put too much nutrient in, if you put it in too fast, if it's too concentrated, you get conditioned aversions. It's very easy to get aversions with food, so you have to be very careful with the rate of nutrient delivery.

DR. DAVID BOOTH (*University of Birmingham, Birmingham, U.K.*): Three short points. The intravenous infusion was in fact done in collaboration with Dr. Nicolaidis with conditioned preferences to odors. Second, food technologists' literature about starch and flours shows you actually leach out the readily digestible forms of the starch from the flour starch by adding water, even in the cold, which fits with your idea that it improves digestion. Third, on the previous questioner's point, it would be even better just to have low carbohydrate drinks readily available to the anorectic so that repletion could take place voluntarily.

Stress-Reducing Effects of Ingesting
Milk, Sugars, and Fats

A Developmental Perspective

ELLIOTT M. BLASS, DAVID J. SHIDE,
AND ARON WELLER

Department of Psychology
Johns Hopkins University
Baltimore, Maryland 21218

This chapter deals with two issues and both are addressed in the title. One issue concerns the remarkable diminution of stress and pain through ingesting small volumes of certain classes of foods. This issue focuses on how food affects behaviors other than ingestion, and thereby allows evaluation of mechanisms underlying feeding control without perturbing the feeding system. The second aim is to demonstrate that analysis of feeding mechanisms from a developmental perspective provides insights into the dynamics of feeding and its consequences that might otherwise continue to go unnoticed through the study of caged adults eating laboratory food in social isolation. These insights can be achieved because, first, the developing animal's behavioral repertoire is often simple relative to that of adults, thereby allowing behavioral isolation and analysis of its component parts. Second, because the social setting in which infant suckling and feeding occur is enormously complex, the effects of various social and physiological factors, alone and in combination, can be assessed through the more accessible motor components of suckling.

The developmental approach also has the virtue of neurological simplification and plasticity that are provided by animals whose central neurology is incomplete relative to its adult target, and whose central organization has not been fully specified. Moreover, feeding patterns during early development have yet to become fully designated. This invites studying the ontogeny of feeding neurology in conjunction with the development of specific appetites and cuisines. Both of these goals can be achieved by carefully considering neonatal behavioral ecology, especially in the nest, and by judiciously manipulating the ecology within the physical and behavioral parameters established by the mother. Thus, concerning the development of neurology subserving suckling, the earliest form of ingestion, Pedersen et al.[1] were able to identify structural changes in the olfactory system based upon Pedersen's[2,3] earlier demonstrations of behavioral change linked to particular olfactory experiences. In a similar vein, it was only after Hall[4-6] isolated the behavioral properties of feeding and drinking systems in infant rats that he was able to identify the neurology underlying sensory, perceptual, and motivational characteristics of these systems[7] in ways that simply have not been previously achieved.

The Hall and Pedersen studies are pioneering research in the development of ingestive neurology. Both share the same strategy of first analyzing behavioral phenomena empirically and then isolating the different behavioral components to identify the underlying neurological mechanism. Both the Pedersen and Hall studies capture the strength of the developmental approach for behavior and brain analysis of ingestion. Pedersen's identified the determinants of infant rats first suckling bout[2] and then the neurology that managed it.[1] By manipulating certain facets of the infant's presuckling experience, Pedersen *et al.*[3] were able to identify different olfactory afferents that gained access to the motor programs that manage search behaviors leading to nipple attachment. Thus, from the perspective of identifying a functional neurophysiology of the earliest form of mammalian ingestion, Pedersen and her colleagues and Leon, Coopersmith, and others[8] have made a significant start.

Hall's analysis, because his animals had never eaten or drunk or experienced dehydration or negative energy balance, serves as a point of reference for analysis in older animals that have eaten different foods on different occasions in different places, and whose functional central neurology presumably reflects these influences as well as those cast by maturation.

Studying infants in the nest also provides a complexity that can offer insights into the dynamics of feeding development as it naturally occurs in a social setting. This setting, which is composed of the infant, its siblings, parents, and nest, is what determines the consequences of the feeding act. That is, a change in state that accompanies milk ingestion occurs within the matrix of maternal contact and sibling competition and contact, among other factors. The present chapter defines the ways in which the mother in particular influences current state and future actions of her young through: (a) her own behavior vis á vis her infants; (b) the stimulus layout provided by her skin, fur, and nipples; and (c) her delivering milk to her infants. Having identified these potential spheres of influence, we then focus on the effects of intraoral infusions of milk, sugars, fats, and polysaccharides on stress-related actions in infant rats and, when appropriate, humans. We next consider some of the properties of one system that is peripherally activated by milk infusion, namely, cholecystokinin. The chapter then identifies potential lasting effects of these early experiences on later food preferences.

MATERNAL BEHAVIORAL INFLUENCES IN EARLY FEEDING

FIGURE 1 presents a photograph of an anesthetized rat mother with her suckling infants. The photo makes a number of important points concerning the possible ways in which mothers, through the nursing setting, can influence infant state and subsequent behavior. Before nursing, rat mothers vigorously lick the anogenital region of the young.[a] This is remarkably activating and apparently rewarding as infant rats prefer an odor associated with such stimulation.[11] Anogenital stimulation is also predictive because it normally occurs when rat mothers hold their infants in opposition to their nipples in such a way that the pup smells the scent that is coating the mother's nipple. Anogenital stimulation of rat pups two to three days of age or amphetamine injection in the presence of an odor allows infant rats to suckle washed nipples bearing that odor[3] and cause rats to markedly prefer the odor in which stimulation occurs. There are longer lasting influences on noningestive behaviors as well. According to Fillion and Blass,[12] the above scenario of repeated anogenital stimulation by the dam as it occurs naturally before nursing influences adult male rat sexual behavior. In short, the mother, through timing and activation surrounding nursing–suckling exchanges,

---

[a] According to Moore,[9,10] licking is distributed differentially according to gender. Rat mothers direct far more licking to male offspring and this is determined by infant hormonal status.

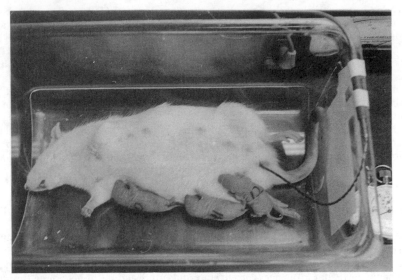

FIGURE 1. Photograph of an anesthetized rat dam and three of her suckling pups. The stimulus array presented by the dam is sufficient for nipple location and apprehension and for serving as a reward in instrumental learning in infant rats. (From Hall, Cramer and Blass[42]; used by permission.)

casts short and long-term influences on: (1) suckling during development, (2) later food selection,[13] (3) later reproductive behavior, and (4) possibly sibling recognition.[14]

TACTILE INFLUENCES AND MECHANISM OF ACTION

Contact is a second means of influence that is often, though not necessarily always, related to infant ingestion. During the first 7–10 days after birth, rat mothers spend over 90% of the time in contact with their litters. The significance of contact has been well documented, of course, in human and nonhuman primates.[15-17] Its importance has recently been established in rodents as well. In particular, contact *per se* with an anesthetized virgin female has the same calming effect for isolated 5–10-day-old rats as does *suckling* without milk delivery.[18] This effect is not blocked by the opioid antagonist naltrexone and is thought therefore to be mediated by nonopioid mechanisms.[19] Contact as a source of comfort has also been recently demonstrated in rats to influence choice behavior.[20] These nonopioid rewarding properties now permit assessments of interactions between mechanisms of reward that utilize opioid pathways, as in mother's milk, for example, and those that do not.

MILK AND ITS INFLUENCE ON RAT PUP BEHAVIOR

The third logical way in which the mother can influence her infants' behavior directly or indirectly is through the milk that she transfers to her infants. In principal, there are multiple pathways through which this can be effective. The suckling act itself, including that aspect concerning withdrawing milk from the nipple is a potential source of reward.[21,22] Nonspecific colligative effects of filling an empty stomach or upper GI tract thereby easing gastric contractions is a second possible candidate. A third general class of changes concern alterations caused by milk in the GI tract. In this regard recent studies in our laboratory have demonstrated a role for cholecystokinin (CCK) in infant quieting.[23] Fourth, caloric repletion in the growing animal may also influence state. A fifth pathway through which milk can influence behavior is through the milk constituents themselves. In particular, morphiceptin, released through β-casomorphine found in the milk of mothers of a number of species may quiet distressed infants.[24] Finally, and this represents our major focus, milk and its constituents of fats and sugars may work directly through taste pathways to cause central opioid release that: (1) is rewarding to infants, (2) relieves distress, and (3) exerts analgesic effects in both rat and human infants.

The developmental approach, therefore, assesses the consequences of ingestion on behavior. The newborn, because of its vulnerability and established behavioral responses to stress, is well suited for revealing the positive consequences of milk or other substance ingestion. Feeding is cast in a broader ecological perspective by this approach as it integrates the act with its naturally arising consequences. According to Leon and his colleagues,[25,26] the mother leaves the nest after nursing owing to thermal reasons and rat pups are abandoned, therefore, for varying periods of time. The issue that arises concerns the effectiveness of milk in helping maintain behavioral equilibrium in nested pups or in pups that have been isolated from the nest as may happen when the dam leaves suddenly or when a pup is dropped during transport from site to site.

The rest of this communication will show that milk can quiet crying pups and elevate their pain thresholds. We will also demonstrate that fat, polycose, and sucrose have calming and antinociceptive effects that are mediated through opioid pathways. These substances are also rewarding to infants as judged by their ability to serve as unconditioned reinforcing stimuli in a classical conditioning paradigm. This property too is opioid dependent.

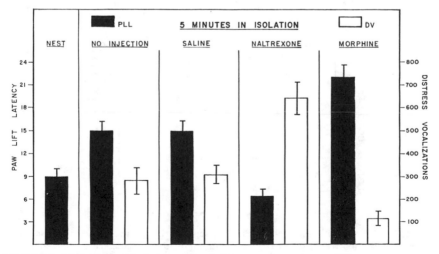

FIGURE 2. The effects of isolation, morphine and naltrexone on pain threshold (filled bars) and distress vocalizations in infant rats. (From Kehoe and Blass[18]; used by permission.)

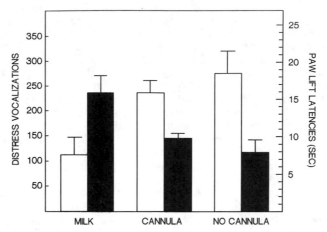

FIGURE 3. The effects of milk on paw-lift latency and distress vocalizations and their reversal by naltrexone. (From Blass and Fitzgerald[28]; used by permission.)

The basis of this approach was the demonstration by Kehoe and Blass[27] that distress vocalizations in infant rats were quieted by morphine administration and markedly elevated by naltrexone, an opioid antagonist. Moreover, isolation was analgesic as it elevated paw-lift latency, an effect that was also normalized by naltrexone. This suggested release on an endogenous opioid that affected both social stress (i.e. isolation) and pain pathways. Evidence for such a relationship is presented as FIGURE 2, in which a negative correlation is expressed between distress vocalizations and paw-lift latency. This correlation implies that an endogenous substance serves to reduce crying level and enhance paw-lift latency. Disruption of this relationship by naltrexone implies opioid mediation.

Because endogenous opioids appeared to modulate these responses in isolated rats,

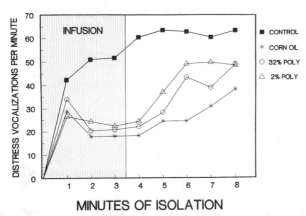

FIGURE 4. The effects of intraoral infusions of vegetable oil, Polycose, and water control on distress vocalizations (expressed as Dv/min). Infusion period is represented by the shaded portion of the figure. Quieting persisted well beyond infusion termination. (From Shide and Blass[29]; used by permission.)

we asked how mothers might ease stress. It followed that contact alone effectively prevents or eases stress because severing contact induced vocalization and establishing contact quieted pups and other infants. The unexplored issue concerned the possible biological role of milk and its constituents in affecting the infant's ability to cope with social or physical stress.

Intraoral infusions of milk had the same effects as morphine injections in 10-day-old rats. As shown in FIGURE 3 they markedly reduced distress vocalizations and increased paw-lift latencies. As with morphine, both effects were naltrexone reversible, suggesting that the taste of milk and its postabsorptive consequences palliated distress and pain by acting through opioid mechanisms. The possible postingestive effect was especially significant because of the dam's protracted absences from the nest.[28]

FIGURE 4 shows that one of the major constituents of milk, fat, has a quieting effect that also persists well past infusion termination. In fact, this long-term quieting effect is characteristic of all substances that appear to calm via an opioid pathway. This is also shown for Polycose. Both of these substances quiet and both effects are naltrexone reversible.[29]

Like morphine, the infused substances also influence positive reward systems and this sphere of influence was also blocked by opioid antagonists. In particular, rats exposed to intraoral infusions of vegetable oil or sucrose in the presence of a mildly aversive orange odor chose this scent over a normally preferred one following conditioning. As shown in FIGURE 5, this was reversed by naltrexone administration at the time of conditioning, suggesting that these substances achieved their effect through the release of endogenous opioids via taste pathways.

Naltrexone administration at the time of testing also eliminated preference for an odor associated with morphine or corn oil but not sucrose. This suggests for the former two substances that the odor is causing the release of endogenous opioids associated with either the injection or oil infusion. The basis of the negative sucrose finding is currently being sought. The general point is clear, however. A number of substances that are known to exert their influence through opioid mechanisms can be associated

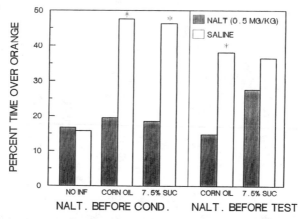

FIGURE 5. Mean percentage time spent on the side of an open test arena that contained orange-scented chips. Rats had previously had orange scent paired with water, sucrose, or vegetable oil. The latter two substances caused a change in performance. This change would be blocked by naltrexone pretreatment at the time of conditioning (left panel). For animals conditioned with corn oil, preference expression could also be blocked with naltrexone administered at the time of testing (D. J. Shide and E. M. Blass, unpublished observations).

with olfactory or gustatory[30] stimuli that are otherwise aversive or neutral. We suggest that in some cases the stimulus that became positive through opioid association sustains choice behavior and protracts ingestion because it now causes the release of endogenous opioids.

These findings are similar to ones obtained with milk infusions but differ in one important regard. Whereas sucrose, polycose, and corn oil exerted an immediate effect on vocalization rate, milk's effect was delayed by 2–3 min.[28] This suggested, at least for the milk that we used (commercial half and half), the possibility of a postingestive effect as opposed to a possibly pure taste phenomenon with sucrose, for example.

To the extent that milk's effectiveness was of a delayed onset but was protracted, we sought a mechanism through which this could occur. Cholecystokinin (CCK) presented a viable candidate because it is thought to be released from the gut by proteins and fats[31] and as a slowly released peptide could have a protracted effect. If milk was working though endogenous CCK among other substances, it followed that some of milk's effects should be obtained by administering exogenous CCK.

According to Weller and Blass,[23] intraperitoneal injections of CCK markedly suppressed ultrasonic vocalizations but did not affect paw-lift latencies. Thus stress and pain systems, although influenced by endogenous and exogenous opioids, are at some level independent and differentially vulnerable to hormonal changes that might naturally occur with milk ingestion.

CCK effects on noningestive behavior are not limited to distress vocalization in preweaning rats. In fact, CCK is rewarding as judged by the clear preference shown in infant rats for an odor associated with very low doses (0.25 and 0.5 μg/kg BW) of CCK. The preference was blocked by the established peripheral antagonist L364,718. We are currently evaluating the action of the antagonist on behaviors that are influenced by infusions of various substances. It is of some interest that the preferences exhibited

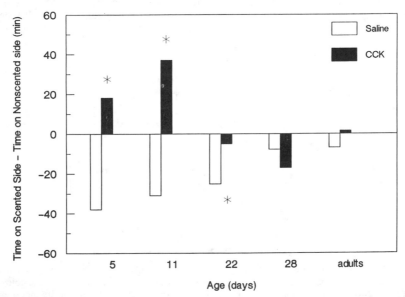

FIGURE 6. Difference in time spent over the orange-scented side versus the unscented side of a maze by rats of various ages that had previously had the orange paired with i.p. injections of CCK or saline.

to an odor paired with CCK did not persist beyond weaning. Specifically, the conditioning effect was obtained in rats 5, 11, and 22 days of age but not in 28-day-old rats that normally would be spontaneously weaned by the dam (FIG. 6). This transition does not require infants to eat solid food at the time of weaning because infants living on mother's milk with a liquid diet supplement also did not exhibit the preference.[32]

Thus, concerning the long-standing debate about the status of CCK as a satiety mechanism,[33-35] the developmental studies strongly suggest that for rat pups, CCK is actually a substance that has rewarding properties in very low doses. In particular CCK can reduce crying and serve as a positive unconditioned stimulus in a classical conditioning paradigm. The fact that CCK in infants, as in adults, acts peripherally provides further grounds for accepting its possible physiological contribution at least prior to weaning. The point here is that there is nothing inherently aversive about the action of CCK. If this is true, then it may provide us with insights about the role for this peptide in ingestive behavior because of the change in status of CCK from rewarding to at least neutral.

DISTINCTIONS BETWEEN OPIOID- AND NONOPIOID-MEDIATED MATERNAL CHARACTERISTICS

We opened this communication with an in-principal distinction between those aspects of the nursing–suckling situation that were opioid-mediated versus those for which nonopioid pathways were the more likely mediators.

There are now two classes of evidence to suggest basic differences between the calm exerted through putative opioid systems versus nonopioid. One class is pharmacological. Naltrexone, at doses that fully reverse the behavioral effects of morphine administration or those caused by the intraoral infusions discussed here, was fully ineffective against quieting caused by maternal contact.[36] It is of interest in this regard, that even a high dose of naloxone (5 mg/kg), an opioid antagonist similar to naltrexone, had no effects on suckling behavior in rats 9–18 days of age. Second, the effects of oral-tactile versus oral–gustatory stimulation on the affective behavior of human infants differs remarkably.

FIGURE 7 presents data from Smith, Fillion, and Blass[37] that show the mean amount of crying exhibited by 1–3-day-old human infants before (filled histogram) or after (open histogram) intervention with either a pacifier (left panel) or sucrose for varying periods of time. In the case of sucrose, as little as two 0.1-ml deliveries of 12% sucrose, each separated by 60 sec, cast an enduring quiet in infants that had been crying for 25% of the baseline period or longer. In this regard, human and rat infant behaviors were quite similar (see FIG. 3). In contrast, even when human infants sucked a pacifier for 14 min, behavior changed after removal of the proximal oral tactile stimulation provided by the pacifier and crying resumed to baseline levels. This is informative because it demonstrates parallels and differences between putative opioid and putative nonopioid pathways. The parallels are that the calming effects are immediate (i.e., within 30 sec of introducing the proximate stimulus) and that they are sustained during stimulation. Differences, at present, focus on the source of stimulation. In both rat and human infants, tactile stimulation, as defined here, is nonopioid mediated. In rats, milk, sucrose, glucose, polycose, and vegetable oil (fat) are all opioid-mediated based on reversibility of effect with very low doses of naltrexone. In humans, based on the parallels in behavior with rat studies, it is now reasonable to infer opioid mediation of the calming effects of sucrose and glucose. Thus, channels for gaining access to opioid mediation differ from nonopioid channels. Also, the time course of decay is

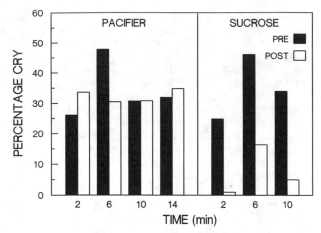

FIGURE 7. Percentage of time spent crying by 1–3-day-old human infants for the 5 min before (filled histogram) and following (open histogram) continuous sucking on a pacifier for 2, 6, 10, or 14 min (left panel) or tasting 0.1 ml 12% sucrose solution once every 2, 6, or 10 min.

different. Changes caused by very modest stimulation of sucrose last well after the taste has presumably worn off. This is not due to a postingestive effect. For tactile stimulation, the decay is immediate as crying resumes within seconds of pacifier removal. The means by which opioid and nonopioid processes are naturally integrated presents a fascinating problem for the development of affect in general and for ingestion in particular.

GENERAL DISCUSSION

These studies have identified certain consequences of ingestion on noningestive behaviors in developing animals. This approach can not help but broaden our appreciation for the larger behavioral pattern in which feeding is embedded and cause us to seriously evaluate the classes of nonphysiological (internal) influences and their mechanisms of action that may influence ingestive behavior quantitatively as well as qualitatively. Accordingly this discussion addresses three issues concerning effects of early ingestion on other behaviors and their mechanisms of actions. They are: (1) The reciprocity between taste systems and those mediating negative affective systems. (2) The emergent relationships between CCK, stress, and positive affect. (3) A model that conceptualizes the influence of stress on feeding and the contribution of opioid and nonopioid mechanisms to this process.

The Relationship between Taste and Stress

To our knowledge, the studies reported in this communication are the first to demonstrate a direct behavioral effect of a taste system on those concerned with pain or stress modulation. This is of particular interest from the perspective of developmental neurology because current technologies will allow identification of pain pathways that are affected by intraoral infusions of sugars, fats, and other substances. For much the same reason, these findings are of interest behaviorally because they establish a functional link through which we can appreciate larger consequences of ingestion. This possibility is placed in sharper relief by the recent finding of analgesic properties acquired by an odor associated with morphine injections.[38] The possible reciprocity between stress and feeding will be addressed below.

Relationship between CCK, Stress, and Positive Affect during Development

We have not yet sufficiently advanced this analysis to conclude with certainty that endogenous CCK, under normal conditions, has a calming influence in rats or any other species. A number of our findings have been informative to us, at least, even at this early stage of analysis. (1) CCK, even in very low doses, has a specific quieting effect on distress vocalizations. It does not affect pain thresholds. (2) CCK acts through a nonopioid pathway to achieve this effect. (3) CCK is also rewarding in rats 22 days of age and younger as judged by its capacity to become classically associated with an odor to induce an olfactory preference. (4) The demise of the ability of CCK to act as a positive reinforcing stimulus in rats 28 days of age and older. These last two sets of findings demonstrate that CCK is *not* intrinsically aversive and in fact is a substance that supports classical conditioning and has positive motivational properties. That is, a normally mildly aversive substance, by virtue of pairing with CCK, is now preferred. This association has caused the rat to overcome the substance's sensory properties.

The change in CCK's rewarding properties occurs at about the time that a rat mother generally weans her young, allowing her to nurse the litter conceived during the postpartum estrus.[39] We can not presently identify an experiential basis for the change in CCK's ability to sustain a preference. We know, however, that it is not the act of eating solid foods *per se* because 22-day-old rats that had been eating solids for 6–7 days exhibit a classically conditioned preference for CCK-associated odors. Moreover, solids do not have to be eaten during the period of 22–28 days of age in order for the preference to disappear. At a different level, one might argue that CCK had a role in helping combat the stress of isolation in suckling-age pups. That might be true, and to the extent that the weaning process is one of increasingly longer periods of absence from the dam, reduced effectiveness of CCK might help the transition. This must remain speculative at present in the absence of a measure that reflects social stress in weaning-age rats. Rate of ultrasonic vocalization is not helpful, because this behavior does not occur in albino rats beyond 15 days of age. It remains of interest, however, that, CCK undergoes a developmental shift from positive to neutral at the time when its physiological effects are becoming manifest in animals that are completing (sometimes abruptly in the case of the birth of a litter conceived during the postpartum estrous) their transition to direct feeding.

Reciprocities between Stress and Feeding

The reciprocity between feeding and stress systems discussed above is new and holds some potential for clinical insights into the relationship between stress and feeding and its nurturance during development. The apparent selectivity of opioid mediation of stress reduction by feeding and its relatively enduring effects take on special interest in light of the report by Vaswani *et al.*[40] that stressed rats preferentially overeat sweets and fats.

This combination of events, the general failure of opioids to enhance feeding of bland diets and of opioid antagonists to interfere with such eating (see Levine, this volume), gives rise to the conceptualization presented in FIGURE 8. The figure depicts a specialized feeding system for preferential ingestion of fats (f), polysaccharides (p), and sugars (s). Central to the figure is a motivational component for f, p, s that is influenced by opioid-mediated events arising either from tasting various substances, alone or in combination, or from stress systems. The outermost portions of the figure (i.e., those enclosed by solid lines) represent factors that have been identified as influencing ingestive behavior that can be operationally defined and experimentally manipulated. They are transduced into signals that gain access to stress and taste systems in the case of heat or isolation and f, p, s, respectively. Internal constraints arising in the oropharynx, the stomach, or from the more distal portions of the gastrointestinal tract are integrated through a comparator to interact antagonistically or synergistically with a feeding system activated to give rise to the integrated motivational state for seeking and eating fat, sugar, or polysaccharides. External constraints reflect the animal's appreciation of the dangers and demands of its environment that facilitate or temper any behavioral inclination including those to eat.

The systems within the dashed lines are inferred from the animal's behavior and from its susceptibility to opioid manipulation. Stress systems influencing feeding are inferred to be opioid modulated, as overeating induced by relatively mild stress can be blocked by opioid antagonists. Moreover, the output characteristics of the stress

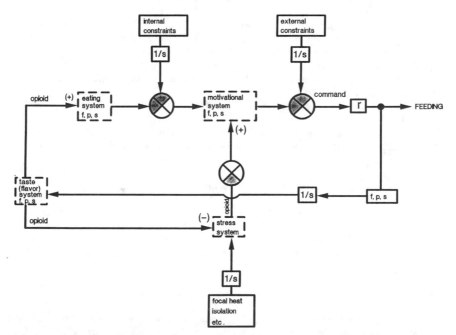

FIGURE 8. Conceptualization of a specialized opioid-mediated feeding system(s) for polysaccharides, and sugars that can be engaged by the flavor of fats, polysaccharides, or sugars or by stress. See text for description of various facets of the figure.

systems, namely vocalization and pain limen, can be modified by ingested substances through pathways that have been shown to be opioid mediated.

The inclusion of an eating system separate from a motivational system is based on Grill's[41] important studies in decerebrate rats that have demonstrated that intake in these animals is sensitive to the same gustatory parameters as in intact rats. The assumption followed here is that these factors coalesce with internal state to give rise to a supraordinate coordinative motivational state. In the present conceptualization this state can be reached through the opioid-mediated taste pathway alone or through the opioid-mediated stress system alone or in combination. It is important to note that the taste system can directly affect the stress system through opioid pathways according to the model as inferred from our studies cited above. Finally, for the purposes of exposition, the constraints imposed by the environment are seen to load into the model conceptually at a supraordinate cognitive level independent of the animal's motivational state. One could conceptualize this as a constraint across states that integrates with the state to give rise to the command to ingest at a particular rate, which is recalibrated through the act and its consequences.

It is worth mentioning a number of factors that have been omitted from the figure. The contribution of CCK has not been presented. We know its effects on stress-related activities in infants but not in adults as they relate to ingestion. In adults, of course, CCK is a well-established inhibitor of feeding. Also, the contribution of morphiceptin or other exorphins, either derived from mother's milk or, in adults, from certain foodstuffs rich with glutins, has not been sufficiently studied to provide a mechanism of action. Finally, and most importantly, we have not indicated the contact points of this system with the environmental stimuli to which it could become associated. To the extent that ingestion of these substances can be associated with neutral or even mildly aversive environmental stimuli and that the association or expression can be prevented via opioid blockade,[38] the points of contact with the model must be elucidated. This is especially important from the developmental perspective.

The developmental contribution to this pattern and to the social quality of eating holds considerable potential. The suckling act itself is governed by nonopioid mechanisms, yet the enduring calming of milk is opioid mediated. Contact and milk delivery occur in social settings, the character of which is determined by the mother, the infant itself, and siblings. Given that certain human feeding disorders such as bulimia and anorexia nervosa seem to reflect developmental and familial tensions, particularly as they surround a meal, an analysis of the dynamics of feeding, using FIGURE 8 as a possible point of departure, may prove useful.

SUMMARY

A developmental approach to the study of feeding is proposed that considers social complexity and its biological mediation as core determinants of later ingestive patterns. Evidence is presented for opioid-mediated influences of milk and its major constituents and for nonopioid-mediated channels for contact comfort. Consideration of these factors might help us better understand some of the determinants of human feeding disorders such as bulimia and anorexia nervosa.

REFERENCES

1. PEDERSEN, P. E., C. A. GREER & G. M. SHEPHERD. 1986. Early development of olfactory

function. *In* Handbook of Behavioral Neurobiology: Developmental Psychobiology and Developmental Neurobiology. E. M. Blass, Ed. Vol. **8:** 163–204. Plenum Press. New York.

2. PEDERSEN, P. E. & E.M. BLASS. 1982. Prenatal and postnatal determinants of the first suckling episode in albino rats. Dev. Psychobiol. **15:** 349–355.

3. PEDERSEN, P. E., C. L. WILLIAMS & E. M. BLASS. 1982. Activation and odor conditioning of suckling behavior in three day old albino rats. J. Exper. Psychol.: Anim. Behav. Proc. **8(4):** 329–341.

4. HALL, W. G. 1979. Feeding and behavioral activation in the infant rat. Science **205:** 206–209.

5. HALL, W. G. 1979. The ontogeny of feeding in rats: I. Ingestive and behavioral responses to oral infusions. J. Comp. Physiol. Psychol. **93:** 977–1000.

6. HALL, W. G. & T. E. BRYAN. 1980. The ontogeny of feeding in rats: II. Independent ingestive behavior. J. Comp. Physiol. Psychol. **94:** 746–756.

7. HALL, W. G. 1989. Neural systems for early independent ingestion: Regional metabolic changes during ingestive responding and dehydration. **103(2):** In press.

8. COOPERSMITH, R. & M. LEON. 1988. The neurobiology of early olfactory learning. *In* Handbook of behavioral neurobiology: Developmental Psychobiology and Behavioral Ecology. E. M. Blass, Ed. Vol. **9:** 283–308. Plenum Press. New York.

9. MOORE, C. 1984. Maternal contributions to the development of masculine sexual behavior in laboratory rats. Dev. Psychol. **17:** 347–356.

10. MOORE, C. & G. A. MORELLI. 1979. Mother rats interact differently with male and female offspring. J. Comp. Physiol. Psychol. **93:** 677–684.

11. SULLIVAN, R. M., M. A. HOFER & S. C. BRAKE. 1986. Olfactory-guided orientation in neonatal rats is enhanced by a conditioned change in behavioral state. Dev. Psychobiol. **19:** 615–623.

12. FILLION, T. J. & E. M. BLASS. 1986. Infantile experience determines adult sexual behavior in male rats. Science **231:** 729–731.

13. LEON, M., B. G. GALEF & J. H. BEHSE. 1977. Establishment of phermonal bonds and diet choice in young rats by odor pre-exposure. Physiol. Behav. **18:** 387–391.

14. HOLMES, W. G. 1988. Kinship and the development of social preferences. *In* Handbook of behavioral Neurobiology: Developmental Psychobiology and Behavioral Ecology. E. M. Blass, Ed. Vol. **9:** 389–413. Plenum. New York.

15. BOWLBY, J. 1969. Attachment and Loss. Vol. 1. Basic Books. New York.

16. HARLOW, H. F. & H. F. HARLOW. 1965. The affectional systems. *In* Behavior of Non-human Primates. A. M. Schrier, H. F. Harlow, and F. Stollnitz, Eds. Vol. 2. Academic Press. New York.

17. HARLOW, H. F. & H. F. HARLOW. 1962. Social deprivation in monkeys. Sci. Am. **207:** 137–146.

18. KEHOE, P. & E. M. BLASS. 1986. Opioid-mediation of separation distress in 10-day-old rats: Reversal of stress with maternal stimuli. Dev. Psychobiol. **19:** 385–398.

19. BLASS, E. M., T. J. FILLION & A. WELLER. 1988. Separation of opioid from nonopioid mediation of affect in neonatal rats. Manuscript under review.

20. ALBERTS, J. R. & B. MAY. 1984. Nonnutritive thermotactile induction of filial huddling in rat pups. Dev. Psychobiol. **17:** 161–181.

21. KENNY, J. T. & E. M. BLASS. 1977. Suckling as an incentive to instrumental learning in preweanling rats. Science **196:** 898–899.

22. KENNY, J. T., M. L. STOLOFF, J. P. BRUNO & E. M. BLASS. 1979. The ontogeny of preference for nutritive over nonnutritive suckling in albino rats. J. Comp. Physiol. Psychol. **93:** 752–759.

23. WELLER, A. & E. M. BLASS. 1988. Behavioral evidence for cholecystokinin-opiate interactions in neonatal rats. Am. J. Physiol. **255:** R901–R907.

24. TESCHEMACHER, H. 1987. Casein-derived opioid peptides: Physiological significance? Adv. Biosci. **65:** 41–48.

25. LEON, M. 1986. Development of Thermoregulation. *In* Handbook of Behavioral Neurobiology: Developmental Psychobiology and Developmental Neurobiology. E. M. Blass, Ed. Vol. **8:** 297–322. Plenum. New York.

26. LEON, M., P. G. CROSKERRY & G. K. SMITH. 1978. Thermal control of mother-young contact in rats. Physiol. Behav. **21:** 793–811.

27. KEHOE, P. & E. M. BLASS. 1986. Opioid-mediation of separation distress in 10-day-old rats: Reversal of stress with maternal stimuli. Dev. Psychobiol. **19:** 385–398.

28. BLASS, E. M. & E. FITZGERALD. 1988. Milk-induced analgesia and comforting in 10-day-old rats: Opioid Mediation. Pharmacol. Biochem. Behav. **29:** 9–13.

29. SHIDE, D. J. & E. M. BLASS. 1989. Opioid-like effects of intraoral infusions of corn oil and polycose on stress reactions in 10-day-old rats. Behav. Neurosci. In press.

30. KEHOE, P. & E. M. BLASS. 1986. Behaviorally functional opioid systems in infant rats: I. Evidence for olfactory and gustatory classical conditioning. Behav. Neurosci. **100(3):** 359–367.

31. ANIKA, S. M. 1983. Ontogeny of CCK satiety. Eur. J. Pharmacol. **89:** 211–215.

32. WELLER, A. & E. M. BLASS. 1989. Cholecystokinin conditioning in rats: Ontogenetic determinants. Behav. Neurosci. In press.

33. VERBALIS, J. G., M. J. MCCANN, C. M. MCHALE & E. M. STRICKER. 1986. Oxytocin secretion in response to cholecystokinin and food: Differentiation of nausea from satiety. Science **232:** 1417–1419.

34. SWERDLOW, N. R., D. VAN DER KOOY, G. F. KOOB & J. R. WEGNER. 1983. Cholecystokinin produces conditioned place-aversions, not place-preferences, in food-derived rats: Evidence against involvement in satiety. Life Sci. **32:** 2087–2093.

35. HOLT, J., J. ANTIN, J. GIBBS, R. C. YOUNG & G. P. SMITH. 1974. Cholecystokinin does not produce bait shyness in rats. Physiol. Behav. **12:** 497–498.

36. BLASS, E. M., T. J. FILLION & A. WELLER. 1988. Separation of opioid from nonopioid mediation of affect in neonatal rats. Manuscript in preparation.

37. SMITH, B. A., T. J. FILLION & E. M. BLASS. 1988. Orally mediated opioid and non-opioid reward mechanisms in human infants. Presented at the International Society of Developmental Psychology meeting, November, 1988. Toronto, Canada.

38. KEHOE, P. & E. M. BLASS. 1989. Conditioned opioid release in ten-day-old rats. Behav. Neurosci. In press.

39. GILBERT, A. N., D. A. BURGOON, K. A. SULLIVAN & N. ADLER. 1983. Mother–weanling interactions in Norway rats in the presence of a successive litter produced by postpartum estrous. Physiol. Behav. **30:** 267–271.

40. VASWANI, K., G. A. TEJWANI & S. MOUSA. 1983. Stress induced differential intake of various diets and water by the rat: The role of the opiate system. Life Sci. **32:** 1983–1996.

41. GRILL, H. & K. BERRIDGE. 1984. Taste reactivity as a measure of the neural control of palatability. *In* Progress in Physiological Psychology and Psychobiology. A. Epstein & J. Sprague, Eds. Academic Press. New York.

42. HALL, W. G., C. P. CRAMER & E. M. BLASS. 1977. Ontogeny of suckling in rats: Transitions toward adult ingestion. J. Comp. Physiol. Psychol. **91:** 1141–1155.

DISCUSSION

DR. ANTHONY SCLAFANI (*Brooklyn College, CUNY, Brooklyn, NY*): Elliott, you didn't mention protein. Is that because you haven't tested it yet or you have tested it and it doesn't have an effect in pups.

DR. ELLIOTT BLASS (*Johns Hopkins University, Baltimore, MD*): The former. To my knowledge, there are no protein sources that we would consider to be palatable, at least to our palates, or cited in the rat literature as palatable. Proteins may have intestinal effects, but I can't comment beyond that.

DR. DAVID BOOTH (*University of Birmingham, Birmingham, U.K.*): Conditioning effects with CCK strike me as bad news for CCK satiety, but perhaps as good news for the food abuse theory of bulimia. What I mean is that you're finding a CCK calming effect and not a specific feeding inhibition effect, which is emotionally conditioned liking for the food. This fades when the CCK satiety effect begins to develop, and we suggested some time ago that you indeed can use the satiating effect as a conditioner of preference. So I think that this is excellent news for the prospects of human application that there are emotional effects of food that may in later life be still capable of influencing our attitudes towards foods.

DR. PAUL ROBINSON (*Kings College Hospital School of Medicine, London*): I'd like to make a comment on the last speaker's question. We have studied food intake in infant rats ingesting milk independently from the floor of an incubator. We found, with rather similar dose ranges to the ones you found earlier, that CCK does selectively inhibit the intake of milk in that experimental situation. Desulfated CCK is ineffective and the behaviors that are affected by CCK are ingestive, or oral behaviors; noningestive behaviors such as pawing, locomotion, and rolling are not affected. So we think we do have a specific effect of CCK on ingestive behavior in the rat at day one.

The second point I'd like to make is to say how exciting I think your results are and to make a comment about the possible site of action. We've looked at CCK-33 receptors in the stomach, in the upper gastrointestinal tract, and CCK-8 receptors in the brain from fetal life to adult life. In the periphery we find that CCK receptors are widely distributed in the gastric mucosa, in the roof of the esophagus, in the antrum muscle, and in the pyloric sphincter in the rat fetus at fetal day 17. These receptors regress during development so that in the adult past day 20, which I notice is the time that you find the change in the responsivity of the animal, the receptors are entirely confined to the pyloric sphincter, highly localized. So we have a situation in which the receptor distribution of a peptide is regressing with development. I'm not sure if there are any other similar examples other than brain opioid receptors which also show this sort of change. I just want to suggest that your effect might be mediated through gastric CCK receptors.

DR. BLASS: We have data to support that point. A peripheral CCK receptor antagonist completely wipes out the preference effect. It's important to also bear in mind, however, that CCK is not effective as an inhibitor of suckling until the animals start to eat normal food. So again there is a dissociation of these two ingestive systems.

Orosensory Self-Stimulation by Sucrose Involves Brain Dopaminergic Mechanisms[a]

LINDA H. SCHNEIDER

Department of Psychiatry
New York Hospital–Cornell Medical Center
White Plains, New York 10605

INTRODUCTION

A substantial body of experimental evidence suggests that the ascending brain dopamine systems serve as the substrate for behaviors that are termed inherently "rewarding." A distinction between relatively "less natural" and "more natural" rewards may be drawn on the basis of the stimulus which is self-administered. In the first category are intracranial electrical self-stimulation (ICSS) and psychoactive drug self-injection.[1–6] In the second category is the ingestion of foods,[2–7] especially those that are highly palatable, such as sweet solutions.[8–25] It is not necessary in supporting a critical role for brain dopamine (DA) in the orosensory reward of sweet solutions that the positive-reinforcing effect of all these stimuli depend upon the activation of the same central dopaminergic pathways and receptor sites.

A critical involvement of the DA systems in the natural reward of the ingestion of foods as well as in lever-pressing for the less natural reward of ICSS and psychoactive drugs was first postulated and demonstrated by Wise.[4–6] Wise elegantly showed that the dopamine receptor antagonist pimozide reduced the positive reinforcing effects of these three classes of stimuli. A common objection was that these drugs produced motor debilitation, which prevented the animal from performing the required task. Wise and his colleagues produced strong evidence against any role of motoric deficits in the present context. After administration of pimozide, rats initially increased their response to ICSS, as if the stimulating current had been diluted or disconnected. Furthermore, for drugs of abuse and dopamimetics, rats' responding rate increased to sustain blood levels if possible, that is, if this was allowed by the experimental paradigm. If not, rats also initially exhibited bursts of lever pressing. Finally, for a reward of palatable food pellets, the inhibition of intake by the DA antagonists was observed only over multiple sessions, in between which the animals were untreated with drugs and ate normally for two days.

Examined together, these results of Wise *et al.* showed two clearly differing patterns of extinction. The first was a very rapid adjustment to dilution or omission of delivery of the unnatural stimuli. The second was typified by the results of the food-pellet experiment; for this natural stimulus, the pattern was a subacute reduction in food intake.

[a] This research has been supported by the National Institute of Mental Health (NRSA Postdoctoral Fellowship MH 90400) and by National Institutes of Health (FIRST award R29 NS 23781).

A more immediate reduction in the intake of sweet solutions by pimozide, for example, significant inhibition within minutes after the start of a test session, has been demonstrated using normal, intact rats[11,12] as well as using rats with an open chronic gastric cannula for sham feeding.[13-15] Sclafani and coworkers[11,12] reported that the "real" (i.e., not sham) consumption by rats of a glucose–saccharin solution was inhibited by pimozide in a dose-related manner. The pimozide-induced inhibition was relatively specific for sweet solutions as compared, for example, with intake of water. Interestingly, the inhibitory effect of pimozide was behaviorally equivalent to simple dilution of the sweet solution. These results suggest that decreased intake reflects decreased positive reinforcement, but this simple interpretation is clouded by possible postingestive satiating effects.

To circumvent this confound, Geary and Smith[13] in this laboratory examined the effects of pimozide upon the *sham* intake of sucrose in rats (see below, FIG. 1, and Smith, this volume) after a mild (4.75-hr) food deprivation. Sham intake in the absence of pimozide was a direct function of sucrose concentration, which supports the position that the sham-feeding paradigm eliminates postingestive effects. The inhibitory efficacy of a fixed dose (0.25 mg/kg, i.p.) of pimozide was an inverse function of increased sucrose concentration. For example, the same amount of a 20% sucrose solution was consumed after pimozide pretreatment as was consumed of a 5% sucrose solution after vehicle pretreatment. Thus, Geary and Smith demonstrated a behavioral equivalent to dilution of the sucrose solution sham fed, as Xenakis and Sclafani[11,12] had previously proposed for the real intake of a glucose–saccharin solution.

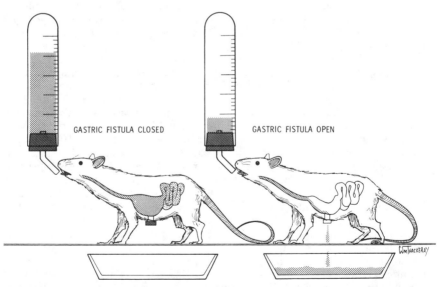

FIGURE 1. When the gastric cannula is closed (*left*), the sucrose solution is tasted and swallowed. Because it accumulates in the stomach and enters the small intestine, postingestive effects occur. When the gastric cannula is open (*right*), the sucrose solution is tasted and swallowed, but it does not accumulate in the stomach and does not enter the small intestine. Thus, postingestive effects are minimized. (From Smith *et al.* 1974. Fed. Proc. Am. Soc. Exp. Biol. **33:** 1146–1149. Reproduced by permission.)

THE ROLE OF DOPAMINE RECEPTOR SUBTYPES IN OROSENSORY SELF-STIMULATION BY SUCROSE

This paper is focused upon the separate and interactive roles of brain D-1 and D-2 receptors, according to the nomenclature of Kebabian and Calne,[26] in the stimulation of ingestion by sucrose solutions as studied in the sham-feeding rat. The findings discussed above implicated D-2 receptors as necessary for sweet taste reward. My experiments first sought to clarify that the observed effects of pimozide were due to its blockade of D-2 receptors. We have subsequently investigated the separate and interactive roles of D-1 and D-2 receptors. This became possible by using agents characterized by *in vitro* neuroreceptor binding assays, which were more selective antagonists of DA receptors than pimozide. These agents included the D-2 antagonists sulpiride as well as its more potent derivatives, sultopride and raclopride.[27-29] The D-1 receptor antagonist, SCH 23390[28-31] was also used. Recently, it has become evident[32] that SCH 23390 has a non-negligible affinity for brain serotonin (5-HT) receptors of the 5-HT_{2A} subtype and therefore can no longer be considered as selective a D-1 receptor antagonist as the benzamides (sulpiride and its derivatives) are selective antagonists of D-2 receptors. Nevertheless, there is sufficient separation for the relative potency of SCH 23390 to inhibit binding to D-1 and 5-HT_{2A} sites *in vitro* to allow its use here.

D-1 OR D-2 RECEPTOR BLOCKADE INHIBITS SHAM-FED SUCROSE

TABLE 1 summarizes the results obtained over a series of experiments that tested the effect of pretreatment with various selective DA receptor antagonists on rats' sham intake of a 10% (0.3 M; wt/vol) sucrose solution. Several aspects should be emphasized in this compilation of previously reported results.[15,16] First, under control conditions rats sham feed this sucrose solution at a mean rate >1 ml/min over a 30-min test even though they are only mildly food deprived. This suggests that our baseline reflects a potent orosensory reward of this sweet solution as our laboratory has shown this rate is still not at a maximal ceiling.[13,14,33] Second, note the wide divergence of doses of the D-2 antagonists necessary to produce half-maximal inhibition. For the D-2-selective receptor antagonists, the estimated doses corresponding to the ID_{50} values of sultopride (racemic) and raclopride [this being (−)-raclopride] are approximately 4- and 300-fold lower than the parent compound [(−)-sulpiride], respectively. This differential potency for the inhibition of sucrose sham feeding by the three D-2-selective receptor antagonists tested is in accord with both the relative potency of these three benzamides for binding in assays using striatal homogenates *in vitro* as well as their relative efficacy in crossing the blood–brain barrier.[27-29,34,35] The other two D-2 antagonists tested, pimozide and haloperidol, were clearly potent in inhibiting sucrose sham feeding [about 300- and 700-fold, respectively, more potent than (−)-sulpiride], as would be expected from the *in vitro* D-2 potency as well as from their relative brain penetrabilities.[28,29] Because neither pimozide nor haloperidol can be considered to be completely D-2 selective,[29,36] the results obtained with the benzamides most strongly supported the conclusion that activation at central D-2 receptors is necessary for the orosensory reward of sucrose in maintaining sham feeding.

While selective antagonism at central D-2 receptors appears to be sufficient to inhibit sucrose sham feeding in a dose-related manner, a similar profile was found for the antagonism of D-1 receptors by SCH 23390 (see TABLE 1 and Schneider *et al.*[16]). At the dose of SCH 23390 corresponding to its ID_{50} of 0.05 mg/kg, it could be considered to be selective at D-1 receptors.[30,37] Our data demonstrated that selective blockade of *either* DA receptor subtype was sufficient to inhibit the positive reinforcing effect of sucrose that maintains sham feeding. The finding that *either* D-1 or D-2 receptor blockade could inhibit a behavior was not surprising. It has been reported that SCH 23390 as well as D-2 antagonists inhibit behaviors such as conditioned avoidance responding, ICSS, and D-1 or D-2 or mixed DA agonist-induced locomotion.[29,30,37,38] Only in animals with compromised (i.e., lesioned or subacutely depleted) ascending brain DA systems is differential D-1/D-2 receptor antagonist selectivity observed.[29,37,38]

POSSIBLE INTERACTIVE ROLES OF D-1 AND D-2 RECEPTORS

The conclusion suggested by the results summarized in TABLE 1 was that central dopaminergic activity at *both* D-1 and D-2 receptors was necessary for the orosensory stimulation of (sham) ingestion by sucrose. There remained the possibility that there was an interaction between D-1 and D-2 receptor mechanisms in the mediation of this effect. This possibility was addressed in a subsequent experiment in which the additivity of inhibition of sucrose sham intake produced by selective blockade of D-1 receptors (by SCH 23390) and of D-2 receptors (by raclopride) was tested.[39] To do so, the effects on the sham intake of sucrose of combined treatments with SCH 23390 and raclopride were compared with the inhibitions produced by each antagonist alone (plus vehicle injection). Using the same protocol as above, four doses of SCH 23390 were administered, two of which were subthreshold, and two of which were administered in combination with two doses of raclopride, which alone yielded significant quarter and half-maximal inhibitions. It was found that the combinations of SCH 23390 with the threshold dose of raclopride did *not* produce a significantly larger inhibition than that dose of SCH 23390 alone. When the raclopride treatment was combined (at the dose corresponding to its ID_{50}) with a dose of SCH 23390 that alone produced more than a 50% inhibition, a similar failure of additivity of selective D-2 and D-1 receptor blockade was observed.

These results demonstrated a failure of additivity of the inhibitory effects on sucrose sham feeding of selective blockade of D-1 and D-2 receptors. The lack of additivity, let alone a possible synergistic interaction, between D-1 and D-2 receptor mechanisms was not due to a floor or ceiling effect. Thus, one plausible interpretation of these data is that the central D-1 and D-2 receptor mechanisms that are critical for the orosensory reward of sham-fed sucrose are functionally related in series rather than in parallel.[39]

RESEARCH TO VALIDATE THE HYPOTHESIS THAT CENTRAL D-1 AND D-2 RECEPTORS ARE CRITICAL TO OROSENSORY SUCROSE SELF-STIMULATION

In behavioral psychopharmacology, whenever a behavioral dependent variable is *reduced* by a drug treatment and a neurochemical substrate is postulated, certain experiments are necessary controls. These include the demonstrations that the inhibition observed was due to a diminished potency of the stimulus (sucrose) to sustain its self-administration (sham feeding). To do this, experiments were undertaken to show that the treatment (D-1 and/or D-2 receptor antagonists) was (a) pharmacologically specific, (b) behaviorally selective, (c) similar to solution dilution, and (d) not due to a motor deficit. I will now summarize the results of research that provide convergent,

TABLE 1. Comparison of the Inhibition of Sucrose Sham Feeding by D-1 and D-2 Receptor Antagonists[a]

Antagonist	Dose (mg/kg)	Sham Intake (ml/30 min⁻¹)	Percent Inhibition	Latency (min)
D-1 Antagonists				
SCH 23390	0	34.1 ($\pm$ 2.4)		
	0.0125	33.1 ($\pm$ 3.8)	2.9	–
	0.025	22.0 ($\pm$ 3.8)*	35.5	18
	0.05	16.4 ($\pm$ 4.2)**	51.9	9
	0.1	6.5 ($\pm$ 3.0)**	80.9	6
D-2 Antagonists				
Raclopride	0	30.8 ($\pm$ 2.5)		
	0.1	24.9 ($\pm$ 2.5)	19.2	–
	0.2	19.6 ($\pm$ 2.1)**	36.4	6
	0.4	12.5 ($\pm$ 2.4)**	59.4	6
	0.8	4.3 ($\pm$ 1.6)**	86.0	3
Sultopride	0	35.0 ($\pm$ 2.2)		
	10	28.9 ($\pm$ 2.5)	17.4	–
	20	19.0 ($\perp$ 4.1)**	45.7	9
	40	13.8 ($\pm$ 4.0)**	60.6	9
(−)-Sulpiride	0	40.3 ($\pm$ 2.6)		
	100	18.7 ($\pm$ 4.2)*	53.6	6
Pimozide	0	34.3 ($\pm$ 2.0)		
	0.25	22.0 ($\pm$ 2.0)**	35.9	9
Haloperidol	0	33.5 ($\pm$ 2.4)		
	0.025	27.3 ($\pm$ 3.3)	18.5	–
	0.05	27.5 ($\pm$ 3.7)	17.9	–
	0.1	21.2 ($\pm$ 2.5)*	36.7	12
	0.2	10.9 ($\pm$ 3.6)**	67.5	6
	0.4	5.4 ($\pm$ 2.9)**	83.9	6

[a] Data are based upon the mean 30-min sham intakes of 11 rats sham feeding a 10% (wt/vol) sucrose solution. The latency of inhibition is the time (in min) until a significant supression in 3-min cumulative intake was found for a drug dose, as compared with vehicle. * represents $p < 0.05$; ** represents $p < 0.01$ as compared with vehicle control treatments. The SCH 23390 and raclopride tests were conducted in a separate group of 11 sham-feeding rats rather than in the initial 11 animals which were tested with the other receptor antagonists. (See references in Schneider *et al.*[15,16] for experimental details.)

strong evidence that central D-1 and D-2 receptor mechanisms exert critical separate and/or interactive roles in the orosensory sucrose self-stimulation paradigm of the sham-feeding rat, operationally defining sweet taste reward.

CONTROL EXPERIMENTS FOR PHARMACOLOGICAL SPECIFICITY

Fortunately, for many D-1 and D-2 receptor antagonists, pharmacologically active and inactive enantiomers exist.[28-30] Rats reduced sucrose sham intake by about 50% after pretreatment with (−)-sulpiride, as compared with either vehicle or (+)-sulpiride.[15] This stereoselectivity for D-2 receptors contributed strong support for their activation being a critical locus for sweet taste reward.

More recently, stereoselectivity for the inhibition of the sham feeding of sucrose has been found for D-1 receptors.[20-22] At a dose of SCH 23390 that halved 30-min sham intake of sucrose solutions, SCH 23388 was without any effect. These control experiments, which utilize microstructural analysis, also demonstrate that the pattern of licking for sucrose solutions was inhibited by the active enantiomer of the selective D-1 receptor antagonist without altering motor competence (see below).

In addition to testing for stereoselectivity, the inhibitory potency of equimolar doses of SCH 23390 and raclopride, when administered into the brain or injected i.p., were compared.[19] For D-2 receptors, infusion of raclopride into a lateral ventricle (i.c.v.) was clearly more potent than the same dose injected i.p. For D-1 receptors, a marginally statistically significant greater i.c.v. than i.p. inhibitory potency was observed. This result suggests that those D-1 receptor mechanisms critical for sweet taste reward are not accessed well after lateral ventricular infusions. Another possible, but less likely, interpretation is that peripheral D-1 receptors are involved. As there is no evidence that significant peripheral D-1 receptor populations are coupled to enteric neuronal or vagal afferent pathways, this interpretation is unlikely, although it cannot be discounted. Further experiments involving intracerebral administration of antagonists directly into defined DA terminal zones will be required to resolve this question.

CONTROL EXPERIMENTS FOR BEHAVIORAL SELECTIVITY

To support the hypothesis that central D-1 and D-2 receptor mechanisms are critical to orosensory self-stimulation by sucrose, a number of studies were conducted to show that sweet taste reward, as quantified by rats' sucrose sham intake, was differentially inhibited; that is, there was behavioral selectivity. This was done primarily in two ways. First, it was shown[15,18] that DA antagonist treatment resulted in a significantly more potent inhibition of sweetened water when rats were mildly hungry (10% sucrose solution, 4.75-hr food deprived) than of tap water when rats were very thirsty (i.e., overnight water deprived) when these two different tests were performed at equivalent baselines (>30 ml/30 min). Second, it was demonstrated that selective D-1 or D-2 blockade is functionally equivalent to dilution of the sucrose solution sham fed (see below). These results lent further strong support for establishing a critical role for DA in orosensory sucrose self-stimulation. These findings will now be summarized.

Sham-Fed Sucrose Reduced More Than Sham-Drunk Water by SCH 23390, Raclopride, Pimozide, or Haloperidol

Using sham intake (ml/30 min) as a dependent measure of the reinforcing potency of 10% sucrose or water, rats when tested mildly food deprived or thirsty (see above) will lick rapidly (about 6 licks/sec) for both of these liquids. Under these experimental conditions, a behavioral selectivity for sweet taste reward to be inhibited more potently by DA antagonist treatment was demonstrated in three separate experiments.[15,17,18] Since this was shown for the selective D-2 receptor antagonist raclopride,[17,18] the results obtained for the preferential D-2 receptor antagonists pimozide and haloperidol[15] were likely produced through their potency at D-2 sites.

For each of these DA antagonists, including those selective for D-1 and D-2 receptors (SCH 23390 and raclopride, respectively), a more significant inhibition of sham intake of the sweet solution (sham feeding; SF) than of water (sham drinking; SD) was observed. This was found in tests employing separate groups of animals for SF and SD[18] or when testing SF and SD (on separate days) using the same group of animals.[15,17]

In either case baselines for sham intake were always >30 ml/30 min, and the effect was not dependent on the details of the experimental paradigm (e.g., home vs. test cage). For each DA antagonist tested across a dose range, there were usually two doses that clearly differentiated SF from SD, the former always being significantly more potently inhibited. If palatability is reflected in the avidity with which a food stimulus is self-administered (e.g., the rate of sucrose sham feeding; see Refs. 13, 33, 40, and 41), these results support the relative behavioral selectivity of treatment with a pharmacologically selective DA receptor antagonist to the attenuation of sweet taste reward. Note that this conclusion does not preclude an important role for DA in the reward of water to a thirsty rat; this is evidenced by results reported from other laboratories (e.g., see Refs. 3, 11, and 12) as well as our own summarized here (see also section on microstructural results below). Rather, it suggests that central D-1 and D-2 receptor mechanisms are involved in orosensory reward produced by sweet solutions.

Analysis of Sham-Feeding Rates: Inferential Evidence that D-1 or D-2 Blockade Reduces Palatability but Not Performance

The hypothesis that antagonism of D-1 or D-2 receptors reduces sham intake by attenuating the orosensory reward of the sucrose solution was further supported by application of the method of Davis et al.[41] to the cumulative sham-intake curves for the experiments summarized in TABLE 1. While TABLE 1 presents only the 30-min intake values following vehicle and DA antagonist treatment, volumes were recorded in all experiments at 3-min intervals. Through this analysis of these data, we found[42] that the effect of the DA antagonists was to decrease the *initial* rate of licking without altering the *rate* of decay of sham intake over the 30-min test. This pattern of results is consistent with a decrease in the palatability of the sucrose solution and is not consistent with an impairment of motor systems following treatment with DA antagonist. Moreover, a similar profile of a reduction in the initial rate of licking without alteration of the rate of decay of licking was found when the model of Davis and Levine[43] was applied to the analysis of cumulative intake functions of rats that were sham feeding sucrose solutions of decreasing concentration without drug treatment.[33,42]

Thus, this analysis provided further evidence, albeit inferential, that the effect of DA antagonist treatment is to reduce selectively the orosensory potency of the sucrose solution sham fed in a manner similar to solution dilution and does so without producing a motor deficit. These analyses, using the method of Davis et al.[41] in conjunction with the relatively greater potency of the DA antagonists for the inhibition of sucrose sham feeding than water sham drinking and the controls for pharmacological specificity (see above), advanced the basic hypothesis that central D-1 and D-2 mechanisms are critical for sweet taste reward. Subsequent experiments through the innovative use of microstructural analysis (see Davis, this volume) have substantially enhanced the direct nature of the evidence collected to support this hypothesis.

ANALYSIS OF THE MICROSTRUCTURE OF LICKING DEMONSTRATES THAT D-1 OR D-2 BLOCKADE REDUCES OROSENSORY SUCROSE REWARD WITHOUT IMPAIRING MOTOR COMPETENCE

The hypothesis that central D-1 and D-2 receptor mechanisms mediate the orosensory reward of sham-fed sucrose has been supported by results summarized above in this paper. All these had been based upon analyses of the effects of experimental manipulations on the volume sham fed over a 30-min test, as recorded by observation at 3-min intervals. This body of research included controls for the pharmacological specificity and behavioral selectivity of the inhibition of sucrose sham feeding by D-1 and D-2 receptor antagonists. Taken together, these results provided strong evidence that dopaminergic blockade reduces sham intake by attenuating the orosensory reinforcing potency of the sweet solution without interfering with the motor control of licking and other ingestive movements.

The ability to demonstrate this more directly became possible through use of microstructural analysis of licking behavior in collaboration with Dr. John D. Davis. In this volume, Dr. Davis presents the details, rationale, and utility of studying the microstructure of ingestive behavior. Here I will summarize the results of experiments we conducted to evaluate whether selective D-2 receptor blockade was functionally equivalent to dilution of a sham-fed sucrose solution[17] and more recent experiments comparing the effects on the microstructure of sucrose sham feeding of SCH 23390 and haloperidol with those of raclopride.[20-22] The implementation of this approach has provided strong evidence that DA receptor blockade decreases the orosensory reward of sham-fed sucrose without impairing the rate, pattern, or efficiency of licking at the high rates seen under our experimental conditions, typically about 6 licks/sec.

Selective D-2 Blockade Is Similar to Sucrose Dilution

The results of an experiment conducted to test whether raclopride treatment at its ID_{50} and 50% dilution of a sucrose solution produced similar effects on the volume and microstructural patterns of sham-feeding rats appear in TABLE 2. In this study, water sham drinking was used as a comparison. The animals ($n = 10$) were also adapted to the sham drinking of water after 18-hour water deprivation; their baseline (saline i.p.) intakes were equivalent for water and for sham feeding a 10% sucrose solution following a four-hour food deprivation to which they had been adapted first. After stable baselines for SF 10% sucrose and SD water were obtained, half the rats were tested with raclopride SF before being tested SD, and the other half were tested in the opposite order. Following these two tests, all rats were given 30-min access to a 5% sucrose solution following a four-hour food deprivation and vehicle administration (saline i.p.). The novel aspect of this experiment was the collection by computer of the entire temporal distribution of licks, so that the microstructural measures of cluster size (number of licks in a cluster or bout of licking), intercluster interval (ICI; secs), number of clusters in the session, distribution of interlick intervals, and licks per milliliter were available for subsequent analysis (a cluster was operationally defined in this experiment as a run of licks separated by less than a two-second pause; see Davis, this volume).

The outcome of this experiment is clearly that D-2 blockade and solution dilution produced similar effects upon several microstructural parameters as well as on the volume intake of sucrose sham fed. The comparability of the reductions in cluster size, number of clusters, and the increase in intercluster interval for sham-fed 10% sucrose after raclopride treatment and for 5% sucrose (saline i.p.) provide strong evidence that behavior after D-2 blockade resembles behavior after dilution of the sweet solution. Not illustrated in TABLE 2 (see Schneider et al. 17) are the results that these two treatments similarly altered the number of licks per milliliter and that although total intake was approximately halved, there was no perturbation of the rapidity of licking during bouts; for example the distribution of interlick intervals (ILIs) was superimposable with that under baseline conditions (10% sucrose, saline i.p.), with mean ILIs peaking at 150 msec.

TABLE 2. Similar Effect of D-2 Receptor Blockade and Dilution on the Microstructure of Sucrose Sham-Feeding Behavior

Test Solution	Drug (i.p.)	Sham Intake (ml/30 min)	Cluster Size (# of licks)	ICI (sec)	# of Clusters (in 30 min)
10% Sucrose	Saline	35.0 (2.6)	81.0 (11.2)	17.1 (1.4)	62 (6.5)
10% Sucrose	Raclopride	13.9 (1.7)	52.8 (8.4)	31.4 (3.8)	44 (4.6)
5% Sucrose	Saline	17.1 (1.5)	58.9 (5.4)	37.2 (5.8)	41 (4.0)
Water	Saline	39.5 (3.7)	154.4 (31.7)	30.3 (4.5)	58 (6.7)
Water	Raclopride	22.0 (3.5)	51.8 (9.1)	19.2 (2.1)	33 (4.5)

[a] All values represent mean ± SEM; $n = 10$). Raclopride significantly decreased the sham intake of 10% sucrose (by $57.9 \pm 6.1\%$; $p < 0.001$) as well as the sham intake of water (by $46.2 \pm 4.2\%$; $p < 0.001$). Raclopride decreased the cluster size for both 10% sucrose ($p < 0.05$) and water ($p < 0.025$) significantly. However, raclopride lengthened the ICI for 10% sucrose significantly ($p < 0.01$), while it shortened the ICI for water ($p < 0.025$).

Note that there were no significant differences in these measurements between sham feeding 10% sucrose after raclopride pretreatment and 5% sucrose after vehicle (saline) pretreatment. (For further details see Schneider et al.[17])

These results provide a strong argument in favor of an attenuation of the orosensory reward of the sucrose solution by raclopride as well as strong evidence against any impairment of rats' motor performance. The comparison of the effects of raclopride on SF sucrose and SD water also support this interpretation. When the volume of water sham intake was about halved by a slightly higher dose of raclopride, a differential effect was found through microstructural analysis in that ICI was reduced; that is, the rats initiated bouts of sham drinking more often under drug than under control conditions (TABLE 2). Thus, the *palatability* of the solution being sham ingested significantly affects the *pattern* of licking behavior. This differential effect is evidence against any generalized motor impairment, as the rats engaged in SD more often under raclopride than under saline pretreatment. Further supporting this is the absence of any effect of raclopride on the distribution of ILIs or licks per milliliter for water sham drinking.[17] In summary, this experiment demonstrates that selective D-2 receptor blockade closely resembles dilution of sucrose solution, clearly indicating that palatability is reduced and motor competence is preserved.

Comparison of the Effects of D-1 with D-2 Receptor Antagonists on the Microstructure of Licking for Sham-Fed Sucrose

Having ascertained to our satisfaction that the effect of selective D-2 receptor blockade by raclopride was functionally equivalent to dilution of a sham-fed sucrose solution by microstructural analysis, subsequent experiments examined the effects of SCH 23390, SCH 23388, and haloperidol on the microstructure of sucrose sham feeding.[20-22] A similar approach was employed, namely, using treatment with the selective D-1 receptor antagonist SCH 23390 and an equivalent dose of its inactive enantiomer SCH 23388, and comparing these results with those produced by raclopride and haloperidol in the same animals. In these studies, all drugs (except SCH 23388) are used at the doses that correspond to their ID_{50} values. It was necessary to offer a 40% rather than a 10% sucrose solution to obtain baselines in excess of 1 ml/min in this group of animals ($n = 12$). Under these conditions, a differential effect of D-1 blockade was found: The duration of sham feeding (first to last lick in the 30-min test) was *shortened* by SCH 23390 but not raclopride.[21] This result would suggest the possibility that the positive reinforcing effect of sucrose were decreased below some critical threshold necessary to sustain licking by blockade at D-1 receptors (by 23390) but not at D-2 receptors (by raclopride). Such a differential D-1/D-2 effect should be further examined in rats ingesting 10% sucrose and should also be compared with the effects of solution dilution (see above). At present, the major conclusions to be drawn are that it is invaluable to utilize the analysis of the changes in the microstructural patterns of licking within a paradigm in which volume intakes are halved. To date, we have found that with 10% sucrose, as with 40% sucrose, SCH 23390 does not alter rats' licking rate or efficiency even when intake is halved by D-1 blockade in these sham-feeding rats. Evidence for pharmacological specificity for D-1 receptors was obtained; at a dose of SCH 23390, which halved the sham intake of 40% sucrose[20,22] or 10% sucrose (Schneider *et al.*, unpublished results), the same dose of SCH 23388 did not alter sham intake or lick patterns. Therefore, for D-1 as well as for D-2 systems, the use of microstructural analysis supports the conclusion that pharmacological blockade of either DA receptor subtype attenuates the orosensory reward, that is, the palatability, without impairing motor competence.

SUMMARY AND CONCLUSIONS

The most convincing body of evidence supporting a role for brain dopaminergic mechanisms in sweet taste reward has been obtained using the sham-feeding rat. In rats prepared with a chronic gastric fistula and tested with the cannula open, intake is a direct function of the palatability of the solution offered as well as of the state of food deprivation. Because essentially none of the ingested fluid passes on to the intestine, negative postingestive feedback is eliminated. Thus, the relative orosensory/hedonic potency of the food determines and sustains the rate of sham intake; long periods of food deprivation are not required. In this way, the sham feeding of sweet solutions may be considered a form of oral self-stimulation behavior and afford a preparation through which the neurochemical and neuranatomical substrates of sweet taste reward may be identified. The results obtained in the series of experiments summarized in this paper clearly indicate that central D-1 and D-2 receptor mechanisms are critical for the orosensory self-stimulation by sucrose in the rat. In conclusion, I suggest that such investigations of the roles of brain dopaminergic mechanisms in the sucrose sham-feeding rat preparation may further our understanding of normal and aberrant attractions to sweet fluids in humans (see Cabanac, Drewnowski, and Halmi, this volume), as an innate, positive affective response of human neonates to sucrose[44] and the sustained positive hedonic ratings for glucose when tasted but not when consumed[45] have demonstrated.

ACKNOWLEDGMENTS

I wish to thank my collaborators and co-workers involved in conducting these experiments, including Drs. Gerard P. Smith, John D. Davis, and James Gibbs and express my thanks for technical support from Chris Watson, Amy Miller, and others. I thank Mrs. Jane Magnetti and Mrs. Marion Jacobson for secretarial assistance. I also wish to thank the following pharmaceutical companies for their generous gifts of dopamine receptor antagonists: Astra (Sweden) for raclopride, Schering-Plough for SCH 23390 and SCH 23388, McNeil Pharmaceutical for pimozide, Ravizza for (−) and (+) sulpiride, and Delegrange International for sultopride.

REFERENCES

1. FIBIGER, H. C. & A. G. PHILLIPS. 1988. Mesolimbic dopamine systems and reward. Ann. N.Y. Acad. Sci. **537:** 206–215.
2. HOEBEL, G. G, L. HERNANDEZ, S. MCLEAN, B. G. STANLEY, E. F. AULISSI, P. GLIMCHER & D. MARGOLIN. 1982. Catecholamines, enkephalin and neurotensin in feeding and reward. *In* The Neural Basis of Feeding and Reward. B. G. Hoebel & D. Novin, Eds.: 465–478. Haer Institute for Electrophysiological Research. Brunswick, ME.
3. STELLAR, J. R. & E. STELLAR. 1985. The Neurobiology of Motivation and Reward. Springer-Verlag. New York.
4. WISE, R. A. 1982. Common neural basis for brain stimulation reward, drug reward, and food reward. *In* The Neural Basis of Feeding and Reward. B. G. Hoebel & D. Novin, Eds.: 445–454. Haer Institute for Electrophysiological Research. Brunswick, ME.
5. WISE, R. A. 1982. Neuroleptics and operant behavior: The anhedonia hypothesis. Behav. Brain Sci. **5:** 39–87.
6. WISE, R. A., J. SPINDLER, H. DEWIT & G. J. GERBER. 1978. Neuroleptic-induced "anhedonia" in rats: Pimozide blocks the reward quality of food. Science **201:** 262–264.
7. ETTENBERG, A. & C. H. CAMP. 1986. Haloperidol induces a partial reinforcement extinction effect in rats: Implications for a dopamine involvement in food reward. Pharmacol. Biochem. Behav. **25:** 813–821.
8. BREESE, G. R., R. C. SMITH, B. R. COOPER & L. D. GRANT. 1973. Alterations in consummatory behavior following intracisternal injection of 6-hydroxydopamine. Pharmacol. Biochem. Behav. **1:** 319–328.
9. SANDBERG, D., M. VAILLANCOURT, R. WISE & J. STEWART. 1982. Effects of pimozide on saccharin and sucrose consumption. Soc. Neurosci. Abstr. **8:** 603.
10. BAILEY, C. S., S. HSIAO & J. E. KING. 1986. Hedonic reactivity to sucrose in rats: Modification by pimozide. Physiol. Behav. **38:** 447–452.
11. SCLAFANI, A., P. F. Aravich & S. XENAKIS. 1982. Dopaminergic and endorphinergic mediation of a sweet reward. *In* The Neural Basis of Feeding and Reward. B. G. Hobel & D. Novin, Eds.: 507–515. Haer Institute for Electrophysiological Research. Brunswick, ME.
12. XENAKIS, A. & A. SCLAFANI. 1981. The effects of pimozide on the consumption of a palatable saccharin–glucose solution in the rat. Pharmacol. Biochem. Behav. **15:** 435–442.
13. GEARY, N. & G. P. SMITH. 1985. Pimozide decreases the positive reinforcing effect of sham-fed sucrose in the rat. Pharmacol. Biochem. Behav. **22:** 787–790.
14. SMITH, G. P. & L. H. SCHNEIDER. 1988. Relationships between mesolimbic dopamine function and eating behavior. Ann. N.Y. Acad. Sci. **537:** 254–261.
15. SCHNEIDER, L. H., J. GIBBS & G. P. SMITH. 1986. D-2 selective receptor antagonists suppress sucrose sham feeding in the rat. Brain Res. Bull. **17:** 605–611.
16. SCHNEIDER, L. H., J. GIBBS & G. P. SMITH. 1986. Selective D-1 or D-2 receptor antagonists inhibit sucrose sham feeding in rats. Appetite **7:** 294–295.
17. SCHNEIDER, L. H., J. D. DAVIS & G. P. SMITH. 1987. Similar effects of D-2 receptor blockade and dilution on the microstructure of sucrose sham feeding behavior. Abstracts, Conference on Appetite, Thirst, and Related Disorders. Official Satellite Meeting of Society for Neuroscience. (San Antonio, TX): 55. Nov. 12–15.
18. SCHNEIDER, L. H., D. GREENBERG & G. P. SMITH. 1988. Comparison of the effects of selective D-1 and D-2 receptor antagonists on sucrose sham feeding and water sham drinking. Ann. N.Y. Acad. Sci. **537:** 534–537.
19. SCHNEIDER, L. H., C. A. WATSON & G. P. SMITH. 1988. Centrally administered D-1 and D-2 selective receptor antagonists reduce sweet taste reward in the rat. Soc. Neurosci. Abstr. **14:** 614.
20. SCHNEIDER, L. H., J. D. DAVIS, C. A. WATSON, J. GIBBS & G. P. SMITH. 1989. Inhibition of sucrose sham feeding by haloperidol: Comparison by microstructural analysis of ID_{50} treatments with haloperidol, SCH 23390, and raclopride. J. Psychophamacol. In press.
21. SCHNEIDER, L. H., C. A. WATSON, J. D. DAVIS, J. GIBBS & G. P. SMITH. 1989. Differential D1/D2 antagonism of sucrose sham feeding. Soc. Neurosci. Abstr. **15:** 655.
22. SCHNEIDER, L. H., C. A. WATSON, J. D. DAVIS & G. P. SMITH. 1989. Microstructural analysis of the inhibition of sucrose sham feeding by SCH 23390. Appetite **12:** 236.

23. SMITH, G. P., K. BOURBONAIS, C. JEROME & K. J. SIMANSKY. 1987. Sham feeding of sucrose increases the ratio of 3,4-dihydroxyphenylacetic acid to dopamine in the hypothalamus. Pharmacol. Biochem. Behav. **26:** 585–591.

24. HEFFNER, T. G., G. VOSMER & L. S. SEIDEN. 1984. Time-dependent changes in hypothalamic dopamine metabolism during feeding in the rat. Pharmacol. Biochem. Behav. **20:** 947–949.

25. BLACKBURN, J. R., A. G. PHILLIPS, A. JAKUBOVIC & H. C. FIBEGER. 1986. Increased dopamine metabolism in the nucleus accumbens and striatum following consumption of a nutritive meal but not a palatable non-nutritive saccharin solution. Pharmacol. Biochem. Behav. **25:** 1095–1100.

26. KEBABIAN, J. W. & D. B. CALNE. 1979. Multiple receptors for dopamine. Nature (London) **277:** 93–96.

27. KOHLER, C., H. HALL, S. O. OGREN & L. GAWELL. 1985. Specific in vitro and in vivo binding of tritiated raclopride: A potent substituted benzamide drug with high affinity for dopamine D-2 receptors in the rat brain. Biochem. Pharmacol. **34:** 2251–2259.

28. CHRISTENSEN, A. V., J. ARNT, J. HYTTEL, J. J. LARSEN & O. SVENDSEN. 1984. Pharmacological effects of a specific D-1 antagonist SCH 23390 in comparison with neuroleptics. Life Sci. **34:** 1529–1540.

29. WADDINGTON, J. L. & K. M. O'BOYLE. 1989. Drugs acting on brain dopamine receptors: A conceptual re-evaluation five years after the first selective D-1 antagonist. Pharmacol. Ther. **43:** 1–52.

30. IORIO, L. C., A. BARNETT, F. H. LEITZ, V. P. HOUSER & C. A. KORDUBA. 1984. SCH 23390, a potential benzazepine antipsychotic with unique interactions on dopaminergic systems. J. Pharmacol. Exp. Ther. **226:** 462–468.

31. HYTTEL, J. 1983. SCH 23390—the first selective D-1 antagonist. Eur. J. Pharmacol. **91:** 153–154.

32. IORIO, L. C., V. RUPERTO, M. GREZLAK, V. COFFIN, R. E. CHIPKIN & A. BARNETT. 1988. SCH 39166 HCl: A specific D-1 receptor antagonist with anti-psychotic potential. Soc. Neurosci. Abstr. **14:** 934.

33. JOYNER, K., G. P. SMITH, R. SHINDLEDECKER & C. PFAFFMANN. 1985. Stimulation of sham feeding in the rat by sucrose, maltose, glucose, and fructose. Soc. Neurosci. Abstr. **11:** 1223.

34. MIZUCHI, A., N. KITAGAWA & Y. MIYACHI. 1983. Regional distribution of sultopride and sulpiride in rat brain measured by radioimmunoassay. Psychopharmacology **81:** 195–198.

35. HONDA, F., Y. SATOH, K. SHIMOMURA, H. SATOH, H. NOGUCHI, S. UCHIDA & R. KATO. 1977. Dopamine receptor blocking activity of sulpiride in the central nervous system. Jpn. J. Pharmacol. **27:** 397–411.

36. LARGENT, B. L., A. L. GUNDLACH & S. H. SNYDER. 1984. Psychotomimetic opiate receptors labelled and visualized with (+)-^{3}H-(3-hydroxyphenyl)-N-(1-propyl) piperidine. Proc. Natl. Acad. Sci. USA **81:** 4983–4987.

37. BRAUN, A. R., P. BARONE & T. N. CHASE. 1986. Interaction of D1 and D2 dopamine receptors in the expression of dopamine agonist-induced behaviors. *In* Neurobiology of Central D1 Dopamine Receptors. G. R. Breese & I. Creese, Eds.: 151–166. Plenum. New York.

38. BREESE, G. R., R. A. MUELLER, T. C. NAPIER & G. E. DUNCAN. 1986. Neurobiology of D1 receptors after neonatal 6-OHDA treatment: Relevance to Lesch-Nyhan disease. *In* Neurobiology of Central D1 Dopamine Receptors. G. R. Breese & I. Creese, Eds.: 197–215. Plenum. New York.

39. SCHNEIDER, L. H. & G. P. SMITH. 1988. Effect of combining selective D-1 and D-2 receptor antagonists on sucrose sham feeding. Eastern Psychol. Assoc. Abstr. **59:** 10.

40. WEINGARTEN, H. P. & S. D. WATSON. 1982. Sham feeding as a procedure for assessing the influence of diet palatability on food intake. Physiol. Behav. **28:** 401–407.

41. BERNZ, J. A., G. P. SMITH & G. P. SMITH & J. GIBBS. 1983. A comparison of the effectiveness of intraperitoneal injections of bombesin (BBS) and cholecystokinin (CCK-8) to reduce sham feeding of different sucrose solutions. Proc. Eastern Psychol. Assoc.: 94.

41. DAVIS, J. D., B. J. COLLINS & M. W. LEVINE. 1978. The interaction between gustatory stimulation and gut feedback in the control of the ingestion of liquid diets. *In* Hunger Models. D. A. Booth, Ed.: 109–142. Academic Press. New York.

42. Davis, J. D., L. H. Schneider, J. Gibbs & G. P. Smith. 1986. D-1 and D-2 receptor antagonists reduce initial rate of intake in sham feeding rats. Soc. Neurosci. Abstr. 12: 1557.
43. Davis, J. D. & M. Levine, 1977. A model for the control of ingestion. Psychol. Rev. 84: 379–412.
44. Steiner, J. E. 1977. Facial expressions of the neonate infant indicating the hedonics of food-related chemical stimuli. In Taste and Development: The Genesis of Sweet Preference. J. M. Weiffenbach, Ed.: 173–187. DHEW (NIH) 77–1068. Bethesda, MD.
45. Cabanac, M. 1971. Physiological role of pleasure. Science 173: 1103–1107.

DISCUSSION

Dr. David Booth (*University of Birmingham, U.K.*): If I remember correctly Jack Davis was asked yesterday whether raclopride affected sweet taste reward or palatability or sweet perception. I wonder what you think of a suggestion that might put your data on sweet together with Steve Cooper and Dave Gilbert's data on salt, that you can take advantage of your data complementing what I would call output analysis, which very nicely excludes a motor component. You can then use input–output relationship analysis to look at the effects of different levels of sweetness or saltiness in comparison with some measure of the ingestive behavior in order to see if you alter the slope of the relationship between the concentration of sweetner or of salt and the measure of ingestive behavior induced by the conditions. This psychophysical analysis coupled with the dose–response analysis would in fact enable you, if you chose your different responses, to distinguish perceptual effects from motivational effects.

Dr. Linda H. Schneider (*New York Hospital–Cornell Medical Center, White Plains, NY*): I should mention that on the basis of this animal work we actually did a human experiment in normal college students, males, injecting a milligram of Haldol intramuscularly and quantifying its effects on magnitude estimation and hedonic ratings of sucrose and salt solutions. We're still analyzing those data, but it appears as if there are effects on both hedonic ratings and magnitude estimation. This provides an example of going from the animal work to normal persons, and obviously I'm interested in testing clinical populations for sweet and salt hedonics and intensity.

Dr. Kenny Simansky (*Medical College of Pennsylvania, Philadelphia, PA*): That's nice work, Linda. I just thought you might comment on my suggestion that you temper with caution the specific mediation by dopamine of this response because all the sham-feeding data come from animals that have been sham fed over, obviously, a number of days or weeks. As I'm sure you are well aware, it is unnecessary for the animals even to taste the food once they have been exposed to what could be considered a discriminative stimulus for the food; nevertheless, the dopamine system will turn on in the hypothalamus. Because we don't know what the unconditional response is in this circumstance, this could be a conditioning of the dopamine reward system, but not necessarily be linked directly to the taste response.

Dr. Schneider: Yes, I agree with you. I certainly am aware of your neurochemical data, and there are also some data from the University of British Columbia. The only thing I would say is because the rats' behavioral data at the microstructural as well as macrostructural level were indistinguishable between raclopride on 10% sucrose and saline or 5% sucrose, that was very convincing. Obviously, it would be good to do neurochemistry under those circumstances, including microdialysis.

DR. DONNA LARSON (*Mental Health Center of Boulder County, Colorado. Longmont, CO*): This is much more of a clinical psychiatric comment, and not an issue directly pertaining to your basic research. I work in a community infant project with failure-to-thrive infants. As you and the last speaker talked, the fact came to mind that these mothers of infants that fail to thrive don't seem able to read their babies' hunger signals. The mothers may be fairly well motivated, and the infant opens its mouth and seeks for the breast and gives what, for any other person, would be very clear cues that it is hungry, but the mother is failing to react to those cues. If that pattern continues, it seems to me that this would greatly affect the development of the stress-reducing responses of the nervous system. The baby is not being fed in response to its own cues to the mother. Its own ability, therefore, to have milk at certain times and get some analgesic effects is impaired. The impairment of these stress-reducing functions would have an impact on the developing brain over a very vulnerable period of time.

DR. SCHNEIDER: Your question has more relevance to Dr. Blass's work, and he unfortunately had to catch a plane. I would agree with you, however; we're also interested in studying the ontogeny of these systems.

DR. MICHEL CABANAC (*Université Laval, Quebec, Canada*): Yesterday, we heard very nice story which almost fits yours, but it was another transmitter, serotonin. So, Is it serotonin or dopamine or both?

DR. SCHNEIDER: And where, I might add, in the brain? In response, I will reiterate a comment I made at the press conference yesterday which is that researchers should not to be tied to one particular neurotransmitter. The brain, as we all know, is redundant, and this is in fact why, when you give a drug chronically, other systems take over. It doesn't have to be either/or, and there are also the complexities of co-existence, interactions, and so forth. I refuse to take a position on sole mediation by dopamine or serotonin. The microdialysis work has shown that, for example, amphetamine releases both.

Benzodiazepine Receptor-Mediated Enhancement and Inhibition of Taste Reactivity, Food Choice, and Intake

STEVEN J. COOPER

School of Psychology
University of Birmingham
Birmingham, B15 2TT, United Kingdom

INTRODUCTION

Benzodiazepines (BZs) are a class of drugs that have found wide clinical application. Some common examples are diazepam, chlordiazepoxide, lorazepam, midazolam, and clonazepam. They are used clinically as anxiolytics, anticonvulsants, hypnotics, and muscle relaxants. Initial pharmacological investigations of chlordiazepoxide, the first of the BZs to be synthesized, indicated that one noticeable effect in animals, at least, was that the drug increased food intake.[1] That observation has been confirmed in many different mammalian species,[2,3] including two primate species, squirrel monkeys and rhesus monkeys.[4,5] There has been a persistent inclination to see the hyperphagic effect of BZs simply in terms of their anxiolytic properties,[6-8] on the grounds that BZs should disinhibit feeding responses that are suppressed by fear, stress, or novelty. The hyperphagic effect, according to this view, is no more than secondary to a more fundamental anxiolytic effect. A counter view is the proposal that the hyperphagic effect reflects a more direct effect on eating behavior, and hence deserves to be studied in its own right.[3,9,10]

This article adopts the latter position and attempts to achieve two aims. First, it will give an account of recent pharmacological developments in the field of BZ research and relate these to empirical investigations of food intake. These developments are not trivial[11,12] and can appear at first sight to be bewilderingly complex. Nevertheless, each point will be illustrated with examples taken from feeding research.[13] Second, I wish to go beyond the mere fact that BZs increase food consumption and will consider the means by which this might occur. Taking the two aims together, I will try to relate what happens at a molecular level in the brain to the behavioral changes that become expressed in terms of the increased ingestion of food. At the end of this development of ideas concerning BZ functions, I shall consider briefly the possible clinical implications.

MOLECULAR BASES OF BENZODIAZEPINE ACTIONS

Benzodiazepine Receptors

The crucial discovery that revolutionized our understanding of the actions of BZs in the brain occurred in 1977. In that year, the presence of high-affinity, specific, and saturable binding sites for BZs in neural tissue was reported.[14,15] These sites, which are present on synaptic neuronal membranes,[16] are recognized to be BZ receptors (BZRs).[17] These receptors are not uniformly distributed in the brain and spinal cord; high densities are found in cerebral cortex, limbic structures, olfactory bulb, and hypothalamus, substantia nigra, and cerebellum. The patterns for receptor distribution are remarkably similar for rat[18] and human[19] brains, although there are differences in detail.

The earlier discovery of specific opiate receptors in the brain led to the further exciting discoveries of several families of endogenously occurring opioid peptides.[20] These are the natural ligands for the opiate receptors. Naturally, investigators were eager to discover endogenous ligands for BZR in the central nervous system. Although several candidate substances have been proposed,[12] there is still no universal agreement that authentic endogenous ligands have been identified. Nevertheless, one very promising line of investigation that pursues this problem will be discussed later.[21]

Drugs That Act as BZR Ligands

The discovery of BZR made possible the rapid screening of many kinds of compounds to see if they also bind to these receptors.[12] Many have been found, and they can be grouped into three main categories according to their characteristic pharmacological actions: agonists, antagonists, and inverse agonists.

Agonists

Agonists produce BZ-like effects. They include not only familiar BZs, like chlordiazepoxide and diazepam, but also certain novel compounds that show high affinity for BZRs. Such compounds include β-carbolines (e.g., ZK 93423 and ZK 91296),[22,23] pyrazoloquinolines (e.g., CGS 9895 and CGS 9896),[24,25] the triazolopyridazine CL 218,872,[26] and cyclopyrrolone derivatives (e.g., zopiclone and suriclone).[27,28] All can elicit BZ-like effects in many different types of test. Differences can occur between these drugs, however, because some have relatively low efficacy and behave as *partial* agonists. When this is the case, the drugs may produce some of the typical BZ effects (anxiolytic and anticonvulsant activity, for example), but fail to elicit others (sedation and ataxia, for example).

Antagonists

Antagonists block BZ-like effects that are due to drug action at BZR. If given alone, antagonists have little or no intrinsic activity. Examples of these drugs include Ro15–1788 (flumazenil)[29] and the β-carboline, ZK 93426.[30]

Inverse Agonists

Strangely enough, inverse agonists bind with high affinity to BZR, but produce effects that are opposite to those associated with BZs.[31,32] Examples include imidazobenzodiazepines, such as Ro15-4513,[33] β-carbolines, such as FG 7142, DMCM,[34] and the pyrazoloquinoline CGS 8216.[25] BZR antagonists block the effects of inverse agonists; effects of agonists and those of inverse agonists cancel one another.

These drug categories are discussed in greater detail by Little *et al.*,[35] and FIGURE 1 provides a classification scheme for several types of BZR ligand.

BZR Ligands and Palatable Food Consumption

The food-intake experiments that we have undertaken involve, in the main, the use of nondeprived adult male rats trained to eat a sweetened mash in a 30-minute test period. Familiarizing the rats with the test procedure is necessary, to avoid interpretation of drug effects couched in terms of "antineophobic" effects and other appeals to novelty as a relevant factor. Consequently, typical baseline levels of intake, in our experiments, usually lie between 15–20 g in the 30-minute test.

Despite the relatively high baseline, BZs are effective, and dose-dependent increases

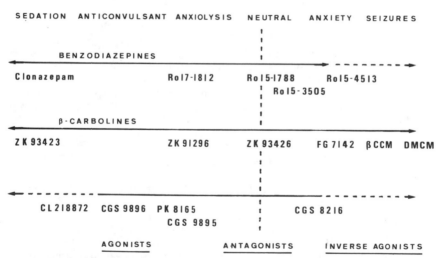

FIGURE 1. Drugs that act at BZR can be arranged in terms of a spectrum of effects. They range from full agonists (far left), through partial agonists and antagonists, to inverse agonists (right-hand side). The first row shows that drugs with benzodiazepine structures can be identified across the spectrum. Similarly, as the second row shows, β-carbolines provide examples of drugs that span the full spectrum. The bottom row identifies the relative positions of pyrazoloquinolines and other, miscellaneous drugs. (Adapted with permission from Little *et al.*[35])

in food consumption are reliably obtained.[36-38] Following BZ treatments, it is not uncommon for individual animals to consume in excess of 30 g of the diet in the 30-minute test, approximately a tenth of their body weight. The increase in food intake could result from a number of behavioral changes, for example, eating faster or eating more often. However, we found that midazolam (a water-soluble BZ of about the same potency as diazepam) increased the duration of individual bouts of eating, but did not increase either the rate of eating or the frequency of eating bouts.[39] Midazolam, over the effective-dose range (3.0–10.0 mg/kg i.p.), has side-effects, and consequently locomotion, rearing, and grooming are reduced.[39] Nevertheless, as I shall show later, these depressant effects are not indirectly responsible for the increase in food consumption.

Pharmacologically, several criteria have to be met before one can be satisfied that increases in food consumption depend on agonist activity at specific BZRs. First, other factors being equal, the potencies of agonists should correspond to their relative affinities for the receptor. Clonazepam has a higher affinity for the BZR than chlordiazepoxide and is more potent in terms of the minimum dose required to increase food intake.[40] Second, the BZ-induced increase in food intake should be blocked by selective BZR antagonists. This point has been demonstrated not only for rats, but also for rabbits and rhesus monkeys.[37,41,42] Third, there is stereospecific binding to BZRs, and the binding site distinguishes, in its recognition, between enantiomeric pairs. We were able to demonstrate that BZ-induced hyperphagia does depend on the stereoselective binding to the receptor.[43]

Hence, BZRs mediate the increase in food consumption that follow benzodiazepine treatments. This analysis can be taken further, however, if BZRs are distinguished into two subtypes: Type 1 (cerebellar-type, because they are characteristic of the BZ sites in the cerebellum) and Type 2 (hippocampal-type, characteristic of sites in the hippocampus).[44] The novel hypnotic compound, zolpidem, binds with high affinity to BZRs, and shows greater affinity for the BZR_1 subtype.[45,46] Its characteristic pharmacological feature is that in addition to its having anxiolytic effects, it is very potent in producing sedative-hypnotic effects.[47,48] We have recently found that zolpidem does not increase palatable food consumption in the rat.[49] Hence, the hyperphagic effect of BZs may depend upon agonist activity at the BZR_2 subtype. However, in the absence of an agonist that is selective for the BZR_2 receptor, this idea has yet to be tested directly.

BZR Partial Agonists

A number of drugs have been identified as BZR partial agonists; they provide a continuum of agents having effects that lie between full agonists at one extreme, and antagonists at the other. Several of these compounds have been tested in relation to palatable food consumption in the rat.[50] The β-carboline ZK 91296 and the imidazobenzodiazepines, Ro16–6028 and Ro17–1812, significantly increase food intake.[51,52] In contrast, the pyrazoloquinolines CGS 9895 and CGS 9896 not only do not stimulate food intake, but, most interestingly, are effective as BZ antagonists.[43]

Each of these drugs produce effects in animal models that are indicative of potential anxiolytic activity.[50] They show a reduced propensity for inducing sedation and ataxia as side effects. Because their pharmacological effects are more restricted than those of full agonists, like diazepam, some important conclusions can be drawn (TABLE 1).

TABLE 1. Comparisons between Several Categories of BZR Agonists Indicate that BZR-Mediated Hyperphagia Is Dissociable from Anxiolytic Activity and Sedative–Hypnotic Effects

Drug	Putative Anxiolytic Activity	Increased Food Consumption	Sedative–Hypnotic
Full BZ agonists			
Diazepam	Yes	Yes	Yes
Midazolam	Yes	Yes	Yes
BZ partial agonists			
Ro16-6028	Yes	Yes	No
Ro17-1812	Yes	Yes	No
Ro23-0364	Yes	Yes	No
Pyrazoloquinolines			
CGS 9895	Yes, weak	No, antagonism	No, antagonism
CGS 9896	Yes	No, antagonism	No, antagonism
Selective hypnotic			
Zolpidem	Yes	No	Yes, strong

First, the hyperphagic effects of BZs can be separated from the induction of sedation and ataxia. Hence, the hyperphagic effect is not secondary to either of these additional effects. This point is reinforced by experiments with zolpidem, which were referred to earlier. Zolpidem induces sedation but does not increase food consumption. Second, there is more than a hint that the anxiolytic properties of BZs are potentially dissociable from their hyperphagic effect. In several animal models of anxiolytic drug activity, the pyrazoloquinolines, CGS 9895 and CGS 9896, produce effects that are quite similiar to those of diazepam,[53-55] yet both drugs antagonize benzodiazepine-induced hyperphagia.[43] Zolpidem is also an effective anxiolytic in some animal models. Therefore, at a molecular level, it may prove possible to tease apart BZR-mediated responses linked to anxiolytic effects of BZs, from those responses that translate into increases in feeding behavior. If this does prove possible, it would of course be of fundamental significance from both basic and clinical points of view.

BZR Inverse Agonists

Inverse agonists were an unexpected discovery.[31,32] Because they exert effects opposite those produced by typical BZR agonists, it seems possible that they would reduce food consumption in the same tests that BZs have been shown to increase intake. Our initial results confirmed this, and demonstrated that the β-carbolines DMCM and FG 7142, and the pyrazoloquinoline CGS 8216, dose-dependently reduced palatable food intake in nondeprived rats.[36] The reduction in food intake produced by FG 7142 was found to be blocked by BZR antagonists, Ro15–1788 and ZK 93426.[36,51]

When an agonist, such as clonazepam, is given in combination with FG 7142, they act competitively.[56] The consequence is that the effect on food intake can vary from marked hyperphagia at one extreme (due to agonist influence) to anorexia at the other (due to the inverse agonist's effects), according to the relative concentrations of the two ligands. Hence, there can be bidirectional control of food intake, mediated by a single type of receptor.[40,57]

Endogenous Ligands

Experiments by Costa and his colleagues in Washington, D.C. indicate that an endogenous polypeptide, which they call DBI (diazepam binding inhibitor) may be a precursor for smaller peptides that bind to BZRs.[21,58] One product of DBI is an 18-amino-acid segment called ODN (octadecaneuropeptide).[59] DBI-like immunoreactivity is found in neurons, but also in some glial cells and in some peripheral tissues. Within neurons, DBI-like immunoreactivity is primarily associated with synaptic vesicles, suggesting that DBI may be released as a possible neuromodulator.[60]

Interestingly, DBI-like immunoreactivity is detected in human brain.[61] Patients suffering from major depression show significantly greater concentrations of DBI-like immunoreactivity in cerebrospinal fluid when compared with control.[62] (No differences are found in schizophrenic patients, or patients with dementia of the Alzheimer's type.)

If peptides derived from DBI do have physiological roles with regard to brain function, what evidence is there which may throw light on those roles? BZR inverse agonists (FG 7142, DMCM, β-CCE) are known to enhance the suppression of licking at a drinking spout produced by a low-intensity shock.[63] In the same test, DBI produced a similar effect, which could be antagonized by Ro15-1788.[64] According to this limited evidence, therefore, DBI should behave like a BZR inverse agonist, leading to the prediction that DBI may have anorectic effects mediated by BZR.

BENZODIAZEPINES, TASTE PREFERENCE, TASTE REACTIVITY, AND FOOD CHOICE

The preceding section was devoted to pharmacological considerations of the BZR-mediated increases and decreases in food consumption. In this section, series of experiments will be described which together suggest that drug actions at central BZRs interact with taste-dependent factors to promote, or retard, ingestional responses. Because extensive pharmacological investigations have not yet been carried out for the several different methods that will be described, the data are limited in pharmacological scope, but gain in behavioral and physiological analysis.

Taste Preference

In early work on chlordiazepoxide, Maickel and Maloney gave 23-hour water-deprived rats access to one of three fluids in a one-hour drinking test.[65] They were water, saccharin solution (0.2%), and tartaric acid (0.5%), respectively. Chlordiazepoxide increased fluid intake in each case, but the authors noted that "chlordiazepoxide works best when the consummatory fluid is a pleasant-tasting saccharin solution" (p. 767). Nevertheless, BZs do induce hyperdipsia,[66] and therefore an alternative approach is needed to determine whether or not BZs have more selective effects on preference.

Recently, we were able to show that the potent BZ, clonazepam, selectively increased saccharin consumption in a two-choice preference test.[67] As FIGURE 2 indicates, clonazepam had no effect on water intake, but dose-dependently increased the consumption of a preferred 0.05% sodium saccharin solution. Thus, clonazepam did not elevate intake nonspecifically, but only affected consumption of the saccharin solution. An interesting, additional aspect of the experiment was that zolpidem, the imidazopyridine that has selective affinity for the BZR₁ subtype,[45,46] did not affect con-

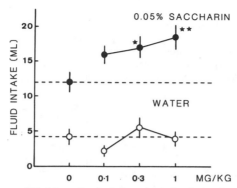

FIGURE 2. Clonazepam (0.1–1.0 mg/kg, i.p.) dose-dependently increased intake of a preferred 0.05% sodium saccharin solution in water-deprived rats.[67] Water intake in the two-choice test was not affected.

sumption in the saccharin preference test. Hence, we can conclude that the Type 2 receptor subtype (hippocampal type) may be of more importance than the Type 1 in relation to changes in saccharin preference.

If BZRs do mediate increases in saccharin preference, it follows from the bidirectionality principle for BZRs[40] that inverse agonists should selectively diminish saccharin intake in a two-choice test. An initial experiment with the β-carboline FG 7142 confirmed the prediction: saccharin preference was abolished (FIG. 3).[68] Nevertheless, FG 7142 is strongly antidipsogenic,[69] and the observed effect on saccharine preference could be confounded by a strong overall effect to reduce fluid consumption. Therefore we turned to a weaker (lower efficacy) inverse agonist, the pyrazoloquinoline CGS

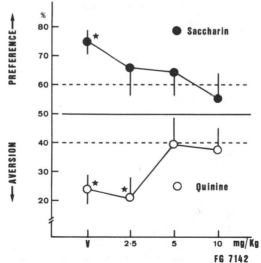

FIGURE 3. The β-carboline inverse agonist, FG 7142 (2.5–10 mg/kg, i.p.), reduced saccharin preference in a two-choice test.[68] Aversion to a quinine solution was reduced. Water-deprived male rats were used.

8216,[25] which does not reduce drinking responses indiscriminately.[69,70] The result showed that CGS 8216 reduced saccharin intake in a two-choice test, without affecting the consumption of water.[71] Hence, given the right compound, it is possible to demonstrate selective reduction of ingestion of a preferred sweet solution, consistent with the bi-directionality principle of BZR-mediated responses.

This result carries some interesting implications. One of these concerns an imidazobenzodiazepine, Ro15–4513, which is currently under intensive investigation as a functional ethanol antagonist.[72,73] Basic pharmacological and biochemical studies indicate that Ro15–4513 is a weak inverse agonist at BZR.[33,74] Hence, we should expect that Ro15–4513, like CGS 8216, will reduce saccharin consumption selectively in a two-choice test. A recent experiment confirms this prediction (TABLE 2). Water intake was not affected by Ro15–4513. So far as we can determine, therefore, intake of a preferred saccharin solution in a two-choice test can be selectively enhanced or reduced by BZR agonists and inverse agonists, respectively.

These results suggest that endogenous substances in the brain, active at BZRs (e.g. DBI), will modulate preference for sweet taste. But there may also be an important link with ethanol preference and consumption. Ro15–4513 not only affects saccharin preference, but it also has ethanol–antagonist properties. This leads one to suspect that DBI, as an endogenous BZR ligand, may be associated with ethanol preference. In support of this possibility, recent evidence indicates that ethanol-preferring rats show increased DBI-like immunoreactivity in hypothalamus and cerebellum, after chronic ethanol consumption.[75]

Taste Reactivity

An important series of taste-reactivity experiments provides further evidence for a link between BZR mechanisms and behavioral responses to tastes. It has been established that certain species-typical reactions (e.g., tongue protrusions, mouth grapes), provide a measure of palatability, and that they can be reliably elicited by intraoral infusions of fluids.[76] Berridge & Treit discovered that chlordiazepoxide selectively increased the number of ingestive responses elicited by a variety of tastes, but had little or no effect on the number of aversive responses elicited by the same tastes.[77] They drew the conclusion that agonists acting at BZRs have the effect of enhancing the positive palatability of tastes. A subsequent experiment confirmed the main result, and also showed that chlordiazepoxide's effects were antagonized by Ro15–1788 and CGS 8216.[78] Most interestingly, the neural substrate for chlordiazepoxide's selective effect on taste reactivity measures appears to lie within the mesencephalon, and/or caudal to it. Ber-

TABLE 2. Effects of the Imidazabenzodiazepine, Ro15-4513 on Saccharin and Water Intake in a Two-Choice Test

Fluid Intake (ml)	Ro15-4513 Dose (mg/kg, i.p.)			
	0	1	3	10
Saccharin (0.05%)	7.9 ± 0.6	$4.3^a \pm 0.5$	$5.0^a \pm 0.5$	$3.1^b \pm 0.4$
Water	5.1 ± 0.6	5.0 ± 0.5	3.7 ± 0.5	5.4 ± 0.5

NOTE: Results are shown in terms of mean $\pm$ SEM; $n = 14$. 30-min test using 22-hour, water-deprived male rats. Levels of significance for comparisons against vehicle control were determined with Dunnett's t-test. (Cooper, Bowyer & Van Der Hoek, unpublished data.)
[a] $p < 0.05$.
[b] $p < 0.01$.

ridge has shown recently that chlordiazepoxide remains effective in chronic mesen-cephalic decerebrate rats.[79] Drugs active at BZR may modulate the positive palata-bility of tastes within neural circuits located within the lower brainstem.

Sham Feeding

Sham-feeding rats, with an open gastric fistula, show marked satiety deficits.[80] Their intake of sucrose solutions provides an important index of diet palatability.[81] Sham feeding in the rat is therefore a very useful model for investigating further the effects of BZR drugs on hedonic aspects of ingestion.

We have observed that the BZ full agonist, midazolam, significantly enhanced su-crose sham feeding in the rat.[82] The BZ antagonist, Ro15-1788, had no effect,[82] whereas several inverse agonists (Ro15-3505, CGS 8216, FG 7142) all significantly reduced sham feeding.[82,83] In the case of CGS 8216, it decreased sucrose sham feeding at doses that did not affect sham drinking of water.[83] Thus, bi-directional effects on sucrose sham feeding can be obtained using agonists and inverse agonists acting at BZR.

Food Preferences

Behavioral tests, in which a variety of foods are available to hungry rats, indicate that BZs do not produce nonspecific increases in food ingestion. For example, given a choice between a single familiar food and a range of novel foods, a small dose of chlordiazepoxide selectively increased the response to the familiar food.[84] When all the foods were familiar, chlordiazepoxide enhanced the response to preferred food.[85] When rats were given a choice of three foods (matched in texture), chlordiazepoxide (5 and 10 mg/kg i.p.) selectively enhanced the consumption of a food to which sac-charin had been added (FIG. 4).[86] The bidirectionality principle of BZR-mediated re-sponses has not been tested in these experiments, but the results do suggest that BZ agonist activity potentiates feeding responses to preferred food items. One of the factors determining food preference may, of course, be taste.

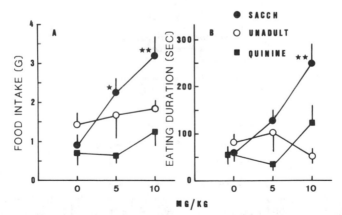

FIGURE 4. Chlordiazepoxide (5.0 and 10 mg/kg, i.p.) selectively increased intake (panel A) and eating duration (panel B) for a saccharin-flavored mash in a three-choice test.[86] Responses to the other choices were not affected. Food-deprived male rats were used.

Scheme for BZR-Mediated Changes in Ingestion

FIGURE 5 illustrates how the behavioral data can be integrated to give an account of BZR-mediated changes in ingestional responses.

As we have seen, BZs specifically enhance taste palatability in test that measure ingestive actions to intraoral infusions of sapid solutions. This effect, an increase in positive hedonic loading of tastes, could lead, in turn, to a selective increase in sweet-taste preference. It could also result in increased consumption of preferred food items, for example, when foods are sweetened. We anticipate that inverse agonists will modulate ingestional responses in opposite ways. Evidence has been reviewed above indicating that inverse agonists reduce food intake, and they also reduce saccharin intake in a two-choice test of preference. Further work is needed to determine if inverse agonists affect taste reactivity responses selectively, or, indeed, if they affect food preferences selectively.

CLINICAL IMPLICATIONS

The authors of a recent review of the neurobiological basis of eating disorders acknowledged that they had neglected to examine the role that hedonic factors (particularly in relation to taste) have in the modulation of feeding behavior.[87] An underlying

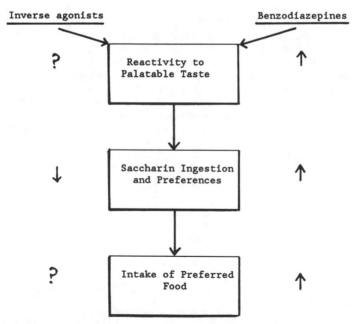

FIGURE 5. BZR agonists and inverse agonists may affect palatability of tastes, bidirectionally. As a result, saccharin preference can be affected by these drugs, and food preferences may be modified.

↑ Increase, ↓ Decrease, ? Not determined.

theme of the present discussion, in contrast, is the emphasis that has been placed on hedonic factors in trying to account for the powerful effects that drugs, active at BZR, have on food consumption. BZR-mediated responses are of considerable interest since bidirectional effects can be obtained depending upon the use of agonists and inverse agonists. Therefore, a unique situation exists in which either pronounced increases in food intake, or equally pronounced decreases, can be obtained from actions at a single receptor. An attractive hypothesis, which deserves further study, is that hedonic-loading of food-related stimuli (e.g. taste) do come under the influence of BZR mechanisms. Some evidence suggests a location for the receptors in the brainstem.[79]

Recent experiments carried out with persons who exhibit eating disorders reveal some interesting taste preferences. Normal-weight bulimic patients prefer sweeter stimuli than controls.[88,89] Anorectic patients like sweet but dislike high-fat stimuli.[89] Relationships between eating disorders and affective disorders have been described,[90,91] and a high incidence of alcoholism in first-degree relatives of bulimic patients has been reported.[90]

So far as I am aware, virtually no clinical data are available at present to implicate BZR-mediated effects with these characteristics of patients with eating disorders. Nevertheless, we have seen that a putative endogenous ligand for these receptors (DBI) has been linked to depression in patients[62] and to ethanol preference in rats.[75] If DBI is confirmed as a neuropeptide with inverse agonist activity, then from the basic experimentation completed to date, we should expect it to exhibit anorectic properties and to reduce hedonic loading of sweet taste. In addition, DBI may give rise to more than one cleavage product that acts as a ligand at BZR,[92] and it is possible that both agonist and inverse agonist effects could occur.

The basic findings described in this chapter indicate that important aspects of the control of food ingestion and preference can be affected bidirectionally by drug actions at BZR. The links with eating disorders affecting humans remain to be demonstrated. However, as more is discovered about the presence of putative endogenous ligands for these receptors in human brain, and in the brains of other animals, the more likely it will be that these basic studies will find clinical application.

ACKNOWLEDGMENT

I wish to thank Mrs. B. Conlon for her preparation of the manuscript.

REFERENCES

1. RANDALL, L. O., W. SCHALLEK, G. A. HEISE, E. F. KEITH & R. E. BAGDON. 1960. The psychosedative properties of methaminodiazepoxide. J. Pharmacol. Exp. Ther. **129:** 163–171.
2. BAILE, C. A. & C. MCLAUGHLIN. 1979. A review of the behavioral and physiological responses to elfazepam, a chemical feed intake stimulant. J. Anim. Sci. **49:** 1371–1395.
3. COOPER, S. J. 1980. Benzodiazepines as appetite-enhancing compounds. Appetite **1:** 7–19.
4. LOCKE, K. W., D. R. BROWN & S. G. HOLTZMAN. 1982. Effects of opiate antagonists and putative *mu*- and *kappa* agonists on milk intake in rat and squirrel monkey. Pharmacol. Biochem. Behav. **17:** 1275–1279.
5. FOLTIN, R. W. & C. R. SCHUSTER. 1983. Interaction between the effects of intragastric meals and drugs on feeding in rhesus monkeys. J. Pharmacol. Exp. Ther. **226:** 405–410.
6. POSCHEL, B. P. H. A simple and specific screen for benzodiazepine-like drugs. Psychopharmacologia (Berlin) **19:** 193–198.

7. TYE, N. C., D. J. NICHOLAS & M. J. MORGAN. 1975. Chlordiazepoxide and preference for free food in rats. Pharmacol. Biochem. Behav. 3: 1149–1151.
8. SHEPHARD, R. A. & L. B. ESTALL. 1984. Anxiolytic actions of chlordiazepoxide determine its effects on hyponeophagia in rats. Psychopharmacology 82: 343–347.
9. WISE, R. A. & V. DAWSON. 1974. Diazepam-induced eating and lever-pressing for food in sated rates. J. Comp. Physiol. Psychol. 86: 930–941.
10. SOUBRIÉ, P., S. KULKARNI, P. SIMON & J. R. BOISSIER. 1975. Effets des anxiolytiques sur la prise de nourriture de rats et de souris placés en situation nouvelle ou familière. Psychopharmacologia (Berlin) 45: 203–210.
11. HAEFELY, W. 1985. Tranquilizers. In Psychopharmacology 2, Part 1: Preclinical Psychopharmacology. D. G. Grahame-Smith & P. J. Cowen, Eds.: 92–182. Elsevier. Amsterdam.
12. HAEFELY, W., E. HYBURZ, M. GERECKE & H. MÖHLER. 1975. Recent advances in the molecular pharmacology of benzodiazepine receptors and in the structure–activity relationships of their agonists and antagonists. In Advances in Drug Research. B. Testa, Ed. Vol. 14: 165–322. Academic Press. London.
13. COOPER, S. J. 1987. Drugs and hormones: Effects on ingestion. In Feeding and Drinking. N. Rowland & F. M. Toates, Eds.: 231–269. Elsevier. Amsterdam.
14. SQUIRES, R. G. & C. BRAESTRUP. 1977. Benzodiazepine receptors in rat brain. Nature (London) 266: 732–734.
15. MÖHLER, H. & T. OKADA. 1977. Benzodiazepine receptor: Demonstration in the central nervous system. Science 198: 849–851.
16. MÖHLER, H., J. G. RICHARDS & J. -Y. WU. 1981. Autoradiographic localization of benzodiazepine receptors in immunocytochemically defined γ-aminobutyrergic synapses. Proc. Natl. Acad. Sci. USA 78: 1935–1938.
17. RICHARDS, J. G. & H. MÖHLER. 1984. Benzodiazepine receptors. Neuropharmacology 23: 233–242.
18. YOUNG, W. S. & M. J. KUHAR. 1980. Radiohistochemical localization of benzodiazepine receptors in rat brain. J. Pharmacol. Exp. Ther. 212: 337–346.
19. ZEZULA, J., R. CORTES, A. PROBST & J. M. PALACIOS. 1988. Benzodiazepine receptor sites in the human brain: Autoradiographic mapping. Neuroscience 25: 771–795.
20. AKIL, J., D. BRONSTEIN & A. MANSOUR. 1988. Overview of the endogenous opioid systems: Anatomical, biochemical and functional issues. In Endorphins, Opiates and Behavioral Processes. R. J. Rodgers & S. J. Cooper, Eds.: 1–23. John Wiley. Chichester, England.
21. BARBACCIA, M. L., E. COSTA & A. GUIDOTTI. 1988. Endogenous ligands for high-affinity recognition sites of psychotropic drugs. Ann. Rev. Pharmacol. Toxicol. 28: 451–476.
22. FILE, S. E. & H. A. BALDWIN. 1987. Effects of β-carbolines in animal models of anxiety. Brain Res. Bull. 19: 293–299.
23. STEPHENS, D. N., H. H. SCHNEIDER, W. KEHR, L. H. JENSEN, E. PETERSEN & T. HONORÉ. 1987. Modulation of anxiety by β-carbolines and other benzodiazepine receptor ligands: Relationship of pharmacological to biochemical measures of efficacy. Brain Res. Bull. 19: 309–318.
24. WOOD, P. L., P. LOO, A. BRAUNWALDER, N. YOKOYAMA & D. L. CHENEY. 1984. In vitro characterization of benzodiazepine agonists, antagonists, inverse agonists and agonists/antagonists. J. Pharmacol. Exp. Ther. 231: 572–576.
25. COOPER, S. J., T. C. KIRKHAM & L. B. ESTALL. 1987. Pyrazoloquinolines: Second generation benzodiazepine receptor ligands with heterogenous effects. Trends Pharmacol. Sci. 8: 180–184.
26. LIPPA, A. S., J. COUPET, E. N. GREENBLATT, C. A. KLEPNER & B. BEER. 1979. A synthetic non-benzodiazepine ligand for benzodiazepine receptor: A probe for investigating neuronal substrates of anxiety. Pharmacol. Biochem. Behav. 11: 99–106.
27. BLANCHARD, J. C., A. BOILEAU, C. GARRET & L. JULOU. 1979. In vitro and in vivo inhibition by zopiclone of benzodiazepine binding to rodent brain receptors. Life Sci. 24: 2417–2420.
28. BLANCHARD, J. C. & L. JULOU. 1983. Suriclone: A new cyclopyrrolone derivative recognising receptors labelled by benzodiazepine in rat hippocampus and cerebellum. J. Neurochem. 40: 601–607.

29. HUNKELER, W., H. MÖHLER, L. PIERI, P. POLC, E. P. BONETTI, R. CUMIN, R. SCHAFFNER & W. HAEFELY. 1981. Selective antagonists of benzodiazepines. Nature (London) 290: 514–516.

30. JENSEN, L. H., E. N. PETERSEN, C. BRAESTRUP, T. HONORÉ, W. KEHR, D. N. STEPHENS, H. SCHNEIDER, D. SEIDELMANN & R. SCHMIECHEN. 1984. Evaluation of the β-carboline ZK 93426 as a benzodiazepine receptor antagonist. Psychopharmacology 83: 249–256.

31. BRAESTRUP, C., M. NIELSEN, T. HONORÉ, L. H. JENSEN & E. N. PETERSEN. 1983. Benzodiazepine receptor ligands with positive and negative efficacy. Neuropharmacology 22: 1451–1457.

32. POLC, P., E. P. BONETTI, R. SCHAFFNER & W. HAEFELY. 1982. A three-state model of the benzodiazepine receptor explains the interactions between the benzodiazepine antagonist Ro15–1788, benzodiazepine tranquilizers, β-carbolines, and phenobarbitone. Naunyn–Schmiedebergs Arch. Pharmacol. 321: 260–264.

33. BONETTI, E. P., P. POLC & L. PIERI. 1984. An azido analogue of the benzodiazepine antagonist Ro15–1788 (Ro15–4513) behaves as a partial inverse benzodiazepine agonist. Neurosci. Lett. (Suppl.) 18: 530.

34. BRAESTRUP, C., R. SCHMIECHEN, G. NEFF, M. NIELSEN & E. N. PETERSEN. 1982. Interaction of convulsive ligands with benzodiazepine receptors. Science 216: 1241–1243.

35. LITTLE, H. J., D. J. NUTT & S. C. TAYLOR. 1987. Kindling and withdrawal changes at the benzodiazepine receptor. J. Psychopharmacol. 1: 35–46.

36. COOPER, S. J., D. J. BARBER, D. B. GILBERT & W. R. MOORES. 1985. Benzodiazepine receptor ligands and the consumption of a highly palatable diet in non-deprived male rats. Psychopharmacology 86: 348–355.

37. COOPER, S. J. & D. B. GILBERT. 1985. Clonazepam-induced hyperphagia in non-deprived rats: Tests of pharmacological specificity with Ro5–4864, Ro5–3663, Ro15–1788 and CGS 9896. Pharmacol. Biochem. Behav. 22: 753–760.

38. COOPER, S. J. & W. R. MOORES. 1985. Benzodiazepine-induced hyperphagia in the non-deprived rat: Comparisons with CL 218,872, zopiclone, tracazolate and phenobarbital. Pharmacol. Biochem. Behav. 23: 169–174.

39. COOPER, S. J. & R. E. YERBURY. 1986. Midazolam-induced hyperphagia and FG 7142-induced anorexia: Behavioural characteristics in the rat. Pharmacol. Biochem. Behav. 25: 99–106.

40. COOPER, S. J. 1985. Bidirectional control of palatable food consumption through a common benzodiazepine receptor: Theory and evidence. Brain. Res. Bull. 15: 397–410.

41. FOLTIN, R. W., S. ELLIS & C. R. SCHUSTER. 1985. Specific antagonism by Ro15–1788 of benzodiazepine-induced increases in food intake in rhesus monkeys. Pharmacol. Biochem. Behav. 23: 249–252.

42. MANSBACH, R. S., J. A. STANLEY & J. E. BARRETT. 1984. Ro15–1788 and β-CCE selectively eliminate diazepam-induced feeding in the rabbit. Pharmacol. Biochem. Behav. 20: 763–766.

43. COOPER, S. J. & R. E. YERBURY. 1986. Benzodiazepine-induced hyperphagia: Stereospecificity and antagonism by pyrazoloquinolines, CGS 9895 and CGS 9896. Psychopharmacology 89: 462–466.

44. SIEGHART, W., A. EICHINGER, P. RIEDERER & K. JELLINGER. 1985. Comparison of benzodiazepine receptor binding in membranes from human or rat brain. Neuropharmacology 24: 751–759.

45. ARBILLA, S., H. DEPOORTERE, P. GEORGE & S. Z. LANGER. 1985. Pharmacological profile of the imidazopyridine zolpidem at benzodiazepine receptors and electrocorticogram in rats. Naunyn–Schmiedeberg's Arch. Pharmacol. 330: 248–251.

46. BENAVIDES, J., B. PENY, A. DUBOIS, G. PERRAULT, E. MOREL, B. ZIVKOVIC & B. SCATTON. 1988. In vivo interaction of zolpidem with central benzodiazepine (BZD) binding sites (as labeled by [^{3}H]Ro15–1788) in the mouse brain. Preferential affinity of zolpidem for the ω_1 (BZD$_1$) subtype. J. Pharmacol. Exp. Ther. 245: 1033–1041.

47. DEPOORTERE, H., B. ZIVKOVIC, K. G. LLOYD, D. J. SANGER, G. PERRAULT, S. Z. LANGER & G. BARTHOLINI. 1986. Zolpidem, a novel nonbenzodiazepine hypnotic. I. Neuropharmacological and behavioral effects. J. Pharmacol. Exp. Ther. 237: 649–658.

48. SANGER, D. J., G. PERRAULT, E. MOREL, D. JOLY & B. ZIVKOVIC. 1987. The behavioral profile of zolpidem, a novel hypnotic drug of imidazopyridine structure. Physiol. Behav. **41:** 235–240.

49. YERBURY, R. E. & S. J. COOPER. 1989. Novel benzodiazepine receptor ligands: Palatable food consumption following administration of zolpidem, CGS 17867A or Ro23–0364, in the rat. Pharmacol. Biochem. Behav. In press.

50. COOPER, S. J., R. E. YERBURY, J. C. NEILL & A. DESA. 1987. Partial agonists acting at benzodiazepine receptors can be differentiated in test of ingestional behaviour. Physiol. Behav. **41:** 247–255.

51. COOPER, S. J. 1986. Hyperphagic and anorectic effects of β-carbolines in a palatable food consumption test: Comparisons with triazolam and quazepam. Eur. J. Pharmacol. **120:** 257–265.

52. YERBURY, R. E. & S. J. COOPER. 1987. The benzodiazepine partial agonists, Ro16–6028 and Ro17–1812, increase palatable food consumption in nondeprived rats. Pharmacol. Biochem. Behav. **28:** 427–431.

53. BENNETT, D. A., C. L. AMRICK, D. E. WILSON, P. S. BERNARD, N. YOKOYAMA & J. M. LIEBMAN. 1985. Behavioral pharmacological profile of CGS 9895: A novel anxiomodulator with selective benzodiazepine agonist and antagonist properties. Drug Dev. Res. **6:** 313–325.

54. BENNETT, D. A. & B. PETRACK. 1984. CGS 9896: A nonbenzodiazepine, nonsedating potential anxiolytic. Drug Dev. Res. **4:** 75–82.

55. BERNARD, P. S., D. A. BENNETT, G. PASTOR, N. YOKOYAMA & J. M. LIEBMAN. 1985. CGS 9896: Agonist–antagonist benzodiazepine receptor activity revealed by anxiolytic, anticonvulsant and muscle relaxation assessment in rodents. J. Pharmacol. Exp. Ther. **235:** 98–105.

56. COOPER, S. J. 1985. The anorectic effect of FG 7142, a partial inverse agonist acting at benzodiazepine recognition sites, is reversed by CGS 8216 and clonazepam but not by food-deprivation. Brain Res. **346:** 190–194.

57. COOPER, S. J. 1986. β-Carbolines and appetite: Evidence for bi-directional control of food intake. Brain Res. Bull. **19:** 427–431.

58. CORDA, M. G., M. FERRARI, A. GUIDOTTI, D. KONKEL & E. COSTA. 1984. Isolation, purification and partial sequence of a neuropeptide (diazepam-binding inhibitor) precursor of an anxiogenic putative ligand for benzodiazepine recognition site. Neurosci. Lett. **47:** 319–324.

59. FERRERO, P., M. R. SANTI, B. CONTI-TRONCONI, E. COSTA & A. GUIDOTTI. 1986. Study of an octadecaneuropeptide derived from diazepam binding inhibitor (DBI): Biological activity and presence in rat brain. Proc. Natl. Acad. Sci. USA **83:** 827–831.

60. FERRARESE, C., F. VACCARINO, H. ALHO, B. MELLSTROM, E. COSTA & A. GUIDOTTI. 1987. Subcellular location and neuronal release of diazepam binding inhibitor. J. Neurochem. **48:** 1093–1102.

61. FERRERO, P., E. COSTA, B. CONTI-TRONCONI & A. GUIDOTTI. 1986. A diazepam binding inhibitor (DBI)-like neuropeptide is detected in human brain. Brain Res. **399:** 136–142.

62. BARBACCIA, M. L., E. COSTA, P. FERRERO, A. GUIDOTTI, A. ROY, T. SUNDERLAND, D. PICKAR, S. M. PAUL & F. K. GOODWIN. 1986. Diazepam-binding inhibitor. A brain neuropeptide present in human spinal fluid: Studies in depression, schizophrenia, and Alzheimer's disease. Arch. Gen. Psych. **43:** 1143–1147.

63. CORDA, M. G., W. D. BLACKER, W. B. MENDELSON, A. GUIDOTTI & E. COSTA. 1983. β-Carbolines enhance shock-induced suppression of drinking in rats. Proc. Natl. Acad. Sci. USA **80:** 2072–2076.

64. COSTA, E., M. G. CORDA & A. GUIDOTTI. 1983. On a brain polypeptide functioning as a putative effector for the recognition sites of benzodiazepine and beta-carboline derivatives. Neuropharmacology **22:** 1481–1492.

65. MAICKEL, R. P. & G. J. MALONEY. 1974. Taste phenomena influences on stimulation of deprivation-induced fluid consumption of rats. Neuropharmacology **13:** 763–767.

66. COOPER, S. J. 1982. Benzodiazepine mechanism and drinking in the water-deprived rat. Neuropharmacology **21:** 775–780.

67. COOPER, S. J. & R. E. YERBURY. 1988. Clonazepam selectively increases saccharin ingestion in a two-choice test. Brain Res. **456:** 173–176.

68. COOPER, S. J. 1986. Effects of the β-carboline FG 7142 on saccharin preference and qui-

nine aversion in water-deprived rats. Neuropharmacology **25:** 213–216.
69. ESTALL, L. B. & S. J. COOPER. 1987. Differential effects of benzodiazepine receptor ligands on isotonic saline and water consumption in water-deprived rats. Pharmacol. Biochem. Behav. **26:** 247–252.
70. KIRKHAM, T. C., D. J. BARBER, R. W. HEATH & S. J. COOPER. 1987. Differential effects of CGS 8216 and naltrexone on ingestional behaviour. Pharmacol. Biochem. Behav. **26:** 145–151.
71. KIRKHAM, T. C. & S. J. COOPER. 1986. CGS 8216, a novel anorectic agent, selectively reduces saccharin solution consumption in the rat. Pharmacol. Biochem. Behav. **25:** 341–345.
72. SUZDAK, P. D., J. R. GLOWA, J. N. CRAWLEY, R. D. SCHWARTZ, P. SKOLNICK & S. M. PAUL. 1986. A selective imidazobenzodiazepine antagonist of ethanol in the rat. Science **234:** 1243–1247.
73. TICKU, M. K. & S. K. KULKARNI. 1988. Molecular interactions of ethanol with GABAergic systems and potential of Ro15-4513 as an ethanol antagonist. Pharmacol. Biochem. Behav. **30:** 501–510.
74. SIEGHART, W., A. EICHINGER, J. G. RICHARDS & H. MÖHLER. 1987. Photoaffinity labeling of benzodiazepine receptor proteins with the partial inverse agonist [³H]Ro15-4513: A biochemical and autoradiographic study. J. Neurochem. **48:** 46–52.
75. ALHO, H., M. MIYATA, E. KORPI, K. KIIANMAA & A. GUIDOTTI. 1987. Studies of a brain polypeptide functioning as a putative endogenous ligand to benzodiazepine recognition sites in rats selectively bred for alcohol related behavior. Alcohol Alcoholism, Suppl. **1:** 637–641.
76. GRILL, H. J. & K. C. BERRIDGE. 1985. Taste reactivity as a measure of the neural control of palatability. *In* Progress in Psychobiology and Physiological Psychology. J. M. Sprague & A. N. Epstein, Eds. Vol. **11:** 1–61. Academic Press. Orlando, FL.
77. BERRIDGE, K. C. & D. TREIT. 1986. Chlordiazepoxide directly enhances positive ingestive reactions. Pharmacol. Biochem. Behav. **24:** 217–221.
78. TREIT, D., K. C. BERRIDGE & C. E. SCHULTZ. 1987. The direct enhancement of positive palatability of chlordiazepoxide is antagonized by Ro15-1788 and CGS 8216. Pharmacol. Biochem. Behav. **26:** 709–714.
79. BERRIDGE, K. C. 1988. Brainstem systems mediate the enhancement of palatability by chlordiazepoxide. Brain Res. **447:** 262–268.
80. YOUNG, R. C., J. GIBBS, J. ANTIN, J. HOLT & G. P. SMITH. 1974. Absence of satiety during sham feeding in the rat. J. Comp. Physiol. Psychol. **87:** 795–800.
81. WEINGARTEN, H. P. & S. D. WATSON. 1982. Sham feeding as a procedure for assessing the influence of diet palatability on food intake. Physiol. Behav. **28:** 401–407.
82. COOPER, S. J., G. VAN DER HOEK & T. C. KIRKHAM. 1988. Bi-directional changes in sham feeding in the rat produced by benzodiazepine receptor ligands. Physiol. Behav. **42:** 211–216.
83. KIRKHAM, T. C. & S. J. COOPER. 1987. The pyrazoloquinoline, CGS 8216, reduces sham feeding in the rat. Pharmacol. Biochem. Behav. **26:** 497–501.
84. COOPER, S. J. & Y. M. T. CRUMMY. 1978. Enhanced choice of a familiar food in a food preference test after chlordiazepoxide administration. Psychopharmacology **59:** 51–56.
85. COOPER, S. J. & A. McCLELLAND. 1980. Effects of chlordiazepoxide, food familiarization, and prior shock experience on food choice in rats. Pharmacol. Biochem. Behav. **12:** 23–28.
86. COOPER, S. J. 1987. Chlordiazepoxide-induced selection of saccharin-flavoured food in the food-deprived rat. Physiol. Behav. **41:** 539–542.
87. MORLEY, J. E. & J. E. BLUNDELL. 1988. The neurobiological basis of eating disorders: Some formulations. Biol. Psychiatr. **23:** 53–78.
88. DREWNOWSKI, A., F. BELLISLE, P. AIMEZ & B. REMY. 1987. Taste and bulimia. Physiol. Behav. **41:** 621–626.
89. DREWNOWSKI, A., K. A. HALMI, B. PIERCE, J. GIBBS & G. P. SMITH. 1987. Taste and eating disorders. Am. J. Clin. Nutr. **46:** 442–450.
90. LEE, N. F., A. J. RUSH & J. E. MITCHELL. 1985. Bulimia and depression. J. Affect. Dis. **9:** 231–238.
91. LAESSLE, R. G., S. KITTL, M. M. FICHTER, H. -U. WITTCHEN & K. M. PIRKE. 1987. Major affective disorder in anorexia nervosa and bulimia. A descriptive diagnostic study. Br. J. Psychiatr. **151:** 785–789.
92. GUIDOTTI, A., A. BERKOVICH, C. FERRARESE, M. R. SANTI & E. COSTA. 1988. Neuronal-

glial differential processing of DBI to yield ligands to central or peripheral benzodiazepine recognition sites. *In* Imidazopyridines in Sleep Disorders. J. P. Sauvanet, S. Z. Langer
& P. L. Morselli, Eds.: 25–28. Raven Press. New York.

DISCUSSION

DR. RALPH E. NORGREN (*Pennsylvania State University, Hershey, PA*): I noticed
on one of your earlier slides that you had some data on quinine aversion. Do the drugs
that reduce saccharine preference also reduce quinine aversion?

DR. STEVEN J. COOPER (*University of Birmingham, Birmingham, U.K.*): The drug
that was tested in that case actually was FG 7142. One prediction was that it might
increase the aversion because it has been suggested it's anxiety producing or aversive.
In fact it reduced the aversion at the doses where there was a decrease in preference.

DR. SARAH LEIBOWITZ (*Rockefeller University, NY*): How do you reflect on this
relative to the broader question of how the neurotransmitter GABA might be acting
on energy balance within the brain and also the broader question of treatment for
the eating disorders that we're looking at?

DR. COOPER: What I'd like to speculate on is DBI. If this really turns out to be
an endogenous ligand, there might be several implications. The work of Costa *et al.*
indicates that you find DBI in neurons, in synaptosomes, and you find DBI colocalized with GABA. Their idea is that DBI is released with GABA and has a modulating
effect. There's some work that indicates that the levels of DBI in CSF are elevated
in depressed patients, so it could be there is an association here with clinical conditions.

My expectation would be that DBI would act like an inverse agonist, and therefore
would have anorectic properties. On the basis of the data I've just shown you, it would
affect sweetness preference. If we have convincing evidence that there is an endogenous
ligand, I think there'll be some important clinical implications.

DR. LEIBOWITZ: Do you link this at all to the role of the GABA neurotransmitter
within the brain locally or do you think it's just a receptor?

DR. COOPER: I think this GABA benzodiazepine complex may be located in taste-
processing pathways. There's binding evidence to indicate that's the case, and what
we'd like to do is to microinject benzodiazepines into, for example, nucleus of the solitary tract to see if we can get these effects on taste preference.

DR. LEIBOWITZ: With flurazepam we found that that when administered into the
medial hypothalamus, it will stimulate feeding.

DR. JOHN BLUNDELL (*University of Leeds, Leeds, U.K.*): It strikes me that there
might be some important implications here for human eating disorders if it is the case
that benzodiazepines increase food consumption and especially increase palatable food
consumption, and also increase sweet food consumption in rats and, as Foltin has shown,
seems to be the case in primates. Then if that occurs in man or in woman there is
a basis here for the iatrogenic class of eating disorders because of the widespread diffusion of these drugs among the population even if they themselves don't induce an eating
disorder. They certainly don't make life any easier for people who are trying to curb
their intake, and they seem to make it a lot more difficult. In fact I know that there
are a number of studies in man showing weight increases with benzodiazepine treatment. Now it seems to me those effects don't go away just because you discover a benzodiazepine receptor, and I wanted to ask you whether or not you thought that the

benzodiazepine receptor and its activity intervenes at some stage between this drug and an output ultimately mediated through amines.

DR. COOPER: The thought that we're actually pursuing at the present time is to take note of the similarity between benzodiazepines and 5-HT$_{1A}$ agonists.

DR. BLUNDELL: Do you know if these are in parallel or in series?

DR. COOPER: I can't tell yet. What we first are doing is characterizing them separately, then we're planning interaction experiments.

DR. ARTHUR CAMPFIELD (*Hoffmann-La Roche, Nutley, NJ*): I want to congratulate Steve on his very careful analysis of this problem and just remind the general audience that this class of compounds came before a receptor. It was an effect and then the receptor was discovered. The search for both other agonists and antagonists has been led by binding and has not been very fruitful. The one that you mentioned, the so-called alcohol antagonist, is something that Hoffmann-La Roche does *not* propose as a use for this drug; I'll go on the record for that. I think Steve has led the way to look at a multiple series of chemical structures that have the same properties and to begin to analyze what's going on with the benzodiazapine receptor and food intake. He has provided a good example of how to do drug studies.

Summary: Part IV

LINDA BARTOSHUK

Pierce Foundation
New Haven, Connecticut 06519

This has been a dazzling group of papers and a wonderful session. First of all it is significant that we started with a sensory paper. We looked at a molecular analysis of the sensory system of taste, we moved through papers that talked about sensory hedonic interactions, and we ended up looking very carefully at a molecular analysis of the hedonic nature of taste. I think that's an extremely interesting trend both historically in the research and in this session.

Ralph Norgren's paper was a beautiful example of some major themes in his work. His work has progressed through strict anatomy into a consideration of some very important behavioral issues. His awareness that we spend far too much time on the tip of the tongue and not enough time on the rest of the mouth is an insight that deserves attention. His development, now, of the awake, unanesthetized preparation and particularly of our ability to analyze sweetness in the awake preparation is an extraordinary accomplishment, and one that I think is going to be very important to this field.

Douglas Mook is a very unusual person in our field because he is a theorist. It is wonderful to have a person in our field who is *both* a theorist and an experimentalist and is capable of bringing the best of both to bear on the problems we examine. What he did today was to grab our attention with a counter-intuitive experiment and introduce us a to a new idea that nevertheless is compatible with current thinking. I was reminded, as he spoke, of some patients that I have seen in the clinic at the University of Connecticut. We occasionally see patients who have lost both the sense of taste and the sense of smell. On the basis of Dr. Mook's work, it is doubtful that these persons would be able to set appropriate criteria for satiety, although they have other cognitive inputs. They know what the foods are, and they have had a lot of learning experience. Nonetheless, I was startled when I thought about these patients, because when we first saw them we thought that these people are not going to be able to regulate intake because taste and smell drive regulation. We learned better, but the interesting thing is that these people fall into two categories. Some of them gain weight, some of them lose weight, and they do seem to have some problems with satiety. I would like to ask Dr. Mook to comment on how compatible his work is with the comments of our other speakers.

As Dr. Sclafani began to talk about the palate, Ralph Norgren whispered to me that we talk about the palate as a general metaphor for taste and for food preference; for example, we say one has or does not have "a palate for" something. He pointed out that maybe in the rat that's really true. The nasal incisor duct on the palate responds magnificently to sweets, which gives some feeling to that metaphor.

I was reminded by this beautiful work on dry sugar versus a sugar solution, of a patient that I evaluated, a policeman from a large city, who claimed to have lost the sense of taste when he was kicked in the head by a horse while performing crowd control. We felt that maybe he wasn't telling us the truth. I brought him into the lab and gave him a lot of sugar solutions including a one-molar solution to taste, and he assured me he could detect absolutely nothing. Then I told him that I was going to give him something really concentrated that I thought he would be able to taste. I gave him some sucrose crystals, which of course, as you know from Dr. Sclafani's work, cannot be tasted as well as the solution. However, he was able to identify the crystals very well. This showed that his taste system was not as impaired as he claimed.

After years of following the experiments on Polycose and being dragged kicking and screaming into this, I am a convert. I think Polycose is absolutely fascinating and clearly represents a phenomenon in rats not shared by humans.

Dr. Elliott Blass has shown us through his extraordinary command of technique what he can do with infant rats. We're familiar with his ability to keep these little rat pups alive and seemingly thriving with interventions that some years ago we would have thought were impossible. One of the things I find fascinating about this paper, which I think is also found in Dr. Schneider's paper, is that we suddenly see oil coming into the picture in sham-feeding. The use of oil in these experiments begins to make it look as if oil has some form of hard-wired palatability that it shares with sucrose. Although I don't think it can possibly be true, I think it is something worth discussing in the future.

The final presentation, an analysis of receptors, was truly a tour de force. The final comments about alcohol and saccharine were particularly important, in the light of anecdotal information about alcoholics who develop cravings for sweets.

That much progress has been made in the understanding of neurologic and behavioral responses to taste stimuli is clear from the work presented in this session. We have also progressed in refining the questions that need to be addressed in future research.

Palatability of Food and the Ponderostat

MICHEL CABANAC

Département de Physiologie
Faculté de Médecine
Université Laval
Québec G1K 7P4, Canada

WHAT IS REGULATION?

Matter and energy continuously flow back and forth between living beings and their environment. Without this exchange, life cannot be sustained. Inflow consists mainly of continuous respiratory oxygen intake, intermittent food and water intake, and occasional heat intake. Outflow consists mainly of the continuous release of sensible and latent heat, carbon dioxide, and water; of intermittent micturition, defecation, and mechanical work; and of occasional lactation.

The overall flows of energy and various constituents are adjusted in such a way as to equalize inflow and outflow. There may be a transient excess or deficit of inflow over outflow resulting in energy or matter storage or depletion, but over the long term, inflow and outflow remain fairly equal. As suggested by Brobeck,[1] the word control should be used to describe the management of inflow and outflow that results in homeostasis. The mechanisms controlling inflow and outflow achieve the stability of tensive variables within the body, for example, blood pressure, core temperature, and calcium concentration. This stability is the result of regulation; thus, regulation is achieved through the control of inputs and outputs.

The last fundamental concept to be described here is set-point.[2] The set-point is the value of a regulated variable at which an organism stabilizes by means of the process of regulation.[3] When the regulated variable strays from the set-point, the regulatory process consists of increasing and decreasing both inflow and outflow in such a way that the regulated variable is driven back to its set-point. Regulation and set-point can be identified if and when a nonlinear corrective response occurs on the controlled inflow and outflow. Figure 1 is an analogue representation of regulation, and Figure 2 is its block diagram model.[4]

Water flows into the tank at a rate determined by the current and flows out of the tank at the same rate. As a result the level of water remains constant. The level of the water is sensed by a float. One loop controls the inflow negatively and another exerts positive control on the outflow. Thus the system goes through a negative feedback loop and a positive feed-forward loop. The regulated system includes an important piece of information: the set-point. The set-point is incorporated into the length of the shafts between the float and the input and output faucets. This model is an analogue of all regulated systems, whether technological or biological.

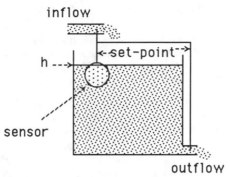

FIGURE 1. Analogue model of regulation.[4] The passive system includes tank and input and output faucets. All the elements are constant when the system is in steady state. The float (sensor of the water level) feeds back negatively to the inflow, and forward positively to the outflow. The water level (h) is the regulated variable, its set-point is fixed by the length of the shafts between float on the one hand and input/output faucets on the other hand.

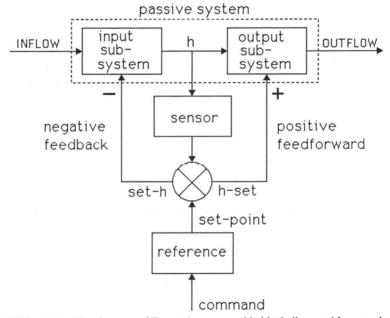

FIGURE 2. The regulated system of FIGURE 1 represented in block diagram.[4] Input and output subsystems are the input and output faucets. The regulated water level is "h." The sensor is the float. The signal produced by the float is fed negatively back and positively forward after being compared with its set value. The new element on the block diagram as compared to FIGURE 1 is the possibility of adjusting the set-point by changing the reference.

IS BODY WEIGHT REGULATED?

All the elements of regulation are present in maintaining energy balance in the biological system. The inflow into the regulated system is food intake. The outflow is heat production. The regulated variable could be body mass. However there is no known sensor of body mass. It is therefore likely that body mass *sensu stricto* is not regulated.

Nevertheless, it is highly likely that the regulated variable(s) is linked to body mass in the same way as the water lever in the tank of FIGURE 1 is linked to the mass of stored water. Hervey[5] and Nicolaidis *et al.*[6] have presented a different hypothesis on the mechanisms that possibly link tensive variables, such as the concentration of steroids or of free fatty acid in the blood with the mass of fat stored in the body. Although the missing link has not been identified, as long as the system behaves as though body mass is regulated, we may proceed under the working hypothesis that this is the case.

Experiments on the system placed in an open-loop situation, as is the case with alliesthesia[a] in humans[7] or the hoarding of food by rats,[8] provide strong indirect evidence that a ponderostat exists and regulates near a set-point. The purpose of this short review is to examine the relationship between the various elements of the ponderostat — inflow of energy, outflow of energy, and the set-point — and the palatability of foods.

Palatability describes the quality of pleasantness as applied to foods. A subject stimulated with palatable food experiences pleasure. Palatability, on first examination, seems to characterize the stimulus. However, palatability also depends on the stimulated subject, as we will see below. Human experiments are reviewed, and animal experiments are referred to only when human information is lacking.

Theoretically, the palatability of food may exert its influence on each element of regulation, that is, inflow, outflow, and set-point. Reciprocally, because palatability depends on the subject, the elements of regulation may also influence palatability. This is indeed the case, as is demonstrated below.

INFLUENCE OF PALATABILITY ON INGESTION

It may appear tautological to measure the influence of the pleasure of eating on the volume eaten. Indeed, common sense reveals that pleasure is the main factor in the control of food intake.[9-11] However, the mere fact that it is possible to refrain from eating, or to overeat, shows that pleasure is not indissolubly united with intake. In fact, the role of pleasure in food intake is even doubted. The influence of the palatability of food on food intake therefore deserves to be measured.

[a] The word alliesthesia (Greek *Allios* changed and -*esthesia* sensation) is applied to the affective component of sensation, pleasure or displeasure. The amount of pleasure or displeasure aroused by a given stimulus is not invariable — it depends on the internal state of the stimulated subject. Factors that can modify the internal state and in turn induce alliesthesia are as follows: internal physiological variables (e.g., deep body temperature or body dehydration modify the pleasure of thermal sensation or taste of water); set points (e.g., during fever the body temperature set point is raised and pleasure defends the elevated set point); multiple peripheral stimuli (e.g., mean skin temperature determines the set point for deep body temperature and in turn generates alliesthesia); and past history of the subject (e.g., association of a flavor with a disease or a recovery from disease renders it unpleasant or pleasant). Positive alliesthesia indicates a change to a more pleasurable senation; negative alliesthesia a change to a less pleasurable one. (From *Encyclopedia of Neuroscience*. 1987. G. Adelman, Ed. Birkhäuser, Boston.)

The experiments must be conducted on fasted subjects, because intake is able to modify palatability, as will be seen later on. Newborn babies show their pleasure or their displeasure by displaying eloquent faces when they are presented with sweet or bitter gustatory stimuli.[12] Their behavior is in conformity with their pleasure as they vigorously suck sweet solutions and reject bitter ones.[13-16] Adults also conform their behavioral choice with their gustatory pleasure.[17-28] The influence of palatability is not only qualitative, because subjects also eat more of what they like.[29-35] As a result of this relationship, the measurement of the pleasure aroused by an alimentary stimulus provides the degree of acceptability of this stimulus.[36] The corrolary is that subjective preference is an excellent index of satiety and hunger motivation.[37] In patients with a duodeno-illeal shunt there is a lowering of the palatability of foods and a diminished food intake.[38]

Some discrepancies, however, have been reported between the pleasure aroused by sweet solutions and the amount of sucrose used by subjects to sweeten their tea,[29] but these discrepancies can be explained by methodological artifacts originating in the sequence of stimuli presentation or from the excessive concentration of sucrose in the sweet solution used as a stimulus.[40] Subjects may also be biased against sweet stimuli in their behavior and in their rating of preferred foods when they are dieting and wish to avoid foods rich in energy.[41-43] When these factors are taken into account and are well controlled, sensory pleasure and food intake are found to be coherently related. The best example of such a confirmation of common sense can be found in the selective appetite for salt displayed by patients with Addison's disease.

Berstein and Borson[44] hypothesized that a decreased palatability of foods causing a decreased food intake might be an important component of anorexia nervosa. An alternative hypothesis on the cause of anorexia nervosa will be discussed later on, but what must be stressed is that these authors implicitly introduce the concept that palatability is an important determinant of intake.

INFLUENCE OF INGESTION ON PALATABILITY

Palatability may be influenced in the minutes and hours following food intake or intake of pharmacological drugs that suppress the effects of food intake. Over the long term, palatability may also be influenced by chronic overfeeding or underfeeding.

The decrease of palatability just after food intake has been reviewed recently by Fantino[45] and will only be outlined here. The influence of food intake has been described using the terms alliesthesia[45] and sensory-specific satiety.[47] Within the couple of hours following ingestion, satiety occurs, then fades away.[48-55] During this process, alimentary stimuli become unpleasant, after which palatability returns to control value. The whole process is specific for alimentary stimuli.[56] The modulation of palatability is also specific for the ingested substance,[57-59] especially when the stimulus is not directly injected into the stomach by the experimenter but rather is ingested via the natural route.[20,47,60]

The opposite situation of postingestive satiety is obtained experimentally when subjects receive an injection of insulin, which produces artificial hunger and is accompanied by positive alliesthesia on the sweet sensation.[61,62] The decrease of intracellular glucose concentration, following injection of 2-deoxy-D-glucose, also results in positive alliesthesia from sweet stimuli[63] and increased food intake.[64]

Eventually, when the flow of nutrients ingested is artificially modified, palatability also is modified, that is, long-term alliesthesia occurs. Chronic forced overfeeding decreases the pleasure normally aroused by sweet stimuli in fasted subjects.[65] On the other hand, chronic undernutrition suppresses the negative alliesthesia for alimentary stimuli occurring normally after a meal or a gastric load of glucose.[7,32,66–68] The intensity of the pleasure, aroused by sweet stimuli during chronic undernutrition, does not seem to be increased as compared with the normal nutritional state.[69]

INFLUENCE OF PALATABILITY ON ENERGY EXPENDITURE

In recent years, there has been a considerable rebound of interest in the postprandial thermogenesis initially described by Rubner[70] under the term "specific dynamic effect" (specifisch-dynamische Wirkung) later translated as "specific dynamic action" (SDA). Two reviews, by Jequier[71] and Keesey and Powley,[72] were recently devoted to the relationship between metabolic activity and the ponderostat. Most studies have looked at either the influence of food intake or palatability on postprandial thermogenesis, but there are good reasons to think that palatability also exerts a chronic influence on basal metabolism, or rather on Nicolaidis's *"métabolisme de fond."*[73]

Postprandial thermogenesis is predominantly influenced by the palatability of the food. A test meal generated three times more heat production than an equivalent intragastric load of synthetic food.[74] Low palatability generated low postprandial heat production.[75] The same test meal eaten as normal food was followed by 50% more heat production than under the form of dry crackers plus water.[76] Finally the mere oral presentation and chewing of food was more thermogenetic than normal eating.[77]

Over a long period, chronic undernutrition decreased the energy expenditure of the subjects under diet restriction,[78–80] whereas chronic excessive food intake was followed by increased heat production.[80–83] Knowing the acute effect of palatability on postprandial thermogenesis, one may hypothesize that an identical effect occurs over the long term to modulate the *métabolisme de fond* as a function of the palatability of the ingested foods.

INFLUENCE OF ENERGY EXPENDITURE ON PALATABILITY

The reciprocal of the above section would be that the level of energy expenditure modulates the palatability of food. Does such an anticipatory effect exist? To date, no experimental study of this question is available. Only common sense or anecdotal knowledge indicates that increased energy expenditure, for example, after prolonged or repeated muscular exercise, is followed by an increase in the palatability of ordinary food. This also implies that decreased energy expenditure, such as prolonged inaction, induces a decrease in the palatability of food.

Chronic exposure to cold and hypothermia are known to increase food intake in animals and there is abundant literature on the subject.[84] Brobeck[85] has suggested that "animals eat to keep warm and stop eating to prevent hyperthermia" and this thermoregulatory theory of hunger could also hold true for humans. Cold exposure and hypothermia delayed or suppressed negative alliesthesia for sweet stimuli, triggered by intragastric glucose loads.[86] This observation would fit with an anticipatory action of energy expenditure on palatability.

INFLUENCE OF SET-POINT ON PALATABILITY

To understand how the set-point may influence palatability, it is first necessary to recall the principle of set-point action. The set-point is only a signal. This signal is compared to another signal emitted by the variable under regulation. The difference between set-point and actual variable is called the error signal. It is the error signal that actuates the regulatory responses. Several consequences follow from the above statements:

   (i) When in a system, the regulated variable is equal to its set value, there is no corrective response;

  (ii) Only when a system presents a regulatory response will the student know that the regulated variable is different from its set value; and

 (iii) When a set-point in a regulation is raised or lowered, the error signal activates the correcting responses only as long as the regulated variable remains different from its set value.

In the case of body weight regulation, therefore, the actuating signal is not body weight but the algebraic difference: body weight minus set-point, and the regulatory responses are modulations of food intake and energy expenditure. This explains the absence of a straight correlation between body weight and "sweet tooth" or between body weight and alliesthesia.

We are concerned here with perception of palatability and its direct relation to food intake. It has been repeatedly reported that when body weight is below its set-point, postgastric load negative alliesthesia tends to disappear, which has the same result as increased palatability of food. This was true in patients during the dynamic phase of obesity when they were gaining weight[65,87,88] as well as in dieting overweight patients.[32,50,68,89–93] Obesity can thus be considered to be a state of elevated set-point. The palatability of foods is adjusted to defend the elevated set-point.

A number of reports do not concur with the above description of an elevated set-point as being the best description of obesity nor with the evidence that the difference between actual body weight and set-point is the subject's determinant of palatability. Two main explanations can be found for the apparent discrepancies of results.

(i) The amount of food deprivation is often not measured and the subjects are just categorized as "dieters" and "nondieters" according to their self report[53,69] or are categorized as "obese" and "controls"[94,95] or no mention is made of body weight, a fortiori of set-point.[96]

(ii) Several authors reported that ingestion of a glucose load was not followed by negative alliesthesia for alimentary stimuli in all their subjects,[95] or negative alliesthesia follows only in a proportion of their population, the "nonshifters."[96,97] A careful examination of these results shows that the "nonshifters" in whom there was no postingestive alliesthesia already regarded sweet stimuli as unpleasant. One would not expect a pleasant sensation to become unpleasant when it was unpleasant in the first place. The point is therefore not the absence of alliesthesia here but rather the existence of dislikers among hungry subjects.[98,99] A likely explanation for these deviant examples of behavior is the cultural bias against sucrose[41] that was reported, especially among overweight persons[100,101] and female subjects[102,103] Drewnowski et al.[104] suggest that the sucrose negative bias has evolved since the seventies, owing to the influence of the media and is now also applied to fats.

Another case where body weight changes drastically is anorexia nervosa. We have seen above that Berstein and Borson[44] have suggested that food aversion might initiate the disease. An alternative hypothesis could be a resetting of the set-point at a lower level of body weight. Such a resetting of the set-point for body temperature has been reported in these patients.[105] A low set-point for body-weight regulation would lower the palatability of foods and reduce food intake as long as actual body weight remains higher than set-point. This hypothesis is not supported, however, by the fact that anorexic patients have no postingestive alliesthesia for sucrose,[104] a result showing that actual body weight was lower than set-point. A possible cause for anorexia may be linked to brain opioids (see Fantino et al.[107]). It is also possible that the different behaviors observed in anorexia and in anorexia-bulemia are the result of a lowered set-point in the former and intact set-point in the latter.

The ponderostat seems to be at a higher set-point during the postovulatory phase than during the preovulatory phase of the ovarian cycle,[108-111] because preovulatory subjects eat more. The fact that subjects presented both higher ratings for sucrose when fasted and clear-cut negative alliesthesia after glucose load[54] confirms that their ponderostats were set at a higher level during the luteal phase.

INFLUENCE OF PALATABILITY ON SET-POINT

Food that is either palatability enriched or impoverished may act to raise or lower the set-point for body weight regulation. Paradoxically, the available experimental evidence is mostly negative: a chronic long-term lowering of the palatability of food, obtained by a monotonous synthetic liquid food[99,112-114] or by chronic intragastric feeding,[115] is followed by a loss of body weight. Postingestive alliesthesia allows the conclusion that the set-point of the ponderostat is lowered in these subjects.

The presence of information on the positive action of palatability (i.e., palatability-raised set-point) is supported only by indirect information.[116] It has been demonstrated that increased variety of foods increases food intake.[20,33,117,118] Such an action could be the result of a raised set-point. This has been demonstrated to be the case in rats.[119,122]

CONCLUSIONS

The analysis of the literature from the point of view of control theory brings about two types of conclusions, methodological and theoretical.

It is possible to study the determinism of food intake through human experiments. This avoids the need for adventurous extrapolations from results obtained in laboratory rats. In spite of ritual protests of caution, it is quite common that conclusions based on rats are extended to humans in the media. Yet these conclusions are perhaps not valid in other rodents or even in wild rats. Human experimentation has obvious ethical limits. There are also some methodological constraints such as the use of a subject as his own control. It is indeed difficult to compare results obtained in different subjects. If these limitations are observed, human cognition and psychophysics provide a tool whose power is out of reach of experiments limited to animal behavior.

One difficulty of the present approach is the apparent circularity presented above between food intake, palatability, and set-point. On first examination, it may appear needlessly complex to state that palatability raises the set-point and, in turn, food intake and body weight, whereas Ocam's razor would make it simpler to state that palatability increased food intake. However, the measurement of alliesthesia opens the feedback loop between food intake and body weight in the same way that the measurement of hoarding behavior opens the same loop in the case of the rat.[8,119]

Sensory pleasure aroused by food provides the subject with information on the usefulness of the stimulus. Pleasure integrates information on the stimulus and the stimulated subject and will therefore anticipate the effects of ingestion. The determination of pleasure is therefore understandably complex. Palatability provides the basis for an instantaneous decision as to whether to consume or reject the stimulus.

An important corrolary of the interrelations between ponderostat and palatability is that it is possible to analyze the stability of body weight in terms of the regulatory process. The reduced thermogenesis observed in obesity[120] can be seen not as the *primum movens* resulting in weight gain, but as the control exerted on energy expenditure to save energy and raise body weight up to the elevated set-point. This is not simply an academic discussion, because therapeutic sanctions will differ depending on whether pathology impairs the set-point or the effectors. If obesity is due to a raised set-point, as is defended in this short review, then therapy should aim at lowering the set-point. If obesity is passive and simply due to increased food intake or decreased energy expenditure, then therapy should aim at better control of input and output. The high percentage of relapse among obese patients who have lost weight[121] is a strong indication of body weight regulation by set-point.

REFERENCES

1. BROBECK, J. R. 1965. Exchange, control, and regulation. *In* Physiological Controls and Regulations. W. S. Yamamoto & J. R. Brobeck, Eds.: 1–13. Saunders, Philadelphia, PA.
2. HARDY, J. D. 1965. The "set-point" concept in physiological temperature regulation. *In* Physiological Controls and Regulations. W. S. Yamamoto & J. R. Brobeck, Eds.: 98–116.
3. IUPS COMMISSION ON THERMAL PHYSIOLOGY. Glossary of Terms for Thermal Physiology. Second edition. 1987. Pflug. Arch. **410**: 567–587.
4. CABANAC, M. & M. RUSSEK. 1982. Régulation et contrôle en biologie. Presses Univ. Laval.
5. HERVEY, G. R. 1969. Regulation of energy balance. Nature **222**: 629–632.
6. NICOLAIDIS, S., M. PETIT & J. POLONOVSKI. 1974. Etude du rapport entre la régulation de la masse adipeuse corporelle et la composition lipidique des centres régulateurs. C. R. Acad. Sci. **278**: 1393–1396.
7. CABANAC. M., R. DUCLAUX & N. H. SPECTOR. 1971. Sensory feedback in regulation of body weight: Is there a ponderostat? Nature **229**: 125–127.
8. FANTINO, M. & M. CABANAC. Body weight regulation with a proportional hoarding response in the rat. Physiol. Behav. **24**: 939–942.
9. YOUNG, P. T. 1959. The role of affective process in learning and motivation. Psychol. Rev. **66**: 104–125.
10. PFAFFMAN, C. 1960. The pleasures of sensation. Psychol. Rev. **67**: 256–268.
11. WYRWICKA, W. 1969. Sensory regulation of food intake. Physiol. Behav. **4**: 853–858.
12. STEINER, J. E. 1977. Facial expressions of the neonate infant indicating the beconics of food-related chemical stimuli. *In* Taste and development. J. M. Weiffenback, Ed. U.S. Department of Health Education and Welfare. Bethesda, Maryland.
13. LIPSITT, L. P. 1977. Taste in human neonates: Its effects on sucking and heart rate. *In* Taste and Development. J. M. Weiffenback, Ed. U.S. Department of Health Education and Welfare. Bethesda, MD.
14. DESOR, J. A., O. MALLER & R. E. TURNER. 1973. Taste in acceptance of sugars by human infants. J. Comp. Physiol. Psychol. **84**: 494–501.
15. ASHMEAD, D. H., B. M. REILLY & L. P. LIPSITT. 1980. Neonates' heart rate, sucking rhythm, and sucking amplitude as a function of the sweet taste. J. Exp. Child Psychol. **29**: 264–281.
16. FOMON, S. J., E. ZIEGLER, S. E. NELSON & B. B. EDWARDS. 1983. Sweetness of diet and food consumption by infants. Proc. Soc. Exp. Biol. Med. **173**: 190–193.
17. MAYER-GROSS, W. & J. W. WALKER. 1946. Taste and selection of food in hypoglycemia. Br. J. Exp. Pathol. **27**: 297–305.
18. BERNSTEIN, I. L. 1978. Learned taste aversions in children receiving chemotherapy. Science **200**: 1302–1303.
19. PORIKOS, K. P., M. F. HESSER & T. B. VAN ITALIE. 1982. Caloric regulation in normal

weight men maintained on a palatable diet of conventional foods. Physiol. Behav. **29:** 293–300.

20. ROLLS, B. J., E. A. ROWE & E. T. ROLLS. 1982. How sensory properties of food affect human feeding behavior. Physiol. Behav. **29:** 409–417.

21. BRALA, P. M. & R. L. HAGEN. 1983. Effect of sweetness perception and caloric value of a preload on short term intake. Physiol. Behav. **30:** 1–9.

22. SHEPHERD, R., C. A. FARLEIGH & D. G. LAND. 1984. The relationship between salt intake and preference for different salt levers in soup. Appetite **5:** 281–290.

23. PANGBORN, R. M. & M. E. GIOVANNI. 1984. Dietary intake of sweet foods and of diary fats and resultant gustatory responses to sugar in lemonade and to fat in milk. Appetite **5:** 317–327.

24. BEAUCHAMP, G. K. & B. J. COWART. 1985. Congenital and experimental factors in the development of human flavor preferences. Appetite **6:** 357–372.

25. CABANAC, M. & C. FERBER. 1986. Sensory pleasure and preference in a bidimensional taste space. Appetite **7:** 245–256.

26. MATTES, R. D. & D. J. MELA. 1986. Relationships between and among selected measures of sweet taste preference and dietary intake. Chem. Senses **11:** 523–539.

27. FERBER, C. & M. CABANAC. 1987. Influence of noise on gustatory affective ratings and preference for sweet and salt. Appetite **8:** 229–235.

28. CONNER, M. T. & D. A. BOOTH. 1988. Preferred sweetness of a lime drink and preference for sweet over non-sweet foods related to sex and reported age and body weight. Appetite **10:** 25–35.

29. GAWECKI, I., M. URBANOWICZ, J. JESKA & B. MAZUR. 1976. Feeding habits and their physiological determinants. Relationship between consumer's preference for sweetness of drinks and certain physiological parameters. Acta. Physiol. Polon. **27:** 455–460.

30. NISBETT, R. E. 1968. Taste deprivation, and weight determinants of eating behavior. J. Pers. Soc. Psychol. **10:** 107–116.

31. PRICE, J. M. & J. GRINKER. 1973. Effects of degree of obesity, food deprivation and palatability on eating behaviors of humans. J. Comp. Physiol. Psychol. **85:** 265–271.

32. RODIN, J. 1975. Effects of obesity and set-point on taste responsiveness and ingestion in humans. J. Comp. Physiol. Psychol. **89:** 1003–1009.

33. ROLLS, B. J. 1979. How variety and palatability can stimulate appetite. Nutr. Bull. **5:** 78–86.

34. BERNSTEIN, I. L. & M. M. WEBER. 1980. Learned taste aversions in humans. Physiol. Behav. **25:** 363–366.

35. BELLISLE, F., R. LUCAS, R. AMRANI & J. LEMAGNEN. 1984. Deprivation, palatability and the microstructure of meals in human subjects. Appetite **5:** 85–94.

36. MOSKOWITZ, H. R. & J. L. SIDEL. 1971. Magnitude and hedonic scales of food acceptability. J. Food Sci. **36:** 677–680.

37. BLUNDELL, J. E. & P. J. ROGERS. 1980. Effects of anorexic drugs on food intake, food selection and preference and hunger motivation and subjective experience. Appetite **1:** 151–165.

38. BRAY, G., R. E. BARRY, J. R. BENFIELD, P. CASTELNUOVO-TEDESCO & J. RODIN. 1976. Intestinal bypass surgery for obesity decreases food intake and taste preference. Am. J. Clin. Nutr. **29:** 779–783.

39. MATTES, R. D. & H. T. LAWLESS. 1985. An adjustment error in optimization of taste intensity. Appetite **6:** 103–114.

40. MCBRIDE, R. L. 1985. Stimulus range influences intensity and hedonic rating of flavour. Appetite **6:** 125–131.

41. FRIJTERS, J. E. R. & E. L. RASMUSSEN-CONRAD. 1982. Sensory discrimination, intensity perception and effective judgements of sucrose sweetness in the overweight. J. Gen. Psychol. **107:** 233–247.

42. LOGUE, A. M. & M. E. SMITH. 1986. Predictors of food preference in adult humans. Appetite **7:** 107–125.

43. LUNDGREN, B., B. JONSSON, R. M. PANGBORN, A. M. SONTAG, N. BARYLKO-PIKIELNA, E. PIETRZAK, R. DOS SANTOS GARRUTI, M. A. CHAIB MORAES & M. YOSHIDA. 1978. Taste discrimination vs hedonic response to sucrose in coffee beverage. An interlaboratory study. Chem. Senses Flavour **3:** 249–265.

44. BERNSTEIN, I. L. & S. BORSON. 1986. Learned food aversion: A component of anorexic syndromes. Psychol. Rev. **93**: 462–472.
45. FANTINO, M. 1984. Role of sensory input in the control of food intake. J. Auton. Nerv. System. **10**: 347–348.
46. CABANAC, M. 1971. Physiological role of pleasure. Science **173**: 1103–1107.
47. ROLLS, B. J., E. T. ROLLS, E. A. ROWE & K. SWEENEY. 1981. Sensory specific satiety in man. Physiol. Behav. **27**: 137–142.
48. BOOTH, D. A., A. T. CAMPBELL & A. CHASE. 1970. Temporal bounds of post-ingestive glucose induced satiety in man. Nature **228**: 1104–1105.
49. PLINER, P., J. POLIVY, C. P. HERMAN & I. ZAKALUSNY. 1980. Short-term intake of overweight individuals and normal weight dieters and nondieters with and without choice among a variety of foods. Appetite **1**: 203–213.
50. GILBERT, G. D. & R. L. HAGEN. 1980. Taste in underweight, overweight and normal-weight subjects before, during and after sucrose ingestion. Additive Behav. **5**: 137–142.
51. BOOTH, D. A., R. P. MATHER & J. FULLER. 1982. Starch content of ordinary foods associatively conditions human appetite and satiation induced by intake and eating pleasantness of starch-paired flavours. Appetite **3**: 163–184.
52. SCHERR, S. & K. R. KING. 1982. Sensory and metabolic feedback in the modulation of taste hedonics. Physiol. Behav. **29**: 827–832.
53. ESSES, V. M. & C. P. HERMAN. 1983. Palatability of sucrose before and after glucose ingestion in dieters and non-dieters. Physiol. Behav. **32**: 711–715.
54. PLINER, P. & A. S. FLEMING. 1983. Food intake, body weight, and sweetness preferences over the menstrual cycle in humans. Physiol. Behav. **30**: 663–666.
55. BIRCH, L. L., M. DEYSHER & C. KENNEDY. 1984. The effect of macronutrient load on satiety and alliesthesia in young children. Fed. Proc. **43**: 4524.
56. DUCLAUX, R., J. FEISTHAUER & M. CABANAC. 1973. Effets du repas sur l'agrément d'odeurs alimentaires et non alimentaries chez l'homme. Physiol. Behav. **10**: 1029–1033.
57. CABANAC, M. & R. DUCLAUX. 1970. Specificity of internal signals in producing satiety for taste stimuli. Nature **227**: 966–967.
58. GUY-GRAND, B. & Y. SITT. 1976. Origine de l'alliesthésie gustative, effets comparés de charges glucosées ou protido-lipidiques. C. R. Acad. Sci. Paris **282D**: 755–757.
59. RABE, E. & M. CABANAC. 1974. Origine de l'alliesthésie olfacto-gustative, effets comparés d'une huile végétale et du glucose intragastrique. C. R. Acad. Sci. Paris **278D**: 765–768.
60. ROLLS, E. T., B. J. ROLLS & E. A. ROWE. 1983. Sensory specific and motivation specific satiety for the sight and taste of food and water in man. Physiol. Behav. **30**: 185–192.
61. MAYER-GROSS, W. & J. W. WALKER. 1946. Taste and selection of food in hypoglycemia. Br. J. Exp. Pathol. **27**: 297–305.
62. BRIESE, E. & M. QUIJADA. 1979. Positive alliesthesia after insulin. Experientia **35**: 1058.
63. THOMPSON, D. A. & R. G. CAMPBELL. 1977. Hunger in humans induced by 2-deosy-D-glucose: Glucoprivic control of taste preference and food intake. Science **198**: 1065–1068.
64. WELLE, S. L., D. A. THOMPSON, R. G., CAMPBELL & U. LILAVIVATHANA. 1980. Increased hunger and thirst during glucoprivation in humans. Physiol. Behav. **25**: 397–404.
65. FANTINO, M., F. BAIGTS, M. CABANAC & M. APFELBAUM. 1983. Effects of an overfeeding regimen on the affective component of the sweet sensation. Appetite **4**: 155–164.
66. GUY-GRAND, B. & Y. SITT. 1975. Gustative alliesthesia: Evidence supporting the ponderostatic hypothesis for obesity. *In* Recent Advances in Obesity Research. Volume 1. A. Howard, Ed. Newman. London.
67. MOSKOWITZ, H. R., V. KUMRAIAH, K. N. SHARMA, H. L. JACOBS & S. D. SHARMA. 1975. Cross cultural differences in simple taste preference. Science **190**: 1217–1218.
68. RODIN, J., H. R. MOSKOWITZ & G. BRAY. 1976. Relationship between obesity, weight loss, and taste responsiveness. Physiol. Behav. **17**: 591–597.
69. FRIJTERS, J. E. R. 1984. Sweetness intensity perception and sweetness pleasantness on women varying in reported restraint of eating. Appetite **5**: 103–108.
70. RUBNER, M. 1902. Die Gesetze des Energieverbruchs bei der Ernahrung. Franz Deuticke. Leipz U. Wien.
71. JEQUIER, E. 1985. Thermogénèse induite par les nutriments chez l'homme: son rôle dans la régulation pondérale. J. Physiol. Paris. **80**: 129–140.

72. KEESEY, R. E. & T. L. POWLEY. 1986. The regulation of body weight. Ann. Rev. Psychol. **37:** 109–133.
73. NICOLAÏDIS, S. & P. EVEN. Mesure du métabolisme de fond en relation avec la prise alimentaire: Hypothèse ischymétrique. C. R. Acad. Sci. Paris **298:** 295–300.
74. LEBLANC, J., M. CABANAC & P. SAMSON. 1984. Reduced postprandial heat production with gavage as compared with meal feeding in human subjects. Am. J. Physiol. **246:** E95–E101.
75. ANTON-KUCHLY, B., M. LAVAL, M. L. CHOUKROUN, G. MANCIET, P. ROGER & P. VARENE. 1985. Postprandial thermogenesis and hormonal release in lean and obese subjects. J. Physiol. Paris **80:** 321–329.
76. LEBLANC, J. & L. BRONDEL. 1985. Role of palatability on meal-induced thermogenesis in human subjects. Am. J. Physiol. **248:** E333–E336.
77. LEBLANC, J. & M. CABANAC. 1989. Cephalic postprandial thermogenesis in human subjects. Physiol. Behav. **46:** In press.
78. APFELBAUM, M. & J. BOTSARON. 1969. Le bilan d'énergie de l'obèse soumis à un régime restrictif. Presse Méd. **77:** 1941–1943.
79. APFELBAUM, M., J. BOTSARON & D. LACATIS. 1971. Effect of caloric restriction and excessive caloric intake on energy expenditure. J. Clin. Nutr. **24:** 1405–1409.
80. SIMS, E. A. H. & E. S. HORTON. 1968. Endocrine and metabolic adaptation to obesity and starvation. Am. J. Clin. Nutr. **21:** 1455–1470.
81. GULICK, A. 1922. A study of weight regulation in the adult human during overnutrition. Am. J. Physiol. **60:** 371–395.
82. HANSON, J. S. 1973. Exercise responses following production of experimental obesity. J. Appl. Physiol. **35:** 587–591.
83. MILLER, D. S. & P. MUMFORD. 1973. Luxuskonsumption. *In* Energy Balance in Man. M. Apfelbaum, Ed. Masson & Cie. Paris.
84. ANDERSSON, B., C. C. GALE & J. W. SUNDSTEN. 1963. The relationship between body temperature and food and water intake. *In* Olfaction and Taste. Proc. First Intern. Sympos. Wenner-Gren Center. Y. Zotterman, Ed. Pergamon Press. Oxford.
85. BROBECK, J. R. 1947–1948. Food intake as a mechanism of temperature regulation. Yale J. Biol. Med. **20:** 545–552.
86. RUSSEK, M., M. FANTINO & M. CABANAC. 1979. Effects of environmental temperature on pleasure ratings of odors and tastes. Physiol. Behav. **22:** 251–256.
87. GUY-GRAND, B. & Y. SITT. 1974. Alliesthésie gustative dans l'obèsité humaine. Nouv. Presse Méd. **3:** 92–93.
88. DOASSANS-WILHELM, M. 1978. Régulation pondérale et obésité. Etude de l'alliesthésie gustative chez 91 sujets obèses. Thèse Doctorat Méd. Univ. Paris. VI.
89. UNDERWOOD, P. J., E. BELTON & P. HUME. 1973. Aversion to sucrose in obesity. Proc. Nutr. Soc. **32:** 93A–94A.
90. HIBSCHER, J. A. & C. P. HERMAN. 1977. Obesity dieting and the expression of "obese" characteristics. J. Comp. Physiol. Psychol. **91:** 374–380.
91. HERMAN, C. P., J. POLIVY & V. M. ESSES. 1987. The illusion of counterregulation. Appetite **9:** 161–169.
92. DREWNOWSKI, A., J. D. BRUNZELL, K. SANDE, P. H. IVERIUS & M. R. C. GREENWOOD. 1985. Sweet tooth reconsidered: Taste responsiveness in human obesity. Physiol. Behav. **35:** 617–622.
93. CABANAC, M. & R. DUCLAUX. 1970. Obesity, absence of satiety aversion to sucrose. Science **168:** 496–497.
94. WITHERLY, S. A., R. M. PANGBORN & J. S. STERN. 1980. Gustatory responses and eating duration of obese and lean adults. Appetite **1:** 53–63.
95. WOOLEY, O. W., S. C. WOOLEY & R. B. DUNHAM. 1972. Calories and sweet taste: Effects on sucrose preference in the obese and nonobese. Physiol. Behav. **9:** 765–768.
96. MOWER, G. D., R. G. MAIR & T. ENGEN. 1977. Influence of internal factors on the perceived intensity and pleasantness of gustatory and olfactory stimuli. *In* The Chemical Senses and Nutrition. M. R. Kare & O. Maller, Eds. Academic Press. New York.
97. THOMPSON, D. A., H. R. MOSKOWITZ & R. G. CAMPBELL. 1976. Effects of body weight and food intake on pleasantness ratings for a sweet stimulus. J. Appl. Physiol. **41:** 77–83.

98. PANGBORN, R. M. 1970. Individual variations in affective responses to taste stimuli. Psychn. Sci. **21:** 125–128.
99. JOHNSON, W. G., T. M. KEANE, J. R. BONAR & C. DOWNEY. 1979. Hedonic ratings of sucrose solutions: Effect of body weight, weight loss and dietary restrictions. Addict. Behav. **4:** 231–236.
100. MEISELMAN, H. L. 1977. The role of sweetness in the food preference of young adults. *In* Taste and Development. J. M. Weiffenbach, Ed. U.S. Department of Health Education and Welfare. Bethesda, MD.
101. DREWNOWSKI, A. 1985. Food perception and preferences of obese adults: A multidimensional approach. Int. J. Obesity **9:** 201–212.
102. ENNS, M. P., T. B. VAN ITALIE & J. A. GRINKER. 1979. Contribution of age, sex and degree of fatness on preferences and magnitude estimations for sucrose in humans. Physiol. Behav. **22:** 999–1003.
103. TUORILA-OLLIKAINEN, H. & S. MAHLAMAKI-KULTANEN. 1985. The relationship of attitudes and experiences of Finnish youths to their hedonic responses to sweetness in soft drinks. Appetite **6:** 115–124.
104. DREWNOWSKI, A., B. PIERCE & K. A. HALMI. 1988. Fat aversion in eating disorders. Appetite **10:** 119–131.
105. LUCK, P. & A. WAKELING. 1982. Set-point displacement for behavioural thermoregulation in anorexia nervosa. Clin. Science. **62:** 677–682.
106. GARFINKEL, P. E., H. MOLDOFSKY, D. M. GARNER, H. C. STANCER & D. V. COSCINA. 1978. Body awareness in anorexia nervosa: Disturbance in "body image" and "satiety." Psychosom. Med. **40:** 487–498.
107. FANTINO, M., J. HOSOTTE & M. APFELBAUM. 1986. An opioid antagonist, naltrexone, reduces preference for sucrose in humans. Am. J. Physiol. **251:** R91–R96.
108. WRIGHT, P. & R. A. CROW. 1973. Menstrual cycle: Effect on sweetness preferences in women. Horm. Behav. **4:** 387–391.
109. WEIZENBAUM, F., B. BENSON, L. SOLOMON & K. BREHONY. 1980. Relationship among reproductive variables, sucrose taste reactivity and feeding behavior in humans. Physiol. Behav. **24:** 1053–1056.
110. DALVIT, S. 1981. The effect of the menstrual cycle on patterns of food intake. Am. J. Clin. Nutr. **34:** 1811–1815.
111. DALVIT-MCPHILLIPS, S. P. 1983. The effect of the human menstrual cycle on nutrient intake. Physiol. Behav. **31:** 209–213.
112. HASHIM, S. A. & T. B. VAN ITALIE. 1965. Studies in normal and obese subjects with a monitored food dispensing device. Ann. N.Y. Acad. Sci. **131:** 654–661.
113. SPIEGEL, T. A. 1973. Caloric regulation of food intake in man. J. Comp. Physiol. Psychol. **84:** 24–37.
114. CABANAC, M. & E. F. RABE. 1976. Influence of a monotonous food on body weight regulation in humans. Physiol. Behav. **17:** 675–678.
115. FANTINO, M. 1976. Effet de l'alimentation intragastrique au long cours chez l'homme. J. Physiol. Paris **72:** 86A.
116. GEISELMAN, P. J. & D. NOVIN. 1982. The role of carbohydrates in appetite, hunger and obesity. Appetite **3:** 203–223.
117. BEAUCHAMP, G. K. & M. MORAN. 1982. Dietary experience and sweet taste preference in human infants. Appetite **3:** 139–152.
118. HILL, A. J., L. D. MAGSON & J. E. BLUNDELL. 1984. Hunger and palatability: Tracking ratings of subjective experience before, during, and after the consumption of preferred and less preferred food. Appetite **5:** 361–371.
119. FANTINO, M., F. FAION & Y. ROLLAND. 1986. Effect of dexfenfluramine on body weight set-point: Study in the rat with hoarding behaviour. Appetite **7(Suppl.):** 115–126.
120. JUNG, R. T., P. S. SHETTY, W. P. T. JAMES, M. A. BARRAND & B. A. CALLINGHAM. 1979. Reduced thermogenesis in obesity. Nature **279:** 322–323.
121. SCHRUB, J. C., B. HILLEMAND, M. DUBVISSON & J. P. JOLY. 1971. Obésité et cure de jeûne. Chute pondérale immédiate et à distance. Sem. Hôp. Paris. **47:** 217–227.
122. KEESEY, R. E. 1988. The relation between energy expenditure and the body weight set-point: Its significance to obesity. *In* Handbook of Eating Disorders. Part 2. Burrows, Beumont & Casper, Eds. Elsevier. New York.

DISCUSSION

GARY ZISK (*Brooklyn College, Brooklyn, NY*): Dr. Stunkard at the University of Pennsylvania feels that the use of anorectic agents will lower the set point on a permanent basis if patients are continued on this medication. Do you have any thoughts on that?

DR. CABANAC (*Université of Laval, Québec, Canada*): I think it's a beautiful hypothesis. I hope it works.

DR. LINDA SCHNEIDER (*New York Hospital–Cornell Medical Center, White Plains, NY*): When I visited Dr. James Gibbs in Dr. Nicolaidis's laboratory last year, we talked about the question of why so many Parisians have such fine body shapes, and Jim was puzzled about why he hadn't figured out how they achieve this. Do you have any comments, given the high palatability of French food?

DR. CABANAC: It's a possibility that those Parisians who are obese are ashamed of their body weight and keep hidden. It could have something to do with the frequency of the meals. The French are still strongly under the influence of their Latin origin and have two big meals with practically no snacking in between. It could have something to do with that; I don't know.

DR. JOHN BLUNDELL (*University of Leeds, Leeds, U.K.*): It seems that the set-point has as its logical status that of the mediating concept or theoretical construct, and it relates to palatability in the way in which you suggest. However, I think one thing that makes people feel uncomfortable is that the existence of a set-point is defined in terms of shifts in palatability, but when you want to explain why are there shifts in palatability, you have to say it's because there's a change in set point. It's a circular set of mutually reinforcing definitions. I wonder if there are any other denotated principles, any other indices, of a set-point that allow us to escape from this circle.

DR. CABANAC: The most useful aspect of the concept of regulation is the set point. As you correctly pinpoint, there is a tendency toward circularity in reasoning, but if you measure what I like to call alliesthesia, you break the circularity because you can measure verbal reports of pleasure without influencing food intake. There is a relationship between pleasure following food intake or previous food intake, but if you measure pleasure at various times after the previous meal, you are likely to find no relationship.

There is another situation you can look at, and that is hoarding behavior in the rat. There is no direct relationship between the hoarding and body weight. You can, again, open the feedback loop by just removing the amount of food hoarded and with this method you can obtain superimposed results. There is no circularity in this study, and, by the way, no cultural bias in rats.

The Functions of Taste and Olfaction

LINDA M. BARTOSHUK

Department of Surgery (Otolaryngology)
Yale University School of Medicine
New Haven, Connecticut 06510

DISTINCTIONS BETWEEN TASTE AND SMELL

Taste and olfaction have different properties and different functions. They appear to be closely related because both are stimulated by chemicals. However, their independence is dramatically illustrated by a routine occurrence in taste and smell clinics. A typical patient reports to the clinic complaining that he/she cannot taste or smell. One of the first questions to ask is whether or not the patient can taste salt, sugar, the sourness of acidic substances like salad dressing and lemon juice, and the bitterness of substances like dark chocolate, black coffee, and medications. Many patients will respond that they can taste these substances but cannot taste anything else. From the point of view of taste, there isn't anything else.

When we eat, foods stimulate taste receptors on the tongue, but in addition, volatiles from the foods rise through the oral and nasal cavities and stimulate the olfactory receptors (located at the top of the nasal cavity just under the brain). Most of the time, the entire perception is referred to the mouth apparently because foods stimulate touch receptors in the mouth and touch mediates much of the localization of taste and smell.[1,2] We probably say that we "taste" foods because the taste receptors are genuinely in the mouth. We need a verb that reflects the perception of flavor, but we do not have one in English. On the occasions when we eat substances that are pungent (e.g. horseradish), we become aware of the path that the volatiles take because touch receptors in the nasal cavity are stimulated by pungent substances. When olfaction is damaged, the sensations produced by foods are diminished because the olfactory component is missing or reduced. In this case, the patient perceives "taste" to be affected even though the taste receptors are functioning in a normal manner. This confusion may make taste and smell seem to be more closely related than they really are.

PROPERTIES OF TASTE AND SMELL

Words Describing Qualities

The taste qualities generally accepted by taste investigators are sweet, salty, sour, and bitter. These are abstract terms that can be used in contexts that have little to do with the sense of taste (e.g., "she has a sweet disposition" or "he has a bitter outlook on life"). In these cases, we have borrowed the affective tone of the taste quality and applied it to some other affective situation.

353

There are a good many distinguishable odors. Although many systems have been proposed, there is no generally accepted list of basic olfactory quality names. Olfactory qualities are concrete and reflect the object that emits the odor (e.g., lemony, rose, minty, chocolate, smokey).

Affect

Taste

Taste affect is "hard-wired," that is, the affect is present at birth before an infant has had experiences with the consequences of ingesting sweet substances like sugar. The inborn affect of taste explains why we are able to use taste terms to express value. The value is unambiguous because it does not change valence based on learning.

The hedonic properties of taste are generally quite robust. In animals, attempts to render bitter substances palatable have not been very successful. Although sweet can be made aversive by pairing with nausea in rats (e.g., Pelchat et al.[3]), sweet aversions are very rare in humans (Bartoshuk and Wolfe, unpublished data). One study successfully induced aversions to mapletoff ice cream (a novel flavor created for the study) in children.[4] The specificity of the aversion was demonstrated by allowing the children to choose between the mapletoff and another flavor. The children significantly avoided the mapletoff but did consume the other ice cream. Because both ice creams tasted sweet, we can see that the children failed to develop a conditioned aversion to the sweetness.

Although it appears to be difficult to produce a conditioned aversion to sweet in humans, the palatability of sweetness can be temporarily altered by manipulating metabolic variables. For example, sweetness can be rendered temporarily less palatable by consumption of a sweet substance.[5] It can be rendered more palatable by an injection of insulin.[6,7]

Similarly, the palatability of NaCl varies with metabolic variables. When the body needs sodium, a craving for the salty taste develops in at least some subjects[8,9] and the palatability of salty tasting foods increases.[10]

Olfaction

Olfactory affect appears to be learned. Studies with children suggest that odors are still neutral to many children even at 1 and 2 years of age.[11,12] One of the most interesting questions yet to be answered in this field concerns whether any odors possess inborn affect. For example, although some have assumed that mammalian pheromones have their hedonic meaning established at birth, many experts believe that the affect of mammalian pheromones is entirely learned.[13]

The hedonic properties of odors show considerably more lability than the hedonic properties of tastes.[14,15] Unpleasant odorants move toward neutrality by exposure.[14] Neutral odors can be rendered pleasant by pairing with sweet[16] or calories.[17] Pleasant and neutral odorants can be rendered unpleasant by pairing with nausea.[3]

Analytic versus Synthetic Mixtures

If we mix colors on a color wheel, a new color results that is qualitatively distinct from the components. An observer cannot tell what the components were from looking at the mixture. This kind of mixing is called synthetic. On the other hand, if we play a chord on a piano (and the notes are not too close together) the component notes retain their distinctive pitches. A listener can hear the individual notes. This kind of mixing is called analytic. There has been some debate about whether taste is synthetic or analytic. Erickson and Covey[18] argued that taste is synthetic because they were able to construct some two-component mixtures that had "unitary" tastes. However, mixture suppression is well known in taste,[19-21] and the synthesis seen by Erickson and Covey appears to reflect simple suppression of one of the components.[22] When the components are equally intense, subjects identify taste qualities correctly in mixtures (e.g., see Bartoshuk[20]). Thus taste mixtures resemble auditory mixtures; they are analytic.

The components in some olfactory mixtures can be identified correctly.[23] However, more typically olfactory mixtures are processed holistically.[15] Cain has compared the ability to identify odors to the ability to identify faces.

The way in which we process mixtures in taste and olfaction suggests very different functions for the two senses. Using taste, we analyze a complex sensation to detect the presence of specific substances (e.g., salt, sugar, the presence of a bitter taste). On the other hand, using olfaction, we perceive the odor emitted by a particular object holistically, and we use it to identify the object.

ARE TASTE AND SMELL TUNED TO DETECT NUTRIENTS?

First, let us consider three categories of nutrients: macronutrients (those from which we derive calories), micronutrients (vitamins and minerals), and poisons or anti-nutrients. Because we know the chemical structures of typical examples of these nutrients, we can apply what is known about taste and smell to evaluate the sensory properties of the nutrients.

Macronutrients

The macronutrients consist of proteins, fats, and carbohydrates. Protein molecules are too large to produce taste and smell sensations. There are a few exceptions that are generally believed to represent cases in which a small group bound to the protein produces a taste. The sweet protein Monellin is such an exception. We consume many protein foods that have distinctive flavors (e.g., beef, chicken, tuna fish); however, the flavor is due to the smell produced by smaller volatile molecules present along with the protein molecules.

Fat molecules are also too large to produce taste and smell sensations. Again, the smells that appear to be produced by fat (e.g., bacon fat) are actually produced by smaller molecules mixed in with the fat. Fat is a good solvent for many odorants. For this reason, fat may seem to be an especially good source of odors.

Carbohydrates include large molecules such as starch but also include smaller molecules such as sugars. The sugars that are biologically important to us tend to taste sweet. For example, sucrose (common table sugar) is a sweet disaccharide that is made up of two monosaccharides, glucose and fructose. Both fructose and glucose also taste sweet. Maltose, a disaccharide made up of two glucose molecules, and lactose, a disaccharide made up of the monosaccharides galactose and glucose, are also sweet.

Starch is made up of a chain of glucose molecules. Humans do not taste chains with more than two glucose molecules, but rats appear to have a taste receptor that enables them to taste chains of as many as four glucose molecules. That is, the rat appears to have a starch detector that the human lacks.[23]

Micronutrients

Vitamins are usually present in such small quantities that any taste or smell they possess is not likely to be detected. In any case, most vitamins do not have distinctive tastes and/or smells that would permit them to be discriminated from other compounds.

Minerals are ingested in the form of salts. Some salts can be detected by the sense of taste. There appear to be some species differences in the taste of salts so the following generalizations should be limited to human subjects until the apparent species differences are better understood. Sodium and lithium salts taste salty; however, the intensity of the saltiness is affected by the anion. When sodium and lithium are paired with a small anion like chloride, the salt formed is very salty. As the anion gets larger (e.g. bicarbonate), it exerts inhibition on the taste of the cation. When the anion gets large enough, its structure determines whether or not it can produce bitter or sweet tastes (e.g., sodium saccharin tastes sweet because of the structure of the saccharin anion).

As cations get bigger than sodium, a bitter taste is added to the salty taste of the cation. For example, potassium salts taste bitter as well as salty. The intensity of the bitterness depends on an individual's genetic status for the ability to taste 6-n-propylthiouracil, also called PROP.[25]

The key point for the present discussion is that many salts taste bitter-salty. The sense of taste does not provide distinctive tastes for each salt.

Anti-nutrients

The bitter taste appears to have evolved as a poison detector. Unfortunately, there are many toxic substances that do not taste bitter; however, most of the substances that do taste bitter are toxic to humans if ingested in sufficient quantities.

Conclusion

Taste is the sense that *is* tuned to nutrients. The salty taste is characteristic of sodium, the sweet taste is characteristic of biologically useful sugars, and the bitter taste is characteristic of a variety of poisons.

Smell *is not* tuned to nutrients. However, the smells emitted by food objects provide cues that can be associated with the consequences of ingesting nutrients.

TASTE AS THE NUTRITIONAL SENSE: WHAT DO WE KNOW ABOUT TASTE STIMULI?

The four taste qualities can be divided into two groups: the electrolytes (acids and salts) and the nonelectrolytes (sweet and bitter substances).

Electrolytes (Salty and Sour)

The taste stimulus in an electrolyte is the positively charged particle. Thus in acids, the hydrogen (H^+) ion tastes sour and in salts, the cation (e.g., Na^+) tastes salty. As noted above, anions (the negatively charged particle) can taste bitter or sweet if they are structurally complex enough to interact with the bitter or sweet receptor sites, and they also exert an effect on the taste of cations. The larger the anion, the more it inhibits the taste of the cation.[26] Monosodium glutamate (MSG) offers a good example of this. MSG crystals taste much less salty than NaCl crystals because the glutamate anion inhibits the saltiness of the sodium cation more effectively than the chloride anion does.

Nonelectrolytes (Bitter and Sweet)

Bitter and sweet are taste qualities associated with organic compounds. The mechanism of these tastes may be of the "lock-key" variety. The shape of the active group on the bitter or sweet molecule "fits" the complementary shape on the taste receptor membrane. There seem to be multiple bitter and sweet receptors and our genes apparently control how many of each we have.

McBurney[27] showed that we possess more than one type of taste receptor for bitterness. This may have resulted from the fact that there are many different poisons. Several receptor types, each tuned to a particular set of poisons, provide the ability to detect just the poisons without thereby detecting nonpoisons as well.

A considerable body of literature supports the idea that we possess more than one type of receptor for sweet taste.[28-32] This may have the function of tuning the taste system such that not all sugars taste sweet. A variety of biologically useless sugars are chemically very similar to the biologically useful sugars. Nature appears to have found a way to allow us to taste the sugars that we can use. Fortunately or unfortunately, depending on your point of view, a variety of other compounds manage to stimulate the sweet receptor(s). Thus, we have artificial sweeteners. Interestingly enough, some other species respond to artificial sweeteners as if they did not taste sweet to that species. In particular, Hellekant[33] discovered that aspartame tastes like sugar only to the higher primates.

The ability to taste PTC (phenythiocarbamide) or its chemical relative, PROP (6-n-propylthiouracil) demonstrates the genetic control of the tasting of bitter. Pieces of paper saturated with PTC or PROP taste intensely bitter to some persons but taste like plain paper to others. The persons that taste PTC/PROP apparently have many receptors on their tongues for this compound. Those who do not taste it have either very few or none at all. The "nontasters" carry two recessive genes for this characteristic. The "tasters" carry either one dominant and one recessive gene or two dominant genes.

Tasters of PTC/PROP taste a variety of bitter compounds as more intense than nontasters do. For example, the bitternesses of saccharin and KCl (the salt substitute available in supermarkets) are more intense to tasters.[25,34] Surprisingly, some sweet compounds are also affected by this genetic mechanism. Sucrose (common table sugar) and saccharin taste sweeter to tasters of PTC/PROP.[34,35] That this genetic trait can affect the ability to taste some sweet compounds as well as bitter ones shows that nontasting is not simply a matter of lacking a particular type of bitter receptor. However, the molecular differences between the taste receptors of tasters and nontasters are not understood at this time.

Speculations on "Wisdom of the Body"

"Wisdom of the Body" was the title of the Harveian Oration delivered to the Royal College of Physicians of London in 1923 by Ernest H. Starling.[36] He used it to refer to various automatic physiological mechanisms (e.g., the heart's ability to increase or decrease the rate at which it beats based on body need). Several years later, Walter B. Cannon wrote a book that extended the ideas in Starling's lecture.[37] Cannon entitled his book *The Wisdom of the Body* out of respect for Starling's pioneering work. Cannon described the maintenance of a relatively constant steady-state in the body as "homeostasis." Curt Richter extended homeostasis to the behavioral sphere in his Harvey Lecture in 1942.[38] Richter proposed that organisms are capable of "total self-regulatory function" in the selection of appropriate nutrients. The initial empirical evidence came from studies on the specific hungers for salt and sugar. Later studies generalized this thinking to vitamins and other minerals.

NaCl

The need for sodium induces consumption of sodium salts. This was demonstrated dramatically in the case of a small boy with adrenal insufficiency who kept himself alive by consuming large amounts of NaCl.[8] Rats can be made sodium deficient by removing the adrenal glands. In this case, rats will increase intake of NaCl and keep themselves alive. Richter initially sought to explain this intake by suggesting that the rat's taste system had become more sensitive to NaCl. Pfaffmann and Bare[39] showed that this was not the case. Later, Contreras[40] showed that adrenalectomy actually renders the rat's taste system *less* sensitive to NaCl. Richter's explanation cannot be true. In fact, the increased intake of NaCl is not a sensory phenomenon but rather a hedonic one. The taste of NaCl becomes more *palatable* as a result of the body's need for it. Rats' facial expressions are an index of palatability.[41] When a rat is made salt hungry, the facial expression it produces when tasting salt becomes increasingly positive. If a rat has never encountered NaCl before, it can still consume it avidly at first exposure because the experience is so pleasurable. With experience comes the possibility of utilizing memory to obtain salt. Once a person or a rat has experienced the increased palatability of NaCl in the presence of NaCl need, he/she/it could experience a craving for the substance when the need is experienced in the future.

Can an organism actually experience a salt craving if it has never experienced NaCl in the presence of NaCl need? Krieckhaus[42] and Krieckhaus and Wolf[43] showed that rats exposed to NaCl and water in the presence of water-need (thirst) but not NaCl need can learn where both stimuli were. Later when a need for the NaCl was produced, the rats unhesitatingly located NaCl. These rats had not previously experienced the increased palatability induced by the salt need. They sought NaCl *as if they knew how pleasant it was going to taste.*

Sugar

Much like NaCl, the palatability of sugar is related to the body's need for it. Consumption of a sugar load renders sugar less palatable.[5,44,45] Injections of insulin render sugar more palatable.[7] Mayer-Gross[6] noted an even more dramatic effect with greater doses of insulin. Some schizophrenic patients given insulin shock therapy were described as going on "sugar riots."

Are There Any Other Specific Hungers?

At first, there seemed to be a specific hunger for thiamin. That is, rats on a thiamin-deficient diet immediately switched to a diet containing thiamin when given the opportunity. However, subsequent research showed that the rats were in fact switching to any novel diet to avoid the diet associated with the deficiency (see Rozin,[46] Rodgers,[47] and Nachman and Cole[48] for reviews).

Rodgers concluded that apparent specific hungers for calcium and magnesium were, like thiamin, actually examples of conditioned aversions for the deficient diet.

The idea that nutrient intake could be regulated by specific hungers is very attractive. As need for a particular nutrient increased, we would be driven to seek and ingest it. Then as the need diminished, the craving would diminish too. Specific hungers for specific nutrients would insure intake of all necessary substances. Nevertheless, there are innate specific hungers only for NaCl and sugar as well as an innate aversion to bitter substances.

Taste and Innate Specific Hungers

It is not an accident that the need-driven, innate specific hungers are for substances perceived via the sense of taste. Consider the characteristics of the taste system that were discussed above. First, NaCl tastes salty and sugar tastes sweet at the concentrations that are biologically useful to us. Poisons taste bitter even when they are very dilute just as required by a poison detector. Second, taste is analytic; that is, we can recognize salt, sugar, or bitter substances even when they are mixed with other substances. Third, the taste qualities salty, sweet, and bitter produce affective reactions at birth. That affect can then be modulated by body-need.

Olfaction and Learned "Specific Hungers"

The ability of an organism to learn to avoid a diet deficient in a nutrient is just as valuable as an innate specific hunger. In this case, we can deal with nutrients that are present in concentrations much too small to be detected by any of our senses (e.g., vitamins in food are neither tasted nor smelled). However, these nutrients can be detected by their effects on our bodies. We can learn to associate the effects of nutrients with the sensory characteristics of the foods in which they are present. Thus an animal made thiamin-deficient with a diet flavored with chocolate can learn to avoid chocolate. Then if the animal is offered a new diet containing thiamin and flavored with vanilla, the animal can learn to prefer the vanilla diet because of its beneficial effects. The characteristics of olfaction are tailor-made for this function. First, olfaction is the sense that identifies foods. The large number of olfactory qualities that can be perceived provides discrete sensory "labels" for a very large number of foods. Second, the lability of the pleasantness associated with odors permits the rapid alterations of palatability required for learning based on the consequences of food in the body.

REFERENCES

1. CAIN, W. S. 1978. History of research on smell. *In* E. C. Carterette & M. P. Friedman, Eds.: 197–229. Handbook of Perception, V. 1A, Tasting and Smelling. Academic Press. New York.
2. ROZIN, P. 1982. "Taste-smell confusions" and the duality of the olfactory sense. Percept. Psychophys. **31:** 397–401.
3. PELCHAT, M. L., H. J. GRILL, P. ROZIN & J. JACOBS. 1983. Quality of acquired responses to tastes by *Rattus norvegicus* depends on type of associated discomfort. J. Comp. Psychol. **97:** 140–153.

4. BERNSTEIN, I. L. 1978. Learned taste aversions in children receiving chemotherapy. Science **200:** 1302–1303.
5. CABANAC, M., Y. MINAIRE & E. R. ADAIR. 1969. Influence of internal factors on the pleasantness of a gustative sweet sensation. Comm. Behav. Biol. Part A **1:** 77–82.
6. MAYER-GROSS, W. & J. W. WALKER. 1946. Taste and selection of food in hypoglycaemia. Br. J. Exper. Pathol. **27:** 297–305.
7. RODIN, J., J. WACK, E. FERRANNINI & R. A. DEFRONZO. 1985. Effect of insulin and glucose on feeding behavior. Metabolism **34:** 826–831.
8. WILKENS, L. & C. P. RICHTER. 1940. A great craving for salt by a child with corticoadrenal insufficiency. J. Am. Med. Assoc. **114:** 866–868.
9. HENKIN, R. I., J. R. GILL & F. C. BARTTER. 1963. Studies on taste thresholds in normal man and in patients with adrenal cortical insufficiency: The role of adrenal cortical steroids and of serum sodium concentration. J. Clin. Invest. **42:** 727–735.
10. BEAUCHAMP, G. K. 1989. Development and modification of human chemosensory preferences. Proc. Abstr. Annu. Meeting Eastern Psychol. Assoc. **60:** 45.
11. ENGEN, T. 1982. The Perception of Odors. Academic Press. Orlando, FL.
12. ENGEN, T. 1979. The origin of preferences in taste and smell. *In* Preference Behaviour and Chemoreception. J. H. A. Kroeze, Ed.: 263–273. Information Retrieval Ltd. London.
13. BEAUCHAMP, G. K., R. L. DOTY, D. G. MOULTON & R. A. MUGFORD. 1976. The pheromone concept in mammalian chemical communication: A critique. *In* Mammalian Olfaction, Reproductive Processes and Behaviour. R. L. Doty, Ed.: 143–160. Academic Press. New York.
14. CAIN, W. S. 1979. Lability of odor pleasantness. *In* Preference Behavior and Chemoreception. J. H. A. Kroeze, Ed.: 303–315. Information Retrieval Ltd. London.
15. CAIN, W. S. 1984. What we remember about odors. Perfum. Flavor. **9:** 17–21.
16. ZELLNER, D. A., P. ROZIN, M. ARON & C. KULISH. 1983. Conditioned enhancement of human's liking for flavor by pairing with sweetness. Learn. Motiv. **14:** 338–350.
17. BOOTH, D. A., M. LEE & C. MCALEAVEY. 1976. Acquired sensory control of satiation in man. Br. J. Psychol. **67:** 137–147.
18. ERICKSON, R. E. & E. COVEY. 1980. On the singularity of taste sensations: What is a taste primary? Physiol. Behav. **25:** 79–110.
19. PANGBORN, R. M. 1960. Taste interrelationships. Food Res. **25:** 245–256.
20. BARTOSHUK, L. M. 1975. Taste mixtures: Is mixture suppression related to compression? Physiol. Behav. **14:** 643–649.
21. LAWLESS, H.T. 1979. Evidence for neural inhibition in bittersweet taste mixtures. J. Comp. Physiol. Psychol. **93:** 538–547.
22. SZCZESIUL, R., H. GRILL & L. M. BARTOSHUK. 1987. Recognition of components in taste mixtures: Analytic or synthetic? (Poster) 95th Annual Meeting of the American Psychological Association. August 28–September 1, 1987. New York.
23. LAING, D. G., H. PANHUBER, M. E. WILLCOX & E. A. PITTMAN. 1984. Quality and intensity of binary odor mixtures. Physiol. Behav. **33:** 309–319.
24. SCLAFANI, A. & S. MANN. 1987. Carbohydrate taste preferences in rats: Glucose, sucrose, maltose, fructose and polycose compared. Physiol. Behav. **40:** 563–568.
25. BARTOSHUK, L. M., B. RIFKIN, L. E. MARKS & J. E. HOOPER. 1988. Bitterness of KCl and benzoate: Related to PTC/PROP. Chem. Senses **13:** 517–528.
26. BEIDLER, L. M.1953. Properties of chemoreceptors on tongue of rat. J. Neurophysiol. **16:** 595–607.
27. MCBURNEY, D. H., D. H. SMITH & T. R. SHICK. 1972. Gustatory cross adaptation: Sourness and bitterness. Percept. Psychophys. **11:** 228–232.
28. SCHIFFMAN, S. S., H. CAHN & M. G. LINDLEY. 1981. Multiple receptor sites mediate sweetness: Evidence from cross adaptation. Pharm. Biochem. Behav. **15:** 377–388.
29. LAWLESS, H. T. & D. A. STEVENS. 1983. Cross adaptation of sucrose and intensive sweeteners. Chem. Senses **7:** 309–315.
30. JAKINOVICH, W. 1982. Stimulation of the gerbil's gustatory receptors by saccharin. J. Neurosci. **2:** 49–56.
31. BARTOSHUK, L. M. & J. F. GENT. 1985. Taste mixtures: An analysis of synthesis. *In* Taste and Olfaction and the Central Nervous System. D. Pfaff, Ed.: 210–232. Rockefeller University Press. New York.

32. BARTOSHUK, L. M. 1987. Is sweetness unitary? An evaluation of the evidence for multiple sweets. *In* Sweetness. J. Dobbing. Ed.: 33–47. Springer-Verlag. New York.
33. HELLEKANT, G., D. GLASER, J. BROUWER & H. VAN DER WEL. 1981. Gustatory responses in three prosimian and two simian primate species (*Tupapia glis, Nycticebus, Galago senegalensis, Callithrix jacchus jacchus, and Saguinus midas niger*) to six sweeteners and miraculin and their phylogenetic implications. Chem. Senses **6:** 165–173.
34. BARTOSHUK, L. M. 1979. Bitter taste of saccharin: Related to the genetic ability to taste the bitter substance 6-*n*-propylthiouracil (PROP). Science **205:** 934–935.
35. GENT, J. F. & L. M. BARTOSHUK. 1983. Sweetness of sucrose, neohesperidin dihydrochalcone, and saccharin is related to genetic ability to taste the bitter substance 6-*n*-propylthiouracil. Chem. Senses **7:** 265–272.
36. STARLING, E. H. 1923. The Wisdom of the Body. H. K. Lewis & Co. Ltd. London.
37. CANNON, W. B. 1939. The Wisdom of the Body. W. W. Norton & Co. Inc. New York.
38. RICHTER, C. P. 1942–1943. Total self regulatory functions in animals and human beings. Harvey Lecture Series **38:** 63–103.
39. PFAFFMANN, C. & J. K. BARE. 1950. Gustatory nerve discharges in normal and adrenalectomized rats. J. Comp. Physiol. Psychol. **43:** 320–324.
40. CONTRERAS, R. J. 1977. Changes in gustatory nerve discharges with sodium deficiency: A single unit analysis. Brain Res. **121:** 373–378.
41. GRILL, H. J. & R. NORGREN. The taste reactivity test. 1978. I. Mimetic responses to gustatory stimuli in neurologically intact rats. Brain Res. **143:** 263–279.
42. KRIECKHAUS, E. E. 1970. "Innate recognition" aids rats in sodium regulation. J. Comp. Physiol. Psychol. **73:** 117–122.
43. KRIECKHAUS, E. E. & G. WOLF. 1968. Acquisition of sodium by rats: Interaction of innate mechanisms and latent learning. J. Comp. Physiol. Psychol. **65:** 197–201.
44. CABANAC, M. 1971. Physiological role of pleasure. Science **173:** 1103–1107.
45. CABANAC, M. 1979. Sensory pleasure. Q. Rev. Biol. **54:** 1–29.
46. ROZIN, P. 1967. Thiamine specific hunger. *In* Handbook of Physiology, Sect. 6, Alimentary Canal, Vol. 1., Food and water intake. C. F. Code, Ed.: 411–431. American Physiological Society. Washington, D.C.
47. RODGERS, W. L. 1967. Specificity of specific hungers. J. Comp. Physiol. Psychol. **64:** 49–58.
48. NACHMAN, M. & L. P. COLE. 1971. Role of taste in specific hungers. *In* Handbook of Sensory Physiology. Vol. IV, Chemical Senses, Part 2. L. M. Beidler, Ed.: 337–362. Springer-Verlag. New York.

DISCUSSION

DR. PAUL ROZIN (*University of Pennsylvania, Philadelphia, PA*): Linda, that wasᶜ one of the most exciting talks I've heard in a long time; it was full of fascinating and inciteful ideas. The one thing I'm going to take issue with is the idea of taste aversion not being about taste. I like the general distinction you're making, however, as almost the entire animal literature is based on using pure tastings. My suggestion is that the reason you don't get "pure taste aversions" in humans is, first, humans rarely eat pure tastings so they're not in a situation like that of laboratory animals. Second, a number of learning phenomena, such as overshadowing and blocking, are going on here. The things that we normally taste have an olfactory component. It may be that, since we get these basic tastes all the time, they are protected from acquiring an aversion, and the more distinctive olfactory component of the flavor is being conditioned. In the case of the rats, in fact, they rarely get pure tastings except when they're in the laboratory, so it may be partly a matter of previous exposure. I still think your point is basically correct about the hard wiring of the taste system and the open-endedness of olfaction.

DR. BARTOSHUK (*Pierce Foundation, New Haven, CT*): I can't disagree with that; you are absolutely right. But let me make a counter-argument that the animal literature takes its knocks, because when I look at the stimuli used to condition taste and smell in the animal conditioned-taste literature, it looks to me like there's an intensity problem. The taste stimuli used always are very intense, while some of the olfactory stimuli are weak. I think that's a problem in that literature.

DR. DAVID BOOTH (*University of Birmingham, Birmingham, U.K.*): I wonder if you'd agree that you could tie together your reference to the biological and to the learned a little more tightly than you did. In the case of multiple sweet taste receptors, a possibility is that they are acquired, we don't need them at birth as much later because they're tuning out this very broadly tuned, bitter aversion to the peptides, amino acids, amino sugars, that we need in human milk. That's on the biological side of the possible function of sweet receptors.

On the learning side with which I'm more concerned, I wonder if it's just the postingestive factors that would change the hedonics to sweet. Clearly, when we've learned to like certain sweets in the context of their textures and appearances, then it is possible to have too much sweet very easily in a sweet food or drink. We can also have too little bitter in a quinine water beverage such as was used in your quinine water taste tests. If we like the beverage, then it could be too weak, or have too little bitter in it. I suggest an effect on biological functioning from social and cultural things we've learned. Toast for breakfast is very boring for most of us without jelly on it, but jelly on the melba toast or the bread on the side plate at supper is pretty revolting, I guess, for most of us.

DR. BARTOSHUK: Your points are well taken and something you said really resonated. You talked about sweet taste being important for very early conditioning. It's something that occurred to me only recently, and I haven't thought about it much, but one of the most important functions of the sweet palatability might be just that, to condition extremely early learning, in the first few months after birth, and to condition a positive affect of those olfactory cues you get from mother.

Quantifying Palatability in Humans

FRANCE BELLISLE

Laboratoire de Neurobiologie de la Nutrition
Université Paris VI
75252 Paris, France

Strickly speaking, palatability has to do with what is "agreeable to the palate or taste" (*Webster's Dictionary*). Indeed, during food stimulation, important sensations arise from the oral cavity. These and other cephalic sensory messages exert a crucial influence on the control of food intake. However, palatability is not a simple function of sensory qualities; it depends on the internal state of the organism and on the nutritive properties associated with a specific configuration of sensory qualities.[1-3]

Palatability is a complex notion and many definitions of it have been proposed by distinguished researchers in this field:

- The hedonic response of an organism to a foodstuff.[4]
- The orosensory action of the food that determines its acceptance.[5]
- The hunger-dependent and sensory-specific stimulation to eat.[3]
- Palatability is the interaction between the orosensory stimulation and internal factors that together determine acceptability of a food.[6]

In spite of differences in relative emphasis, these definitions recognize that food qualities act on an organism so that potential foodstuffs are accepted and feeding is stimulated under specific biological conditions.

How can we best quantify such acceptance? What indicators of the stimulation to eat can we use fruitfully as indices of palatability?

SUBJECTIVE CORRELATES

Palatability has subjective correlates: hedonic value, relative preferences, or sensory pleasure. These correlates are assessable in human subjects and are often measured using category scales, visual analogue scales, magnitude estimation techniques, and so forth. Poor correlation has sometimes been reported between verbal report and behavioral measures.[7,8] However, recent studies have addressed the problem of quantifying the relationship between changes in hedonic ratings and changes in intake[9]: Hedonic ratings did not appear to be good discriminators of intake differences between subjects; however, taste ratings proved reliable guides to consumption differences within a person.

OBJECTIVE INDICATORS

Saliva Flow

Many studies have dealt with salivation as an objective index of palatability. It has been stated that in nondieters, increases in saliva flow rate are a direct function of palatability[10]; in other studies, palatability did not emerge as a significant variable controlling salivation,[11] which responded more directly to the physiological and chemical properties of the foods.

Facial and Body Responses

Gusto-facial reflexes in the human newborn have been documented since the last century. These innate responses to basic tastes have been widely described in infants,[12] and their transformation has been described during growth.[13] Nowadays even the facial responses of rats to taste stimuli are successfully examined and analyzed in terms of food acceptance or rejection.[14]

MEASUREMENTS OF FEEDING BEHAVIOR

All these measures are potentially valuable indicators of the stimulation to eat exerted by foods. A lot could be said about their respective merits. In this talk, I would like to concentrate on some objective measures of intake, a number of which have been developed very recently. Their common element is the notion that in order to know how stimulated feeding is, one ought to measure feeding *per se*. In order to know how acceptable a given configuration of sensory properties is, one ought to test acceptance *per se*.

A simple indicator of the stimulation to eat one particular food is the amount ingested or meal size.

In terms of energy intake and body energy balance, meal size obviously is a crucial factor. In animals and human subjects, the studies that have used amount eaten as an indicator of the stimulation to eat are countless. However, such a simple index appears somewhat crude or insufficient. Definitions of palatability in terms of meal size tend to be circular[15]: If palatability simply amounts to meal size, and therefore meal size to palatability, we are dealing with a circular, sterile proposition that leaves the concept of palatability exhausted. Moreover, palatability is not the only determinant of meal size; the satiating power of foods is a distinct learned characteristic of foods that contributes to bringing the meal to its end.[16-18] Meal size results from a balance between stimulating positive factors and satiating negative factors.[2] These complementary and opposing mechanisms should be discriminated.

Eating Rates

To address this problem, many researchers have looked at eating rates. In humans as in animals, a high stimulation of intake is associated with rapid eating rates. Moreover, eating rate is not uniform during a meal. Studies have shown that eating rates best reflect palatability at the beginning of a meal.[7,20-22] At the start of ingestion, people eat faster when presented with foods that they enjoy; they eat more slowly when the food has low hedonic value.[23,24] In the course of the meal, eating rate decreases progressively until satiation is reached and the meal is terminated. Palatability of a food declines throughout the meal[2] and declines in proportion to the amount consumed of that particular food.[25] It has been suggested that the decline in eating rate reflects normal physiological satiation[24] or else indicates a decrease in the desire to eat.[19] A quadratic equation has been proposed as a good descriptor of the cumulative intake curve in humans.[19] The hypothesis has been advanced that platability operates on a facilitatory process and can be measured by the linear coefficient of the quadratic equation, which reflects the initial rate of eating.[20]

Many studies have reported accelerated eating rates in the obese.[26-32] A few studies have shown that the eating rate in obese persons does not decelerate through the course of a meal or does so less than with controls.[20,24,33]

We know that there is no universal obese eating style. The literature of food intake in obese humans contains many irreconcilable contradictions.[8] However, the above observations of obese persons have inspired constructive reflexions about sensitivity to sensory factors and about failure of satiation mechanisms in the obese. They are potentially important for behavioral treatment because a rapid eating rate has been shown to drive subjects to increased intakes [34,35] and to affect the duration of satiety following a meal.[36]

Lately, the modes of action of various anorexigenic drugs (amphetamine, fenfluramine) have been compared using an analysis of eating rates.[37] Although the compounds produced a similar suppression of food intake, they differed on a number of microstructural parameters.[38] In particular, fenfluramine brought about a noticeable slowing of eating rate and eliminated the characteristic decline in rate of feeding across the course of a meal.[37] This is consistent with the notion, based on neurophysiological evidence, that fenfluramine decreases food reward or palatability.[39]

Microanalyses of Feeding Patterns

The above-described results emphasize the importance of measuring rate of feeding. They also suggest that the microanalysis of feeding behavior provides a tool for understanding systems involved in the modulation of food consumption. For example, one could study how changes in specific meal parameters might have diagnostic value in assessing eating disorders.

Fine analyses of feeding behavior have been performed using a variety of techniques. Both laboratory studies and naturalistic observations (overt or covert) of feeding in humans have dealt with such parameters as

- Number of bites or mouthfulls[21,35,40]
- Average bite size[28,40]
- Eating time[41]
- Average bite duration[28]
- Bites per unit time[35,40,42]
- Total number of chews per meal[40,43]
- Calories per unit time[40]
- Chewing time[21,26,43]
- Chews per bite[26]
- Chews per unit time[40]
- Intrameal pause duration[43-45]
- Drinks[26,40,43]
- Total drinking time[43]

Much has been learned about these parameters in the past 15 years and some of them have been shown to reflect palatability changes. Once again, the comparison between obese persons and controls has provided much impetus in this area of research.

The Edogram

In their search for the mechanisms that control feeding, J. Le Magnen and his colleagues have contributed to the analysis of the meal structure in humans.[22,33,46,47] As a member of this team, I have been involved in a series of studies carried out in the laboratory. We used a recording device that allowed the continuous monitoring of eating responses (chewing, swallowing, pausing) in human subjects presented with standardized food pieces. Jacques Le Magnen termed the resulting recordings the "edogram" (FIG. 1). From such a recording, we were able to read and quantify many parameters of the structure of meals:

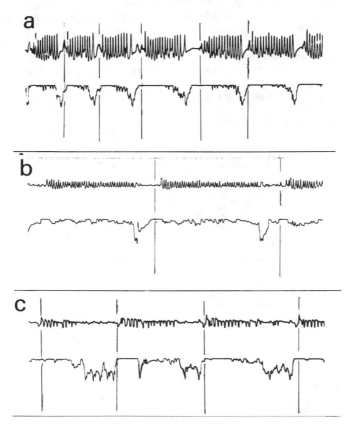

FIGURE 1. Three edograms (**a, b,** and **c**) recorded in different subjects. Vertical lines represent the intake of one piece of food into the subject's mouth. Bursts of chews (top lines of each edogram) have different duration and frequency in these three examples. Swallows are represented by the deep deflections in the bottom lines of each edogram.

- Total number of chews
- Number of chews per food piece
- Chewing rate
- Number of intrameal pauses
- Average intrameal pause duration
- Number of drinks per meal
- Drinking time per meal

Under these rigorous experimental conditions, presenting foods of different palatability induces a configuration of consistent changes in the microstructure of meals (FIG. 2). An increase in palatability is reflected in an acceleration of feeding patterns mainly due to a reduction in chewing activity. This is clear in different single-food meals representing different palatability levels. It is also obvious from the beginning

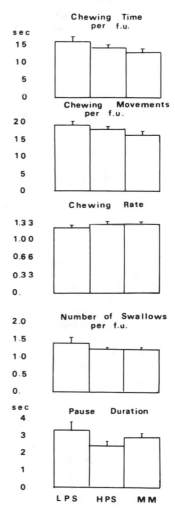

FIGURE 2. Five meal parameters as measured in 10 normal-weight subjects by the edogram method. Chewing time and number of chews per standard bite, as well as average pause duration decreased when palatability increased. LPS = Low preference single-food meals; HPS = High-preference single-food meals; MM = mixed meals; f.u. = standard food unit. Chewing rate is expressed in chews per second (after Bellisle and Le Magnen[46]).

to the end of a given meal. At the beginning of a meal, sensory stimulation is at maximum level; consequently, eating rate is fast, and chewing activity is reduced as compared to the end of the meal, when satiation factors play their inhibitory role. In mixed meals, the palatability effect is greater than in any single-food meal; moreover, sensory-specific stimulation is apparent in variations of chewing activity.[48]

What the edogram allows us to do is to quantify very finely each aspect of the microstructure of the meal. It certainly is more precise than covert observation,[49] but unfortunately its recording is somewhat constrained. It implies the use of very sensitive and to a certain extent burdensome laboratory apparatus. The edogram remains a laboratory tool, and the range of palatability that one can obtain under strict laboratory conditions is limited.

The mouth sensor recently developed by Eliot Stellar and his colleagues will soon allow a precise quantification of the microstructure of varied meals in human subjects in many real-life situations. This work will no doubt be of interest to all students of feeding behavior, especially behavior therapists who need to know more about the aspects of feeding responses that actually require modification.

INDIVIDUAL EATING STYLE

There is another reason why the microstructure of feeding behavior is worth the trouble of quantifying. We students of human behavior know the extreme variability found in all or almost all aspects of human responses. Interpersonal differences are huge and, more importantly, the reliability of many responses in the same person is often questionable.

The parameters that we select as indices of palatability will have to exhibit some internal reliability. It has been remarked that there are large individual differences in rate of eating that are stable over several days.[45] Consistent individual differences in ingestive responses have also been reported in human newborns.[50] In our experience, the edogram bears an individual "signature" which is clearly specific and remains recognizable over years.

FIGURE 1 displays edograms recorded in three different persons, showing important individual differences. These differences are stable over days and over years. When human subjects are retested under the same meal conditions after time intervals of a few weeks or a few years, most parameters of the edograms remain consistent with previous values. FIGURES 3 and 4 present eating rates as well as five meal parameters recorded in four persons in three series of two meals. A few weeks elapsed between the first two series and two to four years between the second and third series. Eating rate and chewing rate (chews per second) exhibited high stability in all four subjects. Chewing time and number of chews per standard bite as well as pause duration were very reliable in three out of four persons. Number of swallows per standard bite appeared stable in two persons, while it varied in the other two subjects. When the experimenter reads the corresponding edograms, these parameter values translate into patterns that can unmistakably be attributed to a specific person.

While one can imagine that certain responses such as meal size can be consciously or unconsciously altered in a human subject under experimental scrutiny, this seems highly unlikely of the meal parameters. The edogram is extremely robust and appears practically unfalsifiable.

Against this background of very reliable responses, what does palatability do?

Changes in palatability make sensitive parameters vary within narrow margins and, in our experience, produce a consistent configuration of microchanges (TABLE 1) that are reliable over years. Thus the microstructure of meals is sensitive and reliable enough to reflect moment-to-moment changes in palatability within the same meal, as well as chronic preferences in an individual.

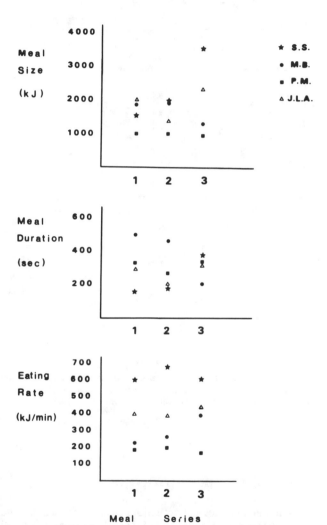

FIGURE 3. Average meal size, duration, and eating rate in four human subjects, in three successive series of meals. The first two meal series were administered within a few weeks of each other; the third one was presented two or four years after the first two. Note the relative stability of eating rates over time.

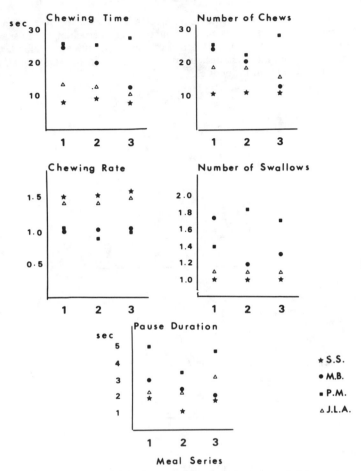

FIGURE 4. Five parameters of the microstructure of meals, as recorded from edograms. Four subjects were tested at a few weeks' interval (Series 1 and 2) and again two to four years later (Series 3). In most cases within-subject variability over time is smaller than between-subject differences.

BEYOND THE TAUTOLOGICAL TRAP

Rather than a circular, tautological definition, we are now facing a multitude of potentially valid responses and microresponses. Do all proposed palatability indices have equal validity? Do they really measure the same phenomenon? If palatability is defined as the stimulation of ingestive responses elicited by the sensory properties of foods, then such stimulation could be translated into various aspects of behavior and take different forms depending on meal conditions.

Correlations have been reported between meal size, hedonic ratings, and various

TABLE 1. Summary of the Effects of Increasing Palatability on Food Intake

Meal size	↑
Meal duration	↑
Eating rate	↑
Chewing time per uniform food piece	↓
Number of chews per uniform food piece	↓
Chewing rate	●
Number of swallows per uniform food piece	●
Duration of intrameal pauses	↓

NOTE: ● Indicates no change.

TABLE 2. Effects of Increasing Palatability

Mixed Meal Type	Traditional	Semiliquid	Sandwich
Hedonic ratings	↗	↗	↗
Meal size (kCal)	↗		↗
Meal weight (grams)	↗	↗	
Meal duration		↗	↗
Total time with food in mouth		↗	↗
Number of mouthfuls	↗	↗	↗
Average time in mouth per mouthful	↘		
Total intrameal pause duration			
Number of pauses		↗	
Average intrameal pause duration			
Average weight per mouthful	↗		
Eating rate			↘

NOTE: Heavy arrows indicate significant change; light arrows indicate insignificant trend (after Lehner[49]).

parameters of the meals.[7,46,48] In this context, consistent variations of many parameters allowed a definition of palatability in terms of a configuration of objective, predictable aspects of consumatory responses.

However, beside this harmonious picture, recent works have underlined situations in which all aspects of feeding behavior apparently do not respond alike to manipulations of the hedonic quality of foods.

For example, the response of various indices of palatability is not independent of the type of meals presented. The liquid/solid food distinction is very important.[51,52] A recent study has been performed on normal-weight French women who were presented with three types of mixed meals of high or low preference value.[49] The types of meals were (1) traditional four-course meals, (2) mixed sandwich meals, and (3) mixed semi-liquid meals. TABLE 2 summarizes the results of this study.

These observations are of obvious importance because many studies of palatability are performed with semiliquid or highly standardized food pieces ("pellets for humans"). They demonstrate that some indices might prove more sensitive than others according to the experimental context or the specific question that is asked. It should also be kept in mind that palatability is a broad continuum.[2,47] Behavioral indices of palatability may be differentially sensitive at various levels of this continuum.

Besides differences in relative sensitivity, discrepancies sometimes appear between candidate palatability indices. For many years, researchers have known that gustatory preferences in humans are different whether a tastant is presented in a solution or in real foods. For this reason many recent tests of palatability in human subjects are performed using real food.[53]

Now, under certain conditions, we have to recognize some discrepancies between hedonic ratings of foods and actual consumption. It has been shown that sensory evaluation tests with short exposure to food stimuli tend to overestimate the preferred sweetness intensity as compared to preferences quantified according to consumption tests.[54] The same discrepancy has been demonstrated in the assessment of the most preferred salt level in a familiar food (mashed potatoes).[55] FIGURE 5 shows that in brief-exposure taste tests, most of the subjects gave best preference ratings to highly salted food stimuli; in consumption tests, most subjects preferred foods of lower NaCl concentrations.

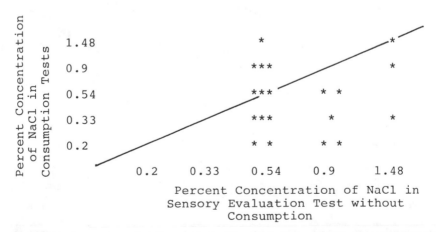

FIGURE 5. Comparison of preferences in the 20 subjects (represented by *) according to the two types of tests. A diagonal shows the isopreference level. r = 0.09; n.s.

CONCLUSION

The tools are many and numerous candidate indicators exist. Our problem is to ask the right question in the right terms and to select a sensitive method to generate the right answer. Palatability is a broad continuum. Some tools may be more valid or more sensitive than others under different experimental conditions or at particular points along the continuum.

It has been convincingly established that, regardless of innate preferences for taste qualities, palatability is acquired and is related both to the nutritive properties of a given food and to the subject's nutritional state. Thus, palatability plays a role in feeding behavior and nutritional homeostasis.[2] The essential goal that will guide an investigator's choice of the correct palatability indicator is its sensitivity with regard to the intricate factors that determine energy regulation.

An important question that may now be addressed with the numerous research tools that have become available is the complex relationship between ingestion responses during sensory stimulation, that is, while the subject is exposed to the palatability of foods and regulatory mechanisms that allow long-term adaptation of energy intake to expenditure. In this task, it will be helpful to track palatability from all viewpoints and in every convergent detail. Research is now in a better position to realize this than it was just a few years ago.

REFERENCES

1. BOOTH, D. A. 1977. *In* Food Intake and Chemical Senses. Y. Katsuki, M. Sato, S. F. Takagi & Y. Oomura, Eds.: 317–330. University of Tokyo Press. Tokyo.
2. LE MAGNEN, J. 1987. *In* Eating Habits. R. A. Boakes, D. A. Popplewell & M. J. Burton, Eds.: 131–154. Wiley. Chichester, England.
3. LE MAGNEN, J. 1987. *In* Progress in Sensory Physiology. Vol. 8: 95–128. Springer-Verlag. Berlin.
4. YOUNG, P. T. 1967. *In* Handbook of Physiology (Sec. 6) Alimentary Canal. Vol. 1: 353–366. American Physiological Society. Washington, D.C.
5. LE MAGNEN, J. 1971. *In* Progress in Physiological Psychology. E. Stellar & J. M. Sprague, Eds. Vol. 4: 203–261. Academic Press. New York.
6. KISSILEFF, H. R. *In* International Encyclopedia of Psychiatry, Psychology, Psychoanalysis, & Neurology. Vol. X: 172. Human Sciences Press. New York.
7. BOBROFF, E. M. & H. R. KISSILEFF. 1986. Appetite 7: 85–96.
8. SPITZER, L. & J. RODIN. 1981. Appetite 2: 293–329.
9. KISSILEFF, H. R. 1986. *In* Interaction of the Chemical Senses with Nutrition. Chapter 15: 293–317. Academic Press. New York.
10. WOOLEY, O. W. & S. C. WOOLEY. 1981. Appetite 2: 331–350.
11. CHRISTENSEN, C. M. & M. NAVAZESH. 1984. Appetite 5: 307–315.
12. STEINER, J. E. 1974. Ann. N. Y. Acad. Sci. 237: 229–233.
13. CHIVA, M. 1978. Ann. Nutr. Alim. 30: 255–262.
14. GRILL, H. J. & R. E. NORGREN. 1978. Brain Res. 143: 263–280.
15. PFAFFMAN, C., V. G. DETHIER & D. M. HEGSTED. 1977. *In* The Chemical Senses and Nutrition. M. R. Kare & O. Maller, Eds.: 463–475. Academic Press. New York.
16. BOOTH, D. A. 1972. Physiol. Behav. 9: 199–202.
17. BOOTH, D. A. 1977. Psychosom. Med. 39: 76–81.
18. BOOTH, D. A., M. LEE & C. McALEAVEY. 1976. Br. J. Psychol. 67: 137–147.
19. KISSILEFF, H. R., J. THORNTON & E. BECKER. 1982. Appetite 3: 255–272.
20. KISSILEFF, H. R. & J. THORNTON. 1982. *In* Changing Concepts of the Nervous System. A. J. Morrison & P. Strick, Eds.: 585–607. Academic Press. New York.
21. HILL, S. W. 1974. J. Comp. Physiol. Psychol. 86: 652–657.
22. PIERSON, A. & J. LE MAGNEN. 1969. Physiol. Behav. 4: 61–67.

23. JORDAN, H. A., E. STELLAR & S. Z. DUGGAN. 1968. Comm. Behav. Biol. 1(Part A): 65–67.
24. MEYER, J. E. & V. PUDEL. 1972. J. Psychosom. Res. 16: 305–308.
25. PLINER, P., J. POLIVY, C. P. HERMAN & I. ZAKALUSNY. 1980. Appetite. 1: 203–213.
26. GAUL, D. J., E. CRAIGHEAD & M. J. MAHONEY. 1975. J. Consult. Clin. Psychol. 43(2): 123–125.
27. GELLER, S. E., T. M. KEANE & C. J. SHEIRER. 1981. Addict. Behav. 6: 9–14.
28. HILL, S. W. & N. B. MCCUTCHEON. 1975. Psychosom. Med. 37: 395–401.
29. MARSTON, A. R., P. LONDON, L. COOPER & N. COHEN. In Recent Advances in Obesity Research. A. Howard, Ed. 1: 207–210. Newman. London.
30. NISBETT, R. E. 1968. J. Pers. Soc. Psychol. 10: 107–116.
31. STUNKARD, A. J. & D. KAPLAN. 1977. Int. J. Obes. 1: 89–101.
32. WAXMAN, M. & A. J. STUNKARD. 1980. J. Pediatr. 96: 187–193.
33. BELLISLE, F. & J. LE MAGNEN. 1981. Physiol. Behav. 27: 649–658.
34. JORDAN, H. A. & T. A. SPIEGEL. 1977. In The Chemical Senses and Nutrition. M. A. Kare & O. Maller, Eds.: 393–407. Academic Press. New York.
35. KAPLAN, D. L. 1980. Psychosom. Med. 42(6): 529–538.
36. WOOLEY, O. W., S. C. WOOLEY & K. TURNER. 1975. In Recent Advances in Obesity Research. A. Howard, Ed. 1: 212–215. Newman. London.
37. ROGERS, P. J. & J. E. BLUNDELL. 1979. Psychopharmacology 66: 159–165.
38. BLUNDELL, J. E., C. J. LATHAM, E. MONIZ, R. A. MCARTHUR & P. J. ROGERS. 1979. Cur. Med. Res. Opinion. 6(Suppl. 1): 34–54, 658.
39. LE MAGNEN, J. 1988. In Baillière's Clinical Gastroenterology. 2(1): 169–182.
40. STUNKARD, A. J., M. COLL, S. LUNDQUIST & A. MEYERS. 1980. Arch. Gen. Psychiatry 37: 1127–1129.
41. WITHERLY, S. A., R. M. PANGBORN & J. S. STERN. 1980. Appetite 1: 53–63.
42. DODD, D. K., H. J. BIRKY & R. B. STALLING. 1976. Addict. Behav. 1: 321–325.
43. ADAMS, N., J. FERGUSON, A. J. STUNKARD & S. AGRAS. 1978. Behav. Res. Therapy 16: 225–232.
44. ALLISON, J. & N. J. CASTELLAN. 1970. J. Comp. Physiol. Psychol. 70: 116–125.
45. MOON, R. O. 1979. Int. J. Obes. 3: 281–288.
46. BELLISLE, F. & J. LE MAGNEN. 1980. Appetite 1: 141–150.
47. BELLISLE, F., F. LUCAS, A. AMRANI & J. LE MAGNEN. 1984. Appetite 5: 85–94.
48. BELLISLE, F. 1984. Thèse de Doctorat d'Etat. Université Paris-Sud Orsay. Orsay, France.
49. LEHNER, V. 1987. Doctoral Dissertation. Université Pierre et Marie Curie. Paris.
50. KRON, R. E., J. IPSEN & K. E. GODDARD. 1968. Psychosom. Med. 30: 151–161.
51. HILL, S. W. & N. B. MCCUTCHEON. 1984. Appetite 5: 73–83.
52. KISSILEFF, H. R. 1985. Am. J. Clin. Nutr. 42: 956–965.
53. DREWNOWSKI, A. & H. R. MOSKOWITZ. 1985. Am. J. Clin. Nutr. 42: 924–931.
54. LUCAS, F. & F. BELLISLE. 1987. Physiol. Behav. 39: 739–743.
55. BELLISLE, F., I. GIACHETTI & A. TOURNIER. 1988. Sciences des Aliments. 8: 557–564.

DISCUSSION

DR. JACK DAVIS (*University of Illinois, Champaign–Urbana, IL*): I'm very impressed with the similarity in the patterns that you're getting with your microstructural measures of eating by human beings to the patterns that we get on responses to palatability variations in the rat. As far as I can tell they are identical.

Furthermore, I'm impressed with the fact that the chewing rate is constant across all conditions. It's very difficult in the rat to modify chewing rate; you can do it with drugs, but you certainly don't do it with variations in palatability.

DR. FRANCE BELLISLE (*Université Paris VI, Paris*): Yes, chewing rate is something very difficult to change. We've tried to modify it with deprivation and a number of manipulations, but it's very, very stable.

DR. DAVID BOOTH (*University of Birmingham, Birmingham, U.K.*): These are very important measures and important lines of experimentation. I wonder if you'd agree that trying to chase the very broad-spectrum concept of palatability and to devise finite measures palatability risks inhibiting progress, and the way forward is to look at the way the different measures are in fact breaking up in the last experiment you described in which you moved to real foods and a variety of foods.

DR. BELLISLE: Yes, I think you're right. We have so many tools in our hands now that we have to learn how to use them most efficiently. Probably there's a lot to learn by using many tools even though we're not able to decide now exactly what they reveal about one another and whether they have equal validity in all cases.

DR. ANTHONY SCLAFANI (*Brooklyn College, CUNY, Brooklyn, NY*): That was a very thorough review of your own work and previous work on measuring palatability. What struck me was the almost exclusive emphasis on quantifying the rate of eating. There was almost no discussion of preference for different foods. It seems to me that rate doesn't always correspond to preference, and clearly humans, even more than animals, are very distinct in their preferences. Is there a particular reason why there has not been as much work done in preference for different foods?

DR. BELLISLE: There has been much work done in preference in humans, preference for different foods, but I make a great distinction between preference and palatability. Preference has to do with relative hedonic response to various foods, whereas the way I view palatability is as a representation of acceptance behavior and acceptance response. This is why I have concentrated on palatability as fact, but obviously relative preferences are also something very important as well as feeding patterns beyond the meal. I think that we should also give some thought to the problem of what we observe when the subject, human subject or animal subject, is under the stimulation provided by food. This must have something to do with feeding patterns on a longer term basis, on satiety, and on the reappearance of hunger later on. This is a very important problem that we have to face now.

DR. JOYCE PRIGOT (*CUNY Graduate Center, Franklin Square, NY*): I have a question about your measures. Which best differentiates your obese from your lean subjects?

DR. BELLISLE: I tested very few obese subjects. What happened was that they ate faster, and they chewed less than the lean subjects. They also did not show any deceleration of eating rates during the meal. But also remember, we were working in a laboratory setting, and they ate very little in front of us, so I don't know whether this shows that the obese subjects that I was testing actually are hypophagic or whether they were not eating as much as they would have if they had been in their natural setting. But the fact is that their intake did not show any deceleration during the meal.

Disorders of Food Selection

The Compromise of Pleasure[a]

PAUL ROZIN

Department of Psychology
University of Pennsylvania
Philadelphia, Pennsylvania 19104

Food and eating are laden with significance with respect to health, pleasure, and so-cial/moral concerns.[6,32,33] In discussing eating and food selection disorders, it is too easy to focus entirely on the health domain. By doing so, we drastically limit the scope and significance of these disorders. The social/moral stigma associated with obesity, and the limitations of pleasure associated with guilt about eating and dieting may be the greatest costs of obesity. When we come to disorders of food selection, much of the justification for using the term disorder derives from compromises in pleasure. It is the thesis of this paper that there are many deviant and maladaptive food selec-tion practices, but that (a) there is little psychobiology as opposed to cultural psy-chology that can be marshaled to explain them, and (b) the main cost of these activi-ties is not directly on health, but on the quality of life.

Disorders of food selection have received almost no attention in the scientific liter-ature, being overshadowed by the salient pathologies of food intake (obesity, anorexia, and bulimia) and by substance abuse. Of course, substance abuse, in some cases, can be viewed as a disorder in food selection. Coffee, tobacco, and most particularly al-cohol, qualify as foods[24] according to some definitions. There is an understandable urgency in dealing with these problems. Nonetheless, it seems appropriate to take stock of food selection more generally, because there is wide variation here, and because the activities involved take up a good part of the waking time of humans (the procure-ment, preparation, and consumption of food).

It is reasonable to define something as a disorder if it meets two of the following three criteria: (1) It is deviant, (2) it is maladaptive, and (3) it can be explained in terms of a known pathology in some system. Diabetes, for example, clearly qualifies on all counts. Obesity meets the first and perhaps the second, but not the third according to the current state of knowledge, while anorexia clearly meets the first two, but not the third criterion. In order to give full scope to abnormality in food selection, I will relax the definition of disorder and require that only one of these three criteria be met. I will also expand the maladaptive criterion to include decrease in the quality of life, as opposed to simply compromise in health. Maladaptiveness in its most objec-tive form means mortality. Death, or length of life, is an unarguable dependent vari-able. Growth rate and size are other nicely measured end points. However, many sig-

[a] Preparation of this paper was supported by grants from the University of Pennsylvania Re-search Fund and from the John D. and Catherine T. MacArthur Foundation Health and Be-havior Network.

nificant events do not map into longevity or growth rate, but affect the quality of life. Quality of life is harder to measure and validate, but these methodological problems have nothing to do with the reality of such effects.

The metabolic versatility of organisms is such that a tiny percentage of all the molecules necessary for existence need to be ingested. For humans and other mammals, the number is in the range of 30 to 40. These substances are present in a wide variety of foods, such that it is probably true that a random selection of foods from the shelves of a supermarket would lead to an adequate diet that would prevent deficiencies. On the other side, overingestion of potentially harmful substances would also be minimized by the simple strategy of eating a wide variety of foods. The result is that, given a variety of foods, serious compromises of health are unlikely to occur, even in the face of a wide range of deviant practices: avoiding meat or fruits, eating only two meals a day, never mixing foods, and so forth. Yet some people behave as if every selection of every bite has grave health implications.

The actual physical health problem is further ameliorated by the fact that the cuisines that guide us in the foods we eat have been shaped over generations and tend to define a balanced set of foods (otherwise the cuisine group in question would be at a serious disadvantage). Thus, peasant Mexican cuisine, lowish in meat protein for economic reasons, includes two staple foods, corn and beans, which together have a balanced amino acid profile.

The maladaptive side of food selection then falls into two domains: (a) the selection of nonoptimal diets that may decrease longevity, and (b) overconcern about food selection, leading to anxiety, dysphoria, and the despoiling of one of the great pleasures of life.

To illustrate, consider the phenomenon of widespread food rejection in childhood. Parental complaints about very narrow food selection, or extensive consumption of a few "undesirable" foods, or insufficient appetite in two- to four-year-olds are among the most frequent concerns encountered by pediatricians.[2] A survey of Canadian mothers of young children records complaints about some aspect of feeding in 49% of cases; 7% of families were judged to have serious food problems.[21] These problems are associated with general difficulty in these children, including aggressiveness and difficulty in toilet training.[21] At this point, we cannot disentangle cause and effect. However, it is a reasonable hypothesis that the main effect of restricted food choice in children is not on their nutritional status (after all, peanut butter and jelly, milk, and a few other favorites need not be an unhealthy diet), but on the interpersonal relations in the family. We all know of families in which parent–child fighting over food has led to difficult relations. The point is that the outcome of a food selection deviance may have serious consequences in other domains.

A BRIEF SURVEY OF DEVIANT FORMS OF FOOD SELECTION

Deviance in food selection can be classified into three categories: excesses, avoidances, and miscellaneous. I will consider instances of each type, with a data base that consists primarily of Americans. Some of the data presented comes from a national mail survey ($n = 123$ responses) done with Maureen Markwith in which a long list of possible deviances were listed (see TABLE 1), and subjects were asked merely to check those that appropriately described their own behavior. To my knowledge, there has been no previous statement of a taxonomy of food selection disorders, so the following may be considered a first, rather primitive attempt.

Excesses

Descriptions of the three types of excesses follow.

Ingestion of Items Not Normally Considered Food

The best example of indiscriminate eating or mouthing is the normal infant. The little evidence available[5,27] suggests that infants, up to about two years of age, will put almost anything in their mouths and chew and swallow almost all of such items (when this is possible). One of the major features of early development in the food domain seems to be to learn what not to eat. The most significant adult form of this type of excess ordinarily goes under the name of pica or geophagy: consumption of earth or clay. It is common in many cultures and in the United States is most associated with pregnant, lower class, Southern women.[4,10] It has been linked, but not definitively, with iron deficiency.[4] Four percent of respondents in our national survey (TABLE 1) indicated ingestion of nonfood items.

Excess Ingestion of or Craving for Specific Foods

It is very common for people to consume a great deal of one food, either because of a strong preference or craving, or for economic/availability reasons. Of course, in extreme forms, such cravings can also be described as avoidances, because a wide variety of foods are *not* eaten. In the same national survey we have referred to,[28] subjects were asked to list any cravings they had, with craving defined as "a strong desire for a particular food or drink. This desire is so strong that it will cause a person to go far out of his or her way to satisfy the craving." Seventy percent of subjects listed at least one food. Sweets (especially chocolate, fruit, soda, and ice cream), vegetables, and animal foods are among the most commonly craved items. A number of studies suggest a particularly high incidence of cravings during pregnancy, with fruit, chocolate, ice cream, and other sweets dominant (and meat products more characteristically viewed aversively than craved).[7,16] On the whole, these cravings have a benign quality.

Excess Variety

A strong desire for a highly varied diet might be considered excessive. Some people may be particularly susceptible to boredom by a monotonous diet; in the national sample, for example, 9% of subjects said that they never eat the same main course two days in a row (TABLE 1).

Avoidances

The most striking and significant phenomenon among the avoidances is extensive neophobia. I described childhood food neophobia above. Such a phenomenon surely exists in some form in adults but has not been documented. The national survey illustrates some "subsyndromes"; for example, 23% of respondents eat exactly the same meal for breakfast every day, and 18% completely avoid a major food group (see TABLE 1; also note other avoidances on the table). Vegetarians are the most prominent group who avoid a specific group of foods, in various degrees (from avoiding only red meat

TABLE 1. Benign Deviances of Food Selection Based on a National Sample of 123 Persons[a]

"Deviance"	n	Percent
High Variation or Excesses		
Never eat the same main course two days in a row	11	9
Eating what is not normally considered food (for example, clay/earth, plaster, ashes, charcoal)	5	4
Low Variation or Avoidances		
Always eat the same meal for breakfast	28	23
Always eat the same meal for lunch	2	2
Completely avoid a major group of foods (for example, meat, vegetables, dairy products, breads or cereals, sweets, fruits)	22[b]	18
Won't eat uncooked food	6	5
Can't stand a particular quality of food (for example, sweet, mushy, crispy, sour, salty)	30[c]	24
Eating Patterns/Combination Rules		
Eat foods separately in the main course (for example, all peas first, all potatoes second, all meats last)	11	9
Won't eat any combination of foods (for example, peas and carrots)	2	2
Never let different foods touch on my plate	2	2
Never put different foods on my fork or spoon at the same time	17	14
Always mix foods on my plate	11	9
Won't drink a beverage without a straw	1	1
Always leave a clean plate	66	54
Never leave a clean plate	3	2
Don't drink while I eat	19	15
Social		
Never eat alone	10	8
Always eat alone	6	5
Never eat a food if I saw someone else touch it	11	9
Never eat leftovers	5	4

[a] National random sample, 300 surveys mailed, 65 with no forwarding address, 123 complete returns.

[b] Most common responses: some subset of animal foods (other than dairy), 8; sweets, 4.

[c] Most common responses: salty, 8; mushy, 8.

through avoiding all animal products). The more extreme forms of vegetarianism (e.g., complete avoidance of all animal products) put the practitioners at potential nutritional risk; that is, some care is required in creating an adequate nonanimal diet. The food restrictions of vegetarians and the motives for them vary greatly; health and ethical/moral motives play differing roles, and the practice can, but need not, engage strong social ties.[8,9] Other less well defined restrictions appear in American culture, such as avoidance of additives or "nonnatural" foods.

Much more specific restrictions, rarely significantly restricting the range of acceptable foods, result from specific taste aversions, traceable to past pairings of ingestion and illness[15] and avoidances consequent upon food allergies. Although both result in avoidances, the mechanisms and manifestations are different. Taste aversions result in a dislike for the taste of the offending food (an acquired distaste[25]) and is usually caused by the postingestional event of nausea.[22] Avoidances based on allergies are not usually accompanied by a dislike for the taste of the food; the food is considered dangerous but desirable. Nausea seems to be the critical event that causes acquired distaste.[22]

Eating Patterns

To my knowledge, there have been no explorations of variations in the patterns of eating. The national survey included a set of items in this domain (TABLE 1). Note that "always leaving a clean plate" is normal, and that there are many ritualized ways of dealing with the confrontation with multiple foods that occurs in most meals. Some people eat all foods separately, one at a time; some will not even allow the foods to touch on the plate. Others may allow some mixing of different foods, but will never combine foods simultaneously on the same fork. Again, some avoid foods touched by others or will not eat leftovers. All of these idiosyncrasies are interesting but not of substantial import for health or the management of life. People feel quite strongly about the way in which they eat but don't much care what other people, including those close to them, do.

CAUSES OF FOOD SELECTION DEVIANCE

Regardless of their ultimate significance, the wide variations in food selection must have causes, and it is appropriate to inquire about them. Looking across the entire human race, it is obvious that the major variations in both what people eat and how they eat it are cultural in origin. Each cuisine emphasizes its own foods, preparations, and rules of eating etiquette. In the traditional Hindu household, it is critical to know who prepared the food and whose leftovers (if any) are being served. The order of serving is a means of reaffirming social and familial relationships.[1] In the American household, these matters are of little significance; indeed, in buying saran-wrapped food in impersonal supermarkets, we surrender the possibility of knowing the origins of our food. This massive difference, relating to the role of food as a social and moral substance, is surely based on cultural tradition and is unlikely to be related to levels of any brain enzyme. The challenge in understanding variation in food selection is to identify some areas where biological factors *are* significant. After all, it is a feature of being both human and omnivorous that what is food and how that food is eaten are open-ended, and specified loosely, if at all, in the genes.

Biological factors are implicated in explaining individual differences at two levels: the identification of foods by means of sensory systems, and the evaluation of foods in terms of their metabolic consequences.

Sensory Factors

Sensory factors are under strong biological control, and are, particularly for the case of taste and smell, of central importance for all humans in the identification of food. However, the question at hand relates to individual differences in sensory systems and related aspects of food selection, not to the overall, general importance of sensory factors. There are only a few well-documented instances of genetically determined differences in chemical sensitivity in humans, with PTC tasting being the most striking example.[11,23,37] The ability to taste phenylthiocarbamide and related compounds is controlled primarily by a single genetic locus; people (and other primates) who are sensitive taste this set of compounds as bitter. The compounds include a number of natural (sometimes antithyroid) substances present in some common vegetables, including cabbage and turnips. The tasting trait varies cross-culturally.[3] Although there are a few studies that indicate a higher level of taste aversions in people with a low threshold for PTC,[12] no study has shown a direct mapping between PTC taste sensitivity and rejection of foods containing PTC-related compounds. Thus, although there are some reported genetic differences in chemical sensitivity (and likely to be more), no specific link to changes in food preferences have been documented.

Metabolic Factors

Both individuals and ethnic groups have genetic differences in metabolism. Because individuals are able to modulate their food intake on the basis of the consequences of ingestion, these biological differences would be expected to appear in both individual food preferences and culinary practices. A number of striking examples are available, the clearest being the link between lactose intolerance and avoidance of milk (and sometimes other dairy products)[34] (also see Katz[18] for other examples). However, the mapping is not simple; many lactose-intolerant persons like milk, and many continue to consume modest levels of milk (discussed in Rozin & Pelchat[30]). The special changes in appetite during pregnancy may well have a hormonal basis, or result from the extra nutritional demands during that period, but solid evidence remains to be produced.

In short, while there are surely biological factors responsible for some food deviances, few have been linked to actual food choice, and most food choice seems very much the result of culture and individual experience.

RISK HYPERSENSITIVITY AND THE COMPROMISE OF PLEASURE

The principal thesis of this paper is that in the United States, where food is plentiful, the major maladaptive response to food is overconcern about the risks of eating. A great deal of money is spent by advertisers and consumers to achieve peace of mind about dietary health risks, and a great deal of anxiety is manifested in this arena. The result is that one of the most pleasant of human activities has become drenched in worry. Tiny increases in mortality risk lead to worry and food avoidances, with no thought for the benefits in terms of quality of life that might result from maintaining certain highly desirable foods in the diet. One gets the impression that some think that eating is more dangerous than not eating. The massive concern and overreaction to minimal threats from the supposed carcinogenicity of cyclamate or saccharine, and the widespread avoidances of fruit following the recent Alar/apple or Chilean grape scares are symptomatic of this state of mind. The question is: What characteristics of humans contribute to this overresponse?

Part of the problem arises because of special features of foods, and part because of general features of human response to risk. Interactions with food are of particular intimacy, because eating involves incorporating something from the outside world into the body. People feel very strongly about this and have very strong reactions to placing foreign substances in their mouths.[26] In particular, cross culturally, there is a tendency to believe that one takes on the properties of the foods one eats ("you are what you eat").[19] The emotional intimacy of eating is probably related as well to the fact that food often takes on moral characteristics, overtly in India and more subtly in American culture. Thus, sugar and sweetness sometimes seem to be associated with sinfulness.[14,31] Some of the great overconcern about very small food risks may result from these special properties of foods.

Most of the problem derives from general problems in risk perception, and the fact that humans are poorly equipped to handle information about very low risks. After all, such risks are not of the sort that any person would experience in a lifetime; they result from population statistics, of the sort that were not available to humans during their evolution. There has been an explosion of important work on lay inference in recent years (e.g., Nisbett & Ross,[20] Kahneman, Slovic & Tversky,[17] and Tversky & Kahneman[38]), which bears directly on overconcern about food. Risk concerns seem to be enhanced by situations that are unfamiliar, have dread outcomes, deal with unknown factors (and delays), and are out of individual control.[35] Concerns about food additives fall into this category; the substances are unfamiliar, there is the dread outcome of cancer, the effects are delayed and not understood, and the individual does not control the addition of these substances. In contrast, the much riskier activities of alcohol ingestion or driving are perceived as less risky than they actually are, because they are familiar, under voluntary control, and, for the case of driving, less associated with unknown, delayed effects. These factors are illustrated in a comparison of rankings of relative risks of 30 activities and technologies by risk experts and college students (TABLE 2).[36] Note the underestimate of risks of alcohol and motor vehicles by the students, and the overestimates of the risk of nuclear power (involuntary, unfamiliar, dread, and unknown). Student ratings of alcohol risk are below those of experts, while the student ratings of pesticide risk are higher than those of experts (TABLE 2).

The study of attitudes to food suggests some additional features of human thinking that lead to overconcern about food. One is a tendency to view the world categorically; to think of foods as either risky or of zero risk; and, of course, to prefer the zero risk, unattainable as it may be. The categorical view leads to what I call dose insensitivity: a tendency to think of foods or additives as good or bad, a property that applies to any dose. Thus, 20% of the same national survey sample referred to above expresses slight or strong agreement with the statement "a pinch of sugar added to one food every day is bad for your health" and 31% agree with the statement "If something can cause harm to the body in large amounts, then it is better not to eat it even in small amounts."[29]

Finally, people and institutions such as the Congress tend to downgrade the benefits, in terms of reduced pleasure, in banning a food or publicizing its risks, and to be dominated by mortality statistics, however miniscule the risk. It is a case of a categorical error: If any risk (e.g., the loss of one human life in the world) can be attached to an activity, then the associated benefits of the activity become irrelevant. It is a tendency to pay little attention to the quality of life.

Overreactions to food risks may be treatable by education. Teaching of cost–benefit modes of thought would be highly desirable. In addition, it may be possible to frame risks so that people can more clearly see the relative riskiness of their activities (see Fischhoff, Lichtenstein, Slovic & Derby[13] for a general approach to this problem). For example, Wilson[39] has produced an equal risk table that makes it easy to compare risks; the low level of the risks is factored out, and only relative risks are presented. TABLE 3 shows a selection from this work, indicating a set of food and nonfood activities calculated to incur equal risks (1 part in one million). One can, of course, dispute any of the specific estimates, but the equal risk framing is surely helpful to an individual in evaluating personal risks.

TABLE 2. Selective Rankings of 30 Activities and Technologies by Experts and College Students[a]

	Rating	
Risk	College Student	Expert
Motor vehicles	5	1
Handguns	2	4
Nuclear power	1	20
Smoking	3	2
Alcohol	7	3
Pesticides	4	8
Food preservatives	12	14
Food coloring	20	21

[a] Adapted from Slovic, Fischhoff & Lichtenstein.[36]

An important message from this table is that there are serious risks of ingestants. Alcohol, cigarettes, high-fat diets, and probably a few more nutritional practices can cause significant harm to health. But when these significant risks are lumped with risks such as that from saccharine, the public has difficulty sorting out what is worth doing something about. From the point of view of public health, the aim should be to distinguish between risks, to focus on the major items, and pretty much ignore the rest.

CONCLUSION AND SUMMARY

Many deviancies exist in food selection. As a group, these are benign and result primarily from cultural forces or individual experiences. Perhaps the major forms of food disorders, outside of substance abuse, have to do with a few nutritional excesses, such as consumption of high-fat diets and the compromise of the pleasure of eating that occurs at the dinner table when little children don't eat what their parents think is good, or that occurs when people worry so much about the low risk of food toxins or imbalances that they deny themselves favorite foods and worry with every bite. The good news is that the compromise in pleasure is treatable by education, and that it is still possible to enjoy a good meal.

TABLE 3. Risks Estimated to Increase Chance of Death in Any Year by One Part in One Million[a]

Activity	Cause of Death
Smoking 1.4 cigarettes	Cancer, heart disease
Drinking 0.5 liter of wine	Cirrhosis of the liver
Spending one hour in a coal mine	Black lung disease
Traveling 150 miles by car	Accident
Traveling 1,000 miles by jet	Accident
Living 2 months with a cigarette smoker	Cancer, heart disease
Living two days in New York or Boston	Air pollution
Eating 40 tablespoons of peanut butter	Liver cancer caused by aflatoxin B
Eating 100 charcoal-broiled steaks	Cancer from benzopyrene
Drinking 30 12-oz cans of diet soda	Cancer caused by saccharin

[a] Adapted from Wilson.[39]

ACKNOWLEDGMENTS

Thanks are extended to Maureen Markwith for assistance in data collection and analysis and to Maureen Markwith and Marcia Pelchat for comments on the manscript.

REFERENCES

1. APPADURAI, A. 1981. Gastro-politics in Hindu South Asia. Am. Ethnol. **8:** 494–511.
2. BAKWIN, H. & R. M. BAKWIN. 1972. Behavior Disorders in Children. W. B. Saunders. Philadelphia, PA.
3. BARNICOT, N. A. 1950. Taste deficiency for phenylthiourea in African Negroes and Chinese. Ann. Eugen. **15:** 248–254.
4. COOPER, M. 1954. Pica. Charles C. Thomas. Springfield, IL.
5. DAVIS, C. 1939. Results of the self-selection of diets by young children. Can. Med. Assoc. J. **41:** 257–261.
6. DEGARINE, I. 1972. The socio-cultural aspects of nutrition. Ecol. Food Nutr. **1:** 143–163.
7. DICKENS, G. & W. H. TRETHOWAN. 1971. Cravings and aversions during pregnancy. J. Psychosom. Res. **15:** 259–268.
8. DWYER, J. T., L. D. V. H. MAYER, R. F. KANDEL & J. MAYER. 1973. The new vegetarians. Who are they? J. Am. Dietetic Assoc. **62:** 503–509.
9. DWYER, J. T., R. F. KANDEL, L. D. V. H. MAYER & J. MAYER. 1974. The "new" vegetarians: Group affiliation and dietary strictures related to attitudes and life style. J. Am. Dietetic Assoc. **64:** 376–382.
10. EDWARDS, C., H. MCSWAIN & S. HAIRE. 1954. Odd dietary practices of women. J. Am. Dietetic Assoc. **30:** 976–981.
11. FISCHER, R. 1967. Genetics and gustatory chemoreception in man and other primates. In The Chemical Senses and Nutrition. M. R. Kare & O. Maller, Eds.: 61–81. Johns Hopkins Press. Baltimore, MD.
12. FISCHER, R., F. GRIFFIN, S. ENGLAND, & S. M. GARN. 1961. Taste thresholds and food dislikes. Nature **191:** 1328.
13. FISCHHOFF, B., S. LICHTENSTEIN, P. SLOVIC, S. L. DERBY & R. L. KEENEY. 1981. Acceptable Risk. Cambridge University Press. New York.
14. FISCHLER, C. 1986. Attitudes towards sugar and sweetness in historical and social perspective. In Sweetness. J. Dobbing, Ed. Springer-Verlag. London.
15. GARB, J. & A. J. STUNKARD. 1974. Taste aversions in man. Am. J. Psychiatry. **131:** 1204–1207.
16. HOOK, E. B. 1978. Dietary cravings and aversions during pregnancy. Am. J. Clin. Nutr. **31:** 1355–1362.
17. KAHNEMAN, D., P. SLOVIC & A. TVERSKY. Eds. 1982. Judgment under Uncertainty: Heuristics and Biases. Cambridge University Press. New York.
18. KATZ, S. H. 1982. Food, behavior and biocultural evolution. In The Psychobiology of Human Food Selection. L. M. Barker, Ed.: 171–188. AVI. Westport, CT.
19. NEMEROFF, C. & P. ROZIN. 1989. An unacknowledged belief in "you are what you eat" among college students in the United States: An application of the demand-free "impressions" technique. Ethos. J. Psychol. Anthropol. **17(1):** 50–69.
20. NISBETT, R. & L. ROSS. 1980. Human Inference: Strategies and Shortcomings of Social Judgment. Prentice-Hall. Englewood Cliffs, NJ.
21. PELCHAT, M. L. & P. PLINER. 1986. Antecedents and correlates of feeding problems in young children. J. Nutr. Educ. **18:** 23–29.
22. PELCHAT, M. L. & P. ROZIN. 1982. The special role of nausea in the acquisition of food dislikes by humans. Appetite **3:** 341–351.
23. RICHTER, C. P. & K. H. CLISBY. 1941. Phenylthiocarbamide taste thresholds of rats and human beings. Am. J. Physiol. **134:** 157–164.
24. RICHTER, C. P. 1941. Alcohol as food. Q. J. Studies Alcohol **1:** 650–662.
25. ROZIN, P. & A. E. FALLON. 1981. The acquisition of likes and dislikes for foods. In Criteria of Food Acceptance: How Man Chooses What He Eats. J. Solms & R. L. Hall, Eds.: 35–48. Forster. Zurich.

26. ROZIN, P. & A. E. FALLON. 1987. A perspective on disgust. Psychol. Rev. **94:** 23–41.
27. ROZIN, P., L. HAMMER, H. OSTER, T. HOROWITZ & V. MARMARA. 1986. The child's conception of food: Differentiation of categories of rejected substances in the 1.4 to 5 year age range. Appetite **7:** 141–151.
28. ROZIN, P. & M. MARKWITH. 1990. Food cravings. Manuscript in preparation.
29. ROZIN, P. & M. MARKWITH. 1990. The monotonic mind: Dose insensitivity in human judgements of risks. Manuscript in preparation.
30. ROZIN, P. & M. L. PELCHAT. 1988. Memories of mammaries: Adaptations to weaning from milk. *In* Progress in Psychobiology, Volume 13. A. N. Epstein & A. Morrison, Eds.: 1–29. Academic Press. New York.
31. ROZIN, P. 1986. Sweetness, sensuality, sin, safety and socialization: Some speculations. *In* Sweetness. J. Dobbing, Ed.: 99–110. Springer-Verlag. London.
32. ROZIN, P. 1988. Social learning about foods by humans. *In* Social Learning: A Comparative Approach. T. Zentall & B. G. Galef, Jr., Eds.: 165–187. Erlbaum. Hillsdale, NJ.
33. ROZIN, P. 1990. Social and moral aspects of eating. *In* The Legacy of Solomon Asch: Essays in Cognition and Social Psychology. I. Rock, Ed.: In press. Lawrence Erlbaum. Potomac, MD.
34. SIMOONS, F. J. 1982. Geography and genetics as factors in the psychobiology of human food selection. *In* The Psychobiology of Human Food Selection. L. M. Barker, Ed.: 205–224. AVI. Westport, CT.
35. SLOVIC, P. 1987. Perception of risk. Science **236:** 280–285.
36. SLOVIC, P., B. FISCHHOFF & S. LICHTENSTEIN. 1980. Facts vs. fears: Understanding perceived risks. *In* Social Risk Assessment: How Safe Is Safe Enough? R. Schwing & W. A. Albess, Jr., Eds.: 181–216. Plenum. New York.
37. SNYDER, L. H. 1931. Inherited taste deficiency. Science **74:** 151–152.
38. TVERSKY, A. & D. KAHNEMAN. 1981. Judgment under uncertainty: Heuristics and biases. Science **185:** 1124–1131.
39. WILSON, R. 1979. Analyzing the daily risks of life. Technol. Rev. **81:** 40–46.

DISCUSSION

DR. LINDA BARTOSHUK (*Pierce Foundation, New Haven, CT*): I was interested in what you had to say about pica having some possible biological significance, because having developed ice pica myself when I became anemic. I got very interested in whether this could have any biological significance. I knew why I was eating the ice; it was because it felt so good. There's a blood rerouting with anemia to keep oxygen coming to the brain. I think it's Cabanac's alliesthesia, your mouth is hot so the ice feels great. I reviewed a lot of other types of literature, and I'm convinced that the pica phenomenon is immediate sensory gratification. Most cases of pica feel good, and that's what maintains the behavior. My speculation is that sensory gratification is the cause, and it isn't nutritional at all.

DR. PAUL ROZIN (*University of Pennsylvania, Philadelphia, PA*): There is a problem that in some cases the clay pica absorbs nutrients and puts the people in trouble. A clear link exists between nutritional deficiency and pica: The question is which way it goes. There may well be the route that you're thinking.

DR. PAUL ARAVITCH (*VA Medical Center, Hampton, VA*): Would it be fair to say that you take a very strong position against the current trend regarding nutrition and health?

DR. ROZIN: Yes.

DR. ARAVITCH: It seems that someone has to defend the opposite position, and I want to ask you how you might account for some of the clear-cut effects that deviant nutrient selections do have pathologically. We could cite any number of substances; let's go with something current, such as dietary fatty acids and blood pressure regulation. There is no unequivocal evidence that saturated fats, when consumed in high proportions, increase blood pressure in and of themselves and potentiate hypertension in a number of different experimental animals as well as in people. It is also true in both people and animals that polyunsaturated omega-6 fats have the opposite effect. It is also true in people and in rats that omega-3 fatty acids contained in free radicals have even more beneficial effects on blood pressure regulation than do the omega-6's. It would seem to me that data of that type suggests that deviant food selections indeed have pathological impass biologically.

DR. ROZIN: I think you don't mean deviant; you mean particular. Some of those choices are among the most common kinds of food selection and therefore are not deviant, but yes, I agree with you. My claim, remember I used cigarettes as an example, is that people should emphasize those relatively few cases where we know there is a real link between food choice and disease. There is a penumbra over it that is just unfounded. My claim is not that we should ignore risks, but that we should focus on those risks that are well established and would make a big difference. Even with the fatty acids and fats issue, compared to driving without a seatbelt or even driving, these are relatively minor risks, most of them. I am not saying therefore we shouldn't go after them. But think about the problem of getting people to put on seatbelts. The savings of using seatbelts are great. Other problems, such as high saturated fat diets, are much harder to change because people like those things. I think the seatbelt problem is the bigger problem, and it's pretty much intractable at the moment. So I agree with you, but I think the point is it is not in the interest of the public health to get people to worry about very low risks at this point. There are substantial risks, and I think the one you are pointing to is a substantial one. We should focus on these and stop giving attention to other things like the sugar business, which is really not well founded.

DR. JOEL GRINKER (*University of Michigan, Ann Arbor, MI*): We did a study in which we looked at food choices by parents during transition from breast or bottle feeding to weaning foods. We found that obese women offered twice as many different foods to their children when they started weaning. I wondered if you knew of any similar data collection in women who have other kinds of eating disorder problems.

DR. ROZIN: No I don't, but the Pelchat and Pliner final result is that, generally speaking, the more variety a child is offered in food the less likely it is that feeding problems will develop. It's a weak relationship.

DR. GRINKER: But on the other hand they might have increased intake at later stages.

DR. ROZIN: They might indeed, but the finding was that this was not related to their obesity; it was related to their food problems.

Sensory-Specific Satiety in Anorexia and Bulimia Nervosa

MARION HETHERINGTON

National Institute of Mental Health
Section of Biomedical Psychiatry
Bethesda, Maryland 20892

BARBARA J. ROLLS[a]

Department of Psychiatry and Behavioral Sciences
The Johns Hopkins University School of Medicine
Baltimore, Maryland 21205

INTRODUCTION

In the diagnoses of the eating disorders anorexia and bulimia nervosa, the eating- and weight-related features of the syndromes have been emphasized.[1,2] Both disorders share the central characteristic of an intense preoccupation with weight and shape.[3] Weight loss in anorexia nervosa is accomplished through strict food restriction or by restriction combined with periodic eating episodes (binges or normal meals) followed by purging. In bulimia nervosa, recurrent cycles of binging and purging prevent weight gain.

Anorexia and bulimia nervosa are thus typified by disturbed eating practices, either through starvation or binging and purging. Despite the clinical descriptions of these practices, only a few experimental studies have attempted to document and understand the eating behavior of eating-disordered persons.

To determine whether anorexics can recognize peripheral signals associated with hunger, studies have been conducted on the perception of stomach fullness[4,5] and gastric contractions.[6] Although no evidence of abnormal or diminished gastric contractions was found, some anorexics tended to deny hunger in the presence of strong gastric contractions[6] and anorexics tended to judge amounts of food introduced into the stomach less accurately than controls.[4]

Clinical reports suggest that anorexics may feel hungry but may be too afraid to eat.[7] Thus, there may be denial of hunger rather than an impairment of hunger perception. More recent studies of hunger and satiety in anorexics[8,9] and in bulimics[10] have demonstrated significant differences between eating-disordered patients and controls in the self-report of hunger and satiety. Both Garfinkel and Chiodo and Latimer found that reports of hunger before and after a test meal did not differ between eating-disordered subjects and controls, but that satiety was experienced differently by the eating-disordered subjects.[8,10] Owen *et al.* found that anorexics displayed considerable

[a] Address for correspondence: Barbara J. Rolls, Ph.D., Department of Psychiatry and Behavioral Sciences, The Johns Hopkins University School of Medicine, Meyer 207, 600 N. Wolfe Street, Baltimore, MD 21205.

confusion over hunger and fullness, and that these ratings did not relate to the amount of liquid diet consumed in the test meal.[9]

Nutritional analyses of diet records kept by anorexics suggested that these patients tend to eat significantly fewer calories and less of all major macronutrients relative to normals.[11] This would suggest that anorexics would eat less in a controlled situation relative to normals.

Rosen et al. found that bulimic subjects consumed less food than normals if they were requested not to vomit after eating.[12] In contrast, Walsh and his colleagues found that bulimic subjects ate more than controls in both a multicourse and a single-course test meal when asked to eat as much as they could, but with no restriction on vomiting.[13]

It may be that the bulimic subjects in each of these studies responded to the instructions given during the experiment, eating less when instructed not to purge and eating more when allowed to "let go." This observation parallels some of the research conducted in chronic dieters, who tend to restrict food intake most of the time to maintain or lose weight, but who periodically overeat.[14-16] It has been suggested that dieting may cause binge eating by producing eating behavior that is influenced more by cognitive rather than physiological cues. Thus dieting itself may be related to the disturbed eating observed in eating-disordered individuals.

Therefore, these preliminary studies indicate that underlying the disordered eating patterns described clinically is a disturbed perception of hunger, appetite, and satiety.

Another method of assessing interoceptive awareness and eating behavior is to investigate hedonic responses to foods and food intake in the eating-disordered population. The hedonic value or pleasantness of a food or drink declines following consumption,[17-19] and this change in pleasantness influences subsequent intake.[19,20] Satiety can be assessed in terms of how much of a particular food is consumed and how pleasant that food is before and after consumption.

Garfinkel et al. investigated the development of satiety in anorexics following a test meal by instructing subjects to rate the pleasantness of the taste of a sucrose solution before and after lunch.[21] Although the controls reported a decrease in the pleasantness of sucrose after the meal, anorexic subjects reported no change in the pleasantness of the sucrose solution. This experiment demonstrated that anorexic subjects failed to show alliesthesia, that is, the decrease in pleasantness of the taste as the physiological need for the substance declined.[22] This experiment raises a number of questions. Can anorexic or bulimic subjects detect and report satiety to complex, solid foods? Also, is the disturbance in satiety specific to alliesthesia, or are all aspects of satiety disturbed?

We have developed methods of studying the changing hedonic response to foods that show that as a food is eaten, the acceptance of that food declines relative to other foods and subsequently that food is less likely to be consumed.[19,23] Because the changing hedonic response to the food that has been eaten depends at least in part on its sensory characteristics, the changes have been termed "sensory-specific satiety."[24] Because sensory-specific satiety can be important for the termination of eating and can influence food selection, its presence or absence in eating-disordered subjects could provide further understanding of any deficit in satiety that these persons might have and the factors that may underlie aberrant eating behavior.

STUDIES OF FOOD INTAKE AND SENSORY-SPECIFIC SATIETY

The following experiments were designed to investigate several aspects of the eating behavior of eating-disordered and dieting subjects. Three main questions were posed.

First of all, is sensory-specific satiety evident in these subjects following the consumption of a meal? This question is of major interest because the phenomenon of sensory-specific satiety plays an important role in food intake and selection and has been observed in a number of animal species as well as in children, adolescents, and adults.[25] Thus, investigating sensory-specific satiety in eating-disordered persons may provide information on the fundamental features of the disordered eating behavior characteristic of the syndrome.

Secondly, do these subjects respond to challenges such as overnight fasting, foods of differing energy density, and preloads differing in calories in an appropriate manner by adjusting intake accordingly? This question is important because it addresses the issues of whether eating-disordered individuals are capable of any kind of regulation, and whether any disturbances in regulation are manifest only in the eating-disordered population or also in the dieting population.

Thirdly, do eating-disordered subjects demonstrate normal hunger, appetite, and satiety in response to these challenges? Using highly structured experimental paradigms, the assessment of hunger, appetite, and satiety can be compared within subjects and across groups under several different conditions. A number of studies have reported aberrant subjective reports of hunger, appetite, and satiety; however, little is understood about their responses to familiar foods and to deprivation.

To answer these questions, three experiments were conducted. Five groups of subjects were recruited: normal-weight, nondieting controls, normal-weight dieters, overweight dieters, normal-weight bulimics, and low-weight restricting and bulimic anorexics. To establish weight criteria, the Metropolitan Life Statistical Tables were employed.[26] Dieting status was assessed using the Eating Inventory[27] such that a score of 10 or above on the cognitive restraint factor indicated high restraint. Attitudes towards weight and eating were evaluated using the Eating Attitudes Test.[28] Non-eating-disordered subjects scoring above 30 on the EAT were not selected for the study and anyone with a previous history of eating disorders as indicated by the Diagnostic Survey for Eating Disorders[29] was excluded. Anorexic and bulimic subjects met DSM-IIIR[3] criteria for anorexia and bulimia nervosa.

Experiment 1: Food Deprivation

Deprivation caused by restricting food intake, fasting and purging, could be an important factor in the excessive eating by dieters and bulimics. It has been suggested that chronic deprivation may be a trigger for overeating and binging.[30] Therefore, by manipulating the level of deprivation in the experiment, food intake, hunger, appetite, and satiety responses could be compared across the different groups.

Subjects came to the laboratory twice. On one occasion, they were instructed to fast overnight from 10:00 P.M. until the test session at 12:00 noon (deprivation condition). On the other occasion, subjects were instructed to have their usual breakfast (no-deprivation condition). In both tests subjects rated their feelings of hunger, fullness, and other subjective sensations. They then rated the pleasantness of the taste of nine sample foods (bread and margarine, tuna with mayonnaise, cheese on cracker, orange segment, cottage cheese, chocolate pudding, corn chip, tomato segment, and chocolate bar).

After these ratings, subjects were offered a first course of low-fat cottage cheese (250 g) and instructed to eat as much as they wanted. After they had eaten this first course, the subjects were requested to re-rate their feelings of hunger, and so forth, and the pleasantness of the sample foods at 2, 20, 40, and 60 minutes. Subjects were

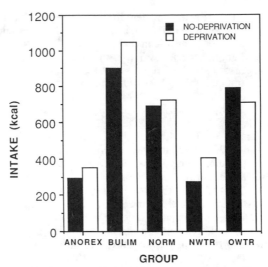

FIGURE 1. Total energy (kcal) consumed in both first and second courses after a standard breakfast (no-deprivation condition) or after overnight fasting (deprivation condition). Intakes for the anorexic (anorex), bulimic (bulim), control (norm), normal-weight restrained (nwtr), and overweight restrained (owtr) subjects are shown.

then offered a variety of foods to choose from following the 60-minute ratings and instructed to eat as much as they wanted. These foods consisted of bread and margarine, tuna with mayonnaise, American cheese, crackers, cottage cheese, chocolate pudding, corn chips, and chocolate confectionery. Thus the cottage cheese was the only low-calorie option.

All subjects except for the overweight dieters consumed slightly, but not significantly, more in the self-selection meal after the overnight fast. Differences in energy intake between groups were significant. Anorexics ($n = 5$) and normal-weight dieters ($n = 5$) ate less than the controls ($n = 5$), the overweight dieters ($n = 5$) and the bulimic subjects ($n = 7$). Post-hoc tests revealed a significant difference in intake only between the anorexics and all other subjects except the normal weight dieters (see FIG. 1).

In general, hunger ratings decreased and fullness ratings increased after the first course in both conditions and for all groups. However, the deprivation condition produced higher initial ratings of hunger relative to the no-deprivation condition, although this had no significant impact on amount consumed. Significant differences between groups indicated that anorexic subjects rated hunger lower and fullness higher than the other subjects. Anorexic subjects tended to rate hunger very low and fullness very high even before the test meals were presented, whereas in the other groups, hunger was high and fullness low before the test meals.

Ratings of the pleasantness of the taste of the cottage cheese tended to decrease relative to the other, uneaten foods overall. However, this pattern of changes in pleasantness, or sensory-specific satiety, was significant only for the anorexic and control subjects. Sensory-specific satiety was not observed in the bulimic and dieting groups (see FIG. 2).

In conclusion, although subjects rated hunger higher as a result of overnight fasting relative to the no-deprivation condition, this did not significantly increase the amount consumed. Anorexic and normal-weight dieters ate less than the other groups. Anorexics also showed the lowest hunger and appetite ratings, yet clearly demonstrated sensory-specific satiety. The only other group to show sensory-specific satiety was the control group.

Experiment 2: **Ad Libitum** *Consumption of High- and Low-Calorie Foods*

The second experiment was designed to investigate the effect of offering free access to foods of different energy density on subsequent food intake, ratings of hunger, appetite, and sensory-specific satiety. This was done to compare responses to foods of different caloric value, because the caloric density of a food or the perception of the food as high or low-calorie may influence eating more in subjects who are overly concerned with calories and their effects on body weight and shape.

The procedure for this experiment was similar to that for Experiment 1 except that both lunch time tests followed a standard breakfast. Subjects were instructed to eat as much as they wanted of a first course of either cottage cheese (250 g) or cheese on crackers (120 g). The self-selection second course followed immediately after a second set of subjective ratings.

Subjects consumed significantly less weight of the first course of cheese on crackers and fewer calories of the first course of cottage cheese. In the self-selection meal, subjects tended to eat less after the cheese on cracker first course, but this effect was only marginally significant (FIG. 3). Following both types of food, hunger ratings decreased in all groups. The magnitude of this decrease was not influenced by the energy density of the foods consumed. However, hunger decreased least of all in the anorexic ($n = 5$) and bulimic subjects ($n = 10$). In addition the anorexic and bulimic subjects rated initial hunger lower than the controls.

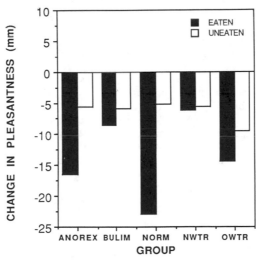

FIGURE 2. Changes (initial − subsequent) in the pleasantness of the taste of the eaten food (cottage cheese) relative to the uneaten foods following the first course of cottage cheese with both deprivation and no-deprivation conditions combined.

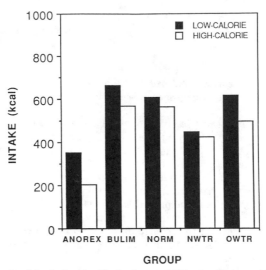

FIGURE 3. Energy (kcal) intake in the self-selection meal following the low-calorie (cottage cheese) and high-calorie (cheese and cracker) conditions.

Following both first courses, controls and anorexics demonstrated sensory-specific satiety. However, the bulimic and dieting subjects failed to show this (see FIG. 4). Although not significant, the overweight dieters tended to report a decrease in the pleasantness of the eaten food relative to the uneaten foods.

Interestingly most of the anorexic subjects chose cottage cheese in the self-selection meal, despite having consumed this food in the first course. This result would not be predicted on the basis of sensory-specific satiety, because the rated pleasantness of the taste of the eaten food decreased after consumption relative to the other foods, and in general, subjects tend to consume less of the food that was previously eaten. All of the bulimic subjects consumed the same food again in the self-selection meal following the cheese on cracker first course, whereas few of the other subjects ($n <$ 2) selected the eaten food again.

These observations indicate a trend for anorexic subjects to select the low-calorie, low-fat food regardless of what was consumed in the first course and in spite of sensory-specific satiety. The bulimic subjects, on the other hand, may have chosen the same food again in the self-selection meal because the eaten food was still rated as pleasant.

This experiment provided further evidence of significant differences between eating-disordered groups and other subjects in terms of eating behavior. As in the first experiment, anorexic subjects rated initial hunger before eating lower than controls, as did the bulimics in the study. Anorexic and normal-weight dieters tended to eat less than the other subjects. Finally, the anorexics clearly demonstrated sensory-specific satiety although this did not influence intake, whereas bulimics failed to show sensory-specific satiety.

Experiment 3: Preloads of High- and Low-Calorie Foods

The third experiment, similar to the previous two, was designed to investigate the responses of eating-disordered subjects to fixed amounts (preloads) of high- and low-calorie foods. The preloading technique was employed for a number of reasons. First of all, giving preloads prevented restriction of intake and ensured that all of the subjects consumed the same amount of food in the first course. This is important because the absence or presence of sensory-specific satiety in some of the subjects may have been due to the amount of the food consumed in the first course. Also, anorexic subjects reported sensory-specific satiety after very small amounts of foods, and so we were interested in their response to a more substantial amount of food.

The preloads consisted of low-calorie cottage cheese (70 g; 50 kcal; preload A), high-calorie cheese on cracker (70 g; 322 kcal; preload B), and low-calorie cheese on cracker (10 g; 50 kcal; preload C). These preloads were chosen to control for weight (preloads A and B), for calories (preloads A and C), and for food type (preloads B and C). In this way, the effects of the same caloric load of different foods, the same weight of different foods, and different portions of the same food could be assessed.

The procedure for this experiment was similar to that described for Experiments 1 and 2. Subjects were tested at lunch time following a standard breakfast, and the self-selection meal was offered one hour after the preload.

Hunger ratings varied according to the preload offered for all groups. Thus following the low-calorie cheese on cracker preload (condition C) hunger changed least, and after the high-calorie cheese on cracker preload (condition B), hunger ratings changed to the greatest extent. Absolute ratings of hunger indicated that the anorexic subjects rated feelings of hunger lower than all other groups before all of the preloads. Similarly, fullness was rated higher by the anorexics relative to the other subjects. Changes in fullness ratings differed according to the preload given, and indicated that the high-calorie cheese on cracker preload (condition B) produced the highest ratings of fullness overall. However, anorexics and bulimics reported only small changes in fullness after the different preloads. The anorexics demonstrated the same magnitude of change in fullness, regardless of condition. This observation may have been due to a ceiling effect, because fullness ratings were already very high before consumption.

The pleasantness of the taste of the food given as the preload declined relative to

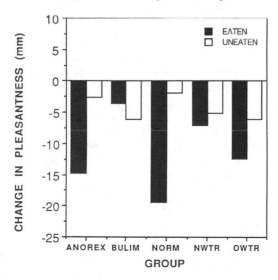

FIGURE 4. Changes in the pleasantness of the taste of the eaten food (cheese on cracker or cottage cheese) relative to the uneaten foods after the first course, with both conditions combined.

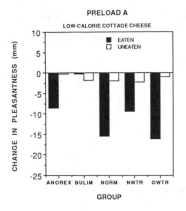

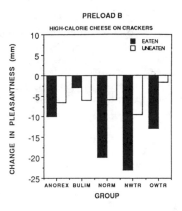

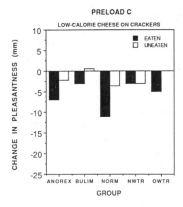

FIGURE 5. Changes in the pleasantness of the taste of the eaten foods relative to the uneaten foods following preload A (low-calorie cottage cheese), preload B (high-calorie cheese on crackers), and preload C (low-calorie cheese on crackers).

the uneaten foods in all groups except the bulimic subjects in both conditions A and B. Thus, sensory-specific satiety was not observed in the bulimic subjects for any of the preloads. In condition C, the only subjects demonstrating sensory-specific satiety were the anorexic and control subjects. The anorexic subjects reported a decrease in the pleasantness of both eaten and uneaten foods following the high-calorie preload (Condition B) and therefore satiety was not sensory-specific in this condition. (FIG. 5).

Food intake in the self-selection meal also provided support for differences between the groups found in Experiments 1 and 2. Anorexic subjects consumed significantly less, in terms of weight and calories, than all other subjects except the normal-weight dieters. Normal-weight dieters consumed significantly less than the bulimic subjects overall. No significant differences were observed in intake related to the preload type. Although subjects received preloads of varying weight, calories, and food type, no significant differences within groups were noted for condition. It is interesting to note, however, that all subjects except the bulimics adjusted their food intake for the high-calorie cheese on cracker preload in the appropriate direction, by consuming less after this preload than after the other preloads. In contrast, the bulimic subjects consumed more following this preload relative to the other preloads (FIG. 6). This finding may reflect counter-regulation[14,15] because subjects ate more in the self-selection meal when the largest caloric preload was given. A de-briefing questionnaire used at the end of the experiment asked subjects to identify any occasion in which their eating had been considered "excessive" or "like a binge." It was found that almost half of the bulimics had binged following the high-calorie preload. Although not a significant trend, this observation may be related to the proposal[31] that counter-regulation is the laboratory equivalent of binging. It is of some interest to note that the pattern of food choice varied markedly among the different groups, such that the anorexics never selected chocolate confectionery or chocolate pudding and were much more likely than the other subjects to choose low-fat cottage cheese in the meal, regardless of having had this food in the preload.

In conclusion, this experiment provided further support for significant differences between the eating-disordered population and both the dieters and controls. In response to three different preloads, anorexics consistently reported lower levels of hunger, desire to eat, and the amount they wanted to eat before and after preloads compared to the other subjects. They rated fullness higher before and after the preloads relative to the other subjects. Sensory-specific satiety was observed in the controls and anorexics across all preload conditions, while it was inconsistently demonstrated in the dieters, and the bulimics failed to report sensory-specific satiety. The anorexics rated both the eaten and uneaten foods as less pleasant after the high-calorie preload. Anorexics also consumed the least amount of food in the self-selection meal relative to the other subjects, and bulimics tended to counter-regulate following the high-calorie preload.

CONCLUSIONS FROM THE EXPERIMENTS

These three experiments have lead to interesting conclusions concerning the eating behavior of eating-disordered subjects. First of all, anorexics clearly demonstrated

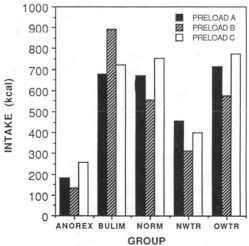

FIGURE 6. Energy (kcal) intake in the self-selection meal following each of the three preloads shown in FIGURE 5.

sensory-specific satiety despite consuming significantly less food than the controls. This suggests that it takes less for these subjects to become satiated on a specific food relative to normals. Such a response may limit food intake in anorexics. Despite sensory-specific satiety, the anorexics selected the eaten food again in the self-selection meal, when that food was low-calorie cottage cheese. These subjects reported normal sensory-specific changes in the pleasantness of this food, but nevertheless choose this as the "safest" option among other, considerably higher calorie foods. Thus, in anorexics sensory-specific satiety may be overridden by beliefs about foods.

In contrast, the bulimics did not show sensory-specific satiety, although in general their food intake did not differ from that of the controls. This result implies that bulimics fail to show sensory-specific satiety to normal amounts of food whether eaten *ad libitum* or as a fixed load. Thus, the failure to report a decrease in the pleasantness of a specific food may enable the bulimics to eat beyond the normal limits of satiety during binge episodes. Because these are preliminary findings, they must be interpreted with caution; nevertheless, it is interesting to note the contrast in the report of sensory-specific satiety in anorexics relative to bulimics.

In terms of the ability of eating-disordered subjects to adjust food intake according to the three different challenges posed, it was clear that although anorexics and normal-weight dieters consistently consumed the least amount of food, they did alter intake in the same direction as the controls. Bulimic subjects, however, overate when given the high-calorie preload, suggesting a similar phenomenon to the counter-regulation observed by Herman and his colleagues.[32] Counter-regulation has been compared to binge eating insofar as eating a "forbidden" or high-calorie avoided food may trigger overeating. This result provides some support for this comparison, since of the ten bulimics, four reported that they considered their intake to have been a binge and had subsequently vomited.

Therefore, although food intakes differed according to group, only the bulimics showed inappropriate adjustment to the preloads, and the anorexics, controls, and dieters tended to show adjustments in the predicted direction.

Finally, in agreement with previous reports,[9,33] anorexics consistently rated variables related to hunger and appetite as low and fullness as high before a meal, relative to the other subjects. It is not yet known if this represents a deficit in subjective assessments of appetite or if this indicates a denial of such feelings.[7]

The results of these experiments illustrate some of the parameters that are aberrant in the eating behavior of eating-disordered persons. Further studies need to be conducted to understand the mechanisms underlying such disordered eating behavior. These studies will not only provide insights into normal processes of hunger, appetite, satiety, and food intake, which are generally under homeostatic control, but will also clarify how such basic processes can become destabilized by disordered eating practices and psychopathological fears about fatness and body shape.

REFERENCES

1. HALMI, K. A. 1985. Classification of the eating disorders. J. Psychiat. Res. **19:** 113–119.
2. RUSSELL, G. F. M. 1979. Bulimia nervosa: An ominous variant of anorexia nervosa. Psych. Med. **9:** 429–448.
3. AMERICAN PSYCHIATRIC ASSOCIATION. 1987. DSM-IIIR: Diagnostic and Statistical Manual of Mental Disorders. 3rd edit. (Revised). American Psychiatric Association. Washington, D.C.
4. CODDINGTON, R. D. & H. BRUCH. 1970. Gastric perceptivity in normal, obese and schizophrenic subjects. Psychosomatics **11:** 571–579.
5. ROBINSON, P. H., G. F. M. RUSSELL, T. H. MORAN, J. D. STEVENSON & P. R. McHUGH.

1989. Gastrointestinal response to food in anorexia nervosa and bulimia nervosa. N.Y. Acad. Sci. New York.

6. SILVERSTONE, J. T. & G. F. M. RUSSELL. 1967. Gastric hunger contractions in anorexia nervosa. Br. J. Psychiatry 113: 257-263.

7. KAY, D. W. K. & D. LEIGH. 1954. The natural history, treatment and prognosis of anorexia nervosa based on a study of 38 patients. J. Mental Sci. 100: 411-431.

8. GARFINKEL, P. E. 1974. Perception of hunger and satiety in anorexia nervosa. Psych. Med. 4: 309-315.

9. OWEN, W. P., K. A. HALMI, J. GIBBS & G. P. SMITH. 1985. Satiety responses in eating disorders. J. Psychiatr Res. 19: 279-284.

10. CHIODO, J. & P. R. LATIMER. 1986. Hunger perceptions and satiety responses among normal-weight bulimics and normals to a high calorie carbohydrate-rich food. Psych. Med. 16: 343-349.

11. BEUMONT, P. J. V., T. L. CHAMBERS, L. ROUSE & S. F. ABRAHAM. 1981. The diet composition and nutritional knowledge of patients with anorexia nervosa. J. Hum. Nutr. 35: 265-273.

12. ROSEN, J. C., H. LEITENBERG, K. M. FONDACARO, J. GROSS & M. WILLMUTH. 1985. Standardized test meals in assessment of eating behavior in bulimia nervosa: Consumption of feared foods when vomiting is prevented. Int. J. Eat. Dis. 4: 59-70.

13. WALSH, B. T., H. R. KISSILEFF, S. M. CASSIDY & S. DANTZIC. 1989. Eating behavior of women with bulimia. Arch. Gen. Psychiatry 46: 54-58.

14. POLIVY, J. & C. P. HERMAN. 1985. Dieting as a problem in behavioral Medicine. In Advances in Behavioral medicine. E. Katkin & S. Manuk, Eds.: 1-37. AIS. New York.

15. POLIVY, J. & C. P. HERMAN. 1985. Dieting and binging — a casual analysis. Am. Psychol. February edition: 193-201.

16. WARDLE, J. 1980. Dietary restraint and binge eating. Behav. Anal. Modification. 4: 201-209.

17. CABANAC, M. 1979. Sensory pleasure. Q. Rev. Biol. 54: 1-29.

18. LEMAGNEN, J. 1967. Habits and food intake. In Handbook of Physiology. C. F. Code, Ed.: 11-13. American Physiology Society. Washington, D.C..

19. ROLLS, B. J., E. T. ROLLS, E. A. ROWE & K. SWEENEY. 1981. Sensory specific satiety in man. Physiol. Behav. 27: 137-142.

20. ROLLS, B. J., P. M. VAN DUIJVENVOORDE & E. T. ROLLS. 1984. Pleasantness changes and food intake in a varied four-course meal. Appetite 5: 337-348.

21. GARFINKEL, P. E., H. MOLDOFSKY, D. M. GARNER, H. C. STANCER & D. V. COSCINA. 1978. Body awareness in anorexia nervosa: Disturbances in "body image" and "satiety." Psychosom. Med. 40: 487-498.

22. CABANAC, M. 1971. Physiological role of pleasure. Science 173: 1103-1107.

23. ROLLS, B. J., M. HETHERINGTON, V. J. BURLEY & P. M. VAN DUIJVENVOORDE. 1986. Changing hedonic responses to foods during and after a meal. In Interaction of the Chemical Senses with Nutrition. M. R. Kare & J. G. Brand, Eds.: 247-268. Academic Press. New York.

24. LEMAGNEN, J. 1971. Advances in studies in the physiological control and regulation of food intake. In Progress in Physiological Psychology. E. Stellar & J. M. Sprague, Eds.: 204-261. Academic Press. New York.

25. ROLLS, B. J. 1986. Sensory-specific satiety. Nutri. Rev. 44: 93-101.

26. METROPOLITAN LIFE INSURANCE COMPANY. 1959. New weight standards for men and women. Stat. Bull. 40: 1-4.

27. STUNKARD, A. J. & S. MESSICK. 1985. The three-factor eating questionnaire to measure dietary restraint, disinhibition and hunger. J. Psychosom. Res. 29: 71-83.

28. GARNER, D. M. & P. E. GARFINKEL. 1979. The Eating Attitudes Test: An index of the symptoms of anorexia nervosa. Psych. Med. 9: 273-280.

29. JOHNSON, C. 1985. Initial consultation for patients with bulimia and anorexia nervosa. In Handbook of Psychotherapy for Anorexia Nervosa and Bulimia. D. M. Garner & P. E. Garfinkel, Eds.: 19-51. The Guilford Press. New York.

30. GARNER, D. M. & P. E. GARFINKEL. 1981. Body image in anorexia nervosa: Measurement theory and clinical implications. Int. J. Psychiat. Med. 11: 263-284.

31. POLIVY, J., C. P. HERMAN, M. P. OLMSTED & C. JAZWINSKI. 1984. Restraint and binge eating. In The Binge-Purge Syndrome. W. J. Fremouw & R. C. Hawkins II, et al. Eds.: 104-123. Springer Publishing Co. New York.

32. HERMAN, C. P. & J. POLIVY. 1984. A boundary model for the regulation of eating. *In* Eating and Its Disorders. A. J. Stunkard & E. Stellar, Eds.: 141–156. Raven Press. New York.
33. ROBINSON, P. H., M. TORTOSA, J. SULLIVAN, E. BUCHANAN, A. E. ANDERSEN & M. F. FOLSTEIN. 1983. Quantitative assessment of psychologic state of patients with anorexia nervosa or bulimia: Response to caloric stimulus. Psychosom. Med. **45**: 283–292.

DISCUSSION

DR. MICHEL CABANAC (*Université Laval, Quebec, Canada*): Off the record, I have nothing against sensory-specific satiety, I just avoided this term in my talk in order not to enter this part of the discussion, but I am aware that it's different from general negative allesthesia. Now your beautiful experiments show how powerful these psychophysical methods are to explore the motivation and the behavior of humans, perhaps more powerful than any experiments on animals. Would you agree that your sorting of low-weight patients between anorectic and bulimic could be described as the anorectic having a lower set point in body weight and the bulimic having a normal set point for body weight? At least that is suggested by the sensory-specific satiety displayed by the anorectic, even after a low internal load, and not by the bulimic. The bulimics would explain how they cannot resist food because they are so far below their body weight set-point that they eat, and then they have to find other ways to get rid of this extra energy ingested.

DR. BARBARA ROLLS (*Johns Hopkins University School of Medicine, Baltimore, MD*): First of all, I'd just like to comment on alliesthesia versus sensory-specific satiety because I suspect some people think that Dr. Cabanac and I disagree, and I don't think we really do. There are two different phenomena. Alliesthesia, by definition, is a change in hedonic response due to the internal state, it takes a long time to come into play. Sensory-specific satiety, by definition, is a very rapid phenomenon. It's due to the sensory properties of food; you can get it with foods with virtually no calories. So the terms are different.

In terms of the set-point, we really haven't thought about it so much in that way. One thing that we want to do in our experiments to try to get at this issue more clearly is to look at individuals at the start of treatment and after their weight is normalized because that, I think, will tell us more about that issue.

DR. EMILY FOX KALES (*Tufts University, Medford, MA*): I do appreciate the complexity of your study because you looked at so many different groups. One question I had was if you want to continue to challenge whether the restraint theories were correct, and, looking at the continuum of pathological eating, would you say that your data suggests that indeed the restrained eater and the bulimic are along that continuum given the fact that they were the two groups that seemed to most counter-regulate?

DR. MARION HETHERINGTON (*National Institute of Mental Health, Bethesda, MD*): Actually, the dieters failed to counter-regulate in our experiment. We've never been able to see counter-regulation as such in the dieting population, although I would say that the normal-weight dieters were somewhat similar to the anorexic. I wouldn't agree that they were similar to the bulimics, although maybe the overweight dieters were more similar. We just don't have the evidence for that at the moment, although I think it's an interesting proposition. I think it is something that is very testable, but that is not what we have been finding.

Taste Responsiveness in Eating Disorders

ADAM DREWNOWSKI[a]

Program in Human Nutrition
School of Public Health
and
Department of Psychiatry
Medical School
University of Michigan
Ann Arbor, MI 48109-2029

Patients with anorexia or bulimia nervosa suffer from disturbances in body weight and nutritional status. Anorexia nervosa is characterized by extreme caloric restriction, avoidance of starches and fats, and a variety of metabolic and neuroendocrine dysfunctions associated with a severe loss of body weight.[1,2] Bulimia nervosa is characterized by uncontrollable eating binges that may be countered by fasting, purging, vomiting, or excessive physical exercise.[3,4] Patients with a combined diagnosis of anorexia nervosa with bulimia alternate periods of near starvation with recurrent eating binges that are followed by purging or self-induced vomiting to lose weight.[5-7]

Both anorexia and bulimia nervosa represent nutritional as well as psychiatric disorders.[8-10] Characteristic patterns of food aversion and uncontrollable food cravings have been linked to the patients' nutritional or metabolic status.[11-13] Evidence is growing that uncontrollable binges are triggered by physiological events, and that food aversions may also have a psychobiological basis. Both physiological abnormalities and psychopathology can be reversed following weight regain and the resumption of normal eating habits.[14]

Taste responsiveness may have a role in mediating food preferences and diet choices of eating disorder patients.[15,16] Some studies suggest that taste functioning of eating disorder patients is characterized by dysgeusia or hypogeusia.[17,18] Prolonged calorie malnutrition and endocrine abnormalities in anorexia nervosa may lead to dysfunctions in taste and smell that depress appetite and contribute to food aversions. Chronic vomiting in bulimia nervosa reduces salivary flow, lowers oral pH, and may lead to a loss of taste sensitivity or sensory functioning.[19,20]

Hedonic aspects of taste responsiveness may also underlie food cravings or food aversions. Anorectic patients profess to dislike sugars and starches and show a calculated avoidance of sweets and desserts.[8,21] However, this phenomenon, sometimes known as "carbohydrate phobia,"[22] is by no means a stable trait of eating disorders. The same patients may consume vast quantities of sweets and desserts in the course of an eating binge. Recent clinical studies have further shown that both anorectic and bulimic women like the taste of intensely sweet solutions presented in the form of not-to-be-ingested taste stimuli.[16] More recent reports based on analysis of cognitive structure[23] indicate

[a] Address for correspondence: Dr. Adam Drewnowski, School of Public Health M-5170, University of Michigan, Ann Arbor, MI 48109-2029.

that anorectic women tend to avoid foods they view as high in calories, that is, foods rich in fat. Consequently, there is some question whether the pattern of food choice in anorexia nervosa is better described in terms of fat avoidance or carbohydrate phobia. This review examines food selection patterns in patients with eating disorders, focusing on the nature of sensory preferences for sugar and fat.

FOOD CHOICES IN EATING DISORDERS

It is commonly believed that anorectic women reject starchy, fattening foods and avoid all carbohydrates, particularly sugar. In reality, dietary intakes in anorexia nervosa can be highly variable. Anorectic patients show many idiosyncratic food choices that may include vegetarianism, avoidance of red meat dishes, and abstinence from some dairy products, sweets and desserts.[3,8,10,24] According to some reports, anorectics are willing to eat vegetables, lettuce, fresh fruit, cheese, and sometimes eggs, but avoid carbohydrates and are disgusted by milk and meat.[3,8]

While some anorectic patients eat diets lacking in basic nutrients, others consume a balanced diet, choosing to restrict calories by eating irregularly, or by severely restricting intake at each meal.[25] Although many anorectics seem to consume mostly vegetables and fruit, the macronutrient content of the typical anorectic diet is open to question. Early studies of hospitalized patients[8] revealed a mean intake of 1,031 kcal/day, with carbohydrates providing only 33% of total daily calories, fat providing 49%, and protein 18%. However, another study[10] based on 24-hour food recalls reported that anorectic patients ate a normal amount of carbohydrate but ate significantly less fat than normal-weight controls.

Anorectic patients often allow themselves to eat only healthy or nutritious foods, and avoid foods perceived as high in calories or rich in fat.[23,24] However, such calorie-dense foods are often the mainstay of eating binges, often defined as the ingestion of large amounts of easily digestible, high-calorie foods consumed in a short space of time.[26] Some investigators have argued that all binges consist of carbohydrate-rich foods, consumed by bulimic women in an attempt to rectify underlying abnormalities in serotonin metabolism.[27] However, as dietary assessment studies show, the macronutrient content of eating binges can again be highly variable.

According to some clinical reports, typical binge foods were bread, cakes, chocolate, yogurt, or cottage cheese.[3] The patients were reported to eat up to 7 lb of food and the magnitude of an eating binge was estimated at 15–20,000 kcal. More recent studies have estimated an average binge at 3,415 kcal (range 1,200–11,500 cal) consumed within 1.2 hours.[28] Observations of hospitalized bulimic women[29] placed the average amount eaten per binge at 4,394 kcal (range 1,436–8,585 kcal), and mean binge duration at just under one hour.

The chief binge foods seem to include ice cream, bread, candy, doughnuts, soft drinks, salads and sandwiches, cookies, popcorn, milk, cheese, and cereal.[28] Bulimic patients monitored in a hospital setting mostly consumed doughnuts, pies, sandwiches, chocolate candy, and carbonated beverages.[29] In contrast, eating bouts not classified as binges included salads, vegetables and fruit, and diet soft drinks. According to some reports, eating binges typically included high fat, moderate carbohydrate, and low-protein foods.[28,29] Other studies estimated binge composition at approximately 50% carbohydrate, 40% fat, and 10% protein.[30] However, none of the studies distinguished between complex carbohydrates and simple sugars: It is likely that some binges are high in sweet, sugar-rich foods.

Although many binges do include dessert-type foods, the notion of what constitutes a binge may be highly subjective. Eating episodes that include snacks or desserts are often described as binges: The consumption of forbidden sweet foods is typically associated with guilt, anxiety, and a desire to vomit.[31] In contrast, meals consisting of vegetables and fruit may not be seen as binges. Self-reports of binge-eating may therefore be subject to attitudinal bias: reported binge frequency may be influenced by what was eaten rather than how much.

Furthermore, bulimic women are not the only group binging on carbohydrate-type snacks. College students who binged made comparable food choices, snacking on pastries, breads, and cookies, as well as other "junk food" items, including salted snacks, pretzels, or potato chips.[32] Quite simply, many commercially available, prepackaged snacks tend to be high-carbohydrate foods that are also high in fat content. Snacking on protein–fat combinations was mentioned less often: Some college men but no women reported binging on hamburgers.[32]

It should also be noted that many snack-type foods tend to be mixtures of only two ingredients: sugar and fat. Although chocolate, cookies, or ice cream are generally regarded as high-sugar and therefore carbohydrate-rich foods, most of their calories are derived from fat rather than carbohydrate.[33] Moreover, the chief carbohydrate present is simple sugar. The nutritional content of selected "carbohydrate-rich" snacks is summarized in TABLE 1. It can be seen that fat and sugar are the principal ingredients, accounting in some cases for up to 98% of snack calories.

PHYSIOLOGICAL ASPECTS OF EATING BINGES

Several investigators believe that eating binges are triggered by physiological events. According to some clinical studies, patients seemed to know that a binge was imminent, and there are reports of buying, hoarding, and preparing foods.[34] Binges typically occurred during the early afternoon or evening, and reported precipitating events included tension, being alone, craving specific foods, thinking of food, or actually eating something.[34]

The taste of food may play a central role in binge-eating behavior. Bulimic patients report that they eat too quickly during a binge to taste anything.[34] However, all patients feel that the taste and texture of food is important, at least at the beginning of the binge. Often the foods of choice are soft, milky, fluid foods that have connota-

TABLE 1. Composition of Selected Snack Foods

Snack Food	Kilocalories			$(S+F)/T^a$ (%)
	Total	Sugar	Fat	
M&M/Mars chocolate candies (package)	237	109	123	98
Hershey dark chocolate (bar)	222	80	108	85
Nestle Crunch bar (bar)	156	60	72	85
Hostess chocolate cupcake (1 cake)	160	60	52	70
Pepperidge Farm Geneva (1 cookie)	63	16	36	82
RJR Nabisco Oreo (1 cookie)	52	16	18	66
Ice cream (16% fat) (1 scoop)	122	39	80	98

[a] Kilocalories from sugar and fat as a percentage of total kilocalories.

tions of high caloric density, satisfaction, and satiety.[29] The drinking of noncaloric soft drinks and eating softer foods (e.g., ice cream) toward the end of a binge may also facilitate vomiting, which is usually planned ahead of time.

TASTE-RESPONSIVENESS STUDIES

Clinical studies on eating disorders have only recently begun to focus on the interaction between nutritional status, taste responsiveness, food preference, and diet selection.[14,15] Among clinical features of anorexia nervosa, some of which are secondary to malnutrition, are endocrine abnormalities, reduced basal metabolic rate, hypokalemia, and impaired regulation of water balance.[1,2,35] Protein and carbohydrate metabolism is said to be relatively preserved, and fasting blood glucose and insulin levels are low-normal or low. Abnormalities in lipid metabolism include hypercholesterolemia, and elevated β-hydroxybutyrate and plasma free fatty acid levels.[35] Because anorectic patients often take vitamin and mineral supplements, zinc, copper, iron, and folic acid have been reported as normal in some studies but not in others.[16,36]

The number of studies on taste psychophysics in anorexia nervosa has been very limited. One study systematically examined the role of trace metals, vitamins, and other biochemical parameters in relation to taste function.[36] The majority of anorectic patients had subnormal taste acuity for sour and bitter substances; taste acuity for salt and sweet was less disturbed. However, taste recognition scores failed to correlate with plasma zinc levels.[36] In a more recent study examining responses to the four basic tastes, a majority of women with anorexia or bulimia nervosa showed evidence of hypogeusia or dysgeusia.[16] Taste functioning improved substantially following weight regain to more than 85% of normal body weight. Although serum zinc and iron of eating disorder patients were depressed, they again failed to correlate with taste recognition and dysgeusia scores.[16]

Normal-weight bulimic patients show little evidence of nutritional trauma, and carbohydrate metabolism is largely intact.[9] However, potential medical complications of binging and vomiting include electrolyte imbalance, erosion on the lingual surfaces of maxillary anterior teeth, pulp exposure, and swollen salivary glands. The consumption of sweet snacks, reduced buffering capacity of saliva, and low oral pH may lead to increased incidence of dental caries.[19] Recent studies of anorectic and bulimic women[18] showed lower magnitude estimate scores for the four basic tastes. The effect was most pronounced for hydrochloric acid, suggesting an impaired gustatory sensitivity for sour. Studies with normal-weight bulimics show a definite loss of sensation in sour receptors on the soft palate: Reflux of vomit damages taste receptors in this area. Taste distortions may be the consequence of chronic vomiting in bulimia nervosa.

TASTE HEDONICS: SUGAR AND FAT

Studies on hedonic aspects of taste responsiveness in anorexia and bulimia nervosa have focused on sensory perception and preferences for sugar and fat.[15,37] The subjects were young women with a diagnosis of anorexia nervosa (restrictor), anorexia with bulimia, and bulimia nervosa, as well as a volunteer group of normal-weight controls. As summarized in TABLE 2, all clinic patients were tested twice, before and after dietary treatment and a substantial gain in body weight. The stimuli were 20 different mixtures of milk, cream and sugar, containing a range of sugar (0–20% sucrose) and fat levels (0–52% fat).

TABLE 2. Subject Weights Pre- and Post-Treatment[a]

Group	Age (yr)	Pretreatment Weight (kg)	Pretreatment BMI (kg/m²)	Post-Treatment Weight (kg)	Post-Treatment BMI (kg/m²)
Anorectic	17	40.5	15.5	49.7	19.0
Bulimic	19	56.8	21.3	57.4	21.6
Normal weight	19	57.8	21.1	–	–

[a] From Drewnowski et al.[16] Reprinted by permission.

The subjects followed the standard sip-and spit technique and were asked to rate the perceived intensity of sweetness, fatness, and creaminess of the stimuli. They also assigned an overall hedonic preference rating to each sample.[38–40] No deficiencies in taste perception for these suprathreshold stimuli were observed between anorectic and bulimic women and normal-weight volunteer controls. Intensity estimates of sweetness and fat content increased as logarithmic functions of sucrose or fat concentration, and no differences in sensory evaluation were observed between patients with eating disorders and the comparison group. These data complement previous studies on taste perception in human obesity, where no differences in sweetness perception were observed between normal-weight, obese, or dieting individuals.[41] It should be noted that this study involved the perception of recognizable sweet stimuli, and combined sweet taste perception with oral sensory evaluation of stimulus texture.

Significant differences between subject groups were observed in hedonic preference scores for mixtures of sugar and fat. Anorectic restrictor and anorectic bulimic patients showed elevated preferences for sweet taste and sharply reduced preferences for the oral sensation of fat relative to the comparison group. Stimulus optimization procedures involving the response surface method (RSM) determined that eating disorder patients optimally liked stimuli containing 16.5% fat and 12.7% sugar. In contrast, control subjects preferred stimuli that were richer in fat (28.7%) but were somewhat less sweet (9.1% sucrose). Three-dimensional projections of the hedonic response surface, and the corresponding isohedonic contours are shown in FIGURE 1.

Hedonic responsiveness as measured by the optimally preferred sugar/fat ratio was negatively correlated with the subjects' body fatness — as measured by the body mass index (wt/ht²). The most underweight subjects showed the highest sensory responsiveness to sweet taste. However, body weight is not the only factor influencing taste responsiveness. A recent study has shown that normal-weight bulimic women presented with samples of sweetened soft, dessert-type white cheese preferred stimuli that were sweeter but lower in fat content than those selected by normal-weight female controls.[38]

TASTE HEDONICS AND BODY WEIGHT

The hedonic response to sweet taste has long been regarded as a useful index of metabolic status or physiological "set-point."[41] Calorie-deprived subjects maintaining body weight below set-point by virtue of constant dieting are expected to find sweet solutions extremely pleasant, a finding reported in some studies, though not in others.[42,43]

The present finding that underweight subjects show elevated preferences for sweet taste seems consistent with the set-point hypothesis. However, as seen in FIGURE 2, this pattern of response remained stable even following six to eight weeks of dietary therapy and weight regain to target levels.[16] Optimally preferred levels of sugar and

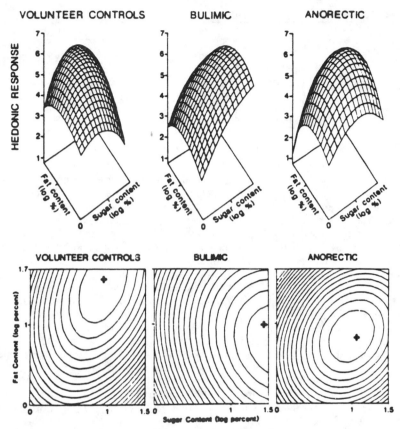

FIGURE 1. Hedonic response surfaces for the average subject expressed in terms of three-dimensional projections (top) and isohedonic contours (bottom). The axes represent sucrose (x-axis) and lipid content (y-axis) of the stimuli, expressed as log percent wt/wt. Regions of optimal preference as predicted by the Response Surface Model are denoted by + signs (From Drewnowski et al.[16] Reprinted by permission.)

fat were approximately the same both before and after weight regain, as summarized in TABLE 3.

One potential explanation for this stability of taste response is incomplete clinical recovery. Physiological or neuroendocrine impairments often persist following the recovery of body weight and the taste response may be equally slow to adjust.[16] Other investigators have also observed that affective responses are surprisingly resistant to changes over time.[44] Neither weight gain[16,44] nor moderate caloric restriction and weight loss[45] have been linked with significant changes in preference for sweet taste.

Measures of hedonic response to sweetness following the consumption of an intensely sweet preload have also failed to reveal significant changes in sweet preference following gains or losses in body weight. In one early study,[46] anorectic women showed slightly elevated preferences for sweet taste relative to controls following the consumption of a 400-kcal meal. However, elevated preferences for sweet taste were also ob-

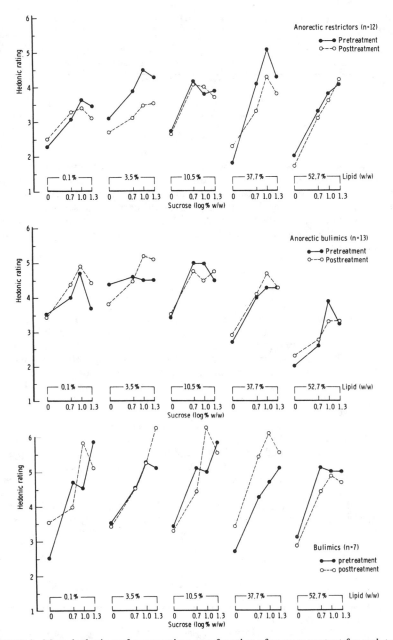

FIGURE 2. Mean hedonic preference ratings as a function of sucrose content for each type of dairy product. Sucrose levels are plotted as log percent wt/wt. The data are for anorectic restrictor patients (top panel), anorectics with bulimia (middle panel), and bulimic patients (bottom panel) tested before and after treatment.

TABLE 3. Optimal Stimulus Composition Pre- and Post-Treatment[a]

Group	n	Pretreatment		Post-Treatment	
		Sugar %	Fat %	Sugar %	Fat %
Anorectic	25	12.7	16.5	10.6	17.8
Bulimic	7	15.3	27.9	13.3	19.3
Normal weight	16	9.1	28.7	–	–

[a] From Drewnowski et al.[16] Reprinted by permission.

served in a follow-up study conducted with the same patients one year following the regain of target body weight.[44] Similarly, studies on obese persons failed to show differences in satiety aversion to sucrose between underweight, normal-weight, and overweight persons.[42,43] It may be that the pleasure response to sweet taste is not a reliable measure of distance from set-point as indexed by fluctuations in body weight. Individual profiles of taste responsiveness appear to be a stable trait that is resistant to short-term shifts in body weight.

CENTRAL MECHANISMS

Taste responsiveness may be linked to indices of metabolic status other than body weight. The relationship between serotonin metabolism, affective disorders, and carbohydrate craving in bulimia has been proposed by a number of previous studies.[12,27] It should also be noted that neuroendocrine dysfunctions and deficits of hypothalamic–pituitary regulation of the adrenal axis may persist for months following weight regain.[47] Both have been linked with altered food preferences and diet choices. Elevated endogenous opioid levels in anorexia nervosa and bulimia[2,48] have in some cases been reported to decline following weight regain.

The relationship between opioid peptides, the pleasure response to sweet taste and uncontrollable binges on sweet foods offers a new and promising avenue of research. Studies on laboratory animals have linked endogenous opioids with nutrient selection, eating behavior, and obesity in both rats and mice.[8,36] Opioid peptides are known to mediate the biological response to stress and are thought to modulate the pleasure response to sweetness.[51] Dieting anorectic and bulimic patients have been reported to show elevated levels of β-endorphin[48] and elevated preferences for the taste of sweet solutions.[16,38] It remains to be seen whether taste responsiveness mediates the presumed link between physiological factors, bulimic episodes, and the selection of sweet foods during a binge.

REFERENCES

1. HALMI, K. A. & J. R. FALK. 1981. Common physiological changes in anorexia nervosa. Int. J. Eating Disord. **1:** 16–27.
2. WEINER, H. 1985. The physiology of eating disorders. Int. J. Eating Disord. **4:** 347–388.
3. RUSSELL, G. F. M. 1979. Bulimia nervosa: An ominous variant of anorexia nervosa. Psychol. Med. **9:** 429–448.
4. JOHNSON, C., C. LEWIS & J. HAGMANN. 1984. The syndrome of bulimia: Review and synthesis. Psychiatr. Clin. N. Am. **7:** 247–272.
5. CASPER, R. C., E. D. ECKERT, K. A. HALMI, et al. 1980. Bulimia: Its incidence and clinical importance in patients with anorexia nervosa. Arch. Gen. Psychiatry **37:** 1030–1035.

6. GARFINKEL, P. E., H. MOLDOFSKY & D. M. GARNER. 1980. The heterogeneity of anorexia nervosa: Bulimia as a distinct subgroup. Arch. Gen. Psychiatry 37: 1036-1040.

7. JOHNSON, C. L., M. K. STUCKEY, L. D. LEWIS & D. M. SCHWARTZ. 1982. Bulimia: A descriptive survey of 316 cases. Int. J. Eating Disord. 2: 3-16.

8. RUSSELL, G. F. M. 1967. The nutritional disorder in anorexia nervosa. J. Psychosom. Res. 11: 141-149.

9. TAYLOR, M. E., R. W. LAWRENCE & K. G. D. ALLEN. 1986. Nutritional assessment of college age women with bulimia. Int. J. Eating Disord. 5: 59-74.

10. BEUMONT, P. J. V., T. L. CHAMBERS, L. ROUSE & S. F. ABRAHAM. 1981. The diet composition and nutritional knowledge of patients with anorexia nervosa. J. Hum. Nutr. 35: 265-273.

11. KAYE, W. E., M. H. EBERT, H. E. GWIRTSMAN & S. WEISS. 1984. Differences in brain serotonergic metabolism between nonbulimic and bulimic patients with anorexia nervosa. Am J. Psychiatry 141: 1598-1601.

12. ROSENTHAL, N. E. & M. M. HEFFERMAN. 1986. Bulimia, carbohydrate craving and depression: A central connection? In Food Constituents Affecting Normal and Abnormal Behaviors. Nutrition and the Brain, Vol 7. R. J. Wurtman & J. J. Wurtman, Eds.: 139-166. Raven Press. New York.

13. LOGUE, A. W., K. R. LOGUE & K. E. STRAUSS. 1983. The acquisition of taste aversions in humans with eating and drinking disorders. Behav. Res. Ther. 21: 275-289.

14. SHERMAN, B. M. & K. A. HALMI. 1977. The effect of nutritional rehabilitation on hypothalamic-pituitary function in anorexia nervosa. In Anorexia Nervosa. R. A. Vigersky, Ed. Raven Press. New York.

15. RODIN, J. 1987. Sweetness and eating disorders. In Sweetness. J. Dobbing, Ed.: 193-204. Springer-Verlag. Berlin.

16. DREWNOWSKI, A., K. A. HALMI, B. PIERCE, J. GIBBS & G. P. SMITH. 1987. Taste and eating disorders. Am. J. Clin. Nutr. 46: 442-450.

17. NAKAI, Y., F. KINOSHITA, T. KOH, S. TSUJII & T. TSUKADA. 1987. Taste function in patients with anorexia nervosa and bulimia nervosa. Int. J. Eating Disord. 6: 257-265.

18. JIRIK-BABB, P. & J. L. KATZ. 1988. Impairment of taste perception in anorexia nervosa and bulimia. Int. J. Eating Disord. 7: 353-360.

19. HURST, P. S., J. H. LACEY & A. H. CRISP. 1977. Teeth, vomiting and diet: A study of the dental characteristics of seventeen anorexia nervosa patients. Postgrad. Med. J. 53: 298-305.

20. MILES, D. A., B. F. GREGG, B. J. GLASS & M. L. VAN DIS. 1985. Bulimic erosion: Dental management and report of cases. J. Can. Dent. Assoc. 10: 757-760.

21. CRISP, A. H. 1967. The possible significance of some behavioral correlates of weight and carbohydrate intake. J Psychosom. Res. 11: 117-131.

22. CRISP, A. H. & R. S. KALUCY. 1974. Aspects of the perceptual disorder in anorexia nervosa. Br. J. Med. Psychol. 47: 349-361.

23. DREWNOWSKI, A., B. PIERCE & K. A. HALMI. 1988. Fat aversion in eating disorders. Appetite 10: 119-131.

24. O'CONNOR, M. A., S. W. TOYUZ, S. M. DUNN & P. J. V. BEUMONT. 1987. Vegetarianism in anorexia nervosa? A review of 116 consecutive cases. Med. J. Aust. 147: 540-542.

25. HUSE, D. M. & A. R. LUCAS. 1984. Dietary patterns in anorexia nervosa. Am. J. Clin. Nutr. 40: 251-254.

26. AMERICAN PSYCHIATRIC ASSOCIATION COMMITTEE ON NOMENCLATURE AND STATISTICS. 1980. Diagnostic and Statistical Manual of Mental Disorders (DSM-III). Washington, DC.

27. KAYE, W. H., H. E. G. WIRTSMAN, D. T. GEORGE, S. R. WEISS & D. C. JIMERSON. 1986. Relationship of mood alterations to binging behaviour in bulimia. Br. J. Psychiatry 149: 479-485.

28. MITCHELL, J. E., R. L. PYLE & E. D. ECKERT. 1981. Frequency and duration of binge-eating episodes in patients with bulimia. Am. J. Psychiatry 136: 835-836.

29. MITCHELL, J. E. & D. C. LAINE. 1985. Monitored binge-eating behavior in patients with bulimia. Int. J. Eating Disord. 4: 177-183.

30. KISSILEFF, H. R., B. T. WALSH, J. G. KRAL & S. CASSIDY. 1986. Laboratory studies of eating behavior in women with bulimia. Physiol. Behav. 38: 563-570.

31. ROSEN, J. C., H. LEITENBERG, C. FISHER & C. KHAZAM. 1986. Binge-eating episodes in

bulimia nervosa: The amount and type of food consumed. Int. J. Eating Disord. **5:** 255–267.

32. LEON, G. R., K. CARROLL, B. CHERNYK & S. FINN. 1985. Binge-eating and associated habit patterns within college student and identified bulimic populations. Int. J. Eating Disord. **4:** 43–57.

33. DREWNOWSKI, A. 1987. Changes in mood following carbohydrate consumption. Am. J. Clin. Nutr. **46:** 703.

34. ABRAHAM, S. F. & P. J. V. BEUMONT. 1982. How patients describe bulimia or binge eating. Psychol. Med. **12:** 625–635.

35. PIRKE, K. M., J. PAHL, U. SCHWEIGER & M. WARNHOFF. 1985. Metabolic and endocrine indices of starvation in bulimia: A comparison with anorexia nervosa. Psychiat. Res. **15:** 33–39.

36. CASPER, R. C., B. KIRSCHNER, H. SANDSTEAD, *et al.* 1980. An evaluation of trace metals, vitamins, and taste function in anorexia nervosa. Am. J. Clin. Nutr. **33:** 1801–1808.

37. DREWNOWSKI, A., F. BELLISLE, P. AIMEZ & B. REMY. 1987. Taste and bulimia. Physiol. Behav. **41:** 621–626.

38. DREWNOWSKI, A. 1986. Sweetness and obesity. *In* Sweetness. J. Dobbing, Ed.: 177–192. Springer-Verlag. Berlin.

39. DREWNOWSKI, A., J. B. BRUNZELL, K. SANDE, P. H. IVERIUS & M. R. C. GREENWOOD. 1985. Sweet tooth reconsidered: Taste responsiveness in human obesity. Physiol. Behav. **35:** 617–622.

40. DREWNOWSKI, A. & M. R. C. GREENWOOD. 1983. Cream and sugar: Human preferences for high-fat foods. Physiol. Behav. **30:** 629–633.

41. CABANAC, M. & R. DUCLAUX. 1970. Obesity: Absence of satiety aversion to sucrose. Science **168:** 496–497.

42. GILBERT, D. G. & R. L. HAGEN. 1980. Taste in underweight, overweight, and normal-weight subjects before, during, and after sucrose ingestion. Addict. Behav. **5:** 137–142.

43. GRINKER, J. 1978. Obesity and sweet taste. Am. J. Clin. Nutr. **31:** 1078–1087.

44. GARFINKEL, P. E., H. MOLDOFSKY & D. M. GARNER. 1979. The stability of perceptual disturbances in anorexia nervosa. Psychol. Med. **9:** 703–708.

45. RODIN, J., H. R. MOSKOWITZ & G. A. BRAY. 1976. Relationship between obesity, weight loss, and taste responsiveness. Physiol. Behav. **17:** 391–397.

46. GARFINKEL, P. E. 1974. Perception of hunger and satiety in anorexia nervosa. Psychol. Med. **4:** 309–315.

47. GOLD, P. W., H. GWIRTSMAN, P. C. AVGERINOS *et al.* 1986. Abnormal hypothalamic-pituitary-adrenal function in anorexia nervosa. N. Engl. J. Med. **314:** 1335–1342.

48. KAYE, W. H., D. PICKAR, D. NABER & M. H. EBERT. 1982. Cerebrospinal fluid opioid activity in anorexia nervosa. Am. J. Psychiatry **139:** 643–645.

49. MARGULES, D. L., B. MOISSET, M. J. LEWIS, *et al.* 1978. Beta-endorphin is associated with overeating in genetically obese mice (ob/ob) and rats (fa/fa). Science **202:** 988–991.

50. BLASS, E. M. 1986. Opioids, sugar and the inherent taste of sweet: Broad motivational implications. *In* Sweetness. J. Dobbing, Ed.: 115–126. Springer-Verlag. Berlin.

DISCUSSION

DR. HARRY KISSILEFF (*St. Luke's-Roosevelt Hospital, New York*): Adam, it was mentioned earlier by Dr. Linda Bartoshuk that fats have volatiles in them that produce odors, but I noticed when you mentioned all the different factors that could discriminate between your various mixtures, you did not say anything about the odor. I think odor is an important component in this carbohydrate-craving phenomenon. If you think about all the foods that are listed, there aren't only fats and sugar mixtures, there are the odor-producing chemicals in them that might be the most important component. Have you any thoughts on that?

DR. ADAM DREWNOWSKI (*University of Michigan, Ann Arbor, MI*): Yes, it is very important. In milk you have esters and lactones, and you have the volatile components. Of course it gets much richer if you are dealing with solid fat, shortening, oils, and so on. In this particular set of studies, we did not use nose clips or any other ways of removing sensory cues other than taste or texture. Dr. Rose Marie Pangborn has done studies like that, and there are weak cues from odor. However, we wanted to have natural conditions and have subjects taste the stimuli under such conditions as they normally would eat sugar and fat foods. But in some cases, I should note, the actual odors in fats are really not all that pleasant. In fact because of the odor, there may be an aversion to specific types of fats in those combinations of sugar and fat. It's a very good point.

DR. BARBARA ROLLS (*Johns Hopkins University, Baltimore, MD*): In your fat preference, obviously, viscosity could be a factor, and I know you have thought about that. I am wondering if we know anything else about texture in relation to eating disorders. I understand texture is an important factor in influencing intake in anorectics and bulimics.

DR. DREWNOWSKI: Anorectics often seem to subsist on a diet of what they call safe foods that seem to be mostly crunchy vegetables. However, many bulimic binges specifically include soft, creamy semi-solid foods, and one of the reasons that has been mentioned is that such foods may facilitate vomiting after the binge. Toward the end of the binge, texture of the food sometimes changes. There is a great deal of drinking of diet sodas and patients eat softer foods. So it is possible that while taste may be the initial stimulus, the texture of foods also plays a role.

Is There An Eating Disorder in the Obese?

HARRY R. KISSILEFF[a]

Department of Psychiatry
Columbia University
College of Physicians and Surgeons, and
Obesity Research Center
St. Luke's-Roosevelt Hospital Center
New York, New York 10025

INTRODUCTION

Because so much effort has been expended on answering this question in the past, any conference on eating disorders would be incomplete without a discussion of eating behavior in the obese. The question addressed in the title immediately requires some clarification. First, much of the controversy surrounding this question may turn on the criteria for obesity. The literature on the problem frequently lumps all obese together and therefore individuals classified as "obese" could range from as little as 20% overweight to those who are morbidly obese. Tables of obesity and overweight are based on both actuarial standards for desirable weights in relation to longevity and on extremes of distributions of indices of body fatness.[1] We shall not draw fine distinctions among the various overweight groups used in the studies cited below, but it is important to note that future work should pay closer attention to the magnitude of overweight and distributions of body fat within the individual than has been paid in the past. Second, an eating disorder will be a variable of eating behavior that is observed to lie outside the "normal" range of such variables among individuals who are not overweight or obese. Once again the criterion for "normal controls" has been variable. In work reported below from our laboratory we have chosen as controls subjects whose desirable weight for height ranges between -5 and $+15\%$ of the values suggested in the Fogarty conference of 1973.[2] Third, it must be recognized that eating behavior in both obese and nonobese people has been studied in a variety of situations with a variety of methods. Consequently, the answer to the question rests on the logical assumption that any positive demonstration of a difference between obese and nonobese persons constitutes an affirmative answer to the question, and that negative results can be regarded as examples of conditions that were inadequate for such a demonstration. Nevertheless, it is instructive to review both the positive and negative evidence, because an extraction of the essential conditions for appearance of a critical difference will help us to identify the appropriate behavioral "cofactors."

[a] Address for correspondence: Harry R. Kissileff, St. Luke's Hospital, 114th St. & Amsterdam Ave., New York, NY 10025.

Three major techniques have been used to study human eating behavior in attempts to determine whether eating disorders are found in the obese: diaries, structured interviews, and direct observation both in natural situations and in laboratories. Therefore, each of these areas (i.e., description, prediction, and techniques of controlled observation with experimental intervention) will be considered. The motivation in each of these areas is that positive evidence would provide a framework for therapy, under the working hypothesis that correction of the disturbance in eating would ultimately correct the disturbance in body composition. This assumption is of course extremely tenuous because it fails to account for the possibility that accumulation of excess body fat can be self-perpetuating, particularly if fat cell proliferation has occurred. In addition, this simple assumption, that correction of an eating disturbance could lead to normalization of body composition, ignores the possibility that changes in body composition lead to changes in energy expenditure that tend to preserve body weight. Nevertheless, it is important to emphasize that evidence for an eating disorder in obesity would be important so that therapeutic measures would be directed at both intake and expenditure controls simultaneously rather than one at a time.

FOOD DIARIES

The earliest methods used to compare intakes in the obese and nonobese were food diaries and dietary histories. These studies[3] showed that, according to records kept by the patients, the obese ate less, though not significantly less, than the nonobese. However, when a skilled interviewer took a diet history, it was found that the obese ate on the average 600 kcal/day more than the nonobese (TABLE 1). The obese apparently underestimated, even more than the nonobese, what they actually ate. They were also unable to record what they ate with sufficient precision for reliable estimates.[4]

LONG-TERM STUDIES WITH INPATIENTS

Because these indirect measures of eating behavior were unreliable and gave conflicting results, investigators undertook direct studies of eating behavior in the laboratory. Two major types of studies have been done, inpatient and outpatient. The inpa-

TABLE 1. Food Intakes of Obese and Nonobese People One Day or More

Intake (kcal)		Sex	Method	Percent Overweight	Reference
Obese	Nonobese				
1964	2198	F	Diary 1 day	–	3
1591	2196	F	Diary 3 day	–	3
2829	2201	F	Diet History	–	3
785	1442	M & F	Vending machine	36 kg/m²	14
2133	1724	F	Platter	70%	16
3418	4131	M	Platter-sugar	24–134%	13
2575	2130	M & F	Normal life	>15%	10
3963	1968	M	Feeding machine	76%	6
475		F	Feeding machine		6
2924		M	Feeding machine		7
2930	3230	M	Formula, conc.	>20%	8
1870	1980	M	Formula, dilute		8

tient studies were initiated by Hashim and Van Itallie,[5] who developed a machine that allowed continuous monitoring of consumption of a formula diet 24 hours a day, indefinitely. These studies initially showed that obese persons ate less than nonobese, but the sex and age of the subjects was not controlled. In later studies[6,7] some obese subjects were found to eat more than nonobese (TABLE 1). Among those obese who had more fat cells than normal, those whose cells were of normal size ate more than those who had enlarged fat cells.

Studies in other laboratories have given different results. Wooley[8] found that the obese ate somewhat less than controls, although both groups ate more when the formula diet they were served was diluted. (Classically,[9] the ability of animals to eat more when the energy density of their diet is diluted by adding nonnutrients to it has been used to determine whether a given type of person or animal adjusts food intake on the basis of its energy content.) On the other hand, Evans and Miller[10] found that the obese ate more than controls. Intake was self-monitored by the subjects who ate their habitual diet. Furthermore, the subjects reduced their intakes 10% when 20 g of guar or methylcellulose was eaten in 10-g amounts twice a day. However, this study suffered from a design problem in that there was no placebo control. A recent study from our own laboratory[11] found no effect of 3 g of guar in comparison to a control on a test meal, although this study tested only one meal a day and was not carried out over an extended period of time. Another problem in the Evans and Miller experiments is that subjects were required to monitor their own intakes, which could have affected their eating behavior.

The problem of monitoring the consumption of normal foods was solved by Porikos et al.[12,13] They provided subjects with an array of palatable foods in the laboratory three times a day, on demand, and snacks were provided ad libitum. Subjects lived on a metabolic ward. All food was measured before and after meals, and the contents of the snack box were measured daily. In this situation, where subjects were well adapted to the setting and appetizing food was available, the obese ate on the average 713 kcal/day more than the nonobese[13] (see TABLE 1). When aspartame (a very high-intensity, low-energy sweetener) covertly replaced the sucrose in these palatable foods, intake stabilized at 15% below baseline in both groups, although the energy concentration had been diluted on the average by 25%. However, it is not possible to determine whether the failure of subjects to completely compensate for the dilution was the result of their initial overeating on these highly palatable foods or whether they were unable to detect the reduction in energy density of the food.

When subjects are allowed to choose freely from a diet containing a variety of foods, some of which have been artificially sweetened and some of which have not, it is impossible to control the amount of dilution. The dilution will be greater the more sweet food is selected by the subject. Therefore, Durrant et al.[14] used a different procedure to test the response to dilution. Subjects lived in the laboratory and fed themselves from a food-dispensing machine,[15] which delivered one of four types of foods when the subject pressed a button. Just before each meal a homogeneous food was given in one of three caloric amounts 300, 600, or 900 kcal. For both obese and nonobese subjects, the more they were given before the meal, the less they ate of the regular foods. However, the difference in intake between high- and low-energy premeal feedings (i.e. preloads) was greater in the nonobese than in the obese, and the obese ate only half as much as the nonobese overall (TABLE 1).

In contrast to the preceding study, and consistent with the Porikos & Van Itallie study,[13] obese subjects did eat more than nonobese (see TABLE 1) when they were tested by Woo & Pi-Sunyer[16] in a platter service paradigm with somewhat less palatable foods than those used by Porikos et al.[12] The obese, however, did not increase their intake when they were forced to increase energy expenditure by 25%, whereas the nonobese did increase their intake. In summary of these long-term inpatient studies, it appears that the obese will eat more than the nonobese when food is readily available and is palatable or neutral, and when sufficient time is allowed for the obese subjects to adjust to the testing situation. When diet palatability is marginal and the food choices restricted as they were in the experiments of Durrant *et al.*,[14] obese individuals are likely to eat less than controls.

OUTPATIENT STUDIES: SINGLE MEALS

Shortly after Van Itallie and colleagues developed the feeding machine for chronic studies of human eating, Jordan and colleagues[17] devised a method of studying short-term eating in the laboratory. They used a liquid dispenser separated from the subject's view by a wall. The experimenter sat behind the wall and read the level of the liquid every minute, while the subject obtained the liquid formula by sucking on the end of the tube. This method was adopted by Meyer and Pudel.[18] They reported that the rate of eating during a meal gradually slowed in nonobese individuals but stayed at a constant rate in the obese. They suggested that the gradual slowing indicated satiety, which was not experienced by the obese, because their rates did not slow.

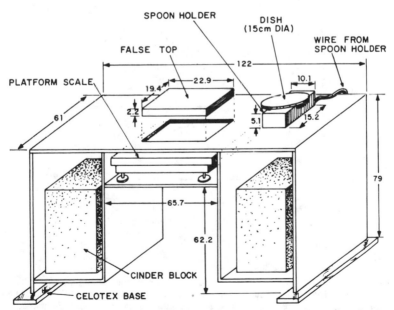

FIGURE 1. Universal eating monitor. Front pieces have been removed revealing the electronic balance in the center drawer, located below a false top cut out of the table. Normally a tablecloth covers the table concealing the balance from the subject's view. (From Kissileff *et al.*[19] Used with permission.)

We were stimulated by this work to develop our own Universal Eating Monitor,[19] which consists of a table containing an electronic balance located under a panel cut in the table top and covered by a table cloth (see FIG. 1). A bowl or large container of food is placed on the table top, and the change in the weight of the container as the subject eats is transmitted to a digital computer that calculates the amount eaten every three seconds. We refer to the resulting curve of intake over time as a "cumulative intake curve." In one of our first studies,[19] we found that a yogurt and fruit mixture, served in semisolid form, produced a cumulative intake curve that showed less deceleration than when the identical food was given after being liquefied in a blender, although the differences in total intake were not significant.

In order to obtain a more quantitative measure of the deceleration of the cumulative intake curve, we fitted it to several different equations and showed that a quadratic provided the simplest equation with adequate fit.[20] Use of the quadratic allowed a simple explanation[20] of the two coefficients that described the curve (see FIG. 2). The equation describes intake as a function of time. The mathematical derivative of the quadratic equation gives the rate of eating during the course of the meal. The linear

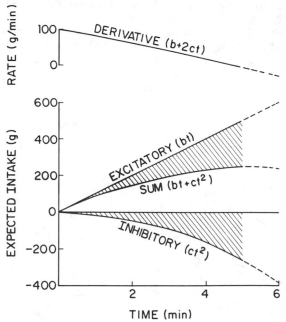

FIGURE 2. Theoretical cumulative intake curve (lower) and mathematical derivative (upper). The curve marked "sum" is partitioned into two components, excitatory and inhibitory. If the curve were determined by excitation alone, intake would rise at a constant rate "b" giving the intake at each point in time as "bt." The addition of the inhibitory component "ct²" reduces the rise at a constant rate of change, "2ct" giving an intake reduction of "ct²." The derivative in the upper portion shows the theoretical rate of eating starting from an initial rate "b" (where the line intersects the ordinate) and dropping at rate "2c" (shown by slope of the line). The actual rate at any time is therefore the sum of the initial rate "b" and the reduction at that point in time "2ct." The linear coefficient of the curve "b" is therefore equal to the initial rate of eating, and the quadratic coefficient "c" is half the rate of deceleration. Time is given by "t." The dotted lines indicate projection of the curves beyond the null point where facilitation and inhibition balance. (From Kissileff & Thornton.[20] Used with permission.)

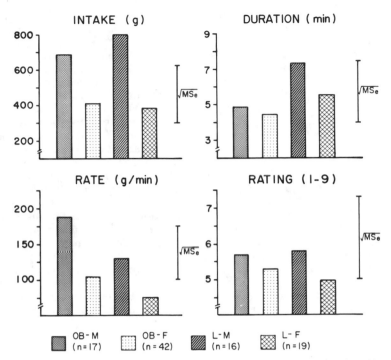

FIGURE 3. Intakes, durations, mean rates of eating, and rating of how much the subject liked the test meal, for the morbidly obese (OB) and nonobese (L) men (M) and women (F). Key at bottom indicates group. $\sqrt{MSe}$ is the square root of the mean square error from the analysis of variance.

coefficient represents the rate of eating at the beginning of the meal, and the quadratic coefficient is half the rate of deceleration. We further speculated that the linear coefficient was a measure of excitation or hunger and that the quadratic coefficient was a measure of inhibition or satiety. However, it is important to keep in mind that these objective measures of behavior do not necessarily map onto such constructs as excitation and inhibition, hunger or satiety, and that these constructs may in fact have little utility in describing or predicting behavior. The variables we measure in the laboratory have validity only insofar as they can be used to explain or predict behavior. Such prediction is largely empirical rather than theoretical. However, there is a danger of being unable to interpret microanalysis of behavior without a theoretical structure to guide it. Although the coefficients of the cumulative intake curve fitted by least-squares regression to a quadratic equation could provide an objective measure of the hunger at the start of a meal and the rate of onset of satiety, the utility of such constructs will depend on the theoretical use to which they are put. In the present case, they allow the further testing of Meyer and Pudel's hypothesis that at least some obese do not experience satiety.

In order to test that hypothesis, we examined cumulative curves from 43 obese and 11 nonobese persons eating a macaroni and beef test meal that both groups found equipalatable and moderately liked (mean rating 7.2 for obese, 7.6 for nonobese).[20]

However, although there were some hints at differences overall, none was significant. On the other hand eight obese persons individually ate more than any of the nonobese persons.

In a further study, Kral and I[21] examined cumulative intake curves from 75 morbidly obese (greater than 100% overweight) patients who were candidates for gastric restrictive surgery. Also tested were 41 normal weight controls. Each patient ate a single liquid meal in the laboratory three hours after a standard 300-kcal breakfast consisting of an English muffin, 250 g of apple juice and 1 1/2 pats of butter. The liquid test meal was a milk shake fortified with casein. It was consumed from an opaque container with a straw. There were no significant differences in intake or meal duration between the obese and nonobese, but there were significant differences between men and women in intake. The men ate 300 g more than the women (see FIG. 3). The average rate of eating (intake divided by duration for each person) was faster in the obese than in the nonobese ($p < 0.05$), and men ate faster than women ($p < 0.05$).

The coefficients of the cumulative intake curves for those individuals whose curves had at least a 95% fit (i.e. $r^2 \geqslant 0.95$) to the quadratic equation were no different between obese and nonobese, but the initial rates of eating were higher ($p < 0.05$) in men (244 g/mil) than in women (151 g/min). The rates of deceleration were not different among the four groups, although obese men had higher rates of deceleration than the other three groups (see FIG. 4). However, there were some unexpected differences. More of the obese than the nonobese failed to exhibit smooth curves of cumulative intake. In the obese, 22 out of 75 exhibited bursts of rapid eating (gulping) separated by long pauses of no eating, while this pattern was seen in only four of the nonobese.

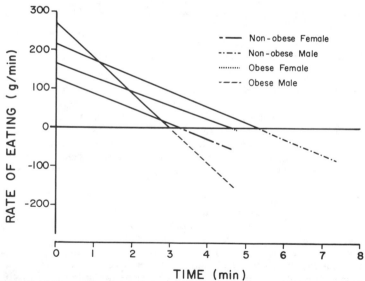

FIGURE 4. Initial rates of eating and deceleration of eating rates derived from coefficients of individual cumulative intake curves for each group. Initial rates of eating (point where line intersects the ordinate) were higher for men than women, but rates of deceleration (slopes of lines) were not significantly different, although the rate of deceleration was more rapid in the obese men. Extensions of below the horizontal zero line simply indicate the duration of the meal for each group and also indicate the group by type of line by means of the key in the upper right. (From Kissileff & Kral.[21])

Finally, seven obese and five nonobese persons had cumulative intake curves that did not slow significantly. These results do not confirm Meyer and Pudel's[18] hypothesis that in general the obese do not exhibit satiety. Rather they suggest that the obese may experience sporadic bouts of excitation manifested in brief periods of rapid gorging.

Our ability to measure eating behavior objectively in the laboratory led us to three other studies involving obese subjects. First we explored the possibility that laboratory test meals could predict the outcome of gastric restrictive surgery. The hypothesis was that the most successful patients would be those who ate small amounts, slowly, and that the operation would be relatively unsuccessful for those who ate large amounts or ate rapidly. Intake in a test meal showed a small but significant correlation ($r = 0.32$) with weight loss at the plateau after a gastric restrictive operation.[22] A subsequent analysis with a larger group showed that this correlation lost significance. Nevertheless, no patient who ate more than 500 g of the test meal lost more than 25% body weight, whereas most of those who ate less than 500 g lost 25% or more.

In another series of studies,[23,24] we found that obese men (30 to 50% overweight) ate 300 g more than nonobese men, but both groups reduced their intakes by 125 g ($p < 0.05$, one-tailed) upon infusion of the putative satiety agent and gut peptide, cholecystokinin. Weight of the subjects, food used, and duration of study were different than in the preceding descriptive study.[21] In another study[25] obese and nonobese women ate the same amounts, but the obese (30–50% overweight) did not reduce their intake immediately after acute strenuous exercise as did the nonobese. More work is still needed to establish the critical conditions under which obese persons will eat more than nonobese persons in a laboratory setting.

Several studies, in addition to ours, have been done of single meals taken by both obese and nonobese subjects. As in the longer term studies, the obese ate more than the nonobese in some studies, and in others they ate less. For example Porikos and Hagamen[26] found that adding fiber to bread increased gram intake in the nonobese to maintain caloric intake, but actually reduced both gram and calorie intake in the obese (see TABLE 2). Bellisle and Le Magnen[27] found that the obese ate less than the nonobese when they were given a variety of foods in a single meal, but the obese ate faster, in agreement with our work. Many other studies have been done to compare eating in obese and nonobese (see Spitzer & Rodin[28] for review.) Type of food, effort required to obtain and eat it, and palatability are all important in determining whether obese individuals will eat more than nonobese in a laboratory setting.

CONCLUSIONS

Although physiological manipulations have shown differences in eating behavior between obese and nonobese persons in the case of exercise, they did not do so under conditions of CCK infusion. Obese-nonobese differences were seen sometimes when

TABLE 2. Single Meal Intakes of Obese and Nonobese Persons

| Intake (kcal) | | | | Percent | |
Obese	Nonobese	Sex	Method	Overweight	Reference
820	380	M	Sandwich low fiber	32%	26
490	400	M	Sandwich high fiber		26
1174	1495	M	Casein shake	127%	21
838	587	F	Casein shake	123%	21

subjects were simply asked to taste foods, or when emotionally charged or effort-requiring instructions were given.[28] Another condition has been neglected in executing these studies: the instructions to the subject. In our studies on women with bulimia in comparison to controls (see Walsh *et al.*, this volume), it was clear that the instructions provide important cues that determined how much the subjects would eat in the laboratory, and whether differences between groups would emerge. Bulimics ate no more than controls when asked to eat "normally" but ate between two and three times more than controls when asked to eat as much as they could. Although obese and nonobese persons do not always exhibit differences in eating behavior, there is a strong possibility that in many experiments the instructions given to the subjects have been inappropriate. It is reasonable, because the obese eat more than the nonobese under some conditions, that the instruction to eat a normal amount, rather than as much as possible, has obscured differences that might have appeared had this alternative instruction been used. We predict that when obese persons are asked to eat as much as they can, they will consistently eat more than controls, in studies such as those described above.

In conclusion, it now seems important to repeat some of the previous types of studies with special attention to the instructions given to the subjects: "eat normally" versus "eat as much you can." If such changes in instructions reveal significant consistent differences in energy intake, further advances could be made in exploring pathology, testing therapeutic interventions, and developing new treatments based on physiological mechanisms for the control of food intake. Because reduction in food intake is the least invasive way of eliminating obesity, a systematic search of food components and/or pharmacological agents that will reduce intake appears to be needed. The technology for carrying out such studies in man has been demonstrated.

ACKNOWLEDGMENTS

I would like to thank my collaborators, T. B. Van Itallie, F. X. Pi-Sunyer, J. Kral, and B. T. Walsh for their invaluable participation in carrying out the studies reported from our laboratory. I would also like to thank T. B. Van Itallie for his helpful critical suggestions on the manuscript. Parts of this report were presented at the Japan Society for the Study of Obesity, November, 1987, and I would like to thank Shuji Inoue for the invitation that provided the initial impetus for preparing it.

REFERENCES

1. VAN ITALLIE, T. B. 1985. Health implications of overweight and obesity in the United States. Ann. Intern. Med. **103:** 983–988.
2. BRAY, G. A. 1975. *In* Obesity in Perspective. Vol 2. Part 2. Washington, D.C.
3. BEAUDOIN, R. & J. MAYER. 1953. Food intakes of obese and non-obese women. J. Am. Diet. Assoc. **29:** 29–33.
4. LANSKY, D. & K. D. BROWNELL. 1982. Estimates of food quantity and calories; errors in self-report among obese patients. Am. J. Clin. Nutr. **35(4):** 727–732.
5. HASHIM, S. A. & T. B. VAN ITALLIE. 1964. An automatically monitored food dispensing apparatus for the study of food intake in man. Fed. Proc. **23(1):** 82–84.
6. CAMPBELL, R., S. HASHIM & T. VAN ITALLIE. 1971. Studies of food-intake regulation in man. N. Engl. J. Med. **285:** 1402–1407.
7. YANG, M. & T. B. VAN ITALLIE. 1983. Relationship of adipose tissue morphology to spontaneous intake of liquid diet in obese humans: Preliminary observations. Paper presented at the Fourth International Congress on Obesity, New York, October, 1983.

8. WOOLEY, O. 1871. Long-term food regulation in the obese and nonobese. Psychosom. Med. **33(5):** 436–444.
9. ADOLPH, E. F. 1947. Urges to eat and drink in rats. Am. J. Physiol. **151:** 110–125.
10. EVANS, E. & D. MILLER. 1975. Bulking agents in the treatment of obesity. Nutr. Metabol. **18:** 199–203.
11. KISSILEFF, H. R., S. MELTZER & T. B. VAN ITALLIE. Guar (3 g) does not reduce single meal food intake in obese women. Poster presented at NAASO meeting, Banff, August, 1988.
12. PORIKOS, K., G. BOOTH & T. VAN ITALLIE. 1977. Effect of covert nutritive dilution on the spontaneous food intake of obese individuals; a pilot study. Am. J. Clin. Nutr. **30:** 1638–1644.
13. PORIKOS, K. P. & T. B. VAN ITALLIE. 1984. Efficacy of low-calorie sweeteners in reducing food intake: Studies with aspartame. *In* Aspartame: Physiology and Biochemistry. L. D. Stegink & L. J. Filer, Jr., Eds.: 273–286. New York and Basel.
14. DURRANT, M., J. ROYSTON, R. WLOCH & J. GARROW. 1982. The effect of covert changes in energy density of preloads on subsequent ad libitum energy intake in lean and obese human subjects. Hum. Nutr. Clin. Nutr. **36C:** 297–306.
15. SILVERSTONE, T., J. FINCHAM & J. BRYDON. 1980. A new technique for the continuous measurement of food intake in man. J. Clin. Nutr. **33:** 1852–1855.
16. WOO, R. & F. Pi-Sunyer. 1985. Effect of increased physical activity on voluntary intake in lean women. Metabolism **34(9):** 836–841.
17. JORDAN, H., W. WIELAND, S. ZEBLEY, E. STELLAR & A. STUNKARD. 1966. Direct measurement of food intake in man: A method for the objective study of eating behavior. Psychosom. Med. **28(6):** 836–842.
18. MEYER, J-E. & V. PUDEL. 1972. Experimental studies on food intake in obese and normal weight subjects. J. Psychosom. Res. **16:** 305–308.
19. KISSILEFF, H. R., G. KLINGSBERG & T. B. VAN ITALLIE. 1980. Universal eating monitor for continuous recording of solid or liquid consumption in man. Am. J. Physiol. **238:** R14–R22.
20. KISSILEFF, H. R. & J. THORNTON. 1982. Facilitation and inhibition in the cumulative food intake curve in man. *In* Changing Concepts of the Nervous System. A. J. Morrison & P. Strick, Eds.: 585–607. New York.
21. KISSILEFF, H. R. & J. G. KRAL. 1986. Abnormal eating behavior in obese men and women. Paper presented at the 6th International Congress on Obesity, Jerusalem, Israel, Sept. 14.
22. KISSILEFF, H. R., P. PRITCHARD & J. G. KRAL. 1983. Eating tests before and after obesity surgery. Paper presented at the Fourth International congress on Obesity, New York, October, 1983.
23. KISSILEFF, H., F. PI-SUNYER, J. THORNTON & G. SMITH. 1981. C-terminal octapeptide of cholecystokinin decreases food intake in man. Am. J. Clin. Nutr. **34:** 154–160.
24. PI-SUNYER, F. X., H. R. KISSILEFF, J. THORNTON & G. P. SMITH. 1982. C-terminal octapeptide of cholecystokinin decreases food intake in obese men. Physiol. Behav. **29:** 627–630.
25. KISSILEFF, H. R., S. MELTZER, K. R. SEGAL & X. F. PI-SUNYER. 1987. Acute strenuous exercise reduces food intake in women. Paper presented at the 27th Annual Meeting for the American Society for Clinical Nutrition.
26. PORIKOS, K. & S. HAGAMEN. 1986. Is fiber satiating? Effects of a high fiber preload on subsequent food intake of normal-weight and obese young men. Appetite **7:** 153–162.
27. BELLISLE, F. & J. LE MAGNEN. 1981. The structure of meals in humans: Eating and drinking patterns in lean and obese subjects. Physiol. Behav. **27:** 649–658.
28. SPITZER, L. & J. RODIN. 1981. Studies of human eating behavior: A critical review of normal weight and overweight individuals. Appetite **2:** 293–330.

Summary: Part V

JOHN E. BLUNDELL

Psychology Department
Biopsychology Group
University of Leeds
Leeds County LS2 9JT, United Kingdom

It seems to me that this morning's session has been one of the most constructive and fascinating of the whole symposium so far. I have attempted to conceptualize a scheme (FIG. 1) which would illustrate the various phenomena that the participants discussed. The simple scheme that makes sense for me is a stepwise scheme starting with the physical characteristics of food, either in individual substances or in foods themselves which register with sensory receptors: taste, tactile, olfactory, or receptors for temperature. As Linda Bartoshuk pointed out, there may be many receptors for different modalities. Food, of course, is consumed and confers a certain metabolic property onto the system.

From the receptor stage we moved to conscious perception, and this relationship is what is known as classical psychophysics: the relationship between the physical quantity of the stimulus and the psychological response at the level of perception of intensity. At this stage it is useful to keep in mind that there are certain attributes that go along with the response at receptors, and in turn one assumes that it is something happening here that determines the hedonic response, the preference or liking for these commodities, which are graded or calibrated on particular scales. At this stage it gets more interesting because there is a translation, possibly, into these mediating concepts of hunger and satiety and the amount of product consumed. Leading from the amount of product consumed in the short term is the question how does that affect changes in the long term; that is, does short-term intake confer properties on a long-term pattern, and do the long-term patterns lead to changes in eating habits and changes in body weight?

I need some sort of system like this to allow me to understand the various concepts and phenomena that have been described, and I will try to place the various authors within this simple scheme. Michel Cabanac, I believe, was speaking about the relationship between hedonic response, preference or palatability, and some fraction of body weight, a set-point indicator. That is a powerful explanatory concept. It seems to me that the question here is what is palatability. This is a key phenomenon. How palatability, even in Michel Cabanac's scheme, is dependent not only upon some parameter of body weight, but also upon metabolic action, energy utilization, and food consumption. Therefore, it is not in itself a unique indicator of a set point, although it may be an attribute of set point.

Linda Bartoshuk spoke in her elegant way about the relationship between taste and olfaction and the conscious response. One question that was raised in my mind is, What is the relationship between these taste characteristics and ultimate food consumption? Is there an abnormality here that could lead to some abnormality in the pattern of consumption either in the short or the long term? It is a little mystifying, because states of dysgeusia and anosmia do not, apparently, lead inevitably to dis-

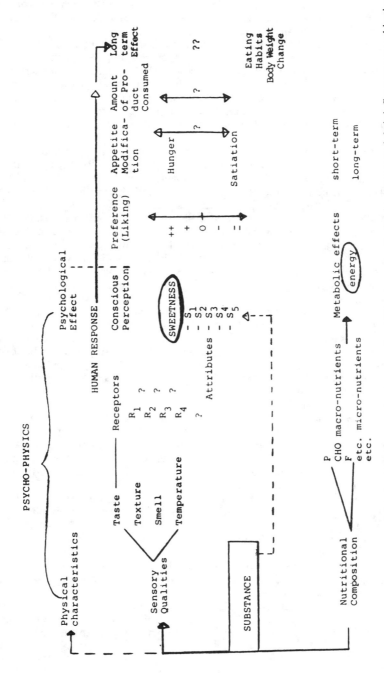

FIGURE 1. Conceptualization of the relationships between the sensory and nutritional aspects of a food substance and their influence upon subjective states and eating behavior.

ordered patterns of eating or to disordered body weight. So although one would like to think that there is some neat relationship between taste receptor activity and intake, I'm not sure that it's really emerging.

France Bellisle spoke about the notion of palatability and about her studies to anchor palatability in some objective index of food consumption, particularly in the microstructure of eating. It's absolutely necessary that at some stage this very elusive term, palatability, is anchored. France also raised the interesting issue of the possible distinction between preference and palatability, so it seems to me that there is still a semantic issue here to be worked out, and it needs to be decided whether or not we are using these two terms interchangeably to refer to the same phenomenon or whether they are quite distinct.

Paul Rozin took an abiological view, and it seems to me that this approach is not embraced by my conceptual scheme (FIG. 1). Although Paul began by stipulating that his approach was strictly nonbiological, I know from his other writings that he does regard culture itself as a biological phenomenon, and I agree with that. It would have been interesting to hear how the cultural system embraces biological states.

The Rolls–Hetherington duo talked again about the concept of sensory-specific satiety, which is now part of the litany of food intake. It seems to me that sensory-specific satiety attempts to link sensory perception with preference and consumption. The argument is that this is a coupled system, with information arising from sensory parameters being reflected in the hedonic response and in turn reflected in consumption. And this is indeed a powerful explanatory device, and it seems to be important to define whether or not this is a tightly or loosely coupled system.

One thought I have about sensory-specific satiety has to do with its logical basis. This was raised by Dr. Rolls herself when she said that in sensory-specific satiety, the satiety itself is a consequence of the sensation. It seemed to me the logical issue here is the fact that if we ate foods that possessed all of the sensory qualities but had no metabolic information, they should carry with them the satiating power. So we should be able to live on tastes and smells forever and feel satiated without getting any of the benefit of nutrients. If we were presented with novel tastes, one after the other, would we go on eating forever?

Adam Drewnowski spoke about the relationship between taste and nutritional composition of foods and how they affect palatability. This is a very interesting triadic relationship. One of the questions that occurs to me is how that relationship eventually impinges on products consumed in the short and long term. Is there an invariant relationship that transcribes that tripartite relationship onto patterns of food consumption? There may already be data that can confirm or deny that.

These are my thoughts and they are really just ways of allowing me to try and understand some very, very complex issues. Finally, I will just mention what might be crucial features to keep in mind. One is the impact of nutrition on the system. We are living in a world in which various novel food commodities are being diffused into our food supply. They carry with them different sorts of sensory delights and different sorts of metabolic properties. It seems to me that our biological systems are being placed under rather severe demands to cope with this wide variety and inconsistent mixture of food commodities.

Second, as I have mentioned before, there are semantic issues to clear up. What do we want to mean by palatability and preference? We have to settle this semantic issue before we can even start to anchor those terms in objective indices.

It would be nice if there were a simple algorithm that we could all carry around with us that would explain fully what happens in this psychobiological system and how it confers characteristics on weight disorders, but I think that is absolutely unrealistic. I don't think there is such an algorithm, and I don't think we should continue to look for it. What seems to me to be appropriate is that everybody should have some sort of concept with which they can begin to understand any particular individual pattern, whatever it might be. Then we would be armed intellectually with conceptualizations, theories, and hypothetical constructs to enable us to understand a complex system.

General Discussion: Part V

HARRY KISSILEFF, *Chair*

DR. BARBARA J. ROLLS (*Johns Hopkins University School of Medicine, Baltimore, MD*): Dr. Blundell's comments on sensory-specific satiety need a response. We have obviously never meant to imply that sensory-specific satiety is satiety, that you stop eating just because of changes in sensory experience. Sensory-specific satiety takes place in the context of all the other factors that go on in the regulation of food intake. Changing hedonic response to a food is something that's very real and that occurs during a meal. It does help to limit the intake of particular foods within a meal, and perhaps it limits selection extending into the next meal. So although it is real, it is very much a short-term effect.

DR. ANTHONY SCLAFANI (*Brooklyn College, CUNY, Brooklyn, NY*): My question is related to that point. You report that your data with the bulimics demonstrate that bulimics don't seem to show sensory-specific satiety. My question is, What in the data suggests that it was a deficit in sensory-specific satiety rather than a deficit in alliesthesia? As Allen Geliebter said the other day, perhaps bulimics have larger stomachs or perhaps they're not getting the same type of postingestive feedback cues. How can you distinguish between sensory-specific satiety and, say, alliesthesia?

DR. ROLLS: One of the distinguishing features of these two conditions is the time course. Alliesthesia, when you look carefully at the literature, doesn't occur for some time. It's a postabsorptive effect; it, by definition, depends on the internal state. We are seeing our biggest effects with sensory-specific satiety two minutes after the end of a meal. I think that the alliesthesia work needs to be done over again in eating disorders. Someone needs to look at what happens when straight sweet solution is given to bulimics — how it changes the internal state in bulimics. That has never been done.

DR. LINDA BARTOSHUK (*Pierce Foundation, New Haven, CT*): Yes it has. Judy Rodin and I did the Cabanac experiment with bulimics, and I can tell you that the Cabanac effect, that is, the reduction in perceived pleasantness of sugar after a sugar load, is reduced in bulimia, and it's extremely drastic.

DR. MICHEL CABANAC (*Université Laval, Quebec, Canada*): Along with Stylianos Nicolaidis, we coined the word alliesthesia, which means changed sensation, in order to avoid the long phrase "a given stimulus can be felt as pleasant or unpleasant according to." At the beginning it was meant to be used only for the thermal sensation where it is obvious and very easily reproducible. Now I am convinced that you have shown something new, sensory-specific satiety, that is a special case of alliesthesia. There is organic support for this, because Dr. LeBlanc in Quebec has shown that when you chew foods and spit them out, you obtain satiety just out of this chewing and sham feeding, comparable to what Dr. Mook or Dr. Sclafani obtain. Therefore, it's probably a special case of alliesthesia, but it deserves to keep its name. It is not necessarily a postabsorptive phenomenon. On the contrary, we have shown with Fantino that alliesthesia is preabsorptive and that the most potent signal for changing this elementary stimulus from pleasant to unpleasant is intraduodenal concentration. Whether it is nutritious glucose or non-nutritious maltose, which is not absorbed, is irrelevant. The concentration is the signal that might be relevant to those, such as Sclafani

424

or Mook, who study direct ingestion within the stomach. This may very well be the source of either sensation, perceived sensations, or nervous nonaversive signals.

DR. ROLLS: I have written a number of reviews now where I have distinguished the two. You can keep calling sensory-specific satiety negative alliesthesia, but we prefer to think of it as a distinct phenomenon. In relation to the experiments using just chewing and spitting out, we have done experiments like that; we do get the effects. We prefer to use foods with virtually no calories to look at this because chewing and spitting out is very aversive and you get a decrease in hedonic response. You don't know whether it's because the people just don't like doing it. You get sensory-specific satiety with foods with virtually no energy, but you don't get alliesthesia with foods with virtually no energy. We wanted to emphasize the sensory properties in calling it sensory-specific satiety, and also we're doing honor to LeMagnen, who defined sensory-specific satiety.

DR. FRANCE BELLISLE (*Université Pierre et Marie Curie, Paris*): There's a very important difference, I believe, between the concepts of alliesthesia and sensory-specific satiety the way I understand them. You get sensory-specific satiety after you have ingested a given amount of a certain food with certain sensory qualities, but you don't overeat the food. You just eat a little of it or more if you feel like it. The way I understand the method for inducing alliesthesia, however, is to administer a glucose load that is aversive.

DR. CABANAC: Not with temperature. Glucose has nothing to do with alliesthesia in temperature.

DR. HARRY KISSILEFF (*St. Luke's–Roosevelt Hospital, New York*): Maybe it would be helpful to define the operations that produce sensory-specific satiety and the operations that produce alliesthesia. I think Dr. Bellisle was saying that Dr. Cabanac originally demonstrated alliesthesia for glucose by intubating a glucose solution that was not tasted.

DR. BELLISLE: Even if the subjects take it by mouth, most of them find that aversive; it's an aversive experience.

DR. KISSILEFF: However, in that case they don't develop a negative aversion for something that was not intubated, like a salt solution for example. Is that correct? In sensory-specific satiety, they're eating a certain food until they feel satiated, and then they're asked to rate the pleasantness of eating that food or some other food. The operations are similar; actually I'm not sure how different they are. We need to establish a committee on terminology to report at the next meeting.

DR. TIMOTHY WALSH (*New York State Psychiatric Institute, New York*): The question I had was about the bulimic experiment of Dr. Hetherington's in which the patients, after the larger preload, clearly overate. To what degree would the patients have rated that overconsumption as a binge, and did they purge afterwards? My question is about the possible significance of vomiting in these kinds of sequences and experiments.

DR. MARION HETHERINGTON (*National Institute of Mental Health, Bethesda, MD*): That is an excellent point. At the end of the three experiments, we conducted an interview with all of the subjects. Included in the interview was the question "Did you consider your intake during the experiment to have been overeating, did you consider that the eating had been a binge, and then subsequently did you void the food by whatever method you use, usually self-induced vomiting?" What we found was that after they overate, after the high-caloric preload, only 4 in 10 subjects that had been tested subsequently considered that a binge and then went on to void the food. After the preloads that were low caloric, 2 out of 10 and 3 out of 10 considered their intake to have been a binge and they went on to vomit, so there was no significant difference in the frequency of binging. However, they had considered their intake to have been overeating, and 4 of 10 considered their intake to have been a binge which they then voided.

DR. WALSH: So I guess it would suggest that whether they vomit or not the abnormality is there.

DR. HETHERINGTON: Yes, I think so, but it needs to be tested further.

LYNN EDLUND-NEZIN (*Albert Einstein College of Medicine, New York*): I had a question for Drs. Rolls and Hetherington about the stimuli they used for that particular experiment. It was confusing to me to evaluate the subjects' choices by bringing in some of the other aspects of culture; for instance, you used a food in the low calorie situation that is stereotypically a dieter's food and "safe." You used a food in the high-calorie situation that has a very different sensory quality to it. It was crispy and creamy and salty and not at all bland and not unitextural. It was also presented in a fashion that would be very easy for someone to exercise portion control, because each portion was an individual cracker with a piece of cheese on it. I had difficulty with the lack of comparability outside of the caloric differences in those two food choices, and I wondered if you thought about that.

DR. HETHERINGTON: First, as a comment on the aspects of texture and taste, the subjects for these studies were selected on the basis of liking cottage cheese and cheese and crackers equally. If they didn't like one or other of the foods they weren't included in the study. In answer to your question about portion size and availability of food, you must remember that in the third experiment, we controlled how much they consumed by giving them a fixed amount of food. So we weren't giving them the option to choose how much they wanted to eat in that situation. Barbara, do you want to comment on that?

DR. ROLLS: Only that the question of what one chooses as "safe" or "dangerous" is something that needs to be explored more. We are going to be continuing this line of work, and certainly our choices in the future will be different. This was a first pass; we were just trying out what we thought would be quite clear-cut and we wanted to use the same food group, dairy.

DR. ALLAN GELIEBTER (*St. Luke's–Roosevelt Hospital, New York*): I have a question for Linda Bartoshuk and Adam Drewnowski. Linda, in your fascinating talk you said that an animal does not use pure taste to discriminate macronutrients. I am wondering whether animals use texture perception to select macronutrients? I mention this in light of Adam's talk that texture may play an important role.

DR. BARTOSHUK: Animals can use any cue they can get, and they *will* use any cue they can get. The point I was trying to make is that logically when you're trying to apportion where the cue is coming from, you really have to know that it can't be coming from the protein and the fat nor from most carbohydrates. However, I do think any conceivable difference that is detectable will be used and in fact will be learned if it is in the animal's interest to do so. I think that is a really good point.

DR. ADAM DREWNOWSKI (*University of Michigan, Ann Arbor, MI*): I want to add one more point to this and that is that the perception of sugar and preferences for sugar can be abstracted from one system to another. Preferences for sweetness, say in a liquid food system, are comparable in the same subject to their preferences for sugar in solid foods. But preferences for fat are very much dependent on texture and to a larger extent system-specific, as though fat was the property of the food itself. So the preferences for fat in one system need not imply that the same person would prefer fat in another system, and in fact there are differences. Typically people prefer higher levels of fat in solid food than in liquid food, whereas the level of preference for sweetness is the same. So I would agree with Linda Bartoshuk here that sweetness has a more direct relation to nutrition and can be abstracted from different food systems. Fat I'm not sure about. Maybe it cannot be, and we do rely on textural use for it.

DR. PAUL ROZIN (*University of Pennsylvania, Philadelphia, PA*): I have a comment that takes this into the cultural context of eating. Remember, sugar is an additive. That is, people add sugar; they adjust the sweetness of foods. They tend not to do that with fat. Therefore, people have a different relationship to sugar because it is something more under their control in the meal.

DR. DONNA LARSON (*Mental Health Center of Boulder County, Longmont, CO*): I have a question about the two-year-olds in the study, about how the affect was not associated yet with olfactory sense. There is a great increase of suspiciousness toward food between the ages of two and four. Is that the same age that the olfactory sense is beginning to be associated with affect?

DR. ROZIN: The answer to that is roughly yes, but the data on both of these points are minimal. For example, there is a recent study done by Hillary Schmidt and Beck, Beecham, and Bonell suggesting that very young children of less than one are responding somewhat negatively to decay odor. The previous literature indicated that decay odors, such as the odors of cheese and so on, were not negative to children until somewhere between three and seven years, depending on the study.

DR. LARSON: I'm probably ignorant of all the previous studies that have been done, but I don't hear much about the visual sense coming into play in food. We spend all kinds of effort trying to make certain things attractive. It accounts for some of the variety when we serve, of course, to put different colors into everything we're eating or serve on different colored dishes.

DR. ROLLS: It's certainly not been ignored, although we haven't yet gotten into visual cues in eating disorders. Katherine Halmi, Jim Gibbs, and the Cornell group have looked at the presence or absence of visual cues and how they affect consumption of a liquid diet. I presume they'll be presenting some of these data later.

DR. DAVID BOOTH (*University of Birmingham, Birmingham, U.K.*): I would like to return to the sensory-specific satiety and alliesthesia distinction, because it is such a basic issue. We have heard a lot about it this morning, and this audience should not go away with the idea that the data are muddy. It seems to me that what is happening has been demonstrated for more than a decade. The Rolls and the Cabanac data make it absolutely clear and are supported by Wooley's data in the early 1970s and some data of our own. We have satiating or nauseating manipulations that are acting postingestionally that have very general effects on the pleasantness of foods, the preference for foods, and the acceptance for foods, and tend to suppress satiety across the board. That's one big effect. We also have found that the food that has just been eaten becomes less appealing. As Barbara said today, you get tired of it; you get bored with it; you get less interested in eating it. You are genuinely satiated by it, and that is a food-specific phenomenon, not a foods-general one, specific to the food you have recently been eating. The distinction is demonstrated in that the tasted glucose load produces effects on sweet water ratings, as Cabanac showed and we showed, which are both sensory specific and postingestionally general. Cabanac showed that odor pleasantness is not suppressed, for example, by a meal-satiety load.

My second and briefer point is that I would suggest that the data indicate that this is not a sensation change and not a sensory change. The perception of sweetness is not changed: What is changed is the reaction specific to that stimulus. To other food stimuli, the alliesthesia is not a change in sensation, it is a change in reaction to the food sensations.

DR. KISSILEFF: I think that is a very important point. It sounds also as though you are saying David, correct me if I'm wrong, that the two conditions are actually pretty similar and may be operating on a common mechanism, would you agree to that?

DR. BOOTH: They're both satiety, but one is by getting tired of the food you have just been eating, the other is satiety by being filled up or nauseated.

DR. KISSILEFF: I believe you have data showing that if you give animals a protein load, they will show satiety for flavor that was paired with protein, but not satiety for flavor paired with carbohydrates. So it's a postingestive-originating satiety, but yet it's sensory specific. So again, what is the distinction?

DR. BOOTH: There is a phenomenon that I notoriously call conditioned satiety, and that is food specific also, but it is also equally and just as much specific to an internal state. I don't know if Dr. Cabanac still holds to this, but he did initially suggest that maybe the post-ingestional glucose satiety was specific to sweet tastes or specific to carbohydrates or something like that. Certainly I'm more convinced by his evidence that the salt-induced alliesthesia is specific to water and thirst because of the salt–water connection. We have had other suggestions in this meeting that there are sweetness–energy deprivation connections. I personally think that is an open question so this issue is muddying discussion because I have an uncertain position. I don't think the data tell us yet whether sweetness is an unpleasant taste preference. Sweetness preference is a carbohydrate-specific appetite, whether learned or unlearned we don't know yet. We have an unlearned salt appetite, and we have learned protein-specific appetite. The protein appetites are not to protein taste, they're to any arbitrary flavor that is provided which repairs the protein need. Liking for that flavor is then tied to not only the flavor but also to the protein need. However, that is a third food-specific phenomenon that is separate from the food-general phenomenon and separate from the recent-eating-induced, food-specific phenomenon.

DR. ROLLS: I just want to reiterate why we say sensory, but then I'm going to go on and qualify that. It occurs very rapidly, this hedonic change, and the time course then shows that over the hour after consumption the pleasantness changes come back up toward baseline, so two minutes after eating is where the biggest change occurs. You get the changes with foods with virtually no calories in them. You get these sorts of changes just between foods with, for example, different textures. You get bigger intake of three different shapes of pasta than just one shape of pasta, for example. But if you read what I've written on sensory-specific satiety, you will see that I then go on to question the sensory part of this. We took that name, as I've already said, from LeMagnen. I'm giving him credit for his earlier work, but I don't think we know whether it is cognitive specific satiety. We are working with humans. People know that they already have had what they have desired of a particular food, and we can't get that out of our experiments at this point. We have not yet tried to separate cognitive versus sensory.

DR. CABANAC: I wish to ask David Booth to add complementary information on the distinction that he makes between the response and the sensation.

DR. BOOTH: The sensation of the intensity of the flavor of the food, as I think you just quoted, may change very, very transiently but that isn't what is explaining the lack of interest in the food. So food-specific or stimulus-specific satiety, whether cognitively mediated or not, is possibly better terminology, but I accept that we originally had the word sensory used. It's okay as long as we don't think it is the sensations that change. The sensations we are referring to relate how strong the sweetness is and are the sensations that the psychophysicists rate. The food scientists and indeed the academic psychophysicists talk about sensory processes that are being monitored by these conscious verbalizations of the sensations. Now the response, if it is associated with a subjective experience, is often associated with affects or hedonics. I am only using what I take other people to be using as a distinction between physical sensations like tastes, and even fullness of the stomach, and affective emotional or active and behavioral response to the situation. I suggest the data are quite clear that the sweetness sensation is not changing your present ratings. It is the affect, and I would say the tendency to eat the food is changing.

DR. CABANAC: Okay, but then we are facing another semantic problem. Not being trained as a psychologist, I looked at the dictionary when I started to be interested in this field, and I was quite confused. Therefore I started to use sensation as the multidimensional experience aroused in your consciousness, which includes qualitative, quantitative, and affective dimensions of the experience. That would include what David calls the response, whereas while I used response only for the behavioral or possibly for the oral response.

DR. BOOTH: Words themselves don't matter. All that matters is in using the words we understand what phenomena we are talking about. So if we want to use sensation to mean broadly subjective experience, fine. Let's understand that we are not referring to a change in the sensation of sweetness, we are referring to a change in the *reaction* to the sensation of sweetness or the other sensations of the food that we just ate.

DR. KISSILEFF: Classically, what Dr. Cabanac is calling sensation was probably called perception, sensation being just the naked stimulus quality and perception being how it is interpreted by the brain. Maybe Dr. Rozin could comment on that.

DR. ROZIN: That is correct, but the affective part does not have a clear place in the sort of array that we are talking about. What you are concerned about is a not very well-stated distinction in the field. The perception–sensation distinction is independent of whether you are going to load affect into perception.

DR. DOUGLAS G. MOOK (*University of Virginia, Charlottesville, VA*): I have two rude questions, so I'm going to address them to the whole panel. First of all, let me present a little bit of data. It sticks in my mind that a paper was published a few years ago that made predictions about hedonic judgments on the basis of set-point theory, but nevertheless obtained data opposite to those predicted and interpreted them in terms of set-point theory. Those were my data. The authors were able to do that by appealing to all the escape routes that come up when hedonic data do not match our preconceptions. The problem is that these objections seem to me to apply with equal force when they do. Maybe the subjects were denying; maybe they were self presenting; maybe they were confusing hedonic judgments with the onset of nausea. I have some data like that in two prepubescent subjects that I had at the time. Maybe they are confusing how good something tastes with how much they intend to eat, or maybe they are making theory-driven judgments about how good the fluid ought to taste under the circumstances. So my first question is, How can we be sure that we are studying a hedonic perception uncontaminated by other variables that might affect hedonic judgments?

My second question is, If we agree that what we have are two response measures, one the hedonic judgments and the other the intake, and that sometimes these can be moved in the same direction by manipulation, do we have any grounds for saying that the subjects eat less because the food tastes less good? That's a statement about causality, and it seems to me that what we have are data that remain stubbornly correlational.

DR. BARTOSHUK: I agree completely with the first part of your comment, and one of my pet gripes is papers that claim to have a hedonic change with no sensory control. You absolutely cannot draw any conclusions about hedonic change. We have not proved that the experience stays stable. Almost nobody does that; they just simply assume it, and occasionally you do it and are confounded. You find out that there was a sensory change, and that is very interesting.

DR. DREWNOWSKI: I agree with Linda that we must use sensory controls always. We don't mention here that hedonic ratings have a double life, because on the one hand they are being used routinely in research and taste psychophysics to denote pleasantness or pleasure, and on the other hand they are used in consumer psychology where they are called the affective component of attitude. This influence of attitude, especially attitudes related to weight and dieting on hedonic preferences, has really not been examined in great detail, and it should be. And I think we are going to be surprised just how much hedonic ratings are colored, in fact, by attitudes.

DR. ROLLS: Now I think, particularly in persons with eating disorders, trying to assess any of this objective response is extremely difficult. They are notorious liars. I was trying to be more tactful. They often don't tell the truth, and all we can do is try. You have to look and see whether what you're getting is consistent and whether it makes sense, whether it relates to food intake. One thing that strikes me in relation to looking at the hedonic changes in food intake, for example, is the data that Marion Hetherington presented on the anorexics. I think they show how the hedonic ratings can be overridden. Here you have the anorexics showing very very strong sensory-specific satiety, yet their beliefs about food completely override that hedonic change, and they go for the food that they know is "safe" regardless of this hedonic response.

DR. ROZIN: I think we all know that eating is multi-determined and preference is multi-determined. However, I believe it is generally true in situations, at least in humans, in which economic constraints are not at work, that liking of the flavor is the single best predictor of what people will choose. So it's not purely correlation. If you know that information ahead of time and you give people a free choice and look at their initial choice, it is, as far as we know, the best predictor, but it does not account for that much of the variance.

DR. ROLLS: Yes, that is what we usually find, Paul. I was citing the anorexics as an exception. Normally we do find that these changes in rating relate to subsequent consumption.

DR. ANTHONY SCLAFANI (*Brooklyn College, CUNY, Brooklyn, NY*): In relation to that, I tried to make two points in my talk. Number one was that preferences change so you could load the situation so that an initially highly unpreferred diet becomes preferred with experience. So if you just do a short-term test, you cannot predict what the long-term intake is going to be, nor can you predict what the long-term preference is. Second, there is at least one unusual situation where the most preferred food of two foods is the food that is eaten less by the rat. This gets back to the issue of preference and palatability. There are conditions under which what initially was the least preferred of the foods comes to be the most consumed.

DR. BOOTH: Added to the list of the things that need to be done and could be done should be finding out what is in fact controlling this response, whatever it is, be it the preference or be it the intake. If you're getting exceptions, then we need to characterize what it is in the bulimic that is actually peculiar about response for that food, be it ratings, be it intake, or whatever. So determining the influences where there are inconsistencies, or indeed characterizing them in full detail even where there are consistencies, is important.

DR. BARRY KEATING (*Bureau of Applied Research, New York*): I would like to make a comment on the use of sensation and perception. It seems to me that most uses of sensation should be perception by standard psychological definitions here. I think if you go back to S. S. Stevens you will see that you get precise definitions of sensation and perception and that he includes affect in perception, not sensation. There are a lot of different kinds of affect and not just one scale, not just a hedonistic scale.

Let me give you an example in market research. A celebrated failure of market research on Coca-Cola and Pepsi-Cola took place here in the last couple of years. When you do a plain taste test and people don't know what they're tasting, Pepsi-Cola wins over Coca-Cola (Classic Coca-Cola now) very readily, because Pepsi-Cola is sweeter. But when Coca-Cola tried to change their mixture to make it sweeter, it was a very spectacular failure of the company because people want the bottle, they want the perception. It isn't the taste; it's the perception. I think with adults and with older children it is always tricky unless you have a very narrowly psychophysical experimental paradigm that will elicit sensations rather than perceptions.

Hunger and Satiety in Anorexia and Bulimia Nervosa[a]

KATHERINE A. HALMI, SUZANNE SUNDAY,
ANGELA PUGLISI, AND PEGGY MARCHI

*Department of Psychiatry
New York Hospital — Westchester Division
White Plains, New York 10605*

Cognitive distortions are common in anorexia and bulimia nervosa. Garner and Bemis[1] described some of these distortions along with effective cognitive therapy techniques. The possibility that distortions in the perceptions of hunger and satiety may occur and be related to the eating behavior in anorexia and bulimia nervosa is a sparsely investigated idea. Grossman[2] emphasized that satiety is a relative rather than an absolute phenomenon and takes hedonic as well as nutritive considerations into account. Blundell[3] postulated that perceptions of hunger and satiety are complex and are formed from interactions between the internal physiological state and environmental conditions. Booth[4] stressed the role of conditioned (learned) components in hunger and satiety responses.

Careful documentation of hunger and satiety responses in anorexia and bulimia nervosa patients under standardized conditions is a necessary first step toward detecting the relationship of these perceptions to the actual eating behavior. In this study eating disorder patients and control persons recorded or tracked hunger and satiety perceptions before, during, and after an experimental meal. Examples of the generated hunger and satiety curves were published[5] and showed distinct differences between the subgroups of eating disorder patients and control persons. A careful scrutiny of these hunger and satiety perceptions provoked a series of questions that form the basis of this investigation. (1) Do the eating disorder patients and control persons begin and end the meal on different levels of hunger and satiety? (2) How do eating-related variables such as amount consumed, rate of consumption, palatability, and degree of restrained eating influence hunger and satiety levels in eating disorder patients and controls? (3) How do psychological variables such as preoccupation with food, urge to eat, willpower to stop eating, and satisfaction influence hunger and satiety levels or perceptions in eating disorder patients and controls?

METHODS

Hunger and satiety responses were examined in three types of eating disorder patients: anorectic-restrictors (AN-R), anorectic bulimics (AN-B), normal weight bulimics (NW-B), and control (C) persons. The clinical characteristics of the eating disorder

[a] This study was supported by National Institutes of Health Grant number 5-KO2-MHOO516-O4 and a grant from General Foods, both to Dr. Halmi.

TABLE 1. Clinical Characteristics of Eating Disorder Patients and Controls[a]

Patient Group	Age	Admission BMI[b]	Discharge BMI	Admission Weight (kg)	Discharge Weight (kg)
Anorectic restrictors $n = 32$	18.31 ± 6.08	15.30 ± 1.82	19.41 ± 0.71	39.35 ± 5.59	50.70 ± 5.17
Anorectic bulimics $n = 28$	22.00 ± 4.72	16.42 ± 2.24	19.73 ± 0.88	43.31 ± 7.57	51.98 ± 5.81
Normal-weight bulimics $n = 29$	22.34 ± 6.34	20.59 ± 2.24	20.87 ± 1.61	55.20 ± 5.29	55.91 ± 3.41
Controls $n = 16$	20.66 ± 3.50	20.77 ± 1.96	21.45 ± 1.75	56.14 ± 5.47	56.21 ± 4.55

[a] All values are given as mean ± SD.
[b] BMI = weight in kg divided by height in m².

patients and control participants are presented in TABLE 1. Anorectic-restrictors are those patients who lose weight only by restricting their food intake and/or by exercising. Anorectic bulimics are emaciated and not only engage in severe dieting, but have periods of binging and purging behavior. All eating disorder patients met DSM-III/R criteria for anorexia nervosa or bulimia nervosa. Control subjects were obtained from the local community and had no history of eating disorders, psychiatric illness, or chronic medical disorders. All subjects were female.

Patients were tested upon admission to an inpatient eating disorder unit and the anorectics again several weeks after weight restoration. Normal controls and normal weight (NW) bulimic patients were tested at a similar time interval. All patients were within a normal weight range, eating normally and free of any binging or purging behavior for at least four weeks at the time of the second examination.

All participants fasted after midnight until the following morning test, which occurred at 10:00 AM. They all received Sustacal, a liquid nutritionally balanced food containing 1 cal/ml. The subjects controlled the rate of intake by pressing a button that controlled a small peristaltic pump. The food was delivered to the participant's mouth via a straw. The subject also controlled the length of the meal and told the examiner when she was finished. Every two minutes the subject made ratings on 10-cm visual analogue scales for hunger and fullness. These ratings began eight minutes before the meal and continued during the meal and for fourteen minutes after the completion of the meal. The participants were also asked to make a taste rating for the Sustacal before and after the test meal using a similar visual analogue scale. On both the pre- and posttreatment testing occasions, two pairs of experimental meals were conducted. On one presentation the reservoir of food was hidden from the subject's view and on the other it was uncovered and the participant could view the amount of food she was taking. The order of presentations was randomized for each pair.

Patients and controls completed the Herman/Polivy[6] restrained eating scale the day before the experimental meal. Immediately after the meal all participants rated four questions on willpower to stop eating, satisfaction at the end of the meal, urge to eat, and preoccupation with thoughts of food on five-point Likert ratings (one = none and five = extreme).

Hunger and fullness curves were graphed for each patient and have been described in a previous publication.[5] Differences between the eating disorder subgroups and controls in hunger and fullness levels at the beginning of the meal, end of the meal, and twelve minutes after the end of the meal were analyzed by analysis of variance (ANOVA) and pairwise contrasts. The effect of amount consumed, rate of consumption, palatability, and degree of restrained eating on hunger and satiety levels was determined by hierarchical regression analyses,[7] in addition to ANOVAs and pairwise contrasts. One of the primary questions we were interested in was the interrelationship between variables; that is, how one variable affected other variables. The statistical procedure of hierarchical regression analysis provides a means to examine such interactions. Likewise, the relationship of body mass index (BMI), urge to eat, preoccupation with food, willpower to stop eating, and satisfaction on hunger and satiety levels was analyzed with a hierarchical regression analysis as well as with ANOVAs and pairwise contrasts. All pairwise contrasts had alpha levels adjusted to 0.05 using the Bonferroni procedure.

Analyses were made separately for the covered and uncovered conditions of the food reservoir. The results were similar in almost all of the analyses. The few differences that did exist were inconsistent and not meaningful. Therefore, results presented here are on one condition, the uncovered condition.

RESULTS

The analysis of hunger levels (TABLE 2) revealed a significant effect of diagnosis $[F(3,75) = 4.83, p = 0.004]$ treatment $[F(1,75) = 9.3, p = 0.003]$, and before/after meal ratings $[F(1,75) = 113.88, p < 0.001]$. There were no significant interactions. The anorectics (AN-R and AN-B) had significantly lower hunger ratings than the other two groups (NW-B and C) before the meal pretreatment $[F(1,75) = 6.32, p < 0.05]$, after the meal pretreatment $[F(1,75) = 5.86, p < 0.05]$ and before the meal post-treatment $[F(1,75) = 5.66, p < 0.05]$.

Satiety levels (TABLE 3) were significantly different across diagnosis $[F(3,75) = 4.22, p < 0.008]$, treatment $[F(1,75) = 6.27, p = 0.01]$ and before/after meal $[F(1,75) = 192.25, p < 0.001]$. Again there were no significant interactions. The anorectic-restrictors had significantly higher satiety ratings than did the NW-bulimics and controls before the meal pretreatment $[F(1,75) = 5.61, p < 0.05]$ and post-treatment $[F(1,75) = 9.95, p < 0.05]$ and after the meal pretreatment $[F(1,75) = 4.2, p < 0.05]$.

Slopes for the hunger and satiety curves from eight minutes before to the beginning of the meal, during the meal, and at the end of the meal for 12 subsequent minutes were calculated for all diagnostic groups (TABLE 4). There were few significant differences. Slopes were calculated for each subject pre- and post-treatment using regression analysis.

The hunger slopes during the meal differed only by diagnosis $[F(3,75) = 3.1, p = 0.03]$ and by time across the meal $[F(2, 150) = 69.79 p < 0.01]$. The AN-R group as compared with all others had a lower decrease in hunger during the meal pretreatment $[F(1,75) = 4.93, p < 0.05]$. Only time across the meal had a significant effect for the satiety slopes $[F(2,150) = 73.86, p < 0.001]$. The AN-R group showed a steeper satiety slope before the meal post-treatment than did the other groups $[F(1,75) = 12.6, p < 0.05]$.

TABLE 5 depicts palatability ratings of the Sustacal. There was a significant effect of diagnosis $[F(3,73) = 2.93, p = 0.04]$. Subjects ratings decreased after the meal $[F(1,73) = 6.25, p = 0.02]$, and there were significant treatment by diagnosis $[F(3,73) = 3.69, p = 0.02]$ and treatment by before/after meal $[F(1,73) = 4.31, p = 0.04]$ interactions on the before-meal ratings. After treatment AN-Rs found the meal to be less palatable than did the others $[F(1,73) = 11.28, p < 0.05]$. Patients with a history of binging

TABLE 2. Hunger Levels[a]

	Anorectic-Restrictors (n = 32)	Anorectic-Bulimics (n = 28)	Normal-Weight Bulimics (n = 29)	Controls (n = 16)
Pretreatment				
Before meal	32.16 ± 30.24	42.36 ± 33.97	50.14 ± 30.68	57.13 ± 23.90
After meal	5.56 ± 7.41	10.75 ± 17.27	17.97 ± 21.85	18.75 ± 19.50
12 Minutes after meal	8.97 ± 12.59	17.89 ± 23.20	17.59 ± 21.28	21.00 ± 17.37
Post-treatment	(n = 26)	(n = 24)	(n = 21)	(n = 8)
Before meal	43.00 ± 23.56	46.58 ± 28.65	62.19 ± 23.10	60.88 ± 27.55
After meal	15.65 ± 14.85	17.63 ± 17.22	22.24 ± 19.78	22.38 ± 22.18
12 Minutes after meal	16.35 ± 16.35	22.83 ± 21.95	17.19 ± 15.66	20.00 ± 16.14

[a] Expressed as mean ± SD.

TABLE 3. Satiety Levels[a]

	Anorectic-Restrictors (n = 32)	Anorectic-Bulimics (n = 28)	Normal-Weight Bulimics (n = 29)	Controls (n = 16)
Pretreatment				
Before meal	46.28 ± 32.72	34.79 ± 31.15	28.28 ± 24.80	17.69 ± 12.23
After meal	85.97 ± 18.53	82.64 ± 19.19	71.00 ± 27.47	63.88 ± 22.53
12 Minutes after meal	78.69 ± 23.72	79.86 ± 20.64	70.86 ± 27.06	64.87 ± 18.51
Post-treatment	(n = 26)	(n = 24)	(n = 21)	(n = 8)
Before meal	38.42 ± 27.29	29.75 ± 22.62	13.71 ± 11.98	23.63 ± 19.85
After meal	70.12 ± 26.66	75.04 ± 23.00	65.71 ± 24.94	67.13 ± 27.18
12 Minutes after meal	70.54 ± 29.30	70.04 ± 25.02	69.29 ± 25.89	71.63 ± 17.14

[a] Expressed as mean ± SD.

TABLE 4. Slopes of Hunger and Satiety Curves[a]

Hunger/Satiety	Anorectic-Restrictors	Anorectic-Bulimics	Normal-Weight Bulimics	Controls
	($n = 32$)	($n = 28$)	($n = 29$)	($n = 16$)
Pretreatment Hunger				
Premeal	-0.26 ± 1.68	-0.0 ± 2.03	-0.13 ± 2.37	0.44 ± 1.18
During meal	-1.9 ± 1.90	-3.99 ± 4.93	-4.71 ± 4.69	-3.81 ± 2.64
Post meal	0.27 ± 0.85	0.45 ± 1.02	0.06 ± 1.12	0.38 ± 0.96
Pretreatment Satiety				
Premeal	0.78 ± 2.66	0.64 ± 3.53	0.46 ± 1.22	-0.08 ± 0.86
During meal	3.44 ± 4.0	5.65 ± 4.89	5.47 ± 5.9	4.48 ± 2.35
Post meal	-0.62 ± 4.5	-0.25 ± 0.65	0.01 ± 1.18	-0.32 ± 1.0
Post-treatment Hunger	($n = 26$)	($n = 24$)	($n = 21$)	($n = 8$)
Premeal	0.04 ± 1.36	0.26 ± 1.1	0.11 ± 0.92	0.57 ± 1.15
During meal	-3.7 ± 4.5	-3.02 ± 3.1	-5.17 ± 4.47	-4.13 ± 2.53
Post meal	-0.03 ± 0.76	0.64 ± 2.01	-0.30 ± 0.89	0.03 ± 1.24
Post-treatment Satiety				
Premeal	1.08 ± 1.89	0.13 ± 0.79	0.04 ± 0.9	-0.44 ± 1.21
During meal	4.3 ± 5.33	4.39 ± 3.37	6.86 ± 5.52	5.14 ± 2.89
Post meal	-0.08 ± 1.2	-0.44 ± 2.11	0.23 ± 0.97	0.24 ± 1.55

[a] Expressed as mean ± SD.

TABLE 5. Palatability and Restrained Eating[a]

Palatability	Anorectic-Restrictors	Anorectic-Bulimics	Normal-Weight Bulimics	Controls
Pretreatment	(n = 32)	(n = 28)	(n = 29)	(n = 16)
Before meal	42.56 ± 31.70	44.21 ± 26.63	57.10 ± 24.07	51.69 ± 23.66
After meal	38.91 ± 34.44	39.43 ± 27.4	45.79 ± 31.81	46.88 ± 22.91
Post-treatment	(n = 26)	(n = 24)	(n = 21)	(n = 8)
Before meal	27.96 ± 24.24	48.61 ± 26.96	60.48 ± 27.28	44.50 ± 21.67
After meal	31.96 ± 27.73	47.33 ± 28.06	57.76 ± 28.45	33.57 ± 11.00
		Restrained Eating		
Pretreatment	(n = 28)	(n = 22)	(n = 14)	(n = 14)
	9.39 ± 6.51	23.64 ± 26.96	24.57 ± 4.35	14.79 ± 5.21
Post-treatment	(n = 23)	(n = 21)	(n = 11)	
	14.52 ± 4.26	18.83 ± 4.63	17.18 ± 5.47	

[a] Mean ± SD.

TABLE 6. Amount and Rate of Liquid Meal Consumed[a]

	Anorectic-Restrictors	Anorectic-Bulimics	Normal-Weight Bulimics	Controls
Amount (ml)				
Pretreatment	($n = 32$)	($n = 28$)	($n = 29$)	($n = 16$)
	270.94 ± 278.05	263.75 ± 212.95	222.24 ± 118.36	294.38 ± 158.33
Post-treatment	($n = 26$)	($n = 24$)	($n = 21$)	($n = 8$)
	182.69 ± 107.95	278.12 ± 245.92	299.52 ± 242.39	318.13 ± 130.55
Rate (ml/min)				
Pretreatment	($n = 32$)	($n = 28$)	($n = 29$)	($n = 16$)
	20.09 ± 16.23	24.68 ± 11.43	29.28 ± 13.8	23.36 ± 9.40
Post-treatment	($n = 26$)	($n = 24$)	($n = 21$)	($n = 8$)
	21.75 ± 13.0	22.17 ± 12.81	35.08 ± 28.42	30.82 ± 11.44

[a] Mean ± SD.

TABLE 7. Anorectic-Restrictors' Variation of Responses to Test Meal

Number	Amount Consumed	Before Meal		
		Hunger	Satiety	Palatability
	>800cc			
n = 4	820	90	17	47
	820	56	2	99
	1000	94	4	54
	930	76	5	96
Mean	892.5	79.0	7.0	74.0
SD	88.5	17.2	6.8	27.3
	400–550cc			
n = 4	480	46	47	57
	520	92	5	96
	450	48	33	14
	420	78	1	72
Mean	467.5	66.0	21.5	59.8
SD	42.7	22.7	22.2	34.5
	<400cc			
n = 24				
Mean	134.6	18.7	57.0	34.5
SD	98.2	18.9	29.6	28.5

(AN-B and NW-B) found the meal more palatable than AN-Rs and Cs after treatment for both before- and after-meal ratings [$F(1,73) = 9.34$, $p < 0.05$; $F(1,73) = 8.61$, $p < 0.05$].

Restraint scores (TABLE 5) were obtained for control subjects only during the first testing period; therefore, two ANOVAs were performed on this data. In the pretreatment condition there was a significant effect of diagnosis [$F(3,74) = 9.91$, $p < 0.001$] with the patient groups (AN-R, AN-B, and NW-B) having higher restraint scores than the controls [$F(1,74) = 21.54$, $p < 0.05$]. The effects of treatment were examined only in the patients' restraint scores, which had declined post-treatment [$F(1,49) = 80.76$, $p < 0.001$].

The amount of meal consumed did not differ among diagnostic groups during pretreatment nor was there a significant effect of treatment (TABLE 6). However, the variation within groups was large. This was especially true of the AN-Rs during the pretreatment period. During the post-treatment phase, AN-Rs consumed significantly less than the other subjects ($F(1,75) = 5.44$, $p < 0.05$). The rate of meal consumption differed among groups only in the post-treatment period; the AN-Rs and AN-Bs had a slower rate compared with NW-Bs and Cs [$F(1,75) = 5.71$, $p < 0.05$].

The enormous variations in the amount of meal consumed by the AN-Rs and the relationship of the amount consumed to hunger and satiety levels and palatability are shown in TABLE 7. It appears that hunger and satiety levels may be significantly influenced by the amount of meal consumed and the palatability. Analyses for this possibility were made across all diagnostic groups.

Hierarchical regression analyses were used to determine the effect of palatability, amount consumed, rate of eating, and BMI on hunger and satiety levels. In each case the variable in question was entered first, diagnosis second, and the interaction of the variable and diagnosis third. There were no significant interaction effects between any of the above variables and diagnosis. During pretreatment, palatability accounted for 19% of the variance of before-meal hunger [$F(1,103)$ = 24.15, $p < 0.001$], 4% of variance of after-meal hunger [$F(1,103)$ = 4.25, $p < 0.04$], and 10.4% of the variance of before-meal satiety [$F(1,103)$ = 12.02, $p < 0.001$]. During post-treatment, palatability accounted for 21% of the variance of before-meal hunger [$F(1,76)$ = 20.16, $p < 0.001$] and 13.6% of the variance of before-meal satiety [$F(1,76)$ = 11.99, $p < 0.001$].

Amount of meal consumed during pretreatment accounted for 17.7% of the variance of before-meal hunger [$F(1,103)$ = 22.18, $p < 0.001$], 10.5% of the variance of before-meal satiety [$F(1,103)$ = 12.09, $p < 0.001$] and 5.8% of the variance of after-meal satiety [$F(1,103)$ = 12.09, $p < 0.05$]. Post-treatment, the amount of meal consumed accounted for 18.6% of the variance of before-meal hunger [$F(1,77)$ = 17.57, $p < 0.001$], 10.6% of the variance of before-meal satiety [$F(1,77)$ = 9.1, p = 0.003], 10.1% of the variance of after-meal satiety [$F(1,77)$ = 8.65, p = 0.004], and 5.7% of the variance of satiety 12 minutes after the meal [$F(1,77)$ = 4.7, p = 0.03].

Rate of eating during pretreatment only accounts for 12.3% of the variance of before-meal hunger [$F(1,103)$ = 14.49, $p < 0.001$]. During post-treatment, rate of eating accounts for 6.1% of the variance of before-meal satiety [$F(1,77)$ = 4.97, $p < 0.05$], 6.1% of the variance of after-meal satiety [$F(1,77)$ = 4.98, $p < 0.05$], and 5.9% of the variance of satiety 12 minutes after the meal [$F(1,77)$ = 4.81, $p < 0.05$]. The amount of time required to complete the meal did not affect hunger and satiety levels.

BMI during pretreatment accounted for 5.9% of the variance of before-meal hunger [$F(1,103)$ = 6.48, $p < 0.012$] and during post-treatment BMI accounted for 14.6% of the variance for before-meal hunger [$F(1,77)$ = 13.18, $p < 0.001$]. BMI during pretreatment accounted for 10% of the variance of before-meal satiety [$F(1,103)$ = 11.4, $p < 0.001$] and during post-treatment BMI accounted for 9.4% of the variance of *before-*meal satiety [$F(1,77)$ = 7.98, $p < 0.006$].

After-meal hunger and satiety levels during pretreatment periods and after-meal hunger levels during post-treatment periods were most strongly affected by before-meal levels of hunger and satiety. The variance accounted for, respectively, is 12.3% [$F(1,103)$ = 14.42, $p < 0.001$], 15% [$F(1,103)$ = 18.25, $p < 0.001$], and 18.6% [$F(1,77)$ = 7.28, $p < 0.009$].

In summary, palatability influences mainly before-meal levels of hunger and satiety. Amount of meal consumed is significantly related to both before-meal levels of hunger and satiety and after-meal levels of satiety. Rate of eating is significantly related to before-meal hunger pretreatment and before- and after-meal satiety levels post-treatment. BMI only effects before-meal hunger and satiety levels, which in turn strongly affect after-meal hunger and satiety levels. After-meal satiety levels are predominantly affected by before meal satiety levels, amount consumed, and rate of eating. Anorectic subjects (AN-R and AN-B) reported lower levels of hunger before and after the meal pretreatment. In addition to the altered hunger levels, AN-Rs also showed higher satiety levels before and after the meal. After treatment the anorectics (AN-R and AN-B) still displayed lower hunger ratings before the meal and the AN-Rs had steeper satiety ratings after the meal. Only after treatment did the groups differ in their palatability ratings; AN-R gave lower ratings while the bulimics (AN-B and NW-B) gave higher ratings.

There was no difference between eating disorder subgroups in the amount of change in hunger and the satiety levels over a meal. However, considerable variations occurred within the groups. There was an effect of diagnosis on change in hunger and satiety levels over treatment only in the before-meal satiety levels [$F(3,74)$ = 3.64, p = 0.017].

Restrained eating had no effect on hunger and satiety levels or amount consumed in this experimental meal paradigm. [Before-meal hunger 3.6% of the variance, $F(1,76)$

= 2.88, NS; after-meal hunger 3.6% of the variance, $F(1,76) = 2.86$, NS; before-meal satiety 2.2% of the variance, $F(1,76) = 1.68$, NS; after meal satiety 1.2% of the variance, $F(1,76) = 0.93$, NS; amount consumed 0.9% of the variance, $F(1,76) = 0.67$, NS].

The above results present the variables that affect hunger and satiety levels. The question then arises whether differences between diagnostic groups in these levels are present over and above the effects of palatability, amount consumed, and rate of eating. The specific findings that follow show that the eating disorder subgroups were distinguished primarily by their differences in before-meal perceptions of hunger and satiety both in the pretreatment and post-treatment periods. Hierarchical regression analysis showed diagnostic group differences were present during pretreatment in before-meal hunger over and above amount consumed [$F(3,100) = 4.05$, $p < 0.01$] and in before-meal satiety over and above palatability [$F(3,100) = 3.44$, $p < 0.05$]. During post-treatment, hierarchical regression analysis showed diagnostic group differences were present in before-meal satiety over and above amount consumed [$F(3,74) = 3.89$, $p < 0.05$], and rate of eating [$F(3,74) = 3.82$, $p < 0.05$].

After-meal perceptions of hunger and satiety for the most part do not discriminate the eating disorder subgroups. Hierarchical regression analysis showed diagnostic group differences were present during pretreatment in after-meal hunger over and above before-meal palatability [$F(3,100) = 2.91$, $p < 0.05$] and after-meal palatability [$F(3,100) = 3.25$, $p < 0.05$] and in after-meal satiety over and above amount consumed [$F(3,100) = 5.13$, $p < 0.05$]. During post-treatment, diagnostic group differences were not present over and above the cognitive factors discussed above that influence after-meal perceptions of hunger and satiety.

Other cognitions or psychological variables related to ending a meal—urge to eat, preoccupation with food, willpower to stop eating, and satisfaction were rated by participants at the end of the experimental meal. The results are presented in TABLE 8. The day before the experimental meal participants rated the same cognitions related to ending a meal but for an imagined major meal of the day.

The effect of these cognitions after the experimental meal on hunger and satiety levels was analyzed by hierarchical regression analysis with the cognitions entered first, diagnosis second, and the interaction of the cognition and diagnosis third.

During pretreatment, urge to eat accounted for 42% of the variance of after-meal hunger [$F(1,102) = 73.77$, $p < 0.001$], 32.7% of the variance of hunger 12 minutes after the meal [$F(1,102) = 49.16$, $p < 0.01$], 15.5% of the variance of after-meal satiety [$F(1,102) = 18.69$, $p < 0.01$] and 10.1% of the variance of satiety 12 minutes after the meal [$F(1,101) = 11.36$, $p < 0.01$]. During post-treatment urge to eat accounted for 27.8% of the variance of after-meal hunger [$F(1,77) = 29.7$, $p < 0.01$], 22.1% of the variance of hunger 12 minutes after the meal [$F(1,77) = 21.82$, $p < 0.01$], 16.6% of the variance of after-meal satiety [$F(1,77) = 15.37$, $p < 0.01$] and 21% of the variance of satiety 12 minutes after the meal [$F(1,77) = 20.49$, $p < 0.01$].

Willpower to end the meal during pretreatment accounted for 5.8% of the variance of after-meal hunger [$F(1,102) = 6.31$, $p < 0.05$]. During post-treatment, willpower to end the meal accounted for 7.4% of the variance of after-meal hunger [$F(1,77) = 6.12$, $p < 0.05$] and 5.1% of the variance of hunger 12 minutes after meal [$F(1,77) = 4.11$, $p < 0.05$].

Preoccupation with food and satisfaction had little effect on hunger and satiety levels. The former accounted for 5.4% of the variance of after-meal hunger during pretreatment [$F(1,102) = 5.87$, $p < 0.05$] and 8.1% of the variance of after meal hunger during post-treatment [$F(1,77) = 6.83$, $p < 0.05$].

The analysis of the after-meal urge to eat revealed a significant diagnosis effect [$F(3,45) = 3.04$, $p < 0.05$] and a significant treatment by diagnosis interaction [$F(3,45) = 5.28$, $p = 0.003$]. Subjects' urge ratings were higher after the imagined meal [$F(1,45)$

TABLE 8. Cognitions Related to Eating at End of Meal

Diagnostic Group	Urge to Eat	Preoccupation with Food	Willpower to Stop	Satisfaction
Anorectic-Restrictor				
Pretreatment, $n = 31$	1.26 ± 0.51	2.13 ± 1.36	1.42 ± 0.76	3.16 ± 1.42
Post-treatment, $n = 26$	1.58 ± 0.70	1.65 ± 0.94	1.19 ± 0.40	3.08 ± 1.19
Anorectic-Bulimic				
Pretreatment, $n = 28$	1.75 ± 1.0	2.57 ± 1.10	2.04 ± 1.26	2.89 ± 1.29
Post-treatment, $n = 24$	1.79 ± 0.78	1.92 ± 1.06	1.75 ± 1.11	3.00 ± 1.09
Normal-Weight Bulimic				
Pretreatment, $n = 29$	2.09 ± 1.00	2.48 ± 1.21	1.93 ± 1.13	2.48 ± 0.99
Post-treatment, $n = 21$	1.76 ± 0.89	1.86 ± 0.91	1.48 ± 0.81	3.00 ± 1.18
Controls				
Pretreatment, $n = 16$	1.69 ± 0.87	1.69 ± 0.60	1.38 ± 0.72	2.50 ± 0.89
Post-treatment, $n = 8$	1.63 ± 0.74	1.63 ± 0.52	1.38 ± 0.52	2.63 ± 0.74

[a] Cognitions were rated on a five-point Likert Scale; 1 = none, 5 = extreme. Results expressed as mean ± SD.

= 9.27, p = 0.004]. AN-Rs had significantly lower urge to eat after the meal pretreatment for both the experimental meal and the imagined meal than did the other groups. [$F(1,45)$ = 6.32, $p < 0.05$, $F(1,45)$ = 9.11, $p < 0.05$]. Pretreatment NW-Bs had a higher urge to eat after the experimental meal than did the other subjects [$F(1,45)$ = 5.39, $p < 0.05$]. The two ratings of urge were not correlated in the pretreatment condition but were correlated post-treatment (TABLE 9).

Preoccupation with thoughts of food decreased after treatment [$F(1,45)$ = 8.33, p = 0.006]. The patients who binged (AN-B and NW-B) were more preoccupied with thoughts of food after the experimental meal before treatment than were the AN-R and controls [$F(1,45)$ = 3.58, $p < 0.05$]. Again the ratings after the experimental meal and after the imagined meal were correlated post-treatment but not pretreatment.

Willpower to stop eating was greater for the experimental meal than for the hypothetical meal [$F(1,44)$ = 5.44, p = 0.02]. The willpower necessary to stop eating decreased after treatment [$F(1,44)$ = 7.31, p = 0.01]. There were no differences between groups. The two measures of willpower were significantly correlated both pre- and post-treatment (TABLE 9).

After treatment the cognitive responses to the experimental meal appeared to be more like those to a typical meal in that a significant correlation was present in all the corresponding cognitive responses of the experimental and imagined typical meal (TABLE 9).

In summary the feeling of urge to eat is very strongly related to after-meal hunger; it accounts for 22% to 42% of the variance. Urge to eat is strongly related to after-meal satiety; it accounts for 10 to 21% of the variance. Willpower to end the meal is weakly associated with satiety after the meal and, along with preoccupation with food and satisfaction, is weakly associated with after-meal hunger. Pretreatment, AN-R had a lower urge to eat before the experimental meal, NW-B had a higher urge to eat after the experimental meal, and the AN-B and NW-B were more preoccupied with thoughts of food after the experimental meal. These differences did not persist after treatment. Comparison of these cognitions after the experimental meal to after an imagined major meal showed differences only in the pretreatment conditions. The urge to eat was greater after the imagined meal than after the experimental meal. Willpower to stop eating was greater after the experimental meal than after the hypothetical meal.

CONCLUSIONS

Eating disorder patients have disturbances in the perceptions of hunger and satiety. The hunger and satiety curves before, during, and after an experimental meal[5] demon-

TABLE 9. Comparison of Experimental Meal to a Typical Major Meal

	r^a	p
Pretreatment — after meal		
Urge to eat	0.236	NS
Willpower to stop eating	0.363	0.01
Preoccupation with food	0.155	NS
Post-treatment — after meal		
Urge to eat	0.353	0.05
Willpower to stop eating	0.540	0.01
Preoccupation with food	0.473	0.01

a Pearson Product Moment Correlation.

strate that anorexia nervosa and bulimia nervosa patients often have difficulty distinguishing between perceptions of hunger and satiety. Some bulimic patients had little change in their satiety curves over the course of the experimental meal. Healthy controls had proportionally inverse hunger and fullness curves that crossed during the meal. These findings suggested that some relationship between the perceptions of hunger and satiety and the clinical descriptions of eating behavior should be present. There are anorexia nervosa patients who maintain their underweight condition exclusively by restricting food intake. It is reasonable to assume these patients may perceive lower hunger and higher satiety levels than healthy persons or bulimics. Other anorexia nervosa patients do not have this control and alternate severe food restrictions with binge eating. These patients should have lower satiety levels after a meal compared with the anorectic-restrictors. The bulimic patients who are normal weight should have the lowest satiety levels after a meal compared with anorectic patients and healthy controls. These patients are unable to achieve an underweight condition even though they purge. The results of this study, for the most part, supported the above postulations. Underweight anorectics had lower hunger levels, higher satiety levels, and less urge to eat than normal-weight bulimics and healthy controls. Subjects who binged and purged were more preoccupied with thoughts of food, and normal-weight bulimics had more urge to eat after finishing a meal. After treatment when all subjects were at a normal weight, the anorectics continued to have lower hunger levels, and the AN-R also continued to have higher satiety levels. In order to determine if these satiety perceptions are a trait phenomenon, the subjects should be tested over time to establish the stability of the satiety responses.

Comparing the hunger and satiety slopes with the best-fit regression line does not seem to be an adequate method of assessing these curves. Especially after the meal, there were so many directional changes that a best-fit line simply did not reflect what was happening.

The palatability results supported clinical predictions. Bulimics found the experimental meal to be more palatable compared with the anorectics and controls. Palatability influenced hunger and satiety levels especially before the meal. Hunger and satiety levels after the meal were primarily determined by before-meal hunger and satiety levels, amount consumed, and rate of eating. Only during the pretreatment period were diagnostic group differences on hunger and satiety levels found after the meal over and above these eating-related variables. The group differences were present primarily in the before-meal hunger and satiety perceptions. Because these differences disappeared after treatment (which includes weight gain for the anorectics), a relationship of hunger and satiety levels to BMI was expected and found. The lower the BMI, the lower the hunger levels and the higher the satiety levels.

The psychological variable, urge to eat, strongly influenced after-meal hunger and satiety levels. The concept "urge to eat" seems to incorporate both the perceptions of hunger and satiety. For future studies, urge to eat may be a better predictor of eating behavior than the perceptions of hunger and fullness.

Treatment altered most of the psychological variables assessed but had less effect on the more direct eating-related variables. For example, the psychological variables of restraint, preoccupation with thoughts of food, and willpower needed to stop eating approximated those of control subjects after treatment. The more physiological or direct eating-related variables of satiety, hunger, palatability, amount eaten, and rate of eating continued to differ among some of the eating disorder subgroups. Specifically, two patterns of responses emerged unaltered by treatment: (1) those patients who were previously underweight (AN-R and AN-B) continued to have lower hunger ratings compared with the other groups, and (2) those previously underweight patients who solely restricted food intake (AN-R) continued to have a higher level of satiety compared with the other groups. After treatment a difference emerged with those patients with a history of binging and purging. These patients had significantly higher palatability ratings compared with the AN-R and controls. In order to determine whether these characteristics represent a state or trait phenomenon we are currently retesting the patients one year after treatment.

REFERENCES

1. GARNER, D. M. & K. M. BEMIS. 1982. A cognitive behavioral approach to anorexia nervosa. Cog. Ther. Res. **6**: 1223–1250.
2. GROSSMAN, J. T. 1979. The Biology of Motivation. Ann. Rev. Psychol. **30**: 209–242.
3. BLUNDELL, J. E. & A. HILL. 1986. Behavioral pharmacology of feeding: Relevance of animal experiments for studies in man. *In* Pharmacology of Eating Disorders. M. O. Carruba & J. E. Blundell, Eds.: 51–70. Raven Press. New York.
4. BOOTH, D. A. 1985. Food-conditioned eating preferences and aversions with interceptive elements: Conditional appetite and satieties. Ann. N.Y. Acad. Sci. **443**: 22–41.
5. HERMAN, C. P., J. POLIVY, P. DLINER, J. THRELKELD & D. MUNIC. 1978. Distractibility in dieters and non-dieters: An alternative view of "externality." J. Pers. Soc. Psychol. **36**: 536–548.
6. OWEN, W., K. HALMI, J. GIBBS *et al.* 1985. Satiety responses in eating disorders. J. Psychiatr. Res. **19**: 279–284.
7. COHEN, J. & P. COHEN, Eds. 1983. *In* Applied Multiple Regression/Correlation Analysis for the Behavioral Sciences: 120–123, 360–366, 508–512. Lawrence Erlbaum Associates. Hillsdale, NJ.

DISCUSSION

DR. PAUL MCHUGH (*Johns Hopkins University, Baltimore, MD*): Katherine, these are wonderful data, and it is important to get these collections out, but of course we all still have a bit of a problem with the analogue scale, particularly in patients who are disturbed and distorted in their minds. I know you are working on the issue of validation here, but do you have other good behavioral methods to demonstrate the validation of these dispositions? Fundamentally, the patient is reporting a disposition to behave in certain kinds of ways. What kind of validations do you have, even behavior itself, to confirm that we are measuring what the words hunger and satiety say.

DR. KATHERINE HALMI (*New York Hospital–Cornell Medical Center*): Well that is what we are trying to do by seeing how hunger and satiety are related to other concepts. The best validation I have in this study is the relationship between hunger and satiety levels within the anorectic-restrictor group and in showing how they are related to the amount consumed, the palatability of the solution, and so forth. With one group we do show a relationship between the amount consumed, the concept of palatability, and hunger and satiety levels.

There are problems with analogue scales, and one of the most serious problems is whether the patients use the whole scale and how they interpret the scale. I have talked extensively with Linda Bartoshuk on this problem and her advice is just to continue as I am with this at the present time. The other validation is control data.

DR. MCHUGH: Yes, but the controls don't have the disorder. Control data are very good in demonstrating what you have told us about the initial states.

UNIDENTIFIED SPEAKER (*CUNY Graduate Center*): I am fascinated with this whole idea that you related to urge to eat; I think it is important for both clinical groups. Did you get any sense about what it was that they were considering, for example, this physiological drive, is it cognitive drive? Did you get any sense there might be different things in the urge?

DR. HALMI: That's a good question. We didn't systematically assess that, no. I do think the urge to eat might possibly mean different things to these patients. Some of the patients described their feeling of hunger as brain hunger, and said they were full, but they had brain hunger. Even though they were full, they had this urge to eat. Some of them described it as the necessity to alleviate anxiety. However, we have not systematically assessed that.

COMMENT: I have heard some patients say, that they were "hungry in the stomach," while at other times they know that they're eating because they want to eat or they're driven to eat.

DR. HALMI: Our patients were full in their stomachs; they had what they call brain hunger.

Eating Behavior in Bulimia[a]

B. TIMOTHY WALSH,[b] HARRY R. KISSILEFF,[c]
AND COLLEEN M. HADIGAN[b]

[b]Department of Psychiatry
College of Physicians & Surgeons
Columbia University
New York, New York 10032

[c]Obesity Research Center
St. Luke's–Roosevelt Hospital
New York, New York 10025

INTRODUCTION

Bulimia nervosa is an eating disorder in which individuals recurrently consume large amounts of food in discrete periods of time (DSM-IIIR[1]). Most patients presenting to clinics with bulimia nervosa are women who report that binge eating episodes occur between 2–20 times per week and are usually followed by self-induced vomiting or the use of some other purgative method. Despite their grossly disturbed eating behavior, most patients who present to clinics for treatment of bulimia are of normal weight.

Although much attention has focused on the psychological and affective characteristics of patients with this syndrome, less effort has been devoted to understanding the salient behavioral feature of this disorder, namely, the disturbance of eating behavior. In recent years, we have developed a paradigm that permits the objective measurement of eating behavior in patients with bulimia in a laboratory setting.[2] This paper reviews the results of experimental studies conducted in this laboratory setting. The specific goals of these studies were (1) to characterize the binge eating and non-binge eating behavior of normal-weight women with bulimia nervosa in the laboratory, in terms of food choice, quantity consumed, and rate of eating, and (2) to compare the eating behavior of bulimic women under standardized laboratory conditions to that of normal controls.

PROCEDURES

Subjects were given four test meals under different conditions on nonconsecutive days. On the first test day, each subject participated in a taste test and then had a standard breakfast consisting of an English muffin and apple juice. Three hours later, a strawberry yogurt shake was served and subjects were asked to eat "as much as you like."

On the other three experimental days, subjects were given an English muffin and apple juice for breakfast and told to eat no other food until they returned to the hos-

[a] This work was supported in part by MH-42206 and Obesity Center Grant AM-26687.

pital at 5:00 in the evening. On the second and third experimental days, subjects were presented with an identical array of foods, including both foods believed typical of a binge (e.g., ice cream, cake) and other foods typical of a dinner meal (e.g., chicken, green beans). On one of these occasions, subjects were asked to eat as much as they would in a normal meal, and, in the other they were asked to binge. ("Let yourself go and eat as much as you can. If you eat so much that you feel sick, there is a bathroom down the hall which no one else will use while you are here.") The order of the instructions was chosen randomly for each pair of subjects. On the last experimental day, subjects were given a single-course meal of ice cream and asked to binge. All the instructions about eating were given by tape recording, so that all subjects, both patients and controls, received identical instructions. All study days were spaced two to three days apart.

Questionnaires describing mood, bodily sensations, and levels of hunger and satiety were given before and after each meal. In addition, the post-meal questionnaires included ratings of the sensory qualities of the meal, how typical of a binge the meal was (5-point scale), how well the instructions were followed (15-cm analogue scale), and how well the subject controlled her eating (15-cm analogue scale). All the foods were weighed before and after each meal. In addition, in the two single-course meals (the first and fourth), the food was placed directly over the scale of a University Eating Monitor so that intake could be recorded every four seconds. The Universal Eating Monitor is a device that permits the amount of food consumed to be covertly weighed be means of an electronic balance located under a false panel in the table.[3] While eating, subjects were also observed by a technician via a closed-circuit video camera; informed consent was obtained for this observation, and no video recordings were made.

INITIAL STUDIES

An initial study of the feasibility of this procedure was conducted in eight normal-weight women who met DSM-III criteria for bulimia. During the multicourse binge meal, all women binged and vomited afterwards. The mean intake was 4477 kcals (range 2083 to 8499), and patients rated the meal as between moderately and very typical of a binge. These data are in agreement with other laboratory studies of bulimic binge eating that have reported average binge sizes of 4394 kcal (range 1436 to 8585 kcal)[4] and 3500 kcal (range 1570 to 6370).[5] When asked to eat normally from the multicourse meal, six of the eight patients consumed large amounts of food (mean 3076 kcals) and then induced vomiting. Thus, although asked to eat normally, these patients binged, and there was a perfect rank-order correlation between the sizes of their multicourse "normal" and multicourse "binge" meals. The other two patients ate only small amounts of food (91 and 353 kcals) during their multicourse normal meals.

Seven of the eight patients participated in the single-item binge meal, and consumed an average of 1336 kcals. There was a highly significant correlation between the amounts consumed in the single-course binge meal and the multicourse binge meal ($r^2 = 0.92$, $p < 0.005$).

The single-course normal meal resulted in markedly variable intake across patients (mean = 637 kcals, range 30–1504). Two patients consumed what appeared to be— even in the absence of control data—very large amounts (1504 and 1103 kcals), and two patients ate very little (30 and 95 kcals).

The use of the Universal Eating Monitor to measure the instantaneous consumption of the single-item meals allows the generation of cumulative intake curves, showing the amount of food consumed over time during the meal. The majority of the patients, during the single-course meals, showed either linear or positively accelerating cumulative intake curves. In contrast, normal individuals typically show decelerating curves, indicating a decrease in the rate of consumption as the meal progresses.[6] These data suggested that patients with bulimia became more, rather than less, motivated to eat as the meal progressed.

In summary, these initial studies provided persuasive evidence that it was possible to examine the disordered eating behavior characteristic of bulimia in the laboratory. The aim of the following study was to replicate the results obtained in the initial feasibility study and to compare the eating behavior of women with bulimia nervosa to that of age- and sex-matched controls.

COMPARATIVE STUDIES

Subjects

Twelve women of normal body weight with bulimia nervosa by DSM-IIIR criteria participated in this study. The results of this study have been reported elsewhere.[7] Ten of the 12 patients participated in the entire four-meal protocol, and the remaining two patients participated in all but the last meal. Seven of the 12 patients were studied during the first 10 days of their admission to an inpatient treatment program, and the other five patients were studied as outpatients.

Controls were recruited from women who responded to a notice. Potential subjects were screened by telephone and then by brief interview to exclude persons with eating disorders and with medical or psychiatric illnesses. Patients and controls were very similar in age and weight.

The protocol was similar to the one described previously, but, in addition to participating in four laboratory meals, all subjects were interviewed by a research dietician. During this interview, they were asked to describe in detail their eating behavior during the previous 24 hours, including both normal eating and, for the patients, binges.

Multicourse Binge Meals

Examination of individual patients' data suggested that instructions were not always followed. For example, one patient, when asked to binge, consumed a small amount of food (217 kcal) and rated her meal as "not at all" typical of a binge. Conversely, two patients, when asked to eat normally, consumed very large amounts of food (3673 and 4881 kcals) and rated these meals as "very" or "extremely" typical of a binge. Therefore, the meals eaten by the patients were classified into two groups on the basis of their response to the question "How typical is the eating you just completed of a binge?" Patient meals rated as "extremely" or "very" typical of a binge were classified as a binge and meals rated as "not at all" or "slightly" typical of a binge were classed as nonbinge meals. Meals taken by the controls were classified by the instructions they were given, because it is not clear what a binge means to a nonbulimic.

Data from the multicourse meals of the patients are compared to the multicourse meals of the controls in TABLE 1. As in the previous study, patients consumed a large amount of food when binge eating (3352 ± 1193 kcals). Although the controls increased their caloric consumption from 856 to 1412 kcals when asked to overeat, the amount of food consumed by the patients when binge eating was still much greater than by the controls. These data clearly document that the binge eating of patients with bulimia is quantitatively different from that of normal persons. In addition, the

TABLE 1. Multicourse Meals in Bulimic Patients and Controls[a]

	kcal	Duration (min)	Rate (kcal/min)	%CHO	%FAT	%PRO	Hunger	
							Pre-Meal	Post-Meal
				Nonbinge Meal				
Patients (n = 9)	679 ± 614^{gmi}	17.3 ± 6.7^{m}	33.4 ± 22.1^{mi}	51.7 ± 24.8	31.5 ± 14.3^{m}	18.1 ± 9.6^{m}	8.8 ± 3.9	3.6 ± 4.2^{g}
Controls (n = 10)	856 ± 265^{gmi}	20.1 ± 6.6^{m}	44.6 ± 14.5^{mi}	41.3 ± 4.4	40.7 ± 4.5^{m}	19.1 ± 3.4^{m}	7.9 ± 3.5	1.1 ± 1.0^{g}
				Binge Meal				
Patients (n = 9)	3,352 ± 1,193^{gmi}	42.6 ± 16.0^{m}	80.3 ± 24.1^{mi}	46.6 ± 4.1	41.0 ± 3.8^{m}	12.2 ± 3.7^{m}	9.7 ± 2.7	2.8 ± 2.8^{g}
Controls (n = 10)	1,412 ± 227^{gmi}	33.9 ± 8.4^{m}	44.0 ± 13.8^{mi}	44.9 ± 4.0	41.5 ± 5.3^{m}	15.5 ± 3.2^{m}	9.8 ± 2.7	0.7 ± 1.0^{g}

[a] Two-factor ANOVA: [g] group (patients vs. controls) effect, $p < 0.05$; [m] meal type (binge vs. nonbinge) effect, $p < 0.05$; [i] group × meal type interaction, $p < 0.05$.

rate of caloric consumption was higher for the patients than for the controls when binge eating (80.3 ± 24.1 vs. 44.0 ± 13.8 kcal/min).

A feeling of loss of control over eating is a salient feature of bulimia nervosa and is one of the diagnostic criteria for the illness in the DSM-IIIR. FIGURE 1 shows the calories consumed versus the subjects' rating of control for all multicourse meals for all subjects. For the control subjects, there was no correlation between the degree of control and the calories consumed. However, in the patient group, these two parameters showed a strong inverse correlation ($r^2 = 0.6$, $p < 0.005$).

FIGURE 2 shows the calorie content of the multicourse binge meal in the laboratory versus the average calorie content of binges described to the research dietician in the 24 hours before the first test meal. There was a significant positive correlation between these two measures ($r = 0.59$, $p < 0.05$).

We believe that these data strongly suggest that the behavior observed in the laboratory bears at least some resemblance to the "naturally occurring" eating behavior of bulimic patients: 10 of the 12 patients rated at least one meal as "very" or "extremely" typical of a binge, and these binge meals, compared to those of the controls, were characterized by a large calorie content, a high rate of eating, and a feeling of lack of control, characteristics that are major features used in the clinical diagnosis of the syndrome. Finally, there was a significant correlation between the reported size of a binge consumed by the patients in their natural environment and the kilocalories consumed during a binge in the laboratory.

Multicourse Nonbinge Meals

Differences between patients and controls were less striking in the multicourse non-

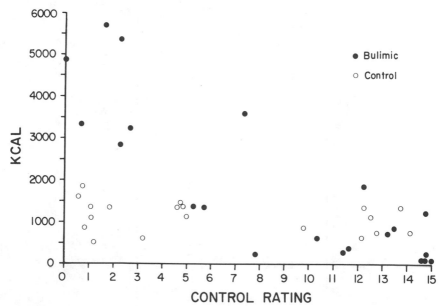

FIGURE 1. Kilocalories consumed versus control rating for multicourse meals for bulimic patients and controls. Both normal-instruction and binge-instruction meals are included.

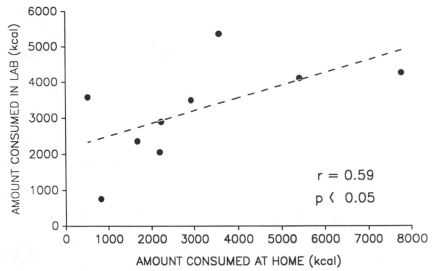

FIGURE 2. Kilocalorie content of bulimic patients' multicourse binge meals versus average kilocalorie content of binge episodes reported to a dietician in a 24-hour dietary recall.

binge meals. Although the mean difference was not significant, the patients tended to consume fewer calories than the controls (679 ± 614 vs. 856 ± 265 kcals). An additional examination of the individual caloric intakes for patients in both the initial feasibility study and the controlled study revealed that the meals that patients rated as "not typical of binge" tended to be smaller than the caloric intake of the controls' normal meals. While all 10 controls ate between 450 and 1325 kcals in their normal meal, half of the patients ate fewer than 450 kcals.

Macronutrient Composition of Multicourse Meals

Patients with bulimia nervosa who present to clinics typically report that binges consist primarily of "junk food" containing large amounts of carbohydrate.[8-10] Despite patients' reports of "craving carbohydrates," there were no major differences between the macronutrient composition of the multicourse meals of patients and that of controls' meals. Compared to their intakes during the nonbinge meals, both groups, when overeating, obtained a smaller fraction of calories from protein and tended to increase the fraction of calories obtained from fat. However, there was no significant group × meal interaction. Both patient and control groups obtained approximately 45% of their total calories from carbohydrates in both types of meals. Thus, although the absolute amount of carbohydrates consumed increased substantially between the patients' nonbinge and binge meals, there was no indication of an increase in relative carbohydrate content during binge eating.

Single-Course Meals

Differences between patients and controls followed a similar pattern for the single-course meals as they did for the multicourse meals. During the single-course binge meal, the patients ate more than twice as much as the controls (1328 ± 874 vs. 530 ± 176 kcal, $p < 0.02$). In the single-course normal meal, the patients ate less (353 ± 289 kcal) on average than the controls (448 ± 262 kcal), although the small difference was not significant.

We examined the correlations between caloric intake and control rating for the single-course meals. As was the case for the multicourse binge meal, there was a significant inverse correlation between intake of the single-course binge meal and control rating for the bulimic group ($r^2 = 0.63$, $p < 0.007$), but not for the controls.

We also examined the cumulative intake curves for all the single-course meals. Although the cumulative intake curves for the binge meals of the patients appeared superficially different from those of the controls, the coefficients of the quadratic equations describing the cumulative intake curves were not significantly different for either the binge or the normal meal. On the other hand, two of the bulimic patients but none of the controls showed positively accelerating curves on the binge meal, and two of the patients versus one of the controls had positively accelerating curves during the normal meal.

There were significant correlations between the sizes of single-course and multiple-course binge meals for the patients ($r^2 = 0.51$, $p < 0.03$), as well as for the controls ($r^2 = 0.46$, $p < 0.05$). The correlations between single- and multiple-course normal meals were not significant.

Hunger Ratings

Subjects rated their hunger before and after each meal (see TABLE 1). The premeal ratings of hunger were similar in patients and controls for all meals, but the patients' average postmeal hunger rating was significantly greater than that of the controls for all four meals. This finding is of particular interest in the multicourse "binge" meal, where even though the patients' average caloric intakes were significantly larger than the caloric intake of the controls, the patients were hungrier after the end of the meal.

SUMMARY

Despite our strong belief in the utility of laboratory studies of eating behavior, we also note several caveats on the data thereby obtained. First, it must be assumed that subjects' behavior is influenced by the laboratory environment and is not identical to eating behavior in a "normal" setting. Second, not all bulimic subjects who were screened for these studies actually participated, so that it is possible that the sample of patients from whom we obtained data differed in some ways from a general clinical population of women with bulimia.

Nonetheless, we believe that our data provide compelling evidence that the disturbed eating behavior characteristic of bulimia nervosa can be profitably studied in the laboratory. Even under structured laboratory conditions, most bulimic patients rated one of their multicourse meals as typical of a binge, and, during that meal, consumed a much larger amount of food and ate more rapidly than did controls who were asked to overeat. The significant correlations between the sizes of the multicourse and single-course binge meals and between the size of laboratory binge meals and the size of the "naturally occurring" binge meals reported to the dietician suggest that a reproducible phenomenon is being examined.

The results of our studies suggest that the abnormalities of eating behavior in bulimia nervosa cannot be viewed simply as a disturbance of carbohydrate consumption or even as the episodic consumption of a certain type of food. Rather, eating behavior in this syndrome appears more generally disturbed. The most striking difference between the binge and the nonbinge meals of bulimic patients and between the binge eating of patients and the overeating of normal persons is the amount of food consumed, not the macronutrient composition of the meals. In addition, for all four meal types, the patients were hungrier after the end of the meal than were the controls, even though the patients' average caloric intakes were generally larger and their average hunger ratings before the meals did not differ from those of the controls. Certainly, self-induced vomiting may contribute to this abnormality, but it was also observed after nonbinge meals when vomiting did not occur.

Together, these data are consistent with the notion that the essential appetitive abnormality in bulimia nervosa lies in the control of the amount of food consumed, not in the consumption of a particular macronutrient or type of food. Patients with bulimia nervosa appear less responsive than normal to the signals that lead to the termination of a meal. In other words, there may be a disturbance in the mechanisms responsible for satiety. Such a disturbance is consistent with patients' reports of their experience while eating[11,12] and would certainly help explain the excessive consumption characteristic of binge episodes. A disturbance in satiety might also be consistent with the tendency of many patients to under-consume when they are not binge eating. This reduction in intake may be the result of a conscious over-compensation for the lack of normal inhibitory influences of satiety. A disturbance in satiety is also suggested in data collected by Halmi,[13] by the work of Hetherington and Rolls on sensory-specific satiety,[14] and by the recent report of Geracioti and Liddle[15] that the release of cholecystokinin (CCK) into plasma following a test meal is impaired in patients with bulimia. It appears to be profitable to test the hypothesis that bulimia nervosa is associated with an abnormality in satiety. Presumably, this disturbance is not innate, but develops during the course of the illness. However, once established, it may become a critical factor in the perpetuation of the abnormal eating behavior that characterizes bulimia nervosa.

ACKNOWLEDGMENTS

We gratefully acknowledge the assistance of Julie Bukar, Janet Guss, Susan Cassidy, Sondra Dantzic, Linda Wong, and Valerie Lukasik.

REFERENCES

1. AMERICAN PSYCHIATRIC ASSOCIATION. 1987. Diagnostic and Statistical Manual of Mental Disorders, Third Edition — Revised. American Psychiatric Association. Washington, D.C.
2. KISSILEFF, H. R., B. T. WALSH, J. G. KRAL & S. M. CASSIDY. 1986. Laboratory studies of eating behavior in women with bulimia. Physiol. Behav. **38**: 563–570.
3. KISSILEFF, H. R., G. KLINGSBERG & T. B. VAN ITALLIE. 1980. Universal eating monitor for continuous recording of solid or liquid consumption in man. Am. J. Physiol. **238**: R14–R22.
4. MITCHELL, J. E. & D. C. LAINE. 1985. Monitored binge-eating behavior in patients with bulimia. Int. J. Eating Disord. **4**: 177–184.
5. KAYE, W. H., H. E. GWIRTSMAN, T. GEORGE, S. R. WEISS & D. C. JIMERSON. 1986. Relationship of mood alteration to bingeing behavior of bulimia. Br. J. Psychiatry **149**: 479–485.
6. KISSILEFF, H. R. & J. THORTON. 1982. Facilation and inhibition in the cumulative intake

curve in man. *In* Changing Concepts of the Nervous System. A. J. Morrison & P. Strick, Eds.: 585–607. Academic Press. New York.

7. WALSH, B. T., H. R. KISSILEFF, S. M. CASSIDY & S. DANTZIC. 1989. Eating behavior of women with bulimia. Arch. Gen. Psychiatry, in press.

8. MITCHELL, J.E., R. L. PYLE & E. D. ECKERT. 1981. Frequency and duration of binge-eating episodes in patients with bulimia. Am. J. Psychiatry **138**: 835–836.

9. MITCHELL, J. E., D. HATSUKAMI & E. D. ECKERT. 1985. Characteristics of 275 patients with bulimia. Am. J. Psychiatry **142**: 482–485.

10. ABRAHAM, S. F. & P. J. V. BEUMONT. 1982. How patients describe bulimia or binge eating. Psychol. Med. **12**: 625–635.

11. WEISS, S. R. & M. R. EBERT. 1983. Psychological and behavioral characteristics of normal-weight bulimics and normal-weight controls. Psychosom. Med. **45**: 293–303.

12. PYLE, R. L., J. E. MITCHELL & E. D. ECKERT. 1981. Bulimia: A report of 34 cases. J. Clin. Psychiatry **42**: 60–64.

13. HALMI, K. A. Taste, hunger, and satiety perceptions in anorexia nervosa and bulimia. *In* Eating Behavior in Eating Disorders. B. T. Walsh, Ed. American Psychiatric Press. Washington, DC.

14. HETHERINGTON, M. & B. J. ROLLS. 1988. Sensory-specific satiety and food intake in eating disorders. *In* Eating Behavior in Eating Disorders. B. T. Walsh, Ed. American Psychiatric Press. Washington, DC.

15. GERACIOTI, T. D. & R. A. LIDDLE. 1988. Impaired cholecystokinin secretion in bulimia nervosa. N. Engl. J. Med. **319**(11): 683–688.

DISCUSSION

DR. KARL M. PIRKE (*Max-Planck Institut, Munich*): I would like to mention that we have conducted, together with Dr. Fichter and with the help of the Department of Nutrition at our university, a study in which patients with bulimia and normal controls kept a diary on what they were eating over a three-week period. We obtained exactly the same results as you have presented here. That is to say, when we compared what they were eating during the binge attacks and what they were eating during binge-free days, there was no change in percentage of carbohydrate and total caloric intake, but there was a significant decrease in protein consumption and a significant increase in fat consumption. When we compared that with the normal controls we got the impression that the patients, on the days without binging, were maintaining a low-caloric diet, or what they thought would be a low-caloric diet, but during the binge attacks they lost control, and added more fat to their eating.

DR. TIMOTHY WALSH (*Columbia University, New York*): Thank you, that's very nice to hear. It's also reassuring that data from the laboratory resembles data from naturalistic studies.

DR. KATHERINE HALMI (*New York Hospital–Cornell Medical Center, White Plains, NY*): I think it's very interesting that the bulimics eat less protein when they binge. You don't differentiate the fats and carbohydrates. As I recall, John Blundell did a study a while ago showing that protein foods induce satiety more readily than fats and carbohydrates. This makes me wonder if we can assume bulimics have any resemblance to normal people. Perhaps they don't want to induce satiety early. Perhaps they want to get on with the binge because there may be some postingestive effects that are beneficial to them, such as relief of anxiety or some other factors that are bothering them. We haven't pinpointed it yet.

DR. WALSH: I think that is a valuable point. An interesting aspect of these data is that when we asked the controls to overeat, they also reduced the percent of calories derived from protein. So, there appears to be a similar pattern in both patients and controls.

DR. G. F. M. RUSSELL (*The Institute of Psychiatry, London*): You rightly, I'm certain, take into account what the patient's objective awareness is of the binge, whether she thinks that she is out of control. Do you, however, allow that to negate the actual caloric measurement that you have? In other words, if you have a patient who eats very little in the way of calories but tells you she's out of control, how do you deal with that?

DR. WALSH: So far we haven't seen that. The patients who report being out of control eat a lot of calories.

DR. RUSSELL: I think you might be prepared for it; it may not be common, but I recently had a patient who told me she had terrible binges. I asked her to explain what she ate. She said, "Well, my piece of toast and my cup of coffee." I said, "What was the binge?" Well, instead of eating white bread it was whole wheat bread, her one piece of toast; instead of having her cup of coffee with skim milk she had ordinary milk: That was her binge.

DR. WALSH: I concur. I too have seen patients like that. The only thing that I would say is that in recruiting patients for this study, and in making the diagnosis of bulimia nervosa, we had to be convinced that patients did indeed consume a large amount of food. So if a patient's only "binge" was whole-wheat toast and cream in her coffee, we would not have included her in the study.

Gastric Function in Eating Disorders[a]

P. H. ROBINSON

Department of Psychological Medicine
Kings College Hospital Medical School
London, SE5, England

DELAYED GASTRIC EMPTYING DUE TO STARVATION IN ANOREXIA NERVOSA

Gastric distension is a potent inhibitor of food intake in rats[1] and rhesus monkeys,[2] and slowing of gastric emptying has been shown, in the rhesus monkey, to contribute to the feeding inhibitory effects of cholecystokinin[3] and fenfluramine.[4] Patients with anorexia nervosa complain of prolonged satiety after meals,[5,6] and while gastric contractions in anorexia nervosa appear to be normal,[7] the demonstration of slow gastric emptying in patients with anorexia nervosa[8-13] has provided a physiological basis for this symptom. Studies that are summarized below[13] have suggested possible mechanisms for the development of delayed gastric emptying in anorexia nervosa.

Three groups of patients and one group of controls were tested. Ten patients fulfilled criteria for anorexia nervosa[14] but were not receiving nutritional treatment. Twelve further patients also fulfilled criteria for anorexia nervosa, but had been treated on an inpatient unit for eating disorders for an average of two weeks, receiving a diet containing 2500–3000 kcal/day. Eight of these patients were retested after reaching normal weight. Ten further patients fulfilled criteria[15] for bulimia nervosa but were not underweight. These groups of patients are referred to as (1) anorexia nervosa, self-selection (or free) diet; (2) anorexia nervosa, refeeding diet (underweight and weight restored); and (3) bulimia nervosa.

Gastric emptying was measured with gastric scintigraphy using three meals: a solid mixed meal containing labeled, poached egg white, bread and butter, and orange juice; an isotonic acaloric liquid meal of 200 ml of physiological saline; and a hypertonic, caloric liquid meal of 200 ml d-glucose solution, 0.5 kcal/ml. All meals were labeled with Technetium-99m, 3.7 MBq (100 microcuries). For the solid meal, anterior and posterior scans were acquired with a gamma camera every 5–10 minutes for two hours and analyzed electronically by drawing a region of interest around the gastric outline, determining the geometric mean of anterior and posterior counts, and generating a curve of decay-corrected gastric counts against time. For the liquid meals, 15-second anterior scans were acquired consecutively for 60 minutes, corrected for decay and plotted against time.

[a] This work was performed with the help of a Lecturership at the Institute of Psychiatry from the Wellcome Trust, London.

456

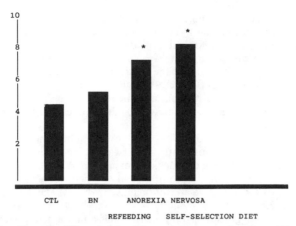

FIGURE 1. Duration of solid meal. Mean time taken to complete the solid meal in controls and patients with eating disorders. * Significantly different from controls and patients with bulimia nervosa, $p < 0.05$, analysis of variance.

Consumption of the solid meal, but not of the two liquid meals, was significantly slower in both groups of anorexic patients compared to controls and patients with bulimia nervosa (FIG. 1). Weight gain on the ward did not significantly affect eating rate. Gastric emptying was significantly delayed compared to controls only in the patients with anorexia nervosa selecting their own diet (FIG. 2). Emaciated anorexic patients who had been on the refeeding diet for about two weeks had normal gastric emptying, and weight gain did not affect emptying rate. Patients with bulimia nervosa who were not underweight also had normal gastric emptying. However, "self-selection diet" patients with anorexia nervosa who also suffered bulimic episodes were found to have delayed gastric emptying. Delayed emptying was therefore only observed in patients who were suffering from short-term starvation whether due to continuous

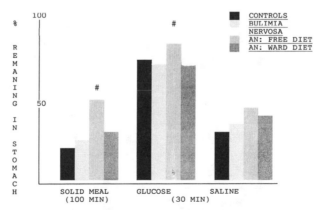

FIGURE 2. Gastric emptying in eating disorders. Mean percentage of the meal remaining within the gastric outline during gastric emptying tests in controls and patients at 100 minutes (solid meal) or 30 minutes (glucose and saline meals). # Significantly different ($p < 0.05$) from other diagnostic groups (analysis of variance).

food restriction, or vomiting of ingested food. Moreover, the nutritional disturbance had to be severe enough to result in emaciation, because delayed emptying was not observed in bulimic patients who were not underweight.

The disturbance in gastric emptying was characterized in a further way. The gastric abnormality was only observed for the solid mixed meal and the glucose solution. Emptying of saline was normal (FIG. 2). Both the solid and glucose meals contained calories and were hypertonic to plasma, and the results suggest that delayed gastric emptying in anorexia nervosa may therefore be determined either by the caloric or osmotic properties of the meal.

Lastly, among the patients with anorexia nervosa or bulimia nervosa, abuse of laxatives was associated with a significantly slower gastric emptying rate of glucose. At 30 minutes, the mean percentage of glucose remaining within the stomach was 85.1% for laxative-abusing patients ($n = 8$) compared to 75.0% in patients not abusing laxatives ($n = 22$). [Two-way (laxative abuse/diagnosis) ANOVA, laxative effect: $F(1,24) = 5.18$, $p = 0.032$.]

The present work suggests that food restriction is a major determinant of delayed gastric emptying in anorexia nervosa. Experiments in rats indicate that similar changes occur during food restriction in animals.[16] Adult male Wistar rats were allowed access to food (powdered rat chow) for two hours per day for three months. Gastric emptying was then measured using 5-gram meals, similar in content to those used in the human studies, labeled with Technetium-99m. The egg meal was eaten voluntarily and the glucose and saline meals were administered by gavage. Scanning was then performed for two hours and gastric emptying rate calculated. Emptying of all three meals was grossly delayed compared to control animals allowed unrestricted access to food (FIG. 3). Delayed gastric emptying therefore occurs in food-deprived rats. Saline emptying was also affected, in contrast to anorexic patients in whom it was normal. After three months of free feeding, gastric emptying of saline had returned to normal. For the solid and glucose meals, emptying in rats on restricted feeding was still significantly slower than in controls, although it had returned toward the normal range.

Delayed gastric emptying is therefore a sequel to severe food deprivation and its occurrence in both rats and patients is consistent with early studies of starvation in

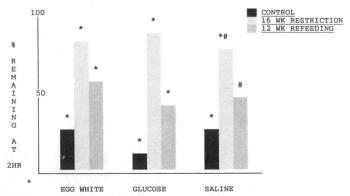

FIGURE 3. Effect of dietary restriction on gastric emptying in rats. Mean percentage of the egg white, glucose, or saline solution meals remaining at two hours in control rats, rats after 16 weeks during which feeding was restricted to two hours per day, and after three months subsequent refeeding. Within each meal, means with the same symbols are significantly different.

human volunteers in whom delayed emptying was observed on barium meal examination.[17] Its adaptive significance for survival during food shortage is uncertain. Under conditions of prolonged intermeal interval, delayed emptying would result in slow but steady energy delivery to the small intestine with, perhaps, an improvement in the completeness of digestion and absorption of certain dietary constituents. The rate at which food leaves the stomach is thought to be a major influence in the control of food intake.[18] Delayed gastric emptying is apparently mediated by starvation, and this suggests that postprandial satiety is modulated by the rate of food intake. If this is indeed the case, then prolonged postprandial subjective gastric fullness is likely to be observed as a result of starvation due, for example, to food shortage. A physiological change that reduces the discomfort associated with starvation, and presumably one incentive to find a source of food, is somewhat counterintuitive, and its biological significance remains to be determined.

VISUAL ANALOGUE SCALE RESPONSES TO FOOD IN EATING DISORDERS

It was suggested by Bruch,[19] a pioneer in the clinical description of anorexia nervosa, that a core feature of the illness was an inability to perceive or interpret accurately either body dimensions or internal sensations. The distortion of body image in anorexia nervosa is well documented[20] and has been confirmed using a variety of techniques. Monitoring of internal state has been assessed only rarely. Coddington and Bruch[21] gave measured amounts of liquid nutrient through a naso-gastric tube and found that 15 obese and 3 anorexic subjects were less accurate on this task than controls.

In the gastric emptying studies described above, subjects were asked to complete 10-cm visual analogue scales every few minutes before and after the solid mixed meal. Because of the position of the camera, a pencil-and-paper test was impractical, and a 10-cm line of 40 light-emitting diodes, controlled by a sliding rheostat, was used. The descriptors used were (1) hungry, (2) sad, (3) full, (4) tense, (5) urge to eat, (6) fat, (7) nausea, (8) urge to be sick, (9) drowsy. The scales were anchored at the ends by the words "not at all" and "extremely." Each rating was scored by noting the distance between the "not at all" end of the scale and the light selected by the subject. Gastric perceptivity was quantified by determination of the Spearman rank correlation coefficient between ratings on the scale "full" and radioactive counts remaining within the gastric outline at that time. Correlations were also determined between gastric contents measured in this way and the other scales. Ratings of stomach fullness correlated fairly well with gastric contents in controls, the mean value of Spearman's ρ being 0.57 (FIG. 4). In patients with anorexia nervosa and bulimia nervosa, the mean value of ρ was not significantly different from controls, suggesting that the patients were able to report gastric fullness with reasonable accuracy. Correlations between the rating "hungry" and gastric contents in anorexic patients (mean $\rho = -0.24$) were significantly lower than in controls (mean $\rho = -0.59$). Correlations between ratings of "urge to eat" and gastric contents were also significantly poorer for patients with anorexia nervosa (mean $\rho = -0.04$) compared to controls (mean $\rho = -0.58$) and to patients with bulimia nervosa alone (mean $\rho = -0.39$). Of the scales related to feeding, therefore, fullness bore a normal relation to gastric contents, but hunger and urge to eat did not. This suggests a disturbance in the interpretation of gastric signals, rather than in their perception.

In this study, it was also found that in the patients, gastric contents were correlated with scales that bore no relation to degree of gastric distension in controls (FIG. 4).

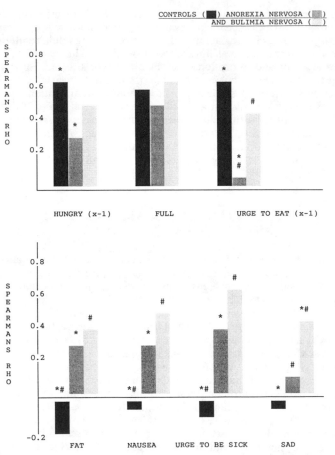

FIGURE 4. Gastric perceptivity. Mean values for Spearman's rank correlation coefficient (rho) between visual analogue scale ratings and radioactive counts remaining within the gastric outline on the scan for each subject individually. Solid meal. Means with the same symbols are significantly different ($p < 0.05$, analysis of variance).

Thus, the scales "fat," "nausea," and "urge to be sick" were not found to be significantly correlated with gastric contents in controls, but frequently were correlated in patients with anorexia nervosa and in those with bulimia nervosa. One patient, for example, was able to give ratings of stomach fullness that related accurately to the amount of isotope-labeled food that remained in her stomach, while her assessment of hunger was not significantly correlated with gastric contents. However, her ratings of "urge to be sick" closely followed the gastric emptying curve. It appears possible that gastric sensations were being processed to modulate symptomatic behavior rather than normal eating. Patients with bulimia nervosa often rated the scale "sad" along with gastric contents as well as those scales describing the other symptoms.

Postprandial gastric discomfort, often described by patients as "bloating," has been described in anorexia nervosa,[22] and this symptom may be linked to delayed gastric emptying. In the present study, absolute ratings of fullness were significantly higher in patients with anorexia nervosa compared to controls and to patients with bulimia nervosa, but the scores did not vary with differences in emptying rate. Patients who, after 100 minutes, had little remaining in the stomach had ratings of fullness as high as those with delayed gastric emptying and more than 50% of the meal remaining. This finding remains to be clarified, and it may represent a "ceiling" effect, as many of the patients were using the top 25% of the scale to indicate their feelings of fullness. However, it also suggests that anorexic patients report sensations apparently related to delayed gastric emptying (i.e., prolonged, exaggerated satiety) when they do not actually show the physiological disturbance, although delayed emptying is likely to have been present in the past.

SUMMARY AND GENERAL DISCUSSION

Patients with anorexia nervosa frequently complain of excessive feelings of satiety after eating. The experimental work described by ourselves and others[8-13] suggests that a disturbance of gastric function, that is, delayed gastric emptying, is responsible, at least partly, for this symptom. The present work demonstrates that this delay is closely associated with severe, acute starvation, a finding that is supported by the observation that rats on a restricted feeding schedule develop delayed gastric emptying. In anorexia nervosa, delayed emptying was only observed after the solid and the glucose meals, suggesting that its pathogenesis might involve alterations in gastric sensitivity to duodenal caloric or osmotic stimuli. This reasoning is challenged by the experiments with rats, showing delayed emptying even of the isotonic, acaloric saline meal. We found that patients who abused laxatives had significantly slower gastric emptying of glucose than those who did not. This finding suggests that laxatives may adversely affect gastric emptying associated with starvation but is, at present, obscure. Control of gastric emptying is complex and involves autonomic, serotonergic, and peptidergic systems acting peripherally and centrally by neural and endocrine mechanisms. The restricted feeding schedule rat promises to be a useful model in which to explore these potential areas of dysfunction and indicate the significant physiological disturbances.

What is the importance of delayed gastric emptying in eating disorders? Its association with starvation suggests that it does not antedate the onset of anorexia nervosa, but is a consequence of the nutritional disturbance. Once a pattern of starvation has been established, gastric slowing may lead to its persistence by producing enhanced satiety and prolonged intermeal interval and thereby contribute to reduced food intake. In some patients, extrapolation of the gastric emptying curve, assuming a monotonic function, suggested that food would remain in the stomach for more than 24 hours after a meal. Delayed gastric emptying may, therefore, act as a perpetuating factor in anorexia nervosa. Starvation-induced delayed emptying may arise in some persons more easily than in others, and this propensity may be genetically determined, a proposition that remains to be tested. Emaciated subjects with anorexia nervosa are at risk for acute gastric dilatation, a potentially fatal complication that can arise during refeeding.[24] Delayed gastric emptying is likely to be an important contributory factor, along with severe malnutrition, causing wasting of the stomach wall.

Gastric emptying of the meals chosen was within the normal range in bulimia nervosa as long as the patient was not severely underweight. In patients with bulimia who were also grossly underweight, gastric emptying was delayed. This indicates that delayed emptying occurs when the amount of nutrient reaching the duodenum is curtailed severely enough to cause marked weight loss, whether by food restriction or vomiting.

It has been suggested that accelerated gastric emptying may contribute to the maintenance of a high weight in morbid obesity.[25] While a similar hypothesis may be advanced to account for failure of satiety in bulimia, our findings do not provide support for failure of satiety in bulimia. Our findings do not support the idea that rapid gastric emptying contributes to the development of bulimia nervosa, although further studies, perhaps using large meals such as are consumed during bulimic episodes, are justified in view of the recent description[26] of reduced secretion in bulimia nervosa of cholecystokinin, a peptide that may have a physiological role in the control of gastric emptying.[27] In patients with anorexia nervosa who also suffer from bulimia nervosa, gastric stasis clearly does not act as a restraint on food intake. However, delayed gastric emptying appears to contribute to the symptoms of anorexia nervosa complicated by bulimia in another way. The longer a bulimic meal stays within the stomach, the longer the interval during which the patient can dispose of most of the meal by vomiting. Patients may make themselves aware of this "safe" interval by swallowing a colored marker, such as a green apple skin, as the first item of a bulimic episode, and vomiting until it appears. By prolonging this interval, delayed gastric emptying in a severely malnourished bulimic patient increases the efficiency of vomiting as a weight control device and therefore contributes to the malnutrition.

Bruch[19] suggested, from clinical experience, that patients with anorexia nervosa have an abnormal perception of their external dimensions and of their internal nutritional status. The first postulate was confirmed and quantified using a variety of measures of body image disturbance.[20] Use of analogue scale ratings during the measurement of gastric emptying has provided quantitative evidence that similarly confirms Bruch's insights. In control subjects, gastric contents were linked to analogue scale measures of hunger and fullness, but not to indicators of symptoms of eating disorder. In anorexia nervosa, hunger was often quite unrelated to stomach contents, and although absolute ratings of fullness were elevated, they did gradually decline as gastric emptying proceeded. This suggests that gastric contents were being perceived, albeit at a greater degree of sensitivity than controls, but that the signals were being misinterpreted. This suggestion is supported by the frequent association between gastric emptying and symptoms of eating disorder, such as the urge to vomit, in patients with anorexia nervosa. The main findings in anorexia nervosa are, therefore, elevated satiety, abnormal hunger, and, apparently, interpretation of satiety signals as symptoms. The increased satiety ratings were observed in both patients who had delayed gastric emptying and in those who had normal emptying. Thus, although ratings of fullness declined with time, absolute scores were just as high 100 minutes after the meal in patients with less than 20% gastric contents remaining as in those with more than half the meal still in the stomach. This suggests that while disturbed physiology may be responsible for prolonged satiety during starvation, other mechanisms (perhaps involving learning during the phase of delayed gastric emptying) lead to the experience of gastric distension when the stomach is actually empty, after refeeding treatment. In bulimia nervosa without severe weight loss, hunger and fullness ratings were normal, but abnormal links between gastric contents and symptoms were also observed in these patients. No word exists to describe this phenomenon, which occurs in both anorexia nervosa and bulimia nervosa. It may be defined as the abnormal interpretation, in terms of morbid symptoms, of sensations arising as a result of a physiological process. A term suggested here is *paraceptivity* (in the sense of disordered perceptivity). Bruch's proposition was that patients with anorexia nervosa had disordered perception or interpretation of internal signals. The present results suggest that these patients manifest both classes of disturbance, namely interoceptive distortion (enhanced satiety) and paraceptive experiences.

ACKNOWLEDGMENTS

The encouragement and support of Professor P. R. McHugh and Dr. T. H. Moran at Johns Hopkins University Medical School, Baltimore, are gratefully acknowledged. The author is also indebted to Professor G. F. M. Russell at the Maudsley Hospital, London, under whose care the patients were treated, to Dr. J. Barrett and Mr. M. Clarke of Kings College Hospital for making available the resources of the Nuclear Medicine and Medical Physics Departments, and to Dr. J. S. Stephenson of the Institute of Psychiatry for expert help with the animal experiments.

REFERENCES

1. GELIEBTER, A., S. WESTREICH, D. GAGE & S. A. HASHIM. 1986. Intragastric balloon reduces food intake and body weight in rats. Am. J. Physiol. 251(Regulatory Integrative Comp. Physiol 20): R794–R797.
2. WIRTH, J. B. & P. R. McHUGH. 1983. Gastric distension and short-term satiety in the rhesus monkey. Am. J. Physiol. 245(Regulatory Integrative Comp. Physiol. 14): R174–R180.
3. MORAN, T. H. & P. R. McHUGH. 1982. Cholecystokinin suppresses food intake by inhibiting gastric emptying. Am. J. Physiol. 242: R491–R497.
4. ROBINSON, P. H., T. H. MORAN & P. R. McHUGH. 1986. Inhibition of gastric emptying and feeding by fenfluramine. Am. J. Physiol. 250(Regulatory Integrative Comp. Physiol. 19): R764–R769.
5. GARFINKEL, P. E., H. MOLDOFSKY, D. M. GARNER, H. C. STANCER & D. V. COSCINA. 1978. Body awareness in anorexia nervosa: Disturbances in "body image" and "satiety." Psychosom. Med. 40: 487–498.
6. ROBINSON, P. H. Self-ratings during measurement of gastric emptying in anorexia and bulimia nervosa. Br. J. Psychiatry, in press.
7. SILVERSTONE, J. T. & G. F. M. RUSSELL. 1967. Gastric "hunger" contractions in anorexia nervosa. Br. J. Psychiatry 113: 257–263.
8. DUBOIS, A., H. A. GROSS, M. H. EBERT & D. O. CASTELL. 1979. Altered gastric emptying and secretion in primary anorexia nervosa. Gastroenterology 77: 319–323.
9. HOLT, S., M. J. FORD, S. GRANT & R. C. HEADING. 1981. Abnormal gastric emptying in primary anorexia nervosa. Br. J. Psychiatry 139: 550–552.
11. McCALLUM, R. W., B. B. GRILL, R. LANGE, M. PLANKY & E. E. GLASS. 1985. Definition of a gastric emptying abnormality in patients with anorexia nervosa. Dig. Dis. Sci. 30: 713–722.
12. STACHER, G., A. KISS, S. WIESNAGROTZKI, H. BERGMANN, J. HOBART & C. SCHNEIDER. 1987. Oesophageal and gastric motility disorders in patients categorized as having primary anorexia nervosa. Gut 27: 1120–1126.
13. ROBINSON, P. H., M. CLARKE & J. BARRETT. 1988. Determinants of delayed gastric emptying in anorexia nervosa and bulimia nervosa. Gut 29: 458–464.
14. RUSSELL, G. F. M. 1983. Anorexia nervosa and bulimia nervosa. In Handbook of Psychiatry. 4. Neuroses and Personality Disorders. G. F. M. Russell & L. A. Hersov, Eds.: 285–298. Cambridge University Press. Cambridge, England.
15. RUSSELL, G. F. M. 1979. Bulimia nervosa: An ominous variant of anorexia nervosa. Psychol. Med. 9: 429–448.
16. ROBINSON, P. H., T. SHIM & J. S. STEPHENSON. 1988. Dietary-induced delayed gastric emptying in rats. J. Physiol. 398: 62p.
17. KEYS, A., J. BROZEK, A. HENSCHEL, O. MICHELSON & H. TAYLOR. 1950. The Biology of Human Starvation. University of Minnesota Press. Minneapolis, MN.
18. McHUGH, P. R. & T. H. MORAN. 1979. Calories and gastric emptying: A regulatory capacity with implications for feeding. Am. J. Physiol. 236: R254–R260.
19. BRUCH, H. 1966. Anorexia nervosa and its differential diagnosis. J. Nerv. Ment. Dis. 141: 555–566.

20. SLADE, P. 1985. A review of body-image studies in anorexia nervosa and bulimia nervosa. J. Psychiatr. Res. 19: 255–265.
21. CODDINGTON, R. D. & H. BRUCH. 1970. Gastric perceptivity in normal, obese and schizophrenic subjects. Psychosomatics 11: 571–579.
22. GARFINKEL, P. E. 1974. Perception of hunger and satiety in anorexia nervosa. Psychol. Med. 4: 309–315.
23. SMITH, B. 1968. Effect of irritant purges on the myenteric plexus in man and the mouse. Gut 9: 139–143.
24. RUSSELL, G. F. M. 1966. Acute dilatation of the stomach in a patient with anorexia nervosa. Br. J. Psychiatry 112: 203–207.
25. WRIGHT, R. A., S. KRINSKY, C. FLEEMAN, J. TRUJILLO & E. TEAGUE. 1983. Gastric emptying and obesity. Gastroenterology 84: 747–751.
26. GERACIOTI, T. D. & R. A. LIDDLE. 1988. Impaired cholecystokinin secretion in bulimia nervosa. N. Engl. J. Med. 319: 683–688.
27. ROBINSON, P. H. 1989. Gastric control of food intake. In Bulimia: Basic Research, Diagnosis and Therapy. M. Fichter, Ed. Enke Verlag. Stuttgart, Germany. In press.

DISCUSSION

DR. MARION HETHERINGTON (*National Institute of Mental Health, Bethesda, MD*): I was wondering, in the light of Tom Geraciotti's work showing abnormal secretion of CCK in bulimics, if you have ever seen individuals with bulimia nervosa of normal weight who had faster gastric emptying.

DR. ROBINSON (*Kings College Hospital Medical School, London*): Yes, that's obviously important. In fact, that was my idea of doing the study at all because I wondered whether bulimic patients would have abnormal satiety related to rapid gastric emptying, particularly after the work of Wright, 1986, where they found that these patients had abnormally rapid gastric emptying. The only bulimic patient in which I did find rapid gastric emptying was a bit overweight. The question that you haven't asked me but that I will answer anyway is that the patients with slow gastric emptying didn't have higher satiety ratings than the ones with rapid gastric emptying.

DR. SCHNEIDER: Thank you and I must congratulate you. This is a major contribution and I think also an example of transferring techniques between animal and human research. This may also help explain why there is immense difficulty in increasing food intake in animals that have been food deprived or in showing increases in food intake when one uses certain drug manipulations.

DR. ALLAN GELIEBTER (*St. Luke's-Roosevelt Hospital, New York*): Paul, I would also like to congratulate you on your fine presentation. I want to pick up on Marion Hetherington's question about whether emptying is even faster in bulimics. We found that there was a tendency for emptying to be slightly faster in bulimics, but it wasn't significantly different. At the same time, we found that when we measured stomach capacity in the bulimics it was significantly different. At the same time, we found that when we measured stomach capacity in the bulimics it was significantly larger than in normals. An interesting correlation that we observed was that subjects that had a larger stomach capacity also had slower emptying. And we think we can explain this as due to the smaller rise in pressure that one sees for a given volume in a larger stomach so that subjects with a large capacity had a smaller rise in pressure. Because the pressure gradient may drive emptying, that could account for a somewhat slower emptying, and this may confound the effect that we saw in emptying between the bulimics and the normals. When one controls for gastric capacity, emptying doesn't seem to be so much faster in the bulimics.

Related to capacity, in your animal data with a two-hour feeding schedule, you might be aware that when you put animals on such a schedule the stomach has a tendency to enlarge. I'm wondering whether or not the enlargement of the stomach might contribute to the slower emptying you see in these rats.

DR. ROBINSON: I think that is an interesting idea and is something we might try to check in some way. Of course the changes in intragastric pressure might have some relevance to liquid emptying, but the solid emptying is mainly controlled by antral function and not by what you would be measuring, which would be fundal function. However, it may be relevant to the liquid situation.

DR. JULIO LICINIO (*New York Hospital–Cornell Medical Center, White Plains, NY*): Your data are very interesting, and they raise major implications about endocrine studies in eating disorders during the course of the meal because eating-disorder patients apparently would absorb nutrients differently from normal persons. Do you have any suggestions about studies in this area, or how we can control for that?

DR. ROBINSON: Yes. I think you have to measure gastric emptying. For instance, if one wants to measure CCK in anorectics, I think one would be foolish not to measure gastric emptying at the same time because the entry of food into the duodenum is the major releaser for CCK. If that is altered you don't know where you are. There are two ways to get around it. One of them is to measure gastric emptying during the test, which is possible, but the other possibility is to insert a duodenal cannula and give a dose of nutrient directly into the duodenum, which would be a constant CCK releaser. The disadvantage of that is it's unphysiological and may be related to nausea and aversive consequences. In fact, I think probably the best answer would be to measure gastric emptying and use the gastric emptying results as covarients.

Summary: Part VI

D. A. BOOTH

School of Psychology
University of Birmingham
Birmingham, England

HOW DO EATING DISORDERS WORK?

To warn you of the longstanding habit I am going to indulge in, all my comments are founded on the view of science as the identification of causal processes. That may seem a resounding truism, and yet it isn't, for it is an approach that is immediately applicable to the development of what we have been hearing this afternoon, and it has been highly relevant throughout the conference.

The key to understanding the eating disorders, I suggest, is to characterise the immediate causally effective input to the momentary behavior that we are observing, whether it be in words or in actions. The measures might be made around or during a binge by a bulimic, for example, or around an occasion when an anorexic is refusing to eat.

We have heard from Dr. Robinson just now, and before lunch from Drs. Rolls and Hetherington and Dr. Drewnowski, examples of what I would call input–output analysis. This morning, it was food-variant input altering the intake or ratings output, and gastric contents relating to ratings just now. The other two papers this afternoon are beautiful examples of what I would call output analysis. Today, these two sorts of study, input–output and output, are in disordered eating behavior itself, not in other conditions that may or may not be relevant.

OUTPUT PATTERNS

My point is that just as yesterday Drs. Schneider and Davis were analyzing the rat's microbehavior in itself as output, so Dr. Halmi is using people's ratings and Drs. Walsh and Kissileff are using their food intake to pick out patterns in the dependent variables. This output pattern identification is the first step, part of the very first step, in characterizing the mechanisms of any normal or abnormal phenomenon, in the present case abnormal appetite. However, output measures by themselves tell you nothing about the causal processes unless you get dissociation among your multiple measures. This is indeed what Schneider and Davis did when they dissociated some microbehaviors from others in the effects of a drug on licking. Faced with such a pattern of data, we must allow that they have evidence that the drug is affecting one eating mechanism and not another.

Yet this still gives us no information on the causes or controls of the differential effect on which the drug acts. Output analysis never identifies the origin of the effect. To do this, we must have input data that relates to the output dissociation. FIGURE 1 shows the principle of input–output analysis, that is, one piece of the evidence that could identify a causal mechanism that is affected by a drug, an eating abnormality,

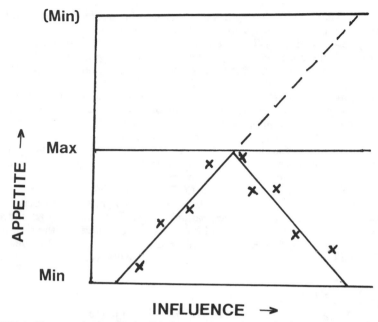

FIGURE 1. The quantitative relationship between learned appetite for food and an influence on it in an individual organism. Differences from the most motivating level of the influence are unfolded and a linear regression calculated through the raw data.[7,8]

or any other condition (compare FIG. 1 in Booth[1]). The output could be one set of various sorts of ratings of appetite (as I would say), which range from abdominal sensations to the global question how hungry you are, the pleasantness of several staple foods, or how much energy is in what someone says they would order from a menu. We showed many years ago[2] that all these ratings tend to correlate highly, and indeed that before/after meal differences also intercorrelate even better.[3,4] This is the same fact that several speakers have mentioned, namely that many of these ratings load highly on a single factor, similar to the factor that Dr. Halmi was detailing for some eating-disordered cases. All of these ratings also correlate with measures of rated preferences, of actual food choice, and of the cumulative results of eating behavior, such as food caloric intake.

This makes a nonsense of the supposition that differently worded ratings measure different experiences or distinguish between the different sorts of objective influences that they refer to, for example, different gastrointestinal processes or metabolic versus sensory influences on eating. Insofar as these output measures all share common variance, insofar as they are all intercorrelated, they cannot be effective discriminators of different influences. Such different causes of appetite may well exist but those ratings provide no evidence of it under the conditions of testing that have confounded, for example, cognitive and physiological influences. As Dr. Robinson put it, they are the same rating even though the words are different.

By the same token, however, when we do dissociate outputs, most interesting and productive questions can be asked. For example, in Dr. Halmi's results, the preoccupation with food was an output measure that was not associated with most of the other direct measures of eating. What is this distinct behavior by these individuals? You know that what the person is saying by this dissociated rating of preoccupation with food is different from "I have an appetite" or "I don't have an appetite." Is it guilt at the food they have just eaten? Is it the respondent appealing to the experimenter to consider what is being done to the long-suffering subject of investigation? That's a genuine scientific and clinical question that obviously could be important to follow up.

Similarly, in the Kissileff and Walsh data, what is the process at the basis of the observed move away from protein during the binge? Is it money-saving habits? Is it perhaps stereotyping the binge as consumption of "junk" food? — that is, picking out the low-protein foods because the binger feels that what she is doing is just eating rubbishy foods in a rubbishy way? There is a real question what the causation is behind this particular output measure, because it is separate from the other responses. Because it works differently from the other measures, it is telling us a whole lot more than masses of data that are all redundant with each other.

So those are examples of real scientific findings and further questions that can arise from multiple output measures. If we show that we have got dissociations, we can ask what is peculiar about the causation of each set of indices of an underlying phenomenon that is different from all the other sets of indices. If the relevance of such an issue to eating disorders needs to be established, the output measure in question has to be associated with another output measure that is characteristic of eating disorders.

DIAGNOSIS OF MECHANISMS

On the other hand, the nature of the influence that exists on a distinct output can only be identified by input–output analysis. This is the nearest, I think, that we can get to what Dr. Blundell was asking for this morning in the way of an "algorithm." We do not need another scientifically indeterminate argument about the definitions of words nor one more conceptual diagram bespattered with boxes and arrows that have no definite relation to data gathering or data analysis. This paradigm, algorithm, or model is the specification of a mental mechanism in appetite in a way that implies how to measure it and how to interpret any relevant observations. Indeed, this approach encapsulates the essentials of individual mental causation by taking the approach that has yielded generalized laws of physical, biological, and economic causation.

The mental mechanism framed in this context is the appetite triangle (FIG. 1) that I described in my paper.[1] When differences from maximum motivation are unfolded around the theoretical peak, an appetite mechanism is measured by the linear psychophysical relationship between any sort of input and any output measure that relates to eating, be it appetite rating or ingestive behavior.

As soon as one faces the basic reality of the mechanistic and quantitative scientific approach, it becomes blindingly obvious that to identify and to measure any influence over the abnormal eating behavior, we must measure the inputs and distinguish the inputs that affect the relevant outputs from those that do not. Furthermore, without this we are not justified in claiming what mechanism it is that the drug, the gastric physiology, or the psychopathology or its therapy is affecting. No diet or rating is a "test" of palatability or preoccupation with food. The test for a mechanism is a discrete set of input–output relationships within behavior. There is no way that we can interpret intercorrelated outputs dissociated from other outputs unless we have some input measure that tightly correlates with the output measure.

Note also that it is not the intercept or the slope of the input–output function (FIG. 1), nor even its correlation coefficient, that measures the strength of influence or the sensitivity of the eating to the influence (and its modulation by an intervention). The more unexplained scatter that there is in the relationship between the input measure and the output measure, then the less we know about what is going on in the situation. Thus, the strength of the observed mechanism is the scatter of the input–output function relative to the slope; the smaller is that ratio, the more of a difference the influence makes to the output.

The approach to this pattern of data is the beauty of Dr. Robinson's results that some of us referred forward to earlier in the conference. As well as getting ratings of fullness or whatever sensation the person is associating with lack of appetite or having eaten recently, he is measuring gastric contents and relating the contents to the ratings of satiety, and getting tight relationships. So this is one form of the absolutely essential second step. First get your output measures; we've heard about pioneering work of that sort for eating-disordered patients from Dr. Halmi. Then seek out potentially causal input–output measures for single cases, as Dr. Robinson is beginning to do.

The third step essential to evidence for a mechanism is to seek out input–output functions systematically and to find dissociations in the relationships between the inputs and the outputs. TABLE 1 shows a result we got with the tastes and flavors of foods.[5] We found that sweetness ratings for sweet, white coffee correlated very tightly (showed very little residual variance) with the sugar content of the coffee, whereas they correlated very poorly with the whitener content, while on the other hand the whiteness ratings correlated rather poorly with the sugar content but correlated very tightly with the whitener content. This is a quantitative double dissociation, using psychophysical techniques. It shows that when people talk about sweetness they are actually talking about sugar or the sweetener in what they're tasting. Anyone would hope that this could be shown, but without data like these we're merely assuming it to be so.

So the third step must be to dissociate between relationships between different sets of inputs and outputs. For example, in Dr. Robinson's data, as he mentioned, there is the problem that knowledge of time since eating is mixed up with the emptying of the contents. It would be nice to know what the people expected as the time course of decay of their satiety after this meal. Then we could attempt to disconfound the perceptivity of the gastric contents from the expectations of the decline of satiety. Measuring the expectations of satiety is no less crucial to understanding the aftereffects on appetite of differences in sweetness or fiber content of food,[6] a point that such experiments have yet to take on board.

Figure 1 in my main paper[1] applies this basic logic for scientific analysis of the effects of conditions on mechanisms. Each panel of the figure gives a pair of input–output functions under a particular condition. We have three levels of each input, the absolute minimum to see whether there is a straight-line relationship between input and output. The output can be whatever measure of appetite is suitable, whether be-

TABLE 1. Median (Range) Percentage Residual Variance of Mean Linear Regressions between Log Concentrations of Constituents and Ideal–Relative Intensity Ratings on Freely Described Off-Ideal Characteristics of Hot Coffee Drinks, in Nine Habitual Drinkers of Sweet, White Coffee[a]

Ratings	Constituent	
	Sugar	Whitener
Sweetness ratings	3 (18)	48 (93)
Whiteness ratings	28 (81)	2 (3)

[a] $p < 0.01$, one-tailed Wilcoxon test, in all comparisons between constituents and ratings.

havioral or verbal. The rows of panels in that figure represent two sorts of conditions. They might be two drug treatments, for example, D1 and D2 dopamine antagonists, and each of three doses. They might be different sorts of people, a restricting anorexic and a bingeing anorexic, an anorexic and a bulimic, or a bulimic and a control. The recovered bulimic, the moderately disordered bulimic, and the acute florid bulimic would be a sort of dose response, as with the drugs. Whatever the overall design, it might be two different foods we're talking about, for example, tomato soup and a cookie, or the two inputs could be constituents of one food; in that case, in each panel of the figure we have the effects on intake or preference of these constituents, sugar and salt, say, in the test food. If we find that, for example, in the acute bulimic the two inputs behave differently, whereas in the normal they behave similarly, this would begin to analyze out a mechanism that operates differently in bulimics from normals. The bulimic's fear of sweetness might be greater than that of saltiness, out of all order to that seen in normal users of food. To take a psychopharmacological example, if a drug makes the same preference measure less sensitive both to saccharin levels and to salt levels, then the drug may be affecting a palatability mechanism, whereas if it affects only the slope for sweetness, then the drug appears to be affecting a taste perceptual mechanism.

In other words, to obtain any sound evidence of the effect of an abnormality or an intervention on a mechanism, we have to hold together three sorts of variables and measure them all at once. The results of a single test, with no measure of differences in influences on the response, cannot advance our scientific understanding of the mechanisms involved. We need not only the differences between the conditions, for example, of the sorts of people, but we also need the differences between the levels of the inputs and outputs, and, furthermore, we need at least two examples of influences to work with that do show dissociable input–output effects (TABLE 1).

CAUSAL RESEARCH AND THERAPY

So, to conclude, this conference has shown that we can do the necessary causal analysis; we have the technology. I hope that we can agree that we should now all move to this fully scientific mode of operation, in the interests of remedying and avoiding eating disorders and the damage and distress they cause. Now we can get information out of ratings in the laboratory; let's do clinical work of this sort as well. Mere demonstrations that we can measure eating behavior or clinical improvement, or even get different effects of drugs on them, are not enough. We do not need just more demonstrations that there are patterns in output or even that we can find a relationship between input and output. We won't discover anything by arguing over semantics or procedures or postulating underspecified theoretical models. We should design our research observations from now on, I suggest, in the way that could in principle help to elucidate the cognitive integration in the individual's behavior and to identify its origins in personal learning, in the biological factors, and in the culture's management of the material realities of bodily shape and an abundance of foods.

REFERENCES

1. BOOTH, D. A. 1989. Ann. N.Y. Acad. Sci. This volume.
2. BOOTH, D. A., P. MATHER & C. MCALEAVEY. 1977. Postintestinal and normal satiety in man. VIth International Conference on the Physiology of Food & Fluid Intake, Paris, July 1977.

3. BOOTH, D. A., P. MATHER & J. FULLER. 1982. Starch content of ordinary foods associa-
    tively conditions human appetite and satiation, indexed by intake and eating pleasantness
    of starch-paired flavours. Appetite 3: 162–184.
4. BOOTH, D. A. 1987. Cognitive experimental psychology of appetite. *In* Eating Habits.
    R. A. Boakes, M. J. Burton & D. A. Popplewell, Eds.: 175–209. Wiley. Chichester, UK.
5. BOOTH, D. A., M. T. CONNER & S. MARIE. 1987. Sweetness and food selection: Measure-
    ment of sweeteners' effects on acceptance. *In* Sweetness. J. Dobbing, Ed.: 143–160. Springer-
    Verlag. London.
6. BOOTH, D. A. 1989. The effect of dietary starches and sugars on satiety and on mental state
    and performance. *In* Dietary Starches and Sugars in Man: A Comparison. J. Dobbing,
    Ed.: 225–249. Springer-Verlag. London.
7. BOOTH, D. A., A. L. THOMPSON & B. SHAHEDIAN. 1983. A robust, brief measure of an indi-
    vidual's most preferred level of salt in an ordinary foodstuff. Appetite 4: 301–312.
8. CONNER, M. T., A. V. HADDON, E. S. PICKERING & D. A. BOOTH. 1988. Sweet tooth demon-
    strated: Individual differences in preference for both sweet foods and foods highly sweet-
    ened. J. Appl. Psychol. 73: 275–280.

Panel Discussion

Progress and Prospects for Research Related to Human Eating Disorders

PAUL R. McHUGH, *Panel Moderator*

Johns Hopkins University
Baltimore, Maryland 21205

PANEL: LINDA BARTOSHUK (*Pierce Foundation, New Haven, CT*);
DAVID BOOTH (*University of Birmingham, Birmingham,
England*); ARTHUR CAMPFIELD (*Hoffmann-LaRoche, Nut-
ley, NJ*); STEPHEN J. COOPER (*University of Birmingham,
Birmingham, England*); KATHERINE A. HALMI (*New York
Hospital–Cornell Medical Center, White Plains, NY*);
HARRY KISSILEFF (*St. Luke's–Roosevelt Hospital, New
York*); JOHN MORLEY (*Sepulveda VA Medical Center,
Sepulveda, CA*); STYLIANOS NICOLAIDIS (*College de France
CNRS, Paris*); PAUL H. ROBINSON (*Kings College Hospital
College of Medicine, London*); GERALD F. M. RUSSELL (*The
Institute of Psychiatry, London*); LINDA SCHNEIDER (*New
York Hospital–Cornell Medical Center, White Plains, NY*).

DR. McHUGH: To start, I would just like to say that it's been an absolutely wonderful meeting with a great deal of intriguing observations being made, observations
at every level from the sociocultural down to the molecular. Certainly progress is going
to continue on all of these levels. Advances may well also arise from the psychiatric
point of view.

One of them will be to emphasize the overriding problem that these persons with
eating disorders suffer from, namely this overvalued idea about their bodily weight.
I was interested that this concept, which derives actually from Karl Wernike, is one
of the Russell criteria for anorexia nervosa.

Paul Rozin, in exploring his views of the cultural aspects, rediscovered the overvalued idea. In fact, what comes out in a culture, often in some of the vulnerable
members of that culture, is that this overvaluing of body weight is an idea of great
importance to those persons and is shared by a portion of society but not to such
a great degree. Others have almost delusional proportions about its importance and
have great affectivity tied to it. All of our patients with anorexia nervosa really are
suffering from this kind of an overvalued idea that then generates portions of their

behavior and produces a lot of the physiological and psychological changes that we have been observing.

The other issue that I was interested in was not discussed here but certainly will be discussed at our next international meeting because of its emergence as an important concept, and that is cancer anorexia, which probably is the most prominent human eating disorder that we see in clinical medicine. I now ask the panel for their thoughts regarding future prospects for progress in eating disorder research.

DR. NICOLAIDIS: The future is bright. Also, I think we don't take enough advantage of clinical pictures such as those seen in new surgery, as I have been seeing during my whole career. For some reason we are very reluctant in using that material, but it's very precious material. Those who have access to neurosurgical traumatic cases can see that there are changes on set point; tremendous changes occur in body weight that are very well defended, just as the previous body weight was defended at the lower or higher level. Usually body weight goes up. I've seen several intensive cases of that type, but it looks like there is no one lesion that can account for that particular jump of set point. Probably I didn't spend enough time for that, and somebody else could do it. Of course, traumas hit the brain differently, and various lesions will end in this change of set point.

DR. SCHNEIDER: I think that one of the things that I would like to see examined more is the interaction between human eating behavior and energy output or exercise anorexia. I feel that is one topic that we have not covered. Also, I'm particularly concerned about education. We haven't spoken much about reaching down to the vulnerable population and trying to communicate what constitutes proper regulation of weight and body imagery, in order to get feedback from them and to get to these especially vulnerable girls at the right age.

DR. CAMPFIELD: Many of the issues that I see as appropriate directions for research, I mentioned in my discussion. I think David Booth has laid down a formidable challenge for all of us to take up the search for mechanism and to be careful about what we consider inputs and outputs and to look for associations and dissociations to lead us along the way. In the poster session last night, we saw several exercise-induced models, restrictive feeding induced models, and various other attempts to be innovative within the confines of studies on rat feeding. We might be able to look among many different laboratories and many different models and see features of the syndrome. Perhaps from this we could put the pieces of the model together and see if we could better understand their mechanisms. We can then come to some ideas about how we might either intervene earlier or more successfully in the human situation.

I also was impressed today, in seeing the human feeding studies, the first on sensory–hedonic aspects, and then the actual confrontation with the disorder in the clinic. I was encouraged, based on what I know about the syndrome of anorexia and what the patients say they want to do, that is, to restrict food intake. In spite of all cues, signals, and urgings, they are able to do that. I think we saw that in the data from Johns Hopkins as well as from Adam Drewnowsky's data on fat selection. These patients were able to recognize what they consider dangerous and avoid it; even though they have sensory-specific satiety, they manage to not eat. Therefore, I think that this work has established the ground floor. I encourage the people working with humans not to simply characterize the syndrome over and over, but to turn to the search for mechanism. We should be encouraged by the fact that this group of patients do provide significant information on rating scales, tell the psychiatrist revealing information, and perform in the eating clinic laboratory. I'm now more encouraged than I was before the meeting began.

DR. BARTOSHUK: Two things that I've seen at this meeting are very exciting, and provide ways in which I would like to see sensory psychophysicists begin to get more involved in this field. For one thing, particularly with purging bulimics, the oral cavity is altered by that pathology. We're only now beginning to look at what the act of purging itself, in the exposure of gustatory tissue to acid, is doing to taste, and I think we're going to be finding that there are very interesting changes. Sensory psychophysics, it seems to me, has a very important role, at least in some branches of the study of eating disorders.

In addition I was very excited by the sensory scaling and the psychophysical scaling that was done, essentially measurement of eating behavior in the laboratory. I think this is a wonderful way to go. There are problems, and Paul McHugh raised one: What do these scales mean with these populations? Distortions exist. These are profoundly interesting problems, but they are not substantially different than the problems that psychophysicists face every day when looking at other questions. The insights from some of these other areas might serve here. What do you do when you're trying to evaluate the psychophysical world of a person who is hearing impaired or vision impaired? Some of the same distortions are involved; some of the same solutions might be applicable to this area.

A third area that interests me a great deal is something that I think hasn't been done yet, and I don't know whether it can be done or not. We talk about distortions in the world of people with eating disorders, and psychophysics provides a wonderful tool to measure distortions. Some wonderful techniques are available to use, which to the best of my knowledge haven't yet been used with eating disorders. I'd love to see us know better what the perceptual world of a person who has an eating disorder is. I think there's a great deal more to be found out.

DR. KISSILEFF: It gets more and more difficult to say something new. Nevertheless, I'll put up my wish list. I was originally trained as a biologist, and I worked on rats for many years. When I came to St. Luke's and began working on the human, I wanted to be able to apply some of those preclinical techniques to the human. I think that we've demonstrated, and other people have demonstrated, that while human eating behavior can be studied in a laboratory, it's not the same as natural eating behavior in the "wild," as Dr. Walsh pointed out. However I'm a little bit depressed by the limitations of what we can actually do with the human. I'd like to know, for example, what's going on in the liver of a human. We don't have any way of doing that now. We can't do biopsies. There aren't any radiotracers that are specific for liver cells, but I think that the kinds of models that David Booth, for example, has generated with energy flows are useful, and gastric emptying, at least, we can measure. For many of the questions of mechanism, of brain neurotransmitters, for example, we can't put probes into the brain and determine where a particular neurotransmitter is being produced. We have to rely on the animal models. As someone said many years ago, man is not a rat; rats are only models, and that makes it very difficult. But I would like to see the human work, as David Booth suggested earlier, move more in the direction of hypothesis testing. Research would be driven by an idea rather than simply seeking further description. Of course, if we find interesting pathological situations that haven't been described before, descriptions are always the first step in getting some idea of where to go, but for many of the eating disorders we've already got those descriptions. It's time to try to develop a mechanistic approach that we can use, but that project is going to require collaborations with colleagues in other fields, such as, physiology, neurobiology, and neuropsychology, so that we can develop techniques to look at the biological processes that are presently hidden from view.

DR. BOOTH: I think I should retrieve one very unfortunate impression that not only I have, but most of us will have been creating, that even though the research requirements are exciting, the prospect of getting on with them is extremely complex and tough. In some cases this is true, but I think a lot of useful work can be done without getting into horrendous statistics, without getting into impossible physical manipulations of human beings, and so on. I really think that the sort of techniques that I've been talking about can in fact be carried out in the clinical interview. Experimental investigations would be better if they were modeled more flexibly and individually, more verbally sophisticated at the level of the clinical interview. When using these purely verbal inputs and purely verbal outputs, the second key point is to analyze them individually. You get all the statistical mess because we're throwing different individuals' data into one pot, it just doesn't fit together, and so the statistics go haywire. We should take interview data, well structured but tuned to the individual, and not only collect it individually but analyze it individually. Then we should seek to generalize only after having understood the individual. This is a technique that many more people should explore and that can be executed quite simply.

DR. ROBINSON: One of the problems with the basic scientific approach is that it's slow and painstaking. It has to be. That often leaves the clinicians wondering what we ought to do in the meantime, for the next hundred years while the basic mechanisms are sorted out, and we're faced with the patients in the clinic. A major effort needs to be made in defining empirical treatments for eating disorders. Many patients with anorexia nervosa still spend their entire lives as chronically starved, chronically ill persons that I'm afraid we can do very little about. It's for those patients that we urgently need to find treatments. This is not to say that the search for empirical causes and basic causes shouldn't go on. The levels at which it should proceed are very wide, very disparate, and one investigator can't encompass them. They obviously extend from the organic, which I personally find very fascinating. The neuropeptide work, looking at CCK, bombesin, and endorphins, and all those transmitters, will be useful, particularly when we can look at the receptors and the positron emission tomography scanning. Although it's been a little bit disappointing until now, tomography scanning might in the future give us a handle on central neuropeptide function. I think the other thing sustaining eating disorders is family determined, the way in which the specific culture within the family can lead to or exacerbate an eating disorder in a family member. Research into that area is in its absolute infancy. There isn't a proper way of assessing a family at the moment, and I think that is another area that needs to be addressed.

DR. MORLEY: We should be aware of a number of things. Not surprisingly, I think we should get away from the sexist approach to eating disorders, the view that it is a disorder of young females. I think eating disorders occur throughout the lifespan, and we have to be more aware of that. I think in addition we have to be more aware of the fact that eating disorders are cross-cultural, and in other cultures eating disorders may present in different ways. I think that is very important. We tend to look at eating disorders as being, perhaps, a spiritual phenomenon in India rather than as anorexia nervosa. On the other hand, spiritual fasting may be no different from anorexia nervosa if you understand the cultural setting. I think we have to look at those things very carefully; we have to be careful not to take our own mindset, and say we see it as this because DSM-IIIR says this is the way it's going to be. In different cultures, in different age groups, subtle differences will occur in the disease and we can become blind to them.

As far as animal models are concerned, I think there is a great future for animal models. The first caveat that we have to understand is that we all should be very careful not to do things in animals that are easily done in humans. I think that's one of the biggest problems animal scientists have. If the work can't be done in humans, animal models become very useful, particularly for dissecting out some of the neurotransmitter-type studies. Clearly we do have a good model that hasn't been brought up at this meeting in the tail-pinch model first started by Dr. Eliot Stellar and his colleagues in cats back in the 1960s and then taken up by others. In fact, tail pinch produces hypophagia but is associated with weight loss over a period of time. So what you have there is a very good model of bulimia nervosa, where you can have intermittent binging but in the end weight loss.

In addition the recent studies by George Bray show that chronic infusion of CRF causes weight loss in animals, but that weight loss is due to a change in energy: an increase in thermogenesis as much as a decrease in feeding. CRF does decrease LH; it also decreases gastric emptying. It has a lot to offer as one of the pathophysiological links, and certainly when I look at the literature I would prefer to see CRF rather than serotonin being studied. I think serotonin doesn't do nearly as much as CRF does to explain some of the eating disorders.

I think we have to be careful not just to look at eating. It is important to realize that there are changes, such as those a meal can have on memory, and that these changes often have the same linkage, they work through the same hormones, as the satiety effect. For instance, Jim Flood and I showed in *Science* last year that perhaps some of the effects of a meal on enhancing memory are mediated by cholecystokinin through the same afferent vagal impulses as are thought to work for satiety. I think one of the things we have to be very careful about is which phenomenon we're looking at. As Dr. Joseph Wortis pointed out to me earlier, what we perhaps should be talking about is irreversible starvation. Whenever you study an anorectic person, you have to study a starving person alongside the anorectic. Otherwise, many of the observations, such as a decrease in CCK seen in bulimics, could just as well be because of the bulimic binge as it could be because it had something to do with bulimia. We have to be very careful.

The one last point is that I think in the eating disorders if we gave up hypothesis-driven research and tried to start our research from looking at the data and then developing the hypothesis there would be an inordinate improvement in the standard of the data and the hypotheses we would generate. Hypotheses cannot be driven without data.

DR. HALMI: The clinical eating disorders are complex disorders, and we have emphasized eating behavior more in this conference. The real challenge is to integrate the cultural, cognitive, and physiological mechanisms that put persons at risk for developing the disorders, that actually produce anorexia nervosa and bulimia and that maintain these conditions, in addition to those factors that bring about relapses. The real challenge to clinicians is not to get the patient well in the hospital setting, which is highly controlled, but to prevent relapses of the disorder. The challenge to research is to integrate all of these complex phenomena that we have been talking about today.

DR. RUSSELL: Because all my colleagues have said so many wise things, out of a sense of perversity I feel obliged to disagree with one or two things that have been said. As our moderator has suggested, we have to look at some of the basic and difficult aspects of the clinical pictures, especially the psychological disturbance in these patients. These patients, and it's part of their illness, are prone to deny, to distort what they say; they indulge in self deception. There's a certain lack of veracity, and investigators, and I mean clinical scientists as well as basic scientists, tend to look upon that as a nuisance and an artifact. It isn't: It's part of what makes that person prone to eating disorders and other disorders as well. In the old-fashioned literature, this is called the hysterical mechanism. It's a word we don't use anymore but is a phenomenon that has been under-researched. For example, when Dr. Bartoshuk says that the psychophysicist's methods can be used and that they are reasonably straightforward, I know she doesn't mean that, because in fact she gave a beautiful example this morning of how to sort out a person who denied he had a sense of taste. It turned out that there was a financial compensation issue in that case. So she's very well aware that it's not easy.

This has been the best conference I've ever attended where I have convincingly seen the interaction between basic scientists and clinical scientists. That reflects very favorably on the organizers, the New York Academy of Sciences, and I want to thank them for holding this conference.

Long-Term Perspectives on the Study of Eating Behavior

ELIOT STELLAR

Department of Anatomy and
Institute of Neurological Sciences
School of Medicine
University of Pennsylvania
Philadelphia, Pennsylvania 19104-6058

Because I am now one of the oldest living members in our field still standing on two feet, I have a long-term perspective on the control of food intake to offer. I have lived through most of the relevant history. While I recognize it is easy to distort history by taking a subjective approach, I also know it is possible to get at fundamental truths that way.

So let's look at history through my eyes. How is it that we have made such tremendous advances in our knowledge of the physiological controls of food intake in animals, and yet we have very few effective ideas of how to treat obesity, bulimia, or anorexia nervosa? I can't answer that question, except to say that we still don't have an understanding of why animals eat and what controls the amount they eat and the choices they make. We have a lot of new facts and some general guiding principles, but no comprehensive theory that permits real understanding and the transfer of knowledge to the human clinical case. We are still waiting for someone to put it all together, even in a heuristic concept that could yield testable hypotheses for treatment. Perhaps the new insights we will gain from this conference will move us along the way, but a conference won't do it. It still will wait for one person to try to put it all together.

The history of our field is interesting and instructive, and it may help us see the future. When I first became interested in these questions, I was an undergraduate working under Cliff Morgan's tutelage in Lashley's laboratory at Harvard. The year was 1938, 50 years ago, and Lashley had just published his paper "The Experimental Analysis of Instinctive Behavior."[1] In it, he tried to show two things: (1) that hunger and the regulation of food intake, along with thirst, sexual behavior, migration, and so forth, were part of a broader category of motivated behavior that he called instinctive behavior in the terminology of his day and (2) that some excitatory state of the brain had to be aroused to produce the switch from lack of motivation to motivation, for example from nonhungry behavior to hungry behavior. He recognized that hormones and the internal environment as well as external and internal sensory stimuli played a role, and that it all had to be integrated in the central nervous system to yield specific organized, goal-directed behavior. His problem was that in 1938, he had no idea where in the brain this excitatory and integrative mechanism might be.

Lashley's views were a radical departure from previous history, for up until his paper, the predominant view was that hunger was a sensation that humans experienced, and that it was produced by sensory input arising in the stomach, the so-called gastric contraction or hunger pang. Cannon[2] was the chief proponent of this peripheral theory, and it fit right in with William James's more general theoretical concept of emotion in which he said that when we experienced the peripheral vascular and skeletal changes that the emotional circumstance produced, that *was* the emotion.[3] So there began a dichotomy of those who supported the mainstream peripheralist view and the newly arrived centralists, championed by Lashley.

Philip Bard, working in Cannon's laboratory, was a centralist, and he was convinced that emotion was a central brain state, probably of thalamic origin, and that the peripheral effects were the output of that central state and not the major cause of it.[4] He even convinced Cannon of it.[5] Richter, on the other hand, showed that the periphery was much more complicated than gastric contractions and vasomotor responses, and he directed our attention to the contribution of the internal environment to both physiological regulation and the control of motivated behavior, which he called self-regulatory behavior.[6] Particularly important for Richter were the endocrine glands and their secretions which recent advances in techniques had made accessible to experimental manipulation by endocrine gland extirpation and replacement therapy. Thus Richter was able to show that adrenalectomy radically increased salt appetite and that replacement therapy with aldosterone eliminated the salt hunger if the dose wasn't too high. That this was the mechanism in humans as well as rats was tragically illustrated by the case of a three-year-old boy that Wilkins and Richter reported in 1940 who had an enormous craving for salt from birth. He ate it by the spoonful and died when restricted to a standard hospital diet. It turned out that his adrenal glands had been destroyed by tumors and that he had kept himself alive by his excessive salt appetite.[7]

In 1943, Morgan tried to put all these peripheral and central factors together in his first edition of the textbook *Physiological Psychology*,[8] but he still didn't have a handle on the central nervous system. Instead, he referred to a humoral motive factor and a central motive state, comparable to Sherrington's central excitatory state but without reference to anatomical locus. It was not until 1950, when I collaborated with Morgan on the second edition of *Physiological Psychology*[9] that it became apparent that the hypothalamus was a candidate for the focal point of a widespread neural system in the brain that yielded motivated behavior in general and hunger and satiation in particular. This enabled me in 1954 to build on Lashley's and Morgan's conceptions and propose a general "physiology of motivation"[10] that put the hypothalamus at the center of a neuronal system (FIG. 1) that was under multifactor control, with both external and internal sensory inputs and internal environmental influences, and which was expressed on the output side through an unspecified response mechanism that was downstream in the neuraxis from the diencephalon, somewhere in the final common path for the behavior.

The intent of the 1954 paper was to present a balanced picture of peripheral and central factors, but not surprisingly attention focused on the hypothalamus, and everyone went out and bought a stereotaxic instrument and began making lesions or implanting electrodes or cannulas. Other parts of the nervous system were hardly looked at, and no one focused very much experimental attention on what the peripheral input, other than taste, might be. Yet theories abounded that the peripheral signals for hunger and satiation were glucose or glucose utilization[11]; fat, ingested or deposited in adipocytes[12]; protein[13]; or some aspect of energy metabolism, perhaps best indicated by body temperature changes.[14] Furthermore, it seemed clear at the time that the ventromedial and lateral hypothalamus were involved as part of the satiation and hunger mechanisms because lesions there were believed to lead directly to overeating or starvation, and stimulation led to the inhibition or arousal of eating, respectively. The metabolic and visceral outputs of the hypothalamus were largely ignored and so were the elusive metabolic and visceral inputs to the brain.

But the pendulum slowly swung as we began to appreciate these peripheral effects and inputs and the role of the hypothalamus in their operation. Now we know that medial hypothalamic lesions (more likely involving PVN than VMN) result in visceral,

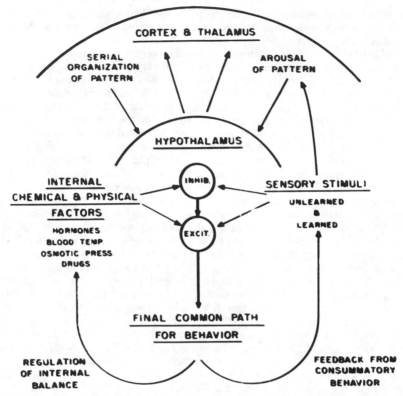

FIGURE 1. Diagram of the physiology of motivation proposed in 1954, emphasizing the inter-action of central neural, and peripheral sensory and internal environmental influences in activating the final common path to the behavior. (From Stellar.[10] Used by permission.)

metabolic, and endocrine changes, particularly hyperinsulinemia, that contribute to the obesity and indirectly to the hyperphagia.[15] The question of whether we should think of hypothalamic hyperphagia in terms of a primary or secondary hyperphagia has been most graphically suggested by Marci Greenwood in connection with her meta-bolic studies of the genetically obese Zucker rat. This animal's metabolic defect is that it preferentially deposits ingested nutrients as fat, thereby depriving itself of nutrients for energy expenditure, so it is driven to eat more. FIGURE 2 shows a direct effect on food intake in the left cartoon and an indirect effect in the right cartoon where the "pacman" adipocytes gobble up the nutrients.[16] Could something like this be happ-ening in the rat with medial hypothalamic lesions? Could something like this happen in human cases of obesity? Recently, there has been an increasing interest in the meta-bolic basis of human obesity, either due to genetic factors or to past history of dieting cycles or to other life experiences. We know that a genetic factor plays a role in the obesity of the Zucker rat. That a genetic factor may well play a role in human obesity is indicated by the Danish adoption[17] and twin studies [18] of Mickey Stunkard and his colleagues. For example, in the Danish adoption study (FIG. 3), they found a good correlation of the children's body mass index with that of the biological parents they left in infancy and a poor correlation with the adoptive parents who raised them from infancy.

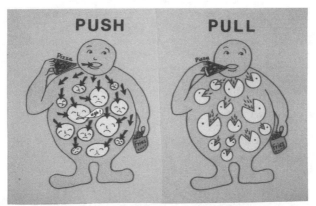

FIGURE 2. Cartoons illustrating two ways in which hyperphagia and obesity may be generated. On the left, the hyperphagia is primary, leading to obesity; on the right, the hyperphagia is secondary, following the preferential depositing of nutrients in the adipocytes (provided by M.R.C. Greenwood and based on concepts reviewed in Greenwood and Pittman-Waller[16]).

Given the major role of metabolic factors in such cases as the genetically obese rat, we are still left with the specific question of why they overeat. What signals does the metabolic and humoral periphery provide to the brain to start and stop eating in the Zucker rat, and for that matter, in the normal rat or human. In recent years, clear evidence of a role of metabolic events in the liver have been brought forward by Mark Friedman.[19] In fact, he now believes that a very specific signal of oxidative metabolism is generated in the liver that might be crucial.

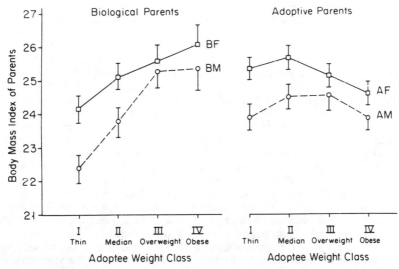

FIGURE 3. Results of a Danish adoption study, showing that the body mass index of adopted children correlated highly with the body mass index of their biological parents and poorly with the body mass index of their adoptive parents. (From Stunkard *et al.*[18] Used by permission.)

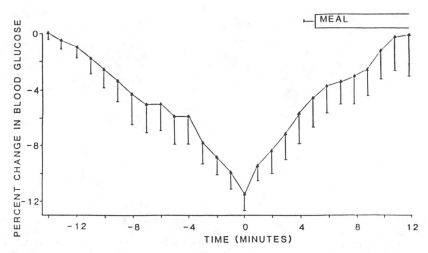

FIGURE 4. Blood sugar measurements, showing that there is a drop and then a rise in blood sugar before a meal is initiated in the normal meal-taking of the laboratory rat. (From Campfield *et al.*[20] Used by permission.)

In a different vein, Art Campfield has shown that a specific temporal pattern of change in blood glucose may be the initiator of bouts of eating in the rat.[20] As FIGURE 4 from his work shows, it is a drop in blood sugar followed by a rise that precedes the initiation of eating. So the pattern the brain sees may be fairly complex. As Stylianos Nicolaidis suggests, such information from the blood could theoretically be detected directly in the brain by brain cells that witness body states. He has made the case for brain cells that witness fundamental metabolism, or *"métabolisme de fond"* once gross bodily activity is subtracted.[21] Or signals could be picked up by chemical sensors in the blood stream or metabolic sensors in the liver and transmitted over visceral afferents like the vagus to the hindbrain.

Quite possibly both peripheral-neural and direct-CNS effects are involved simultaneously. Certainly, as Rich Miselis has shown (FIG. 5), the brain circuitry is there to provide connections between the termination of the vagus in the hindbrain and the hypothalamus, amygdala, and other parts of the limbic system and back down again from the hypothalamus to the caudal medulla.[22] Certainly there are windows in the blood–brain barrier (FIG. 6) in the hypothalamus and caudal brainstem areas that would permit direct influences of the internal environment on the diencephalic and brainstem circuits.[23] We know, however, from Harvey Gills' work[24] that the caudal medulla does a lot of processing of information having to do with food acceptance and food rejection and the animal's responsiveness to its own internal state. For example, the decerebrate rat, fitted with an oral cannula, accepts sucrose solutions dripped into its mouth only when it is food deprived. If recently fed, it rejects sucrose. Under all conditions, hungry or not, it rejects quinine. It does all of this with the hypothalamus cut off from the response mechanism, so the brainstem is a very important integrator of information about hunger and satiation and the control of food intake.

Quite clearly, we have greatly enriched our understanding of the circuitry of the brain mechanisms involved in the control of eating and the peripheral sensory, metabolic, and humoral signals that are put into it. We know that genetic and metabolic factors operate in both animal and human eating and in obesity. We also know from

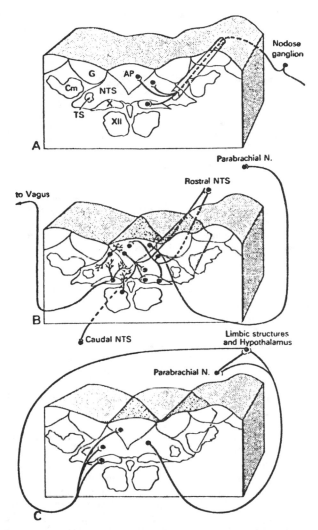

FIGURE 5. Central connections of the vagus, showing (**A**) its terminations in the caudal medulla, (**B**) the secondary connections with the rostral medulla and pons, and (**C**) the further connections with the hypothalamus and other limbic structures which, in turn, send connections to the caudal medulla. AP, area postrema; NTS, caudal medial nucleus of the solitary tract; X, dorsal motor nucleus of the vagus; XII, hypoglossal nucleus; TS, tractus solitarius; CM, medial cuneate nucleus; G, gracile nucleus. (From Hyde & Miselis.[22] Used by permission.)

both animal and human studies that habit and conditioning play an important role in both hunger and satiety.

But where are we in the understanding and treatment of eating disorders? We are not very far, and we have not yet been able to take much advantage of the advances in basic sciences. Anorexia nervosa and bulimia are just being addressed experimentally, as this conference demonstrates. The hope that lateral hypothalamic starvation

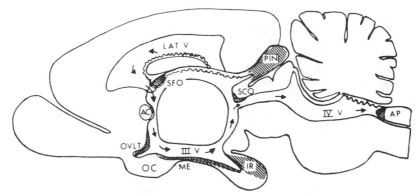

FIGURE 6. The seven circumventricular organs that have little or no blood–brain barrier, shown in a lateral view of the rat's brain: SFO, subfornical organ; OVLT, organum vasculosum of the lamina terminalis; ME, median eminence; IR, infundibular recess and neuropypophysis; SCO, subcommissural organ; PIN, pineal gland; AP, area postrema. (From Phillips.[23] Used by permission.)

might teach us something about clinical anorexia has not been realized; nor has hypothalamic hyperphagia shed much light on bulimia. Treatment of both disorders is empirical and depends on whether the therapist has a behavior modification or psychodynamic orientation, or both; or whether pharmacological interventions are used. Although some efforts have been made to relate these disorders and their treatment to hormonal and metabolic factors, none of the current interventions, as far as I know, is based in any significant way on an understanding of the mechanisms that control either food intake or obesity.

Obesity has had a longer and more checkered history of treatment than anorexia or bulimia. Because we don't understand obesity scientifically, everything has been tried at one time or another in repeated cycles of empirical trial and error including a great deal of quackery. Most people entering any treatment program lose weight, probably because their motivation to diet and exercise is at a peak. But most of them gain it back in a year or even less because motivation flags. Behavior modification helps in the maintenance of motivation and the maintenance of weight loss, but the losses are small. So efforts have been made to combine behavior modification with the greater weight losses produced by pharmacological therapy and very low calorie diets. For the morbidly obese patient, where metabolic factors may play a major role, gastric bypass surgery has had some success, but the method is a drastic one and doesn't always work for long periods of time.

The problem facing us is twofold: (1) to understand the physiological and behavioral controls of food intake and obesity and (2) to transfer that knowledge to the clinical problems of obesity, bulimia, and anorexia in a practical way. To make progress in the first, we need someone to pull together the welter of experimental information currently available about animals into a comprehensive theory of appetite and obesity and their controls. To make progress in the second, we need more experimental work on appetite and obesity in human food intake laboratories, and we particularly need well-designed investigations of the efficacy of various treatments with emphasis on long-term follow-up of the maintenance of *both* the behavioral change in response to food and the weight loss.

New anatomical, physiological, metabolic, neurochemical, and behavioral methods give us new data and open new windows for our conceptual perspectives on the psychobiology of human eating disorders, and we are hearing a lot about these advances at this meeting. But there remains that crucial first step that I throw out as a challenge to all of you: Some one person has to put it all together in a multifactor scheme of peripheral–central interactions, involving metabolic and visceral inputs to the brain, affecting widespread systems throughout the neuraxis, systems whose properties originate in the cellular and molecular properties of the neurons involved and that yield an output that controls metabolism, visceral function, and eating behavior, both appetitive and consummatory. It has to be a comprehensive theory that is both testable in the laboratory and applicable to the human clinical problem of eating disorders. That's a big order, but I believe we are up to it.

REFERENCES

1. LASHLEY, K. S. 1938. An experimental analysis of instinctive behavior. Psychol. Rev. **45:** 445–771.
2. CANNON, W. B. 1932. The Wisdom of the Body. Norton. New York.
3. JAMES, W. 1884. The physical basis of emotion. Psychol. Rev. **1:** 516–529.
4. BARD, P. 1928. A diencephalic mechanism for the expression of rage with special reference to the sympathetic nervous system. Am J. Physiol. **84:** 490–515.
5. CANNON, W. B. 1927. The James-Lange theory of emotion: A critical examination and alternative theory. Am. J. Physiol. **39:** 106–124.
6. RICHTER, C. P. 1942–43. Total self-regulatory functions in animals and human beings. Harvey Lect. Ser. **38:** 63–103.
7. WILKINS, L. & C. P. RICHTER. 1940. A great craving for salt by a child with cortico-adrenal insufficiency. J. Am. Med. Assoc. **114:** 866–868.
8. MORGAN, C. T. 1943. Physiological Psychology. McGraw-Hill. New York.
9. MORGAN, C. T. & E. STELLAR. 1950. Physiological Psychology. McGraw-Hill. New York.
10. STELLAR, E. 1954. The physiology of motivation. Psychol. Rev. **61:** 5–22.
11. MAYER, J. 1953. Glucostatic mechanism of regulation of food intake. N. Engl. J. Med. **249:** 13–16.
12. KENNEDY, G. C. 1953. The role of depot fat in the hypothalamic control of food intake in the rat. Proc. R. Soc. London Ser. B. **140:** 578–592.
13. MELLINKOFF, S. M., M. FRANKLAND, D. BOYLE & GREIPEL. 1956. Relationship between serum amino acid concentration and fluctuations in appetite. J. Appl. Physiol. **8:** 535–538.
14. BROBECK, J. R. 1948. Food intake as a mechanism of temperature regulations. Yale J. Biol. Med. **20:** 545–552.
15. NOVIN, D. & D. A. VANDERWEELE. 1977. Visceral involvement in feeding: There is more to regulation than the hypothalamus. *In* Progress in Psychobiology and Physiological Psychology. J. M. Sporague & A. N. Epstein, Eds. Vol. **7:** 193–241. Academic Press. New York.
16. GREENWOOD, M. R. C. & V. A. PITTMAN-WALLER. 1987. Weight control: A complex, various, and controversial problem. *In* Obesity Handbook. Complete Guide to Understanding and Treatment. R. Frankle & M. Yang, Eds. 3–15. Aspen Systems. Rockville, MD.
17. STUNKARD, A. J., T. I. SØRENSEN, H. C. TEASDALE, R. CHAKRABORTY, W. J. SCHULL & F. SCHULSINGER. 1986. An adoption study of human obesity. N. Engl. J. Med. **324:** 193–198.
18. STUNKARD, A. J., T. I. A. SØRENSEN, C. HANIS, R. W. TEASDALE, R. CHAKRABORTY, W. J. SCHULL & F. SCHULSINGER. 1986. An adoption study of human obesity. N. Engl. J. Med. **314:** 193–198.
19. FRIEDMAN, M. I. & E. M. STRICKER. 1976. The physiological psychology of hunger: A physiological perspective. Psychol. Rev. **83:** 409–431.
20. CAMPFIELD, L. A., P. BRANDON & F. J. SMITH. 1985. On-line continuous measurement

of blood glucose and meal pattern in free-feeding rats: The role of glucose in meal initiation. Brain Res. Bull. **14:** 605–616.

21. NICOLAIDIS, S. & P. EVEN. 1984. Mesure du metabolisme de fond en relation aves la prise alimentaire: Hypothese ischymetrique. C. R. Acad. Sci. (III) **298:** 295–300.

22. HYDE, T. M. & R. R. MISELIS. 1983. Effects of area postrema/caudal medial nucleus of the solitary tract lesions on food intake and body weight. Am. J. Physiol. **244:** R577-R587.

23. PHILLIPS, M. I. 1978. Angiotensin in the brain. Neuroendocrinology **25:** 354–377.

24. NORGREN, R. & H. GRILL. 1982. Brainstem control of ingestive behavior. In The Physiological Mechanisms of Motivation. D. W. Pfaff, Ed.: 99–131. Springer-Verlag. New York.

Dietary Fat-Induced Overeating

Influence of Fat Composition

KAREN ACKROFF, FRANÇOIS LUCAS, AND
ANTHONY SCLAFANI

Department of Psychology
Brooklyn College of CUNY
Brooklyn, New York 11210

In rats, high-fat diets have been shown to promote obesity[1,2] However, the weight gains are often small, and the diets do not always induce overeating.[2] One explanation for these results may be that different forms of fat produce different degrees of hyperphagia and obesity.[3]

The present study compared two fat sources, corn oil and vegetable shortening. They were provided as options to a complete diet so that the animals could control the amount and proportion of fat consumed. In addition, the effect of supplementing the shortening with micronutrients was examined, because a pilot study had shown considerable hyperphagia and weight gain with an enriched-fat option.

Four groups of adult female Sprague–Dawley rats ($n = 8$ or 9) were given 30 days of *ad libitum* access to water and one of the following diets: chow only, chow and corn oil, chow and plain vegetable shortening, or chow and vegetable shortening enriched with micronutrients (AIN vitamin and mineral mixes, choline bitartrate, and celluflour). The fat options and chow were presented in separate containers.

The average daily caloric intakes of the four groups were compared with analysis of variance (the first six days were excluded due to spillage problems in the oil group). As shown in the upper panel of FIGURE 1, the enriched shortening group ate more fat than the plain shortening group, and both shortening groups ate more fat and less chow than the oil group. The oil, plain shortening, and enriched shortening groups selected 38%, 64%, and 73%, respectively, of their total caloric intakes from the fat option. The total intakes of the two shortening groups were similar and reliably exceeded the total intakes of the oil and chow groups.

The percentages in the upper panel of FIGURE 1 indicate the degree of overeating by the fat option groups compared to the chow group. Note that the oil group was not hyperphagic, while shortening promoted considerable overeating that was further enhanced by micronutrient enrichment.

The lower panel of FIGURE 1 shows body weight gains during the 30-day study period. By the end of the study, the enriched shortening group had clearly outgained the other groups; their total weight gain was three times that of the chow group. The plain shortening group gained twice as much weight as the chow group, while the oil group's gain did not reliably exceed control values.

To determine whether the differential intakes of the fat sources were due to rats' greater flavor preferences for particular fats, pairs of fat sources were offered, in separate studies, to naive animals. Both fats, as well as chow and water, were available *ad libitum* for at least 10 days.

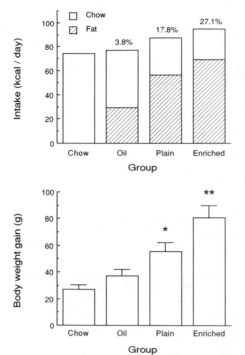

FIGURE 1. Upper panel: Average daily caloric intakes of the four groups during the last 24 days of the study. Intakes of chow and the fat option are shown separately. Percentages indicate the amount of overeating (total calories/day) relative to the chow group. Lower panel: Average 30-day body weight gains of the four groups. Asterisks indicate significant difference from chow group; *$p < 0.05$; **$p < 0.01$.

The rats consumed somewhat more oil than shortening at first; however, a significant preference for the shortening developed (51 kcal/day versus 21 for oil). The rats ate slightly more enriched than plain shortening (53 versus 40 kcal/day); however, the two sources were consumed equally at first and no significant preference emerged over 18 days.

CONCLUSIONS

The nature of the fat source is an important determinant of fat selection, total caloric intake, and body weight gain. Under these conditions, vegetable shortening promoted overeating and weight gain, but corn oil did not. Enriching the shortening with micronutrients further enhanced fat intake and weight gain; the supplementation may permit the animals to consume more fat by preventing the "dilution" of vitamins and minerals in their diet.

The results of the preference tests suggested that orosensory factors alone do not account for the differential consumption of the fat sources. However, the rats did tend over time to prefer the fat source that induced the most hyperphagia. Taken together, these data suggest that postingestive factors account for the differential overeating and weight gain produced by different forms of fat.

REFERENCES

1. SCHEMMEL, R., O. MICKELSON & J. L. GILL. 1970. Dietary obesity in rats: Body weight and body fat accretion in seven strains of rats. J. Nutr. **100:** 1041–1048.
2. JEN, K. C., M. R. C. GREENWOOD & J. A. BRASEL. 1981. Sex differences in the effects of high-fat feeding on behavior and carcass composition. Physiol. Behav. **27:** 161–166.
3. BARBORIAK, J. J., W. A. KRAHL, G. R. COWGILL & A. D. WHEDON. 1958. Influence of high-fat diets on growth and development of obesity in the albino rat. J. Nutr. **64:** 241–249.

Glucoprivic Feeding and Activity-Based Anorexia in the Rat[a]

PAUL F. ARAVICH,[b,c,d] LEE E. DOERRIES,[d,e] ERIC STANLEY,[e]
ARTHUR METCALF,[e] AND THOMAS J. LAUTERIO[c,d]

[b]Department of Anatomy and Cell Biology and
[c]Department of Internal Medicine
Eastern Virginia Medical School
Norfolk, Virginia

[d]Veterans Administration Medical Center
Hampton, Virginia 23667

[e]Department of Psychology
Christopher Newport College
Newport News, Virginia

Anorexia nervosa is characterized by numerous abnormalities, including β-endorphin (BE) alterations[1] and an impaired appetitive response to the glucose antimetabolite, 2-deoxy-D-glucose (2DG).[2] Because of interest in exercise and anorexia nervosa, we are beginning a systematic examination of the phenomenon of activity-based anorexia (ABA), which is produced by superimposing activity-wheel exercise on a restricted-feeding schedule in normal rats.[3] The purpose of this investigation was to determine if ABA is associated with abnormal appetitive and pituitary BE responses to 2DG.

The subjects were 76 male adolescent Sprague–Dawley rats (7–10 rats per group) maintained on Purina chow and a 12/12 light/dark cycle. The treatments were an ABA condition (1.5 hrs/day access to food and 22.5 hrs/day activity wheel access); a body-weight (BW) matched control condition (achieved by food restriction); an exercise control condition (free access to activity wheels and free access to food); and a condition involving no exercise and no food restriction (*ad libitum* control). Within each condition, rats were injected with 2DG (600 mg/kg; 100 mg/ml, i.p.) or with an equal volume of the vehicle (injectable water). Testing began when the ABA and BW controls reached a 25% weight-loss criterion. Exercise controls were tested after four days of running, which was the mean number of days necessary for the ABA rats to reach the criterion. For one to two hours before the injection and six hours after the injection, running wheel access was prevented in the ABA and EXR groups. All rats were given food after the injection. The animals were sacrificed and trunk blood was collected six hours later. Plasma BE was extracted using an anti-BE–sepharose affinity column; radioimmunoassay was performed with a commercial kit (Incstar, Stillwater, MN).

The 2DG challenge caused a paradoxical reduction in food intake in the ABA rats, which was not specific to ABA since the BW-matched controls showed a similar response (FIG. 1). By contrast, 2DG produced a reliable increase in the exercise control

[a] Supported by Eastern Virginia Medical School Institutional Support Grant 188–16.

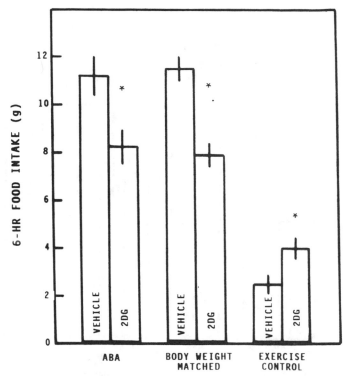

FIGURE 1. Mean ± SEM six-hour food intake (g) following 2-deoxy-D-glucose or vehicle injections in activity-based anorexia (ABA), body-weight matched control, and exercise control conditions. *$p < 0.05$ relative to vehicle treatment (via independent t-tests).

group. The ABA treatment also had abnormal plasma BE concentrations, which were elevated compared to *ad libitum* controls under basal (vehicle) conditions and which, unlike *ad libitum* controls, did not increase following 2DG stimulation FIGURE 2. It should be noted that while the effects of general emaciation were well controlled in this experiment, the exercise control group ran significantly less than the ABA group (not shown).

This experiment demonstrates that ABA is associated with abnormal appetitive and β-endorphin responses to a 2DG challenge. The paradoxical suppression of food intake is importantly related to the general consequences of emaciation; the specific contribution of *intensive* exercise remains to be determined. The elevated basal levels of plasma BE replicate other data reported by us (this meeting) utilizing different gender, control, and sacrifice times. Finally, the failure of 2DG to increase plasma ABA in comparison to *ad libitum* rats may be due to a ceiling effect.

ACKNOWLEDGMENTS

We thank Mark Sutton for his dedicated help with this project.

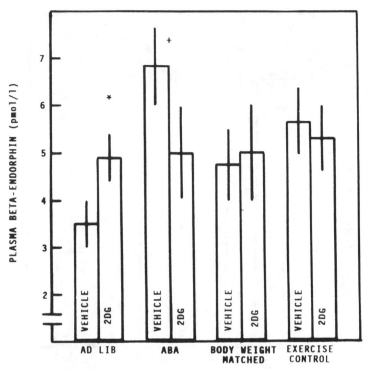

FIGURE 2. Mean ± SEM plasma β-endorphin concentrations (pmol/1) 6 ± 1 hours after 2-deoxy-D-glucose (2DG) or vehicle injections in freely fed, nonexercised rats (*ad libitum* control), activity-based anorexia (ABA), body-weight matched control, and exercise control conditions. *$p < 0.05$ relative to vehicle treatment (via independent t-test). +$p < 0.05$ relative to *ad libitum* vehicle treatment (via a one-way analysis of variance on the vehicle scores followed by Newman–Keuls posthoc tests).

REFERENCES

1. KAYE, W. H. *et al.* 1987. Reduced cerebrospinal fluid levels of immunoreactive pro-opiomelanocortin related peptides (including beta-endorphin) in anorexia nervosa. Life Sci. **41:** 2147–2155.
2. NAKAI, Y., F. KINOSHITA, T. KOH, S. TSUJII & T. TSUKADA. 1987. Perception of hunger and satiety induced by 2-deoxy-D-glucose in anorexia nervosa and bulimia nervosa. Int. J. Eating Disorder. **6:** 49–57.
3. SPEAR, N. E. & W. F. HILL. 1962. Methodological note: Excessive weight loss in rats living in activity wheels. Psychol. Rep. **11:** 437–438.

Serotoninergic Drug Potentiates the Satiating Capacity of Food

Action of d-Fenfluramine in Obese Subjects

JOHN E. BLUNDELL AND ANDREW J. HILL

BioPsychology Group
Psychology Department
University of Leeds
Leeds, LS2 9JT, United Kingdom

Food is the natural agent that reduces motivation to eat and generates satiety. This is achieved by means of a number of intermediate processes that form a structure for the satiety cascade.[1] The dilemma arises because anorexic drugs reduce the amount of material (food) which itself gives rise to satiety. Therefore an effective drug would be one that not only reduced calorie intake but also permitted the remaining consumed calories to exert an enhanced satiating capacity. In other words, the drug should amplify, rather than weaken the satiating power of food. This issue is important because numerous authors have suggested that the capacity of food to bring about satiation is weak in obese people. The problem can be investigated directly by using obese experimental subjects and by means of research designs that exploit the interactions among nutrition, pharmacology, and behavior.

In a previous study we have demonstrated that initially low levels of hunger in obese subjects were reduced by a glucose load and further suppressed in the presence of d-fenfluramine.[2] This finding suggested that the drug was augmenting the capacity of a nutrient (glucose) to induce satiety (i.e., depress hunger). This study was designed to examine the satiating capacity of a high-protein or high-carbohydrate challenge meal in obese subjects ($n = 8$; mean body mass index $= 34.5$) after three days of treatment with d-fenfluramine or placebo. The design was similar to that employed in a previous study on the interaction between nutrients and another serotoninergic compound, tryptophan. The obese subjects were asked to eat lunchtime meals of fixed energy values and nutrient composition (either high carbohydrate — 63% total energy — or high protein, 54%). Three hours after this challenge meal, a free-selection test meal was offered. Subjective motivation to eat and food preferences were sampled at intervals throughout the experimental period. The major outcome of the study is shown in TABLE 1. The high-protein challenge meal had a greater satiating effect than the high-carbohydrate meal. In the presence of d-fenfluramine, the satiating power of the food in both meals was enhanced. In a parallel study we have demonstrated a similar effect in lean subjects. Therefore the obese subjects did not show any noticeable deficiency in their satiating responses to the foods presented. Both lean and obese subjects are sensitive to the action of d-fenfluramine.

The notion of the "turnover" of behavior[5] implies a recognition that the effects of one eating episode will be carried forward to influence succeeding episodes. This concept draws attention to the interaction between nutrition and pharmacology and means that the action of any anorexic drug upon the pattern of ingestion should be

TABLE 1. Food Intake in a Free-Selection Test Meal[a]

	High Carbohydrate Meal		High Protein Meal	
	Placebo	d-Fenfluramine	Placebo	d-Fenfluramine
Weight of food (g)	479.0	427.9	414.1	365.7
x̄ ± SEM	(33.3)	(33.4)	(34.6)	(33.6)
Energy consumed (kcal.)	873.7	781.2	709.3	633.4
x̄ ± SEM	(68.6)	(70.6)	(72.9)	(44.5)

[a] Test meal followed a high-protein (54% total energy) or high-carbohydrate (63%) challenge meal given three hours earlier to obese subjects (x̄ BMI = 38.0). The challenge meals were presented following three days of pretreatment with d-fenfluramine (30 mg) or placebo. There is a significant main effect of challenge meal [$F(1,7) = 21.2, p < 0.01$] and drug treatment [$F(1,7) = 9.8, p < 0.05$] on energy consumed.

interpreted in relation to the nutritional impact of the modulated eating profile, that is, the interaction between the drug action and the satiating power of food. This action is schematically represented in FIGURE 1. Because d-fenfluramine is believed to exert its anorexic action by activating serotoninergic elements,[6] these results implicate a serotonin mechanism at some stage in the satiety cascade that modulates the pattern of food consumption.

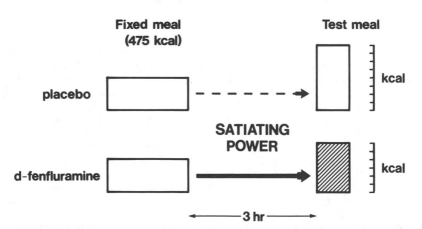

FIGURE 1. Schematic representation of the satiating power of a fixed-calorie test meal in the presence of d-fenfluramine (30 mg/day) or placebo. d-Fenfluramine amplifies the satiating power of the meal in these obese subjects. This effect was brought about by an average dose of approximately 0.3 mg/kg.

REFERENCES

1. BLUNDELL, J. E., P. J. ROGERS & A. J. HILL. 1987. Evaluating the satiating power of foods: Implications for acceptance and consumption. *In* Chemical composition and sensory properties of food and their influence on nutrition. J. Solms, Ed.: 205–219. Academic Press. London.
2. BLUNDELL, J. E. & A. J. HILL. 1988. On the mechanism of action of dexfenfluramine: Effect on alliesthesia and appetite motivation in lean and obese subjects. Clin. Neuropharmacol. **11(Suppl. 1):** S121–S134.
3. HILL, A. J. & J. E. BLUNDELL. 1988. Role of amino acids in appetite control in man. *In* Amino Acid Availability and Brain Function in Health and Disease. G. Huether, Ed.: 239–248. Springer-Verlag. Berlin.
4. BLUNDELL, J. E. 1987. Serotoninergic modulation of the pattern of eating and the profile of hunger-satiety in humans. Int. J. Obesity **11(Suppl. 3):** 141–155.
5. BLUNDELL, J. E. 1988. Turnover of behaviour: A conceptualization for feeding research. *In* Eating Behaviour in Eating Disorders. B. T. Walsh, Ed.: 2–16. American Psychiatric Press. Washington, D.C.
6. GARATTINI, S., T. MENNINI & R. SAMANIN. 1987. From fenfluramine racemate to *d*-fenfluramine: Specificity and potency of the effects on the serotoninergic system and food intake. Ann. N.Y. Acad. Sci. **499:** 156–166.

Responses to the Visual Perception of Food in Eating Disorders

SABINE BOSSERT, CAROLINE MEILLER,
REINHOLD LAESSLE, HEINER ELLGRING,
AND KARL-MARTIN PIRKE

Max-Planck-Institute of Psychiatry
Munich, Federal Republic of Germany

Preoccupation with food and dieting are typical manifestations of anorexia and bulimia nervosa. Food intake is mainly determined by the presumed nutritive value resulting in a rejection of food that is assumed to be highly nutritious.[1,2] It is also well established that the duration of consumption is changed in eating disorders.[3,4] Some of these alterations have also been described in fasting volunteers.[5] At present it is unknown whether these abnormalities merely represent biological correlates of malnutrition or specific psychopathological characteristics in eating disorders.

The few psychological studies available assessed the responses toward food mostly by questionnaires, and *in vivo* studies using behavior observation techniques are rare due to methodological obstacles. Moreover, differences in bulimics and anorexics had not always been scrutinized.

Visual presentation of 19 food items on slides was used in order to investigate the cognitive and emotional responses in 20 normal-weight bulimic and nine restrictive anorexic patients (DSM-IIIR), aged 19 to 25 years, at the beginning and at the end of hospital treatment. The control group consisted of nine age-matched women at the maximum of weight loss ($100.8 \pm 4.8\%$ IBW) during a four-week diet and at normal weight ($106.6 \pm 5.3\%$ IBW).

It was examined whether the degree of rejection, the ratings of nutritive value, and hypothetical duration of consumption of food, categorized according to its nutritive value and ease of consumption, is different in these groups and whether the severity of the eating disorder, that is, the state of malnutrition, is related to these variables. Additionally, the influence of the perception of food items on ratings of appetite directly before and after the experiment was investigated in the groups.

RESULTS

The main findings are presented in TABLES 1 and 2 and FIGURE 1.

The results support clinical and empirical evidence, suggesting a more pronounced rejection of nutritious food and longer hypothetical duration of consumption in anorexics when compared to bulimics and controls. Nutritive value of different food items was more realistically estimated by bulimics than by anorexics, and a period of dieting induced the physiological but not the cognitive and emotional abnormalities of malnutrition. Inconsistency of both findings with other reports[5-7] can be explained by methodological differences. Whether the visual presentation of food is a more reli-

TABLE 1. Ratings of Appetite and Hunger (100-mm Visual Analogue Scale) before (1) and after (2) the Visual Presentation of 19 Food Items in Anorexics and Bulimics at the Onset of Treatment and in Controls at the Maximum of Weight Loss

Subject Group	Appetite				Hunger			
	1	2	p 1 – 2	Difference	1	2	p 1 – 2	Difference
Anorexics ($n = 9$)								
x̄	15.3[a]	25.5[a]	< 0.5	10.2	8.0	21.9	< 0.05	13.9[c]
Sd	15.0	21.2		8.5	7.5	23.0		16.0
Bulimics ($n = 20$)								
x̄	18.0[b]	27.6[b]	ns	9.6	17.6	16.2	ns	-1.3[c,d]
Sd	21.9	28.1		21.8	22.9	24.7		11.5
Controls ($n = 9$)								
x̄	45.8[a,b]	60.2[a,b]	< 0.01	14.4	25.2	37.1	< 0.05	11.9[d]
Sd	27.8	33.4		11.3	29.5	36.4		12.2

[a] Anorexics versus controls, $p < 0.01$; *t*-test, two-tailed.
[b] Bulimics versus controls, $p < 0.05$; *t*-test, two-tailed.
[c] Anorexics versus bulimics, $p < 0.05$; *t*-test, two-tailed.
[d] Bulimics versus controls, $p < 0.01$; *t*-test, two-tailed.

TABLE 2. Ratings of Appetite and Hunger (100-mm Visual Analogue Scale) before (1) and after (2) the Visual Presentation of 19 Food Items in Anorexics and Bulimics at the End of Treatment and in Controls at Normal Weight

Subject Group	Appetite				Hunger			
	1	2	p 1 – 2	Difference	1	2	p 1 – 2	Difference
Anorexics (n = 7)								
x̄	37.3	32.1	ns	−5.1	21.0	19.0	ns	−2.6
Sd	33.8	27.1		17.9	31.2	25.8		16.9
Bulimics (n = 17)								
x̄	27.3[a]	34.5[a]	ns	8.4	26.5	33.1	ns	7.8
Sd	30.2	35.2		21.3	32.9	35.2		18.1
Controls (n = 9)								
x̄	13.8[a]	17.2[a]	ns	3.4	12.6	23.2	ns	10.7
Sd	12.4	20.0		12.3	9.7	24.6		15.5

[a] Bulimics versus controls, $p < 0.1$; t-test, two-tailed.

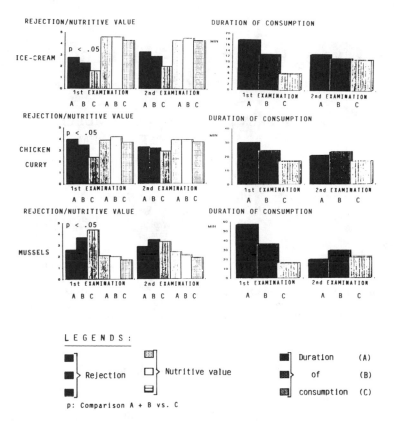

FIGURE 1. Rejection, estimated nutritive value, and duration of consumption of three food items at the first and second examination in (A) anorexics, (B) bulimics, and (C) controls (MANOVA).

able method than other methods for the assessment of cognitive and emotional responses of patients with eating disorders has to be further investigated.

REFERENCES

1. ROSEN, J. C., H. LEITENBERG, C. FISHER & C. KHAZAM. 1986. Int. J. Eating Disord. **5:** 255–267.
2. MORGAN, H. G. & G. F. M. RUSSELL. 1975. Psychol. Med. **5:** 355–371.
3. ABRAHAM, S. F. & P. J. V. BEUMONT. 1982. Psychol. Med. **12:** 625–635.
4. MITCHELL, J. E. & D. C. LAINE. 1985. Int. J. Eating Disord. **4:** 177–183.
5. KEYS, A., J. BROZEK, A. HENSCHEL, O. MICKELSEN & H. L. TAYLOR. 1950. The Biology of Human Starvation. University of Minnesota Press. Minneapolis, MN.
6. BEUMONT, P. J. V., T. L. CHAMBERS, L. ROUSE & S. F. ABRAHAM. 1981. J. Hum. Nutr. **35:** 265–273.
7. LASSLE, R., U. SCHWEIGER, U. DAUTE-HEROLD, M. SCHWEIGER, M. M. FICHTER & K. M. PIRKE. 1988. Int. J. Eating Disord. **7:** 63–73.

Dysregulation of 5-HT Function in Bulimia Nervosa

TIMOTHY BREWERTON,[a] EDWARD MULLER,
HARRY BRANDT, MICHAEL LESEM,
ARLENE HEGG, DENNIS MURPHY,
AND DAVID JIMERSON

National Institute of Mental Health
Laboratory of Clinical Science
Bethesda, Maryland

Bulimia nervosa, which is related to anorexia nervosa and affective illness, is likely to involve serotonin (5-HT) dysregulation.[1] In double-blind, randomized fashion, age-matched women with bulimia nervosa and healthy female controls were challenged with m-chlorophenylpiperazine (m-CPP, 0.5 mg/kg p.o.), a postsynaptic 5-HT agonist, and L-tryptophan (L-TRP, 100 mg/kg i.v.), the dietary precursor of 5-HT. Subjects and methods have been described in detail elsewhere.[1,2]

PROLACTIN RESPONSES

Patients with bulimia nervosa, regardless of weight or mood, had blunted prolactin (PRL) responses to m-CPP ($n = 36$, 5.7 ± 5.4 ng/ml) in comparison to controls ($n = 15$, 27.3 ± 28.7 ng/ml, $p \leq 0.0002$, Mann-Whitney test). PRL responses following L-TRP were not significantly different from controls in the total group of bulimia nervosa patients; however, blunted PRL responses were observed in those bulimics with concurrent anorexia nervosa ($n = 10$, 7.2 ± 6.8 ng/ml, $p \leq 0.006$, unpaired t-test) or major depression ($n = 8$, 9.9 ± 7.4 ng/ml, $p < 0.005$, unpaired t-test). Seasonal variations in PRL responses were also found that are compatible with other evidence for circannual changes in 5-HT function.[3] After Bonferronni corrections, peak delta PRL following m-CPP was significantly lower in summer compared to winter in all subjects and in fall compared to winter in the patients alone ($p \leq 0.05$). Peak delta PRL following L-TRP was significantly lower in summer compared to fall and winter in the normal-weight bulimics and in summer compared to fall in the controls ($p \leq 0.05$).

TEMPERATURE RESPONSES

Peak delta temperature (TEMP) following m-CPP was significantly higher in patients with bulimia nervosa ($0.44 \pm 0.22°C$) in comparison to controls ($0.29 \pm 0.25°C$,

[a] Current address: Department of Psychiatry and Behavioral Sciences, Medical University of South Carolina, 171 Ashley Avenue, Charleston, SC 29425–0742.

$p \leqslant 0.05$, unpaired t-test), whereas the hypothermia induced by L-TRP was equivalent across diagnostic groups. Peak delta TEMP remained significantly higher in patients than in controls ($p = 0.05$) after an analysis of covariance using peak m-CPP concentration as the independent variable.

HEADACHE RESPONSES

Severe headaches with features of common migraine were noted in 54% of subjects 8–12 hours after receiving m-CPP, but not placebo or L-TRP.[2] Headache ratings were greater in subjects with a personal or family history of migraine, and they were significantly correlated with peak concentrations of m-CPP in plasma occurring several hours earlier. Although the frequency of the migraine-like headaches was not significantly different between normal-weight bulimics, anorexics, and controls, patients with bulimia nervosa, regardless of weight or migraine history, demonstrated a greater susceptibility to the development of "severe migraine-like headaches" than controls. This suggests a possible pathophysiological relationship involving 5-HT dysfunction between bulimia nervosa and migraine. Mean maximum headache ratings after m-CPP were significantly higher in patients with negative histories (1.8 ± 1.3) than their control counterparts (0.5 ± 1.2, $p < 0.02$, Mann–Whitney test). These patients also had a significantly greater number of migrainous symptoms ($p \leqslant 0.001$, Mann–Whitney test). More personal and family history negative patients (8/19) than matched controls (1/12, $p < 0.05$, Fisher's exact test) developed "severe migraine-like headaches" (headaches rated as "severe" and associated with two or more migrainous symptoms, for example, nausea, vomiting, photophobia, unilaterality, and throbbing quality[4]). Although the patients without a predisposition to migraine had higher peak m-CPP concentrations than comparable controls ($p \leqslant 0.02$), this factor alone is not likely to account for the severity of headaches experienced by the bulimics. From a purely clinical perspective, these headaches were extremely incapacitating. Such headaches have not been reported by other investigators in either controls[5,6] or other nonbulimic patients[6] who achieved similar or higher peak m-CPP concentrations (the original samples having been assayed in the same laboratory). This is also true for studies of subjects without migraine histories using intravenous m-CPP, which results in much higher concentrations than those produced by oral administration (D. Murphy, personal communication). The mechanism by which m-CPP induces migraine-like headaches is discussed in detail elsewhere[2] but may involve a "rebound" vasodilatory response to stimulation of 5-HT receptors in vascular tissues.

DISCUSSION

The reasons for the discrepancies in the various response measures following m-CPP and L-TRP may relate to differential involvement of pre- and postsynaptic mechanisms and/or of 5-HT receptor subtypes. Taken together, these findings support the concept of altered postsynaptic 5-HT receptor sensitivity in bulimia nervosa, regardless of the presence of anorexia nervosa or affective illness; however, these conditions may be associated with other disturbances in 5-HT function, perhaps presynaptic.

REFERENCES

1. BREWERTON, T. D., H. A. BRANDT, D. T. LESEM, D. L. MURPHY & D. C. JIMERSON. 1989.

Serotonin in eating disorders. *In* Serotonin in Major Psychiatric Disorders. E. Coccaro, D. Murphy, Eds.: In press. American Psychiatric Press. Washington, D.C.

2. BREWERTON, T. D., D. L. MURPHY, E. A. MUELLER & D. C. JIMERSON. 1988. The induction of migraine-like headaches by the serotonin agonist., *m*-chlorophenylpiperazine. Clin. Pharmacol. Ther. **43:** 605–609.

3. BREWERTON, T. D., W. H. BERRETTINI, J. I. NURNBURGER & M. LINNOILA. 1988. As analysis of seasonal fluctuations of CSF monoamines and neuropeptides in normal controls: Findings with 5-HIAA and HVA. Psychiatry Res. **23:** 257–265.

4. AD HOC COMMITTEE ON CLASSIFICATION OF HEADACHE. 1962. Classification of headache. Arch. Neurol. **6:** 173–176.

5. MULLER, E. A., D. L. MURPHY & T. SUNDERLAND. 1985. Neuroendocrine effects of *m*-chlorophenylpiperazine, a serotonin agonist, in humans. J. Clin. Endocrinol. Metab. **61:** 1179–1184.

6. ZOHAR, J., MUELLER, E. A., T. R. INSEL, R. C. ZOHAR-KADOUCH & D. L. MURPHY. 1987. Serotonergic responsivity in obsessive-compulsive disorder. Arch. Gen. Psychiatry **44:** 946–951.

Central Nervous System Opioid Mechanisms That Mediate Stimulation-Induced Feeding in the Rat[a]

KENNETH D. CARR

Department of Psychiatry
New York University Medical Center
New York, New York 10016

In the experiments to be described, lateral hypothalamic electrical stimulation was used to elicit feeding behavior in rats. To investigate the involvement of opioid receptors and their endogenous ligands in the mediation of feeding, receptor antagonists and highly specific antibodies to opioid peptides were administered *in vivo*. All subjects were male Sprague–Dawley rats prepared with chronically indwelling monopolar stimulating electrodes aimed at the lateral hypothalamic "feeding area." Rats were trained in a threshold procedure in which the frequency of 0.1-msec pulses was varied while intensity was held constant. Trials were of 20-seconds duration, separated by 30-second intervals, and the criterion response was five seconds continuous eating of wet mash during stimulation. For experimental testing, a method of limits was employed such that four or six determinations of threshold were obtained over the course of each 15- to 35-minute test session.

EXPERIMENT 1

Repeated measurements were taken on six rats that received either naloxone (0.2 and 1.0 mg/kg, s.c.), quaternary naloxone (2.0 and 10.0 mg/kg, s.c.), or saline vehicle 20 minutes before testing. Naloxone elevated the feeding threshold in a dose-related manner while quaternary naloxone, which does not readily penetrate the blood–brain barrier, had no effect.[1] Moreover, naloxone produced a progressive elevation of threshold over the course of a test session such that each serial determination was higher than the preceding one (FIG. 1). Difference scores for serial determinations taken under naloxone and vehicle conditions described a significant linear trend. This trend contrasts with that produced by other appetite suppressants such as amphetamine (0.25 mg/kg) and phenylpropanolamine (10.0 mg/kg), which elevate threshold uniformly across the session. Follow-up behavioral testing suggested that the progressive elevation may reflect a naloxone-induced reduction in the positive reinforcement of consummatory behavior.[2]

[a] Supported by Grant DA03956 from the National Institute on Drug Abuse.

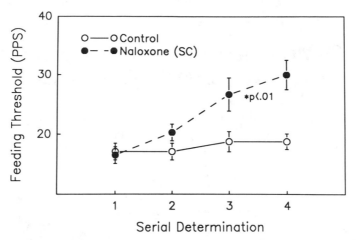

FIGURE 1. Four determinations of frequency threshold (expressed in pulses per second) for stimulation-induced feeding were obtained in serial order following administration of naloxone (1.0 mg/kg, s.c.) and saline vehicle. Difference scores for serial determinations taken under naloxone and saline treatment conditions describe a statistically significant linear trend, indicating the progressive elevation of threshold.

EXPERIMENT 2

Repeated measurements were taken on seven rats that received lateral ventricular infusions of antibodies to either β-endorphin (provided by Dr. Jean Rossier) or dynorphin A (1–13) (provided by Dr. Avram Goldstein) two hours before behavioral testing.

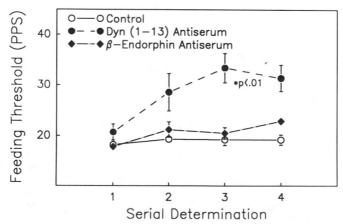

FIGURE 2. Four determinations of frequency threshold (expressed in pulses per second) for stimulation-induced feeding were obtained in serial order following lateral ventricular infusions of antibodies to dynorphin A (1–13), β-endorphin, or buffer control. Difference scores for serial determinations taken under dynorphin antibody and control treatment conditions describe a statistically significant linear trend, indicating the progressive elevation of threshold.

Dynorphin antibodies elevated the feeding threshold while β-endorphin antibodies had no effect. Moreover, dynorphin antibodies produced a naloxone-like pattern of progressive elevation in serially determined thresholds (FIG. 2). These findings suggest that central dynorphin A is involved in the mediation of electrically elicited feeding and that the anorectic action of naloxone may result, at least in part, from antagonism of dynorphinergic transmission.[3]

EXPERIMENT 3

The dynorphin antibodies used in Experiment 2 display complete cross-reactivity with dynorphin (1-17) and 0.25% cross-reactivity with dynorphin (1-8). Both of these prodynorphin products are believed to be biologically active while the 1-13 fragment is not. Thus, highly specific antibodies to dynorphin (1-17) and (1-8) (provided by Dr. Eckard Weber) were infused into the lateral ventricle or mesopontine aqueduct to investigate the CNS level and dynorphin fragment that mediate feeding. In the ten rats with lateral ventricular cannulae, both antibodies elevated feeding threshold while normal serum did not. In the six rats with aqueductal cannulae, only the antibodies to dynorphin (1-8) elevated threshold. Of all these treatments, only dynorphin (1-8) antibodies infused into the aqueduct produced a significant linear trend of progressively rising thresholds. Thus, dynorphin A (1-17) and (1-8) may both be involved in feeding with dynorphin A (1-8) preferentially active within caudal periventricular structures. The similar linear trends produced by systemic naloxone and aqueductal antibodies to dynorphin (1-8) suggest that dynorphin (1-8) activity in some periventricular brainstem structure(s) may contribute prominently to the opioid mediation of feeding as reflected in systemic naloxone antagonism.

REFERENCES

1. CARR, K. D. & E. J. SIMON. 1983. Effects of naloxone and its quaternary analogue on stimulation-induced feeding. Neuropharmacology 22: 127-130.
2. CARR, K. D. & E. J. SIMON. 1984. Potentiation of reward by hunger is opioid mediated. Brain Res. 297: 369-373.
3. CARR, K. D., T. H. BAK, T. L. GIOANNINI & E. J. SIMON. 1987. Antibodies to dynorphin A (1-13) but not β-endorphin inhibit electrically-elicited feeding in the rat. Brain Res. 422: 384-388.

Evidence for a Tonic Inhibition of Food Consumption and Body Weight by the Striatum in Female Rats

Effects of Castration[a]

A. WALLACE DECKEL[b]

Department of Psychiatry
UMDNJ—New Jersey Medical School
Newark, New Jersey 07103

INTRODUCTION

Kainic acid lesions (ka) of the anterior striatum in male rats result in a temporary adipsia and aphagia as well as a minor reduction in body weight that persists and is not made up until several weeks post surgery.[1,2] Preliminary evidence suggests that identical lesions in female rats lead to significant increases in body weight and food consumption for long periods of time post lesion.[3,4] This experiment examined the effects of anterior medial striatal ka lesions in female and male rats on food consumption and body weight, and further assessed if castration in female rats altered the response of the animal to the ka lesion.

METHODS

Young adult Sprague–Dawley rats (200–300 gms) were placed one to a cage, fed *ad libitum* rat chow pellets (Purina) and exposed to a 12-hour light/dark cycle. Six groups of rats were involved in this experiment, including two groups of males and four groups of females. Males were assigned to a lesion (les) or nonlesion (nles) condition. Two groups of females were similarly assigned to either a les or nles condition, while the remaining two groups were first subjected to bilateral ovariectomies (ovx) and then underwent sham (nles) or ka lesion (les). All ka lesions were made bilaterally into the dorsal medial striatum at coordinates (from Bregma) A 1.5, L 2.2, H 4.5. Injections of 0.4 µl of 0.8 µg kainic acid in phosphate-buffered saline (pH = 7.4) were stereotaxically made into the striatum over the course of three minutes; nles received injections of vehicle only. Ovx animals had bilateral removal of the ovaries one week before kal; all other animals received sham ovx surgery.

Body weight and food consumption were measured on a weekly basis for all animals before and for the week after ovx, and during the eight weeks post ka lesion.

[a] This work was supported by grants from the Huntington's Disease Foundation of America and from the Foundation of the University of Medicine and Dentistry of New Jersey.

[b] Address for correspondence: A. Wallace Deckel, Department of Psychiatry, UMDNJ—New Jersey Medical School, 185 S. Orange Avenue, Newark, NJ, 07103.

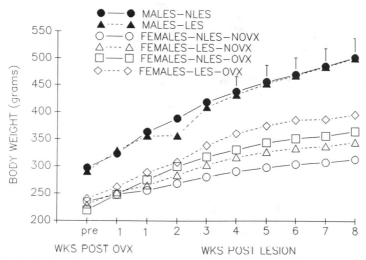

FIGURE 1. Body weight changes pre-ovx and for the one week post ovx, and for the eight weeks post kainic acid lesions of the dorsal medial striatum. NLES, nonlesioned; LES, lesioned; NOVX, nonovariectomized; OVX, ovariectomized. Bars represent standard deviations.

RESULTS

No initial differences were found in body weight within same sex groups. As FIGURE 1 illustrates, male rats showed little effect of the ka lesion aside from a small, statistically nonsignificant decline in food consumption and body weight over the first one to two weeks post ka lesion.

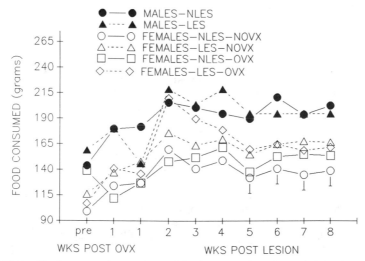

FIGURE 2. Food consumption pre-ovx and for the one week post ovx, and for the eight weeks post kainic acid lesions of the dorsal medial striatum. NLES, nonlesioned; LES, lesioned; NOVX, nonovariectomized; OVX, ovariectomized. Bars represent standard deviations.

Nonlesion ovariectomized females (nles-ovx) gained more weight than nles intact females (nles-novx) over the course of the experiment [$F(1,34) = 30.2; p < .00001$]. Les females, regardless of the presence of ovx, gained more weight than nles [$F(1,34) = 13.32; p = 0.009$; FIG. 1]. No ovx × les interaction effects were detected [$F(1,34) = 0.06; p = $ ns].

Similar findings existed with weekly food consumption. Aside from a one-week period of adipsia and aphagia (FIG. 2), les males were nonsignificantly different from nles, while les females ate significantly more than nles [$F(1,41) = 6.70; p = .013$] regardless of the presence of ovx. Ovx consumed more than novx, while no significant ovx × les effects were detected.

DISCUSSION

These results suggest that removal of the small-cell, intrinsic striatal neurons by ka lesion in female rats causes an increase in body weight and food consumption that is independent of estrogen-mediated body weight regulation. Identical lesions in male rats lead to a temporary adipsia and aphagia that quickly remits and is followed by eventual normalization of body weight in les males. Previous work[3-4] indicated that ka lesion animals, during a period of food deprivation, lose less weight than nles animals while being as active as nles animals. These findings suggest that striatal ka lesion may subtly disturb metabolic regulation in addition to increasing food consumption, and that these two effects together might account for the increased body weights in female rats.

In summary, this experiment suggests that the dorsal medial striatum in female rats is tonically inhibitory to body weight gain and food consumption, and that this regulation is independent of estrogen-mediated regulation, as it is found both in intact and ovx females. This effect appears to be sexually dimorphic as it is not seen in identical lesions of male rats.

ACKNOWLEDGMENTS

The author expresses his gratitude to Dr. Ann Bartlett and Jeffrey Jennings for their assistance in the surgical procedures and technical support, and to Albert W. Deckel, Sr. for the construction of the graphs.

REFERENCES

1. PETTIBONE, D. J., N. KAUFMAN, M. C. SCALLY, E. MEYER, I. ULUS & L. D. LYTLE. 1978. Striatal nondopaminergic neurons: Possible involvement in feeding and drinking behavior. Science 200: 1173–1175.

2. SANBERG, P. R. & H. C. FIBIGER. 1979. Body weight, feeding, and drinking behaviors in rats with kainic acid-induced lesions of striatal neurons. Exp. Neurol. 66: 444–466.

3. DECKEL, A. W. & R. G. ROBINSON. 1987. Receptor characteristics and behavioral consequences of kainic acid lesions and fetal transplants of the striatum. Ann. N.Y. Acad. Sci. 495: 556–580.

4. DECKEL, A. W., T. H. MORAN & R. G. ROBINSON. 1986. Striatal DA systems regulate body weight in female rats. Proceedings and Abstracts of the Annual Meeting of the Eastern Psychological Association. 57: 72.

Seasonal Variations in Bulimia Nervosa

VICTOR M. FORNARI,[a,b] DAVID E. SANDBERG,[a,b]
JULIANA LACHENMEYER,[b] DEBORAH COHEN,[b]
MICHAEL MATTHEWS,[b] AND GERARDO MONTERO[b]

[a]Department of Psychiatry
[b]Department of Pediatrics
North Shore University Hospital
Manhasset, New York 11030

This study was designed to determine whether patients with bulimia nervosa (BN), an eating disorder characterized by binge eating, exhibit seasonal variation in their symptoms similar to patients with seasonal affective disorder (SAD). SAD is characterized by regular fall and winter depressions alternating with nondepressed periods in the spring and summer. Changes in eating patterns, including binge eating and weight gain, are major components of SAD. To ascertain the specificity of any effects observed, patients with anorexia nervosa (AN) and normal controls (NC) were included in the comparisons.

METHODS

Of the 62 patients referred to an eating disorders (ED) program, 35 met DSM-IIIR criteria for a current or past episode of BN (18 of these also had a current or past episode of AN), and 27 met criteria for a current episode of AN alone. Psychiatric diagnoses were made using structured and semistructured interview schedules. All subjects completed the Seasonal Patterns Assessment Questionnaire (SPAQ),[1] an 18-item, retrospective self-report measure assessing the presence of seasonal variations in mood and vegetative symptoms. Subjects with eating disorders were compared to 149 patients with SAD and 46 NC subjects who had been screened for the absence of psychopathology. Summary statistics for the SAD and NC groups were made available by the authors of the SPAQ (N. Rosenthal, personal communication). For data-analytic purposes, all patients with BN (either alone or in the presence of AN) were contrasted with the AN, SAD, and NC groups.

RESULTS

Sample Characteristics

All four groups were predominantly or totally composed of women. The mean ages of the BN ($\pm$ AN; 19.7 $\pm$ 4.3 yr) and AN only (17.5 $\pm$ 4.0 yr) groups were significantly younger than the SAD (38.6 $\pm$ 8.8 yr) and NC (32.8 $\pm$ 9.5 yr) groups. Ninety-one percent of the BN group and 60% of the AN group also met criteria for a lifetime diagnosis of major depressive disorder.

SPAQ Findings

One section of the SPAQ assesses the degree to which the patient feels that she or he has experienced seasonal variation in the following areas: sleep length, social activity, mood, weight, appetite, and energy level. Subjects responded on a five-point Likert scale (0 = no change; 4 = extremely marked change), which was subsequently dichotomized for data analysis. In general, the SAD group received significantly higher scores than all the other groups, followed, in descending order, by the BN, AN, and NC groups. The BN group, however, was significantly different from the NC group on the mood ($p < 0.001$), weight ($p < 0.002$) and appetite ($p < 0.003$) scales, whereas the AN group was not (for example, see FIG. 1). In a subsequent item assessing month-by-month symptom variability across several dimensions, the SAD group uniformly showed the greatest inter-month variability followed by the BN group (for example, see FIG. 2).

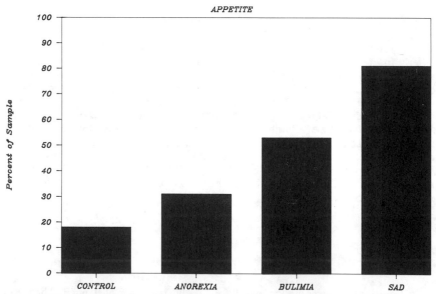

FIGURE 1. The proportion of SAD ($n = 149$), BN ($n = 35$), AN ($n = 27$), and NC ($n = 46$) subjects indicating "moderate change" to "extremely marked change" in appetite across the seasons. Chi²: SAD > BN ($p < 0.002$); BN > NC ($p < 0.003$); BN > AN ($p > 0.10$).

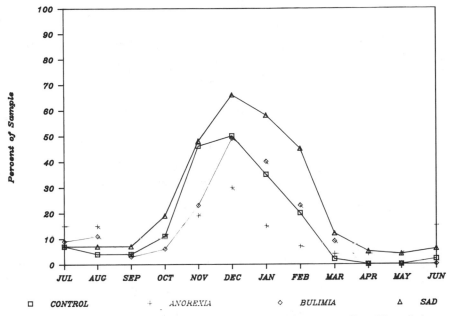

FIGURE 2. The proportion of SAD, BN, AN, and NC subjects responding affirmatively to the question, At what time of year do you eat most? Subjects were permitted to indicate a single month or a cluster of months, if applicable.

CONCLUSIONS

The findings of this study suggest that seasonal variation in symptoms among patients with BN more closely resembles those observed in patients with SAD than in patients with AN or NC. The possibility exists that some SAD patients, additionally, have BN, and some BN patients are subject to seasonal variations in affective and eating symptoms. The extremely high lifetime rate of affective disorder among BN patients may help to explain the overlap between the BN and SAD groups in the seasonality of their symptoms. The commonality between SAD and BN may be seasonal mood variations that, in turn, affect eating behavior. Given the reported later age of onset of SAD, perhaps younger BN patients with seasonally variable eating patterns later develop SAD.

REFERENCE

1. ROSENTHAL, N., G. H. BRADT & T. A. WEHR. 1987. Seasonal affective disorder and its relevance for the understanding and treatment of bulimia. *In* The Psychobiology of Bulimia. J. I. Hudson & H. G. Pope, Eds. American Psychiatric Press. Washington, DC.

The Stomach's Role in Appetite Regulation of Bulimia

ALLAN GELIEBTER, PAMELA M. MELTON,
DONNA ROBERTS, RICHARD S. McCRAY,
DENNIS GAGE, AND SAMI A. HASHIM

Departments of Medicine and Psychiatry
St. Lukes-Roosevelt Hospital
Columbia University
New York, New York 10025

Little is known about the physiological mechanisms associated with bulimia nervosa. Our study focused on the role of the stomach in the control of food intake. A group of nine bulimic and six normal women, similar in age, height, and weight, participated in the study. The bulimics met the criteria of DSM III-R but were otherwise healthy. In this study, the bulimics all purged by vomiting.

Stomach capacity was estimated by oral insertion of a gastric balloon that remained attached to a tube.[1] The balloon was gradually filled with water at the rate of 100 ml per minute with one-minute pauses for measuring intragastric pressure. Subjects rated their hunger, satiety, nausea, and discomfort on a scale from 1–10 after each 100 ml. When subjects rated their stomach discomfort as 10, this was considered their capacity and deflation of the balloon began. Changes in intragastric pressure were also used as an index of capacity. On another day, a liquid meal (Pro-Cal) was ingested by straw from a concealed container until subjects felt extremely full. Finally, gastric emptying rate was determined followed a 500-ml liquid meal (Pro-Cal) containing 200–250 µCi of technetium-99m DTPA, a radioactive tracer.

As seen in FIGURE 1, bulimics had a significantly larger stomach capacity than the normals (t = 2.1, $p < 0.05$). Using a rise of 7 cm H_2O as a criterion for capacity, the volume (x ± SEM) required for bulimics, 893 ± 125 ml, was also larger than for normals, 646 ± 152 ml, although the difference was not significant (t = 1.25, n.s.). The bulimics ingested about 50% more of the liquid meal, 788 ± 130 ml, than the normals, 521 ± 82 (t = 1.7, n.s.). Gastric emptying rate was somewhat faster for the bulimics, T 1/2 = 44 ± 3, than for the normals, T 1/2 = 50 ± 5 (t = 1.5, n.s.).

For all subjects, the correlation between gastric capacity and the amount of meal ingested was significant (r = 0.45, $p < 0.05$) as seen in FIGURE 2. There was also a significant inverse correlation between gastric capacity and rate of emptying (r = 0.46, $p < 0.05$). For a given stomach capacity, emptying for bulimics was faster than for normals as reflected by separate regression lines for the two groups. For the bulimics, there was a significant correlation between the calories ingested in a binge (self-report) and capacity (r = 0.71, $p < 0.05$). There was also a significant correlation between cumulative binge frequency (number of years with bulimia × frequency of binges per week) and gastric capacity (r = 0.51, $p < 0.05$).

This study provides evidence of a larger stomach capacity in bulimics. Gastric capacity may increase due to repeated binging, with the cumulative number of binges and the size of binge correlating positively with capacity. Because these bulimics also

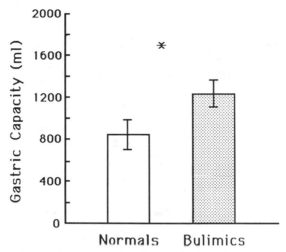

FIGURE 1. Gastric capacity was significantly larger in bulimics than normal subjects (t = 2.1; *p* < 0.05).

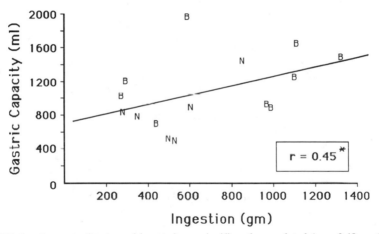

FIGURE 2. Amount of test meal ingested was significantly correlated (r = 0.45; *p* < 0.05) with gastric capacity in normal (N) and bulimic (B) subjects.

ingested more test meal, it is possible that a larger stomach capacity helps perpetuate binging by requiring more food to feel full. There was a tendency toward more rapid emptying in bulimics, especially if one controls for gastric capacity. This suggests an adaptive physiological response by the body to conserve nutrients by propelling them more quickly into the intestine where they cannot be withdrawn by vomiting.

REFERENCE

1. GELIEBTER, A. 1988. Gastric distension and gastric capacity in relation to food intake. Physiol. Behav. **44:** 665–668.

Cortisol Responses to Meals in Human Subjects Living without Time Cues

JUDITH GREEN

Psychology Department
William Paterson College of New Jersey
Wayne, New Jersey 07470

CHARLES P. POLLAK

Department of Psychiatry
Institute of Chronobiology
New York Hospital–Cornell Medical Center
White Plains, New York 10652

Several studies in humans have shown that meals are often followed by a blood cortisol rise that is most prominent around noon[1-3] and may be most related to the protein content of the meal.[3,4] In the previous studies, subjects have been young adults living the usual 24-hour day who were fed standardized meals at scheduled times.

We have examined cortisol responses to meals eaten *ad libitum* by subjects who lived without knowledge of time for several weeks in the laboratory of the Institute for Chronobiology. The subjects were seven women and one man in good health and of normal or near-normal weight (BMI values 18.2 to 28.7), ranging in age from 20 to 77 years. The subjects were allowed to free-run, that is, to determine when to sleep, rise, and eat in the absence of time cues or social prompting. Subjects chose the content of their meals, requesting them of a technician who prepared, served, and recorded the meals. Bloods for cortisol analysis (radioimmunoassay method) were drawn on an average of 20-minute intervals (range 16–24 minutes, randomly distributed). A meal-related cortisol response was defined as an increase of blood cortisol above the baseline level at the time of meal onset. It had to occur within 75 minutes following meal onset.

Subjects varied widely with respect to the frequency and extent of cortisol responses to meals (see FIG. 1). For example, individual subjects showed cortisol increases of at least 0.5 µg per 100 ml (µg%) in 41 to 81% of their meals and their mean cortisol increases ranged from 0.1 to 4.1 µg%. Like others, we found little cortisol response following breakfast: only 36 percent of these meals evoked a postprandial cortisol increase of at least 0.5 µg%. However, in our study, a high rate of nonresponses (< 0.5 µg%) also occurred after lunch (36%) and dinner (32%). The well-known high morning cortisol level was found at the time breakfast was begun (14.5 µg%). Although mean cortisol response to meals for the group as a whole increased as baseline cortisol values fell (see TABLE 1), no significant correlation was found between individual subject's baseline cortisol values and cortisol response to lunch or dinner.

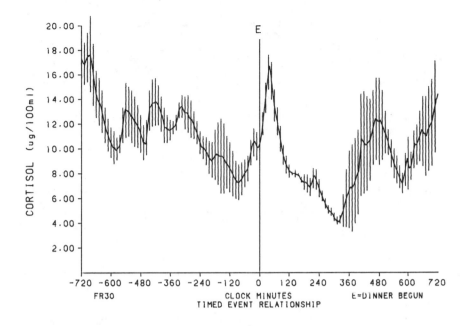

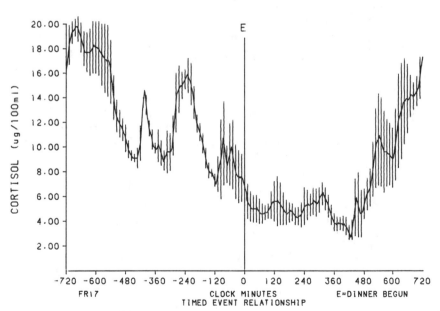

FIGURE 1.   Timed event relationship plots show that when successive dinner onsets are aligned, one subject typically shows a cortisol response (upper graph) while another subject does not (lower graph).

TABLE 1. Mean ± SD Meal and Meal-Related Values in Eight Subjects

Parameter	Breakfast	Lunch	Dinner
Baseline cortisol (µg per 100 ml)	14.5 ± 3.3	9.5 ± 4.9[a]	8.0 ± 4.8[a]
Cortisol change (µg per 100 ml)	1.4 ± 1.1	2.8 ± 1.5	3.4 ± 2.0
Cortisol response: % meals	36	64	68
Meal–cortisol correlations[b] (r values)			
kCalories-cortisol		−0.27 ± .32	0.27 ± .38
Protein-cortisol		−0.16 ± .30	0.14 ± .33
CHO-cortisol		−0.18 ± .45	0.19 ± .39
Fat-cortisol		−0.18 ± .33	0.15 ± .38
Meal size (kcalories)	498 ± 137	601 ± 165	715 ± 188
Protein (grams)	17 ± 6	29 ± 6	42 ± 10
CHO (grams)	76 ± 24	64 ± 2	69 ± 23
Fat (grams)	16 ± 6	27 ± 9	30 ± 8

[a] Significantly different from breakfast, $p < 0.05$.
[b] Breakfast omitted because of the high proportion of cortisol nonresponses.

Within a given subject, the same meal type (breakfast, lunch, or dinner) varied greatly in potency as a cortisol secretogogue. To explain this, we examined the role of differences in meal size and macronutrient content. We found no significant positive correlation between the size of the cortisol response and the caloric, protein, carbohydrate, or fat content of meals, or the percent of total calories represented by protein. These results suggest that the cortisol response is not related to meal size or protein content, certainly not in a simple dose-dependent manner.

In conclusion, our data show wide intra- and intersubject variation in the occurrence and magnitude of cortisol responses to meals. The variation cannot be accounted for by meal size, macronutrient content, or baseline cortisol level. Factors influencing the digestion and absorption (and therefore the signal value) of foodstuffs may contribute to the variation. In addition, sensory and cognitive meal factors (e.g., the sight and smell of food) are sometimes important,[1] and these would be unlikely to correlate with size or macronutrient content of the meal.

REFERENCES

1. FOLLENIUS, M., G. BRANDENBERGER & B. HIETTER. 1982. J. Clin. Endocrinol. Metab. **55:** 757–761.
2. QUIGLEY, M. E. & S. S. C. YEN. 1979. Clin. Endocrinol. Metab. **49:** 945–947.
3. SLAG, M. F., M. AHMED, M. C. GANNON & F. Q. NUTTALL. 1981. Metabolism **30:** 1104–1108.
4. ISHIZUKA, B., M. E. QUIGLEY & S. S. C. YEN. 1983. J. Clin. Endocrinol. Metab. **57:** 1111–1116.

The Satiating Effect of Fats Is Attenuated by the Cholecystokinin Antagonist Lorglumide[a]

DANIELLE GREENBERG,[b] NORBERTO I. TORRES,
GERARD P. SMITH, AND JAMES GIBBS

Department of Psychiatry
Cornell University Medical College
and
Edward W. Bourne Behavioral Research Laboratory
The New York Hospital–Cornell Medical Center
White Plains, New York 10605

INTRODUCTION

Yox *et al.*[1] recently reported a partial reversal of the satiating effect of intraduodenal infusions of oleic acid with Lorglumide (CR1409).[2] Because Lorglumide specifically antagonizes the action of cholecystokinin (CCK) at peripheral, type A CCK receptors, the attenuation of the satiating effect of oleic acid by Lorglumide is evidence that CCK released from the small intestine mediates part of the satiating effect of oleic acid. Reidelberger *et al.*[3] and we[4] have observed a similar satiating effect of intraduodenal infusions of an emulsified mixture of long-chain triglycerides (Intralipid, Kabi Vitrum, Inc. CA). To investigate the possibility that the satiating effect of Intralipid is also mediated in part by CCK, we administered Lorglumide in a similar protocol to that of Yox *et al.*[1] before intraduodenal infusions of Intralipid. We also did similar experiments with oleic acid in order to be certain that our experimental conditions were adequate to detect the antagonistic effect of Lorglumide.

METHOD

Male Sprague–Dawley rats ($n = 7$) were fitted with gastric cannulas for sham feeding and duodenal catheters for infusions.[5] After a 17-hour overnight food deprivation, rats were permitted to sham feed a high-carbohydrate liquid diet (BioServ diluted 40% vol/vol with deionized water). Intraperitoneal injections of 600 µg/kg Lorglumide vehicle were given five minutes before intraduodenal infusions. Infusions (10 ml) of oleic acid (6.5 kcal), Intralipid (10 kcal), or NaCl (0.15 M) vehicle began 12 minutes after

[a] This research was supported by The Weight Watchers Foundation, St. Luke's–Roosevelt Institute for Health Sciences, National Institutes of Health Grant DK38757 (to DG), and National Institute of Mental Health Grant MH40010.
[b] Address for correspondence: Dr. Danielle Greenberg, E. W. Bourne Behavioral Research Laboratory, 21 Bloomingdale Road, White Plains, NY 10605.

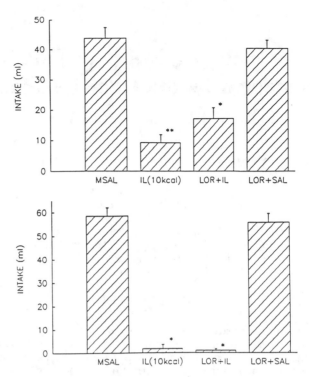

FIGURE 1. The top panel shows mean intakes ± SEM for the time period during duodenal Intralipid (10 kcal) or 0.15 M NaCl infusions. When 0.15 M NaCl was injected i.p. before duodenal infusions of 0.15 M NaCl (MSAL) and when Lorglumide was injected before 0.15 M NaCl was infused (LOR + SAL), rats sham fed equivalent amounts. When 0.15 M NaCl was injected before duodenal infusions of Intralipid (IL 10 kcal) sham feeding was reduced by 77% from baseline ($p < 0.01$), and was significantly different (22% change) from when Lorglumide was injected before duoendal infusions of Intralipid (LOR + IL) as indicated by the ** ($p < 0.05$). Intralipid infusions subsequent to Lorglumide injection resulted in a suppression of sham feeding of 55%, which was still significantly different from saline as indicated by the * ($p < 0.05$). The bottom panel shows mean intakes ± SEM for the time period following duodenal infusions for these same conditions. Again Lorglumide injections did not effect sham feeding compared to vehicle (MSAL compared to LOR + SAL). When Intralipid was infused duodenally preceded by 0.15 M NaCl injection (IL 10 kcal) intakes differed from baseline (96% reduction) as indicated by the * ($p < 0.01$). Lorglumide injections followed by Intralipid infusions also differed from baseline (97% reduction) as indicated by the * ($p < 0.01$). Thus Lorglumide *failed* to reduce this suppression of sham feeding by duodenal Intralipid for this time period.

sham feeding began. Duodenal infusions were given at a rate of 0.44 ml/min for 24 minutes. Sham intakes were measured every five minutes for 90 minutes.

RESULTS

Intraduodenal infusions of Intralipid and oleic acid decreased sham feeding while the duodenal infusions were administered and also after the infusions (FIGS. 1 and

2). For the time period *during* the duodenal infusion (12 to 36 min), injection of 600 µg/kg Lorglumide significantly attenuated the suppression of sham feeding induced by both Intralipid [$F(2,9) = 85.3, p < 0.0001$] (FIG. 1 top) and oleic acid [$F(2,9) = 35.4, p < 0.0001$] (FIG. 2 top). For the time period *following* the infusion (36 to 90 min), injection of 600 µg/kg Lorglumide (CR1409) failed to reverse the suppression of sham feeding induced by duodenal infusions of Intralipid, but attenuated the suppression of feeding induced by duodenal infusions of oleic acid [$F(2,9) = 5.33, p < 0.02$] (FIGS. 1 and 2, bottom).

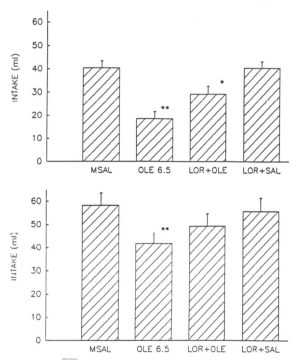

FIGURE 2. The top panel shows mean intakes ± SEM for the time period during duodenal oleic acid (6.5 kcal) or 0.15 *M* NaCl infusions. When 0.15 *M* NaCl was injected i.p. before duodenal infusions of 0.15 *M* (MSAL) and when Lorglumide was injected before 0.15 *M* NaCl was infused rats sham fed equivalent amounts. When 0.15 *M* NaCl was injected before duodenal infusions of oleic acid (OLE 6.5), sham feeding was significantly different from baseline (54% reduction $p < 0.01$) and was significantly different (27% change) from when Lorglumide was injected before duodenal oleic acid infusions (LOR + OLE) as indicated by the ** ($p < 0.05$). Lorglumide injection before oleic acid infusions still reduced sham feeding significantly (27% reduction), as indicated by the * ($p < 0.05$). The bottom panel shows mean intakes ± SEM for the time period following duodenal infusions. Again Lorglumide injections did not affect sham feeding compared to vehicle (LOR + SAL compared to MSAL). When oleic acid was infused duodenally preceded by 0.15 *M* NaCl injection (OLE 6.5) intakes differed from baseline (28% reduction, $p < 0.05$) and from when Lorglumide preceded the duodenal infusions of oleic acid (22% change, $p < 0.05$) as indicated by the **. Lorglumide injections followed by oleic acid infusions did not differ from baseline measures. Thus for this time period a reversal of the satiating effect of oleic acid was observed.

DISCUSSION

Lorglumide (CR1409) significantly attenuated the suppression of sham feeding induced by duodenal infusions of Intralipid and of oleic acid during the duodenal infusions. These results replicate and extend the findings of Yox *et al.*[1] For the time during the infusion the ability of the specific CCK antagonist Lorglumide to attenuate the suppression of sham feeding supports the hypothesis that fat-induced satiety is mediated, at least in part, by CCK. For the time following the infusion, CCK appears to mediate (in part) satiety induced by oleic acid. The failure of Lorglumide to attenuate the suppression of sham feeding induced by duodenal infusions of Intralipid following the infusion suggests that other, perhaps postabsorptive, mechanisms mediate the satiety effect of Intralipid for this time period.

ACKNOWLEDGMENTS

We wish to express our thanks to Kabi Vitrum Inc. for their generous gift of Intralipid.

REFERENCES

1. Yox, D., H. Stokesberry & R. C. Ritter. 1988. Soc. Neurosci. Abstr. **13:** 588.
2. Makovec, F., R. Chiste, M. Bani, M. A. Pacini, I. Setnikar & L. A. Rovati. 1985. Arzneim.-Forsh. Drug Res. **35:** 1048–1051.
3. Reidelberger, R. D., T. J. Kalogeris, P. M. B. Leung & V. E. Mendel. 1983. Am. J. Physiol. **244:** R872-R881.
4. Greenberg, D., J. Gibbs & G. P. Smith. 1984. Soc. Neurosci. Abstr. **10:** 531.
5. Greenberg, D., J. Gibbs & G. P. Smith. 1986. Brain Res. Bull. **17:** 599–604.

Effects of Parental Weight and Fatness on Relative Weight and Fatness of Young Children
Comparison of Cross-Sectional and Prospective Clinical Data[a]

JOEL A. GRINKER,[b] STANLEY M. GARN,[c]
AND KAREN R. ROSENBERG[d]

[b]Human Nutrition
School of Public Health
Department of Pediatrics
University of Michigan
Ann Arbor, Michigan 48109

[c]Human Nutrition
School of Public Health
Center for Human Growth and Development
University of Michigan
Ann Arbor, Michigan 48109

[d]Department of Anthropology
University of Delaware
Newark, Delaware 19716

Fatness follows family lines. Twin and adoption studies suggest that genetic factors play a major role in the familial transmission of fatness,[1-14] although environmental influences are also recognized.[5] The fatness of young children as a function of the fatness of their mothers is examined in data selected from a cross-sectional epidemiological study (Ten-State Nutrition Survey) and a prospective clinical study. Only data from obese (O) or nonobese white women and children were included.

TEN-STATE DATA

Anthropometric data (tricep and subscapular skinfolds, weight and height) were available from mothers and children aged 1 to 12 years. Maternal fatness was defined

[a] Supported in part by National Institutes of Health Grant #AM32944 and Gerber Foods. National Center for Health Statistics data made available by Ken Guire, Dept. of Biostatistics, School of Public Health, University of Michigan, Ann Arbor, MI.

TABLE 1. Triceps Skinfold of White Children in Ten-State Survey by Fatness[a] of Their Mothers

Age of Children	Lean Mothers			Medium Mothers			Obese Mothers		
	n	Mean	SD	n	Mean	SD	n	Mean	SD
BOYS									
0–1	15	8.1	3.23	61	8.9	2.97	12	10.5	4.08
1–2	20	8.2	3.15	94	10.8	5.67	19	10.6[b]	1.95
2–3	23	9.5	2.45	98	9.2	2.36	24	10.5	3.05
3–4	27	8.1	2.14	120	9.4	2.87	23	9.9[b]	2.76
4–5	30	7.9	2.52	115	9.4	3.11	37	10.3[b]	3.73
5–6	30	8.0	2.48	139	8.5	2.63	38	10.6[b]	4.59
6–7	33	7.9	2.85	150	8.7	3.13	38	8.8	2.98
7–8	42	7.7	2.74	156	8.6	3.51	48	10.0[b]	3.59
8–9	42	8.8	3.68	154	9.9	5.32	27	11.4[b]	5.43
9–10	25	9.3	3.93	148	9.9	5.25	43	12.9[b]	7.40
10–11	33	8.8	3.97	164	11.3	5.38	39	13.7[b]	6.42
11–12	27	9.8	3.99	168	11.9	6.38	45	14.4[b]	7.66
GIRLS									
0–1	19	8.1	2.65	80	10.0	9.19	15	9.8	4.47
1–2	20	9.0	2.32	96	10.1	2.80	17	9.2	2.73
2–3	22	8.8	2.52	90	9.9	2.35	26	10.2	3.73
3–4	19	8.0	2.95	103	10.2	2.66	24	10.4[b]	3.05
4–5	31	9.0	2.96	116	10.3	6.23	26	10.8[b]	3.36
5–6	28	8.3	3.85	133	10.2	2.98	25	11.1[b]	3.57
6–7	29	8.6	1.88	142	9.8	3.30	45	11.5[b]	3.73
7–8	41	9.0	2.98	150	10.6	3.62	38	11.5[b]	3.95
8–9	33	10.4	5.33	146	11.5	4.18	43	14.6[b]	6.50
9–10	28	11.1	4.70	133	12.1	4.74	39	15.9[b]	8.31
10–11	27	10.8	6.11	136	13.4	5.72	34	16.7[b]	8.32
11–12	37	11.3	4.94	146	14.1	5.85	33	18.5[b]	8.65

[a] Fatness of mother is defined with reference to triceps skinfold.
[b] $p < 0.05$. Comparison: mean obese versus lean.

in reference to the Z-score for tricep (TRI) skinfolds and reduced to three groups: (1) Lean = < -1 Z score; (2) medium = -1 to 1 Z score and (3) obese = > 1 Z score. The children of obese women are systematically heavier than those of lean women by age three (boys) and two (girls) and significantly fatter (TRI) by age four (see TABLE 1). No systematic height differences were found between children of obese or lean mothers. Children of lean and obese mothers have different patterns of fatness ($<$ and $>$ TRI) from those of medium mothers by ages two to three.

MICHIGAN DATA

Anthropometric data were obtained from healthy middle-income mothers and term healthy infants at delivery and follow-up data (1–48 months) from pediatricians' examinations. Mothers were selected to meet obesity or normal-weight/fatness criteria that were defined on the basis of prepregnancy weight/height standards and *postpartum* skinfold measures.[6] Each infant's weight and height were converted to the appropriate percentiles for weight/age, height/age and weight/height using computerized programs based on National Center for Health Statistics values, and normalized Z scores were

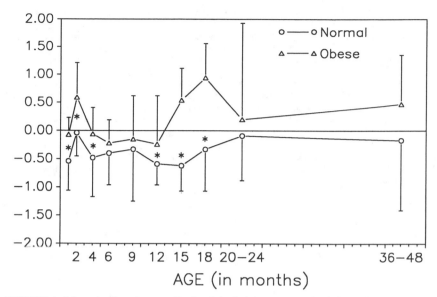

FIGURE 1. Mean (variance) normalized weight/height Z scores for infants from obese and normal-weight/fatness mothers during a longitudinal study from birth to 48 months. Obesity was defined on the basis of >85th percentile height/weight TRI and MAC measurements. Sample sizes at different time points vary as a function of number of infants for whom data were available from pediatricians; n = 17 obese and 20 medium at one month, 24 and 26 at 2 months, 23 and 21 at 4 months, 20 and 27 at 6 months, 16 and 19 at 9 months, 17 and 20 at 12 months, 12 and 16 at 15 months, 5 and 11 at 18 months, 14 and 14 at 20–24 months, and 15 and 14 at 36–48 months.

derived.[7] Infants of obese mothers were significantly heavier and fatter at birth and remained heavier than infants of normal-weight/fatness (M) mothers.[6,8] Infants of obese mothers had consistently larger weight/age Z scores (significantly so at 1, 2, 6, 9, 12, 15, 18, and 36–48 months) and weight/height Z scores (significantly so at 1, 2, 4, 12, 15, and 18 months) than infants of median mothers (see FIG. 1). Height/age Z scores were not different at any age. Five infants of obese mothers and no infants of medium mothers met the criteria for obesity during the first six months. Combined paternal and maternal obesity produced significantly larger weight/height Z scores (2, 12, 15, and 20–24 months) compared with the Z scores of infants of obese only and medium mothers.

Systematic effects of maternal fatness on early childhood fatness were obtained in both studies supporting genetic and environmental explanations in the development of childhood fatness. Results demonstrate that even small sample sizes (19–23 within sex and age groups in the first study and 12–16 in the second study) can illustrate the strong familial transmission of fatness.

REFERENCES

1. BORJESON, M. 1976. The aetiology of obesity in children. Acta. Paediatr. Scand. **65:** 279–287.

2. STUNKARD, A. J., T. T. FOCH & Z. HRUBEC. 1986. A twin study of human obesity. J. Am. Med. Assoc. **256:** 51–54.
3. STUNKARD, A. J., T. I. A. SORENSON, C. HANIS *et al.* 1986. An adoption study of human obesity. N. Engl. J. Med. **314:** 193–198.
4. PRICE, R. A., R. J. CADORET, A. J. STUNKARD *et al.* 1987. Genetic contributions to human fatness: An adoption study. Am. J. Psychiatry **144:** 1003–1008.
5. GARN, S. M., S. M. BAILEY & P. E. COLE. 1976. Similarities between parents and their adopted children. Am. J. Phys. Anthropol. **45:** 539–544.
6. GRINKER, J. A. & K. BOSE. 1987. Obesity prospectives: . . . in familial obesity. *In* Recent Advances in Obesity Research: V. Berry, E. M., S. H. Blondheim, H. E. Eliahou *et al.*, Eds.: 383–390. Libbey & Co. London.
7. HAMILL, P. V. V., T. A. DRIZD, C. L. JOHNSON *et al.* 1979. Physical growth: National Center for Health Statistics percentiles. Am. J. Clin. Nutr. **32:** 607.
8. GRINKER, J. A., J. G. RUBIN & K. BOSE. 1986. Sweet preference and body fatness. Nutr. Behav. **3:** 197–211.

Which Subtype(s) of 5-HT Receptor Mediates the Anorectic Effects of Drugs That Act via the 5-HT System?

G. HEWSON, G. E. LEIGHTON, R. G. HILL,
AND J. HUGHES

Parke-Davis Research Unit
Hills Road
Cambridge, CB2 2QB, United Kingdom

Following the discovery of the anorectic agent DL-fenfluramine, which acts by releasing 5-HT and inhibiting its reuptake,[1] it has become clear that activation of the 5-HT system can markedly reduce food intake. The role of multiple subtypes of 5-HT receptor, as defined by Bradley and coworkers,[2] in this effect is less clear. The aim of this study was to further investigate the involvement of multiple 5-HT receptors in the anorectic effects of compounds that act via the 5-HT system.

Hooded Lister rats (Olac, U.K.) that had starting weights in the range of 175–200 g were used in all experiments. They were housed individually under standard animal house conditions. Training consisted of presenting each rat with 20–30 g of a palatable diet, similar to that used by Cooper et al.,[3] in the home cage for 30 minutes each day over a five-day period. Standard rat chow and water were removed during this 30-minute period. Drugs used were m-chlorophenylpiperazine dihydrochloride (mCPP, Sigma), α-methyl 5-hydroxytryptamine maleate (αMe-5-HT, Parke-Davis), 1-(2,5 dimethoxy-4-iodophenyl)-2-aminopropane hydrochloride (DOI, RBI), ketanserin tartrate (Janssen) and (±) cyanopindolol (Sandoz). All drugs were injected by the i.p. route in a volume of 1 ml/kg and doses refer to the weight of free base. Statistical significance was accepted for $p < 0.05$.

The anorectic effects of αMe-5-HT and DOI were antagonized by the selective 5-HT$_2$ receptor antagonist ketanserin (FIG. 1). Neither ketanserin nor (±) cyanopindolol antagonized the reduction in food intake produced by mCPP (FIG. 2).

The ability of ketanserin to block the anorectic effects of αMe-5-HT and DOI suggests that the anorectic effects of these compounds are mediated by activation of 5-HT$_2$ receptors. These results are consistent with those of Schecter and Simansky[4] who reported that ketanserin and LY53857, another selective 5-HT$_2$ receptor antagonist, blocked the reductions in food intake produced by DOI. Similarly, the effects of 5-HT administered by the i.p. route were antagonized by ritanserin.[5] The anorectic effects of mCPP were not blocked by ketanserin or (±) cyanopindolol, which blocks some of the effects mediated at 5-HT$_{1B}$ receptors, suggesting that the anorectic effects of this compound are mediated at 5-HT receptors other than the 5-HT$_2$ or 5-HT$_{1B}$ subtypes.

Taken together, the results from this study suggest that it is possible to reduce food intake by activation of more than one subtype of 5-HT receptor.

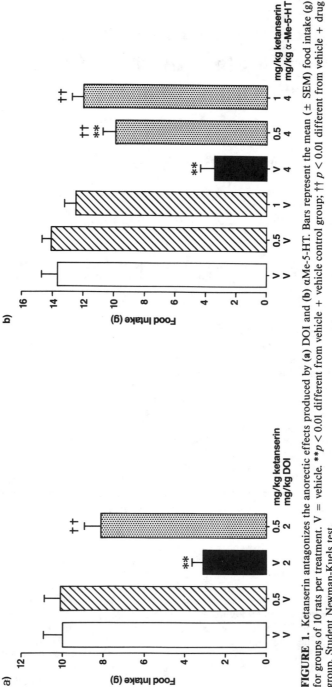

FIGURE 1. Ketanserin antagonizes the anorectic effects produced by (a) DOI and (b) αMe-5-HT. Bars represent the mean (± SEM) food intake (g) for groups of 10 rats per treatment. V = vehicle. **$p < 0.01$ different from vehicle + vehicle control group; †† $p < 0.01$ different from vehicle + drug group, Student Newman-Kuels test.

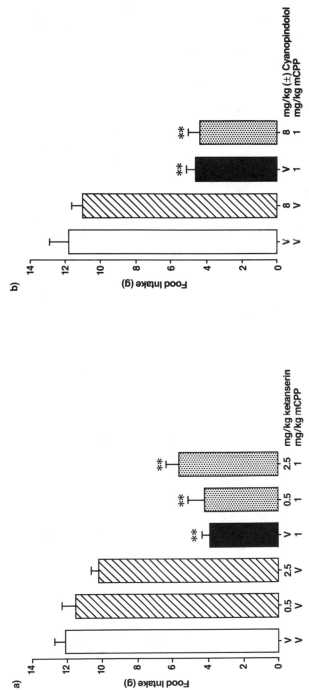

FIGURE 2. Failure of (a) ketanserin or (b) (±) cyanopindolcl to antagonize the anorectic effects of mCPP. Bars represent the mean (± SEM) food intake (g) for groups of 10 rats per treatment. V = vehicle, **$p < 0.01$ different from vehicle + vehicle control group, Student Newman-Kuels test.

ACKNOWLEDGMENTS

M. Northam provided excellent technical assistance. The gifts of drugs by Janssen and Sandoz are gratefully acknowledged.

REFERENCES

1. GARATTINI, S. *et al.* 1986. Appetite **7(Suppl):** 15–38.
2. BRADLEY, P. B. *et al.* 1986. Neuropharmacology **25:** 563–576.
3. COOPER, S. J. *et al.* 1985. Neuropharmacology **24:** 877–883.
4. SCHECHTER, L. E. & K. J. SIMANSKY. 1988. Psychopharmacology **94:** 342–346.
5. MASSI, M. & S. MARINI. 1987. Pharmacol. Biochem. Behav. **26:** 333–340.

Comparison of the Action of Macronutrients on the Expression of Appetite in Lean and Obese Human Subjects

ANDREW J. HILL AND JOHN E. BLUNDELL

BioPsychology Group
Department of Psychology
Leeds University
Leeds LS2 9JT, United Kingdom

Comparisons of the eating behavior of obese and normal-weight individuals have generally failed to identify those features that lead the obese to greater energy intakes. Certainly, there is little evidence of states of excessive hunger in the obese. Rather, subtle differences in the development of satiation and state of satiety are implicated by two experimental findings. First, the obese do not lower their liking of sweet taste stimuli following the ingestion of a glucose load.[1] This absence of glucose-induced negative alliesthesia may indicate a resistance to change in the hedonic value of food stimuli. Second, cumulative intakes of obese people often describe a fixed rate of eating, with no slowing in the rate of ingestion toward the end of a meal.[2] In order to further explore possible differences in the appetite control system, the following studies compared the responsiveness of obese and lean individuals to preloads or small meals containing particular profiles of macronutrients.

In the first study, the pleasantness (and intensity) of a sucrose solution and ratings of hunger motivation were sampled before and at 10-minute intervals for an hour after the ingestion of 50 g glucose in water or the same volume of water (200 ml). FIGURE 1 shows that this group of 11 obese subjects (mean BMI = 39) experienced no glucose-induced negative alliesthesia, but that ingestion of glucose (188 kcal) consistently reduced hunger ratings. In contrast, glucose ingestion reduced both hunger motivation and the pleasantness of sucrose in a group of 10 lean subjects (BMI = 21). In a second study, hunger motivation was tracked in eight obese women (BMI = 38) and nine lean women (BMI = 21), before, during, and for three hours after two small (475 kcal) lunches, either high in carbohydrates (63%) or protein (54%). Obese and lean groups were characteristic in their response to caloric loading, with hunger rapidly decreasing during the meal and steadily returning during the three hours after lunch. It is of note that these profiles of intermeal and postmeal ratings of hunger motivation were similar in both groups. Furthermore, both obese and lean persons displayed sensitivity to the macronutrient content of the lunches, ratings of hunger being consistently lower after eating the high-protein lunch. When subjects were offered a self-selection meal three hours after the lunches, the reduction in subjective hunger after the protein lunch was confirmed by significant reductions in energy intake in obese (19%) and lean (22%; smallest $t(7) = 3.35$, $p < 0.05$) compared with intakes after the carbohydrate lunch (FIG. 2).

A number of differences in response were apparent, however. For example, ratings made of the pleasantness of food during eating were, unlike those of lean individuals, resistant to change and remained at high levels. In addition, baseline ratings indicated lower tonic levels of hunger motivation. In conclusion, the obese appetite control system does possess regulatory properties, but subtle and perhaps important differences in response can be detected. Further detailed investigation of the process of satiation in obese persons is clearly warranted.

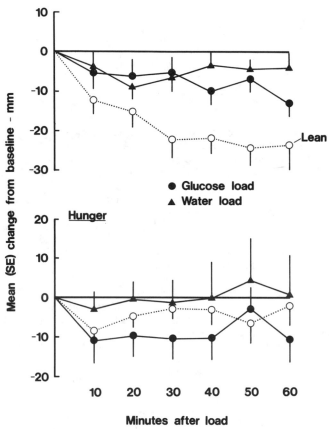

FIGURE 1. The effect of ingesting 50 g glucose in solution (circles) or the same volume of water (triangles) on ratings of the pleasantness of sucrose (20% solution) and hunger in obese (closed symbols) and lean subjects (open symbols).

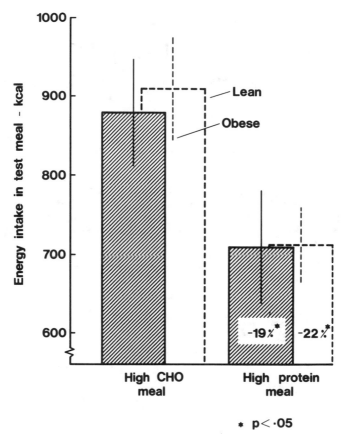

FIGURE 2. The effect of consuming a high carbohydrate or high protein lunch on energy intake from a self-selection meal offered three hours later in obese (shaded columns) and lean (open columns) subjects.

REFERENCES

1. CABANAC, M. & R. DUCLAUX. 1970. Obesity: Absence of satiety aversion to sucrose. Science **168:** 496–497.
2. PUDEL, V. E. & M. OETTING. 1977. Eating in the laboratory: Behavioural aspects of the positive energy balance. Int. J. Obesity **1:** 369–386.

Comorbidity of Eating Disorders in Comparison with Mood Disorders

WOLFGANG HiLLER AND MICHAEL ZAUDIG

Max-Planck-Institute of Psychiatry
Munich, Federal Republic of Germany

Close psychopathological relationships between eating disorders and major affective disorders have been frequently demonstrated along with neuroendocrinological and psychobiological similarities.[1,2] Competing theories were proposed, suggesting that eating disorders represent variants of affective disorder, or that depression could occur

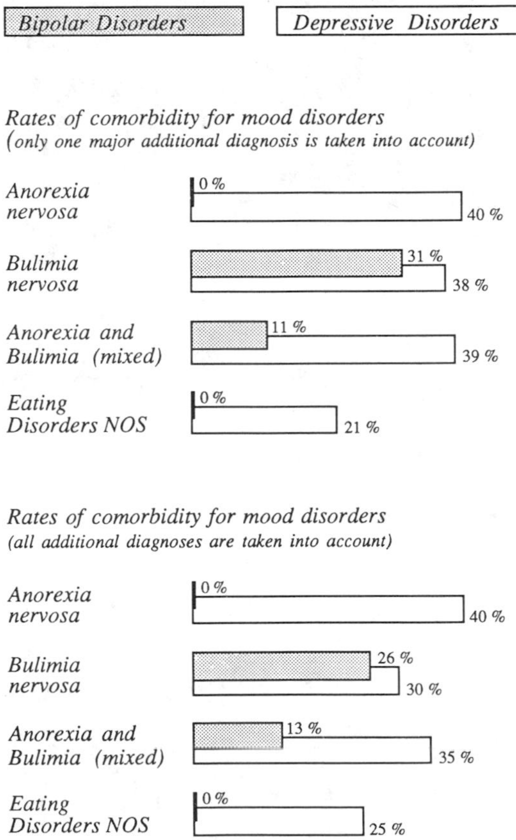

FIGURE 1. Comorbidity of eating disorder: comparison of bipolar and depressive disorders.

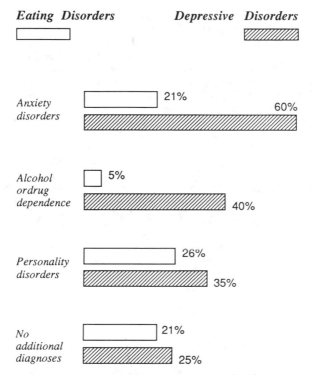

FIGURE 2. Comorbidity of eating disorder and depressive disorders.

secondary to eating disorders. As an extension to studies of psychopathological relations, psychiatric comorbidity of specific and unspecific eating disorders was further evaluated, focusing on the following issues: (1) Is comorbidity of eating disorders comparable with comorbidity of depressive disorders? (2) To what extent are bipolar disorders important in eating disorders?

DSM-IIIR lifetime psychiatric disorders were assessed among 53 outpatients (all female; age: 17 to 30 years) with active bulimia, anorexia, anorexia plus bulimia, and eating disorders nos (residual category for atypical symptomatology) by means of structured diagnostic interviews. A comparison group consisted of 20 patients with DSM-IIIR major depression and/or dysthymia, comparable to the eating disorder sample in age and sociodemographic characteristics. Exclusion criteria were certain or probable organic mental disorders and any sign from the schizophrenia-related sections of DSM-IIIR.

Results showed that 45% of all patients with eating disorders received a lifetime diagnosis of major depression and/or dysthymia. Depressive disorders were equally common in anorectic, bulimic, and mixed anorectic-bulimic subjects. In 17% of the total sample, we found anxiety disorders, drug and alcohol dependence in 6%, and personality disorders in 21%. An increased frequency rate of 39% could be demonstrated for coexisting borderline or avoidant personality disorder in bulimia plus anorexia.

Comorbidity profiles contrasting depression and bipolar disorders are shown in FIGURE 1 for the individual groups of eating disorders. In the upper diagram, only *one* major additional diagnosis was considered. Bipolar disorders (including bipolar conditions with hypomanic or other atypical manic symptoms, and cyclothymia) were most often found in bulimic patients (31%). In this group, the rate of bipolar disorders was almost as high as the rate for unipolar depressive disorders (38%). In contrast, no bipolar disorders were found in anorexia and in the residual group of eating disorders. As can be seen from a comparison of both diagrams in FIGURE 1, the pattern of comorbidity does not depend on the method of assessing comorbidity (i.e., taking only *one* or *all* additional diagnoses into account).

FIGURE 2 gives a comparison of comorbidity rates between eating and depressive disorders. A clearly increased number of coexisting anxiety disorders was found for the depressed group (60% vs. 21%; $\chi^2 = 7.52^*$; sign. at $\alpha = 0.05$). The same result was obtained for alcohol and/or drug dependence (40% vs. 5%; $\chi^2 = 9.08^*$). Coexisting personality disorders did not differ significantly ($\chi^2 = 0.20$), and there was also a comparable proportion of subjects with no additional diagnoses in both groups ($\chi^2 = 0.00$).

To summarize, substantial differences of comorbidity do not suggest that eating disorders and depression are both part of a common psychiatric illness, but validity of the different forms of eating disorders is supported by specific profiles of coexisting diagnoses.

REFERENCES

1. LAESSLE, R. G., S. KITTL, M. M. FICHTER, H.-U. WITTCHEN & K. M. PIRKE. 1987. Major affective disorder in anorexia nervosa and bulimia. Br. J. Psychiatry 151: 785-789.
2. KATZ, J. L. 1987. Eating disorder and affective disorder: Relatives or merely chance acquaintances? Compr. Psychiatry 28: 220-228.

A Laboratory Study of Cognitive Factors in Bulimia

Abstinence Violation Effect

EMILY FOX KALES

Department of Psychology
Tufts University
Medford, Massachusetts 02155

Previous research has established a role for cognition in the counterregulatory behavior of normal-weight and obese restrained eaters.[1] One such cognitive factor is the abstinence violation effect (AVE),[2] which results in the suspension of intake control following the perceived violation of self-imposed dietary restraint. Researchers have used the forced preload paradigm to demonstrate AVE in the cognitive disinhibition of restrained eaters.[3,4] To investigate AVE in the eating behavior of bulimic persons, we conducted a laboratory study using preloads of foods previously rated as "safe" or "forbidden" by bulimic subjects based on caloric density and identification as binge-episode precipitants.

Subjects were 21 normal-weight women who met DSM-IIIR criteria for bulimia; all subjects practiced self-induced vomiting (TABLE 1). Subjects and normal controls completed the Eating Attitudes Test [5] and the Eating Inventory.[6] Controls were screened for dietary restraint and previous eating disorder history. Subjects were tested on two days spaced one week apart. On each test day subjects received a standardized pretest meal. Three hours later, subjects were instructed to consume one of two preloads. Preloads were presented in counterbalanced order. The "safe" preload was 470 g of citrus fruit (217 kcal). The "forbidden" preload was 100 g of ice cream (221.4 kcal). Fifteen minutes after completion of the preload, subjects were given *ad libitum* access to a tray of snack pastries that served as test meal units.

TABLE 1. Subject Characteristics[a]

Variable	Bulimics (n = 21)		Normals (n = 24)	
	Mean	SD	Mean	SD
Age	23.2	4.6	18.1	.5
Weight	130.1	5.5	117.5	15.3
Dev. from average wt (%)[b]	+ 2.8	12.9	− 6.6	7.3
Vomiting/day	1.4	1.2		
Daily binge eating	1.6	1.1		
Duration of bulimia (yrs)	7.1	4.4		

[a] College freshmen.
[b] National Center for Health Statistics, 1979.

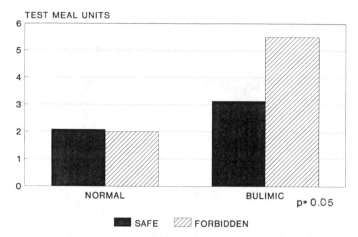

TEST MEAL UNITS

p= 0.05

FIGURE 1. Comparison of test meal intake in bulimic subjects and controls in two preload conditions.

As FIGURE 1 indicates, bulimic subjects showed a significant increase in test meal unit intake following the forbidden preload ($p < 0.05$). In contrast, control subjects showed no such difference in test meal intake, consuming virtually the same amount in both preload conditions. These results suggest that the abstinence violation effect contributes to eating behavior patterns in bulimia.

Because these results were consistent with previous studies of restrained eaters, they suggest that cognitive disinhibition models from restraint theory may be applicable to bulimia.[7] Clinical implications point to the use of cognitive–behavioral therapy for the prevention of AVE-induced relapse.[8] Finally, the study demonstrates the possibility of monitoring binge eating behavior under experimental conditions, a key consideration in research methodology in eating disorders.

ACKNOWLEDGMENT

The author wishes to express appreciation to Elizabeth Baker for her valuable assistance in this study.

REFERENCES

1. HERMAN, C. P. & J. POLIVY. 1980. Restrained eating. *In* Obesity. A. J. Stunkard, Ed. W.B. Saunders Company. Philadelphia, PA.
2. MARLATT, G. A. 1979. Alcohol use and problem drinking: A cognitive-behavioral analysis. *In* Cognitive-Behavior Interventions: Theory, Research, and Procedures. P. C. Kendall & S. C. Hollon, Eds. Academic Press. New York.
3. SPENCER, A. J. & W. FREMOUW. 1979. Binge eating as a function of restraint and weight classification. J. Abnorm. Psychol. **88:** 262–267.

4. RUDERMAN, A. J. & H. C. CHRISTENSEN. 1983. Restraint theory and its applicability to overweight individuals. J. Abnorm. Psychol. **94:** 78–85.
5. GARNER, D. M. & P. E. GARFINKEL. 1979. The eating attitudes test: An index of the symptoms of anorexia nervosa. Psychol. Med. **9:** 273–279.
6. STUNKARD, A. J. & S. MESSICK. 1985. The three-factor eating questionnaire to measure dietary restraint, disinhibition, and hunger. J. Psychosom. Res. **49:** 71–83.
7. HERMAN, C. P. & J. POLIVY. 1984. A boundary model for the regulation of eating. *In* Eating and its Disorders, A. B. Stunkard & E. Stellar, Eds. Raven Press. New York.
8. JOHNSON, C. 1987. The Etiology and Treatment of Bulimia Nervosa. Basic Books. New York.

Weight Loss and Eating Behavior with a Gastric Balloon

THERESA A. SPIEGEL, F. MATTHEW KRAMER,
AND ALBERT J. STUNKARD

Department of Psychiatry
University of Pennsylvania
Philadelphia, Pennsylvania 19104

This study evaluates the effectiveness of the Garren–Edwards Gastric Bubble without adjunctive therapy for weight control. Ten women averaging 111 kg and 91% overweight received the bubble for a 12-week period. Mean weight change was 2.5 kg with a range from −8.8 kg to +1.6 kg. Four patients lost more than 3.5 kg, three lost less, and three gained weight over the 12-week treatment period. (See Kramer *et al.*[1] for more detailed data on weight changes.)

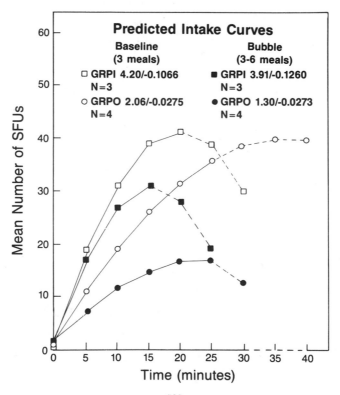

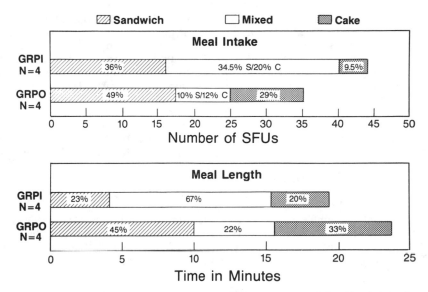

FIGURE 2. This figure shows how patients in GRP1 and GRP0 (defined by their intake patterns during the three baseline meals shown in FIG. 1) distributed their food choices between the sandwich and cake SFUs. (Patients were free to eat their four different varieties of SFUs in any order they chose.) All patients began their meals with sandwich SFUs (sandwich phase). They subsequently introduced cake SFUs and alternated between sandwich and cake SFUs (mixed phase). All patients finished their meals by eating cake with no sandwich SFUs (cake phase). The top panel presents the number and percentage of sandwich and cake SFUs eaten during each of the three phases of patients' meals. The bottom panel presents the percentage of the total meal time that patients spent in each of the three phases.

Reported daily caloric intake decreased from 1724 ± 219 kcal during a four-week baseline period (mean ± SEM) to 1294 ± 167 kcal during the bubble treatment (p < 0.05). Mean number of caloric intakes per day did not change from the baseline period (3.26 ± 0.24) to the bubble treatment (3.11 ± 0.19).

The eating behavior of eight of the patients was observed in laboratory meals consisting of four different kinds of solid food units (SFUs), bite-sized pinwheels of bread with sandwich fillings and sponge cake with sweet fillings. Cumulative intake curves of each patient were fitted with quadratic equations as described by Kissileff *et al.*[2]

FIGURE 1. Patients' predicted cummulative intake curves during laboratory meals in the baseline (three meals/subject) and bubble treatment periods (three to six meals/subject), based upon the linear and quadratic coefficients of the quadratic equations, are presented. The actual intake is depicted by the solid lines. The dashed lines show the continuation of the predicted curves. The numbers in the key are the mean linear coefficient over the mean quadratic coefficient for each curve. There were four patients with the pattern shown by GRP1 during the baseline period, but the laboratory meal intake of one patient in this group was not affected by the bubble. Her data are not included in the figure. Laboratory meal intake was reduced from 39.7 ± 1.6 SFUs during the baseline period to 26.9 ± 4.2 SFUs during the bubble treatment, p < 0.002.

FIGURE 1 shows that the cumulative intake curves of four of the women (GRP1) were typical of those described by Meyer and Pudel[3] for subjects of normal weight. The curves of the other four women (GRP0) were characteristic of obese subjects, with more gradual slowing at the end of meals. The bubble enhanced the development of satiation in patients in GRP1. In contrast, the bubble reduced the rate of intake throughout meals without affecting the rate of deceleration or meal length in patients in GRP0.

FIGURE 2 shows that the two groups also had different patterns of sandwich and cake SFU intake. Patients in GRP1 introduced cake SFUs into their meals sooner, spent more of their meals alternating between sandwich and cake SFUs, and ate fewer cake SFUs at the end of their meals than patients in GRP0. These patterns of food choices did not change with the bubble treatment.

Patients with the normal-weight intake pattern (GRP1) were more likely to lose weight. Three of the four patients in GRP1 lost more than 3.5 kg while only one of the patients in GRP0 lost more than 3.5 kg.

Although the bubble had a modest impact on eating behavior, the effect was insufficient to produce meaningful weight loss in most patients. The results of this study show, however, that obese patients can have very different eating patterns within meals. These different patterns may affect how patients respond to a particular treatment.

REFERENCES

1. KRAMER, F. M., A. J. STUNKARD, T. A. SPIEGEL, J. J. DEREN, M. G. VELCHIK, T. A. WADDEN & K. A. MARSHALL. 1989. Limited weight losses with a gastric balloon. Arch. Intern. Med. 149: 411–413.
2. KISSILEFF, H. R., J. THORNTON & E. BECKER. 1982. A quadratic equation adequately describes the cumulative food intake curve in man. Appetite: J. Intake Res. 3: 255–272.
3. MEYER, J. E. & V. PUDEL. 1972. Experimental studies on food intake in obese and normal weight subjects. J. Psychosom. Res. 16: 305–308.

Effect of Intravenous Branched Chain Amino Acids on Eating Behavior and Brain Biogenic Amine Levels of Rats

AKIO KUBOTA, MICHAEL M. MEGUID,
ANTONIO C. CAMPOS, TING-YUAN CHEN,
AND DAVID HITCH

Surgical Metabolism & Nutrition Laboratory
Department of Surgery
University Hospital
Syracuse, New York 13210

It is postulated that some brain biogenic amines, such as serotonin (5-HT), influence the behavior of dietary intake, and conversely they are influenced by the availability of their dietary precursors, such as tryptophan (Trp). On the other hand, it is well known that branched chain amino acids (BCAA) and other large neutral amino acids (LNAA) compete with Trp to cross the blood–brain barrier (BBB), and a change in blood BCAA concentration should alter the brain Trp level. We observed the effect of intravenous BCAA on eating behavior of rats and their brain biogenic amines.

MATERIALS AND METHODS

Six male Fischer 344 rats were anesthestized and catheters were inserted into right jugular vein, and normal saline (NS) was infused continuously (3 ml/hr). After a six-day recovery period, postoperative days 7–9 served as control (NSC-I). On days 10–12, a 4.4% imbalanced BCAA (IBCAA) solution (Ile = 1.3%, Leu = 1.3%, Val = 1.8%) was given. This was followed by a further three days of NS. Then a 4.4% BCAA-enriched (EBCAA) solution (Ile = 0.5%, Leu = 1.0%, Val = 0.5% and other amino acids) was given on days 16–18 and followed by another three-day NS control period (NSC-II). The order of infusing IBCAA and EBCAA was reversed with each rat. Daily food intake and eating pattern were monitored by previously reported Computed Eater-Meter.[1] Rats were sacrificed at the end of the experiment and brain biogenic amines, such as Nor, Epi, DOPAC, DA, 5HIAA, HVA, 5-HT were measured using HPLC and compared to control rats. Data was evaluated using Student's t-test.

TABLE 1. Spontaneous Food Intake[a]

NSC-I	IBCAA	NSC-II	EBCAA
12.1 ± 0.5	8.0 ± 0.7^b	14.9 ± 0.4	11.9 ± 0.5^b
$p < 0.0001$		$p < 0.0001$	

[a] Results expressed in mg/day; X ± SE; $n = 6$.
[b] $p < 0.0001$ compared to IBCAA.

TABLE 2. Biogenic Amine Levels in Brain[a]

	Nor	Epi	DOPAC	DA	5HIAA	HVA	5HT
BCAA	5.3 ± 0.3	9.9 ± 0.6	0.1 ± 0.1	6.9 ± 0.9	2.9 ± 0.3	1.8 ± 0.2	4.4 ± 0.4
0.9% NS	4.6 ± 0.1	7.6 ± 0.5	0.1 ± 0.1	6.2 ± 0.2	2.7 ± 0.1	1.3 ± 0.3	3.7 ± 0.1
p Value	ns	0.02	ns	ns	ns	ns	ns

[a] Results expressed in ng/10 mg wet tissue.

RESULTS

Spontaneous food intake is shown in TABLE 1. Infusion of either IBCAA or EBCAA decreased food intake ($p < 0.0001$). However, a greater decrease was observed with IBCAA ($p < 0.0001$). A decrease of feeding frequency and meal size was also observed with both solutions. There was no difference in the brain biogenic amines between these two solutions (TABLE 2).

DISCUSSION

Infusion of 4.4% BCAA solution decreased rather than increased spontaneous food intake of the rats significantly, and a greater decrease was observed with the IBCAA relative to the EBCAA, suggesting a disproportionate amino acid pattern caused the depression of food intake.[2] However, brain serotonin level, believed to result in decreased feeding,[3] was not increased, at least not by the end of the experiment. Simultaneous measurement of blood, brain amino acids, and brain biogenic amines and comparison to ordinary amino acid solution may be necessary to verify the relationship between intravenous BCAA and eating behavior.

CONCLUSION

The infusion of IBCAA and EBCCA decreased the food intake of rats, and the decrease with IBCAA was greater than that with EBCAA. Although brain epinephrine increased significantly with BCAA, other brain biogenic amines cannot be implicated with this solution.

REFERENCES

1. MEGUID, M. M., Y. KAWASHIMA & H. LIU. 1987. Computerized eatometer for continuous measurement of rat feeding pattern. Am. J. Clin. Nutr. **45**: 830.
2. ANDERSON, G. H. 1981. Diet, neurotransmitters and brain function. Br. Med. Bull. **37**: 95–100.
3. BENEVENGA, N. J., A. E. HARPER & O. R. ROGERS. 1867. Effect of an amino acid imbalance of the metabolism of the most-limiting amino acid in the rats. J. Nutr. **95**: 434–444.

Cognitive Processing in Bulimia Nervosa

Preliminary Observations

REINHOLD G. LAESSLE,[a] SABINE BOSSERT,
GERTI HANK, KURT HAHLWEG, AND
KARL M. PIRKE

Max-Planck-Institute of Psychiatry
Division of Psychoneuroendocrinology
Munich, Federal Republic of Germany

Neuropsychological performance patterns in patients with anorexia nervosa pointed to attention or vigilance deficits that may indicate some central nervous system dysfunction.[1] Patients with bulimia nervosa are usually within the normal weight range. However, they show the same biological alterations as anorectic patients to a somewhat lesser degree as a consequence of their intermittent dieting behavior.[2] Because altered eating behavior may lead to alterations in central neurotransmitter systems, specific cognitive impairment in eating disorders in the acute stage of illness could well be interpreted as a consequence of starvation. Therefore, we hypothesized deficits in cognitive processing in normal weight bulimic patients, particularly when they show metabolic signs of starvation. Thirty female patients fulfilling DSM-IIIR criteria for bulimia nervosa (age: 24.9 ± 4.0 years, body mass index: 19.6 ± 2.4 kg/m^2, duration of illness: 76.7 ± 47.9 months, binge frequency: 15.1 ± 13.2 per week) were studied. Twenty-three women (age: 25.0 ± 4.8 years) with no evidence of any medical or psychiatric disturbance served as controls. Vigilance performance was measured using a degraded-stimulus continuous performance test (CPT) as reported by Nuechterlein.[3] Hit rate and false alarm rate were used to calculate the signal detection indices, perceptual sensitivity, and response criterion, respectively. As an index of metabolic adaptation to starvation, β-hydroxibutyric acid (BHBA) was measured on three days within one week during a two-week period before the CPT study.

The average hit rate and perceptual sensitivity for bulimic patients was significantly lower than for the controls (TABLE 1). Although false alarm rate did not differ between groups, the response criterion level was significantly higher in the bulimic patients. The patients with metabolic signs of starvation had a significantly lower hit rate than patients without such signs (TABLE 2). Similarly, perceptual sensitivity was significantly lower in the starving patients. Duration of illness, frequency of binging/vomiting, and severity of current psychopathology were not significantly related to vigilance performance. However, bulimic patients with a history of anorexia nervosa showed a higher response criterion level than patients with no past diagnosis of anorexia ($p < 0.08$).

[a] Address for correspondence: Reinhold G. Laessle, Max-Planck-Institute of Psychiatry, Div. of Psychoneuroendocrinology, Kraepelinstr. 10, 8000 München 40, F.R.G.

TABLE 1. Vigilance Performance in Bulimic Patients and Normal Controls

Measure	Bulimia Nervosa ($n = 30$)		Normal Controls ($n = 23$)		$p <$ [a]
	M	SD	M	SD	
Hit rate	0.534	0.230	0.712	0.244	0.02
False alarm rate	0.023	0.019	0.031	0.031	ns
Sensitivity	0.865	0.066	0.909	0.076	0.05
Response criterion	0.790	0.184	0.626	0.305	0.05

[a] Mann–Whitney U-test, two-tailed.

TABLE 2. Vigilance Performance for Bulimic Patients with and without Metabolic Signs of Intermittent Starvation[a]

Measure	With Intermittent Starvation ($n = 12$)		Without Intermittent Starvation ($n = 12$)		p < [b]
	M	SD	M	SD	
Hit rate	0.460	0.214	0.631	0.200	0.03
False alarm rate	0.020	0.014	0.021	0.014	ns
Sensitivity	0.849	0.055	0.892	0.063	0.02
Response criterion	0.776	0.231	0.817	0.131	ns

[a] At least two BHBA values > 0.17 micromol/ml within one week.
[b] Mann–Whitney U-test, two-tailed.

These results support the hypothesis that a substantial part of the poorer vigilance performance in bulimic patients can be explained by consequences of starvation. Because starvation is associated with alterations in CNS transmitter systems, these changes might be involved in a general reduction of the available cognitive processing capacity or in disturbances of control functions for task-relevant processing.

Contrary to the expectation from an impulsive personality style, our bulimic patients were more cautious before deciding that a signal occurred. However, a closer look at subgroups defined according to presence or absence of a medical history of anorexia nervosa revealed the highest response criterion in patients with a history of anorexia nervosa. This is consistent with the assumption that a more rigid, controlled cognitive style, which is typical for anorexia nervosa, is still present in patients who have developed bulimia.

REFERENCES

1. HAMSHER, K. DE S., K. A. HALMI & A. L. BENTON. 1981. Prediction of outcome in anorexia nervosa from neuropsychological status. Psychiatry Res. **4:** 79–88.
2. PIRKE, K. M., J. PAHL, U. SCHWEIGER & M. WARNHOFF. 1985. Metabolic and endocrine indices of starvation in bulimia: A comparison with anorexia nervosa. Psychiatry Res. **15:** 33–37.
3. NUECHTERLEIN, K. H. 1983. Signal detection in vigilance tasks and behavioral attributes among offspring of schizophrenic mothers and among hyperactive children. J. Abnorm. Psychol. **92:** 4–28.

Anorexia Nervosa as an Auto-Addiction

Clinical and Basic Studies

MARY ANN MARRAZZI[a,b,d] AND ELLIOTT D. LUBY[c,d]

[b]*Department of Pharmacology and*
[c]*Department of Psychiatry*
Wayne State University School of Medicine
Detroit, Michigan 48201

[d]*Department of Psychiatry*
Harper-Grace Hospitals
Detroit, Michigan 48201

We have proposed that anorexia nervosa is an addiction to dieting, an auto-addiction.[1,2] During an initial period of dieting, endogenous opioids are released that then get the patient "high" on dieting and addicted to it. The opioids play a dual role in responding to starvation. (1) They increase food intake to correct it. (2) They adapt for survival in the face of starvation until it is corrected, by down-regulating function to an essential minimum. If these responses become uncoupled, addiction can occur to one without the other. In anorexia nervosa, the addiction is to the elation and/or the adaptation to starvation; whereas in bulimia, the addiction is to the opioid drive to eat. Further evidence for our auto-addiction hypothesis includes changes in endogenous opioid levels induced by food deprivation in animal studies, elevated total endogenous opioid activity in the CSF of anorexia nervosa patients, the addiction characteristics of the clinical behavior, and the effectiveness of narcotic antagonists in treatment.

Use of opiate blockade to interrupt the addictive cycle may be therapeutically useful in both anorexia nervosa and bulimia. Our initial studies look very promising.[2,3] TABLE 1 summarizes the initial eight case studies on the use of naltrexone in hospitalized anorexia nervosa patients. In the seven patients with a 4–10 year history of anorexia nervosa, six showed improvement attributable to the drug, including one who is now recovered for over two years. Improvement attributable to the drug is based on comparison of treatment with and without the drug in each patient, using each patient as her own control: Improvement is not based on weight gain alone. Decreases in anxiety over weight gain, in resistance to treatment, and in hyperactivity were not as easily measured but accompanied the weight gain. A double-blind controlled clinical trial is in progress.

Initial case studies on the use of naltrexone in the treatment of bulimia also look very promising. Five patients ages 18–63 years with 7–40-year histories were examined. Four were typical binge-purgers with frequencies of 1–2, 3–5, or 10 episodes per day, and one binged but did not purge once per week. Naltrexone reduced the frequency to zero in four subjects and from three per day to less than one per day in the fifth.

---

[a] Address for correspondence: Dr. Mary Ann Marrazzi, Department of Pharmacology, Wayne State University, School of Medicine, 540 E. Canfield Ave., Detroit, Michigan 48201.

TABLE 1. Initial Case Studies of Naltrexone Treatment of Anorexia Nervosa[a]

Patient Description	Evidence for Improvement Attributable to Naltrexone
33-yr. old female 10-yr history of weight between 70–90 lbs and 20–30 Correctol daily	Maintain ideal body wt. over 2 years now Reached ideal wt. as outpatient on drug
36-yr-old female 4-year history Threatened loss of marriage and custody of 3 children	Comparison of 3 admissions to our unit Drug better than Li⁺ plus Elavil As outpatient, gained 20 lbs reached 96½ lbs Reached highest nonpregnant wt. (96½ lbs) Own cross-over: (secretly) stopped taking the drug, lost 10 lbs., resumed drug, regained weight
22-yr-old female 5-yr history 69 lbs., jogged 10 miles/day Minimal participation in psychotherapy, could not account for improvement	Comparison of 3 admissions to our unit Drug comparable to TPN treatment Began participating in outpatient psychotherapy, began improving and less resistant to treatment
18-yr-old female 4-yr history	Comparison of 2 admissions to our unit Drug comparable to TPN treatment
21-yr-old female 5-yr history, 3 prior hospital admissions Highest adult wt. 80 lbs Admitted from forensic center where sent for petty thefts of food	Continue weight gain seen with TPN about same slope of weight gain Change naltrexone to antipsychotic, lost weight again
17-yr-old female 4-yr history, 2–9-mo hospital stay	Refused to continue drug because of weight gain. On stopping drug, resumed weight loss, hyperactivity, and other anorexic behaviors
18-yr-old female History < 1 year	None
36-yr-old male, 105 lbs. Known at work as "Dr. Death"	None (TPN and drug too intermixed to determine effect of either alone)

[a] Naltrexone is a long-acting, orally active narcotic antagonist used to produce opiate blockade and interrupt the addictive cycle. Because it is a competitive antagonist, lack of improvement attributable to the drug could be due to dosage, which needs to be titrated in each patient, and does not negate our hypothesis. TPN is total parenteral nutrition. Notice three patients had multiple admissions to our unit so that treatment with and without the drug could be compared, one patient secretly did a crossover, one patient continued about the same slope of weight gain that had been achieved with TPN, and one is now recovered for over two years.

When naltrexone was discontinued, the symptoms recurred. A double-blind controlled clinical trial is in progress.

A biological predisposition to eating disorders may result from atypical endogenous opioid systems. Species and strain differences and agonists selective for the subtypes of opioid receptors may be useful in understanding these systems. Morphine activation of the opioid system increases food intake and causes sedation in most species including rats and normal humans. In contrast in BALB/C mice, morphine causes

TABLE 2. Effect of Opiate Agonists on Food Intake and Motor Activity in the Rat and the Mouse

| Species/Strain | Morphine | | U50,488 |
	Food Intake	Activity	Food Intake
Rat			
Sprague–Dawley	↑	↓	↑
Wistar	↑	↓	
Mouse			
BALB/C	↓	↑	↑
CF-1: low dose	↑	–	↑
high dose	↓	↑	↑
DBA/J	↓	–/↓	↑
C57BL/J	↓		↑

[a] The acute effects of morphine or U50,488 on food intake, motor activity, and blood glucose (not shown) were determined in a four-hour test period at the beginning of the light cycle (from 9 AM–1 PM), when the baseline is the lowest. These effects are not meant to simulate anorexia nervosa but to demonstrate the typical or atypical responses when acutely activated by these agonists. The methods are as previously described.[4] Food intake was measured as the difference in the weight of Purina Laboratory Chow pellets made available at the beginning and still remaining at the end of the test period. Motor activity was measured using two matched locomotor activity sensor platforms with body capacity sensors. Drugs were injected five minutes before the beginning of the test period.

anorexia and hyperactivity. This atypical opioid system may be representative of that in the anorexia nervosa patient.[2,4] As summarized in TABLE 2, other atypical patterns are seen in other mouse strains, which may reflect a spectrum of biological predispositions. In all mouse strains, morphine causes anorexia that may or may not be accompanied by hyperactivity. In one strain (CF-1), the food intake changes are biphasic. Morphine is preferential for the μ receptor, whereas U50,488 is selective for the κ receptor. U50,488 increases food intake in all strains of both species (TABLE 2), thus acting similarly in the typical and atypical systems, in contrast to morphine, with which the action in a typical system is opposite that of the atypical system.

REFERENCES

1. MARRAZZI, M. A. & E. D. LUBY. 1988. Int. J. Eating Disorders **5:** 191–208.
2. MARRAZZI, M. A. & E. D. LUBY. 1989. *In* The Brain as an Endocrine Organ. P. Foa & M. Cohen, Eds.: 46–95. Springer-Verlag. New York.
3. LUBY, E. D., M. A. MARRAZZI & J. KINZIE. 1987. J. Clin. Psychopharmacol. **7:** 52–53.
4. BUCK, M. & M. A. MARRAZZI. 1985. Life Sci. **41:** 765–773.

Gustatory Perceptions and Preferences in Young Ballerinas

CHRISTINE MARTIN AND FRANCE BELLISLE

Laboratoire de Neurobiologie de la Nutrition
Universités Paris-Sorbonne and Paris VI
75252 Paris, France

Female ballet dancers must remain thin throughout their careers to satisfy the aesthetic demands of their art. In order to achieve and maintain low body weight, they are frequently engaged in fad and restrictive diets.[1] Excessive weight loss and peculiar nutritional habits have even raised the problem of anorexia nervosa.[2] Body weight status and nutritional habits have been shown to influence gustatory perceptions and preferences; for example, preferences for sweet taste are enhanced in bulimic women.[3] In the present study, we first observed the eating attitudes of female dance students, then their gustatory perceptions of and preferences for the sweet and fat dimensions of foods.

Twenty-three dance students took part in the study. Their mean age was 18.3 years (SD = 4.05). Control groups of normal weight young female subjects, free of eating disorders, were used ($n = 23$ for the Eating Attitudes Test and $n = 12$ for the gustatory perceptions and preferences).

A 40-item questionnaire screening eating attitudes, often used in anorexia nervosa, was administered, the Eating Attitudes Test 40 (EAT 40). For each subject, a score was calculated, the higher the score, the more "anorexic" the attitudes. The mean EAT score was 51.2 (SD = 24.1) for dancers and 12 (SD = 7.3) for controls (FIG. 1).

For brief-exposure taste tests, stimuli were 20 semiliquid mixtures of soft white cheese (0, 3, or 7 grams of fat per 100 grams) or heavy cream (30% fat), sweetened with 1, 5, 10, 20, or 40% sucrose. Subjects tasted each stimulus, then used a nine-point scale to rate the perceived sweetness, fat content, and hedonic value of the stimulus.

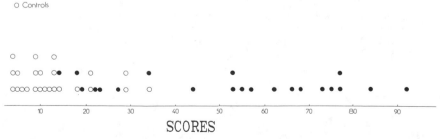

FIGURE 1. Eating Attitudes Test 40: Frequency distribution of scores in 23 ballerinas and 23 controls.

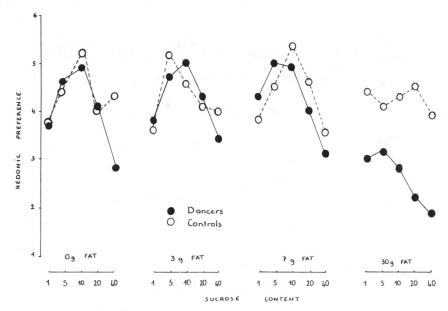

FIGURE 2. Preferences: Mean hedonic ratings as a function of sucrose content for each type of dairy product.

Perceptions of sweetness were comparable for dancers and controls. Perceptions of fatness were slightly better for dancers, especially in very sweet stimuli (10% sucrose and over). Preferences were different for the two groups, with dance students showing clear aversion for heavy cream (FIG. 2).

The EAT 40 revealed that dancers were more preoccupied with weight and food than controls. It also revealed that while dancers shared common traits with anorexia nervosa patients (elective food restriction, dieting, food preoccupations, delayed menarche, and amenorrhea), they also showed differences (no vomiting, no laxative abuse, no desire to cook for or to feed others). Besides, dancers proved to have peculiar gustatory preferences: They had a strong aversion for the fattest stimuli though they could appreciate less fat products. No sign of altered preference for sweetness was found, as in bulimic subjects. The fear of the kilos might have developed a specific sensitivity and repulsion for alimentary fats among dancers.

REFERENCES

1. BRAISTED, J., L. MELLIN, E. GONG & C. IRWIN. 1985. J. Adolescent Health Care **6:** 365–371.
2. MICHAEL, J. & M. D. MALONEY. 1983. Clin. Sports Med. **2(3):** 549–555.
3. DREWNOWSKI, A., F. BELLISLE, P. AIMEZ & B. RÉMY. 1987. Physiol. Behav. **41:** 621–626.
4. GARNER, D. & P. GARFINKEL. 1979. Psych. Med. **9:** 273–279.

Effect of Intravenous Glucose Load on Food Intake and Brain Bioamine Levels

MICHAEL M. MEGUID, YOSHITO KAWASHIMA,
AND ANTONIO CARLOS L. CAMPOS

Surgical Metabolism and Nutrition Laboratory
Department of Surgery
SUNY Health Science Center
Syracuse, New York 13210

We have previously shown that rats given total parenteral nutrition (TPN) intravenously, significantly suppress spontaneous food intake (SFI).[1] The purpose of this study was to see if the observed effect was due to the quantity of calories given.

METHODS AND MATERIALS

Twenty Fischer 344 rats (265 ± 5 g) had a central venous catheter inserted using sterile techniques. Rats were individually housed in metabolic cages and catheter patency maintained with a constant infusion of 3 ml/hr of normal saline. Rats had free access to chow (Purina chow #5008, Ralston Purina, St. Louis, MO) and water, and SFI was

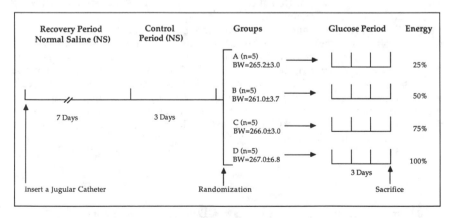

FIGURE 1

TABLE 1. Spontaneous Food Intake (g/day) + Total Caloric Intake (mean ± SD)

Groups	Control Period (3 days)	Study Period (3 days) SFI (g/day)	IV (kcal/day)		Total Intake (kcal/day)
25%	14.9 ± 1.4	12.1 ± 1.7	14.4	=	66.6 ± 5.7
50%	14.5 ± 1.1	10.6 ± 1.0	28.8	=	66.0 ± 3.4
75%	14.9 ± 1.2	9.6 ± 1.2	43.2	=	76.4 ± 4.0
100%	14.8 ± 0.7	8.0 ± 1.9	57.6	=	85.6 ± 6.5

measured daily. Precatheter insertion SFI level was reached by day 7; rats were given three more days of normal saline (control period, FIG. 1). Rats were then randomized into four groups; each receiving i.v. glucose for three days, providing the equivalent of 25%, 50%, 75%, or 100% of the rat's mean SFI during the control period. SFI was measured throughout the experiment using a computerized Eater-Meter.[2] Rats were then decapitated, brains were harvested using freeze-clamp technique, and blood was collected. Blood was analyzed for glucose (G), insulin (IRI), free fatty acids (FFA), and albumin (ALB) using standard techniques. Plasma and whole-brain amino acids were determined using Beckman 6300 Amino Acid Autoanalyzer and biogenic amines measured using HPLC techniques. Data were analyzed using Student's *t*-test and ANOVA.

RESULTS

SFI during the control period remained constant (TABLE 1). SFI fell significantly ($p < 0.01$) as quantity of i.v. glucose calories increased. Mean plasma glucose at the time of sacrifice was elevated, and rose progressively with each infusion group: 25% = 164.7 ± 5.3 mg/dl; 50% = 135.8 ± 4.1 mg/dl; 75% = 169.2 ± 12.9 mg/dl and 100% = 184.8 ± 20 mg/dl. Plasma insulin changes also rose significantly with increases in i.v. glucose infusion being: 25% = 41.6 ± 4.3 µU/ml; 50% = 24.8 ± 1.0 µU/ml; 75% = 40.3 ± 4.0 µU/ml; and 100% = 78.6 ± 15 µU/ml. With a progressive rise in plasma insulin, FFA fell significantly from 0.974 ± 0.233 mEq/l at 25% glucose to 0.235 ± 0.038 mEq/l at 100% glucose. Serum albumin was unchanged in each group being 3.37 g/dl.

TABLE 2. Biogenic Amines in Brain[a]

Index	25%	50%	75%	100%
Plasma Trp: LNAA	0.094 ± 0.003	0.076 ± 0.005	0.095 ± 0.006	0.114 ± 0.005
Brain Trp: LNAA	0.102 ± 0.008	0.079 ± 0.003	0.087 ± 0.015	0.056 ± 0.015
Norepinephrine (NE)	162.9 ± 5.13	145.4 ± 10.31	137.7 ± 4.25	175.7 ± 9.70
Dopamine (DA)	367.1 ± 17.97	353.2 ± 33.68	307.3 ± 16.93	314.7 ± 7.50
Serotonin (5-HT)	302.7 ± 16.37	300.3 ± 21.71	211.2 ± 4.72	279.5 ± 8.62

[a] Results expressed in mg/g wet tissue (M ± SE).

The ratio of tryptophan to large neutral amino acids in the plasma (TRP:LNAA) and thus tryptophan's availability for brain serotonin synthesis gradually increased from 0.094 to 0.114 ($p < 0.05$; TABLE 2).

CONCLUSION

SFI decreased with increasing intravenous glucose loads and appears to be under the influence of brain serotonin synthesis, being depressed by increasing caloric i.v. loads.

REFERENCES

1. GINER, M., K. SNYDER, L. SILLIN & M. M. MEGUID. 1987. Effect of TPN and its components on food intake and GI motility. Surg. Forum 37: 33–36.
2. MEGUID, M. M., Y. KAWASHIMA & H. LIU. 1987. Computerized eatometer for continuous measurement of rat feeding pattern. Am. J. Clin. Nutr. 45: 831.

Amelioration of Anorexia Induced by Food Restriction in Vasopressin-Deficient Rats by Altering Food Intake Schedules

HELEN M. MURPHY AND CYRILLA H. WIDEMAN

Departments of Psychology and Biology
John Carroll University
Cleveland, Ohio 44118

Brattleboro rats lack the hormone vasopressin and have the pathological disorder of diabetes insipidus; hence, Brattleboro rats are referred to as DI rats. It has been proposed that DI animals are more susceptible to stress than normal animals. In 1986, Wideman and Murphy[1] demonstrated that DI rats with 22 or 23 hours of food restriction have a greater percent decrease in body weight, food intake, and water intake than control Long–Evans (LE) rats. In addition, DI rats survive for a shorter period of time and develop more glandular stomach ulcers than controls. In that study, the rats subjected to 22 hours of food restriction were allowed two hours of continuous access to food each day. The purpose of the present study was to determine whether or not two separate feeding periods, each with one hour of access to food, would ameliorate the deleterious effects noted in DI rats subjected to 22 hours of continuous food restriction.

The subjects used were 30 male homozygous DI and 30 male LE rats that were five weeks old and weighed between 80 and 100 g at the start of the habituation period. Subjects from both DI and LE strains were randomly divided into three subgroups each. The experiment contained six treatment groups: (1) DI and (2) LE rats with 24 hours of access to food; (3) DI and (4) LE rats that were food restricted for 22 hours and fed during the second and third hours of the light cycle; and (5) DI and (6) LE animals that were food-restricted for 22 hours and fed during the second and eighth hours of the light cycle (split-feeding).

Animals were subjected to a habituation period for seven days and given *ad libitum* access to food and water. This was followed by an experimental period in which groups 1 and 2 had *ad libitum* access to food and water and groups 3–6 had the previously described paradigms of food restriction. Body weight, food intake, and water intake were recorded daily during both periods. At the end of the experimental period or at death, stomachs were examined for ulcers. Survival time was also noted. Statistical comparisons of the groups and parameters were made through an analysis of variance and Tukey T tests.

As shown in TABLE 1, significant differences were obtained between and among the two strains and subgroups with respect to percent increase or decrease in body weight, food intake, and water intake. (Data in this table are comparisons of the first three experimental days with the last day of habituation. This procedure was used because some animals died on day four.) DI food-restricted rats in the split-feeding para-

TABLE 1. Mean Percent Increase or Decrease in Body Weight, Food Intake, and Water Intake on the First Three Experimental Days Compared with the Last Day of Habituation (± SEM)

Treatment Group	Body Weight Day			Food Intake Day			Water Intake Day		
	1	2	3	1	2	3	1	2	3
DI *ad libitum*	+12.2 ± 3.3	+6.3 ± 2.6	+19.0 ± 2.0	+20.9 ± 7.1	+39.8 ± 6.4	+15.5 ± 6.1	−5.9 ±15.0	+10.7 ± 7.4	+15.8 ± 4.9
LE *ad libitum*	+5.2 ± 0.3	+7.1 ± 0.3	+14.2 ± 0.2	+14.6 ± 8.1	+27.4 ±14.4	+19.2 ± 9.0	+4.6 ± 3.3	−4.5 ± 5.3	+11.3 ± 4.5
DI 2-hr continuous	−18.5[a,d] ± 1.3	−25.2[a,d,e] ± 0.4	−30.1[a,d,e] ± 1.3	−92.3[a,e] ± 4.2	−72.3[a,e] ± 2.6	−69.8[a,e] ± 2.3	−68.3[a,e] ± 2.5	−60.2[a] ± 3.4	−59.9[a,d,e] ± 3.1
LE 2-hr continuous	−12.2[a] ± 1.6	−15.9[a] ± 0.6	−20.2[a] ± 1.1	−91.4[a] ± 4.5	−78.2[a] ± 2.4	−70.2[a] ± 3.1	−70.1[a] ± 2.2	−59.8[a] ± 4.1	−40.2[a] ± 5.1
DI 2-hr split	−16.0[a,d] ± 2.4	−21.2[a,c,d] ± 1.3	−16.9[a,b] ± 2.2	−59.2[a,b,d] ± 4.3	−48.6[a,b,d,e] ± 2.5	−51.1[a,b,d,e] ± 2.4	−65.3[a] ± 2.9	−48.8[a,b] ± 3.5	−36.8[a,b] ± 1.8
LE 2-hr split	−16.8[a,c] ± 1.3	−21.8[a,c] ± 0.5	−20.0[a] ± 1.2	−60.3[a,b] ± 6.7	−59.7[a,b] ± 2.3	−61.6[a,c] ± 1.9	−70.2[a] ± 1.8	−55.2[a] ± 5.4	−37.7[a,b] ± 4.9

[a] Significantly different from *ab libitum* controls of the same strain ($p < 0.01$).
[b] Significantly different from 2-hr continuous feeding of the same strain ($p < 0.01$).
[c] Significantly different from 2-hr continuous feeding of the same strain ($p < 0.05$).
[d] Significantly different from LE rats with 2-hr continuous feeding ($p < 0.01$).
[e] Significantly different from LE rats with 2-hr split feeding ($p < 0.01$).

TABLE 2. Mean Survival Time and Mean Total Length of Ulcers ($\pm$ SEM)

Treatment Group	Mean Survival Time (9-Day Experimental Period)	Mean Total Length of Ulcers (mm)
DI *ad libitum*	9.0	0.0
LE *ad libitum*	9.0	0.0
DI 2-hr continuous	5.6 $\pm$ 1.3^{a,c,d}	10.2^{a,c,d} $\pm$ 2.8
LE 2-hr continuous	9.0	6.8^{a,d} $\pm$ 1.3
DI 2-hr split	9.0	2.6^{a,b,c,d} $\pm$ 0.9
LE 2-hr split	9.0	0.5^{a,b,c} $\pm$ 0.9

[a] Significantly different from *ad libitum* controls of the same strain ($p < 0.01$).
[b] Significantly different from 2-hr continuous feeding of the same strain ($p < 0.01$).
[c] Significantly different from LE rats with 2-hr continuous feeding ($p < 0.01$).
[d] Significantly different from LE rats with 2-hr split feeding ($p < 0.01$).

digm were better able to maintain body weight and ate and drank more than DI animals in the two-hour consecutive feeding situation. In comparing DI and LE food-restricted rats on the split-feeding paradigm, there were no differences in percent decrease in body weight or water intake; however, these DI rats had a lower percent decrease in food intake than their LE counterparts. There was a difference in body weight between DI and LE rats on the consecutive feeding paradigm. As TABLE 2 indicates, survival time and ulcer development were significantly different among the subgroups. DI rats that were fed for two hours consecutively had a shorter survival time than any of the other subgroups. With the split-feeding paradigm, all rats survived throughout the testing period. DI rats in the two-hour consecutive feeding paradigm developed more ulcers than any of the other subgroups and DI rats in the split-feeding paradigm developed more ulcers than their LE counterparts.

The results of this study demonstrate that vasopressin deficiency and food restriction do not necessarily lead to severe anorexia and the demise of the organism. Anorexia can be significantly ameliorated in vasopressin-deficient animals that are food-restricted by short, separated feeding periods.

REFERENCE

1. WIDEMAN, C. H. & H. M. MURPHY. 1986. The pathological effects of limited feeding in vasopressin-deficient animals. Bull. Psychonom. Soc. **24:** 225–228.

Perception of Hunger and Satiety Induced by 2-Deoxy-D-Glucose in Anorexia Nervosa, Bulimia Nervosa, and Obesity

YOSHIKATSU NAKAI, FUMIKO KINOSHITA,
TOSHIKIYO KOH, SATORU TSUJII,
TOSHIHIKO TSUKADA, SHIGEO NAKAISHI,
JUNICHI FUKATA, AND HIROO IMURA

Department of Medicine
Kyoto University
Faculty of Medicine
Kyoto, 606, Japan

The physiological control of food intake in man is complex and not fully understood. In the experiments reported here, we studied the effect of glucopenia induced by 2-deoxy-D-glucose (2-DG), a competitive inhibitor of glucose utilization, on the feelings of hunger and satiety in patients with anorexia nervosa, bulimia nervosa, and obesity.

The subjects were six anorectic patients, three bulimic patients, and eight female obese patients. There were six female volunteers also examined. All subjects received either 2-DG (50 mg/kg) or saline at 9 A.M. on separate days. The subjects gave hunger ratings from a visual analogue scale taken every 30 min before, during, and after 2-DG or saline infusion.[1,2] In normal subjects, hunger ratings increased significantly at 30 min and remained elevated until food intake relieved hunger after 185 min, as shown in FIGURE 1. On the contrary, all anorectic patients exhibited a paradoxical response to hunger ratings; the hunger ratings significantly decreased at 90 and 120 min after 2-DG infusion. When saline solution alone was infused as a control in the same subjects, hunger ratings did not change significantly during the experiments. Three anorectic patients were retested after they had gained weight. The responses of hunger ratings to 2-DG infusion were normalized. Two bulimic patients with normal body weight exhibited normal responses in hunger ratings. One anorexic bulimic patient, whose body weight was only 54% of ideal body weight, however, had a paradoxical response in hunger ratings. These results suggest that the paradoxical responses of hunger ratings in anorectic patients may be secondary to starvation effects.

Beginning at 185 min after 2-DG infusion, the subjects ate a 20-min lunch consisting of a liquid diet containing 1.06 kcal/ml. The satiety questionnaire[3] was used to examine the perception of satiety. The volume of the 20-min lunch was significantly smaller in anorectic patients (98.0 ± 33.5 ml), but that of the bulimic patients (617.3 ± 52.9 ml) was significantly larger than that in normal controls (240.6 ± 32.6 ml), even in an emaciated bulimic patient. All six normal subjects experienced a feeling of satiety and gastric fullness after the intake of the 20-min lunch. However, neither the anorectic patients nor the bulimic patients felt satiety or gastric sensations after

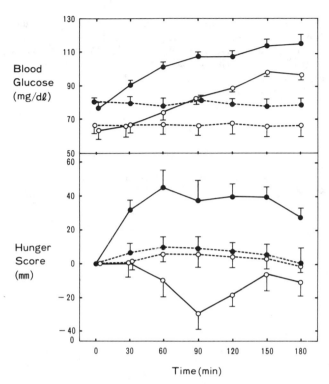

FIGURE 1. The effect of 2-DG (50 mg/kg, solid line) or saline (dotted line) on blood glucose concentrations, hunger ratings from a visual analogue scale in normal subjects (solid circle), or patients with anorexia nervosa (open circle). Means and standard errors of the mean are plotted.

TABLE 1. Clinical Records and Feeding Behaviors after 2-DG Infusion in Eight Patients with Obesity[a]

Case	Age	BL cm	BW kg	Percent IBW	W/H	Volume ml	Hunger	Satiety
Sae	34	160.0	88.0	163.0	0.94	610	+ +	+ +
Oba	17	158.0	83.0	156.0	0.89	650	+ +	+ +
Tan	19	157.9	81.2	152.6	0.89	600	+ +	+ +
Suz	27	155.3	82.0	157.7	0.92	200	±	+
Kit	40	156.3	80.0	152.7	0.81	150	±	+
Nis	29	150.4	84.8	169.6	0.88	580	±	+
Ino	43	157.5	93.0	174.8	0.79	400	−	−
Sai	19	144.5	67.5	150.0	0.76	190	−	−

[a] BL, body length; BW, body weight; IBW, ideal body weight; W/H, the ratio of waist to hip; volume, size of the 20-min lunch; hunger, intensity of response after 2-DG infusion; satiety, intensity of response after 2-DG infusion and 20-min lunch.

lunch. Feeding behaviors in obese patients were heterogeneous; hunger ratings after 2-DG infusion in some obese subjects markedly increased, whereas hunger ratings in some obese subjects did not change significantly. The former subjects experienced a feeling of satiety after lunch, although the latter did not feel satiety after lunch (TABLE 1).

This study demonstrated that the perception of hunger and/or satiety in anorectic patients, bulimic patients, and some obese patients are disturbed.

REFERENCES

1. NAKAI, Y., F. KINOSHITA, T. KOH, S. TSUJII & T. TSUKADA. 1987. Int. J. Eating Disord. 6(1): 49–57.
2. THOMPSON, D. A. & R. G. CAMPBELL. 1977. Science 198: 1065–1068.
3. GARFINKEL, P. E. 1974. Psychol. Med. 4: 309–315.

Sleep States and Body Temperatures in Patients with Anorexia Nervosa

MICHAEL M. NEWMAN, KATHERINE HALMI,
EVELYN SATINOFF, JACK KATZ,
AND CHARLES POLLAK

Department of Psychiatry
New York Hospitals–Cornell Medical Center
White Plains, New York 10605

Previous sleep EEG studies of patients with anorexia nervosa have consistently reported disturbances in sleep continuity and, in some patients, shortened REM latencies. These sleep disturbances are frequently present in patients with major depressive disorders, and there has been the suggestion that sleep disturbances present in anorectic patients may indicate an association between eating disorders and affective illness.[1] Alternatively, the sleep disturbances present in anorectic patients have been attributed to the poor nutritional status and starvation state of these patients.[2]

Measurements of nocturnal body temperature (Tb) in depressed patients have revealed changes in thermoregulation such that depressed patients have higher nighttime body temperatures.[3] To date, no studies of sleep and body temperature have been completed in patients with anorexia nervosa. The aim of this study was to examine sleep EEG recordings and continuous rectal body temperatures in anorectics before and after weight restoration.

Hospitalized patients with a diagnosis of anorexia nervosa were studied on admission and after one month of maintaining ideal body weight (IBW). None of the patients met criteria for major depressive disorder. Subjects spent two days and nights in the Chronobiology Laboratory. Sleep EEG was monitored in six patients for two nights and Tb was monitored continuously in four of those patients. The first day and night in the lab was considered adaptation and data from the second day and night of each test period were used for analysis.

Results showed that before treatment, patients ranged from 60–77% IBW, and had significantly less stage-4 sleep ($\bar{x}$ = 32.9 ± 20.0 minutes versus 77.6 ± 25.0 minutes; $p < 0.02$) and significantly longer REM latencies (110.3 ± 44.4 minutes versus 66.1 ± 26.6 minutes; $p < .05$) compared with one month following weight restoration. Measurements of Tb showed that before treatment, anorectics were able to achieve essentially normal high daytime temperatures which changed little with weight gain. Nighttime sleeping Tbs fell to lower levels in each patient before treatment compared with one month following weight restoration. Abnormally low nighttime Tbs were always accompanied by sleep disturbances. This is in contrast to the association of higher nighttime TBs and sleep disturbances reported on in depressed patients.

REFERENCES

1. KATZ, J. L., A. KUPFERBERG & C. P. POLLAK. 1984. Is there a relationship between eating

disorders and affective disorders? New evidence from sleep recordings. Am. J. Psychiatry **141:** 753–758.
2. CRISP, A. H., E. STONEHILL & G. W. FENTON. 1971. The relationship between sleep, nutrition and mood: A study of patients with anorexia nervosa. Postgrad. Med. **47:** 207–213.
3. AVERY, D. H., R. WILDSCHIODTZ, D. MARTIN & O. J. RAFAELSON. 1986. REM latency and core temperature relationships in primary depression. ACTA Psychiatr. Scand. **74:** 269–280.

Behavioral Model of Anorexia Nervosa

Characteristics of Young Female Rats with Restricted Feeding in Activity-Wheel Cages

NOBUYA OGAWA, CHIAKI HARA, AND
KOUKI WATANABE

Department of Pharmacology
Ehime University School of Medicine
Shigenobu-cho, Onsen-gun
Ehime-ken 791-02, Japan

INTRODUCTION

Young male rats with daily one-hour feeding under the activity-wheel cage housing are reported to develop stomach ulcers[1,2] as well as immunodeficiency[3-5] accompanied by body weight loss, high running activity, and low food consumption resulting in death. Anorexia nervosa is mostly found in adolescent women and is characterized by the following symptoms: anorexia, amenorrhea, body weight loss, and hyperactivity. Therefore, in order to develop the animal model of anorexia nervosa, the present study investigated characteristics of young female rats housed in the activity-wheel cages under food-restricted conditions for aspects of the estrous cycle and behavioral changes.

METHOD

Female Wistar strain rats (6 weeks old) were used. The animals were divided into four groups of five rats each; (1) daily two-hour feeding, (2) daily three-hour feeding, (3) daily four-hour feeding, and (4) free feeding. They were housed in a room with 12:12 LD cycle (lights on 7:00–19:00). Following confirmation of regular estrous cycle using the vaginal smear technique, they were individually housed in the activity-wheel cages. After adaptation to the activity-wheel cage for three days, the restricted feeding schedule was started and continued for three weeks. Food was supplied at 20:00 each day in powder form. During the restricted feeding period, running activity, body weight, food consumption, and estrous cycle were daily recorded. Estrous cycle was checked between 11:00–12:00. After completion of the experiment, the animals were sacrificed and the stomach, thymus, spleen, and adrenals were removed to inspect for stomach ulcers and measure the wet weights.

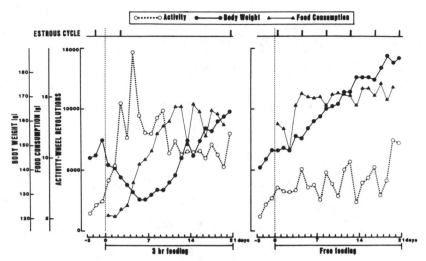

FIGURE 1. Typical behavioral and estrous cycle changes of the rats with a three-hour feeding schedule in comparison with those rats with free feeding.

RESULTS

FIGURE 1 illustrates typical behavioral and estrous cycle changes of the rats with a three-hour feeding schedule in comparison with those rats with free feeding. FIGURE

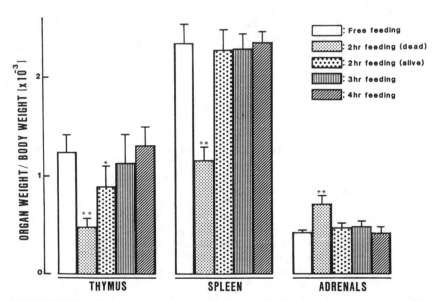

FIGURE 2. The relative organ weights of each group. Each value represents mean ± SD; *p < 0.05, **p < 0.01: statistical difference from free-feeding group (Student t-test or Welch t-test).

2 represents the relative organ weights of each group. The food-restricted groups exhibited high running activity, body weight loss, low food consumption, and disappearance of the estrous cycle. However, only the two-hour feeding group revealed organ weight changes (FIG. 2), and three rats in this group developed stomach ulcers and died. The food intake [$F(3,13) = 5.76$, $p < 0.01$] and body weight [$F(3,13) = 14.78$, $p < 0.001$] in the food-restricted groups on the 21st day were significantly lower than those of the free feeding group.

DISCUSSION

Young female rats housed in the activity-wheel cages under daily three- or four-hour feeding schedules exhibited characteristics similar to typical symptoms of anorexia nervosa without ulcer production and atrophy of the lymphoid organs. The finding that the three-hour feeding group was ulcer-free during the restricted feeding period has been confirmed by the endoscopic observation.[6] The concomitant disappearance of the estrous cycle with augmentation of running activity seems to be a physiological facet of coping behavior under the food-restricted condition, because the phenomenon was in accordance with attenuation of body weight. Because anorexia nervosa is implicated in the psychological factor, the young female rats with the mild food restriction in this study may be applicable to the behavioral model rather than the disease model.

REFERENCES

1. BARBORIAK, J. J. & H. W. KNOBLOCK, JR. 1972. Gastric lesions in food-restricted young rats. Proc. Soc. Exp. Biol. Med. **141:** 437–438.
2. PARE, W. P. & V. P. HOUSER. 1973. Activity and food-restriction effects on gastric glandullar lesions in the rat: The activity-stress ulcer. Bull. Psychon. Soc. **2:** 213–214.
3. HARA, C., K. MANABE & N. OGAWA. 1981. Influence of activity-stress on thymus, spleen and adrenal weights of rats: Possiblity for an immunodeficiency model. Physiol. Behav. **27:** 243–248.
4. HARA, C., N. OGAWA & Y. IMADA. 1981. The activity-stress ulcer and antibody production in rats. Physiol. Behav. **27:** 609–613.
5. HARA, C. & N. OGAWA. 1983. Influence of maturation on ulcer-development and immunodeficiency induced by activity-stress in rats. Physiol. Behav. **30:** 757–761.
6. WATANABE, K., C. HARA & N. OGAWA. Estrous cycle and behavioral changes of female rats exposed to a long-term restricted feeding in activity-wheel cages. Physiol. Behav. Submitted for publication.

Relationship between Taste and Food Preferences in Eating Disorders

BEVERLY PIERCE, K. A. HALMI,
AND SUZANNE SUNDAY

Department of Psychiatry
Cornell University Medical College–New York Hospital
White Plains, New York

Eating-disorder patients in taste studies have demonstrated a strong dislike for high-fat stimuli.[1] Likewise, in a study of self-reported food preferences, eating-disorder patients disliked high-fat foods.[2] This study examines the relationship between preference for sweetness or fat in a taste test and the patients' reported food preferences.

METHODS

Subjects included 33 anorectic restrictors (AN-R), 32 anorectic bulimics (AN-B), 24 bulimics (B), and 24 normal weight controls (C). Taste stimuli included commercially available skim milk (0.1% fat wt/wt), whole milk (3.5% fat), half-and-half (10.5% fat), heavy cream (37.6% fat), and heavy cream with a 15% admixture of safflower oil (52.6% fat). These products were combined with added sucrose at levels 0, 5, 10, and 20% wt/wt. Subjects rated pleasantness on a standard nine-point scale, ranging from "dislike extremely" to "like extremely." Perceived sweetness and fat content were rated using unipolar nine-point scales ranging from absent to extreme. Subjects spit the samples out and rinsed between tastings. Subjects rated their preference for 66 common foods that varied in macronutrient content. Subjects used a nine-point hedonic preference scale ranging from "dislike extremely" to "like extremely." Subjects were tested on admission to a hospitalized eating-disorder program and retested near discharge.

Comparisons between eating-disorder subgroups and controls on intensity of sweetness and fatness and preferences were made by analysis of variance. To determine macronutrient preference, common foods were divided into three categories of carbohydrate/fat content; high carbohydrate/low fat, low carbohydrate/high fat, and high carbohydrate/high fat. Comparisons were made by analysis of variance. Post hoc comparisons were made using Bonferroni corrections.

RESULTS

Taste Test

No significant differences between eating disorder subgroups and controls in perception of intensity of sweetness or fat content. AN-R showed an aversion to pure

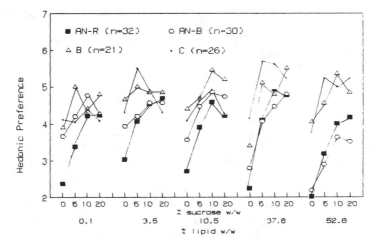

FIGURE 1. Taste preferences: pretreatment.

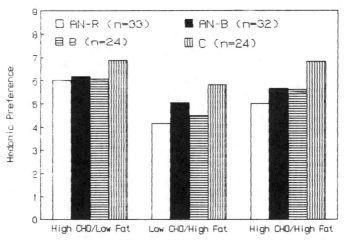

FIGURE 2.. Carbohydrate/fat preferences: common foods.

fat at all concentrations. AN-B showed an aversion to high-fat stimuli (see FIG. 1). B and C showed no differences in their preferences for sweetness and fat stimuli. There was no effect of treatment except in B who, after treatment, showed higher preferences for moderately sweet solutions.

Common Food Preferences

AN-R disliked foods in the low carbohydrate/high fat and high carbohydrate/high fat category when compared with controls. B differed from control subjects only in the low carbohydrate/high fat category, which they disliked compared to C. There were no changes in food preferences over treatment (see FIG. 2).

DISCUSSION

The preference for fat content shows strong consistency in the results from the taste test and common food preferences. AN-R disliked all high-fat taste stimuli and all high-fat-containing foods. B disliked high fat content only when it was not masked by sweetness in the taste test or by high carbohydrate content in the common foods. Fat is the most significant determinant of taste and food preferences in eating-disorder patients, while sweetness and carbohydrate content are minor contributors.

REFERENCES

1. DREWNOWSKI, A., K. A. HALMI, B. PIERCE, J. GIBBS & G. P. SMITH. 1987. Taste and eating disorders. Am. J. Clin. Nutr. **46:** 442–450.
2. DREWNOWSKI, A., B. PIERCE & K. A. HALMI. 1988. Fat aversion in eating disorders. Appetite **10:** 119–131.

Outcome and Prognostic Factors after 20 Years of Anorexia Nervosa

R. H. RATNASURIYA,[a] I. EISLER, G. SZMUKLER, AND G. F. M. RUSSELL

Institute of Psychiatry
London SE5, England

Forty-one patients with a diagnosis of anorexia nervosa admitted consecutively to the Maudsley Hospital between 1959 and 1966 were followed up about 20 years after their admission. Information was gathered on 40 patients.[1] An assessment of general outcome using weight and menstrual function as described in other studies[2-4] indicated that 30% had a good outcome, 32.5% had an intermediate outcome, and 37.5% had died (TABLE 1). Three deaths were related to anorexia nervosa, and three deaths were due to suicide. One patient was unlawfully killed. However, if bulimia is included in the assessment[5] those with a good outcome number 27.5%, intermediate outcome 30%, and poor outcome 42.5%. When other areas of functioning were looked at, only 27.5% were eating normally, normal menstruation occurred in 40%, 47.5% were psychiatrically normal, 42.5% were functioning normally psychosexually, and only 30% were functioning normally psychosocially. Unlike the results in short-term studies,[6] the subjects' economic productivity suffered with time.

Of all the factors mentioned in the literature, those found to be prognostically significant were (1) age of onset of illness, (2) length of illness on admission, (3) a history of neurosis, (4) history of personality problems, and (5) disturbed relationship in the family before the onset of the illness. In the majority of cases the illness took a chronic course though individual patients recovered throughout the 20-year follow-up period. Initially the rate of recovery was constant but decreased sharply after 12–15 years of

TABLE 1. General Outcome at 20 Years

Outcome	Using Morgan and Russell Scales n (%)	Including Bulimia in Assessment n (%)
Good	12 (30)	11 (27.5)
Intermediate	13 (32.5)	12 (30)
Poor		
Chronically ill	8 (20)	10 (25)
Dead	7 (17.5)	7 (17.5)

[a] Deceased.

its duration. An interesting trend that warrants further research was that patients who achieved a higher maximum weight in the hospital tended to do better in the long term.

These findings highlight the need for an early therapeutic endeavor to prevent the illness from becoming chronic.

REFERENCES

1. RATNASURIYA, R. H. 1986. Prognostic Factors and Outcome After 20 Years in Anorexia Nervosa. M. Phil. Thesis. University of London.
2. MORGAN, H. G. & G. F. M. RUSSELL. 1975. Value of family background and clinical features as predictors of long term outcome in anorexia nervosa. Psychol. Med. 5: 282–287.
3. HSU et al. 1979. Outcome of anorexia nervosa. Lancet 1: 61–65.
4. HALL et al. 1984 Anorexia nervosa: Long term outcome in 50 female patients. Br. J. Psychol. 145: 407–413.
5. RUSSELL, G. F. M. 1979. Bulimia nervosa: An ominous variant of anorexia nervosa. Psychol. Med. 9: 429–448.
6. HSU, L. G. K. 1980. Outcome of anorexia nervosa. A review of the literature (1954–1978). Arch. Gen. Psychol. 37: 104–106.

Uncoupling Sweet Taste and Calories

Effects of Saccharin on Hunger and Food Intake in Human Subjects

PETER J. ROGERS AND JOHN E. BLUNDELL

Biopsychology Group
Psychology Department
Leeds University
Leeds LS2 9JT, United Kingdom

Sweetness is a powerful psychobiological phenomenon that has major influences on food preference and patterns of consumption. Intense sweeteners (e.g., saccharin and aspartame) provide a means of sweetening foods and beverages without adding significantly to their energy value and are perceived by consumers as aids to dietary control. Investigations using intense sweeteners to uncouple sweet taste and high caloric content therefore have important theoretical and practical implications. Laboratory studies have a clear role to play provided that they are guided by sound methodology.[1]

Under certain conditions intense sweeteners have been found to stimulate subjective hunger. Compared with the effect of water, consumption of intense sweetener solutions resulted in increases in hunger ratings while glucose solutions of equivalent sweetness reduced hunger.[2,3] The experiment described below examined the effects of saccharin incorporated into a food medium.

The study took the form of a preload manipulation followed by the measurement of hunger (visual-analogue ratings) and food intake. The subjects were male and female, nondieting young adults of normal weight for height. Details of the composition of the preloads and experimental procedure are given in the caption to FIGURE 1. Consumption of the preloads brought about immediate decreases in hunger ratings. Subsequently, hunger following the saccharin preload increased above baseline and after one hour was significantly higher than after the plain, starch, and glucose preloads (*t*-test, all *p* values < 0.02). Food intake at lunchtime was also greatest following the saccharin preload (see FIG. 1). This effect of saccharin was not transitory, and indeed further increases in intake relative to the other preloads occurred during later intervals. Food intake was lowest following the high-energy preloads, with the starch preload producing somewhat the largest suppression of intake.

These results confirm and extend previous findings showing that intense sweeteners do not possess the same satiating capacity as glucose and sucrose.[4] Thus *substitution* of saccharin for glucose failed to reduce overall food intake. Furthermore, *addition* of saccharin to the plain preload led to significant increases in hunger and food intake, indicating that sweetness *per se* can stimulate subsequent appetite.[4] The further increase in intake brought about by saccharin after the test meal may be due to postingestive action(s) of this substance.[4] Such an interpretation is supported by data from the first cohort of 12 subjects in a replication of this study, which indicated that aspartame had a similar effect on intake in the short term (i.e., in the test meal) but not in later intervals (unpublished). Different postingestive effects of these sweeteners may

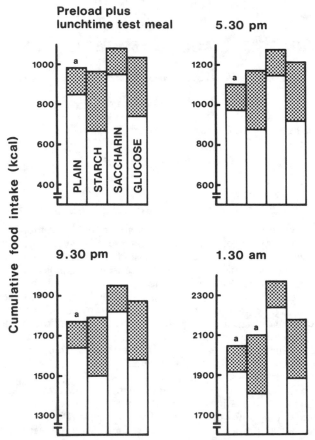

FIGURE 1. Food intake at intervals after the consumption of a low-fat, nonsweet yogurt preload (plain, energy value = 131 kcal) and the same yogurt supplemented with 50 g of starch (295 kcal), 163 mg of saccharin (131 kcal), or 50 g of glucose (295 kcal). The volume of each of the four preloads was 210 ml, and they were all equally liked. The plain and starch preloads, and the saccharin and glucose preloads were equisweet. The study was conducted according to a within-subjects design (n = 21), and food intake was measured in a test meal begun at 1:00 P.M. (and ending at approximately 1:30 P.M.) one hour after the preload was consumed. Thereafter, subjects completed a food-intake diary until bedtime that night. These cumulative intakes *include* the preloads (indicated by the stippled areas); "a" denotes significantly different from saccharin (t-test, $p < 0.05$, 2-tail). The difference between food intakes following the plain and saccharin preloads increased significantly over time [$F(3,60)$ = 2.81, $p < 0.05$].

be expected on the basis of their differing chemical structures. Consequently, it should not be assumed that intense sweeteners will all have equivalent effects on appetite.

REFERENCES

1. BLUNDELL, J. E., P. J. ROGERS & A. J. HILL. 1988. Appetite. **11(Suppl.1):** 54–61.
2. BLUNDELL, J. E. & A. J. HILL 1986. Lancet **i:** 1092–1093.
3. ROGERS, P. J., J-A. CARLYLE, A. J. HILL & J. E. BLUNDELL. 1988. Physiol. Behav. **43:** 547–552.
4. ROGERS, P. J. & J. E. BLUNDELL. 1989. Evaluation of the influence of intense sweeteners on the short-term control of appetite and calorie intake—a psychobiological approach. *In* Progress in Sweeteners. T. H. Grenby, Ed.: 267–289. Elsevier Applied Science. Barking.

Modulation of Nocturnal Free Feeding by Drugs Acting on Serotonergic Neuronal Processes in Rats[a]

KENNY J. SIMANSKY

Department of Pharmacology
Medical College of Pennsylvania at Eastern Pennsylvania
Psychiatric Institute
Philadelphia, Pennsylvania 19129

Drugs that directly stimulate postsynaptic serotonin (5-HT) receptors[1,2] or release neuronal 5-HT[3] decrease food intake. These data suggest that 5-HT normally inhibits feeding. Nonetheless, selective inhibitors of 5-HT uptake have not consistently produced anorexia. For example, fluoxetine,[4,5] ORG 6582,[5] FG 4963,[5] and sertraline[6] reduced food intake and the anorectic action of sertraline was prevented by blocking serotonergic receptors or depleting brain 5-HT.[6] However, fluoxetine[4] and sertraline[6] only transiently decreased feeding with the rats ultimately compensating for the initial anorexia. Furthermore, indalpine failed to reduce feeding even initially despite potently blocking 5-HT uptake.[7]

Each of these studies tested whether inhibiting 5-HT uptake reduces feeding during the light photoperiod after substantial food deprivation. Rats, however, eat primarily during the dark with much smaller intervals between meals. Some data already suggest that inhibiting 5-HT uptake reduces eating rate over 24 hours in freely feeding rats.[5] This study examined whether 5-HT uptake inhibitors might specifically alter nocturnal feeding.

FIGURE 1 compares the anorectic effects of 30-min pretreatment with sertraline on food intake using typical conditions during the light period[6] with the actions of this drug on nocturnal feeding. Sertraline reduced food intake in a dose-related manner during both the first hour, [$F(3,24) = 19.2$, $p < 0.01$, and the first four hours [$F(3,24) = 26.9$, $p < 0.01$] after the onset of darkness. Despite this anorexia, the groups ate similar amounts during the next 20 hours: Vehicle, 23.9 ± 0.6 g; 3.3 µmol/kg, 23.4 ± 1.1; 10.0 µmol/kg, 24.2 ± 1.2 g; 30.0 µmol/kg, 22.7 ± 0.4 g). Thus, sertraline caused a more potent and persistent anorexia, without compensatory overeating, when tested in nocturnal free feeding. In a separate experiment, equimolar doses of fluoxetine reduced nocturnal feeding compared to controls by 10, 25, and 87% during the first hour (controls, 5.2 ± 0.3 g) with the highest dose reducing four-hour intake by 67% (controls, 11.3 ± 0.7 g). This latter dose (*ca.* 10 mg/kg) failed to reduce four-hour intake in a previous study that tested deprived rats during the light period.[4]

These results show that drugs which presumably enhance acute effects of endoge-

[a] This work was supported by United States Public Health Service Grant No. MH 41987.

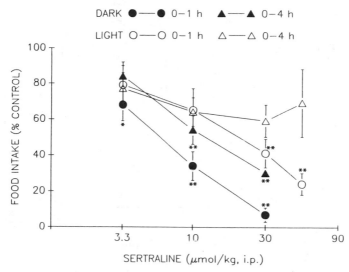

FIGURE 1. Anorectic effect of sertraline in male Sprague–Dawley rats given access to dry pellets after 24-hour food deprivation during the light period (open symbols) or after being deprived for only 30 min before the onset of the dark period (filled symbols). Each data point represents the mean ± SEM of a separate group of rats (n = 7–8 per group). Data are presented as percentages of the cumulative intakes for controls during the first hour and the first four hours of the testing period. Vehicle-injected controls ate 4.6 ± 0.8 g during the first hour and 7.4 ± 0.6 g for the entire four hours when tested during the light. In the nocturnal testing, controls ate 4.0 ± 0.5 g and 9.8 ± 0.5 g during those test periods. Food intakes were corrected for spillage. The ED_{50} for anorexia during the first hour was 19 µmol/kg during the light and 6 µmol/kg during the dark. Data for rats tested in the light period are calculated from results in Lucki *et al.*[6] Asterisks indicate significant difference from respective controls by Duncan's Multiple Range Test, *$p <$ 0.05; ** $p <$ 0.01.

nous 5-HT in central synapses inhibit normal feeding in rats. Conversely, during the light, 8-hydroxy-2-(di-*N*-propylamino) tetralin (8-OH-DPAT) reportedly decreases synaptic 5-HT and increases food intake by activating somatodendritic 5-HT receptors.[8] The results in FIGURE 2 demonstrate that rats also eat more when administered this drug at night. Note, however, that the higher baseline in the dark makes it easier to detect an anorectic effect, whereas the lower control intake in the light more readily reveals increases. The role of stereotyped behaviors in the anorectic effects of 8-OH-DPAT[8] during the night remains to be determined. Overall, it appears that nocturnal free feeding provides a useful model for further exploring serotonergic function in eating behavior.

ACKNOWLEDGMENT

Fred C. Sisk provided excellent technical assistance in these experiments.

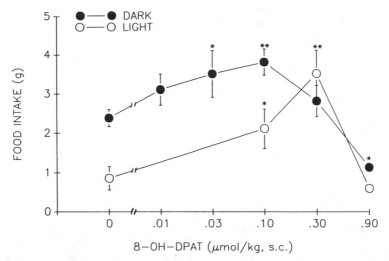

FIGURE 2. Increase in consumption of dry pellets during the first hour after injecting non-deprived rats with 8-OH-DPAT either at the beginning of the dark cycle or in the middle of the light period (6 hours after onset of light). Food was removed and separate groups of 7–15 rats were injected s.c. with the indicated doses of 8-OH-DPAT 15 min before a measured amount of pellets was replaced in each cage. Intakes were corrected for spillage. Size of symbols at 0.90 μmol/kg dose exceeded mean ± SEM. Asterisks signify difference from control value (0 dose) by Duncan's Multiple Range Test: $*p < 0.05$, $**p < 0.01$.

REFERENCES

1. SCHECHTER, L. E. & K. J. SIMANSKY. 1988. Psychopharmacology **94:** 342–346.
2. KENNETT, G. A. & G. CURZON. 1988. Psychopharmacology **96:** 93–100.
3. GARATTINI, S., T. MENNINI, C. BENDOTTI, R. INVERNIZZI & R. SAMANIN. 1986. Appetite **7(Suppl.):** 15–38.
4. GOUDIE, A. J., E. W. THORNTON & T. J. WHEELER. 1976. J. Pharm. Pharmac. **28:** 318–320.
5. BLUNDELL, J. E. & C. J. LATHAM. 1978. *In* Central Mechanisms of Anorectic Drugs. S. Garattini & R. Samanin, Eds.: 83–109. Raven Press. New York.
6. LUCKI, I., M. S. KREIDER & K. J. SIMANSKY. 1988. Psychopharmacology **96:** 289–295.
7. SAMANIN, R., S. CACCIA, C. BENDOTTI, F. BORSINI, E. BORRONI, R. INVERNIZZI, R. PATACCINI & T. MENNINI. 1980. Psychopharmacology **68:** 99–104.
8. DOURISH, C. T., P. H. HUTSON, G. A. KENNETT & G. CURZON. 1986. Appetite **7(Suppl.):** 127–140.

Cognitive Sets toward Foods

Eating Disorders versus Restrained and Unrestrained Eaters

SUZANNE R. SUNDAY, KATHERINE A. HALMI,
AND BEVERLY D. PIERCE

Department of Psychiatry
Cornell University–New York Hospital
White Plains, New York 10605

It has been found that dieters (restrained eaters) and nondieters (unrestrained eaters) differ in their attitudes toward foods. Dieters were more likely than nondieters to associate guilt with foods.[1] People suffering from anorexia and bulimia are highly restrained in their eating. It was the purpose of the present study to examine attitudes toward foods among eating-disorder patients and restrained and unrestrained subjects.

METHOD

The subjects were 19 recently hospitalized eating-disorder patients and normal-weight subjects who were restrained eaters ($n = 19$) or unrestrained eaters ($n = 17$). Restraint was based on Dutch Eating Behavior Questionnaire scores. All subjects were given questionnaires that examined attitudes toward 66 common foods, which differed in calorie, carbohydrate, fat, and sweetness content. Subjects rated each food on a nine-point scale for preference, guilt, danger, and preference if the foods were "calorie-free." For analysis (ANOVAs), the foods were grouped into three calorie, two sweetness, and three carbohydrate/fat categories. All significant pairwise comparisons have corrected alpha levels of 0.05 using the Bonferroni procedure.

RESULTS

Guilt ratings across carbohydrate/fat categories appear in FIGURE 1. Eating-disorder subjects felt significantly more guilt toward all foods (regardless of category) than did unrestrained eaters, and significantly more guilt toward low carbohydrate/high fat foods than did restrained eaters. The patients associated significantly more guilt with low carbohydrate/high fat and high carbohydrate/high fat foods than with high carbohydrate/low fat foods. Restrained eaters associated significantly more guilt with moderate and high calorie foods and with low carbohydrate/high fat and high carbohydrate/high fat foods that did unrestrained eaters. Restrained eaters also felt significantly more guilt toward moderate and high calorie than toward low calorie foods and toward high carbohydrate/high fat than toward high carbohydrate/low fat foods. With respect to danger, eating-disorder subjects saw moderate and high calorie foods and low carbo-

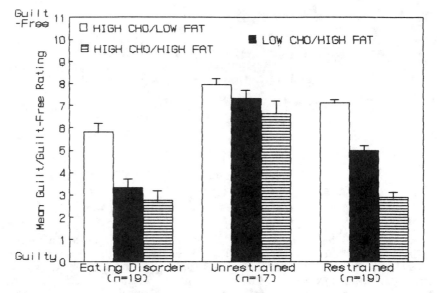

FIGURE 1. Guilt ratings associated with carbohydrate/fat categories among common foods. Mean guilt (1) to guilt-free (9) responses to high carbohydrate/low fat, low carbohydrate/high fat, and high carbohydrate/high fat foods are shown for eating-disorder subjects, unrestrained eaters, and restrained eaters.

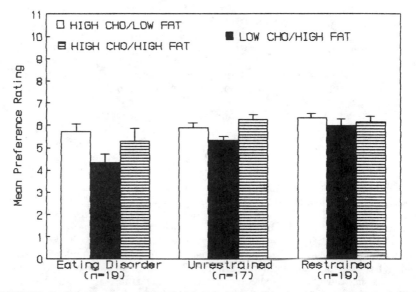

FIGURE 2. Preference ratings associated with carbohydrate/fat categories among common foods. Mean preference responses to high carbohydrate/low fat, low carbohydrate/ high fat, and high carbohydrate/high fat foods are shown for eating-disorder subjects, unrestrained eaters, and restrained eaters.

hydrate/high fat and high carbohydrate/high fat foods as significantly more dangerous than did unrestrained controls. They also found low carbohydrate/high fat foods to be significantly more dangerous than did restrained eaters. There were no differences between groups in preference for calorie or sweetness content of the foods. FIGURE 2 shows preference ratings across carbohydrate/fat categories. Eating-disorder subjects disliked low carbohydrate/high fat foods more than either restrained or unrestrained eaters. There were no differences between preference and "calorie-free" preference.

DISCUSSION

The most pronounced differences in attitudes toward foods were seen in guilt. Eating-disorder subjects associated guilt with all foods while restrained eaters associated guilt with foods that were higher in fat and calories. Unrestrained eaters did not associate guilt with any food. Only eating-disorder subjects regarded any foods as dangerous. Preferences and "calorie-free" preferences generally did not differ between groups, except for low carbohydrate/high fat foods. Restrained eaters were most similar to eating-disorder subjects with respect to the guilt they associated with foods but responded like unrestrained eaters on the other attitude scales. Therefore, when studying cognitive sets toward foods among people suffering from eating disorders, it is necessary to include both restrained and unrestrained control groups.

REFERENCE

1. KING, G., P. HERMAN & J. POLIVY. 1987. Food perception in dieter and non-dieter. Appetite **8**: 147–158.

Failure of Pizotifen (BC-105) to Stimulate Appetite in Rats

ARTUR H. SWIERGIEL

Department of Psychology
University of Wisconsin
Madison, Wisconsin 53706

GEORGES PETERS

Institute of Pharmacology
University of Lausanne
Lausanne, Switzerland

Pizotifen (BC-105), a relatively specific serotonin (5-HT) antagonist with affinity for 5-HT$_2$ receptors, is used as an appetite and weight enhancer (Mosegor®-WANDER, Switzerland) in anorectic and convalescent humans. Its supposed mechanism of action is via 5-HT competitive receptor blockade and antagonizing the feeding-suppressive effects of endogenous 5-HT.[1,2] It is assumed that both peripheral and central 5-HT mechanisms can be manipulated by pizotifen administration. However, increase in appetite in man has been observed after administration of another 5-HT antagonist, cyproheptadine, and almost never after other 5-HT antagonists, methysergide and metergoline.[3-5] Also, there has been some difficulty in confirming the orexigenic effect of pizotifen in animals, particularly in rats.[5] In human treatment pizotifen is given to increase total calorie consumption rather than to affect intake of any particular macronutrient. Therefore, in the present study diets of different caloric density were used with an aim to observe effects of pizotifen on ingestion of both amount of food and energy.

METHODS AND RESULTS

Two-month-old Wistar–Swiss male rats were used. The influence of repeated subcutaneous injections of pizotifen (BC-105: a tricyclic benzocycloheptathiopen derivative with a basic side chain resembling that of cyproheptadine) on intake of different diets and on body weight gain was observed. Doses employed were 0.1, 0.3, 1.0, 5.0, and 10.0 mg/kg body weight per day, with saline as a control. Rats were given a normal diet (ND: 14.5 kJ/g, 26.0% protein, 44.7% carbohydrate, 5.2% fat, 9.3% fiber, 14.8% water, minerals, vitamins) or a low energy content diet (LD: 7.3 kJ/g, 29.0% protein, 0.0% carbohydrate, 5.5% fat, 47.3% fiber, 18.2% water, minerals, vitamins).

Experiment 1 examined intake of the normal diet 1, 3, 6, 18, and 24 hours after a single pizotifen administration. Pizotifen had no effect on food intake, and if any, it rather tended to depress intake of the normal diet in comparison with saline treatment. A massive dose 30 mg/kg of pizotifen depressed ($p < 0.001$) food intake during 18 and 24 hours.

Experiment 2 aimed to establish daily food and energy intakes and body weight gains in untreated rats fed either ND or LD for 14 days. By the fifth day of the access to LD, the rats increased intake of LD so that they ingested the same amount of energy as the rats fed ND.

Experiment 3 studied the effects of the seven-day-long pizotifen treatment on intake of familiar, either normal or low energy content diet and body weight gains. All groups of rats ingested similar seven-day accumulated amounts of energy, although a dose of 1.0 mg/kg of pizotifen seemed to diminish intake of energy in LD. Both in rats fed ND and LD pizotifen depressed ($p < 0.05$) accumulated seven-day body weight gain.

Experiment 4 examined the effects of pizotifen on intake of an unfamiliar diet and body weight gains. The rats habituated to the colony and maintained on laboratory chow were treated with pizotifen for seven days and during that time allowed access to either an unfamiliar ND or unfamiliar LD. Pizotifen had no significant effect on accumulated seven-day energy intake in the unfamiliar ND or LD, although on particular days it seemed to affect intake. Changes, however, were inconsistent and bidirectional. Pizotifen administration resulted in a considerable delay in increasing intake of the unfamiliar LD and on the seventh day of habituation to the diet the rats on LD still consumed less energy than the rats on ND. Pizotifen had no significant effect on daily or seven-day accumulated weight gain in rats fed either ND or LD.

SUMMARY

In none of the experiments did pizotifen stimulate appetite or body weight gains in rats, nor did it shorten the period of initial depression of intake of an unfamiliar diet. On the contrary, pizotifen seemed to diminish intake of the LD and weight gain. Because it has been reported that other 5-HT antagonists can potentiate appetite,[4] it is of some interest that pizotifen failed to modulate appetite or weight in rats. The results suggest that either mechanisms of action of pizotifen in rats differ from those in humans, or that pizotifen only potentiates intake of particular, calorically and carbohydrate rich, diets.

REFERENCES

1. SPEIGHT, T. M. & G. S. AVERY. 1972. Drugs 3: 159–203.
2. FOZARD, J. R. 1987. Trends Pharmacol. Sci. 8: 501–506.
3. MITCHELL, J. E. 1987. Psychopharmacology of anorexia nervosa. In Psychopharmacology: The Third Generation of Progress. H. Y. Meltzer, Ed.: 1273–1276. Raven Press. New York.
4. SILVERSTONE, T. & E. GOODAL. 1986. Appetite 7(Suppl.): 85–97.
5. GARATTINI, S., T. MENNINI, C. BENDOTTI, R. INVERNIZZI & R. SAMANIN. 1986. Appetite 7(Suppl.): 15–38.

Behavioral and Biological Correlates of Restrained Eating

REINHARD J. TUSCHL,[a] REINHOLD G. LAESSLE,
BRITTA C. KOTTHAUS, AND
KARL MARTIN PIRKE

Max-Planck-Institute for Psychiatry
Division of Psychoneuroendocrinology
Munich, Federal Repulic of Germany

Permanent or periodic dieting induces psychobiological alterations that disturb intake regulation. As a consequence, binge eating may occur.[1,2] For the understanding of its high prevalence and its cause, the concept of "restrained eating" may be of great relevance.[3] However, up to now "restrained eaters" have been identified on the basis of questionnaires. It is not known to what degree their intention to restrict food intake is reflected in everyday eating behavior. Are psychometrically classified "restrained eaters" in fact inconspicuous dieters? If so, is their mode of dietary restraint sufficient to affect biological systems susceptible to fasting, for example, metabolism and menstrual functions?

Fifty-eight unselected, healthy, normal-weight women (age 18–26 years) completed the Three Factor Eating Questionnaire.[4] According to its restraint scale, subjects were subdivided by median split into the groups "restrained" and "unrestrained" eaters. Eating behavior was assessed by means of a seven-day food diary and a semistructured interview. Blood samples were taken to analyze concentrations of β-hydroxybutyric acid (β-HBA) and triiodothyronine (T3), which indicate metabolic adaptation to acute starvation. From another collection of healthy, normal-weight women with regular menstruation (age 19–24 years), subjects were selected according to their restraint score. Thirteen were classified as "unrestrained" and nine as "restrained" eaters. Serum concentrations of the ovarian hormones estradiol (E2) and progesterone (P4) were determined daily (except for weekends) throughout one menstrual cycle.

Results concerning body mass index (kg/m²), daily caloric intake, and meal pattern are given in TABLE 1. Restrained eaters reported to diet excessively an average of two days a month. They consumed more food with reduced calorie content (e.g., defattened dairy products) and reported a lower frequency of consumption for sweets (except artificial sweeteners), processed foodstuff, and fat (with the exception of margarine). No differences were found for the categories fruits/vegetables and meat/sausages. Although β-HBA and T3 concentrations did not differ between groups in the expected direction, menstrual function was impaired in restrained eaters (TABLE 2). Replicating the previous study, the restrained eaters were heavier, though consuming fewer calories. The results indicate that the concept of restrained eating is valid for several aspects of every-day eating behavior, that is, energy intake, meal pattern and food selection.

---

[a] Address for correspondence: Dr. Reinhard Tuschl, MPI f. Psychiatrie, Kraepelinstr. 2, D-8000 München 40, Federal Republic of Germany.

TABLE 1. Body Mass Index, Average Daily Caloric Intake and Meal Characteristics[a]

Characteristics	Unrestrained Group ($n = 29$)	Restrained Group ($n = 29$)	p (t-test)
BMI (kg/m^2)	20.3 ± 1.8	21.3 ± 1.8	< 0.05
kCal (per day)	2317 ± 436	1958 ± 354	< 0.01
Daily number of meals	4.7 ± 0.8	4.1 ± 0.7	< 0.01
Average meal size (kcal)	477 ± 107	460 ± 93	ns
Average inter-meal interval (min)	190 ± 34	209 ± 44	< 0.10

[a] Values are means ± SD.

TABLE 2. Metabolic Indices of Starvation and Ovarian Hormone Concentrations (Longitudinal Means During the Luteal Phase)[a]

	Unrestrained Group ($n = 29$)	Restrained Group ($n = 29$)	p (t-test)
β-HBA (μmol/ml)	0.09 ± 0.07	0.07 ± 0.05	ns
T3 (ng/ml)	1.4 ± 0.3 ($n = 13$)	1.7 ± 0.4 ($n = 3$)	ns
E2 (pg/ml)	211 ± 66	171 ± 82	ns
P4 (ng/ml)	11.1 ± 5.3	5.8 ± 4.6	< 0.05
Duration of luteal phase (days)	12.5 ± 3.2	8.6 ± 3.8	< 0.05

[a] Values are means ± SD.

Restrained eaters permanently practice an inconspicuous form of dieting. Nevertheless, they met their actual caloric requirements, because no metabolic signs of acute starvation were found. Despite the lower caloric intake of restrained eaters, their body weight was relatively elevated. These results could be explained by a reduced level of energy expenditure. Energy expenditure may have adapted to intermittent dieting or a constantly reduced energy supply. The impairment of menstrual cycle demonstrates that the alterations in the eating behavior of restrained eaters affect biological functions susceptible to caloric intake.

REFERENCES

1. POLIVY, J. & C. P. HERMAN. 1985. Am. Psychol. **40:** 193–201.
2. WARDLE, J. 1987. Br. J. Clin. Psychol. **26:** 47–55.
3. RUDERMAN, A. J. 1986. Psychol. Bull. **99:** 247–262.
4. STUNKARD, A. J. & S. MESSICK. 1985. J. Psychosom. Res. **29:** 71–81.

Insulin, Sham Feeding, Real Feeding, Glucostasis, and Flavor Preferences in the Rat

DENNIS A. VANDERWEELE

Department of Psychology
Occidental College
Los Angeles, California 90041

RHONDA OETTING DEEMS

Monell Chemical Senses Center
Philadelphia, Pennsylvania 19104

In previous work[1] we had shown insulin to be capable of reducing the amount of milk that rats would sham feed without producing an aversion to the taste of milk paired with insulin injections. Indeed, in that experiment, animals preferred insulin-paired flavors to saline-paired flavors of milk. In earlier work[2] others, however, had found no effect of even large doses of insulin on the real feeding of milk. In this study we returned to these findings and assessed the effects of insulin in real- and sham-feeding rats following modest doses of insulin and an overnight fast.

In two separate, parallel experiments, rats were allowed to sham or real feed a flavored, sweetened condensed milk solution following an overnight, 17½-hour fast. Coincident with the offering of the milk were injections of varying doses of insulin (0.4, 08 U/rat) or saline (0 U/rat). Insulin was without effect on milk intake in the *real* feeding situation, even at doses as large as 5.0 U/rat; however, flavors of milk paired with insulin injections were avoided relative to those paired with saline, at doses greater than 0.8 U/rat. Insulin at these higher dose levels also produced reliable hypoglycemia in these animals (FIG. 1a for intake and preference data and TABLE 1 for glycemic changes).

Insulin significantly reduced the amount of milk *sham* fed by rats at 0.8 U/rat; however, here the flavors paired with insulin were preferred over those paired with saline (see FIG. 1b). Insulin produced a relatively greater hypoglycemia in *sham*-feeding animals than in those real feeding the milk solutions. Additionally, *sham* feeding in saline-injected animals did not produce hypoglycemia, consistent with earlier reports.[3]

It appears that insulin-paired flavors of milk may be preferred when they are ingested in the absence of a filled stomach or significant gastric emptying (as would occur in the sham-feeding animal when ingested food is draining out of the gastrointestinal system through an open cannula). When real feeding milk, rats seem to avoid flavors paired with insulin injections. Some preliminary work in our laboratory indicates that insulin accelerates gastric emptying, even at the low or modest doses used here. Perhaps, this presents to the small intestine a load too calorically dense and unprepared for absorption, as there is no indication of a repair of the hypoglycemic condition in the real-feeding animal, even at 30 minutes postinsulin (see TABLE 1). If insulin in real-feeding rats is accelerating gastric emptying, an aversive state similar to "dumping"

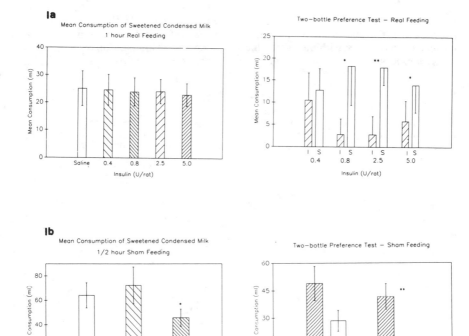

FIGURE 1. Top two panels (**a**) show mean intake of flavored, sweetened condensed milk in food-deprived rats following the doses of insulin depicted (real feeding). Right, top panel shows preferences of these animals for saline-paired flavors in a two-bottle preference test. Each bar represents results for at least 10 animals and * indicates difference significant at the 0.05 level while ** indicates difference significant at the 0.01 level. Bottom two panels (**b**) show mean intake of flavored, sweetened condensed milk in rats sham feeding under the same testing conditions. Right, bottom panel shows preferences of these animals for insulin-paired flavors in a two bottle preference test. Each bar represents results for at least seven animals.

TABLE 1. Mean Plasma Glucose Levels (mg/dl) at 1, 15, and 30 Minutes after Insulin Injections at the Dosages Listed in Rats Real and Sham Fed

Elapsed Time (min)		Insulin Dose	
	Saline	0.4 U/rat	0.8 U/rat
Real Fed			
1	130.4 ± 13.6	133.5 ± 13.0	129.8 ± 17.1
15	153.1 ± 9.4	118.8 ± 18.2	102.3 ± 20.0[a]
30	134.0 ± 9.1	94.7 ± 13.2[a]	83.0 ± 7.7[a]
Sham Fed			
1	108.6 ± 8.8	94.2 ± 17.2	107.3 ± 16.2
15	103.6 ± 10.2	88.2 ± 12.9	91.1 ± 16.4
30	101.3 ± 10.3	76.0 ± 7.9[a]	69.7 ± 14.4[a]

[a] Indicates significantly different from 1-minute level at that dose, $p < 0.01$.

may account for the avoidance of flavors paired with insulin. In the absence of this potential aversive cue, insulin-paired flavors may be preferred over saline-paired ones, as insulin is associated with increased glucose clearance and attenuation of sweet-taste-evoked responses,[4] both responses consistent perhaps with the hedonics of satiation.

REFERENCES

1. OETTING, R. L. & D. A. VANDERWEELE. 1985. Physiol. Behav. **34:** 557–562.
2. BOOTH, D. A. & T. BROOKOVER. 1968. Physiol. Behav. **3:** 439–446.
3. BERTHOUD, H. R. & B. JEANRENAUD. 1982. Am. J. Physiol. **242:** E280–E285.
4. GIZA, B. K. & T. R. SCOTT. 1987. Am. J. Physiol. **252:** R994–R1002.

Cognitive and Physiological Effects on Hunger and Food Intake

JANE WARDLE AND JANE OGDEN

Institute of Psychiatry
University of London
London SE5 8AF, United Kingdom

Abnormalities of hunger perception have long been implicated in the etiology of eating disturbances. Restraint theory has extended this idea to restrained eaters in the normal population, who have been characterized as sensitive to cognitive rather than physiological cues.[1] There has, however, been little direct evidence for this view.

The present study used the method developed by Wardle[2] to manipulate the physiological cues (the actual calorie content of a snack) and the cognitive cues (the believed calorie content) independently. This permitted a direct comparison of sensitivity to internal and external cues.

METHOD

Twenty normal-weight women (10 classified as unrestrained and 10 as restrained on the Dutch Eating Behaviour Questionnaire[3]) took part in the study. Data were also collected on a small sample of eight anorexic women. All subjects took part in each of the four conditions, in which they were given a midmorning drink. This was either orange juice and gelatin (50 kcals) or a similar-tasting drink made of orange juice and a tasteless, colorless starch additive (300 kcals). The subjects were either correctly or incorrectly informed of the calorie content. They then rated their hunger and satiety responses at half-hour intervals, and two hours later were given a test meal at which their food intake was measured.

RESULTS

Both the restrained and the unrestrained eaters showed a significant effect of the physiological manipulation with a slower rise in hunger ratings [$F(4,72) = 3.11$, $p < 0.05$) and a faster fall in fullness ratings [$F(4,72) = 2.62$, $p < 0.05$) after the high-calorie than the low-calorie drinks, irrespective of what information subjects were given (see Fig. 1 for the effects of the physiological manipulation on fullness ratings). The anorexic patients were similar to the normal subjects in showing some differentiation in their hunger ratings after the different caloric loads, although they gave strikingly lower hunger ratings overall.

The restrained eaters were also sensitive to the belief manipulation, with a significant time-by-belief-by-restraint level interaction for the hunger ratings [$F(4,72) = 4.68$, $p < 0.01$), with the restrained eaters showing a more rapid rise in hunger ratings and

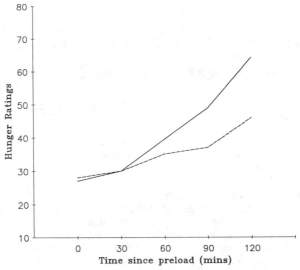

FIGURE 1. Sensitivity to physiological cues. Restrained eaters (*n* = 10): (——) low calorie, (— — —) high calorie.

fall in fullness ratings in the "believed low" than in the "believed high" conditions (see FIG. 2). The preliminary data on the anorexic patients similarly suggested lower hunger ratings when they believed that the drink was high in calories than when they believed it was low calorie.

The food intake results showed substantially higher food intake in the normal subjects than the anorexic patients, but no effect of either the physiological or the cognitive cue manipulations.

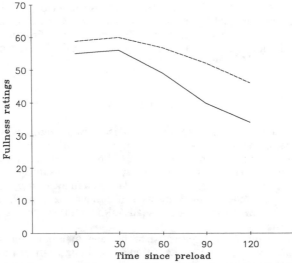

FIGURE 2. Sensitivity to cognitive cues. Restrained eaters: (——) believed low calorie, (— — —) believed high calorie.

SUMMARY

These results provide evidence for sensitivity to cognitive cues in restrained eaters compared with unrestrained eaters. The preliminary data suggest that anorexic patients show a similar cognitive sensitivity. They also support the prediction that in normal eaters, hunger perception is physiologically regulated. However the results conflict with the widely held view that restrained eaters and anorexics are insensitive to internal cues of hunger and satiety. In this study sensitivity to physiological cues was found in both the normal subject groups, and trends in the same direction were shown in the anorexic patients.

REFERENCES

1. HERMAN, P. & J. POLIVY. 1980. *In* Eating and Its Disorders. A. J. Stunkard & E. Elliot, Eds. Raven Press. New York.
2. WARDLE, J. 1987. Physiol. Behav. **40:** 577–582.
3. VAN STREIN, J., J. E. FRIJTERS, G. P. BERGERS & P. B. DEFARES. 1986. Int. J. Eating Disord. **5:** 295–315.

Eating Restraint, Presentation Order, and Time of Day Are Related to Sweet Taste Preferences

ZOE S. WARWICK, PHILIP R. COSTANZO,
JAMES M. GILL, AND SUSAN S. SCHIFFMAN

Departments of Psychology and Psychiatry
Duke University
Durham, North Carolina 27706

This study was conducted to determine whether women differing in degree of eating restraint show different preference profiles for sweet taste. In addition, these preference profiles were studied to assess whether they are stable or are context-dependent. The contexts studied in this experiment were the time of day (morning vs. evening) and the presentation order of the stimuli.

METHODS

Subjects

Forty-eight college-age females completed the Restraint Scale.[1] Subjects who scored 14 or less were classified as "low restraint" (LR), while subjects who scored 15 or higher were classified as "high restraint" (HR). Twenty-five subjects participated in morning testing; fifteen were LR (mean score = 9.9 SD = 3.4) and ten were HR (mean score = 18.4 SD = 2.5). Twenty-three additional subjects were tested in the evening; this group consisted of eleven LR (mean score = 9.9 SD = 3.0) and twelve HR (mean score = 18 SD = 2.5).

Stimuli

The stimuli were six concentrations (0.075 M, 0.15 M, 0.3 M, 0.6 M, 0.9 M, 1.2 M) of reagent-grade sucrose dissolved in deionized water.

Procedure

All six sucrose concentrations were presented in three conditions during morning testing; ascending, descending, and random order of concentration. A 20-ml sample of each stimulus was tasted and then expectorated and rated on a standard nine-point scale of perceived pleasantness. The twenty-five subjects who participated in morning testing rated the stimuli in all conditions. Each test condition was separated by at least

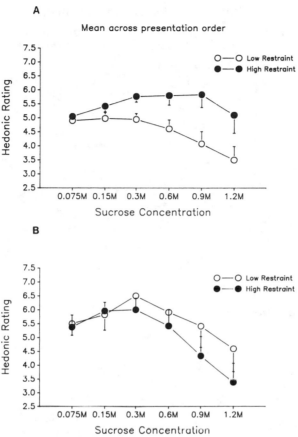

FIGURE 1. (**A**) Morning testing. High-restraint subjects had significantly greater preference for 0.3 *M*, 0.6 *M*, and 0.9 *M* sucrose relative to low-restraint subjects ($p < 0.025$). Preference for the most highly sweet stimuli (1.2 *M*) was marginally significantly preferred by high-restraint subjects ($p = 0.055$).

(**B**) Evening testing. In contrast to morning testing, high-restraint subjects showed marked *dislike* of the most concentrated sucrose stimuli, relative to their preference for the least concentrated stimuli.

48 hours, and order of conditions was balanced across subjects. Evening preference profiles were assessed in ascending order of concentration.

RESULTS

The data were analyzed for morning and evening test sessions using *t*-tests for repeated measures.

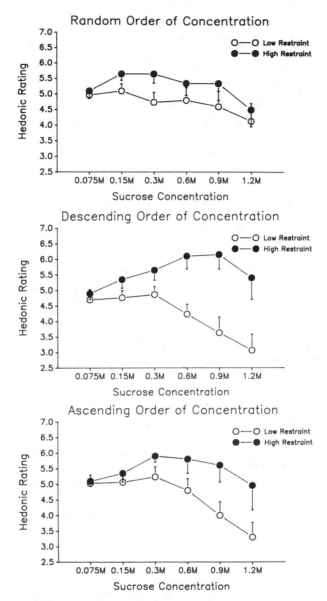

FIGURE 2. The presentation order of the stimuli appears to influence the degree of difference between the preference profiles of high- and low-restraint subjects.

Morning Testing

A mean preference rating (averaged across all orders of presentation) was determined for each subject tested. HR subjects showed a significantly greater preference

($p < 0.025$) for sucrose concentrations of 0.3 *M*, 0.6 *M*, and 0.9 *M* relative to the preferences of LR subjects (see Fig. 1).

The mean preference profiles of LR subjects were characterized by similar preference for the lower concentrations of sucrose followed by a decline in preference with increasing concentrations ("Type I response" as described by Thompson *et al.*[2]). Figure 2 illustrates the effect of presentation order on the preference ratings; the ratings of HR subjects were most sensitive to presentation order. The presentation order of the stimuli influenced the degree of difference between the preference profiles of HR and LR subjects.

Evening Testing

HR subjects tested in the evening showed a very different response profile to the profile determined for HR subjects during morning testing. The HR evening-test profile was characterized by a marked decrease in preference for the higher concentrations of sucrose (see Fig. 1). LR subjects showed the same Type I response as had been found during morning testing. No significant differences were found between the preferences of high- and low-restraint subjects at any concentration of sucrose.

DISCUSSION

The present data reconcile a difference in the literature concerning the relation of sweet taste preferences and eating restraint. The finding that high-restraint subjects have a significantly higher preference for high levels of sweetness relative to low-restraint subjects, when tested in the morning, is in accordance with an earlier report[3] that anorectic and bulimic females (a presumptive HR population) have a maximally preferred sweetness level that is higher than the level preferred by non-eating-disorder subjects. The data on evening preference profiles is also consistent with the finding[4] that there is no difference between the sweetness preference profiles of HR and LR when tested in the evening.

REFERENCES

1. HERMAN, C. P. & J. POLIVY. 1980. Restrained eating. *In* Obesity. A. J. Stunkard, Ed. Saunders. Philadelphia, PA.
2. THOMPSON, D. A., H. R. MOSKOWITZ & R. CAMPBELL. 1976. J. Appl. Psychol. **41**: 77–83.
3. DREWNOWSKI, A., K. A. HALMI, B. PIERCE, J. GIBBS & G. P. SMITH. 1987 Am. J. Clin. Nutr. **46**: 442–450
4. FRIJTERS, J. E. R. 1984. Appetite **5**: 103–108

Doses of Cholecystokinin and Glucagon That Combine to Inhibit Feeding Do Not Affect Gastric Emptying in the Rat

SALLY C. WEATHERFORD[a] AND SUE RITTER

Department of VCAPP
College of Veterinary Medicine
Washington State University
Pullman, Washington 99164

Cholecystokinin[1] (CCK) and glucagon[2] (GL) are proposed endogenous satiety signals. In a recent study by Geary and coworkers a combined injection of these two peptides was found to decrease feeding in a synergistic manner.[3] The mechanism(s) by which these peptides inhibit(s) feeding is not known; however, a proposed hypothesis suggests that CCK inhibits feeding by decreasing gastric emptying.[4] Because GL[5,6] like CCK, is known to inhibit gastric emptying, we hypothesized that the satiating effect of combined injections may be related to retardation of gastric emptying rates.

EXPERIMENT 1

Six male, Sprague–Dawley rats (315 ± 7 g) were trained to eat vanilla wafer cookies during the early part of the light cycle after one hour of food deprivation. Once stable baseline intakes (intake after 0.9% saline, i.p.) were established, peptide testing was initiated. Rats received CCK (0.3 µg/kg, i.p.), or these doses given in combination (separate injections, total volume 1 ml/kg), and food intake was measured every 15 minutes for one hour after presentation of cookies. Four baseline tests preceded each peptide test and each dose, or combination of peptide doses, was tested on two occasions. Data from each repeated dose were averaged and post hoc comparisons were made using a matched-pairs Student's t-test (two-tailed) following a significant analysis of variance (ANOVA).

We found that CCK (0.03 µg/kg) and GL (100 µg/kg) given alone did not affect food intake at any time after injection (see FIG.. 1). Combined injections, however, did decrease food intake relative to a vehicle injection ($p < 0.01$, see FIG. 1A and TABLE 1), but the suppression of feeding was not greater than the predicted additive effect.

[a] Current address and address for correspondence: Sally C. Weatherford, Hoffmann–LaRoche, Department of Neurobiology and Obesity Research, 340 Kingsland St., Nutley, NJ 07110.

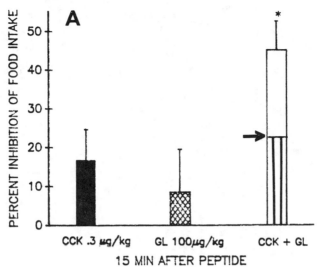

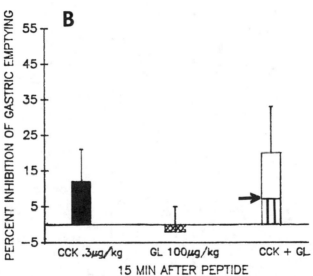

FIGURE 1. Top panel (**A**) shows cookie intake 15 minutes after injection of CCK (0.3 µg/kg), GL (100 µg/kg), or these doses of CCK and GL combined, expressed as percent inhibition relative to 0.9% saline injection. Each peptide dose or combination of peptides was tested two times. Data are the average of two tests. Data are mean ± SEM. $p < 0.01$, peptide vs. saline injection. Predicted additive effect (→) was calculated by adding the precent inhibition produced by each peptide individually.

The bottom panel (**B**) shows gastric emptying expressed as percent inhibition 15 minutes after peptide. Date are mean ± SEM.

TABLE 1. Cookie Intake (G) and Milliliters Emptied from Stomach 15 Minutes after Injection of Saline, CCK, GL, or CCK and GL Combined[a,b]

	CCK		GL		CCK + GL	
	0	0.30	0	100	0	0.30 + 100
Intake (g)	5.9 ± 0.40	4.9 ± 0.40	5.6 ± 0.40	5.0 ± 0.60	5.7 ± 0.40	3.1 ± 0.42*
ml Emptied in 10 min	7.6 ± 0.42	6.7 ± 0.70	6.5 ± 0.30	6.6 ± 0.60	7.4 ± 0.70	5.5 ± 0.90

[a] Data are mean ± SEM, * $p < 0.01$ peptide vs. 0.9% saline.
[b] Doses are expressed in μg/kg.

EXPERIMENT 2

In the second experiment, a new group of rats ($n = 9$, 373 ± 8 g) were implanted with chronic stainless steel gastric cannulas and allowed two weeks to recover. Gastric emptying experiments were conducted every other day during the light cycle after 2–5 hours of food deprivation. Rats were removed from their home cages and their stomachs were lavaged with warm water until the drainage was free of food particles. A latex drainage tube was attached to the cannula and rats were placed in specialized Plexiglas testing cages. Gastric emptying was measured five minutes after an i.p. injection of 0.9% saline (1 ml/kg) by giving an intragastric bolus of 10 ml 0.9% saline containing phenol red. Ten minutes later the saline remaining in the stomach was collected and measured. Gastric emptying rates were determined using a method described previously.[7] Rats were adapted to this procedure four times before peptide testing was initiated. Rats received CCK (0.3 µg/kg) and GL (100 µg/kg) alone or in combination. A baseline test preceded and followed each peptide test. Data were analyzed using a paired Student's t-test.

These doses of CCK and GL were ineffective in altering gastric emptying when given alone or in combination (see FIG. 1B and TABLE 1).

This study demonstrates that doses of CCK and GL that combine to inhibit feeding are ineffective in decreasing rates of gastric emptying. Thus, it is unlikely that the inhibition of feeding observed after these peptides is related to retardation of gastric emptying rates. This is a tentative conclusion, however, because the testing conditions for feeding and gastric emptying were different (i.e., a solid diet vs. a saline load, respectively). Regarding the satiety effect of CCK, these results have two potential implications: (1) the mechanism underlying the satiety effect observed after CCK alone is separate and distinct from the satiety effect observed after combined injections of CCK and GL; or (2) the satiety effect of CCK given alone is not strictly due to inhibition of gastric emptying as previously proposed.[4] Finally, it is interesting to note that GL has been reported to slow gastric emptying in several human studies.[5,6] In the present study, however, GL failed to alter gastric emptying, even at the relatively high dose of 100 µg/kg. It would appear from our results that GL is ineffective in retarding gastric emptying in the rat.

REFERENCES

1. GIBBS, J., R. C. YOUNG & G. P. SMITH. 1973. Cholecystokinin decreases food intake in rats. J. Comp. Physiol. Psychol. **84:** 488–495.
2. GEARY, N. & G. P. SMITH. 1982. Pancreatic glucagon and postprandial satiety in the rat. Physiol. Behav. **28:** 313–322.
3. HINTON, V., M. ROSOFSKY, J. GRANGER & N. GEARY. 1986. Combined injection potentiates the satiety effects of pancreatic glucagon, cholecystokinin, and bombesin. Brain Res. Bull. **17:** 615–619.
4. MORAN, T. H. & P. R. MCHUGH. 1982. Cholecystokinin suppresses food intake by inhibiting gastric emptying. Am. J. Physiol. **242:** R491–R497.
5. CHERNISH, M., R. R. BURNELLE, B. D. ROSENAK & S. AHMADZAI. 1978. Comparison of the effects of glucagon and atropine sulfate on gastric emptying. Am. J. Gastroenterol. **70:** 581–586.
6. FECZKO, P., S. M. SIMMS, J. IORIO & R. HALPERT. 1983. Gastroduodenal response to low-dose glucagon. Am. J. Roentgenol. **140:** 935–940.
7. DEBAS, H. T., O. FAROOQ & M. I. GROSSMAN. 1975. Inhibition of gastric emptying is a physiological action of cholecystokinin. Gastroenterology **68:** 1211–1217.

Feeding-Associated Alterations in Striatal Neurotransmitter Release

IAN N. ACWORTH, KERRY RESSLER, AND
RICHARD J. WURTMAN

Department of Brain and Cognitive Sciences
Massachusetts Institute of Technology
Cambridge, MA 02139

Published evidence suggests a role for dopaminergic (DA) brain pathways in feeding-associated behaviors. Using the novel technique of brain microdialysis of striatal extracellular fluid (ECF) as an index of DA release, Church et al.[1] described increases in levels of DA when animals had limited access to pellets, but not with free access. Dopamine release from the nucleus accumbens did increase with free access to pellets post starvation[2] or after food reward.[3] We used permanently implanted microdialysis probes to measure ECF levels of DA, DOPAC, HVA, and large neutral amino acids (LNAA) for up to 72 hours after implantation among rats experiencing different dietary regimens.

Animals (final weight 300–400 g) were allowed *ad libitum* access to water, but limited access to powdered diet (4 hours per day, noon start) for four weeks before undergoing surgery. Rats were anesthetized with Nembutal (65 mg/ml; 50 mg/kg) and a guide cannula was fixed in place above the right striatum (A +0.5mm, R 2.5mm, V −3.0) and held in place with dental acrylic. Rats were then attached to a liquid swivel and allowed to recover. Three to four days later animals had probes (4 mm) placed into the right striatum, and ECF samples (1.5 µl/min, 20-min periods) were collected outside the cage for up to three days. Samples were analyzed for monoamines and amino acids by standard liquid chromatographic techniques.

The animal's daily food intake was 15 ± 1g/day, and rats maintained approximately 75% of the weight of free-feeding controls. When rats were allowed limited access to powdered diet, striatal levels of DOPAC and HVA peaked 60 minutes after the start of feeding, 30–40% above prefeeding values. Dopamine levels decreased progressively each day (Fig. 1). Levels of LNAA increased by 40 to 116% (methionine and tyrosine, respectively) after the start of eating and showed a similar time-course to dopamine's metabolites (Fig. 2). In contrast, when meal-fed animals had access to pellets instead of powdered diet, then DA levels increased by more than 50% within 15 minutes. (Levels of DOPAC and HVA also increased; data not presented.) Also there was a marked increase in DA release when animals were allowed to chew on nonnutrient items (data not presented).

These data suggest that (1) feeding-associated behaviors *per se* affect striatal dopamine release; (2) meal-feeding animals powdered diet and allowing meal-fed rats access to pellets or nonnutrient items all affect the levels of DA, DOPAC, and HVA in striatal ECF; (3) changes in the levels of dopamine's metabolites DOPAC and HVA need not predict parallel changes in DA release.

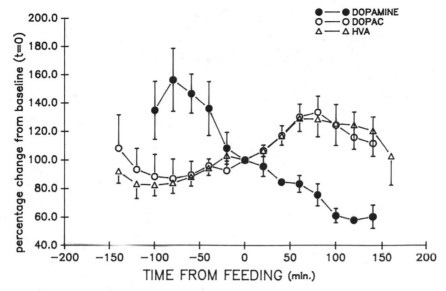

FIGURE 1. Changes in striatal ECF levels of dopamine, DOPAC, and HVA when animals have limited access to powdered diet. Results are presented as percentage change from baseline (value at t = 0); mean ± SEM; n = 2 averaged over three days post probe implant.

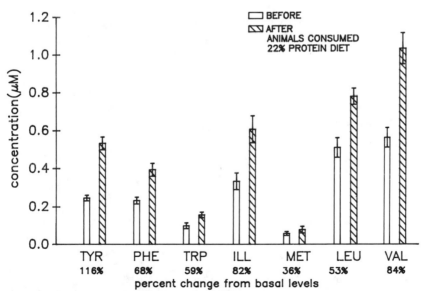

FIGURE 2. Changes in striatal ECF levels of all the large neutral amino acids when rats have limited access to powdered diet. Results are presented as prefeeding (mean of three samples 11:00 A.M. to 12:00 noon) and after (mean of three samples 1:00 to 2:00 P.M.) animals consumed powdered diet; n = 2 averaged over three days post implant.

REFERENCES

1. CHURCH, W. H., J. B. JUSTICE & D. B. NEILL. 1987. Brains Res. **412:** 397–399.
2. RADHAKISHUN, F. S., J. M. VAN REE & B. H. C. WESTERINK. 1988 Neurosci. Lett. **85:** 351–356.
3. HERNANDEZ, L. & B. G. HOEBEL. 1988. Life Sci. **42:** 1705–1712.

Estrogen-Induced Food Aversion in the Rat

Relevance to Anorexia Nervosa

JOHN K. YOUNG

Department of Anatomy
Howard University
Washington, D.C. 20059

CARL R. GUSTAVSON AND JOAN C. GUSTAVSON

University of Texas
Medical Branch at Galveston
Galveston, Texas

One poorly understood aspect of anorexia nervosa is the sex difference in incidence: Most anorexics are female. Because the female sex hormone, estrogen, has pronounced effects upon feeding, we were prompted to investigate the role of estrogen in anorexia.

STUDY I: COMPARISON OF ESTRADIOL- AND LITHIUM CHLORIDE-INDUCED TASTE AVERSIONS IN RATS

In this study, 60 female rats were given oil vehicle s.c., estradiol cypionate (E, 0.4 mg/kg), or lithium chloride (LiCl, 2% of body weight, 0.12 M solution) four hours before or immediately after one-half-hour access to apple juice contained in drinking tubes and were tested for consumption 2, 4, 6, 8, and 24 hours later. Female rats responded to both LiCl and E with comparable decreases in intake (FIG. 1). These parallel results with estradiol and LiCl suggest that nausea or malaise is responsible for E-induced anorexia.

STUDY II: ETHINYL ESTRADIOL-BASED CONDITIONED TASTE AVERSION IN A 16-YEAR-OLD GIRL

In this study, a recovering anorexic girl, hospitalized for chronic nausea nine months after onset of taking an EE-based birth control pill, was examined. She was advised to stop taking the EE pills; within three to four days the patient's chronic vomiting had subsided, and she began more normal social activities. One month later, we conducted a blind placebo and single estrogen exposure study. Consumption of orange-flavored water was followed by a sucrose tablet; two weeks later, peppermint-flavored water was followed by a 0.5-mg EE tablet. The patient reported nausea three hours after taking EE and resumed vomiting over the next four days. FIGURE 2 shows that the EE tablet, but not the placebo tablet, induced a flavor aversion.

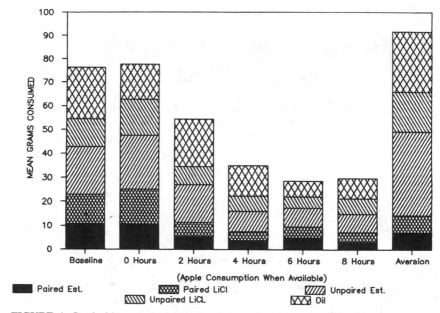

FIGURE 1. Stacked-bar graph showing pooled results of experiment 3.

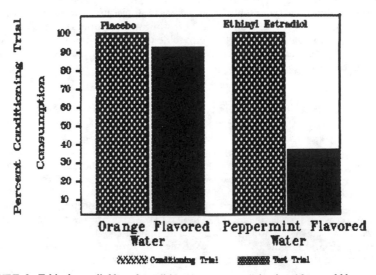

FIGURE 2. Ethinyl estradiol based conditioned taste test aversion in a 16-year-old human female.

SUMMARY

Estrogen appears to provoke taste aversions in both rats and humans.[1,2] Accordingly, we propose that in anorexia (AN), endogenous estrogens produce exaggerated food aversions and chronic malaise. This aversive state is only alleviated when weight loss reduces ovarian function and estrogen output; thus, weight loss in AN may be self-reinforcing by reducing malaise. Other features of AN (obsession with food, hyperactivity) may be secondary to starvation. Even a distorted "body image," often viewed as a basic cause of AN, is not unique to AN and is present in chronically dieting girls.[3] Thus, the sex difference in incidence and an abnormal response to estrogen may be some of the few primary features. An abnormal response to estrogen may arise through an error in development involving the steroid environment of the brain, for example, as in the enhanced ability of estrogen to provoke anorexia in Turner's syndrome.[4] An abnormal function of steroid-sensitive brain regions in anorexics is suggested by hypothalamic tumors that closely mimic the symptoms of AN.[5] Further study is needed to see if (1) developmental exposure to steroids correlates with AN and (2) blockers of the anorexic effect of estrogen, (e.g. progesterone) would reverse the appetite and body weight deficits of anorexics.[6]

REFERENCES

1. BERNSTEIN, I., L. COURTNEY & D. J. BRACET. 1986. Estrogens and the Leydig LTW(m) tumor syndrome: Anorexia and diet aversions attentuated by area postrema lesions. Physiol. Behav. **38:** 159–163.
2. MIELE, J., R. A. ROSELLINI & B. SVARE. 1988. Estradiol benzoate can function as an unconditioned stimulus in a conditioned taste aversion paradigm. Horm. Behav. **22:** 116–130.
3. COUNTS, C. R. & H. E. ADAMS. 1985. Body image in bulimic, dieting, and normal females. J. Psychopathol. Behav. Assess. **7:** 289–300.
4. DOUGHERTY, G. C., W. J. K. ROCKWELL, G. SUTTON & E. H. ELLINWOOD. 1983. Anorexia nervosa in treated gonadal dysgenesis. J. Clin. Psychol. **44:** 219–221.
5. WELLER, R.A. & E. B. WELLER. 1982. Anorexia nervosa in a patient with an infiltrating tumor of the hypothalamus. Am. J. Psychol. **139:** 824–825.
6. TCHEKMEDIYAN, N. S., N. TAIT, M. MOODY & J. AISNER. 1987. High-dose megestrol acetate. A possible treatment for cachexia, J. Am. Med. Assoc. **257:** 1195–1198.

Effects on Feeding Responses of the Selective Dopamine D-1 Antagonist SCH 23390 and the Selective D-2 Antagonist YM-09151-2 in the Rat

PETER G. CLIFTON

Laboratory of Experimental Psychology
University of Sussex
Falmer, Brighton BN1 9OG, United Kingdom

ILENE N. RUSK AND STEVEN J. COOPER

Department of Psychology
University of Birmingham
Birmingham, B15 2TT, United Kingdom

Our aim was to study the effects of selective dopamine antagonists in two different situations and compare the results with those previously reported for relatively non-selective antagonists such as pimozide. Pimozide decreases operant responding for food[8] and, in free-feeding animals, decreases feeding rate, yet increases meal size.[2] Both effects have been attributed to an interference with reward processes.

OPERANT STUDIES

Nine rats were trained to respond for sweetened food pellets during a 20-minute session by bar-pressing on an FR8 schedule using previously described techniques.[6] They were then tested after injection with either saline or 0.01–0.1 mg/kg SCH 23390, a selective D_1 antagonist.[4] In a second experiment we studied the effects of saline or 0.01–0.1 mg/kg YM-09151-2, a selective D_2 antagonist.[7]

After saline administration, the animals responded fairly constantly over the 20-minute session (FIG. 1). The lowest dose of SCH 23390 had little effect on rate, but the two higher doses almost completely abolished responding in the final 15 minutes of the session and substantially reduced it in the first 5 minutes. YM-09151-2 also had substantial effects on response rate with the highest dose (0.1 mg/kg) almost abolishing responding and the intermediate dose (0.03 mg/kg) reducing the number of responses by about one-half. Overall, therefore, SCH 23390 was a little more effective in disrupting responding than YM-09151-2.

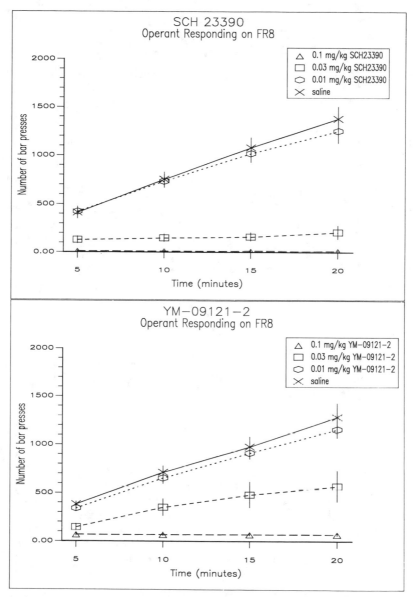

FIGURE 1. Effect of 0–0.1 mg/kg SCH 23390 (above) or 0–0.1 mg/kg YM-09151-2 (below) on operant performance of an FR 8 schedule for a sweetened pellet reward.

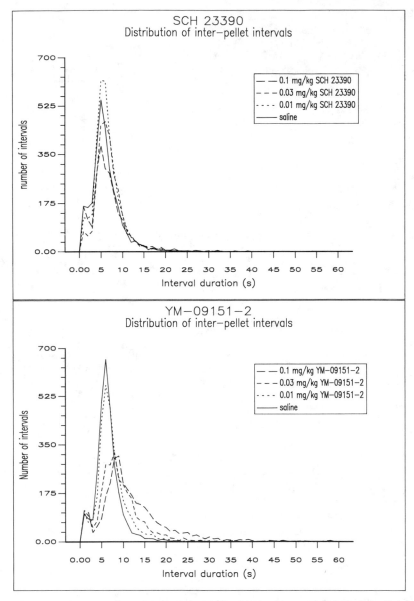

FIGURE 2. Distribution of inter-pellet intervals for the 23.5-hour period following administration of either 0–0.1 mg/kg SCH 23390 (above) or 0–0.1 mg/kg YM-09151-2 (below).

MEAL-PATTERNING STUDIES

The temporal patterns of feeding and drinking were recorded for eight rats over successive 23.5-hour periods using previously described methods.[3] Food was provided as singly presented 45-mg pellets. The records were analyzed either by summing food and water intake over three-hour periods or by dividing the records into a series of "meals." A meal was taken to have terminated after the animal failed to eat or drink for two minutes.

SCH 23390 has relatively little effect on food intake over the twenty-four-hour period following administration. There was only a marginally significant dose-related reduction in feeding rate and the remaining meal parameters were unaffected. There were, however, larger effects on water intake with 0.1 mg/kg significantly reducing the latency to drink and also reducing the size of subsequent water "meals." YM-09151-2, by contrast, had strong effects on meal patterning, although cumulative food intake over the twenty-four-hour period was unaffected. There was a very substantial reduction in feeding rate, seen in FIGURE 2 as a rightward shift of the inter-pellet interval distribution. Meal size was substantially increased, most noticeably at the intermediate dose of 0.03 mg/kg (mean meal size, saline: 33.8 pellets; 0.03 mg/kg YM 09151-2: 48.8 pellets).

SUMMARY

The results show a clear dissociation between reductions in operant responding and on free-feeding meal parameters. The implication is that attempts to explain all of the effects of nonselective dopamine antagonists, like pimozide, within a single theoretical framework[1,8] are likely to require some revision. Instead, it would be appropriate to consider several separate effects of dopamine D_1 and D_2 receptor blockade. D_2 receptor blockade might reduce feeding rate because of direct interference with the rewarding processes that mediate positive feedback at the beginning of a meal and also contribute to the enhancement of meal size by interfering with the influence of preabsorptive cues on satiety. Dopamine D_1 receptor blockade, by contrast, results in animals being more sensitive to reductions in reward produced by a learned response, such as bar-pressing. Hence the effects of D_1 receptor blockade are much more pronounced on leaner schedules[5] and do not correlate well with the small reduction in free-feeding rate seen in the present study.

REFERENCES

1. BLACKBURN, J. R., A. G. PHILLIPS, & H. C. FIBIGER. 1987. Dopamine and preparatory behavior: I. effects of pimozide. Behav. Neurosci. **101:** 352–360.
2. BLUNDELL, J. E. & C. J. LATHAM. 1978. Pharmacological manipulation of feeding behaviour: Possible influences of serotonin and dopamine on fold intake. *In* Central Mechanisms of Anorectic Drugs. S. Garratini & R. Samanin, Eds.: 83–109. Raven Press. New York.
3. CLIFTON, P. G. 1987. Analysis of feeding and drinking patterns. *In* Methods for the Study of Feeding and Drinking. F. M. Toates & N. R. Rowland, Eds.: 19–35. Elsevier. Amsterdam.
4. HYTTEL, J. 1984. Functional evidence for selective dopamine D-1 receptor blockade by SCH 23390. Neuropharmacology **23:** 1395–1401.
5. NAKAJIMA, S. 1986. Suppression of operant responding in the rat by dopamine D-1 receptor blockade with SCH 23390. Physiol. Psychol. **14:** 111–114.
6. RUSK, I. M. & S. J. COOPER. 1989. Profile of the selective dopamine D-2 agonist N-0437: Its effects on palatability- and deprivation-induced feeding, and operant responding for food. Brain Res. Bull. In press.
7. TERAI, M., S. USUDA, I. KUROIWA, O. NOSHIRO & H. MAENO. 1983. Selective binding of YM-09151-2, a new potent neuroleptic, to D2-dopaminergic receptors. Jpn J. Pharmacol. **33:** 749–755.
8. WISE, R. A. 1982. Neuroleptics and operant behaviour: The anhedonia hypothesis. Behav. Brain Sci. **5:** 39–87.

Central and Peripheral 5-HT Receptors Mediate Reductions in Sucrose Sham Feeding in the Rat

STEVEN J. COOPER AND JOANNA C. NEILL

School of Psychology
University of Birmingham
Birmingham, B15 2TT, United Kingdom

Previous work had shown that both central and peripheral serotonergic mechanisms are involved in the control of food intake in the rat.[1] We have recently demonstrated that "5-HT$_1$-like" receptors are involved in d-fenfluramine-induced anorexia[2] and, furthermore, that serotonergic agonists reduce sucrose sham feeding in the gastric-fistulated rat.[3] In order to investigate 5-HT involvemennt in sham feeding further, we have (i) tested if peripherally administered 5-HT itself reduces sham feeding; and (ii) examined the effects of xylamidine (a peripheral 5-HT receptor antagonist) in conjunction with either 5-HT or d-fenfluramine.

METHODS

Twenty-three adult male rats were fitted with a chronic gastric cannula, using a procedure adapted from Kissileff.[4] Following recovery from surgery, the animals were trained to sham feed a 5% solution until intakes had stabilized. On experimental days, rats were food deprived from 10.00 hr. At 13.45 hr, the cannulas were opened, and stomachs rinsed with tepid water to remove all food. Either 5-HT creatinine sulphate (2 mg/kg) or d-fenfluramine hydrochloride (3 mg/kg) were administered i.p. 30 minutes before testing. For control tests, vehicle injections were administered. After 10 minutes, the stomachs were rinsed again, and animals were placed in the test cages. At 14.00 hr they were given access to 5% sucrose. Intakes were reported volumetrically at intervals throughout a two-hour test period. Xylamidine tosylate (3 mg/kg) or its vehicle was injected i.p. three hours before the start of the sham-feeding test.

RESULTS

Peripheral injection of 5-HT significantly reduced 5% sucrose sham feeding ($p <$ 0.01). The peripheral 5-HT antagonist, xylamidine, completely blocked this effect (FIG. 1). d-Fenfluramine induced a marked suppression in sucrose sham feeding ($p < 0.001$); this effect was partially attenuated by xylamidine (FIG. 2). Xylamidine had no effect on sucrose sham feeding when administered by itself.

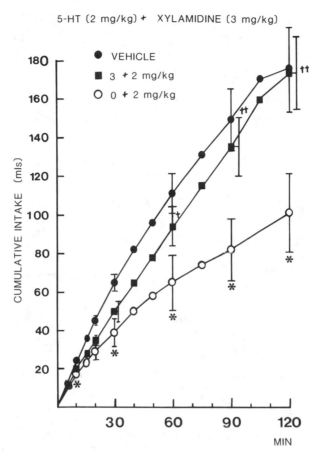

FIGURE 1. Cumulative sucrose feeding over two hours following 5-HT alone and in combination with xylamidine (n = 8 per group). Mean ± SEM (ml). Levels of significance: *p < 0.01, compared with vehicle condition; †p < 0.05, ††p < 0.01, compared with 5-HT alone condition (Dunnett's t-test).

SUMMARY

Peripherally administered 5-HT does not cross the blood–brain barrier,[5] and hence any effect it has on ingestion depends on activation of peripheral 5-HT receptors. We found that 5-HT reduced sucrose sham feeding, and this effect was completely blocked by xylamidine. Hence, activity at peripheral receptors is sufficient to reduce sham feeding. The finding that xylamidine only partially attenuated d-fenfluramine's effects suggests that part of its effect must be mediated by activity at central 5-HT receptors.

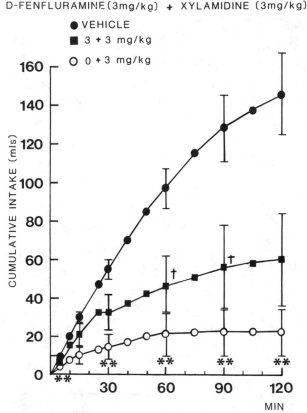

FIGURE 2. Cumulative sucrose sham feeding over two hours following *d*-fenfluramine alone and in combination with xylamidine ($n = 7$ per group). Mean ± SEM (ml). Levels of significance: **$p < 0.001$, compared with vehicle condition; $^†p < 0.05$, compared with *d*-fenfluramine alone (Dunnett's *t*-test).

Sucrose sham feeding, therefore, appears to be sensitive to drug effects at both central and peripheral 5-HT receptors.

REFERENCES

1. CARRUBA, M. O., P. MANTEGAZZA, M. MEMO, C. MISSALE & P. F. SPANO. 1986. Peripheral and central mechanisms of action of serotonergic drugs. Appetite 7(Suppl.): 105–113.
2. NEILL, J. C. & S. J. COOPER. 1989. Evidence that *d*-fenfluramine anorexia is mediated by 5-HT$_1$ receptors. Psychopharmacology 97: 213–218.
3. NEILL J. C. & S. J. COOPER. 1988. Evidence for serotonergic modulation of sucrose sham feeding in the gastric-fistulated rat. Physiol. Behav. 44: 453–459.
4. KISSILEFF, H. R. 1972. Manipulation of the oral and gastric environments. *In* Methods in Psychobiology, Vol. 2. R. D. Myers, Ed.: 125–154. Academic Press. New York.
5. OLDENDORF, E. H. 1971. Brain uptake of radiolabelled amino acids, amines and hexoses after arterial injection. Am. J. Physiol. 221: 1629–1639.

β-Endorphin and Activity-Based Anorexia in the Rat[a]

Influence of Simultaneously Initiated Dieting and Exercise on Weight Loss and β-Endorphin

LEE E. DOERRIES,[b] PAUL F. ARAVICH,[c,d]
ARTHUR METCALF,[b] JAMES D. WALL,[b] AND
THOMAS J. LAUTERIO[c,d]

[b]Department of Psychology
Christopher Newport College
Newport News, Virginia 23606

[c]Eastern Virginia Medical School
Norfolk, Virginia 23501
and
[d]Veterans Administration Medical Center
Hampton, Virginia 23667

The superimposition of exercise upon restricted feeding may precipitate anorexia nervosa (AN). Once precipitated, there is evidence that AN may be perpetuated by differential changes in specific brain opioids.[1] β-Endorphin (BE) is the endogenous opiate that has been most extensively studied in AN.

Our research examines the conjoint effects of exercise and restricted feeding on endogenous opioid concentrations in the rat. Specifically we will exploit a phenomenon known as activity-based anorexia (ABA),[2,3] the consequence of a paradigm that simultaneously introduces normal-weight rats to a restricted feeding schedule and allows them free access to a running wheel.[4] The behavioral consequences of the ABA paradigm are well established.[2-4] Rats progressively increase their activity levels while concomitantly decreasing food intake to a point of self-starvation for many animals. Less apparent is the relationship of ABA to plasma and central concentrations of β-endorphin, the primary focus of this study.

Subjects included 20, 41-day-old, female Sprague–Dawley rats, randomly assigned to either Wahmann Running Wheels or standard wire mesh cages. Experimental rats were fed 90 minutes daily following which they were allowed free access to the running wheel for 22.5 hours. Control rats were fed 90 minutes daily but not allowed the opportunity to run. Animals were on a 12/12 light/dark cycle.

Rats were sacrificed by decapitation when they reached an average of 70% of their

[a] Supported by Eastern Virginia Medical School Institutional Support Grant I88-16.

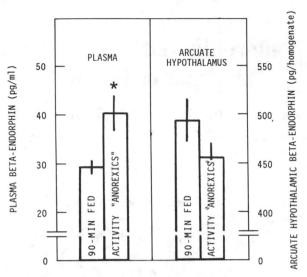

FIGURE 1. Mean ± SEM plasma (pg/ml) and arcuate hypothalamus (pg/homogenate) β-endorphin concentrations in activity "anorexics" and non-running controls fed 90-min/day (* $p < 0.05$).

original body weight. Accurate hypothalami were microdissected and radioimmunoassays performed on plasma and arcuate hypothalami using a standardized kit supplied by Incstar (Stillwater, MN).

Experimental rats progressively increased wheel running to a maximum of 18,000 turns, decreased food intake compared to controls, and reached the 70% weight loss criterion in an average of six days. Nonrunning control rats lost weight at the same rate as experimental animals over the first four days. However on the fifth day, control rats begin to stabilize or regain their weight.

The results of the radioimmunoassays (FIG. 1) show elevated plasma concentrations of β-endorphins for ABA animals compared to controls t(13) = 2.98 ($p < 0.05$). Arcuate hypothalamic concentrations did not vary reliably.

The data support the results from another of our studies[5] showing elevated plasma concentrations of β-endorphin for male ABA rats compared to *ad libitum* fed nonexercised controls. This second study measured BE levels six hours after the removal of the rats from the running wheel, thus suggesting that food restriction and exercise result in chronic elevation of BE.

REFERENCES

1. KAYE, W. H., W. H. BERRETTINI, H.E. GWIRTSMAN, M. CHRETIEN, P. W. GOLD, D. T. GEORGE, D. C. JIMERSON & M. H. EBERT. 1987. Life Sci. **41**: 2147–2155.
2. SPEAR, N. E. & W. F. HILL. 1962. Psychol. Rep. **11**: 437–438.
3. EPLING, W. F. & W. D. PIERCE. 1984. Nutr. Behav. **2**: 37–49.
4. ROUTTENBERG, A. & A. W. KUZNESOF. 1967. J. Comp Physiol. Psychol. **64**: 414–421.
5. ARAVICH, P. F., L. E. DOERRIES, A. METCALF & T. J. LAUTERIO. 1988. Glucoprivic feeding and activity-based anorexia in the rat. Ann. N.Y. Acad. Sci. This volume.

A Residential Laboratory for the Study of Human Eating Behavior

RICHARD W. FOLTIN, MARIAN W. FISCHMAN,
AND THOMAS H. KELLY

Division of Behavioral Biology
Department of Psychiatry and Behavioral Sciences
The Johns Hopkins University School of Medicine
Baltimore, Maryland 21205

Human subjects, participating in studies on feeding behavior, lived continuously in a residential laboratory, consisting of three efficiency apartments and a social area, for up to 14 days. The day was divided into two periods: a private period during which subjects were required to engage in structured work tasks, and a recreation period during which subjects could remain in their private rooms engaging in private activities, for example, reading, or they they could interact with other subjects in the social area. They were given unlimited access to readily available noninstitutional foods including a large variety of snack, meal, and beverage items. The time and amount of consumption of all food items was recorded, allowing the determination of daily patterns of food intake as well as the differentiation of intake into calories consumed as snack items and calories consumed as meal items, that is, items requiring preparation.

In a study on the effects of marijuana on food intake,[1] six healthy adult male research volunteers, in two groups of three subjects each, after providing written consent lived in the residential laboratory for 13 days. Two cigarettes containing active marijuana (2.3% Δ^9 THC) or placebo were smoked during both the private work period and the period of access to social activities. Smoked active marijuana significantly increased total daily caloric intake by 40%. Increased food intake was evident during both private and social periods. The increase in caloric intake was due to an increased consumption of snack foods as a consequence of an increase in the number of snacking occasions. There was no significant change in caloric consumption during meals. The principle increase within the category of snack foods was in the intake of sweet solid items, for example candy bars, compared to sweet fluid, for example soda, or savory solid items, for example potato chips.

In a study on compensation for covert caloric dilution,[2] six healthy adult male volunteers, in two groups of three subjects each, after providing written consent resided continuously in the residential laboratory for 14 days. On days 6 through 11, reduced-calorie versions of food items were covertly substituted for approximately one-third of the regular caloric content items. This manipulation decreased intake from the reduced-calorie group of foods by 500 kcal. The subjects immediately and completely compensated for the loss of calories by increasing the number of non-calorie-manipulated food items consumed. When regular calorie foods were again available during the last three days of the experiment, subjects failed to compensate for this increase in caloric intake. Subjects did not discriminate changes in the caloric status of the available food items. Thus, under conditions of unlimited access to food, human volunteers completely compensated for caloric dilution, but were less accurate in responding to increases in caloric intake. By measuring the food consumption of humans, in this naturalistic laboratory over extended intervals, the conditions under which humans alter the type and amount of food they consume can be investigated with greater reliability and generalizability than with other available research technologies.

REFERENCES

1. FOLTIN, R. W., M. W. FISCHMAN & M. F. BYRNE. 1988. Effects of smoked marijuana on food intake and body weight of humans living in a residential laboratory. Appetite **11:** 1–14.
2. FOLTIN, R. W., M. W. FISCHMAN, C. S. EMURIAN & J. J. RACHLINSKI. 1988. Compensation for caloric dilution in humans given unrestricted access to food in a residential laboratory. Appetite **10:** 13–24.

Hypothalamic α_2-Noradrenergic Receptor System

Relation to Dietary, Genetic, and Hormonally Induced Obesity

M. JHANWAR-UNIYAL,[a,b] J. A. GRINKER,[c]
J. A. FINKELSTEIN,[d] W. BLOCK,[c]
AND S. F. LEIBOWITZ[b]

[b]The Rockefeller University
New York, New York 10021

[c]University of Michigan
Ann Arbor, Michigan 48109

[d]Northeastern Ohio Universities
Rootstown, Ohio 44272

Variables relating to diet, hormones, and genetic background are major factors in the development of obesity. Moreover, hypothalamic neurotransmitter systems are known to influence food intake, appetite, metabolism, and body weight. In particular, the catecholamine, norepinephrine (NE), has been shown in animals to potentiate food intake in satiated subjects, enhance appetite specifically for carbohydrate, affect circulating hormones and nutrients, and reduce energy expenditure.[1] This neurotransmitter, which produces hyperphagia and increased body weight gain with chronic administration, is found to act via α_2-noradrenergic receptors specifically in the hypothalamic paraventricular nucleus (PVN). Circulating substances, such as the glucocorticoid hormone corticosterone (CORT) and glucose, have been shown to influence these PVN α_2 receptors, as well as eating behavior.[2,3] Moreover, evidence suggests that this α_2-receptor system becomes most active and exerts its maximum physiological effects precisely at the start of active cycle, when circulating CORT levels normally peak and when eating behavior, and in particular carbohydrate preference, is strongest.[1-3]

This report reviews the results of three studies that have used radioligand receptor binding techniques to examine the α_2-noradrenergic receptors in discrete hypothalamic sites, including the PVN, of rats that are: (i) maintained for six weeks on a high-fat diet (Purina lab chow mixed with 30% wt/wt Crisco) versus lab chow; (ii) lean (FA/−) versus obese (fa/fa) genetically controlled animals of the Zucker strain; and (iii) adrenalectomized rats treated with either cholesterol or CORT or sham-operated rats treated with cholesterol.

[a] Address for correspondence: Dr. M. Jhanwar-Uniyal, Box 278, The Rockefeller University, 1230 York Avenue, New York, NY 10021.

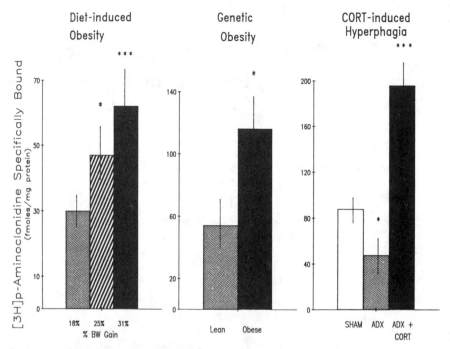

FIGURE 1. [³H]*p*-aminoclonidine binding (fmoles/mg protein $\pm$ SEM) to α_2-noradrenergic receptors in the paraventricular nucleus (PVN) of rats that became moderate to severely obese when kept on high-fat diet (left panel), of lean and genetically controlled obese Zucker rats (middle panel), and of rats receiving either SHAM ADX + cholesterol implants (200 mg), ADX + cholesterol, or ADX + CORT (200 mg) (right panel). * $p < 0.05$, ** $p < 0.01$, and *** $p < 0.001$ for direct comparisons between groups.

METHODS

A standard radioligand binding technique, using the α_2-noradrenergic receptor agonist [³H] *p*-aminoclonidine ([³H]PAC; 45.8 Ci/mmol), was employed to determine the α_2-receptor density in seven micropunched hypothalamic areas. Nonspecific binding was determined in the presence of phentolamine, and the results are expressed as [³H]PAC specifically bound in fmoles/mg protein.

RESULTS

Experiment 1: α^2 Receptors in Relation to Diet-Induced Obesity

The exposure to a high-fat diet for six weeks caused variable changes in body weight in individual rats, ranging from low to severe levels of obesity. Analyses of hypothalamic α_2 receptors (FIG. 1) indicated a significant increase in [³H]PAC binding in the PVN of moderate ($+50\%$; $p < 0.05$) and severely ($+100\%$; $p < 0.001$) dietary-induced obese rats, and also in the dorsomedial nucleus of severely obese rats, as compared to dietary-resistant and chow-fed rats ($+100\%$; $p < 0.01$). In contrast, the density of α₂-noradrenergic receptors in other hypothalamic areas remained unchanged.[4]

Experiment 2: α₂-Noradrenergic Receptors in Genetically Controlled Obese and Lean Zucker Rats

FIGURE 1 presents the [³]PAC binding results for the PVN of lean and obese Zucker rats. As shown here, genetically obese rats had a significantly greater number of available α₂-noradrenergic receptors in the PVN ($+120\%$; $p < 0.05$) than did their lean littermates. Other hypothalamic areas, however, exhibited no group differences in their α₂-receptor density.

Experiment 3: α₂-Noradrenergic Receptors in Relation to Circulating Levels of CORT

As shown in FIGURE 1, the loss of circulating CORT through adrenalectomy (ADX) caused a significant decrement (-46%; $p < 0.05$) in [³]PAC binding to α₂-noradrenergic receptors, specifically in the PVN.[2] Subcutaneous CORT implants, which raised circulating CORT levels to 14 µg%, totally and significantly reversed the [³]PAC binding in the PVN ($p < 0.001$). This down regulation of PVN α₂ receptors in ADX rats, associated with a dramatic decline in eating behavior, was completely reversed by chronic subcutaneous CORT implants, which raised circulating hormone levels to 14 µg% and significantly increased food intake. The only other hypothalamic area affected was the supraoptic nucleus, which exhibited the opposite pattern of changes in α₂-receptor binding.

CONCLUSION

The results of these studies demonstrate that the α₂-noradrenergic receptors specifically in the PVN, which are known to have a role in the control of energy intake and expenditure, exhibit dramatic changes in relation to dietary, genetic, and hormonal factors that are known to contribute to the onset and maintenance of obesity. Further research is needed to establish whether these receptor changes precede or are consequent to the development of hyperphagia and weight gain.

REFERENCES

1. LEIBOWITZ, S. F. 1988. Hypothalamic paraventricular nucleus: Interaction between α₂-noradrenergic receptor system and circulating hormones and nutrients in relation to energy balance. Neurosci. Biobehav. Rev. **12:** 101–109.
2. JHANWAR-UNIYAL, M. & S. F. LEIBOWITZ. 1986. Impact of circulating corticosterone on α₁- and α₂-noradrenergic receptors in discrete brain areas. Brain Res. **368:** 404–408.
3. JHANWAR-UNIYAL, M., M. PAPAMICHAEL & S. F. LEIBOWITZ. 1989. Glucose-dependent changes in α₂-noradrenergic receptors in hypothalamic nuclei. Physiol. Behav. **44:** 611–617.
4. GRINKER, J. A., W. D. BLOCK, M. JHANWAR-UNIYAL & S. F. LEIBOWITZ, 1987. High fat dietary responsiveness: Relationship between catecholamine and sensory responsiveness to carbohydrate and fat. Fed. Proc. **46:** 881.

Ingestion of Highly Palatable Sucrose Induces Naloxone Supersensitivity in the Sham-Feeding Rat

T. C. KIRKHAM AND S. J. COOPER

School of Psychology
University of Birmingham
Birmingham B15 2TT, United Kingdom

The opioid receptor antagonist naloxone stereospecifically attenuates sucrose sham feeding in rats,[1] suggesting that the drug reduces sucrose palatability.[2] Intriguingly, naloxone's anorectic potency is increased twofold in rats sham feeding very palatable 30% sucrose, relative to its effects at lower sucrose concentrations. This change may result from a downregulation of opioid receptors in response to a sucrose-stimulated elevation of brain opioid levels.[3-6] To test this possibility, repeated sham feeding of 30% sucrose was paired with chronic antagonist administration, a treatment known to induce opioid receptor upregulation.[7,8]

METHOD

Two groups ($n = 8$) of male hooded rats were implanted with acrylic gastric cannulas[9] and trained to sham feed 30% (wt/vol) sucrose during one-hour intake tests performed at 14:00 on five successive days. Control data were obtained on day four after i.p. saline. On days one through four, rats in group one received 5 mg/kg (i.p.) naloxone at 09:00 and 17:00. Control animals (group two) were injected with saline. On day five, the 09:00 injection was omitted: Both groups were retested (at 14:00), 30 minutes after pretreatment with 5 mg/kg naloxone.

RESULTS

Both groups displayed similar baseline sham intake of the 30% sucrose (FIG. 1). Naloxone pretreatment on day five produced a marked attenuation of one-hour sham intake in both groups. However, there was a significant interaction between chronic treatment and the degree of intake suppression ($p < 0.05$). Controls showed the expected enhanced sensitivity to the drug; total intake was reduced by 70% ($p < 0.01$). In contrast, one-hour intake of rats in group one was reduced by only 42% ($p < 0.01$).

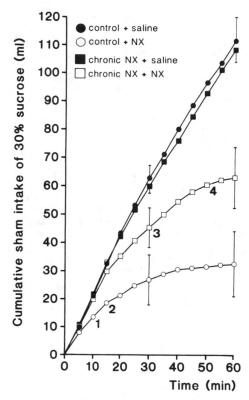

FIGURE 1. The enhanced anorectic potency of acute 5 mg/kg naloxone (NX) in rats sham feeding 30% sucrose solution under control conditions (chronic saline) is prevented by prior chronic naloxone administration (5 mg/kg bi-daily for 4 days). 1: $\bigcirc < \bullet$, $p < 0.05$; 2: $\bigcirc < \bullet$, $p < 0.01$; 3: $\square < \blacksquare$ $p < 0.05$; 4: $\square < \blacksquare$, $p < 0.01$. All values are means for 8 rats (bars indicate SEM).

SUMMARY

This experiment has confirmed that sham feeding of 30% sucrose can induce extreme sensitivity to the acute anorectic effect of the drug. That this enhanced anorexia is prevented by chronic naloxone administration provides indirect evidence that repeated sham feeding of 30% sucrose can induce downregulation of opioid receptors. This may occur as a homeostatic response to overstimulation by opioids released as a consequence of sucrose ingestion. Specific binding/autoradiographic studies are required to test the accuracy of this account. Overall, these findings (i) emphasize the importance of palatability in naloxone anorexia; (ii) support opioid involvement in orosensory reward; and (iii) are indicative of neural plasticity in systems regulating ingestive behaviors.

REFERENCES

1. KIRKHAM, T. C. & S. J. COOPER. 1988. Attenuation of sham feeding by naloxone is stereospecific: Evidence for opioid mediation of orosensory reward. Physiol. Behav. **43:** 845–847.
2. KIRKHAM, T. C. & S. J. COOPER. 1988. Naloxone attenuation of sham feeding is modified by manipulation of sucrose concentration. Physiol. Behav. **44:** 491–494.
3. BATTISTINI, N., L. GIARDINO & L. CALZA. 1987. Opiate receptor autoradiography in fasting rats. Int. J. Obesity **11(Suppl. 3):** 17–21.
4. BLASS, E. M., E. FITZGERALD & P. KEHOE. 1987. Interactions between sucrose, pain and isolation distress. Pharmacol. Biochem. Behav. **26:** 483–489.
5. BRADY, L. S. & M. HERKENHAM. 1987. Dehydration reduces κ-opiate receptor binding in the neurohypophysis of the rat. Brain Res. **425:** 212–217.
6. DUM, J., C. GRAMSCH & A. HERZ. 1983. Activation of hypothalamic β-endorphin pools by reward induced by highly palatable food. Pharmacol. Biochem. Behav. **18:** 443–447.
7. TEMPEL, A., E. L. GARDNER & R. S. ZUKIN. 1985. Neurochemical and functional correlates of naltrexone-induced opiate receptor up-regulation. J. Pharm. Exp. Ther. **232:** 439–444.
8. ZUKIN, R. S., J. R. SUGARMAN, M. L. FITZ-SYAGE, E. L. GARDNER, S. R. ZUKIN & A. R. GINTZLER. 1982. Naltrexone-induced opiate receptor supersensitivity. Brain Res. **245:** 285–292.
9. KIRKHAM, T. C. & S. J. COOPER. 1987. The pyrazoloquinoline, CGS 8216, reduces sham feeding in the rat. Pharmacol. Biochem. Behav. **26:** 497–501.

Impact of Hypothalamic Serotonin on Macronutrient Intake

N. ROGACKI,[a] G. F. WEISS,[a] A. FUEG,[a] J. S. SUH,[a]
S. PAL,[a] B. G. STANLEY,[a] D. T. WONG,[b]
AND S. F. LEIBOWITZ[a]

[a]The Rockefeller University
New York, New York 10021

[b]Lilly Research Labs
Eli Lilly & Co.
Indianapolis, Indiana

The indoleamine serotonin (5-HT) has been suggested to act as an inhibitory neurotransmitter in the control of feeding behavior. Recent evidence[1,2] has demonstrated that 5-HT injected into the paraventricular nucleus (PVN) selectively suppresses carbohydrate ingestion, without affecting intake of either protein or fat, and this effect occurs specifically at the start of the active cycle (nocturnal period for the rat) when a carbohydrate-rich meal normally occurs.[3] This review summarizes the results of studies that have employed a variety of techniques, namely, PVN cannulation, peripheral (i.p.) injections, electrolytic lesions, and microdialysis procedures, to analyze the actions of various serotonergic drugs that affect eating behavior. These drugs are the 5-HT releasing agent *d*-fenfluramine (DF), its active metabolite *d*-norfenfluramine (DNF), and the 5-HT reuptake blocker fluoxetine (FLUOX) in freely feeding rats.

METHODS AND PROCEDURES

Male, albino, Sprague–Dawley rats, weighing 360–380 g at the start of the experiments, were maintained on pure sources of carbohydrate, protein, and fat. The animals were individually housed under a constant 12:12-hour light–dark cycle, during which time testing occurred either at the onset of the dark (early dark, hours 1–2) or in the late dark (hours 11–12). Those rats receiving central injections were stereotaxically implanted with chronic cannulae aimed at the PVN. Animals peripherally injected received bilateral PVN lesions using AC current of 1.0 mA/15 sec through epoxy-coated 00-size insect pins. Animals in the microdialysis experiment had a 200-µ probe aimed at the PVN and HPLC analyses of extracellular 5-HT after local injection of DNF.

RESULTS

In accordance with prior research, macronutrient preferences varied as a function of the nocturnal cycle. In vehicle-injected rats, the data revealed that the diet most preferred in the first hour of the dark was carbohydrate (5.1 kcal), as compared to protein (2.0 kcal) and fat (3.5 kcal). In contrast, during the late dark period, the rats' diet preferences changed, such that the amount of protein and fat increased significantly ($p < 0.01$) to 4.5 kcal and 6.0, respectively, while carbohydrate intake declined to 1.5 kcal ($p < 0.001$).

The serotonergic compounds, injected either into the PVN or peripherally, dramatically altered this pattern of macronutrient preference in the early dark period (TABLE 1). At this time, PVN injection of DNF (3.2–50 nmoles) and FLUOX (3.2–100 nmoles), like 5-HT, suppressed carbohydrate intake in a dose-related manner ($p < 0.01$), while having no effect on ingestion of protein and fat. Total kcal intake was not significantly affected. Similarly, systemic administration of FLUOX selectively and dose-dependently reduced ($p < 0.01$) carbohydrate intake and had no effect on protein or fat intake, leaving total kcal intake unaffected, even at high doses of 10 mg/kg.

In the late dark period, in contrast, a quite different pattern of effects was observed. Specifically, after PVN injection of DNF and FLUOX, little or no suppression of any of the diets was observed. Following systemic administration of FLUOX, however, similar to results reported with peripheral DF,[2] a suppression (-35%) of fat intake and a less significant suppression of protein intake was detected at the higher doses tested (2.5–10.0 mg/kg).

The importance of the PVN in mediating serotonergic inhibition of feeding is demonstrated in an additional study with animals maintained on a single mash diet. While sham-operated animals exhibited a strong, 65% reduction in food intake after i.p. injection of DF (1.0 mg/kg), animals with bilateral electrolytic lesions of the PVN were almost completely unresponsive to this anorexic drug, and animals with unilateral PVN lesions exhibited a mild attenuation of this effect.

Consistent with behavioral results, microdialysis procedures have confirmed a dose-related rise in extracellular 5-HT in the PVN in response to local injection of DNF. As described above, PVN injection of this agonist (5 and 50 nmoles), immediately before the onset of dark, produced a significant increase above baseline ($+482\%$ and $+1,614\%$, respectively) in extracellular levels of 5-HT.

CONCLUSIONS

This study provides strong support for the role of PVN 5-HT in controlling macronutrient intake and in mediating the central action of DNF, FLUOX, and DF. The

TABLE 1. Effect on Diet Intake of Injections of Serotonergic Drugs[a]

| | PVN Injection | | | i.p. Injection |
Diet	5-HT (2.5 nm)	DNF (6.3 nm)	FLUOX (6.3 nm)	FLUOX (2.5 mg/kg)
Carbohydrate	-41%[b]	-56%[b]	-35%[b]	-43%[b]
Protein	$+20\%$	$+8\%$	0%	-5%
Fat	-6%	-5%	$+10\%$	-6%
Total	-9%	-17%	-8%	-18%

[a] While drugs were tested at a variety of doses, and their effects found to be dose dependent, results summarized here were obtained from a single, moderate dose that is representative of the general pattern of effects obtained at lower and higher doses. In all cases, these drugs had no reliable effect on total kcal intake but did produce a selective suppression of carbohydrate intake.
[b] $p < 0.01$.

dose-depentent, time-dependent, and macronutrient-specific results produced by PVN administration of serotonergic agonists agree with those exhibited in response to exogenous 5-HT injection and suggest that endogenous 5-HT may be most active in controlling carbohydrate intake at the onset of the active period. Lesion and microdialysis procedures provide further confirmation of the significance of the PVN and endogenous 5-HT in the control of natural feeding patterns.

REFERENCES

1. LEIBOWITZ, S. F., G. F. WEISS, U. A. WALSH & D. VISWANTH. 1989. Medial hypothalamic serotonin: Role in circadian patterns of feeding and macronutrient selection. Brain Res. **503:** 132–140.
2. LEIBOWITZ, S. F. 1990. Serotonin in medial hypothalamic nuclei controls circadian patterns of macronutrient intake. *In* Serotonin: From Cell to Pharmacology and Therapeutics. R. Paoletti & P. M. VanLoutte, Eds. Kluwer Academic Publishers. In press.
3. TEMPEL, D. L., G. SHOR-POSNER, D. DWYER & S. F. LEIBOWITZ. 1989. Feeding patterns and macronutrient selection during the active cycle of the freely-feeding and food-deprived rat. Am. J. Physiol. **256:** R541–R548.

Developmental Patterns of
Eating Behavior

G. SHOR-POSNER, G. BRENNAN, R. JASAITIS,
C. IAN, B. LEIBOWITZ, AND S. F. LEIBOWITZ

The Rockefeller University
New York, New York 10021

Work from this laboratory has examined patterns of food intake in adult rats and revealed distinct temporal shifts in preference for specific macronutrients across the daily cycles.[1] The present experiment expanded these studies to include young animals in order to understand the relationship of their patterns of eating to adult feeding behavior. Our knowledge of this relationship is important, as several variables, including birth weight, rate of growth and development, and sex, may be predisposing factors in the development of certain eating disorders.

In this study, Sprague–Dawley weanling rats (males $n = 24$, females $n = 22$), were permitted to select their food from separate sources of pure macronutrient diets, protein, carbohydrate, and fat, each mixed with vitamins and minerals in proportion to caloric values. Following a one-week adaptation period, measurements of total intake and macronutrient selection were recorded daily from weanling (28 day) to the adult (84 day) stage.

RESULTS AND DISCUSSION

Analyses of food intake and diet selection indicates striking differences in appetite for specific macronutrients as a function of sex and age (TABLE 1). Initially, male and female weanling rats (28 day) display a similar pattern of eating behavior, ingesting approximately 48 total kcal and consuming significantly more protein relative to carbohydrate and fat ($p < 0.05$). With maturation, specific alterations in feeding behavior are demonstrated. At puberty (42 day), an increase in total intake is exhibited in rats of both sexes in association with an enhanced intake of all three diets. Males ingest significantly more total kilocalories, attributed to a sharp rise in protein intake. Females, in contrast, consume a greater proportion of their diet as carbohydrate at this stage.

From puberty to the adult stage (weeks 7–12), significant shifts in preference for particular macronutrients are observed. In rats of both sexes, a decline in protein consumption is demonstrated along with a rise in fat ingestion ($p < 0.02$); carbohydrate intake remains stable. These changes are reflected in the feeding pattern of young adult males and females (84 day), who consume approximately equal proportions of all three diets. Males, however, ingest a greater amount of protein and total caloric diet than do females.

TABLE 1. Developmental Stages of Macronutrient Intake[a]

Age	Total		Protein		Carbohydrate		Fat	
	Male	Female	M	F	M	F	M	F
Weanling	49.1	45.6	22.6	22.0	15.2	15.2	11.3	8.4
(28 day)			(47%)	(48%)	(31%)	(33%)	(23%)	(18%)
Puberty	81.2[b]	71.1[b]	41.2[b]	29.4[b]	24.5	27.5	15.5	14.3
(42 day)			(52%)[b]	(41%)[b]	(30%)[b]	(39%)[b]	(18%)	(20%)
Adult	98.7[b,c]	75.0[b]	35.5[b,c]	24.2[b,c]	30.4	26.6	32.8[c]	24.3[c]
(84 day)			(36%)[c]	(33%)[c]	(31%)	(35%)	(33%)[c]	(31%)[c]

[a] Given are kilocalories, with SEM ranging from 1–4 kcal, and percent concentration reflecting macronutrient intake relative to total intake. With both sexes, a significant increase ($p < 0.05$) in all diets occurred from weanling to puberty.
[b] $p < 0.05$ for differences between males and females.
[c] $p < 0.02$ for differences from puberty to adult.

These results indicate that, while young rats exhibit similar patterns of feeding behavior and macronutrient selection at the weanling stage, eating patterns of males and females diverge sharply with the onset of puberty. At this stage of development, males display a strong increase in protein intake. This contrasts with females who exhibit an enhanced preference for the carbohydrate diet. These changes at puberty are consistent with the findings of Wade and Zucker,[2] revealing a large postpubertal increase in the females' preference for saccharin. They are also compatible with the Geiselman et al.[3] observations of increased carbohydrate intake at estrus in intact animals and decreased carbohydrate consumption in ovariectomized rats.[3] Together, these results provide strong support for the proposal that sexual differences in macronutrient selection may be mediated by physiological changes in association with maturity.[2] The present findings also indicate that patterns of macronutrient selection vary as a function of age, suggesting that this factor as well as the animals' sex may be critical in predicting the development of natural eating patterns.

REFERENCES

1. TEMPEL, D. L., G. SHOR-POSNER, D. DWYER & S. F. LEIBOWITZ. 1989. Am. J. Physiol. **256:** R541–R548.
2. WADE, G. N. & I. ZUCKER. 1969. J. Comp. Physiol. Psych. **69:** 291–300.
3. GEISELMAN, P. N. J., J. R. MARTIN, D. A. VANDERWEELE & D. NOVIN. 1981. Appetite **2:** 87–101.

Index of Contributors